THE LONG SHADOW

The Great War and the Twentieth Century

DAVID REYNOLDS

**SIMON &
SCHUSTER**

London · New York · Sydney · Toronto · New Delhi

A CBS COMPANY

First published in Great Britain by Simon & Schuster UK Ltd, 2013
This paperback edition published by Simon & Schuster UK Ltd, 2014
A CBS COMPANY

1 3 5 7 9 10 8 6 4 2

Simon & Schuster UK Ltd
1st Floor
222 Gray's Inn Road
London WC1X 8HB

www.simonandschuster.co.uk

Simon & Schuster Australia, Sydney
Simon & Schuster India, New Delhi

A CIP catalogue record for this book is available from the British Library

Paperback ISBN: 978-0-85720-637-4
eBook ISBN: 978-0-85720-638-1

Typeset in Bembo by M Rules
Printed and bound by CPI Group (UK) Ltd, Croydon, CR0 4YY

David Reynolds is Professor of International History at Cambridge University, where he is a Fellow of Christ's College. He has held visiting appointments at Harvard, Nihon University in Tokyo and Sciences Po in Paris, and was elected a Fellow of the British Academy in 2005. The author of twelve books, including *In Command of History: Churchill Fighting and Writing the Second World War* (2004), which was awarded the Wolfson Prize, he has also written and presented nine historical documentaries for BBC Television as well as an award-winning series for BBC Radio 4, *America, Empire of Liberty*.

Praise for *The Long Shadow*:

'Scores of books are planned to commemorate the remorseless battles, the fetid trenches, the mass slaughter, the broad disillusionment, and the grave implications of the conflict that stretched from 1914 to 1918 and haunts us to this day. But few of those volumes will have the breadth and depth of *The Long Shadow*, David Reynolds's masterly look at what the war meant and how its meaning changed decade by decade. *The Long Shadow* isn't a history as much as a meditation on the place of the war in history – and the implications of the war for the future.' *The Boston Globe*

'[Reynolds] looks at [the war's] effect upon nations, democracy, empire, capitalism, civilization and peace. All of these areas have been analysed before, but never with such depth of perception or range of understanding. Reynolds is able to speak with authority on economics and philosophy; literature and art; politics, diplomacy and memory. He is a historian of immense skill, utterly confident of his wisdom and deservedly so.' *Washington Post*

'Reynolds's call to move the understanding of World War I out of the trenches and into broader contexts is a fundamental challenge as the centennial begins.' Dennis Showalter, *Military History Quarterly*

'David Reynolds's most recent book does a remarkable job of explaining why people should know more about the First World War – and why it is so difficult to fully grasp its legacy. *The Long Shadow* is not simply a history of a century-old conflict. Reynolds documents its profound impact on world powers as well as on embryonic nations, politics, warfare, the world economy, culture and literature … *The Long Shadow* transcends conventional histories about World War I. At times, it is almost a psychoanalysis of a world that was profoundly changed by a collective and horrific trauma. But that is no criticism. It is the kind of book that challenges readers to think.' *Dallas News*

'As compelling as *The Long Shadow* is on the topics of war and colonialism, the book truly (and unexpectedly) takes flight when Reynolds turns his eye toward art and culture. If y̶o̶u̶ ̶t̶h̶i̶n̶k̶ ̶o̶f̶ ̶W̶o̶r̶l̶d̶ ̶W̶a̶r̶ ̶I̶ ̶related art begins with Otto Dix and ends with Britai̶n̶ ... ̶ditional works, movement̶s̶ ̶ ̶ ... ̶Cubism to war memorials ... ; impact on the future.' *Th̶...*

Henry George Reynolds
(1882–1959)

James Kay
(1891–1928)

The Tiger : "Curious! I seem to hear a child weeping!"

A premonition of the future for Georges Clemenceau ('The Tiger')
and the other Peacemakers of 1919.

We step from days of sour division
Into the grandeur of our fate.

Laurence Binyon (1914)

Remember me when I am dead
And simplify me when I'm dead.

Keith Douglas (1941)

Never such innocence
Never before or since . . .
Never such innocence again.

Philip Larkin (1964)

Every nation has its own Great War.

Jay Winter and Antoine Prost (2005)

CONTENTS

List of Illustrations   xi
Acknowledgments   xiii

Introduction – Great War   xv

PART ONE – LEGACIES

1   Nations   3
2   Democracy   41
3   Empire   85
4   Capitalism   127
5   Civilization   161
6   Peace   209

PART TWO – REFRACTIONS

7   Again   247
8   Evil   281
9   Generations   315
10 Tommies   359
11 Remembrance   385

Conclusion – Long Shadow   419

Notes   437
Permissions   490
Index   493

LIST OF ILLUSTRATIONS

Frontispiece: 'Peace and Future Cannon Fodder', cartoon by Will Dyson for the *Daily Herald*, 13 May 1919. Photo: Cartoon Archive, University of Kent at Canterbury

PLATE SECTION ONE

1. *Statesmen of the Great War*, painting by Sir James Guthrie, 1924–30. © National Portrait Gallery, London
2. Tomáš Masaryk and President Woodrow Wilson on a postcard of Czech origin, c.1918–25. Courtesy of the Woodrow Wilson Presidential Library, Staunton, Virginia
3. John Redmond on a poster issued by the Central Council for the Organisation of Recruiting in Ireland, 1915. Reproduced by courtesy of the National Library of Ireland (Ref. EPH F113)
4. Eamon de Valera taken prisoner in Richmond Barracks after the Easter Rising, 1916. Reproduced by courtesy of Kilmainham Gaol Museum (Ref. 19PC 1A44–01)
5. President Eamon De Valera inspects military units on O'Connell Street in Dublin, during the 50th anniversary parade of the Easter Rising, 10 April 1966. Photo: PA Photos
6. 'Nothing Doing', cartoon by Bernard Partridge for *Punch*, 12 June 1929 © Punch Ltd
7. 'Nazi Movement – Local Version', cartoon by Will Dyson for the *Daily Herald*, 30 March 1933. Photo: Mirrorpix
8. Advertisement for Halifax Building Society, 1930s. Image Courtesy of The Advertising Archives
9. Advertisement for HMV, 1930s. Image courtesy of the Advertising Archives
10. *Wounded soldier – Autumn 1916, Bapaume*, etching by Otto Dix, 1924. Collection of the National Gallery of Australia, Canberra. Photo: Bridgeman Art Library. © DACS 2013
11. *La Mitrailleuse*, painting by Christopher Wynne Nevinson, 1915. © Tate, London 2013

12.   *The Menin Road*, painting by Paul Nash, 1919. Imperial War Museum, London. Photo: The Art Archive. Crown Copyright
13.   *Gassed*, painting by John Singer Sargent, 1919. Imperial War Museum, London. Photo: The Art Archive
14.   The Peace Ballot, 1935. Courtesy the Library of the London School of Economics & Political Science (Ref. LNU/8/15)
15.   Soldiers marching to Cambridge station pass the 1914–18 war memorial, photograph published in the *Cambridge Daily News*, 21 October 1939. Courtesy the Cambridgeshire Collection, Cambridge Central Library

PLATE SECTION TWO
16.   Front page of the *Daily Mirror*, 5 July 1945, featuring the Zec cartoon 'Don't Lose it Again', originally published on VE Day. Photo: Mirrorpix
17.   J.P. Morgan confronts Senator Gerald P. Nye during the Senate Munitions Committee hearing, Washington, DC, 4 February 1936. Photo: AP/PA Photos
18.   Poster for the movie *Wilson*, 1944
19.   'The Atlantic Area'. Reprinted by permission of 'Foreign Affairs, July 1941 issue. © 2013 by the Council on Foreign Relations, Inc. www.ForeignAffairs.com
20 & 21. Opening captions from the BBC TV series *The Great War* (1964). © BBC Worldwide Ltd
22.   A ration party of the Royal Irish Rifles in a communication trench during the Battle of the Somme, July 1916. © Imperial War Museum, London (Q 1)
23.   Front cover of Anthem for Doomed Youth by John Stallworthy. Published by the Imperial War Museum / Constable & Robinson, 2002
24.   Edmund Blunden. Photo: Topfoto
25.   The Central London Recruiting Depot, August 1914. Photo: Topfoto
26.   The Island of Ireland Peace Tower, near Mesen/Messines, Belgium. Photo: Alamy
27.   Dedication of the Island of Ireland Peace Tower by President Mary McAleese and Queen Elizabeth II, 11 November 1998. Photo: Topfoto
28.   Three tablets record the dead from the Ulster division and two Irish divisions who fought alongside each other in 1917, Mesen, Belgium. Photo: Margaret Reynolds
29.   Memorial to the Missing of the Somme, by Sir Edwin Lutyens, Thiepval, France. Photo: Alamy
30.   Detail from the Memorial showing inscription, Thiepval. Photo: Margaret Reynolds
31.   Headstone commemorating a British soldier, Thiepval. Photo: Margaret Reynolds
32.   Inscriptions on the arch and crosses commemorating French soldiers, Thiepval. Photo: Alamy

ACKNOWLEDGMENTS

The genesis of this book goes back over a decade, to a conference paper I gave in 2002 about how the discourse of what have become known as the First World War and the Second World War developed in various countries. The arguments outlined there formed the embryo of this book and I am grateful to the conference organizers, Richard J. Evans and Emma Rothschild, for the opportunity they provided. More recently I have been able to try out some of my ideas at various seminars and conferences, including Sciences Po in Paris (Maurice Vaïsse), the European Academy in Berlin (Andreas Etges), the Boltzmann Institute in Graz, Austria (Stefan Hauner and Barbara Steltz-Marx) and Deakin University, Melbourne (David Lowe).

I am especially grateful to friends and colleagues who commented on the whole manuscript, notably John Thompson and Zara Steiner, or who discussed some of the chapters and the ideas behind them, particularly Chris Clark, Martin Daunton, Niamh Gallagher and Meike Wulf. The title I owe to Janice Hadlow. I have also learned a great deal from my colleagues on the Imperial War Museum's Academic Advisory Committee for the new First World War galleries: Hew Strachan, David Stevenson, Dan Todman and Deborah Thom. Their scholarly work and that of Jay Winter – not least his Humanitas lectures in Cambridge in 2012 – have been essential foundations for my endeavours. Both James Taylor and James Wallis at the Imperial War Museum have helped with various inquiries.

The research could not have been conducted without the wonderful Cambridge network of libraries: the University Library, a copyright depository where, uniquely, one can borrow and browse, the Seeley Library in the History Faculty, and the library of Christ's College. Gratitude also to Ségolène and Hervé Le Men for much generous hospitality in Marigny and for hours of talking and walking La Grande Guerre. As usual, my family have been essential – supportive, tolerant, diverting and impatient in appropriate measures. Thank you Margaret, Jim and also Emma. Some of Margaret's photographs of the Western Front also appear in the illustrations section.

Particular thanks to my editor Mike Jones and my agent Peter Robinson, both for reading the draft and for much helpful advice. Also to the production staff at Simon & Schuster, especially project editor Jo Whitford, and to copy editor Serena Dilnot and photo-researcher Cecilia Mackay.

It seems customary for historians of my generation to dedicate books about the Great War to the memory of soldierly grandparents. Both of my grandfathers did not fight, being in reserved occupations – Henry Reynolds in the postal telegraphy service in London and Jim Kay as a pattern-maker for Mather & Platt, the great engineering firm in Manchester. But, for a book that aspires to shift our view of the Great War out of the trenches, these two men seem rather apt dedicatees.

Introduction

GREAT WAR

In Britain we have lost touch with the Great War. That may seem a strange assertion given the popularity of novelists such as Pat Barker and Sebastian Faulks and the canonical status of Wilfred Owen and other war poets in the school curriculum. But 1914–18 has become a literary war, detached from its moorings in historical events. 'My subject is War and the pity of War,' Owen declared. 'The Poetry is in the pity.' Our overriding sense now is of a meaningless, futile blood-bath in the mud of Flanders and Picardy – a tragedy of young men whose lives were cut off in their prime for no evident purpose. But by reducing the conflict to personal tragedies, however moving, we have lost the big picture: the history has been distilled into poetry.[1]

This process has been accentuated by the 'cultural turn' in academic history as a whole which, in the case of 1914–18, has resulted in a fascination with the public memory and memorialization of the conflict. Since the 1980s numerous scholars have illuminated the Great War's cultural legacies, especially attitudes to death and mourning that had been ignored by traditional military historians. Yet the cult of memory, like many new historiographical trends, has sometimes been pushed too far, obscuring the direct, material impacts of the war – political, military, economic, social and intellectual.[2] *The Long Shadow* is a book about the living as much as the dead because life went on after 1918. Indeed, as Woodrow Wilson's propaganda chief George Creel put it in 1920, this was a world turned 'molten' by the volcano of war.[3] Most of post-war Europe was not frozen in perpetual mourning; the 1920s and 1930s were not predominantly a 'morbid age'.[4]

Part One develops this perspective by exploring the impact of the Great War on the next two decades, which were perceived by contemporaries as the 'post-war' years and not, as we see them now, the 'interwar' era. In other words, before perspectives on 1914–18 were transformed by the onset of another global war. A series of thematic chapters examine in turn the new national map of eastern Europe, the challenges to liberal democracy, the future of colonial empires, the dislocation of the world economy, the ferment of cultural values and the overarching problem of international peace. Some of the Great War's legacies were negative and pernicious but others proved transformative in a positive sense: the twentieth century was not solely an 'age of hatred'.[5]

By exploring these themes through the 1920s and 1930s, I want to show that the United Kingdom's experience of the conflict differed in significant respects from that of continental Europe – of France and Germany, let alone Russia and the Balkans. This is a major argument of the book. The UK was spared invasion or serious bombing; it was not engulfed in revolution or wracked by civil war and paramilitary violence. In fact, despite folk memories of the General Strike and the Slump, Britain in the 1920s and 1930s was politically and economically much more stable than its continental neighbours. There is, however, an exception: Ireland in the years after the Easter Rising of 1916. The Irish experience of the Great War era was much more continental than that of mainland Britain. The legacies of 1916–23, of Ireland's war of independence, its civil war and partition, would sour the rest of the twentieth century.[6]

The Great War also had global ramifications, reshaping the Near East, colonial Africa and East Asia.[7] Here, too, the British experience was unusual: while other great empires collapsed, the Pax Britannica (like the *Empire Français*) reached its peak after 1918. Yet the unexpected expansion, especially into Palestine and Mesopotamia, created hostages to fortune for the future. As new war clouds loomed on the horizon in the 1930s, the Great War also guided British reactions – not just in pursuing the diplomacy of appeasement to keep the peace but also in making contingency plans for a possible war. Rather than preparing to send another mass army of cannon fodder to the continent, policymakers focused on the air defence of Britain itself. In the 1930s the British were trying to avoid a new Great War and this almost undid them in 1940 when the next war turned out to be quite different from the last.

The United States was even more distant from the Great War, both geographically and emotionally, and its growing disillusion about what the conflict had achieved paralleled that of the United Kingdom. The crucial difference, however, was the body count. The UK death toll was 723,000, the US figure 116,000 – and over half of them were actually soldiers who fell victim to the influenza pandemic of 1918.[8] America's 'great war' was its appalling Civil War of 1861–5 during which 620,000 Americans died, far more than in both World Wars combined. It was the imbalance between, on the one hand, the magnitude of British losses and, on the other, the remoteness of the issues apparently at stake which created the sense of anguish in Britain about the Great War. For Americans, who suffered much less and more briefly, the war of 1917–18 was then overshadowed by the titanic struggles of 1941–5 and the Cold War. Yet the Great War was the United States' first serious encounter with European conflict and global diplomacy and it would prove a benchmark all through the twentieth century for American leaders as they wrestled with the political burdens and moral dilemmas of being a world power.

The various impacts of the Great War were clear and pervasive in the 1920s and 1930s but this 'war to end war' took on a different meaning when it was followed less than a quarter of a century later by a second, even more horrendous conflict in which Britain was heavily bombed, faced imminent invasion and found its Asian empire undermined. The 1920s and 1930s now became the interwar era and the Great War itself was relabelled the First World War. For two decades it was largely obscured by the Second World War and the Cold War, by the even greater horrors of the Holocaust and the Bomb, before being rediscovered in the 1960s around the time of the fiftieth anniversary. This was when 1914–18 became for the British supremely a story of trenches and poets.

As the direct material impacts of 1914–18 diminished after 1945 the cult of memory did become more important, but remembrance was constantly shaped by contemporary concerns – for instance the 1960s youth revolt against the establishment in Britain and against the 'silent generation' in Germany, complicit in Nazi crimes. More recently the war has been redefined anew by post–Cold War efforts at international bridge-building – evident in shared memorials on the Somme and at Caporetto and in the Island of Ireland Peace Tower near Ieper, formerly Ypres. Yet the British view of the conflict has remained stuck in the mud and stalled on the Somme. In a set of chronological chapters, Part Two therefore traces the shadows cast by 1914–18 over the second half of the twentieth century, with the light now not direct but refracted: first through the prism of 1939–45 and then through that of 1989–91 – the Cold War's denouement but also the end of the long post-war era since 1945. In these chapters I seek to connect various books, films and events with which readers are familiar in a random way into an integrated argument about the ever-changing presence of the past.[9]

This book therefore uses the Great War as a way not just to explore the immediate legacies of 1914–18 but also to illuminate important features of the century that followed. The chapters range across a variety of historical sub-disciplines, from military history to cultural studies, from ideology to economics, and also engage with recent trends in historical research. Above all, by setting the UK's experience of the Great War within a European context, I hope to offer a much-needed corrective to narrowly Anglocentric conceptions of what the hell it was all about. In short I shall try to explain why the British now have such a problem with this great but perplexing war.

A way into the problem is to expand our sense of the war's chronology. Popular British conceptions of the Great War are fixated with 1916, indeed with one day of that year – the opening of the battle of the Somme on 1 July. Yet the conflict lasted nearly four years and it fell into several phases, of which the last and most neglected is of particular importance if we want to understand the impact of the conflict on subsequent decades. For the purposes of this book, how the war ended matters more than why it began. And that 'molten' aftermath was a consequence of the volcanic pressures built up through years of stalemate.[10]

The initial phase of the war fits neatly into 1914. Despite premonitions and tensions, the July crisis came out of the blue and gained a momentum of its own. The question of who was to blame – indeed, whether any one nation was to blame – will be explored throughout this book: suffice to say here that what began as a short, sharp strike by the Habsburg Empire, backed by Kaiser Wilhelm's Germany, to deal once and for all with its troublesome neighbour, Serbia, rapidly sucked in Tsarist Russia and its ally the French republic. After anguished debate, Britain's Liberal government threw in its lot with France and Belgium, whose neutrality the UK was pledged to defend. What followed in 1914, it is often forgotten, was a war of movement as the French thrust into Alsace and Lorraine, the Russians surged into East Prussia and the Germans pressed grimly towards Paris. Each government gambled on a quick and decisive victory but their troops soon outran command, control and supply networks. Worse still, they totally underestimated the devastating effect of modern artillery and machine guns on attacking infantry. For most of the belligerents the casualty rates in 1914 were the highest of the war – half a million in the case of France. On its worst day of the war, 22 August 1914, the advancing French army lost 27,000 men – a far larger death toll than the British suffered on the first day of the Somme. Attacking in their massed lines and bright uniforms (blue tunics and red trousers), the French *poilus* of 1914 were easy targets for German machine-gunners.[11]

By 1915 the war in the west had settled into its long second phase, defined by lines of trenches from Switzerland to the North Sea. This is the muddy, bloody stalemate that we now take as axiomatic. In fact, all the belligerents still entertained hopes of a decisive stroke that would bring dramatic victory on the battlefield and shatter the enemy's will to fight. The British and French tried this against Germany's ally, the Ottomans, in April 1915 but the result was disaster at

Gallipoli. Italy had the same hope in May when it attacked Austria-Hungary, only to become locked in a grim war in the icy foothills of the Alps. Germany enjoyed more success in 1915, overwhelming Serbia and seizing much of Poland from the Russians, but even these victories did not deliver a knockout blow: Russian morale held firm. Indeed a feature of the first half of the Great War was the strength of all the home fronts – contrary to fears beforehand about the corrosive effects of socialism and pacifism. As the costs of war soared, so did the price of peace. Only clear-cut victory seemed acceptable; anything less, in the words of the German chancellor in November 1914, 'would appear to the people as absolutely insufficient rewards for such terrible sacrifices.'[12]

Perpetually hopeful that one last push would prove decisive, the belligerents geared up again in 1916. Defence spending soared in most countries to over half of GDP and governments reorganized economy and society for what was being called 'total war'. Politics also hardened: in Germany the truce of 1914 broke down, with dissident socialists openly opposing an imperialist war. Britain finally imposed conscription, breaching sacred Liberal principles, and a new coalition government under David Lloyd George galvanized the war effort. On the battlefield the German High Command targeted the strategic city of Verdun, hoping to 'bleed France white', but its campaign failed and the German army bled almost as much as the French. The death toll for both sides at Verdun has been estimated at between 400,000 and 600,000. A precise figure is impossible because many soldiers were literally blown to bits – the harvest of bones from the battlefield can still be seen in the grisly Ossuary at Douaumont. Hoping to relieve Verdun the Allies mounted an offensive on the Somme. British losses on the opening day were unprecedented – nearly 60,000, a third of them killed – and 1 July 1916 has become, for the British, the most infamous date of the war. Yet the offensive was maintained till November because Field Marshal Sir Douglas Haig still hoped for a dramatic breakthrough. In the whole Somme campaign British casualties totalled 420,000, and France lost half that number, but the cost to the Germans was also enormous, maybe close to the British and French losses combined.[13]

On 13 November 1916, as the battle of the Somme subsided into the winter mud, Lord Lansdowne, a former foreign secretary, asked the British Cabinet to consider a negotiated peace. 'Generations will have to come and go before the country recovers from the loss which it has sustained in human beings and from the financial ruin and the destruction of the means of production which are taking place.' Casualties had already topped 1 million and the war was costing Britain £5 million a day. 'All this it is no doubt our duty to bear,' Lansdowne went on, 'but only if it can be shown that the sacrifice will have its reward. If it is to be made in vain, if the additional year, or two years, or three years, finds us still unable to dictate terms, the war with its nameless horrors will have been needlessly prolonged, and the responsibility of those who needlessly prolong such a war is no less than those who needlessly provoke it.' Lansdowne's plea fell on deaf ears but the question he posed – two years almost to the day before the eventual Armistice – about the point of carrying on still gnaws at the British conscience.[14]

In 1916 each side's knockout blow (Verdun and the Somme) had failed, at enormous cost, while domestic remobilization for an even bigger effort imposed huge strains on their home fronts. During 1917 cracks began to open up and the war entered a third, more volatile phase. The Germans shortened their line in the west, withdrawing to new and well-fortified positions. The United States still maintained a stance of formal neutrality but the British war effort was now heavily dependent on supplies purchased from across the Atlantic using loans raised from American banks and private investors. So the German High Command took the momentous decision to mount unrestricted U-boat warfare in the Atlantic – provoking, as anticipated, American entry into the war. The Germans were gambling that their submarines could sever Britain's vital transatlantic supply line before the United States mobilized effectively, and for a while the gamble seemed to be paying off. In April 1917 elements of the French army mutinied after a suicidal offensive against strong German positions along the Chemin des Dames ridge. The troops, if not their hubristic commander, General Robert Nivelle, could see what was coming: many of them went into battle, up the muddy slope in pouring rain, baaing like sheep. Although the mutinies were quelled, thereafter the French army was rarely risked in all-out offensives. In October the Italians fell apart when defeat on the Alpine foothills at Caporetto turned into a rout. And the British army's thrusts along the Western Front, from Arras in the spring to Passchendaele in the autumn, gained little mud at great cost, exacerbating friction between the politicians and the generals.

The only glimmer of light came from the east, where the Ottoman Empire was also cracking: British Empire troops took Palestine and oil-rich Mesopotamia. But that could not offset the collapse of the Eastern Front in Europe during 1917. In February fury against the war in Russia reached fever pitch. In the capital city of Petrograd it took only a couple of weeks of food riots and army mutinies to topple the Tsar. The Romanov dynasty, absolute rulers of Russia for three centuries, was now consigned to the rubbish heap of history. Although the new Russian government fought on during the summer, the Bolshevik seizure of power in October quickly led to a ceasefire on the Eastern Front. For the first time in the war Germany was free to concentrate on the west.

In the final phase, 1918, the war became mobile again, as it had been in 1914, and both sides went for broke. Having gambled on U-boat warfare in 1917, General Erich Ludendorff and the German High Command, now effectively Germany's military dictatorship, gambled again with a succession of hammer-blows, intended to break the Western Front before the new US army could be deployed in earnest. Ludendorff's initial assault in March 1918 nearly split the British armies from the French and the ensuing crisis quelled strikes and anti-war talk back in Britain. But by going on to the attack for the first time since 1916, Ludendorff exposed his troops to massive Allied firepower. Each of the five German offensives during the spring and summer proved weaker than the last, as casualties and desertion took a formidable toll. By now the Allied blockade was beginning to bite: Berliners scavenged the rubbish heaps for scraps of meat and rotten vegetables as they tried to keep working on a thousand calories a day, less than half the official minimum. During the summer of 1918 the British and French divisions, backed by a million fresh Americans, started to advance. The prospect of a decisive American offensive if the war continued into 1919 helped break German morale but the Doughboys were still learning the nature of modern war in 1918 and their bravado victories were won at huge cost. It was in the autumn of 1918 that the British army finally came into its own. Haig was now commanding nearly sixty divisions, the biggest force ever deployed by the British Empire. At last he was using infantry, tanks, planes and artillery in a coordinated yet flexible way to blast through enemy defences and exploit successes wherever they opened up – all very different from the rigid shell-and-march tactics of 1916. Recent British military historians have insisted that Haig's triumphant last 'Hundred Days' and the 'forgotten victory' of 1918 were the culmination of what they euphemistically call a 'learning curve' that began on the Somme.[15]

Whether the learning was worth all the bleeding remains a matter of intense debate but that final phase of the war is absolutely critical as prologue to this book. The outcome in November 1918 was not merely military victory for the Allies and defeat for the Central Powers: the price of defeat in total war was total collapse. When Ludendorff asked the Allies for an armistice, exposing to astonished citizens the gravity of Germany's plight, the imperial navy and army mutinied and the Reich collapsed in four weeks like a house of cards. The Kaiser was forced to abdicate. Then, as plain Wilhelm Hohenzollern, he slipped into exile in the Netherlands, ending five hundred years of his family's rule in Berlin. The Habsburg Empire also fell apart. On 8 November the thirty-one-year-old Emperor Karl stood for the last time in the vast ballroom of Schönbrunn Palace in Vienna, a rather pathetic young man lost amid the Baroque splendours of Maria Theresa. For one watching politician it was a sight that symbolized 'the deepest tragedy of earthly fame and human power'.[16]

Yet the price of victory was also high: the Allies would find it almost as hard to adjust to the post-war world. Had the fighting ended in 1916 with a negotiated peace, as Lansdowne urged, its impact would have been much less cataclysmic. By going for broke the belligerents broke Europe's old order.

This last tumultuous phase of the Great War sets the scene for the chapters that follow. What would replace the fractured empires of the Habsburgs, Romanovs and Hohenzollerns – previously rulers of most of central and eastern Europe? Could the challenges of Bolshevik revolution and mass democracy be contained in countries where millions of new voters were trained killers? How to manage the colonial empires, whose peoples had been aroused by the new rhetoric of nationalism and democracy? On what basis should the Allies try to reconstruct the shattered structures of global capitalism? How, after four years of mass slaughter, could one dare to affirm the values of civilization? And, above all, was it possible to sustain the peace settlement crafted in Paris in 1919? These questions provide the themes for the first half of this book, as we explore Britain's response to 1918 from an international perspective.

PART ONE

LEGACIES

1

NATIONS

The Prussian Junker is the road-hog of Europe ... if we had stood by when two little nations were being crushed and broken by the brutal hands of barbarism our shame would have rung down the everlasting ages.

David Lloyd George, 19 September 1914

... all well-defined national aspirations shall be accorded the utmost satisfaction ... without introducing new, or perpetuating old, elements of discord and antagonism that would be likely in time to break the peace of Europe and consequently of the world.

Woodrow Wilson, 11 February 1918[1]

During the Paris peace conference the American President and his wife were housed in the Hôtel du Prince Murat – a splendid nineteenth-century palace in the rue de Monceau, full of mementoes from the era of Napoleon. Edith Wilson retained vivid impressions of the red, white and blue sentry box at the gate, the 'great sweep of the stairs' and the 'liveried lackeys' in attendance – lamenting in her memoirs that 'if only some of the costs of this sort of useless attention could be diverted to those who stand in need of the necessary things of life, this would be a better world.' Nor did she forget once entering one of the grand salons to find her husband and his advisers on hands and knees on the floor. They were poring over huge maps of Europe, trying to work out its new frontiers. 'You look like a lot of little boys playing a game,' she laughed. The President turned to her gravely. 'Alas, it is the most serious game ever undertaken, for on the result of it hangs, in my estimation, the future peace of the world.'[2]

Wilson and his fellow statesmen at Paris in 1919 have often been blamed for creating the mess of post-war Europe but, in reality, the problems were already beyond their control. Never had the map of Europe been redrawn so dramatically. The crisis of 1917–18 destroyed the great dynastic empires that had ruled central, eastern and south-eastern Europe for centuries – the Romanovs, Habsburgs, Hohenzollerns and Ottomans. In August 1914 Europe contained only three republics (Switzerland, France and Portugal); by the end of 1918 there were thirteen. One of them was Germany itself, where the Kaiserreich had been shattered by defeat and revolution. The other nine were states that did not even exist at the start of the war, among them Czechoslovakia, Poland and Yugoslavia.[3]

The challenge was to combine independence with interdependence or, as Wilson put it on 11 February 1918, to promote 'national aspirations' within a framework of peace and order. But to achieve such goals at the end of the Great War would have required an alchemist not a statesman. This chapter reflects on the fractious new multinational states that were cobbled together on the ruins of empire, often through brutal paramilitary violence. Their fragility would destabilize the continent for much of the twentieth century.[4]

The United Kingdom of Great Britain and Ireland was also an empire albeit on a small scale – created by centuries of expansion by England – and it did not escape this tornado of empire-breaking and nation-building. The Irish experience of the Great War had many similarities with events on the continent. Ravaged by brutal violence Ireland shattered into two rival states, one fiercely independent, the other sheltering within the UK. But in England, Wales and Scotland the conflict generated a renewed sense of British identity, which would endure for much of the twentieth century.

What is a nation? The French intellectual Ernest Renan posed that question back in 1882, and the debate still rumbles on.[5] People's sense of identity can take many forms, defined by gender or class or religion. In the past identity was often very local and concrete, expressed through friendship groups, churches or clubs. To feel that one is part of a nation requires a big imaginative leap and national consciousness has often been sharpened, or even generated, by fear of what historians have identified as a hostile 'Other' against which to counterpose one's own nation and its values. But nationalism also needs expression in a political structure – a state – in order to gain the legal and emotional leverage over people that is necessary to shape the sense of national identity. In 1800 Europe comprised some five hundred political units, varying hugely in size and viability; by 1900 there were only about twenty.[6] During the nineteenth century states were forged largely by people's wars, fought in the name of the nation and involving mass armies raised by conscription, for which the prototype was France during the revolution and the Napoleonic Empire. France's wars aroused national consciousness elsewhere, especially in the lands that became Italy and Germany. To quote Thomas Nipperdey's history of modern Germany, 'in the beginning was Napoleon'.[7]

From these nineteenth-century struggles scholars developed a distinction between a civic nation and an ethnic nation. The former signified a community of laws, institutions and citizenship within a defined territory, whereas an ethnic nation was defined as a community of shared descent, rooted in language, ethnicity and culture. France was seen as the embodiment of civic nationalism, forged by the ideology of the revolution (*liberté, égalité, fraternité*), Germany as the classic example of ethnic nationalism, steeped in Romantic conceptions of the *Volk*. This stark contrast between civic and ethnic nations has been questioned by some recent scholars yet the general distinction remains useful.[8]

Before the Great War nation-states were mainly found in western and northern Europe. The late nineteenth century did, however, see a surge of nationalist feeling in central and eastern Europe, rooted in a heightened sense of ethnicity. Initial stirrings were largely cultural, through music and folk myths (sometimes fused together, as Smetana did for the Czechs or Sibelius in Finland). Even more important was the process of systematizing a written national language and teaching it in schools. This idea of a nation was then picked up as propaganda by small groups of politicized intellectuals and agitators before taking off as a genuine mass movement with political clout. By the 1900s some nationalists were more 'advanced' in this process than others – the Poles, say, compared with the Slovenes – but hopes of full national independence were largely utopian. In 1914 the big empires, though rickety, still seemed in control. It was the demands of total war that eventually brought them down.[9]

Consider the example of the Habsburg Empire. This was Europe's third most populous state, with over 50 million people, but they included eleven major national groups, several of which harked back to historic states that had been suppressed by the Habsburgs. Allegiance was essentially dynastic, in this case to the phenomenally long-lived Emperor Franz Joseph, who had ruled since 1848. The empire had never recovered from its catastrophic defeat by Bismarck's Germany in 1866, which obliged Franz Joseph to concede what the British would have called Home Rule to Hungary, the largest king-dom in his empire. Henceforth he ruled over a Dual Monarchy, with separate Austrian and Hungarian parliaments and even separate armies alongside the imperial armed forces. Increasingly Hungary proved a dead weight on the operations of the empire, reluctant to pay its share of taxes, especially for the army. In the Austrian domains of the empire, the Germans were the ruling elite – with Bohemians, Moravians and other ethnic groups kept in their place. Within Hungary Romanians, Slovaks, Slovenes, Serbs and Croats – about half the population – were at the mercy of the Magyars who tried with increasing brutality to impose their own language and culture while resisting demands for universal male suffrage. 'The government will never be able to satisfy every national group,' sighed Franz Joseph wearily. 'This is why we must rely on those which are strongest . . . that is, the Germans and the Hungarians.'[10]

The greatest challenge for the Habsburgs was the kingdom of Serbia, freed from Ottoman rule since 1878 and determined to bring all the Serbs into a Greater Serbia. Quite who constituted the Serbs was left extremely vague and Serbdom potentially stretched from Macedonia to Hungary. This 'mythscape' reflected a capacious definition of the Serbian language and a romanticized folk history dating back to the seminal confrontation between Serbs and the Ottoman Other in 1389 at Kosovo Polje (the field of the Black Birds). Serbia's expansive ambitions, promoted by the Karadjordjević dynasty and by various terrorist groups, culminated in the assassination of the heir to Franz Joseph's throne in Sarajevo on 28 June 1914. Vienna's determination to deal once and for all with the Serbian menace ignited the July crisis.[11]

Before the war some Croat and Slovene intellectuals within the Habsburg Empire had talked of sharing a common South Slav (Yugoslav) identity with the Serbs but they were a minority. The striking point about 1914, however, was that imperial loyalties held firm. In the Habsburg campaign to crush Serbia in the autumn of 1914, many of the soldiers were of South Slav extraction. Notwithstanding occasional nationalist outbursts, for most of the war the Habsburg army hung together and fought well, despite an ethnic diversity that seems ludicrous today. For every hundred men in the imperial army in 1914, there were on average 25 Germans, 18 Magyars, 13 Czechs, 11 Serbs and Croats, 9 Poles, 9 Ruthenes, 6 Romanians, 4 Slovaks, 2 Slovenes and 2 Italians. The language of command was German, with a repertoire of eighty different orders, but officers were expected to know the *Regimentssprache*, the language or languages spoken by their men. Many units operated with two languages, some as many as five. Not so much an army, more a tower of Babel, one might think, yet this polyglot command hung together until 1918 when most soldiers effectively went on strike.[12]

A similar story may be told of the Russian Empire. In 1914 the Romanov dynasty ruled about 170 million people (nearly four times the UK population) across one-sixth of the world's land mass, yet less than half of them were ethnic Russian. The regime failed to create a sense of overall imperial identity, or even a sense of nation among the core Russian population. Belated and often brutal attempts by the last two tsars, Alexander III and his son Nicholas II, to impose Russian language and Orthodox religion served only to inflame nationalist sensitivities. Then, after the abortive revolution of 1905, the government reversed itself with half-hearted political concessions that gave national groups a voice in the new parliament, the Duma. Particularly sensitive was the issue of Poland – a historic state that had been partitioned since 1772 and was now largely under Russian control. Yet, despite a few anti-draft riots, war mobilization in 1914 proceeded relatively smoothly, with nearly 4 million men conscripted on schedule. In all 18.6 million men served in the Russian army during the war, over a tenth of the total population and from all ethnic groups.[13]

During the Great War people from the borderlands of Europe – Poles, Czechs and Croats, even Serbs and Italians – fought on both sides. As conscripts, they had little choice. Discipline was harsh and brutal, propaganda played up the threat from the enemy, and there were significant inducements for continued service. In the Russian army, for instance, a soldier's family would lose their allowance from the state if he deserted or 'voluntarily' entered captivity. In any case most troops from rural eastern Europe, where literacy was limited, did not conceive of their identity in clear-cut national terms. 'Were one to ask the average peasant in the Ukraine his nationality', scoffed a British diplomat in 1918, 'he would answer that he is Greek Orthodox; if pressed to say whether he is a Great Russian, a Pole, or an Ukrainian he would probably reply that he is a peasant; and if one insisted on knowing what language he spoke, he would say that he talked "the local tongue" ... he simply does not think of nationality in the terms familiar to the intelligentsia.'[14]

The deepening conflict did help sharpen national consciousness. On the Eastern Front prisoners of war were separated by nationality and then formed into special units to fight against the empire they had previously served. The Central Powers (Germany and Austria-Hungary) organized a Polish Legion, as well as special Finnish and Ukrainian units to fight against the Tsar. The Russians formed their Habsburg prisoners into Polish, Czech and Slovak units. Their Czech Legion was bloodied at Zborov in Galicia on 2 July 1917 – in itself a minor engagement but elevated into a founding national myth because the legion routed several Czech regiments that were fighting for the Habsburgs. The result of all this was a keener sense of national identities right across eastern Europe, as well as a brutalized soldiery who would eventually form the core of post-war paramilitary groups.[15]

Yet flirting with nationalism in this way did not signify any grand plan for a post-imperial Europe. The Entente Powers (Britain, France and Russia) wanted to preserve the Austro-Hungarian monarchy in slimmer form to balance Germany in central Europe. Nor did the British and French initially support Polish national aspirations, since that would infringe the interests of their Tsarist ally. After America entered the war, Wilson's 'Fourteen Points' in January 1918 envisaged 'an independent Polish state' but proposed only 'the freest opportunity of autonomous development' for the peoples of the Habsburg Empire. It was Lenin and the Bolsheviks who coined the radical phrase 'national self-determination', to encourage the break-up of empires in Europe and beyond. Wilson picked up the term but usually without the adjective 'national': for him 'self-determination' was almost a synonym for 'popular sovereignty' or 'consent of the governed'.[16]

By the autumn of 1918, however, statements by the Allies became irrelevant, as the Habsburg and Ottoman armies collapsed and Russia disintegrated in civil war. What exactly would replace them and fill the looming power vacuum depended on a mixture of local power and international influence.

A classic example was the new Czechoslovakia. For Tomáš Masaryk 1918 was spectacular payoff for earlier gambles. An imposing philosophy professor turned Czech nationalist politician, Masaryk already had a predisposition to the West: his academic work was on British and French empiricist philosophy (Hume, Mill and Comte) and, having married the daughter of a wealthy New Yorker, he spoke fluent English. Masaryk fled Prague in late 1914, settling for two years in London where he lived in Hampstead, catching the bus into town to teach Slavonic studies at London University and cultivating his contacts with British officials and journalists. After the fall of the Tsar, he travelled to Russia on a British passport to organize the Czech Legion and then in 1918 to the United States to mobilize

American support. He met Wilson on several occasions in the White House and, in a brilliant propaganda coup, read out a Declaration of Common Aims of the Independent Mid-European States from the steps of Independence Hall, Philadelphia – shrine of America's Declaration of Independence in 1776. Thanks to this blend of influence in high places and shrewd public relations, Masaryk had already secured Allied recognition for an independent Czechoslovakia several months before Habsburg rule collapsed. The revolution in Prague at the end of October was 'a bloodless, gentle takeover of power from officials who no longer wanted to be responsible for the administration of a Habsburg province'. Four years after he had fled Prague, Masaryk returned in triumph as president of a new republic – a position he would hold for seventeen years.[17]

Prague's velvet revolution (strangely similar to another in 1989) was emulated across much of the former Habsburg Empire, with committees of local nationalist parties assuming power. By the time the peace conference convened in Paris in mid-January 1919, the shape of post-Habsburg Europe was clear on the ground. Independence had successfully been proclaimed for Czechoslovakia and for a kingdom of the Serbs, Croats and Slovenes (later renamed Yugoslavia), leaving Austria and Hungary as rump states. On the Tsarist borderlands, however, the pattern was different. There nationalist movements had been weak or non-existent before 1917, but the anarchy caused by the Tsarist collapse and the Russian civil war suddenly made possible the establishment of independent states in Poland, the Ukraine, Estonia, Latvia, Lithuania and Finland.[18] These national revolutions were bloody rather than velvet, with wars and civil wars that rumbled on into the 1920s. For millions across eastern Europe the Armistice of November 1918, so important in the west, was of relatively little consequence.

Here the paradigmatic case was Poland, whose leader Jósef Piłsudski had managed to play off both sides during the Great War. The son of an impoverished Polish-Lithuanian noble family, staunchly Catholic, Piłsudski had been forced in his youth to speak Russian and attend Orthodox worship. He joined the anti-Russian terrorist underground and organized paramilitary units which, when war began, he put at the disposal of Germany as a Polish Legion. In the summer of 1915 Piłsudski's gamble seemed to be paying off as the Germans conquered most of Poland, but this reduced him to a virtual puppet. When he tried to bargain over the use of his troops, the Germans threw him into prison. Unlike Masaryk, who was free to build international support for a Czechoslovak state in the crucial months of 1917–18, Piłsudski languished behind bars from July 1917 until the last days of the war. But what he lost in diplomatic influence he gained in political stature, being seen as a Polish patriot who had fought Russia and then stood up to Germany. When Piłsudski was released by the Germans in November 1918, he returned to Warsaw as a popular hero and the Regency Council made him the provisional head of state. With his high forehead, drooping moustache and magnetic eyes, invariably dressed in a simple grey legionnaire's tunic, Piłsudski was a commanding figure. 'In appearance so striking as to be almost theatrical' remarked one British diplomat. 'None of the usual amenities of civilized intercourse, but all the apparatus of sombre genius.' By fair means and foul Piłsudski would dominate Polish politics until his death in 1935.[19]

But only after fighting for national survival: in the years 1918, 1919 and 1920 Piłsudski waged no fewer than six wars. Partly this was out of vaulting ambition: mindful of his own Lithuanian roots, he wanted to recreate the vast Polish-Lithuanian Commonwealth of the late sixteenth century and to ensure an independent Ukraine under Polish influence. But any Polish leader in 1918 would have been forced to a fight in order to define a country that had virtually no natural frontiers. In the city of Lwow a Pole pointed out the war damage to an American visitor: 'You see these little holes? We call them "Wilson's Points". They have been made by machine guns . . . We are now engaged in self-determination, and God knows what and when the end will be.'[20]

For Piłsudski the vital struggle was against the Bolsheviks. In bitter fighting that ebbed and flowed dramatically during 1920, the Poles penetrated as far east as Kiev, only to be driven back three hundred miles to the edge of Warsaw. In mid-August foreign governments evacuated their embassies from the panic-stricken city. The 'Polish

Army seems for the time being almost to have ceased to exist as a coherent force,' reported the London *New Statesman*.[21] But a desperate surprise attack by Piłsudski into the Russian rear, celebrated in Polish national mythology as the 'Miracle on Vistula', turned the tables again and routed the Bolsheviks. The Treaty of Riga in March 1921 left Poland with the western parts of Byelorussia and Ukraine – both hostages to fortune.

Elsewhere on the Russian borderlands state-building was equally violent. Ukraine enjoyed a brief taste of freedom before most of it was absorbed into the new Soviet Union. The Baltic states did hang on to independence, albeit after bloody struggles in 1919–20 against various Russian armies. In Finland, formerly a Grand Duchy enjoying autonomy in the Tsarist Empire, independence was sealed after a savage civil war in the first half of 1918 where the real divisions were not ethnic or religious but along class lines. This pitted the Reds, backed by Bolshevik Russia, against the Whites, aided by imperial Germany. Terror was ubiquitous and mutual animosity endured for decades after the White victory. Survivors from each side lived in almost separate communities, with their own newspapers, entertainments and sports clubs.[22]

Whether peaceful or violent this new spasm of European state-building after 1918 was different from that of the mid-nineteenth century. Whereas Italy and Germany had been created through the *unification* of various local polities with similar language and culture, state-building in eastern and south-eastern Europe occurred through *secession* from dynastic empires that had hitherto controlled a volatile mix of ethnic groups in various stages of national self-consciousness and political mobilization.[23] In the vanguard were shrewd nationalist politicians like Masaryk and Piłsudski, who harked back to an ancestral kingdom as the core of the new state. But because of the process of secession and fragmentation, they had to use what they could get from the imperial rubble heap, and their jerry-built new states were a mix of various ethnic groups who had previously lived cheek by jowl. Not so much nation-states as mini-empires, with the ethnic tensions of pre-war now exacerbated by four years of brutal fighting. A process of state-building and national mobilization that had taken decades, even centuries, in western Europe occurred almost overnight from the Baltic to the Adriatic, often with horrific violence.

The statesmen at Paris were not, therefore, architects of the new Europe – more like firefighters desperately trying to pour water on the flames. Maps and statistics were woefully inadequate, and the competing states dressed up the demographic evidence to their own advantage. As Wilson and his advisers began to realize, poring over their beautiful maps in the elegant Hôtel Murat, neat, clean lines could not be drawn through ethnically mixed regions whose inhabitants were now angrily self-conscious.

One small but revealing example is the small Duchy of Teschen – less than 900 square miles in area, equivalent to a middling English county such as Derbyshire, but including part of the Silesian coalfield and a strategic railway junction. After the Habsburg collapse, the duchy became a bone of contention between Poland and Czechoslovakia. On ethnic grounds the Poles had a strong case but the Czechoslovaks argued that coal from the mines was essential for their industries and that the railway was a vital link between the two halves of their new state. Although Polish-speakers constituted a majority of the population, relations between them and the Czechs, Germans and Silesians had been reasonably tolerant before 1914, but in January 1919 troops from the rival countries moved in. Fighting ensued, followed by riots among the populace. With tensions too high to allow a plebiscite, the Allies partitioned the duchy in July 1920. The Czech state got most of the coalfield (even though the miners were largely Poles) while the city of Teschen was split in two, with the old quarter allocated to Poland and the suburbs, including the railway station, to the Czechoslovaks. According to one frustrated American participant, 'the electric light plant goes to the one state, but the gas works to the other, and I do not recall what was to become of the municipal water-works'. These rows could have been resolved by economic and transit agreements but that would have required a modicum of trust between Poland and Czechoslovakia which simply did not exist after 1918. The Teschen settlement further poisoned relations between Poland and Czechoslovakia, two new states that should have felt a common interest in containing German revanchism.[24]

Germany maintained its identity when the Hohenzollern dynasty was overthrown but the Reich had its wings severely clipped, losing 13 per cent of its pre-war territory and 10 per cent of its population.[25] On the south-west Alsace and Lorraine, won in the Franco-Prussian war of 1870, were handed back to France. To the east, Germany surrendered most of Poznan, West Prussia and the Upper Silesian coalfield to the new Poland, plus a corridor allowing Poland access to the Baltic Sea but thereby separating East Prussia from the rest of Germany. Three million Germans remained in the new Czechoslovak state, while the peace treaty with Austria explicitly barred its now overwhelmingly German population from a union with Germany (*Anschluss*). None of this was easy to square with the principle of self-determination. Similarly, 3 million Hungarians lived outside the rump state of Hungary, half of them in Transylvania which was occupied by Romania in 1918. The Allies duly ratified this land grab: their dislike of Hungarian autocracy was compounded by the country's brief but alarming Bolshevik revolution in 1919. The German and Hungarian settlements were reminders that the peacemakers had other objectives in mind apart from self-determination, especially punishment for the defeated and security for the victors.

The new states of central and eastern Europe had been able to emerge because of the vacuum created by the collapse of German and Russian power. But, as those two countries revived in the 1920s and 1930s, they resumed their struggle for territory and influence, with Poland, Ukraine and the Baltic states again the battleground. Although Russo-German antagonism ignited eastern Europe's next war in 1941, its fuel was the ethnic animosities of the post-imperial era – the disputed borders and oppressed minorities. Consider some simple demographic statistics from 1930. In Poland 65 per cent of the population were Poles, 16 per cent Ukrainian and 10 per cent Jews. Czechs constituted only 51 per cent of the people of Czechoslovakia; 23 per cent were German and 16 per cent Slovak. In Yugoslavia the ruling Serbs (44 per cent) were not even a majority, 30 per cent of the population being Croats and 9 per cent Slovenes. This was not the demography of stability.[26]

The peacemakers did require the successor states to guarantee minority rights but these treaties soon proved a dead letter. Piłsudski's Poland was unapologetically racist, while most Serbs regarded Yugoslavia as a convenient disguise for Greater Serbia. Even Czechoslovakia, the most tolerant and democratic of these states, did not treat its minorities well. Masaryk, the Czech nationalist son of a Slovak father, was convinced that the cultural and linguistic differences between the two peoples were relatively insignificant. But for three centuries the Czechs had lived under German rule, opening them to Protestantism, the west and industrialization. The Slovaks, by contrast, had lived even longer under the Hungarians: their Catholic, largely rural society was intertwined economically with Hungary and Ukraine. Such fundamental differences could not easily be bridged and the Slovak nationalist leader Father Andrej Hlinka was soon clamouring for Slovak autonomy. The German question was handled even more autocratically by Masaryk and his inner circle. They moved quickly to break up the large estates, mostly German-owned, which Czechs applauded as long-overdue reparation for the Habsburg conquest of 1620. Foreign minister Eduard Beneš told a British diplomat bluntly, 'Before the war, the Germans were here' (pointing to the ceiling) 'and we were there' (pointing to the floor). 'Now,' he declared, reversing his gestures, 'we are here and they are there.' Land reform, Beneš insisted, was 'necessary' to teach the Germans a 'lesson'.[27] But it was a lesson the Germans would not accept, as Beneš would learn the hard way in 1938.

The declarations of independence in 1918, validated at the Paris peace conference, made the so-called national principle the prime test of state legitimacy, rather than dynastic inheritance or imperial rule. Here indeed was a 'seismic shift' in European history.[28] Yet the principle of nationalism was an artificial construct, almost an anthropomorphic fantasy. Consider some of its cognate terms – national *consciousness*, national *will*, *self*-determination: in each case the nation is treated as analogous to an individual human being. But this postulates a unity and coherence that does not exist in any state, and certainly not in the new 'national' states born in 1918. In any case, by the 1900s the person, the self, was understood in much more complex ways through modern psychology. Viewed in a darker light, the national 'self' seemed like a bundle of unconscious herd-like instincts, which needed to be controlled through international institutions.[29] Whether nationalism was a blessing or a curse lay at the heart of debates about peace and security in the 1920s and 1930s. Although nationalist frenzy was more consequence than cause of the Great War, the war-makers had let the genie out of the bottle and the peace-makers could not put it back.

Where does the United Kingdom fit into these patterns? Essentially as a civic nation (Britain) with an ethnic Achilles heel (Ireland). Here the dynamics of nationalism were very different from central and eastern Europe where the explosion occurred in 1918. In the UK ethnic nationalism was hotting up *before* the Great War but then it simmered down – except in Ireland where it came to the boil from 1916 with tragic and enduring consequences.

The UK originated as a 'composite monarchy' on the pattern of Spain after the dynastic marriage of Ferdinand of Aragon and Isabella of Castile in 1469.[30] Thanks to Edward I the English Crown was in control of most of Wales by the late thirteenth century; in 1542, after the English conquest of Ireland, the Irish parliament declared that Henry VIII and his heirs would henceforth be kings of Ireland as well; and in 1603 the childless Queen Elizabeth of England was succeeded by James VI of Scotland, who became James I, King of Great Britain (his preferred title was Emperor). In time dynastic fusion was rein-forced by political union. The Welsh had already been incorporated (unilaterally) in the English parliament in 1536; likewise the Scots after negotiating the Act of Union of 1707, and the Irish were included in panic after a major nationalist rising of 1798 that had been backed by an invasion force from revolutionary France.

The United Kingdom of Great Britain and Ireland, which came into being on New Year's Day 1801, was primarily a union of parlia-ments. Administratively there was much less uniformity. Wales had been brought completely under English law and administration by Henry VIII but the Scots, even after 1707, preserved separate legal and educational systems and their own established Presbyterian Church. After 1801 Ireland also retained its own administrative structure but this was more analogous to the 'pro-consular' regimes of the British colonies, with a viceroy, his court and a tangle of government departments that coexisted uneasily with the Anglo-Irish landed elite imposed on Catholic Ireland as part of the Protestant Ascendancy.[31]

Providing some kind of cement for the Union was an ideology of 'Britishness', prefigured by James I but largely the product of a series of world wars against Catholic France, especially during the long reign of George III (1760–1820). This new British patriotism was expressed in various ways – through songs, prints and cartoons, the iconography of Britannia, the cult of Nelson and new rituals of monarchy, not least the adoption of 'God Save the King' as the 'National Anthem'. France became 'the haunting embodiment of that Catholic Other' which the people of England, Wales and Scotland had been taught to fear since the Reformation. 'Confronting it encouraged them to bury their internal differences in the struggle for survival, victory and booty.'[32] Booty reminds us of the other cement of the Union apart from the Protestant faith and parliamentary government, namely the British Empire. Foreign trade, colonial administration and the army (one of the few truly British institutions) all depended disproportionately on non-English manpower, especially from Scotland. In part this reflected the superiority of Scottish universities – training grounds for doctors, lawyers and engineers – but the British Empire had a special allure for adventurers who felt excluded from the London establishment. It is not much of an exaggeration to say that 'England made the Union, but Scotland made it work.'[33]

Victorian stability and prosperity fostered the idea that Britain had become a 'constitutional nation', grafting on to the shared state structure a new sense of transcendent identity built around parliamentary government and Protestant religion. So Britishness was a form of civic nationalism, seeking to subsume conflicting ethnicities in larger political and ideological values, and this ideology helped mitigate the continued dominance of England, which accounted for three-quarters of the UK's 45 million people in 1910. But Britishness never took hold across the Irish Sea except among the Protestant elite, for whom it became a vital prop of their supremacy. Among the largely Catholic population of Ireland, opposition to British rule had become increasingly vocal in the late nineteenth century. The catalyst was a cultural revival akin to the pattern in eastern Europe. The Gaelic League, founded in 1893, sought to rekindle a sense of Irish identity, through sports such as hurling and Gaelic football and also through language and literature. One of the league's founders, Douglas Hyde, spoke of 'de-Anglicizing' Ireland: he deplored the way Irish sentiment 'continues to apparently hate the English and at the same time continues to imitate them.'[34] Hyde's campaign for a cultural renaissance was taken up by the Irish avant-garde writing in English – figures such as W.B. Yeats and J.M. Synge, pioneers of an Irish National Theatre in Dublin. The political expression of this cultural nationalism was the Sinn Féin movement ('We Ourselves'), founded in 1905. Its leader, Arthur Griffith, initially advocated a Hungarian-style form for Irish independence, modelled on the Habsburg Dual Monarchy of 1867.

This backlash against Britishness began to spread to the Celtic fringes of Britain itself. In the 1880s the Welsh revitalized the annual arts festival (*eisteddfod*); new University Colleges at Aberystwyth, Cardiff and Bangor were fused in 1893 into the National University of Wales. In Scotland the tartan-clad Highlanders – once derided as primitives not just by the English but also by Lowland Scots – were now extolled and romanticized, while the poet Robert Burns and the medieval patriot William Wallace became cult figures. This pan-Celtic revivalism was part of a Europe-wide celebration around 1900 of rural traditions against urbanized modernity – evident even in England in the 'Wessex' novels of Thomas Hardy or the folk songs embedded in the music of Ralph Vaughan Williams. But on the Celtic fringe, cultural pride had a political edge, sharpened by extensions of the UK franchise in 1867 and 1884–5 which made both local and national politics less easy for London to control. In the Habsburg domains, democracy had been kept on a leash; in the United Kingdom the fusion of democracy and nationalism helped to ignite a major political crisis.

The national question was most intractable in Ireland, which accounted for 101 of some 580 seats in the House of Commons. In the late nineteenth century four-fifths of the Irish seats were routinely won by the Irish Parliamentary Party (IPP), a tightly disciplined caucus bent on regaining Ireland's self-governing parliament. Gladstone's Liberal governments responded with Home Rule bills in 1886 and 1893, neither of which became law. In April 1912 the Liberals, now reliant on the IPP for their Commons majority, introduced a third Home Rule bill. This drove party members who wanted to maintain the Union into alliance with the Conservative Party, now renamed the Unionist Party – reflecting Tory claims that the unity and identity of the kingdom were at stake.[35]

The Irish bill of 1912 rekindled the Home Rule movement in Scotland, championed by the Young Scots – a group of social reformers within the Liberal Party. Blaming English reactionaries and the packed parliamentary timetable for blocking their efforts, they argued that there was 'not one single item in the whole programme of Radicalism and social reform today, which, if Scotland had powers to pass laws, would not have been carried out a quarter of a century ago.' Scottish radicals introduced their Home Rule bill in the Commons and in May 1913 it passed its second reading with government support. In Wales, calls for a national parliament were less clamorous: the Young Wales movement (Cymru Fydd) had collapsed in the mid-1890s. Instead passions were directed against the established Anglican Church in Wales whose endowments reinforced the power of largely English landlords. A bill to disestablish the Welsh church and take away its endowments was introduced in the spring of 1912. Devolutionists advocated what was then called 'federalism', or Home Rule All Round, envisaging parliaments in Wales and England. William Cowan, a leader of the Scottish Home Rulers, even predicted that from this 'federation of the United Kingdom' would spring 'a truly Imperial Parliament in which representatives of the Overseas Dominions' would sit 'on terms of absolute equality.' Liberal enthusiasts, including Winston Churchill (whose elaborate scheme envisaged no fewer than seven parliaments for the English regions) believed devolution was essential in the modern world to preserve union and empire, whereas diehard Unionists regarded it as the start of the destruction of both.[36]

The stakes therefore seemed huge. What's more, after a bitter political struggle in 1909–11, Asquith's Liberal government had pushed through the Parliament Act which removed the Lords' veto over legislation. Bills passed by the Commons in three successive sessions would now become law whether the Lords approved or not. In response, Unionists in Ireland and England turned to extra-legal means of opposition. Ulster Protestants, asserting that Home Rule meant Rome Rule, organized paramilitary units, the Ulster Volunteers, and nationalists responded in kind with the Irish Volunteers. Little was done by London to stop the growing militarization. The so-called Curragh Mutiny in March 1914 suggested that the British army, many of whose officers were staunchly Unionist, could not be relied upon to impose Home Rule by force. Most ominous was the increasing bellicosity of political rhetoric. The Unionist leader Andrew Bonar Law warned portentously, 'I can imagine no length of resistance to which Ulster can go in which I should not be prepared to support them.' From the other side Churchill accused the Unionists of upholding the law only when this suited their 'appetite or ambition'. The 'veto of violence', he thundered, 'has replaced the veto of privilege.'[37]

A possible way out was to exempt Ulster, home to most of Ireland's Protestants, from Home Rule but the IPP rejected partition while Irish Unionists had covenanted to keep all Ireland within the UK. In any case, in Ulster as with Czechs and Germans in Bohemia, no neat dividing line could be drawn on the ground. Catholics constituted a majority in the counties of Fermanagh and Tyrone, while in working-class areas of Belfast and Londonderry the two communities often lived in adjacent streets. On 25 May 1914 the Irish Home Rule bill passed the Commons for the third and constitutionally final time. Asquith offered Ulster a six-year opt-out but this was dismissed by Ulster Unionists: 'We do not want a sentence of death with a stay of execution for six years,' declared their leader Sir Edward Carson. In late July cross-party talks hosted by the King at Buckingham Palace broke up without agreement and jumpy British troops fired on a hostile crowd in Dublin, killing three people. The stage seemed set for civil war.[38]

What happened next was colourfully evoked in Churchill's war memoirs. On 24 July, the Cabinet, still exploring the outlines of Ulster exclusion, 'toiled around the muddy byways of Fermanagh and Tyrone' for much of the afternoon. As the meeting ended, the foreign secretary Sir Edward Grey read out a note that he had just received. Grey had been speaking for several minutes, recalled Churchill, 'before I could disengage my mind from the tedious and bewildering debate which had just closed.' The note was Vienna's ultimatum to Serbia following the assassination in Sarajevo. As Churchill took in its unyielding words, 'the parishes of Fermanagh and Tyrone faded back into the mists and squalls of Ireland, and a strange light began immediately, but by perceptible gradations, to fall and grow upon the map of Europe.'[39]

The outbreak of war transformed domestic politics. The Liberal government still forced the Irish Home Rule on to the statute book in September 1914, together with disestablishment of the Anglican Church in Wales, but implementation of both pieces of legislation was suspended for the duration of the war. The Scottish Home Rule bill failed to get a third reading through pressure of wartime business. In May 1915 Asquith formed a coalition with Unionist and Labour representation – an equivalent of the political truces in France and Germany and something that would have been quite inconceivable amid the political rancour a year before. This paved the way for a real government of national unity under David Lloyd George in December 1916.[40] So Churchill's account did prove poetically true: once war broke out, the map of Ireland and the general crisis of Britishness receded into the background as attention shifted across the Channel.

Hardliners in the Cabinet like Churchill had little doubt that Britain must enter the continental conflict. Germany's support for Austria-Hungary, which escalated rapidly into a pre-emptive war against the Franco-Russian alliance, could easily threaten the Channel ports and upset the balance of power. For them this was an echo of earlier struggles against Louis XIV and Napoleon, coming almost a century since the final defeat of Bonaparte in 1815. But their Liberal Party was deeply divided: for most of its MPs what tipped the balance on 4 August, the day Britain declared war, was the German invasion of France via Belgium, whose neutrality Britain was pledged by treaty to uphold. 'Little Belgium' became the defining ideological marker. The Kaiser's armies had flagrantly invaded a neutral nation and then flouted conventional distinctions between soldiers and non-combatants, burning the university town of Louvain and shelling the cathedral at Reims. Some 6,500 Belgian and French civilians were killed, often brutally and without provocation, by German troops during the invasion of 1914.[41]

Reports and pictures in those opening weeks of the war had a powerful effect on British opinion: 'The Oxford of Belgium burnt by the German "Huns"' proclaimed the *Illustrated London News*; 'Holocaust of Louvain' screamed the *Daily Mail*. During the autumn there were real fears that the terror would spread across the Channel. The people of Essex dug trenches in preparation for possible invasion; Scarborough, Hartlepool and other east coast towns were shelled by German warships, killing women and children. Germany's image as a nation of 'baby killers' (Churchill's phrase) was heightened in May 1915 by the sinking of the passenger liner *Lusitania*, with nearly 1,200 dead. In the face of such evidence of Hunnish militarism and barbarism, there was a broad conviction that the British stood for freedom and civilization. In Britain the reason for war was presented as essentially an issue of morality rather than self-interest. As we shall see, this would have far-reaching consequences after 1918.[42]

Lloyd George provides an instructive example of this moral nationalism. Brought up as a Welsh-speaker in rural Caernarvonshire, Lloyd George initially applied his sharp mind and silver tongue to the cause of Welsh nonconformists, attacking the privileges of the Anglican Church. Although he flirted with Cymru Fydd, asserting that the Welsh were treated like 'the niggers of the Saxon household', once he entered the Commons as a Liberal in 1890, aged only twenty-seven, he became a supporter of Home Rule All Round and won national notoriety in 1900 as a critic of the way the Boer War in South Africa was being conducted, denouncing 'this infamy which is perpetuated in the name of Great Britain' and proposing that after the war the Dutch settlers should be given 'full local autonomy'. Lloyd George was not a pacifist or an anti-imperialist – he believed in the British Empire and its place in the world – but in 1914, as the July crisis unfolded, his preference was to stay out of war. Yet, he told his wife on 3 August, 'if the small nationality of Belgium is attacked by Germany all my traditions & even prejudices will be engaged on the side of war.'[43]

It was, however, several weeks before Lloyd George spoke out in public, partly because of his immersion as chancellor of the exchequer in the financial crisis that followed the outbreak of war but also because of his own private turmoil. Eventually on 19 September – feeling, as he put it, 'about to be executed' – he gave a major speech at the Queen's Hall in London, developing the moral case for war with all the fire and fluency of his youth as a lay preacher. The German Chancellor had derided the Belgian treaty as only 'a scrap of paper'. That reminded Lloyd George of the new £1 notes he had just introduced to prevent a run on gold coins. 'They are only scraps of paper,' he declared. 'What are they worth? The whole credit of the British Empire.' He lauded the resistance of Belgium and Serbia – like Wales 'little 5 foot 5 nations' who were 'fighting for their freedom' against the great big 'Prussian Junker' storming along like 'the road-hog of Europe'. This, he told his audience, was 'a great war for the emancipation of Europe from the thraldom of a military caste' which was 'now plunging the world into a welter of bloodshed and death.'[44]

Lloyd George was typical of millions across the country. Patriotic fervour was a consequence of the war rather than a cause but, as it swelled in those first months of fighting, so political debate was refocused. The national question which (unusually in early-twentieth-century Europe) had exploded *before* the war in the UK thanks to the detonator of parliamentary politics, now seemed to fizzle out. Or rather, ethnic nationalisms were increasingly subsumed in a rejuvenated civic nationalism as the conflict pitted British values against a new and menacing Other – militaristic Germany.

In Wales, disestablishment and disendowment of the Anglican Church had satisfied the main demand of nationalists, and Lloyd George's elevation to the premiership in 1916 showed that Welshmen as well as Scots could scale the summit of the British state. Welsh-language newspapers were overwhelmingly pro-war, many peddling what historian Kenneth Morgan has described as 'a crude anti-Teutonic racism', and war orders fuelled an economic revival in the mines, factories and ports of south Wales.[45]

In Scotland, too, coal, steel and shipbuilding all boomed. By 1916 Dundee, home of the British jute industry, was producing 6 million sacks a month for sandbags in trenches along the Western Front. The war, crowed one manufacturer, had turned jute fibres into 'strands of gold'.[46] Scotland paid a big price for such profits. In proportion to its population, the country had the highest rate of army volunteering in the whole of the UK – one in six of the British soldiers of the war were Scottish – and also the highest death rate among those who enlisted. The city of Glasgow also boasted the record for war loans, contributing a staggering £14 million in one Tank Week in January 1918, eclipsing the previous weekly record (£3.5 million) set by London. Scotland's special fervour for the Great War is not easily explained, though it may have been a reflection of the country's warrior past and competing martial traditions (Highland and Lowland); but it showed that distinctively Scottish pride could be incorporated and expressed within the British war effort.[47]

In Scotland and Wales, the war boom followed by post-war recession would create real social and political tensions but, as we shall see in the next chapter, these were seen as issues of class not nation. The National Party of Scotland, precursor to the SNP, was founded in 1928, three years after Plaid Cymru in Wales, but neither had much impact. It is reasonable to suppose that 'had there been no war, some measure of Home Rule would have been on the statute book by 1920' for Scotland. Instead, participation in the struggle against Germany had strengthened a sense of Britishness in both Scotland and Wales. This would be reinforced by an even more titanic struggle in 1939–45. Only from the late 1960s, when Germany was no longer a threat, did the English Other become a bogey again and Scottish and Welsh nationalism start to revive as serious political movements.[48]

*

In Ireland, however, the story was very different. There 1914–18 had a profoundly divisive effect, generating a war for national independence and a civil war, both of which left deep and enduring scars.

In 1914 the omens had looked favourable: Britain's declaration of war on Germany did have a pacifying effect in Ireland, as Churchill said. The leader of the Irish Parliamentary Party, John Redmond, was a committed federalist, aspiring to an eventual place as a dominion within the British Empire, rather like Australia or Canada. Although a devout Catholic, his sense of Irishness was inclusive, embracing Catholic and Protestant alike, and he had not been caught up in the Gaelic revival. A stocky, serious man, Redmond was deeply affected by both the outbreak of the war and by Britain's concession of the principle of Home Rule. In September 1914 he offered the British government the manpower of the Irish Volunteers – 'not only in Ireland itself, but wherever the firing line extends'. In part this was a tactical ploy, emulating nationalist leaders on the continent who hoped that fighting for their imperial masters would win them greater autonomy. But Redmond genuinely believed Britain was waging a struggle for civilization against Prussian despotism. For him, the passing of Home Rule and the decision to fight for Belgium showed that the British leopard had now changed its spots – standing up for the liberty of small nations rather than stamping on them, as it had done with the Boers in South Africa fifteen years earlier. Redmond also hoped that if Irish Catholics and Irish Protestants fought alongside each other, rather than against each other, 'their union in the field may lead to a union in their home', so that 'their blood may be the seal that will bring Ireland together in one nation.' Dissident Irish Volunteers who broke away were dismissed by him as a bunch of 'isolated cranks' with 'no policy and no leader' who 'don't count to a row of pins as far as the future of Ireland is concerned.'[49]

Redmond might have been proved right if the war had finished quickly: Irish volunteering rates in autumn 1914 were better than in parts of England, such as the south-west and East Anglia. But as the conflict dragged on and the carnage mounted, recruitment among Irish Catholics fell away and Redmond's gamble seemed increasingly like a sell-out. 'We've Home Rule now the statute book adorning,' ran one nationalist ditty. 'We brush the cobwebs off it every morning.'[50] Nor could Redmond cash in his political chips. When Asquith formed his coalition in May 1915 the Unionist members included inveterate foes of Home Rule such as Bonar Law and Edward Carson, a leading Ulster Unionist. Redmond was offered a post but, in line with hallowed IPP policy, he refused to serve – thereby forfeiting any chance of exerting a balancing influence.

Then, in April 1916, the 'isolated cranks' cut the ground from under his feet. Their Easter Rising was intended as a desperate bid to keep the flame of Irish nationalism alive. Its principal leader, Padraig Pearse – a tall, imposing orator, usually dressed in black, and a fervent apostle of the Gaelic revival – was described by the poet William Butler Yeats as 'a man made dangerous by the Vertigo of Self-Sacrifice.' Some of Pearse's colleagues represented the rising as a serious military campaign – Joseph Plunkett, for instance, insisting that if the German spring offensive came off, tying down the British army, the rebels might hold out for up to three months after which 'the English would have to make peace'[51] – but in reality the whole operation was a quixotic gesture, botched in many of its essentials. Vital heavy weapons from Germany were intercepted by the British; the rising was delayed from Easter Sunday to the next day, throwing mobilization into chaos; and the rebels failed to seize key points such as the ill-defended Dublin Castle, establishing their HQ instead in the General Post Office, from where they proclaimed an Irish Republic. Their movement attracted little support outside Dublin and by the following weekend British troops had regained control of the city. Some 60 insurgents were killed, plus 130 troops and police, and another 300 civilians died, many of them caught in crossfire.[52]

Seen within a European context, the Irish nationalists were not unusual in trying to play off one side against another: Piłsudski did the same for Poland. What made the Dubliners of 1916 unique was mounting a rebellion against the established government while the war was at its height.[53] Initial reactions in Ireland were perplexed, even hostile. Some local women, married to soldiers in the British army, were furious that they could not collect their normal 'separation allowances' from the besieged Post Office. But there was much admiration for the courage of the rebels. The 'poor foolish young fellows made a clean and gallant fight,' wrote one Redmondite clergyman in Kilkenny. 'Hence a great wave of sympathy has gone out to their memory from every true Irish heart.'[54] Admiration then turned to anger after the ineptly brutal treatment of the prisoners by British military commanders, who were left virtually to their own devices for several weeks until Asquith got a grip on the situation. In the interim martial law was declared, 3,000 people were arrested, 90 sentenced to death and 15 executed, some of them minor figures in the rising. James Connolly, one of the leaders, was so badly wounded that he was reckoned to have only a few days to live. Yet the execution went ahead. Being unable to stand before the firing squad, Connolly was tied to a chair and then shot. The executions turned 'foolish young fellows' into national martyrs, hallowed in iconic photographs and mourning badges, while the rubble of Dublin was often likened in words and pictures to the ruins of Ypres. Pearse's suicidal gesture had worked.

Finally grasping the magnitude of the disaster, Asquith tried to implement the Home Rule Act of 1914, putting Lloyd George in charge of the negotiations. Lloyd George, conscious of Britain's growing dependence on American supplies and loans, feared that the Irish-American lobby could 'force an ignominious peace on us' unless the issue of 'Irish freedom' was settled. But even more potent were fears that some diehard Unionists would resign from the coalition Cabinet. The crunch point in July 1916 was the exclusion of Ulster from the provisions of Home Rule: Redmond would at most tolerate only a temporary exclusion, while diehards like Lord Lansdowne insisted this must be permanent. Ultimately Lloyd George and Asquith were not willing to face down the Unionists, further weakening Redmond's position in Ireland.[55]

A major reason for their circumspection was that these negotiations coincided with the start of Britain's great, hopefully war-winning offensive on the Somme. But there on the bloody slopes of Thiepval Ridge another Irish tragedy unfolded, very different from the Easter Rising but equally fateful. On 1 July the 36th (Ulster) Division lost a third of its 15,000 men, killed, wounded or missing in courageous charges against the German lines. Many of the dead had been Protestant paramilitaries in the Ulster Volunteers in 1914. By the old calendar, 1 July was the anniversary of the Battle of the Boyne in 1690, which Ulster loyalists commemorated as a famous victory over the Catholic French, and the 36th went into battle tanked up on a heady cocktail of prayers, hymns and liquor, with many officers wearing sashes of the Orange Order. Unionists contrasted the Ulster Division's self-sacrifice for civilization (including four Victoria Crosses) with the Judas-like betrayal perpetrated in Dublin. For both nationalists and Unionists, therefore, 1916 was a year of blood sacrifice but, contrary to Redmond's hopes, the bloodshed drove them further apart. The Easter Rising and the first day of the Somme would become markers for the rival ideologies.

For many Irishmen and women, the suppression of the Dublin rising unmasked the Old Adam in their historic foe, proving, contrary to Redmond, that the British Empire would still stamp on small nations. 'All changed, changed utterly,' Yeats marvelled in his poem 'Easter 1916': 'A terrible beauty is born.' Thomas Kettle, a prominent Redmondite and an officer in the 16th (Irish) Division, reflected gloomily that Pearse and his fellows 'will go down to history as heroes and martyrs, and I will go down – if I go down at all – as a bloody British officer.' Kettle, a renowned barrister and writer, was killed on the Somme in September 1916.[56] In June 1917 John Redmond's charismatic brother Willie, a major in the 16th (Irish) Division though in his mid-fifties, also died leading his men at the battle of Messines. Willie was still sure that the blood of war could heal Ireland's wounds and men of the Ulster Division did indeed form a guard of honour at his burial. But it was all too late. During 1917 the rejuvenated Sinn Féin trounced the IPP in a string of by-elections. One of the victors was Éamon de Valera, the most senior surviving commander from Easter Week, who won Willie Redmond's vacant seat. De Valera's conduct during the rising remains a matter of controversy but, like Piłsudksi in Poland, his name was made by incarceration in an imperial jail, and in 1917 he was elected Sinn Féin president. Gone was the old talk about a Hungarian-style solution to the Irish question, with separate parliaments but the same monarch: Sinn Féin was now committed to full independence as an Irish republic.

The crisis escalated in April 1918 when the British government, panicked by the great German offensive, decided that conscription, imposed on the mainland in 1916, should now be extended across the Irish Sea. The British authorities in Dublin warned that this would totally alienate nationalist opinion – 'we might as well recruit Germans', declared the army commander, who predicted 'the loss of Ireland' – but the Cabinet believed the move essential to convince British opinion that the burdens of the war were being fairly shared. The Irish Parliamentary Party had always claimed that, by holding seats at Westminster, it could protect Irish interests, so passage of the new conscription bill destroyed its last shreds of credibility.[57] Strikes and protests spread across Ireland, with most of the Sinn Féin leadership ending up in jail; even Catholic bishops came out openly against conscription. Although the crisis on the Western Front abated and Irish conscription was never seriously enforced, the political damage was irreparable. When the UK went to the polls in December 1918 the IPP was reduced to only seven MPs. Sinn Féin won 73 of Ireland's 105 seats but declined to take them up, instead convening as a revolutionary assembly in Dublin (Dáil Éireann) which proclaimed an independent Irish republic on 21 January 1919, just after the peace conference had opened in Paris. Sinn Féin couched its case in a European context, arguing that Ireland should be treated on a par with other historic, now rejuvenated nations such as Poland and Finland, but the peacemakers did not intend to apply self-determination within their own states. One nationalist complained that 'the blacks and yellows, all colours and races, may be heard before the conference, except the Irish.'[58]

So Irish independence, like that of countries across eastern Europe, was won not at the peace conference but on the battlefield, in a vicious guerrilla war against the British that lasted two and a half years. By violence and intimidation the newly formed Irish Republican Army (IRA) gradually undermined British administration – tax collection, the jury system and especially the Royal Irish Constabulary

(RIC), the largely Catholic police force – across most of rural Ireland. The British government bolstered the army and the RIC with paramilitary units raised from former British soldiers: the Black and Tans and the Auxiliary Division. Named for their initially makeshift uniforms, the Black and Tans, some 9,000 in all, were 'all English and Scotch people', an RIC veteran recalled, 'very rough, f-ing and blinding and boozing and all.' Many regarded service in Ireland as a continuation of the war. 'It was the same ribaldry and the same give and take as in the trenches,' according to one Tan. But this was a different enemy from the one on the old Western Front – shadowy, elusive and in civilian dress – so the paramilitaries soon treated all Irish as potential enemies.[59]

The 2,200 men who served in the Auxiliaries – supposedly an elite British unit recruited from ex-officers and including three VCs – were not much better. After one shoot-out, a senior British army officer noted, 'They all had the wind up, blood up, and did what they used to do in the trenches in France. In the circumstances you cannot hold them criminally responsible, but they are not fit to be policemen – but are any Auxiliaries?' An examination of personnel records suggests that the Auxiliary Division was a haven for 'psychological casualties: schoolboys who had become killers instead of going to university, working-class men disorientated by wartime promotion to the status of officers and gentlemen, fractured personalities whose childhood maladjustments had found temporary relief in the 1914–18 war and whose outward stability depended on the psychic reassurance of a khaki tunic on their back and a Webley .455 on their hip.'[60]

On the IRA side, too, many of the activists were brutalized former British soldiers – men such as Tom Barry, an ex-sergeant in the Royal Munster Fusiliers, who declared that in 1915 'I was not influenced by the lurid appeal to fight to save Belgium or small nations. I went to the war for no other reason than that I wanted to see what war was like, to get a gun, to see new countries and to feel a grown man.' Ambitious and unstable, Barry used his army training to execute some of the IRA's most cold-blooded operations. The worst area was County Cork, where over 700 people were killed between 1917 and

1923 – a third of them civilians who had no involvement with police or guerrillas. 'The political arena was transformed into a nightmare world of anonymous killers and victims, of disappearances, massacres, midnight executions, bullets in the back of the head, bodies dumped in fields or ditches.'[61]

In November 1920 the British government imposed martial law across much of the country – a propaganda own-goal comparable to the executions after the Easter Rising. The conflict escalated that winter, with most of the casualties coming not in direct clashes between rival units but through ambushes and surprise raids on soft targets. This was a dirty war of terror and counter-terror. The policy of reprisals was sanctioned by Churchill, now secretary of state for war, even though his wife, a staunch Liberal, deplored this resort to what she called 'the rough, iron-fisted "Hunnish" way'.[62] It was an apt phrase: the British authorities were using methods never sanctioned on the mainland, including paramilitary mercenaries reminiscent of the German Freikorps in the Baltic states. Martial law was never applied in Britain itself but it was in Ireland (1798, 1803, 1916 and 1920) and also in the colonies – another sign of underlying British attitudes to the Irish question.[63]

The damage this policy was doing to Britain's international image as well as its evident failure in Ireland eventually forced Lloyd George into a dramatic U-turn – accepting a ceasefire that led to the Anglo-Irish Treaty of December 1921. This conceded Dominion status to the twenty-six counties, putting them on a par with the white elite of the British Empire – Canada, Australia, New Zealand and South Africa – who remained subordinate to Britain only in foreign and defence policy. Irish supporters of the treaty argued pragmatically that this was the thin end of the wedge towards complete independence but many IRA men were irreconcilable, not because the treaty 'failed to provide a united Ireland, but because it failed to deliver the "Republic"' and required them to swear fidelity to the hated British Crown. The rift over the treaty proved unbridgeable and led in June 1922 to a ten-month civil war during which more Irish died than in the conflict with Britain. The estimated figure of 1,500–2,000 people killed included 77 republicans executed in cold blood by pro-treaty forces. Principle was involved here but so were less elevated motives: personal animosities, gang rivalries and a revolt by the young against a stratified society run by fathers, priests and employers. The civil war 'created a caesura across Irish history, separating parties, interests and even families, and creating the rationale for political divisions that endured.'[64] Historically it has been very unusual for a war of independence to be followed by a civil war: the only European example after 1914–18 was Finland and that conflict also left enduring scars. Here is another parallel between the Irish experience of the Great War era and that of eastern Europe.[65]

There are continental parallels, too, in Ulster – six counties of which were partitioned from the Irish Free State and, uniquely within the UK, given their own Home Rule parliament. The British government had hoped that partition would be a cooling-off device to allow eventually a devolved all-Ireland parliament but nationalists remained committed to independence for the whole of Ireland and so temporary expedients hardened into durable realities. The new government was bankrolled by Britain, receiving four-fifths of its income direct from the Treasury in London. As in 1914 the precise border was still disputed, especially in the largely Catholic counties of Fermanagh and Tyrone, and a Boundary Commission agreed under the Anglo-Irish Treaty toured disputed areas rather like the investigations sponsored by the Paris peacemakers in hotspots such as Teschen. In the end, however, Dublin caved in and accepted the existing border in December 1925.

Nationalists within Ulster now had to come to terms with the reality of partition, but the new statelet of Northern Ireland was structured against them. The Government of Ireland Act in 1920 had imposed proportional representation (PR) in order to protect minority interests. This did have some effect: in the 1925 general election, for instance, official Unionists were down from 40 to 32 of the 52 seats at Westminster. But nationalists continued to boycott Ulster's own parliament and this made it easy for Unionists to abolish PR, first for local elections and then for the UK Parliament. London acquiesced for fear of bringing down the Ulster government and provoking a new crisis. Unionists also had the constituency boundaries redrawn to suit their interests, bombarding the commission of inquiry with dubious maps and statistics of the sort concocted by eastern European nationalists for the Paris peacemakers. In Belfast, for instance, the Unionist constituencies each comprised fewer than 20,000 voters, whereas nationalists were piled into one mega-constituency of over 30,000. Catholics were also largely excluded from the police and civil service, under the beady eye of prime minister Sir James Craig, Ulster's bull-necked political boss. As the South became what he called a 'Catholic state', with the church's special position enshrined in the constitution, Craig boasted that 'we are a Protestant Parliament and a Protestant State.'[66]

In some ways the partition of Ireland had an air of historical inevitability about it, rooted in the seventeenth-century plantation of Scottish Protestants on the north-east of Catholic Ireland. Across the rest of the island Britishness had never taken hold and partition was under discussion well before 1914. Nevertheless the Easter Rising and the conscription crisis entrenched existing divisions, turning a fraught debate about Home Rule into a bloody war for independence and the stalemate of partition. Craig's Ulster was reminiscent of Masaryk's Czechoslovakia, with one ethno-religious group abridging minority rights to keep itself on top. The victorious British state had not been able to stop Irish independence but it did safeguard the position of Protestant Unionists, though also storing up huge problems for the future. It is interesting to imagine what could have happened if the British Empire had ended up on the losing side in 1918. Ulster Protestants, as in their worst nightmares, might then have been reduced to second-class citizens within a united Ireland, like Germans in the new Czechoslovakia. Idle speculation perhaps, but it reminds us again of why the Great War is 'the single most central experience of twentieth-century Ireland.'[67]

So the United Kingdom of Great Britain and Ireland became the United Kingdom of Great Britain and Northern Ireland, with Britain more united than before 1914 but Northern Ireland an uneasy outpost of Britishness in a largely independent but fiercely hostile island of Ireland.

Ignoring the Irish question (which most people in mainland Britain were very happy to do after 1921), what strikes one most about the British experience of 1914–18 is the contrast with that of continental Europe. Despite the panic of late 1914, Britain was never invaded or in serious danger of invasion (unlike 1940). The British were also the only civilian population virtually out of the firing line: deaths from sea and air bombardment, including the notorious raids on London by Gotha bombers were 1,266 (compared with 60,595 in 1939–45).[68] In eastern Europe, however, countries such as Poland, Romania and Serbia became killing fields – the Serb death toll of nearly a quarter of males between the ages of 15 and 49 being the worst of any belligerent. Even France and Italy, Britain's victorious allies, had to fight on their own soil: north-eastern France was ravaged, while Italy's failure to seize all the land that nationalists regarded as rightfully Italian caused a grave political crisis. Germany was not invaded, but after the war Allied troops occupied the Rhineland and the French took back Alsace and Lorraine, the spoils of 1870–1.

Britain's relative immunity from the fighting had a potentially troubling side, however. The French lost 1.3 million dead (13 per cent of males aged between 15 and 49) but this sacrifice could be 'justified' as the cost of redeeming French territory, whereas the British and Irish death toll of 723,000 (6 per cent of males aged 15–49) was not linked in the public mind to any concrete national goals – only to abstract ideals such as civilized values and even the eradication of war. As those ideals soured in the 1920s and 1930s, so doubts were aired about the point of the sacrifice. In the second part of this book we shall see how these doubts intensified after 1939–45, which became enshrined in national memory as a true war of national survival – won, moreover, at roughly half the human cost.

Only one major belligerent was more detached from the conflict than Britain – the United States, which was 3,000 miles from the battlefields of Europe. Although 4.7 million Americans were mobilized and half of them travelled to Europe, the US army saw combat for less than six months. During that short time, however, its losses in proportion to the number of soldiers engaged were actually comparable to Verdun or the Somme. The US commander John J. Pershing was sure that American-style 'open warfare' – bravura infantry attacks with rifle and bayonet – could break through where the plodding French and British had failed. The results were predictable. During the Meuse-Argonne offensive in October 1918 one American division was totally routed by a German counter-attack; another lost 5,000 men from enemy artillery before even reaching the front; while a third attacked with 12,000 men and came back with only 2,000. By the time Pershing grasped the lessons his allies had painfully learned about close cooperation between infantry, artillery, tanks and airpower, he had lost 26,000 dead in little more than a month – carnage far worse than the Civil War battles of Shiloh, Antietam, Gettysburg and Cold Harbor put together. Fortunately for Pershing the death toll never sank in at home, unlike in Britain after the Somme, thanks to a combination of tight military censorship, embedded reporters who maintained an 'enthusiastic silence' about the body count, and a crescendo of front-page speculation about the impending armistice.[69] So America's Great War was as bloody as Britain's but far shorter. As a result the official death toll was only 116,516 (0.4 per cent of males aged 15–49). Even that is a misleading figure because combat deaths accounted for only 53,402 of the total. More Doughboys succumbed to influenza than to German bullets and roughly half the 'flu victims died in the United States.[70]

For Americans the Great War was 'peculiarly an affair of the mind,'[71] evident above all in the country's sense of national identity. Many Americans regard 'nationalism' as a vice evident in others; some scholars of that 'ism' even omit the USA from their analysis.[72] Yet the United States exhibits a recognizable form of civic nationalism, akin to Britain's though with distinctive twists. The essence of its identity lies not in common ethnicity but in shared civic values: Americans, to quote Eric Hobsbawm, are 'those who wish to be'.[73] These values (for which a shorthand is 'liberty') were transplanted to the American colonies from England and then politicized by the spread of democracy, which embraced nearly all white males by the 1830s – far earlier than in Europe. Despite their English origin, these political values were trumpeted as pre-eminently American amid the anti-British frenzy that fuelled two wars of independence (1776–83 and 1812–14).

During the nineteenth century the United States became a 'nation of immigrants' originating from all over continental Europe, but the core of US citizenship remained these democratic liberties and also the use of English as the country's official language.

The infant United States was not, however, a unitary state like France or Britain but a loose federal polity, wracked for its first eighty years by secessionist forces and shamed by the persistence of racial slavery in a so-called land of liberty. These tensions culminated in the Civil War of 1861–5. The South claimed to be fighting a war of independence, akin to 1776, for what in later Wilsonian parlance would be called 'self-determination'. The North's initial aim was to stop Southern secession from what it asserted to be an indissoluble union. But, as the struggle deepened, this became for the North a war to free the slaves. At Gettysburg in 1863 President Abraham Lincoln redefined America as a single democratic nation now undergoing 'a new birth of freedom' to ensure that 'government of the people, by the people, for the people shall not perish from the earth.' His assertion that America's democracy should be a model for the whole world would be taken up fifty years later by Woodrow Wilson.[74]

Wilson's early career had been spent at Princeton – first as a professor of politics, then as president of the university – but his ambition was always to do politics for real. He was fascinated by the challenge of political leadership in an age of democracy, believing that presidents should listen to the public mood but not be constrained by it. Frankly contemptuous of Congress, which he regarded as a forum for small-minded local interests, he favoured a British-style prime ministerial approach in which the president led from the front, especially on foreign policy. Wilson was the son of a Presbyterian minister and Calvinist religion helped shape his thinking, which included a strong sense of Providence, especially where his own country was concerned. Although often depicted as an uptight academic, he was more exactly an intellectual – fluent with words (usually speaking from notes rather than a text) and often seduced by his own slogans. Nowhere was this more fatefully true than in foreign policy.

When war broke out in Europe, Wilson adopted a stance of studied neutrality. Over 8 million of America's 105 million people had been born in Germany or had at least one German parent; conversely many Czechs and Serbs in America sought the defeat of the Habsburgs to promote national liberation back home. 'The people of the United States are drawn from many nations, and chiefly from the nations now at war,' Wilson observed. 'Some will wish one nation, others another, to succeed in the momentous struggle.' To enter the war in Europe might therefore mean civil war at home and the President did not wish rival ethnic nationalisms to imperil America's overriding civic nationalism. He justified American neutrality by treating the war as a typical Old World feud, devoid of morality. One-liners about 'nothing in particular started it' and America being 'too proud to fight' did not go down well in London and Paris.[75]

When Germany's desperate resort to unrestricted U-boat warfare in 1917 forced Wilson into war, he explained his policy shift in the language of civic nationalism. His war message of 2 April envisioned a world 'made safe for democracy' (perhaps his most famous slogan), with peace 'planted upon the tested foundations of political liberty'. The enemy, Wilson insisted, was not the German people but 'Prussian autocracy'; similarly he welcomed the collapse of Tsarism as the end of a 'terrible' autocracy which had repressed the 'democratic' instincts of the Russian people. So, Wilson declared, the United States would fight 'for democracy, for the right of those who submit to authority to have a voice in their own governments, for the rights and liberties of small nations'.[76]

In short, to recast the world in America's self-image. There was, of course, more than a touch of self-deception here, given the racial discrimination endemic in the United States. When Wilson lectured Queen Marie of Romania about how her country should treat its minorities, she replied archly that of course the President must be well aware of minority issues because of the Negro and Japanese questions in the United States.[77] But, after a ruinous war in which 10 million had died, Wilson and most Americans were more conscious of Europe's defects than their own. He went to Paris in a position of great influence, yet he was venturing into uncharted waters. He was the first US president to leave the western hemisphere while in office, and none of his predecessors had been centrally involved in a European war. 'Lacking adequate guidance from the American diplomatic tradition, he internationalized the heritage of his country.' His overriding aim in Paris was to create a new framework for international relations, based on a League of Nations that would reflect the reality of nationalism yet regulate its warlike tendencies within a world that was, he believed, moving inexorably toward the triumph of democracy.[78]

But in 1919 Wilson's ideological soundbites collided with European realities. 'When the President talks of "self-determination" what unit has he in mind?' asked his frustrated secretary of state Robert Lansing. 'Does he mean a race, a territorial area, or a community?' The phrase, Lansing warned, was 'simply loaded with dynamite': it would 'raise hopes which can never be realized' and 'cost thousands of lives'. Rather plaintively Wilson told senators in 1919 that when he stated that 'all nations had a right to self-determination' he had spoken 'without the knowledge that nationalities existed, which are coming to us day after day.'[79] He also backed off from the implications of his democratic slogans, telling journalists testily, 'I am not fighting for democracy except for the peoples that want democracy. If they want it, then I am ready to fight until they get it. If they don't want it, that is none of my business.'[80]

Nor had Wilson thought through what he meant by a League of Nations. The idea originated among British Liberals, especially Sir Edward Grey. Haunted by the utter failure of diplomacy to halt the slide to war in 1914, the British foreign secretary advocated a forum for international discussion that would require nations to talk before they fought. This minimalist version of the league was always the preference in London. But on that foundation Wilson built a more elaborate edifice, whose heart was article ten of the league covenant. This committed the league to 'preserve as against external aggression the territorial integrity and existing political independence' of all member states. Breaches of this principle could be met by economic sanctions and even military force. The British and French governments went along with article ten because it signified an unprecedented and vital American engagement in global affairs. The

Foreign Office, however, was wary of such a rigid commitment to 'territorial integrity' and 'political independence' when the borders of the new Europe were so problematic but it was unable to get an equally strong commitment in the treaty for the league to promote territorial revisions if these seemed desirable in the interests of peace. Wilson regarded article ten as 'the key to the whole Covenant', considering the pledge as essentially a deterrent, so strong that it would not need to be invoked, and he did not want its wording weakened in any way.[81]

The President's intransigence became a major stumbling block when he tried to bulldoze the league through the US Senate, controlled by his Republican political opponents. They were not persuaded by his casuistic arguments about how league membership would allow America to shape world affairs without abridging its freedom of action. Wilson's arch-rival, Senator Henry Cabot Lodge, did not oppose specific commitments in Europe – for instance an Anglo-American guarantee of French security against future German aggression – but he objected 'in the strongest possible way to having the United States agree, directly or indirectly, to be controlled by a league which may at any time ... be drawn in to deal with internal conflicts in other countries, no matter what those conflicts may be.'[82] In frustration, Wilson tried to whip up popular support through a whirlwind speaking tour across the American heartland but his frenzied efforts eventually laid him low with a paralysing stroke. The administration was unable to secure the two-thirds majority in the Senate necessary to ratify the peace treaty. So the League of Nations came into existence without the most powerful of the victor nations. This left the British and French to try to make it work despite a central principle that they had not wanted – a commitment now to a new map of the Old World designed not by reason in the salons of Paris but by blood across the battlefields of Europe.

Wilson's underlying conviction, born of the tragedy of world war, was that the United States must now play a decisive role in shaping world affairs, breaking out of its isolationist tradition. He attempted to sell that to his sceptical people through the language of principle rather than interest – much as British leaders had presented the war to their own people, semi-detached from the continental cauldron. In both these countries during the 1920s and 1930s the bright language of idealism would struggle against dark post-war realities. But Wilson's seductive soundbites, expressing America's distinctive civic national-ism, would echo down the twentieth century. And the most resonant, even more than 'self-determination', was 'democracy'.

2

DEMOCRACY

The world must be made safe for democracy

Woodrow Wilson, 1917

We have got to make democracy safe for the world

Stanley Baldwin, 1928[1]

At the end of the war, declared H.G. Wells, Woodrow Wilson 'was transfigured in the eyes of men. He ceased to be a common statesman; he became a Messiah.'[2] The President was welcomed ecstatically in London on 26 December 1918, en route to the peace conference in Paris. Standing on the balcony of Buckingham Palace with George V, he acknowledged the cheers of a huge crowd. Next evening he attended a state banquet at the Palace to celebrate the Allied victory. The guests – hundreds of generals and politicians, ambassadors and ministers – represented all parts of Britain and the empire. They were resplendent in uniforms and official dress adorned with medals and jewels. 'All of the table service is of solid gold, bearing the royal arms,' Wilson's physician noted: its value was reputedly $15 million. But the guest of honour cut a very different figure. The President wore an ordinary black suit, without medals or braid. His speech of thanks was clipped and cold, making no mention of the role of the British Empire in defeating Germany. 'There was no glow of friendship or of gladness at meeting men who had been partners in a common enterprise,' Lloyd George recalled. This almost Cromwellian visitation at the pageant of princes was a dramatic sign that the President of the United States had his own agenda. The end of 1918 was the 'Wilsonian moment.'[3]

Wilson had talked of making the world 'safe for democracy' but democracy was an embattled ideal after the Great War. The crisis of 1917–18 ignited the Bolshevik revolution in Russia, offering a very different political programme which threatened to spread across Europe. The backlash against it fuelled Mussolini's fascist movement, which gained power in Italy in 1922. By the 1930s fascist or right-wing authoritarian regimes, backed by military force, had become the norm across central and eastern Europe, and above all in Germany. Even France became polarized between right and left. In this new age of communism and fascism, of mass politics and political 'supermen', the liberal variant of democracy seemed antiquated and irrelevant.

Yet, bucking the trend, Britain remained a liberal polity, adapting its representative institutions to the era of mass electorates and class politics. Socialism was domesticated and constitutional monarchy survived. Equally important, Britain retained a robust two-party system, at a time when continental politics were characterized by either a monolithic totalitarian party or by a kaleidoscope of factions. Even Ireland transcended the violence of civil war to become a stable, constitutional two-party state. Across the Atlantic in the United States not only communism but also socialism failed to take hold – divorcing the American experience from that of all Europe, Britain included.

In February 1917, the Romanovs, Europe's most repressive dynasty, were overthrown in less than two weeks. Lenin was still exiled in Zurich. 'It's so staggering,' he exclaimed to his wife. 'It's so completely unexpected.' The poet Alexander Blok likened the sudden collapse of Tsarism to 'a train crash in the night'.[4] The spark had been Russia's dire food crisis: in early 1917 a combination of military demands and appalling weather paralysed supplies, provoking bread riots in the major cities. Yet the February Revolution was largely the story of just one city, Petrograd (the wartime, de-Germanized name of St Petersburg). Measured against the rest of urban Europe, it was a very unusual city.

Petrograd was the fifth largest metropolis in Europe. A seething industrial sweatshop of 2.4 million people set in a predominantly rural country, 70 per cent of its workers were employed in factories of over one thousand people. This proportion was unmatched even in the conurbations of America or Germany. Sucked in by the war boom, the proletariat lived in the most appalling squalor. Every cellar or single-room apartment was occupied by more than three people on average – double the figure for Berlin or Paris – and roughly half the homes lacked a water supply or sewage system. A quarter of all babies died in their first year. Yet wealth and privilege stared these workers in the face – leered at them, you might say – because the main factory district, Vyborg, lay just across the Neva River from fashionable Nevsky Prospekt and the Imperial Palace. Other European capitals were also industrial centres but in Berlin, Paris and London suburbanization was more extensive: workers lived in their own slums some miles from the centre of government.[5] Equally important, Petrograd was a vast military garrison, with over 300,000 soldiers in the city and its immediate environs. One eyewitness likened this to placing 'kindling wood near a powder keg'.[6] What turned the bread riots into full-scale revolution was the mutiny of these peasant soldiers, who first refused to fire on the protestors and then took their side. Once the army command lost control of the capital, it panicked and persuaded Nicholas II to abdicate. The Tsar's brother then rejected the poisoned chalice, and so the Romanov dynasty, rulers of Russia for three centuries, came to an abrupt end. The whole business had taken ten days.

The fragility of the old order can be explained in large part because, uniquely among European states, Tsarist Russia remained essentially a personal despotism. Nicholas, like his father Alexander III, had revived the old Byzantine traditions of the Tsar as parent of his people, the embodiment of God on earth, the feudal landowner of the whole domain of Russia. Suspicious not merely of parliament but also of bureaucracy and the rule of law as fetters on their personal rule, father and son obstinately upheld their coronation oath to the principles of 'Autocracy'. As symbols of the state and its glory, the Romanovs therefore got the blame for the escalating catastrophe of the Great War. And, when the dynasty fell apart in 1917, so did the whole fabric of political and social order. Russia's problem after the February Revolution was not simply the existence of two rival power centres – the Provisional Government, based in parliament, and the Petrograd Soviet of Workers' and Soldiers' Deputies – but the general political paralysis of which this gridlock of dual power was a part. Police, judges, priests, teachers, bureaucrats, village elders, even husbands all lost their authority without the Tsar. As the country slid into anarchy, Lenin saw his chance. Far from being swept to power by the masses, as celebrated in Eisenstein's tenth-anniversary epic film *October*, he gained it through a daring, small-scale coup, over the doubts of many of his Bolshevik colleagues. The ensuing social revolution swept away the remaining vestiges of the old order, while at the top Lenin gradually centralized all power in his party. 'As a form of absolutist rule the Bolshevik regime was distinctly Russian,' observes historian Orlando Figes. 'It was a mirror-image of the Tsarist state.'[7]

The Russian revolutions of 1917 were therefore rooted in the peculiarities of Romanov rule. That was not, however, how they seemed to many contemporaries. What brought the Tsarist regime to its knees was the crisis of war mobilization, many features of which were common to Europe as a whole. Across the continent millions of men had been enlisted into the armed forces – 15 per cent of the population of the Habsburg Empire by November 1918, 17 per cent of the Kaiserreich and 21 per cent in the case of France. The strain on soldiers was immense: France's army mutinied in 1917, followed in 1918 by those of Germany and Austria-Hungary. Millions more men and women were sucked into war industries but the housing stock proved totally inadequate and pay rates failed to keep pace with raging inflation. By 1917–18 all the belligerent states were wracked by shortages of food, coal and other necessities and industrial centres such as Milan, Paris and Berlin became hotbeds of labour radicalism.

Although the pressures were mostly contained during the war, other than in Russia, after the Armistice they exploded in violent strikes and protests across Europe. Exacerbating these tensions was the demobilization, often very rapid, of millions of soldiers, schooled in violence and facing little prospect of employment as the war boom tailed off.[8]

At the time, therefore, the parallels between Russia and the rest of Europe appeared more striking than the differences. What happened in Germany in November 1918 had evident similarities with Russia's surprise revolution of February 1917.[9] Here too mutiny in the armed forces was the catalyst, although the trouble started in the provinces, rather than the capital, with an uprising among sailors in Kiel. Unrest then spread rapidly across northern Germany, the Rhineland and the south, spawning workers' and soldiers' councils (*Räte*) on the Bolshevik model, before challenging the regime in Berlin itself. Less than two weeks after the Kiel mutiny began, Germany had become a socialist-led republic and the Kaiser fled into exile in Holland. In January 1919 the German Communist Party (KPD) capitalized on the crisis by mounting its own Lenin-style bid for power in Berlin. The rising was brutally put down, the socialist government relying heavily on the army and volunteer veterans, the Freikorps, to restore order. But strikes and protests spread across Germany during the spring, with a Bolshevik republic proclaimed in Bavaria. 'It may be assumed that the rest of Germany will follow,' asserted the novelist Thomas Mann, and then 'the proletariat of the Allied countries' would have 'no choice but to do the same.'[10]

In fact, the Bavarian republic lasted only a month before being suppressed after bloody street fighting but by then Hungary had raised the Red Flag. This Soviet government was led by Bela Kun, a radical journalist before the war who had thrown in his lot with Lenin after the revolution and was bankrolled by Bolshevik money. Neither Kun nor his regime looked impressive: British diplomat Harold Nicolson described him as a 'shifty' little man with a 'puffy white face and loose wet lips' – the looks of 'a sulky and uncertain criminal'.[11] Through a frenzy of reform including the nationalization of businesses, the break-up of landed estates, a ban on alcohol and compulsory sex education in schools, Kun managed to alienate almost everyone in quick time.

The Hungarian Soviet Republic survived only for three and a half months, from March to August 1919, before it was toppled by the Romanian army.

The upheavals in Germany and Hungary, though brief, were deeply alarming. Revolution, it seemed, was not peculiar to Asiatic Russia; it could also explode in the heart of modern Europe. Contemporaries, mindful perhaps of the global pandemic of influenza in 1918–19, spoke of Bolshevism as a virus or a plague against which they had to erect a *cordon sanitaire*. This anxiety pervaded European politics immediately after the war, including in Britain. In the event, however, Bolshevism failed to take root outside the Soviet Union and strong communist parties developed in only two European states during the 1920s. One of these was Germany, where the KPD peaked with nearly 17 per cent of the vote in the November 1932 elections. But German communists failed to exploit their popular support, willing neither to participate in government nor to embark on revolution, and then they were destroyed by Hitler in 1933. During the 1920s French communists (PCF) generally won around a tenth of the vote, surging to over 15 per cent in 1936. This breakthrough was partly the result of a change of strategy, from KPD-style sectarian isolationism in the 1920s to Popular Front cooperation with other anti-fascist parties. But communist success also reflected the unique place of revolution in French political culture, going back to 1870, 1848 and 1789. In no other European country could communism be fused so powerfully with nationalism.[12]

More important in the long term than the threat of communist revolution was the new strength of the socialist left and the consequent reaction from the right. This took place amid the biggest revolution of all, the explosion of mass democracy. In France all men had exercised the vote since 1848, in Germany since 1871, while in the United States adult male suffrage (for whites) dated back to the 1830s. But in 1918 the franchise was dramatically expanded across Europe – mainly to reward the workers for their war efforts though it was also a hasty response to the precedent set by Bolshevik Russia. Many of the states of the former Habsburg Empire adopted adult male suffrage; likewise Italy and the United Kingdom. America and Germany also granted the vote to women, and the UK enfranchised females over the age of thirty. (Female suffrage was not conceded in France and Italy until after the Second World War.) The result of these changes, mostly enacted in 1918, was a dramatic expansion of the electorate – nearly threefold in both Britain and Germany. Political elites feared that workers and women would fortify the parties of the left.

Democracy was not defined simply by the franchise; it also involved the method of government. In Germany and across the former Habsburg Europe, parliaments, whatever the franchise, had previously enjoyed little say over how the polity was governed. Government ministers in imperial Germany, for instance, had been responsible to the Kaiser and not to the Reichstag. But the German revolution of 1918 harnessed the existing democratic franchise (plus women) to a new parliamentary government. In Britain and Italy the dynamic worked in the opposite direction: both states had a liberal tradition of parliamentary government which they now had to adapt for a hugely enlarged electorate. There was an added complication in most of the new states of east and south-east Europe – the constitution. With all the attention given to the 'Wilsonian moment' it is often forgotten that the constitutions of these new democracies were modelled not on America but on Europe's most renowned democracy, France – in other words a weak executive and strong legislature, with ministries formed from the balance of forces in the assembly. In such a system political stability depended on building coalitions among a mix of rival parties and the adroit use of limited governmental powers – no easy task.

Coping with the new mass democracy was Europe's great political challenge of the post-war era. On the continent, the forces of the right would prove more successful than those of the left. The two countries that mattered above all were Italy and Germany.[13] Germany's crisis has received more attention, because it laid the powder trail for another war, but Italy's rightist revolution happened more than a decade before Hitler took power and it influenced politics across Europe.

The victory of fascism in Italy reflected deep social cleavages opened up by the war. The country had remained neutral in August

1914: the decision for war in May 1915 was taken by a few political leaders against the wishes of most of the population and without even consulting the general staff. Rallying to the patriotic cause, interventionists, backed by much of the press, clamoured for the government to complete what was seen as the redemption of Italian lands from Habsburg rule, especially the north-eastern province of Trentino and the city of Trieste. Passionate *interventisti* even glorified war as an end in itself: Gabriele d'Annunzio, the flamboyant author, rewrote Christ's Sermon on the Mount to declare: 'Blessed are the young who hunger and thirst after glory, for they shall be sated.'[14] But most Catholics were lukewarm and the Italian Socialist Party – uniquely in Europe – openly opposed the war. Throughout 1916 and 1917 the army chief of staff, General Luigi Cadorna, drove his troops forward in futile offensives in the Alpine foothills along the Isonzo River, maintaining discipline by savage punishments and random executions – until the twelfth battle of Isonzo in October 1917, better known as Caporetto after the nearby town. The Habsburg army had been stiffened by German storm troopers, among them an audacious young company commander called Erwin Rommel. Their surprise attack, swooping up and down the ridges, routed the bemused Italians, who fell back to within thirty kilometres of Venice: 300,000 were taken prisoner, another 350,000 deserted. Caporetto entered the Italian language as a synonym for shambolic collapse.

Although the Italians regained most of the Trentino when the Habsburg armies collapsed, the Armistice left a sour taste. Socialists and Catholics felt grimly vindicated by the appalling losses; the military and the right blamed them for all that had gone wrong, dubbing them the 'red and black defeatists'. In October 1918 Mussolini was already damning the 'evil brood of *caporettisti*' who had 'stabbed the nation in the back'.[15] And Italy's death toll of nearly 600,000 encouraged extravagant demands, including the city of Fiume and much of the eastern Adriatic coast, to compensate for the 'mutilated victory' (*vittoria mutilata*). In September 1919 d'Annunzio, who had gained new fame as a wartime fighter pilot, took matters into his own hands. He marched into Fiume with 2,000 'legionaries' and reigned there in swaggering splendour for fifteen months. His internationally notorious act of defiance dramatized the feebleness of the Italian state.

Somewhat desperately Italy's traditional ruling elite of liberal politicians tried to play the democratic card. In December 1918 they conceded universal male suffrage to reward the troops; the following summer they introduced proportional representation, hoping to placate moderate Catholics and socialists and thereby head off extremism. Neither gamble worked: 1919 and 1920 have gone down in Italian political folklore as the Two Red Years (Biennio Rosso), with bitter strikes among tenant farmers in Tuscany and the Po Valley and in the north-west industrial triangle of Milan, Genoa and Turin. After the elections of November 1919, Italy's most open to date, the new chamber was dominated by two new mass parties: the Partito Socialista Italiano (PSI) which won a fifth of the vote and the Catholic Partito Popolare Italiano (PPI) with a third. Henceforth, any liberal government would need the support of one of them, but the PSI was committed (at least rhetorically) to revolution while the PPI was an unstable and inexperienced amalgam of different classes and did not stay long in government.

With the Italian state therefore ineffectual, a leading role in suppressing the left, as in Germany, was taken by paramilitary groups. Italy's equivalent of the Freikorps was the Fasci di Combattimento, often war veterans but also militant students, led by the former socialist editor Benito Mussolini. In the summer of 1920 his armed squads struck back in the strongly socialist provinces of north and central Italy, beating up local union members, restoring landlord power and bolstering the middle class. Hoping to co-opt this new political force into traditional politics, the liberal politico Giovanni Giolitti incorporated the fascists in his National Bloc in the May 1921 elections but that simply gave Mussolini political respectability. During 1921 he rebranded his movement as a mass party, the Partito Nazionale Fascista (PNF), while retaining the squads, who now enjoyed near immunity from police restraint. The PNF was therefore a complicated hybrid – both 'political party' engaged in the parliamentary game and also 'military organization' using applied violence.[16] And it was this dual-track approach that finally brought Mussolini to power in October

1922. With the Catholic PPI still on the margins and the PSI mount-ing a general strike, the liberal elite had nowhere else to turn. Fascist squads marched on the provincial capitals and threatened Rome: the liberal elite caved in under this intimidation and the King appointed Mussolini prime minister. The squaddies then entered the capital in triumph – an event celebrated henceforth by fascists as the March on Rome.

Hitler's success derived from a crisis of state legitimacy that was even more profound than in liberal Italy. Its roots lay in Germany's abrupt collapse after the failure of the great offensives of spring 1918. Ludendorff's panicked demand for an armistice shocked troops and public alike, who had been kept in the dark about the gravity of the situation, and it sparked the revolutions across Germany in early November. Yet the German army, though retreating, had not been routed: in the west it was not even fighting on German soil. Hence the plausibility of claims that Germany had been the victim of a 'stab in the back' (*Dolchstoss*) by socialists and revolutionaries at home. This image had Wagnerian overtones: when Ludendorff told his staff that Germany must seek an armistice, one officer tearfully recalled Siegfried at the end of *Götterdämmerung*, 'with his death wound in the back from Hagen's spear'. Ludendorff insisted that a new civilian gov-ernment 'must now clean up the mess they've got us into', even though it was his call for an armistice that started the avalanche.[17] Ludendorff's Machiavellian ploy paid off: it was the new socialist-led republican government that had to carry the can for the Armistice and the hated Treaty of Versailles. Weimar was born in original sin that nothing and nobody could redeem.

Anger was particularly intense among the extreme right-wing veteran groups such as the Steel Helmets (Stahlhelm), whose Brandenburg branch declared in 1928 that 'we hate with all our soul the present constitution of the state' because 'it deprives us of the prospect of liberating our enslaved Fatherland' and 'gaining necessary living-space in the east'. Most of the 3 million plus members of Germany's veterans' associations (*Kriegsvereinen*) in 1930 also believed that Germany had been stabbed in the back and entertained little affection for the republic. Here was fertile soil for Hitlerite dogma. Weimar's armed forces were determined to break the humiliating shackles of Versailles – a tiny army, no air force, tanks, battleships or submarines – and restore Germany to the rank of a great power. In the medium term that would mean conflict with France, eventually with Britain and America. The military considered that a republican Germany and a castrated army were 'anomalies' born of military defeat and political collapse. None of this implied automatic support for Hitler: most of the political right and the officer corps were nostalgic monarchists but they had no affection for the republic and were susceptible to firm militaristic leadership.[18]

In Germany, like Italy, the left proved ineffectual – the communists being unready to mount a revolution and the socialists reluctant to exercise constitutional power in the new republic. The socialists were, in fact, the largest party in the Reichstag for almost all the 1920s but they generally shunned coalition with the bourgeois parties. The Weimar Republic's centre of gravity therefore lay with the Centre Party, largely Catholic, and the liberal People's Party. Although post-war Germany was also plagued by street violence – the state being restricted to an army of only 100,000 under the Treaty of Versailles – this subsided after the Munich putsch of November 1923 when the Nazis tried and failed to emulate Mussolini's March on Rome. Learning the dual-track lesson, Hitler reconstructed his movement as a mass political party, the National Socialists, while also retaining the paramilitary thugs.

In Germany the turning point, quite different from Italy, was the disastrous depression of 1929–33 which, at its nadir, left over one-third of the workforce unemployed. The crisis of capitalism will be examined more fully in Chapter Four; what matters here are its political consequences. Few polities could have survived Germany's level of unemployment: voters deserted the centre for the extremes, both left and right, where the National Socialists were the big beneficiary from the election of 1930. Increasingly the Nazis seemed to offer Germany's political and military elites the equivalent of the fascists in Italy a decade earlier: a serviceable mass party to help turn back the swelling leftist tide – hence the appointment of Hitler as chancellor in January 1933. 'Don't worry, we've hired him,' joked former chancellor Franz von Papen. 'If Hitler wants to establish a dictatorship in the Reich,' predicted General Kurt von Schleicher, 'then the army will be the dictatorship within the dictatorship.' This was fatal complacency. Papen survived, just; Schleicher was murdered eighteen months later.[19]

The cult of a strong leader was central to both Mussolini's Italy and Hitler's Germany. It embodied, in vulgarized form, the ideas of Friedrich Nietzsche, whose craggy face and great drooping walrus moustache had become a cultural icon by 1900. Nietzsche was a protean thinker, whose rambling discourses and pungent slogans could be interpreted in numerous ways: talk of the 'death of God' and of a new morality 'beyond good and evil' endeared him to the radical left and the avant-garde before the Great War.[20] But increasingly it was the militaristic right who adopted Nietzsche, attracted by his contempt for 'herd-like' democracy, his insistence on the 'will to power' as life's central principle and his adulation of the *Übermensch*. That word is almost impossible to translate into English: higher man, overman and superman have all been used. Nietzsche's core meaning was probably self-mastery – in the words of biographer Walter Kaufmann, 'The man who has overcome himself has become an overman' – but Nietzsche's writings also extolled the opportunities offered by mass democracies for mastery of others. 'Men who learn easily, who submit easily, are the rule: the herd-animal, extremely intelligent, has been prepared. Whoever can command will find those who must obey.'[21]

Mussolini was an ardent admirer of Nietzsche who, he said, filled him with 'spiritual eroticism', and from whom he derived favourite phrases such as 'the will to power' and 'live dangerously'. Although formally eschewing any idea of dictatorship, he 'deliberately developed the myth of *mussolinismo* as the one essential dogma of his regime'. In 1929 he was simultaneously prime minister and the head of eight other ministries, from foreign affairs to public works. During the 1920s the cult of the DUCE (in capital letters) became a civic religion in Italy.[22]

The term *Führer* was first applied by Nazis to Hitler in the general sense of 'our leader'; but after Mussolini's March on Rome in 1922 he was lauded as '*the* leader' for whom all Germany had been waiting –

'our Mussolini'. Once the Nazis gained power, Goebbels imposed a new German greeting, modelled on Mussolini's Roman salute – right arm raised while declaiming 'Heil Hitler'. After the death of Hindenburg in 1934, the offices of chancellor and president were merged and Hitler's messianic stature was confirmed by the epic Nuremberg Party Rally, when he descended from heaven, his plane casting a cruciform shadow over the marching troops, as Rudolf Hess intoned, 'Hitler is Germany, just as Germany is Hitler.'[23] The rally was commemorated in Leni Riefenstahl's film *Triumph of the Will*, whose Nietzschean title was personally chosen by Hitler. The Führer, unlike the Duce, was not himself much influenced by Nietzsche but during the 1930s the philosopher was Nazified as a bellicose German nationalist and the apostle of an Aryan master race. The Third Reich increasingly labelled its enemies and outsiders as *Untermenschen* – a term Nietzsche had used infrequently but which, as the antonym of *Übermensch*, now became shorthand for the Jews and Slavs who had to be eliminated.[24]

How to define fascism, whether indeed any definition is possible, has engendered endless historical debate[25] but certain general features are clear from this discussion of Italy and Germany: the cult of the dynamic leader, shrewd manipulation of the new mass politics, a fierce nationalism feeding on the bitter fruits of war, and the celebration of willpower and violence. Although only three other countries – Austria, Hungary and Romania – spawned fascist movements with significant popular support, Europe in the 1930s saw a surge of anti-left politics. These included radical rightist regimes based on military rule and also conservatives who favoured nineteenth-century elitism buttressed by traditional religion. Their common denominator was a profound reaction against the failings of parliamentary democracy. In Poland, for instance, where there were 26 Polish parties and another 33 among the ethnic minorities, Piłsudski mounted a military coup in 1926 to break the political deadlock. The result was not a one-party fascist state but controlled parliamentarianism of a pre-1914 sort, regulated by the armed forces. This was a common pattern across eastern Europe, sometimes imposed – as in Bulgaria, Yugoslavia and Romania – by the monarch, whose standing had revived as the passion for democracy waned. In places this took the form of 'pre-emptive authoritarianism' – the restriction of parliamentary democracy by the elites to avert a full-scale fascist challenge from outside. Romania in 1938 was one example, following Estonia and Latvia in 1934. Only two of the 'new' states invented on the continent of Europe in 1918–19 survived to 1939 as something like liberal democracies – Finland and Czechoslovakia.[26]

During the 1930s instability spread to western Europe. French politics were hamstrung by the Third Republic's constitution (1875) which, fearful of another Napoleonic Empire, ensured a weak executive and a strong assembly, from which a variety of parties formed short-lived coalition governments. Between the triumphant Armistice of 1918 and its humiliating successor in 1940 France had no less than 42 separate cabinets.[27] In the deepening depression, French politics became polarized as the country's socialist and communist left, now the most significant in Europe, was challenged by quasi-fascist 'leagues', notably the royalist Action française and the veterans' organization Croix de Feu, which had nearly half a million members by early 1936.[28] Its leader, François de la Rocque, a retired colonel from a royalist family, deployed motorized paramilitaries to terrorize 'red districts'. With the country apparently sliding towards fascism, and mindful of the rifts among the left that had helped Hitler to power, socialists and communists forged an unprecedented Popular Front which won a majority of Assembly seats in May 1936. The new socialist premier Léon Blum pushed through long-overdue reforms – a forty-hour week with paid holidays and legalized recognition of unions – but the right was appalled. 'Behind the Popular Front', declared General Maurice Gamelin, 'one saw the spectre of Bolshevism.' Obsessed by the leftist challenge from within, France was ill-prepared to confront the threat from Hitler's Germany.[29]

In Spain political polarization resulted in all-out civil war. In 1914 the country had been a corrupt parliamentary monarchy, stabilized by Italian-style deal-making. Although Spain remained profitably neutral in the Great War, this did not save it from spasms of revolutionary violence between 1917 and 1923, during which fifteen governments came and went,[30] until stability of sorts was imposed by military dictatorship under General Miguel Primo de Rivera. So far, it seemed, Spain was following the general European pattern, but the collapse of the dictatorship in 1930 and the overthrow of the monarchy the following year ushered in Spain's Second Republic. Mass political parties took off for the first time and the pendulum lurched left and then right before a Popular Front coalition of socialists and communists gained power in February 1936. Its radical programme of land reform and seizure of estates provoked elements of the army to mount a coup in July. This unleashed a civil war that lasted nearly three years, cost over half a million lives and came, for many contemporaries, to symbolize Europe's political crisis as a whole.

The conflict is now usually depicted as a Manichean struggle between fascism and democracy. Yet General Francisco Franco was essentially a military strongman, who included the Spanish fascists (the Falange) in a Unity Party of rightists and nationalists to avoid what he deemed Primo de Rivera's 'error' of establishing military rule without a party base or ideology.[31] And on the other side the Republicans became a truly revolutionary force in many areas, enacting new rights for women, collectivizing farms and factories, and, more darkly, stirring up political terror, especially against the clergy. 'It should be clearly understood that we are not fighting for the democratic republic,' the anarcho-syndicalist union declared. 'We are fighting for the triumph of the proletarian revolution.'[32] With Soviet Russia supporting the Republic, many governments, including Britain, adopted a policy of so-called 'non-intervention', fearful that Republican victory would spread the Bolshevik virus, not least into France. But this benefited Franco, since he was backed by Germany and Italy.

The crises of 1936 in France and Spain were savage reminders of the fragility of parliamentary democracy in western Europe as well as in Germany, Italy and eastern Europe. So why was the British story significantly different? How did the United Kingdom manage a relatively smooth transition to mass democracy, with a socialist party twice forming a government, and without generating a fascist backlash?

*

A large part of the answer, again, is victory. The huge sacrifices of blood and wealth made by Britain during the war did not end in abject defeat. It was the war's losers – Russia, Germany, Austria-Hungary and the Ottomans – who descended into revolution, and also Italy, where the victory was seen as 'mutilated'.[33]

Victory had certainly not been taken for granted in Britain: indeed in the spring of 1918 politics were conducted 'under the shadow of defeat'.[34] After a winter of escalating labour protests, the German breakthrough had a sobering effect on public opinion. Official reports in mid-April spoke of 'the magical disappearance of labour opposition' and of the 'almost entire cessation of public meetings to advocate an immediate peace'. The populace in Britain (though not in Ireland) now accepted a draconian extension of the conscription laws – 'measures which only that crisis rendered psychologically possible', in the words of Lloyd George. 'Had any attempt been made to enforce them previously, it would have provoked civil disturbance and domestic collapse.' The change of mood, combined with the sudden disintegration of the enemy, helped see the government through.[35]

But if Ludendorff's hammer blows had succeeded in driving Haig's army back to the Channel, 1940-style, maybe even forcing Britain to sign a compromise peace, then the ingredients of a British stab-in-the-back myth were already there. One can see it in wartime animosity to aliens and Jews as well as growing middle-class anger about how, supposedly, industrial workers – exempt from conscription – were profiting from wartime pay rises while they paid the 'blood tax' at the front. Had Britain been engulfed in the rancorous atmosphere of defeat, observes historian Adrian Gregory, it was not inconceivable that an opportunistic journalist could have leveraged himself to power, like Mussolini, on the back of middle-class rage. Someone such as the unscrupulous jingoist Horatio Bottomley whose paper *John Bull* was predicting in May 1918 'the impending collapse of parliamentary government' because the politicians had 'sold the pass'. Such counterfactual speculation should not be pushed too far, of course, but it underlines the point that victory really mattered.[36]

However, resentment at the war's outcome is not the whole explanation for political instability across continental Europe because, as we have seen, neutral Spain and victorious France were also in turmoil by the 1930s. We have to dig deeper into the British experience to understand how the country's institutions came to terms with mass democracy.

The British elite were not complacent about the challenge facing them at the end of the war. The fall of the Tsar had been applauded by the British left: H.G. Wells demanded that Britain also throw off 'the ancient trappings of throne and sceptre', lamenting that the country had to struggle through the war under 'an alien and uninspiring Court'. Wells' jibe incensed George V. 'I may be uninspiring,' he grunted, 'but I'll be damned if I'm alien.' On a personal level this was fair comment: the King acted and sounded like a crusty English country gentleman. But many of his relatives were German princes, not least his cousin the Kaiser, and his dynasty was formally known as the House of Saxe-Coburg-Gotha – hardly ideal when London was being pounded by Gotha bombers. So concerned was Lord Stamfordham, the King's private secretary, that he invented a Shakespearean-sounding alternative, the House of Windsor, which was formally adopted in July 1917. The King persuaded his English relatives to anglicize their names and titles: the Battenbergs became the Mountbattens, for instance, and the Duke of Teck was reinvented as Marquis of Cambridge. Henceforth, it was decreed, the monarch's children would marry suitable British stock rather than foreign royalty. 'We stand at the parting of the ways,' warned Lord Esher, a trusted royal adviser, in November 1918. 'The Monarchy and its cost will have to be justified in the future in the eyes of a war-worn and hungry proletariat, endowed with a huge preponderance of voting power.'[37]

The Representation of the People Act in 1918 almost tripled the electorate to 21.4 million, or nearly 80 per cent of people over the age of twenty-one. Previously the franchise had been closely tied to the ownership or occupancy of property, on the grounds that this gave a man a stake in his locality. But the 1918 Act gave the vote to most males over twenty-one, plus most females over thirty, and no one could predict the political consequences. Lord Bryce, the distinguished constitutional historian, called it 'the wildest revolutionary change' in Britain since the Civil War of the 1640s. In the general election on 14 December 1918, the first under the new rules, the Labour Party won nearly 23 per cent of the vote and 57 of the 707 seats. This was half its target but still a momentous breakthrough.[38]

In several ways the events of 1914–18 helped resolve problems that had seemed intractable during the fraught pre-war years. For one thing there was now a coalition government which forged new working relationships 'with the men we have been fighting bitterly for years', in the words of Lord Selborne, a leading Unionist. And the franchise issue was eventually handled through a Speaker's Conference, bringing together senior backbenchers from all the main parties, who thrashed out a compromise quietly behind the scenes during the autumn and winter of 1916–17. By this time the war had changed the terms of debate about franchise reform. A quarter of the adult male population of the UK, 5.7 million men, had served in the British army during the conflict, of whom 2.45 million (43 per cent) were volunteers. Giving the vote to unpropertied working men, once seen as a rootless proletariat, was now viewed as just reward for patriotic soldiers, many of whom had chosen to risk life and limb. 'What property would any man have in this country if it were not for the soldiers and sailors who are fighting our battles?' declared Sir Edward Carson, the Ulster Unionist leader and erstwhile diehard. 'If a man is good enough to fight for you, he is good enough to vote for you.' The slogan 'one gun, one vote' proved compelling: when in 1918 the vote was given to virtually all men over twenty-one and soldiers of any age, it was also denied to conscientious objectors.[39]

This principle of useful service for the war effort also transformed the argument about women's suffrage. At least 800,000 women worked in the munitions industry during the war, winning nicknames such as 'Tommy's sister' and 'the girl behind the man behind the gun'. Hundreds of thousands more worked in factories, clerical jobs or public transport, filling the places vacated by soldiers and turning out essential supplies. 'Tents are munitions, boots are munitions, biscuits and jam are munitions,' insisted Susan Lawrence, a union leader. The 'canary girls' in the explosives factories, so-called because their skins turned jaundice yellow from the poisonous chemicals, attracted particular public sympathy. Former opponents of votes for women now conceded the principle. 'How could we have carried on the War without them?' admitted Herbert Asquith, the former prime minister, in 1917, though he argued that women had changed as well by abandoning their 'detestable' pre-war campaign of violent agitation. *Tatler*, a high-society magazine, ran a cartoon showing a female munitions worker unlocking the door of Parliament with a key marked 'National Work', having dropped the axe of 'Militancy'.[40]

Ironically, many of those canary girls did not actually gain the vote in 1918 because Parliament limited the franchise to women over the age of thirty who were householders or the wives of householders.* This, scoffed Lord Curzon, was like saying to women war workers 'we are so grateful to you' that 'we propose to give the vote to your elder sister, to your mother, to your grandmother, and to your maiden aunt'. The aim was to avoid an electorate with more females than males and also to exclude young single women who, supposedly, would vote 'more by sentiment than reason' or go for 'the best-looking candidate'. So wartime service was the criterion for conceding votes to young males but not, ultimately, to young females. While moving away from household suffrage for men, Parliament introduced what has been called 'housewife suffrage' for women. Enfranchisement of all females over the age of twenty-one had to wait until 1928.[41]

Even so, the tripling of the electorate in 1918 presaged a much more volatile pattern of politics. At the same time the country was wracked by protests on a massive scale. January 1919 saw disturbances at various army camps about the slow and unfair procedures for demobilization, including a full-scale mutiny among soldiers in Calais. Mass delegations of troops lobbied Whitehall. Pushing his way through them, Sir Henry Wilson, chief of the Imperial General Staff, told the Cabinet that the men 'bore a dangerous resemblance to a soviet'. The demobilization crisis coincided with major strikes by engineering workers on Clydeside, demanding shorter working hours, and in the spring of 1919 there were threats, as before 1914, of a

---

* Also enfranchised were women who were university graduates or who occupied property where the rent was more than £5 a year.

Triple Alliance of the coal, rail and transport unions. Since the mines and the railways had been brought under government control during the war, Lloyd George saw this as a direct syndicalist-style challenge. 'Once the strike begins it is imperative that the state should win,' he told the Cabinet. 'Failure to do so would inevitably lead to a Soviet Republic.' In the event the government bought off the miners with higher wages and shorter hours rather than 'take risks with Labour', as the Prime Minister put it, and thereby 'create an enemy within our borders'. He warned his colleagues darkly that there were now in Britain 'millions of men who had been trained to arms' and also 'plenty of guns and ammunition available'.[42]

During 1919 nearly 35 million days were lost to strikes; in 1920 close to 29 million. Taking 1917–20 as a whole 'more workers undertook strike action in those four years than in any comparable span of time in the history of British industrial relations'. This was partly a reflection of the new power of organized labour: between 1914 and 1920 union membership had doubled to 8.3 million people, nearly half the workforce.[43]

On closer inspection, however, the threat from the left was less menacing than it seemed. Despite shortages and complaints, the rationing and transport systems worked adequately: Britain did not experience the shortages of bread, coal and other essentials that undermined Tsarism in 1917 and the Central Powers in 1918. Although Britain lost 6 million work days to strikes in 1918, four times the German figure, the Kaiserreich was effectively under martial law from 1914, whereas British civil liberties had not been abridged to anything like that extent. Most British strikes were about pay and conditions, with very few of the politicized protests seen on the continent. In fact, Britain's really big strike wave began in the second half of 1918 and then peaked in 1919: workers were demanding not revolution but a recompense for victory.[44]

The coalition's dominant instinct in 1918–19, despite occasional use of force, such as on Clydeside, was to placate the workers. Aware that real wages had fallen substantially since 1914, Lloyd George and his colleagues approved large pay rises, judging for the moment that the main threat to social order stemmed from industrial militancy rather than rising inflation. Even more important, the coalition slashed working hours despite the post-war economic downturn. During 1919 over 6 million workers had their working week reduced by an average of six and a half hours – with 60 per cent of the cuts occurring between January and April when the political mood was at its most febrile. The two years after the Armistice saw 'the most marked and widespread drops ever in the length of the basic working day in British industry'. Lloyd George's mixture of general appeasement and selective toughness drew the sting of labour protest. The threat of a general strike by the Triple Alliance fizzled in 1919 and again in 1921 when the miners were deserted by the railwaymen and the dockers. In the slump of 1921–2 union membership fell sharply: it would not regain the 1920 peak (8.3 million) until after the Second World War.[45]

The strikes of 1918–20 were therefore much more economic than political in motivation. This is confirmed by the comparatively conservative temper of workers in Britain which, alone among major European states in the early twentieth century, did not produce a mass Marxist party. For this a number of reasons have been advanced. Most plants and factories were small: there were few giant companies on the scale of Vickers shipbuilders in Barrow-in-Furness or the engineering giant Armstrong-Whitworth on Tyneside. In fact, in the 1900s only half a dozen heavy industrial firms in the UK employed more than 10,000 people – unimpressive by the standards of Petrograd, Turin or Essen. Even in big companies there were strict demarcations of craft and status and this physical and social fragmentation of the workforce made it difficult to foster an overall sense of working-class solidarity. Nor did British workers feel alienated from the wider popular culture of churches, chapels and sports clubs. The Labour Party was deeply rooted in nonconformist Protestantism and its membership transcended class lines. Arthur Henderson, for instance, was not only an ironworker and union organizer who became party leader; he was also one of the country's leading lay Methodists, not to mention a founder of Newcastle United Football Club and an aficionado of lawn bowls. In Germany, by contrast, socialists (and Catholics) often lived in self-contained 'communities of solidarity' with their own schools, choirs and sports clubs.[46]

The exception that proves the rule was Red Clydeside, whose radicalism was rooted in a profound sense of alienation. Scottish industry had lagged behind England in the acceptance of collective bargaining. Employers denied union recognition, kept wages lower than south of the border and exploited ethnic divisions within the workforce, often using a loyal core of non-union Lowland skilled labour with Highlanders and Irish for more basic tasks. The employers were also prominent in the Presbyterian elite which dominated politics. On Clydeside formal trade union structures were less important than collective solidarity in the workplace, where local shop stewards wielded inordinate power during the war. Most workers were employed by a few big companies, notably John Brown shipbuilders, and lived nearby in squalid tenements: 70 per cent of Glasgow's housing stock took the form of one- or two-bedroom flats at extortionate rents. This all smacked more of Petrograd than most of Britain: the result was a stark confrontation between capital and labour, as articulated in Marxist theory. The big strike of January 1919 was carefully planned by the so-called West of Scotland Soviet under John Maclean, a former schoolteacher, who had served for a while as Bolshevik Russia's consul in Glasgow. Although the immediate demand was for a forty-hour week, Maclean saw this as a popular way to build up support for a general strike to challenge state power. Troops with machine guns were eventually deployed to restore order and the strike leaders put in jail, which the *Glasgow Herald* welcomed as a blow against 'that squalid terrorism which the world now describes as Bolshevism'. But even after Red Clydeside was crushed, Glasgow's proletarian culture remained a seedbed of radical Marxists including Britain's longest-serving Communist MP Willie Gallacher and Labour militants such as Jimmy Maxton and Emanuel Shinwell.[47]

But most of British Labour was not Marxist; in fact party members and their leaders were strongly supportive of the existing parliamentary order. Henderson took the lead in reorganizing the Labour Party in 1917 and giving it a socialist constitution with the famous Clause IV commitment to 'the common ownership of the means of production'. This was not a revolutionary gesture, however, but the very opposite. After visiting Russia that summer, Henderson returned home alarmed by the Bolshevik challenge yet convinced that radical change could be achieved through politics not revolution. A properly constituted Labour Party, he argued, was now vital to show that 'the Democratic State of tomorrow can be established without an intervening period of violent upheaval and dislocation'. In subsequent years Labour rebuffed all requests for affiliation with the party from British communists. They were, asserted the miners' leader Frank Hodges in 1922, simply 'slaves of Moscow' who were 'taking orders from the Asiatic mind'. John Clynes, the party's post-war leader, recalled that when he started in politics Labour supporters were derided as cranks. A former worker in the Lancashire cotton mills, Clynes took exception to the term. 'A crank is a little thing that makes revolutions,' he pointed out. 'We were not cranks, and we staved off a British revolution by giving British workmen a hand in the legislation by which their lives were ruled.'[48]

Workers had been given the vote in other countries after the war but the way it was done also mattered. In Italy, as we have seen, the combination of universal male suffrage and proportional representation (PR) completely destabilized the old parliamentary system. In Britain PR was being pushed in 1918 – but mainly by the unelected House of Lords, who hoped it would moderate extremist forces in the new electorate and thereby prevent a repeat of the radical Parliament of 1906–14. But the Commons firmly rejected the idea. This renewed commitment to the first-past-the-post system, at a time when proportional representation was all the rage on the continent, helped in the long run to preserve a robust two-party system in Britain.[49] The early 1920s did see a brief revival of the Liberal Party, freed from the incubus of coalition and the rift between Asquith and Lloyd George. In the 1923 election Labour and Liberals each gained around 30 per cent of the vote. But in 1924 the Liberals slipped to the position of a third force, as British politics realigned permanently into a struggle between Labour and Conservatives. The Tory decision in 1925 to abandon the title Unionist, the party's official name since 1912, was testimony not only to settlement of the Irish question but also to the centrality of anti-socialism in the Tories' new identity.[50]

On 22 January 1924, thanks to Tory miscalculation and Liberal complicity, Labour was able to form a minority government led by Ramsay MacDonald, the illegitimate son of a Scottish farm labourer. It was twenty-three years to the day, King George noted sadly in his diary, since the death of 'dear Grandmama', Queen Victoria. 'I wonder what she would have thought of a Labour Government!'[51] The right issued apocalyptic warnings – the 'sun of England seems menaced by final eclipse', lamented the *English Review* – while patriots noted that MacDonald had opposed Britain's involvement in the Great War. George V was particularly disturbed by a public reminder from Labour MP George Lansbury that 'some centuries ago a King stood against the common people and he lost his head'. But that remark lost Lansbury a seat in the Cabinet: MacDonald's paramount concern was to show how 'respectable' the party was and dispel suspicions of imminent revolution.[52] Jimmy Thomas, the former railwaymen's leader and new Colonial Secretary, expressed his 'gratitude to the constitution that enables the engine cleaner of yesterday to be the Minister of today. That constitution, so broad, so wide, so democratic, must be preserved, and the Empire which provides it must be maintained.' The evident pleasure of MacDonald, Thomas and others at hobnobbing with princes, peers and tycoons disgusted the left and titillated the right but Labour's leaders mirrored the conservative political culture of British workers. A reverence for the fundamentals of King, Parliament and empire distinguished the Labour Party from most of the European left.[53]

Although Britain's first Labour government was undermined by right-wing smears about supposed links with Bolshevism, its nine months in office in 1924 showed that the party could govern responsibly. In June 1929 MacDonald formed a second minority Labour government, this time as the largest single party in the Commons, which lasted more than two years until overwhelmed by the financial crisis of 1931. Radical slogans from 1918, such as the nationalization of land and the abolition of the House of Lords, disappeared from the party's agenda. This was partly tactical prudence, but MacDonald also genuinely believed that British socialism was lost if it degenerated into 'a guerrilla fight with capitalism'. He stuck to his pre-war conviction that true socialism came from 'the growth of society, not the uprising of a class'; it meant getting everyone to 'think and act socialistically'. Here was an essentially organic and evolutionary view of Labour's mission. Though stigmatized as a class traitor by many of the left for leading a crisis coalition government in 1931–5, MacDonald proved vital in persuading millions of ex-Liberal voters that Labour was not just a bunch of rabid socialists and class-conscious workers but was now the 'great progressive party' for modern Britain, the only realistic alternative to the Tories.[54]

The emergence of Labour, with its idiosyncratic mix of radical policies and conservative culture, was one element in the stabilization of British politics in the 1920s. The other, even more important, was the revival of the Tories but as a party of democracy. Before the war the party had lost three elections in a row, allowing the Liberals in concert with Irish Nationalists to rewrite the constitution by emasculating the House of Lords and enacting Home Rule for Ireland. But 1918, apart from franchise reform, also saw a redrawing of constituency boundaries to reduce the gross disparity between the smallest and largest seats (in 1910 the Irish constituency of Kilkenny had a few hundred electors, Romford in suburban Essex over 50,000). The redistribution of 1918 was worth about thirty seats to the Tories; even more important was the removal of some seventy guaranteed opponents after Ireland gained its own parliament in 1921. The cumulative effect of these changes was to transform the Tories from 'the natural minority party they had been before 1914 to a natural majority party until the Second World War'. Apart from the Labour governments of 1924 and 1929–31, the Tories held office for all of that time, either independently or in governments they dominated.[55]

Yet structural changes alone are not sufficient to explain the new Tory hegemony: the party also reached out to the newly enfranchised masses. Initially Tories regarded the 1918 franchise with deep apprehension – none more so than Stanley Baldwin, the shrewd, bluff Worcestershire businessman who was party leader for fourteen years from 1923 to 1937 and prime minister on three occasions (1923–4, 1924–9 and 1935–7). Although the family's iron and steel business made Baldwin a very wealthy man, his approach to both business and politics was paternalistic and inclusive – in short, a 'One Nation'

Tory. And from his mother's more cultured family (the painter Edward Burne-Jones was an uncle and Rudyard Kipling one of his cousins) Baldwin derived a keen, often romanticized sense of England's heritage. In his opinion the Great War had revealed 'how thin was the crust of civilisation': during those four years men 'climbed to the doors of heaven' but also 'sank to the gates of hell', toppling historic structures and unleashing ruinous savagery. In particular he dreaded the sudden explosion of mass politics. 'Democracy has arrived at a gallop in England', he mused in 1928, 'and I feel all the time that it is a race for life; can we educate them before the crash comes?' Here was the central plank of Baldwin's political philosophy – not to make the world 'safe for democracy', as Wilson had proclaimed in 1917, but to 'make democracy safe for the world'.[56]

Baldwin's tactical thinking was both negative and positive. The negative aspect was his readiness to attack Labour as a narrow, class-driven movement in which dangerous extremism lurked behind MacDonald's constitutional veneer. The threat of a General Strike in 1925–6 therefore proved a propaganda godsend, allowing Baldwin to claim that it was the Tories who upheld 'the lifted torch of democracy' against those making 'no secret of their desire to undermine the Constitution by revolutionary threat'. Although ready to negotiate over the underlying issue of pay and conditions in the coal industry, Baldwin was unyielding about the strike itself when this was finally declared in May 1926. 'The General Strike is a challenge to Parliament,' he told the public in a special radio broadcast: it was 'the road to anarchy and ruin.' The strike collapsed after ten days and the following year Baldwin pushed through Parliament a Trade Disputes Act to eliminate general strikes in the future through restrictions on sympathy strikes and on mass picketing.[57]

While attacking union power, however, Baldwin sought more positively to woo the new working-class voters. His initial ploy was to revive the policy of Joseph Chamberlain who had offered the new working-class voters of the 1880s a single big idea, tariff reform, to turn the British Empire into a protected trading bloc, which supposedly meant 'cheap food'. But when Baldwin espoused tariff reform again in 1923, it proved an electoral disaster – squandering a huge

Tory majority and letting in Labour. Thereafter Baldwin, backed by
progressive Tories such as Neville Chamberlain, Joseph's son, grasped
the importance of breaking down the 'working class' into interest
groups such as savers, taxpayers and ratepayers and wooing each with
targeted policies and benefits. The Tory aim, he declared, was not to
'depress' the people into a 'society of State ownership' but to raise
them up into 'a society in which, increasingly, the individual may
become an owner'. At a time when Labour was trying to address the
housing crisis through government-funded houses and flats for rent,
Baldwin insisted that 'we differ profoundly from the Socialists' in
wanting 'the people to own their own homes'. In the 1930s he started
using the phrase 'a property-owning democracy' – today a cliché but
at the time suggesting a radical new way to cope with mass politics.
Under the old householder franchise, only the few with a stake in
society were allowed the right to vote; now the Tories were offering
millions of new voters a stake in society.[58]

In fact the interwar years saw spectacular growth in home ownership. Before the Great War most accommodation, for people of all
classes, was rented from private landlords. Although exact figures are
problematic, owner-occupancy rose from about 10 per cent of the
total housing stock in England and Wales in 1914 to roughly 35 per
cent in 1938. Initially much of the increase stemmed from the sale of
rented property to sitting tenants but by the 1930s private house-
building took over as construction costs fell dramatically. A
three-bedroom semi-detached house cost £800 to build in 1920 but
less than £300 in the early 1930s. Building societies, previously
strongest in northern cities such as Leeds and Halifax, now spread
across the south and Midlands: between 1910 and 1940 their total
assets increased tenfold to £756 million. Flush with funds, they were
able to loan 90 or even 95 per cent of the total purchase price. On the
continent, by contrast, states tended to shore up the private rental
market: the housing norm in Russian, French and German cities
remained large tenements, such as the notorious *Mietskasernen* of
Berlin. In Scotland, too, where there was much less new construction,
grim multi-storey tenements remained the norm for city housing. So
England and Wales were very unusual in seeing such a dramatic

growth of owner-occupancy in urban areas: this was a 'silent' revolution behind the stereotypes about the grim 1930s.[59]

Ironically, given claims that owner-occupancy would help head off working-class militancy, the principal beneficiaries were middle class. Yet that in itself was a stabilizing force because in continental countries such as Italy in the early 1920s and Germany a decade later, it was not so much the rise of a proletariat that proved revolutionary as the political backlash against it, supported by an anxious, impoverished middle class. As we shall see in Chapter Four, Britain's post-war economy was more stable and more affluent than those on the continent (despite the slump) but the Tory bid to consolidate the middle class, attract better-off workers and stigmatize Labour as envious sectarian socialists played a significant part.[60]

Apart from the workers, the other unknown force unleashed by franchise reform was the power of women and here, too, the Tories proved successful. Before 1914 it was assumed that women did not matter politically. 'DON'T be satisfied with seeing the wife,' Tory canvassers were instructed. 'She may talk, but remember that the husband is the voter.' After 1918, however, women over thirty were also voters and ten years later it was the Tories who enfranchised all females over twenty-one, giving them parity with men. Again Baldwin moved with the times, arguing that democracy was 'incomplete and lopsided' until it embraced the 'whole people'. Equalization of the franchise became law in June 1928 despite vehement opposition from the Daily Mail which howled that 'votes for flappers' would add millions of 'irresponsible' young girls to the electoral roll and probably mean 'the exclusion of the Conservatives for a generation and the misgovernment of the country at a most critical point in English history'. Such scaremongering was an expression of the fevered anti-socialist mind of the paper's owner Lord Rothermere: after 1928 women formed a majority of the electorate and they proved highly susceptible to Tory policies, especially on domestic issues concerning the family, housing and morality. Women also proved far more active than men in party work for local constituencies.[61]

The conservative inclinations of British female voters were not atypical: the same pattern is evident in Germany where women over twenty were enfranchised at the end of the war. This was an even more explosive 'big bang' than in Britain but again with fallout that favoured the right. During the 1920s it was conservative and Catholic parties in Germany that gained disproportionately from women's suffrage. In the early 1930s 'women's votes played a substantial part in bringing Hitler to power' but that was because the Nazis had become a major political party as a result of the depression. In Britain, however, no such extreme option existed because national politics responded very differently to the economic crisis.[62]

The sustained run on sterling in the summer of 1931 obliged MacDonald's government to seek financial support from Wall Street. But the deflationary terms demanded, including a cut in unemployment benefit, split the Labour Cabinet. On 24 August MacDonald went to the Palace to tender his resignation, only to return to Downing Street a few hours later as premier of an emergency National Government, to incredulous anger among his colleagues. In this constitutional crisis George V played a significant role by dissuading MacDonald from resigning as premier: it was his appeal to patriotic duty that 'turned the scales'. The King's intervention left Baldwin with little choice but to join the National Government, despite his aversion to coalitions after the Lloyd George government of 1918–22. A delighted George V commented that 'while France and other countries existed weeks without a Government, in this country our constitution is so generous that the leaders of Parties, after fighting each other for months in the House of Commons, were ready to meet together under the roof of the Sovereign and sink their own differences for a common good'. This remark, although sententious and somewhat naïve, contained a hard kernel of truth.[63]

The party leaders formed an Emergency Cabinet comprising four Labour ministers, four Tories and two Liberals in order to push through an agreed package of deflationary measures. This, it was assumed, would take a month or so, after which a general election could be held which each party would contest on its own. But the financial crisis deepened, eventually forcing sterling off the gold standard on 21 September, and most of MacDonald's Labour colleagues moved into official opposition against the National Government. In

October 1931 the National Government went to the country as a united force, campaigning like the coalition of November 1918 on a patriotic, anti-socialist platform. With capitalism apparently in ruins, Labour abandoned MacDonald-style moderation and demanded radical socialist policies, including nationalizing the banks and key industries, while Philip Snowden, now the 'National Labour' chancellor of the exchequer, attacked his former comrades for advocating 'Bolshevism run mad'. As in 1918, anti-leftist rhetoric worked and the coalition won a massive victory, capturing two-thirds of the vote and 554 of the 615 seats; Labour ended up with only 52. Over 80 per cent of the National Government MPs were Tories. 'In effect the British nation has done through the ballot box what Continental countries can only do by revolution,' exclaimed J.C.C. Davidson, the Tory Party chairman. 'We have a Dictatorship.'[64]

The Tory-dominated National Government ran Britain for the rest of the 1930s, initially under MacDonald – shattered and ailing but a totem of its National character – and then under Baldwin and Chamberlain. In the crisis of 1940 this National Government was replaced by a genuine coalition, in which Labour abandoned its stance of official opposition to work with Churchill in the war against Germany. When one takes into account the coalitions of 1915–22 led by Asquith and Lloyd George, a larger point emerges. Between August 1914 and July 1945, the United Kingdom was ruled by coalitions for twenty-one of those thirty-one years.[65] In other words, the periods of acute national crisis – the Great War, post-war reconstruction, the crash of 1931, the depression and the Second World War – were faced by governments with some degree of cross-party support. Admittedly the Tories were generally the dominant partner but the fact that the British ship of state was a broad-bottomed vessel helps explain why it did not lurch disastrously either to port or to starboard during the storms of 1914–45.

The contrast between Britain and Germany in the early 1930s is particularly marked. The German depression proved the making of the Nazi Party as a political force; its rise to power was abetted by conservative elites, who thought Hitler could be managed, and by the head of state, President Paul Hindenburg, a retired field marshal and war hero who despised parliamentary politics. In Britain, however, the economic crisis resulted not in a government of the extreme right but an all-party coalition forged with the encouragement of the head of the state. That coalition was certainly conservative-dominated, but Britain's riposte to the socialist left in 1931 took the form of ballots not bullets. If the result was something like a dictatorship, at least it was 'Parliamentary Dictatorship' in the words of Tom Jones, deputy cabinet secretary, who voted Tory for the first time in his life because Labour 'had to be thrashed'.[66]

Was fascism ever a possibility in Britain? As on the continent, there were rumblings of discontent in the 1920s about the pernicious effects of democracy and the corruption of party politics. The right was entranced by Mussolini: in 1924 St Loe Strachey, editor of *The Spectator*, commended his 'Fascist counter-revolution' for restoring Italy's morale and unity, calling it 'one of the most notable events in the social and political history of the modern world'.[67] The nearest to a British Mussolini was the demagogic politician Sir Oswald Mosley. The son of minor Staffordshire gentry, Mosley served with distinction during the Great War and then used his brains, eloquence and wom-anizing charm for political advancement. Mosley was as promiscuous in politics as he was in bed – shifting from coalition Tory to inde-pendent and then Labour, before forming his own New Party in 1930–1 and finally heading his British Union of Fascists (BUF) from 1932, attired in trademark black shirts. Mosley advocated a larger role for the state in economic management and welcomed women into the BUF. But what really drove Mosley was not ideology but ego. When he lauded Mussolini in 1932 as 'the great Italian' who represented 'the first emergence of the modern man to power', he saw himself in the same mould.[68]

In January 1934 the BUF won the support of the *Daily Mail* whose proprietor Lord Rothermere told readers, 'At the next vital election Britain's survival as a Great Power will depend on the existence of a well-organized Party of the Right, ready to take responsibility for national affairs with the same directness of purpose and energy of method that Mussolini and Hitler have shown. ... That is why I say Hurrah for the Blackshirts!'[69] But Rothermere's passion for the BUF was another of his madcap campaigns, like the crusade against the so-called 'Flapper Vote', and it cooled rapidly after violent scenes at the BUF's big London rally in July 1934 and Mosley's shift to rampant anti-Semitism. The BUF never numbered more than a few thousand activists and it depended heavily on covert funds from Mussolini's Italy. Apart from the fact that Mosley's authoritarian, charismatic politics did not fit Britain's political culture, he was also frustrated by the timing of events. The surprise formation of a National Government in 1931 cut the ground from under his New Party, and he then pulled the BUF back from contesting the 1935 election, conscious that the worst of the depression was over. Even in the worst moments of the 1910s and 1930s, Britain's economic situation was never as dire as that of Italy or Germany: this, as well as the persistence of a coalition government, limited the appeal of extremism.[70]

Coalition politics also managed to squeeze out the most charismatic and radical figures of the political mainstream. In the 1900s the playwright George Bernard Shaw had popularized Nietzsche's idea of a superman, though he stated that he did not seek the 'salvation of society' in the 'despotism' of a 'Napoleonic' figure. The two Napoleons of interwar British politics were Lloyd George and Churchill – both of whom put policies and self-promotion before party loyalty but who also, unlike Mosley, managed to stay in the parliamentary game. Lloyd George's Machiavellian skills kept him on top of a largely Tory coalition for four years after the war: when the Tories broke away in 1922 Baldwin described Lloyd George as a 'dynamic force' which had 'smashed to pieces' the Liberal Party and could do the same to the Tories. For another decade a Lloyd George comeback still seemed possible but 1922 was really his last hurrah.[71]

The dynamic superman whom Baldwin now feared was Churchill, whose career in the 1920s and 1930s in fact points up key themes of this chapter. As we have seen, many traditionalist politicians anguished about franchise enlargement, votes for women and the socialist challenge. What marked out Churchill was the intemperateness of his reactions. In 1918–19 he was the Cabinet's leading advocate of intervention in the Russian civil war in order to suppress what he called the 'foul baboonery' of Bolshevism. He insisted that 'of all the tyrannies in history the Bolshevik tyranny is the worst, the most destructive, the most degrading' – in fact 'far worse than German militarism'. So intense and persistent was Churchill that Lloyd George warned that this 'obsession' was 'upsetting your balance'. Churchill was equally agitated by the leftist challenge at home. This prompted his return to the Conservative fold, which he had deserted in 1904 for the Liberals, thereby earning himself a lasting reputation as a turncoat. The 'enthronement of a Socialist Government', he warned in 1924, would be 'a serious national misfortune such as usually befallen great states only on the morrow of defeat in war.' In 1926 Churchill was so exercised about the General Strike that Baldwin put him in charge of the government newspaper, the *British Gazette*, on the grounds that it would 'keep him busy and stop him doing worse things.' Visiting Rome in 1927 Churchill lavished extravagant praise on Mussolini, declaring that fascist Italy had 'provided the necessary antidote to the Russian poison' and declaring, 'If I had been an Italian I am sure that I would have been wholeheartedly with you from start to finish in your triumphant struggle against the bestial appetites and passions of Leninism.'[72]

Churchill's antipathy to socialism reflected his residual Liberalism – dislike of state control and commitment to basic freedoms – but by the 1930s he began to sound openly anti-democratic. 'Democratic governments drift along the line of least resistance', he warned in 1931, 'taking short views, paying their way with sops and doles.' Out of office since 1929, Churchill seemed to be intent on stirring up all possible trouble for the National Government to force his way back into the Cabinet. He opposed proposals for greater autonomy and a broader franchise in India, calling them 'faded flowers of Victorian Liberalism which, however admirable in themselves, have nothing to do with Asia and are being universally derided and discarded throughout the continent of Europe.' In the abdication crisis he was Baldwin's leading foe, talked of as an alternative premier at the head of a 'King's Party' if Edward VIII toughed it out and forced Baldwin to resign. When the Spanish civil war broke out, Churchill tilted to Franco because of the danger of a 'Communist Spain spreading its snaky tentacles through Portugal and France'. He even told the Commons in

April 1937 that, although detesting both creeds, 'I will not pretend that, if I had to choose between Communism and Nazism, I would choose Communism.'[73]

Not surprisingly, relations between Churchill and Baldwin became seriously strained. During one of many bitter Commons debates, Churchill popped into the Gents. Only one space was vacant and he found himself standing next to Baldwin. There was an embarrassed silence, even more so than is usual on such gentlemanly occasions. Then Baldwin said, 'I am glad there is still one platform where we can meet together.'[74]

Although Baldwin never applied the phrase 'dynamic force' to Churchill, he undoubtedly perceived him as a man whose formidable will and energy was potentially destructive. He joked that when Churchill was born fairies swooped down to shower his cradle with gifts – imagination, eloquence, industry, ability and so on – all except the gifts of 'judgment' and 'wisdom'. And that, said Baldwin, is why 'while we delight to listen to him in the House, we do not take his advice.' It was also why Baldwin kept Churchill out of government throughout the 1930s, though he did make this striking observation in private in 1935: 'If there is going to be a war – and no one can say that there is not – we must keep him fresh to be our war Prime Minister.'[75]

In British politics the 1920s and 1930s were not the era of Lloyd George and Churchill, would-be supermen. This was instead the age of MacDonald and Baldwin, two leaders who pulled their rival parties towards the centre ground, trying to make socialism and democracy safe for Britain, if not the world. The political culture over which they presided, especially the cultural conservatism of Labour, helps explain why Britain was more successful than the continent in coping with the destructive legacies of the Great War.

The other important force for stability in this period was the British Crown, which rebranded itself astutely as an integral part of democratic Britain. This was all the more remarkable given the catastrophic decline of the British aristocracy, of which the monarchy formed the apex. The war itself played a part in that decline. Of all the British and Irish peers and their sons who served, one in five was killed: the death toll among the armed forces as a whole was one in eight. 'Not since the Wars of the Roses had so many patricians died so suddenly and so violently.' At the same time the aristocracy's landed wealth was decimated by taxation which, Charles Masterman declared floridly in 1922, 'is destroying the whole Feudal system as it extended practically but little changed from 1066 and 1914.' Estate duties were first imposed in 1894, with a levy of 8 per cent on estates with an inheritance value of over £1 million, but the rates soared after the war: 40 per cent from 1919, 50 per cent after 1930 and 60 per cent by 1939. At the same time the ever-rising income tax and the new Super Tax on higher incomes added to the aristocracy's burdens, leading to the break-up of many large estates across the UK, especially in Ireland and Wales. Oscar Wilde had seen the writing on the wall in the 1890s. As Lady Bracknell put it in *The Importance of Being Earnest*, 'What between the duties expected of one during one's lifetime, and the duties exacted from one after one's death, land has ceased to be either a profit or a pleasure. It gives one position, and prevents one from keeping it up.'[76]

Except, that is, if one was the monarch. From the very start the Crown was exempt from estate duties. Income tax had been dutifully paid by Queen Victoria but this burden was also gradually removed during the reign of George V. Lloyd George, when chancellor before the war, had been keen to conciliate the sovereign during the crisis over the House of Lords, and the precedent he set was extended during the 1920s and 1930s, eventually exempting from income tax both the Crown's private income as well as public money from the Civil List. So the monarchy quietly fattened while the rest of the aristocracy was cut to the bone.[77]

At the same time George V gave the Crown a new acceptability after those edgy years at the end of the war. Personally he was not very attractive: a martinet father, obsessed about Court protocol, and also rather thick. His official biographer Harold Nicolson noted (privately) that in the future king's youth 'for seventeen years he did nothing at all but kill animals and stick in stamps.' But George V had a genuine love of his country and a paternalistic feeling for his people. Coached by shrewd courtiers he learned to speak to the nation via the new medium of radio: his first Christmas broadcast in 1932 was delivered with a thick cloth on the table, to muffle the sound of pages rustling in his trembling hands. The King's charismatic, Americanized son wooed a younger generation while Prince of Wales, and was then squeezed out by Baldwin before he could do too much damage as a hands-on king, whereupon his earnest younger brother restored the decorum of family monarchy as George VI. Back in 1918 Lord Esher had noted the American threat to monarchy as well as that posed by Bolshevism: 'The strength of Republicanism lies in the *personality* of Wilson! and the use he has made of his position. It is a lesson. He has made the "fashion" of a Republic. We can "go one better" if we try.' By the end of the 1930s the new House of Windsor had personalized monarchy and made it, if not fashionable, at least acceptable in a democratic age. When one considers the damage done by continental heads of state such as Hindenburg, this was not a trivial achievement.[78]

Democratic stability was the last thing one would have predicted for Ireland in 1923. The war of independence against Britain had cost some 1,200 Irish dead; four or five thousand more were killed in the subsequent civil war of 1922–3.[79] This internecine conflict left enduring hatreds. The pragmatists who accepted the Anglo-Irish Treaty as the best deal possible for the moment – giving effective independence though within the British Empire – formed the government of the new Irish Free State. But their defeated opponents, backed by the rump of the Irish Republican Army, accepted neither the legitimacy of the Irish Free State nor the partition of the country – treating both as relics of British colonial rule at odds with the republican ideals of the 1916 Easter Rising. Consequently they would not sit in the Irish parliament, the Dáil, making Ireland effectively a one-party state dominated by the ruling Cumann na nGaedheal, or Society of the Gaels (CnaG). Here, surely, was fertile soil for continental-style fascism? Yet, by the mid-1930s, Ireland had established a viable two-party system of democratic politics, which squeezed fascism to the margins.

The architect of the new Irish state was William Cosgrave, who became CnaG leader and head of government in August 1922, following the shock deaths in ten days first of Arthur Griffith, from a heart attack, and then Michael Collins, whose head was blown off in an IRA ambush. The burly, handsome Collins was a charismatic leader; Cosgrave, by contrast, was a quiet, dapper little man who had fought in the Easter Rising but later prospered as an insurance sales-man. His priority was to create an efficient administration after the trauma of civil war. 'I am not interested in a Republican form of gov-ernment,' he declared. 'I don't care what form it is, so long as it is free, independent, authoritative and the sovereign government of the people.'[80] Cosgrave helped establish key institutions such as an unarmed police force, moving beyond the hated Royal Irish Constabulary; an effective civil service, building on British legacies; and a functioning system of taxation to recoup the country's ravaged finances. By the mid-1920s the leader of anti-treatyites, Éamon de Valera, could see that, having lost the civil war, they were now losing the political struggle as well: rigid ideological opposition to the Irish Free State served only to exclude them from influence and strengthen the gunmen.

De Valera – tall, bespectacled and austere, another charismatic – was a disciple of Machiavelli who could play both the lion and the fox. He now applied his persuasive talents to bring the bulk of the anti-treatyites in from the cold, forming a new political party, Fianna Fáil (Warriors of Destiny). In 1927 they contested an election for the first time, performing almost as well as CnaG. But in order to take up their seats in the Dáil they were obliged under the constitution to sign the hated oath of allegiance to the British Crown. De Valera huffed and puffed but eventually conformed, claiming that signing was just an 'empty formality' required in order to enter the parliament building. A devout Catholic he moved the Bible to the other end of the room, covered up the words of the oath and wrote his name in the official book, 'in the same way', he said, 'as I would sign an autograph'.[81]

Although taking a hard line with the gunmen, Cosgrave was deter-mined to forge a parliamentary democracy. 'We have been in power too long,' he admitted in 1928 to an American journalist. 'What I would like to see before long is the present Government stepping down and the other fellow taking the reins.' Rare words from a politician, especially one whose career had been forged on the anvil of civil war. The transfer of power was not quite as magnanimous as that: Cosgrave's party fought the February 1932 election almost entirely on a Red threat to law and order, with de Valera portrayed as a front for gunmen and communists. But after the votes were counted, Fianna Fáil ended up by far the largest single party; talk in parts of the army about a pre-emptive coup came to nothing. The peaceful transfer of power from the victors of the civil war to the vanquished was a landmark in Irish history. It gave people 'a new sense of *legitimacy* in the institutions of the new State,' reflected Conor Cruise O'Brien. 'Up to 1932, the State and the pro-Treaty party had seemed one thing' and this tarnished the quality of Irish independence. Now the Irish state was bipartisan property. Even de Valera later acknowledged (in private) that Cosgrave and his colleagues 'did a magnificent job'.[82]

If Cosgrave was the architect of the Irish state, de Valera shaped its sense of national identity. During the 1920s Cosgrave had avoided clashes with Britain, aware that his country's economy was still almost entirely reliant on trade across the Irish Sea. De Valera, by contrast, affirmed Ireland's national self through confrontation with everything British. He embarked on a damaging trade war, presenting it as a continuation of the war of independence: 'If the British succeed in beating us – then we'll have no freedom.'[83] He also used the abdication to sever residual constitutional links with Britain, though Ireland remained nominally within the empire. His new Irish constitution asserted jurisdiction over 'the whole island of Ireland' and, although stipulating freedom of religion, it affirmed the 'special position' of the Catholic Church, banned divorce and lauded the family as the 'fundamental unit group of Society'. A woman's place was definitely in the home.

The constitution bore de Valera's personal imprint. Even some Cabinet colleagues opposed its pinched religiosity, and secularists claimed that Catholicism was itself a form of 'colonialism' in Ireland – the land where, in James Joyce's words, 'Christ and Caesar are hand in glove'. In their view true independence required a break from Mother Church as much as Mother England. Many women also considered that de Valera had betrayed the gender equality proclaimed in 1916.

The constitution was not even 'a return to the Middle Ages' declared Mary Hayden, a leading feminist: 'It is something much worse.' In a referendum on the constitution in July 1937 only 56 per cent of valid votes were in favour. And the Catholic cast of the constitution further alienated Ulster Protestants: one of de Valera's leading critics, Frank MacDermot, said that it 'might have been specially designed to consolidate Partition.'[84]

Ireland did flirt with fascism but this proved ephemeral. In September 1933 the remnants of CnaG allied with other opponents of Fianna Fáil in a new party, Fine Gael (Gaelic Nation), led by Eoin O'Duffy, who had been sacked as police chief by de Valera. O'Duffy developed distinctly fascist tendencies: his blue-shirted paramilitary units engaged in marches and rallies, greeting their leader with 'Hoch O'Duffy' salutes. But despite his boasts that he was 'the third greatest man in Europe' after Hitler and Mussolini, Ireland did not go down the same path. O'Duffy was in fact an alcoholic who lacked political judgment: Fine Gael quickly realized its mistake and Cosgrave took over the party leadership. Although the Blueshirt membership surged to nearly 50,000 by mid-1934, this was driven by economics more than ideology. Most of the support came from County Cork and the south-west where cattle farmers had been hard-hit by the trade war that de Valera was waging with Britain. When that dispute was resolved at the end of 1934, Blueshirt numbers collapsed.[85]

A threat still lurked on the left: the IRA, though banned by both CnaG and Fianna Fáil, had not been extinguished and that legacy of the civil war would also endure. But although Ireland, unlike Britain, had a long tradition of anti-state violence which 1916–23 had exacerbated, the country lacked other key preconditions for continental fascism – notably powerful socialist and communist parties, destabilizing ethnic tensions and profound economic crisis. Between them Cosgrave and de Valera had proved Ireland's commitment to parliamentary democracy, itself a legacy of British rule, and de Valera's constitution was a conservative document, affirming traditional Catholic values shared by much of the population. It might be going too far to say that Irish history after 1918 was driven by 'great hatreds over small differences' but beneath the obsessive political discourse about right and wrong, rather than right and left, there lay a deeper consensus in Ireland about parliamentary democracy.[86]

Across the Atlantic, the United States was even less threatened than Great Britain by serious challenges from the left or right. But, paradoxically, as shown in the Red Scare of 1919, the fear of political radicalism was much greater.

As in continental Europe, so rapid industrialization in the late nineteenth century had provoked severe social conflict in the United States. The railroad strike of 1894, for instance, sparked mob violence in the streets of Chicago. Yet left-wing politics never caught on in the United States. The American Socialist Party, even at its peak in the election of 1912, won only 6 per cent of the popular vote. Eugene Debs, the party's leader and five-time presidential candidate, never advocated a 'labour party' on British lines let alone a Bolshevik uprising. In his view the real revolution America needed was a return to the spirit of 1776, which had been perverted by ruthless plutocrats and corrupt politicians. American working men, he declared, were not 'hereditary bondsmen' but the sons of 'free born' fathers who had the ballot and could use it to 'make and unmake presidents and congresses and courts'. Debs' analysis was correct but it undercut the socialist case. In Britain and Germany the rise of socialism was inextricably entangled with the struggle of working men to win the vote. In America, however, most white males had been enfranchised since the 1830s and they participated in a lively two-party system. Workers therefore saw little need for a new class-based party to advance their goals.[87]

America's major unions also operated within the political system. The most significant was the American Federation of Labour (AFL), led for forty years by Samuel Gompers, a Jewish immigrant from London's East End. Gompers had no time for socialists, convinced they cared only for their party. He believed that unions were an integral part of American business, like management, rather than a subversive force, and declared that 'we American trade unionists want to work out our problems in the spirit of true Americanism.' Gompers wanted to foster unions for individual trades rather than creating a single union for a whole industry; he also concentrated on skilled craftsmen and did little to organize unskilled workers in manufacturing industry. Even after a wartime surge in numbers, there were only 4 million union members in the United States in early 1919 – half the total in the UK, a country with less than half America's population.[88]

So Debs and Gompers managed to Americanize socialism and unions, undermining their radical potential. But there were deeper social reasons why socialism failed to catch on in America. The German commentator Werner Sombart noted the high standard of living there relative to Europe: 'this prosperity was not in spite of capitalism but because of it.' American workers, he declared, were too comfortable to be radical: 'All Socialist utopias came to nothing on roast beef and apple pie.' Sombart was painting too rosy a picture because millions of American workers lived in grinding poverty, but many did eventually rise into the middle class, or watched their children do so. Even more important, hundreds of thousands of workers moved to better jobs in another city or in the burgeoning suburbs. The United States had an unusually high degree of geographical mobility compared with Europe and this helped to undermine the sense of local working-class community that sustained socialism in urban Britain and Germany.[89]

An equally significant obstacle to class consciousness was racial and ethnic division. Wartime demand for industrial workers drew several hundred thousand blacks from the rural south into northern cities such as Chicago, Pittsburgh and Detroit. Yet America's strict racial divide cut across any sense of mutual solidarity with white workers. Many of the latter were recent immigrants from Europe, part of an unprecedented influx of 15 million people during the quarter-century from 1890 to 1914. Whereas earlier migrants had come mainly from Britain, Ireland, Germany and Scandinavia, most of these New Immigrants originated from Italy, Russia, the Balkans and the Austro-Hungarian Empire. They included future household names such as Irving Berlin and Sam Goldwyn, both of them Jews fleeing the Russian Empire. Although some new immigrants – such as Jewish garment workers in New York – became ardent socialists, most had little sense of class consciousness, being divided from their fellows by language, religion and lifestyle and inhabiting their own tight ethnic communities. In the dark alleys and dank courtyards of Lower Manhattan, reporter Jacob Riis noted, one might find little colonies of Italians, Germans, French, Africans, Spanish, Bohemians, Russians, Scandinavians, Jews and Chinese – a 'queer conglomerate mass of heterogeneous elements, ever striving and working like whiskey and water in one glass.' Since these immigrants were eligible after five years to become naturalized US citizens and therefore voters, they were much keener to keep their jobs and avoid a police record than to agitate for a left-wing utopia.[90]

So the failure of European-style radicalism to develop in the United States reflects the deep structures of American politics and society. Yet the aftermath of the Great War was also hugely significant. American workers, like those in Britain, demanded a payback for victory. One of the achievements was the Nineteenth Amendment, finally giving the vote to women, but 1919 also saw a surge of industrial militancy with one worker in five out on strike – a higher level of unrest than ever before in US history. And on 2 June parcel bombs exploded at the homes of prominent figures in cities from Boston to Pittsburgh. The US Attorney General, A. Mitchell Palmer, had the whole front of his Washington home blown in. In response the Justice Department rounded up several thousand radicals, mostly foreigners, often arresting them without warrant and beating them up. The 'Palmer Raids' broke the American communist movement, a mere 70,000 strong, and the Industrial Workers of the World (IWW), a revolutionary syndicalist union of similar strength.[91]

The Red Scare, though brief, left lasting scars. In American politics communism was now firmly off-limits and socialism marginalized. Union membership slumped from a peak of 5 million in 1920 to 3 million in 1933 and the unionization of heavy industry did not take off until the late 1930s. Although there were marked differences between Republicans and Democrats, ideologically these two mainstream parties would have fitted on the centre to right of the European political spectrum. Left-wing politics European-style were virtually unknown to Americans and therefore easily stigmatized as Bolshevik.

In foreign policy, too, American reactions to the Russian revolution were extreme. Unlike the countries of western Europe, the United States, though trading with Russia, did not extend diplomatic recognition to the new Soviet government all through the 1920s. Instead it stuck to a line enunciated in August 1920 that no diplomatic relations were possible with a government whose leaders had declared that 'the maintenance of their own rule' depended on 'the occurrence of revolutions in all the other great civilized nations, including the United States.' This non-recognition policy failed to achieve its aim of promoting regime change within Russia, so in 1933 President Franklin Roosevelt accepted that the Soviet Union was a reality and initiated formal diplomatic relations. He was struck by his wife's experience when opening a rural school. On the wall was a world map with a 'great blank place' where the Soviet Union should have been; the teacher said they were even forbidden to speak about it. In 1933 Roosevelt finally put the USSR on the map, but in the American mind it would remain a blank space, and one that became deeply sinister after 1945.[92]

When Woodrow Wilson spoke in 1917 of making the world safe for democracy, he envisaged the export of political values already deeply rooted in American life. Although the Soviet Union began to function as a new Other for American political identity, symbolizing what the United States was not, overall the Great War had a limited political impact in America. In Europe, however, the introduction of a democratic franchise, coupled often with parliamentary government, amounted to a political explosion, shaking some states to their foundations. Hence Baldwin's assertion that the real problem was making democracy safe for the world. As we have seen, Britain was more successful in doing so than most of continental Europe, where liberal democracy had withered by the early 1930s. But the Wilsonian challenge was global in its implications. Outside Europe, the debates about nationalism and democracy would be played out in a global arena where empires still held sway.

3

EMPIRE

The War demonstrated – I might say revealed – to the world, including ourselves, that the British Empire was not an abstraction but a living force to be reckoned with.

David Lloyd George, 1921

The problem of the twentieth century is the problem of the color-line, – the relation of the darker to the lighter races of men in Asia and Africa, in America and the islands of the sea.

W.E.B. Du Bois, 1903[1]

In Britain the Great War is now remembered mainly as a European conflict. The images that lodge in our minds are the rubble of Ypres, the glutinous Flanders mud and the ravaged landscape of the Somme. Rupert Brooke's famous lines in 'The Soldier' about 'some corner of a foreign field / That is for ever England' evoke verdant cemeteries along the old Western Front, even though Brooke himself was buried on a dusty island in the Aegean. The consequences of the war are also viewed largely through a European prism. As we saw in the previous two chapters, the collapse of the Romanov,

Hohenzollern and Habsburg empires in 1917–18 spawned a tribe of fractious nation states whose instability and enmities were at the root of another European conflict.

Yet the Great War was also a world war, with global repercussions. It ended with a carve-up of Germany's colonies in Africa and Asia and the disintegration of the Ottoman Empire which had ruled the Near East for four hundred years. The German colonies were simply redistributed among the main victors, to lasting anger in China, but on the ruins of Ottoman rule five new states were created on putatively national lines – Syria, Lebanon, Iraq, Palestine and Transjordan. From empire to nation – the pattern seemed similar to Europe, except that in the Near East the 'nations' were even more artificial and they existed only within a new imperial framework, imposed by Britain and France.

In this story the United States, despite its 'Wilsonian moment', was largely a bystander. Although Wilson's slogans about self-determination and democracy spurred anti-colonial nationalists, it is too much to claim that 1919 marked 'the beginning of the end of the imperial order in international affairs'.[2] On the contrary the Great War proved to be an 'imperial moment' when the British and French empires lurched to their zenith. The British were 'the principal victor in this war of empires', observes historian John Darwin. 'They lost less and gained more than all the other original combatants', snatching 'an imperial triumph' from what seemed as late as June 1918 to be 'the jaws of a continental defeat.'[3] But this frenzy of 'war imperialism' would have lasting consequences for Britain and for the countries under its sway.

To a degree unimaginable today, British leaders of the early twentieth century were 'at home' with the empire.[4] They thought imperially, conceiving of Britain as an imperial nation: indeed that was central to their conception of Britishness. But it is equally important to note that their empire did not accord with the modern stereotype of imperialism as the West's iron rule over the Rest. Although the British Empire embraced some 400 million people in the 1900s – 10 per cent of them in Britain and 75 per cent in India – it was actually something of a ragbag. There were a few colonies of British settlement such as Canada and Australia, which had evolved towards self-government on the Westminster model. More common were colonies of rule, ranging from India to Nigeria, where British officials tried to secure key strategic and economic benefits in collaboration with local elites. The empire included fortresses such as Gibraltar, zones of military occupation (Egypt) and remote islands such as the Pacific outcrop of Pitcairn (a mere two miles wide). Canada and India dated back to the eighteenth-century wars against France, whereas British Africa had mostly been acquired in the partitions of the late Victorian era.

Many of these heterogeneous 'possessions', notably India, had started out as areas of commercial influence whose governance Britain had gradually, often reluctantly, assumed. In fact British global hegemony derived in large measure from a web of trade and shipping, investment and financial services that spread out from the City of London across the world to countries that were in no sense formal colonies, such as China, Argentina and the United States (which accounted for one-fifth of British foreign investment in 1914). Britain's 'invisible empire'[5] was far more extensive and economically important than that of France, whose merchant navy amounted to only 12 per cent of Britain's tonnage. In line with its Eurocentric defence priorities, France invested more heavily in Tsarist Russia than in its colonies – 25 per cent against 9 per cent of total French foreign investment in 1914.[6]

Britain's empire, visible and invisible, proved vital for waging the Great War. In 1904 military planners predicted that a future conflict between Germany and Britain would be like 'a struggle between an elephant and a whale' because each, 'though supreme in its own element, would find it difficult to bring its strength to bear on its antagonist'. When war did come a decade later, Germany, the continental land power, developed whale-like capabilities in the form of a formidable U-boat fleet but Britain, the traditional maritime power, eventually proved a more versatile amphibian, using its command of the seas to mobilize massive armies from the empire as well as the UK and to deploy them not just in France but also in Africa and the Middle East. Five million of the 7 million troops that the British government moved overseas were British and Irish (roughly 70 per cent) but 15 per cent came from India and the other 15 per cent from the four main settler colonies – Canada, Australia, New Zealand and South Africa – known as the 'White Dominions'. Although France mobilized significant forces from black Africa, no other belligerent relied so heavily on colonial manpower. For Britain this imperial war effort was also the means for empire-building. In November 1918 54 of the 67 British divisions were fighting in France; likewise 10 of the 12 Dominion divisions, increasingly used as crack assault troops. It was mainly South African troops who seized the vast German colonies of south-west and east Africa. And it was a largely Indian army, nearly a million strong, which conquered much of the Ottoman Empire in 1917–18.[7]

Yet this imperial moment was unforeseen and largely unplanned. The day after war was declared in 1914 a British Cabinet committee stated firmly that the objective of the war was not to acquire more territory and that any land campaigns outside Europe must be undertaken by 'local' forces because no British troops could be spared from the Western Front.[8] The Royal Navy was determined to neutralize the threat from German cruisers to Britain's lines of supply and communications, so Berlin's global network of cable and wireless stations, of naval bases and coaling stations, was therefore an important target. But the forces Britain used for these operations, being 'local', had their own local ambitions. In the Pacific, Samoa and New Guinea were captured within a few weeks by troops from New Zealand and Australia, whose governments wanted permanent annexation. And Britain's ally Japan, who had defeated both China and Russia over the previous two decades, exploited the European crisis in 1914 to expand further in East Asia. Instead of merely dealing with German cruisers, as Britain intended, the Japanese quickly seized the German naval base of Tsingtao in China and the German-owned railway that ran through the Shandong peninsula. They followed up with a series of Twenty-One Demands for commercial and economic rights in China as a whole. Impotently, the British Foreign Office advised the Cabinet to 'bide our time in China till the war is over and trust to being then able to repair the damage', but this would prove a vain hope. Within a few months of the start of the European war, German territory in Asia and the Pacific had fallen to local forces that had no intention of pulling out.[9]

In Africa it was a similar story of opportunistic escalation. Britain's initial objectives were specific strategic targets but within a few weeks of the outbreak of war British forces in West Africa had seized not merely Germany's radio station at Kamina but the whole of its colony of Togoland. The French authorities in equatorial Africa had grander ambitions. Acting without authorization from Paris, they overcame tenacious German resistance to take all the Cameroons by early 1916. Further south, the British Dominion of South Africa had its eye on territorial gains, like Australia and New Zealand in the Pacific. During 1915 South African forces overran German South-West Africa (present-day Namibia) but German East Africa (roughly modern Tanzania), proved a much harder nut to crack. Jan Smuts, the South African commander, had hoped to keep this a white man's fight but he was obliged to make use of black troops from West Africa. Even so German East Africa did not surrender until two weeks after the Armistice in November 1918.[10]

It was in the Middle East that the most significant imperial legacies of the war are to be found. The decline of the Ottoman Empire had been a recurrent headache for nineteenth-century European diplomats and in retrospect it is easy to see 1914–18 as the inevitable last rites for Europe's notorious 'Sick Man'. Only in the 1920s was Turkey reborn under Mustafa Kemal as a 'modern' secular state. Recent scholarship has, however, painted a more complex picture of the late Ottoman Empire, galvanized by the so-called 'Young Turk Revolution' of 1908 and given a new Islamic coherence after losing the Christian Balkans in 1912–13. During the Great War the reconstituted Ottoman army performed surprisingly well, sustaining several fronts spread over hundreds of miles from Armenia to Sinai, from Baghdad to Beirut. It is going too far in the opposite direction to assert that in 1914 'the Ottoman Empire was not sick; it was wounded by its enemies, and finally murdered,'[11] but recent revisionism has highlighted the fatal consequences of total war for the Ottomans, as for the Habsburgs. Otherwise Ottoman rule, which allowed considerable cultural and religious autonomy to non-Muslims, might have staggered on. Certainly its collapse would not have been as abrupt and total as happened in 1918.[12]

The term 'Young Turks' conjures up in the West an image of liberal, modernizing reformers; in fact the officers who led the Committee of Unity and Progress (CUP), to use the proper name of their movement, were essentially Turkish nationalists. Their ideology, inspired by the invented ethnicities of contemporary Europe, stood in tension with the loose civic nationalism of the traditional Ottoman Empire, which rested on the loyalty of all ethnic and religious groups to the Sultan and his household (for whom 'Turk' signified a yokel from the backwoods of Anatolia). The CUP called for a new 'national awareness' that was 'Turkish, Muslim, and modern'.[13] Not only was this new nationalism internally divisive (Christian Armenians were massacred in hundreds of thousands in 1915), it was also fiercely expansionist. Ismail Enver, the Young Turk leader, saw the war as a chance to liberate the Turkic peoples of Asia from Russian rule and forge a Greater Turkey. His obsession with the Caucasus, especially after the Russian revolution, was a prime reason why the Ottoman armies in the Levant in 1918 were left too weak to hold back the British.

By then Britain had built up the Middle East into a major theatre of war, to an extent inconceivable in 1914. It is also at odds with our modern fixation on the Western Front, apart from the apparently bizarre but tragic sideshow of Gallipoli. In fact the Gallipoli campaign started out in the spring of 1915 as a quick-fix plan to send warships through the Dardanelles and shell Constantinople, on the assumption that the rickety Ottoman government would panic and sue for peace. Even after the operation had escalated to a troop commitment of 400,000 men, only to end with humiliating evacuation in January 1916, the British still underestimated Ottoman fighting power. In late 1915 Indian army units were sent up the Tigris valley from Basra, where they were protecting Britain's oil interests on the Persian Gulf, on the assumption that they could soon capture Baghdad and redeem the shame of Gallipoli. Instead tough Turkish resistance and the collapse of supply lines forced 13,000 troops to surrender at the town of Kut in April 1916 – a humiliation that was likened to Yorktown in 1781. The outcry in Britain about the debacles at Gallipoli and Kut helped topple the Asquith government. This marked a turning point: henceforth Britain's war against the Ottoman Empire became a serious operation fuelled by revenge. One British army, now properly supplied, marched up the Tigris into Baghdad in 1917 while another slogged up the coast from Egypt into Palestine. These were major campaigns, involving nearly a million men. During the course of the whole war the British Empire deployed about a third of its troops on the various Ottoman fronts.[14]

Revenge aside, ideology also featured in the Middle Eastern war. To boost morale at home when the Western Front was deadlocked, the government played up the 1917 victories in Palestine as 'the last Crusade' which had finally ended 400 years of Ottoman oppression in 'the Holy Land'. These were themes that resonated with a populace steeped in biblical Protestantism. Lloyd George, raised a strict Baptist in Wales, celebrated a campaign in which 'every hamlet and hill' – places such as Beersheba and Hebron, Bethany and Bethlehem – 'thrills with sacred memories'. He confessed, 'I was brought up in a school where I was taught more about the history of the Jews than about the history of my own land.' But the crusading theme was soft-pedalled in the Middle East. When General Sir Edmund Allenby entered Jerusalem in December 1917 he did so on foot, in a deliberate contrast with the Kaiser's visit in 1898 on horseback wearing a white cloak and plumed helmet. With his eye on Muslim opinion, so important in the Indian Empire, Allenby promised to protect the holy places sacred to all faiths. The Palestine campaign was therefore presented to show the superior morality of Britain's empire compared with that of its enemies.[15]

Geopolitics also loomed large for the British. In the spring of 1918 Russia's exit from the war, Germany's victories in France and Ottoman capture of the oil port of Baku on the Caspian Sea conjured up nightmare visions of the Kaiser and his allies driving across the Caucasus towards India. 'We must stop the wave of German influence sweeping right into the heart of Asia,' a panic-stricken Lord Milner warned Lloyd George.[16] During the autumn, of course, British fears were dispelled by the sudden collapse of Germany and the Ottomans, leaving British armies in control of Syria, Palestine and Mesopotamia. But by now policymakers in London were convinced that the Middle East, hitherto a minor British interest, must henceforth be treated as the fulcrum of imperial defence. This new and, as it proved, durable strategic imperative was a direct result of the Great War.

Keenest to exploit the new situation was Lord Curzon, foreign secretary from 1919 to 1924. A grandee with 'enamelled self-assurance', to quote Margot Asquith, Curzon had been Viceroy of India for nearly seven years at the turn of the century and this shaped his conception of British foreign policy. 'As long as we rule India we are the greatest power in the world,' he pontificated in 1901. 'If we lose it we shall drop straight away to a third rate power.' Viewing the empire from this India-centric perspective Curzon saw Britain's victories in the Middle East as a golden opportunity to strengthen the forward defences of the Raj. He even wanted a British protectorate in Persia and 'strong independent states' on the ruins of the Tsarist Empire in the Caucasus, backed by British power. Balfour, Curzon's predecessor as foreign secretary, objected. The gateways of India were 'getting further and further from India' he remarked sardonically. 'We are not going to spend all our money and men in civilizing a few people who do not want to be civilized.' The Cabinet agreed with Balfour, ruling out a long-term British presence in Georgia or Azerbaijan.[17]

But even if Curzon's position was extreme, in 1919 there was heady optimism in London that British occupation of much of the Middle East could be turned into a permanent sphere of influence. The Cabinet envisaged new client regimes to control Palestine, Syria and Mesopotamia. There was also general agreement that the oppressive Turks must be completely crushed, and even driven from Constantinople – now under Allied occupation. Lloyd George, fired with Gladstonian passion about Turkish barbarities, wanted to build up the Greeks once again as a force in Asia Minor – as they had been before the Turks destroyed the Byzantine Empire in 1453. It was as if half a millennium could simply be expunged from the annals of humanity.

This can-do belief in British might and right – reminiscent in our own time of hubristic American neo-cons – even brought Britain into confrontation with its main wartime ally. In December 1918, just three weeks after the end of an epic European war in which the British had fought alongside the French, Curzon warned the Cabinet that 'the great power from whom we have most to fear in future is France'. At the Paris peace conference Lloyd George took a keen personal interest in advancing Britain's position in the Middle East whereas France's prime minister, Georges Clemenceau, focused on Germany and Europe. French diplomats and colonial lobbyists were furious, complaining of 'a total capitulation' over French interests in Syria, and eventually even Clemenceau took up the cudgels, outraged at what he called Britain's 'unbridled avarice'. During one furious row the French premier offered his British counterpart a choice of swords or pistols.[18] But during 1919 the two governments gradually reached a modus vivendi because London's champagne moment turned into a painful hangover. The heady mood of war imperialism was dispelled by international realities – particularly the new Wilsonian constraints on empire, the mounting evidence of British overstretch, and the conflicting promises made to Britain's wartime allies. Each of these three factors deserves closer attention because they would define Britain's new empire in the Middle East.

Wilson's slogans about 'self-determination' and the 'equality of nations' were seized on by anti-colonial agitators in 1918. On Armistice Day the US consul general in Cairo reported 'a tendency in all classes of Egyptians to believe that President Wilson favors self-government throughout the world and that he will champion the right of the people of this country to govern themselves.' An Indian nationalist reckoned that if Wilson had visited Asia he would have been greeted like 'one of the great teachers of humanity, Christ or Buddha'.[19]

But, as we saw in Chapter Two, the President had given little thought to the implications of his words. Sharing the racial prejudices of most Americans of his era, he believed that self-determination in the non-white world should come through gradual reform not sudden revolution. In any case, he had enough problems at Paris adjudicating the fate of post-war Europe. As colonial nationalists lobbied the peace conference, parroting his slogans, an alarmed Wilson deleted from the League's draft Covenant a clause to apply the principle of self-determination to future claims for territorial adjustment. He also shied away from challenging the empires of his allies – acquiescing in the British protectorate in Egypt, sending only a polite acknowledgment to a nationalist petition from India and reluctantly allowing Japan to retain Shandong rather than hand back the province to China. The President privately defended this settlement as 'the best that could be had out of a dirty past' but he was denounced internationally for violating his own principles. In Beijing the deal over Shandong provoked a mass demonstration at the Tiananmen Gate on 4 May 1919 by 3,000 students, who went on to ransack the houses of 'national traitors' in cahoots with Japan. Protests spread to other cities and Chinese delegates in Paris refused to sign the Treaty of Versailles. The May Fourth Movement became a nationalist legend in China, for right and left alike.[20]

Too late Wilson glimpsed the 'tragedy of disappointment' that his seductive words would set in motion. 'People will endure their tyrants for years', he mused in November 1918 on the boat across to Europe, 'but they will tear their deliverers to pieces if a millennium is not created immediately.' Resentment was certainly pervasive by mid-1919. In Egypt Wilson's endorsement of British rule came as 'a bolt of lightning' journalist Muhammad Haykal recalled: it seemed like 'the ugliest of treacheries'. In China Mao Zedong likened Wilson in Paris to 'an ant on a hot skillet'. He just 'didn't know what to do' when surrounded by 'thieves' such as Clemenceau and Lloyd George. Mao was one of many disillusioned Chinese nationalists who turned to communism in the wake of the May Fourth Movement. Right across the colonial world, in fact, Leninism gained from Wilson's shattered credibility. But the discourse of self-determination, which Lenin and Wilson had both popularized, was now part of the discourse of international politics.[21]

A more lasting legacy of Wilsonianism was the institution of mandates. Unlike all Britain's previous wars for empire the territorial gains from the Great War were not to be annexed outright but held as 'mandates' from the League of Nations in trust for the native inhabitants. On this the President was adamant, insisting that otherwise the League would become a 'laughing stock' if it simply allowed the Great Powers to share out 'the helpless parts of the world'. Whereas the French tried to oppose the President outright, Jan Smuts of South Africa believed that British imperial interests could be dressed up in Wilsonian garb and he developed the idea of mandates. His original scheme did not apply to Germany's colonies in Africa and the Pacific because, he claimed, they were 'inhabited by barbarians' who 'cannot possibly govern themselves'. Smuts wanted to annex German South-West Africa (roughly the size of England and Wales) to his own country; similarly Australia coveted New Guinea, and New Zealand eyed Samoa. At Paris Wilson was particularly offended by the Australian premier Billy Hughes, a crass little nationalist who, waving a grossly distorted map, insisted that 'the Pacific Islands encompassed Australia like fortresses' and that they were as vital to his country 'as water to a city'.[22]

The President dug in, so Smuts refined his scheme into three classes of mandates, graded in terms of supposed readiness for self-rule. Class C amounted to virtual annexation, with minimal League accountability, and most of the Pacific conquests fell into that category – giving virtually a free hand to Japan, Australia and New Zealand. The B mandates were little different, apart from League supervision of open trade; under this scheme the French and British (including Smuts) got most of what they wanted in German Africa. But the A mandates covered peoples deemed close to self-rule where the mandatory powers, instead of governing, would simply provide 'administrative advice and assistance'. This was the category into which the Ottoman Middle East fell, which meant that, although the British and French were free to partition the region between them, they had to engage in what has been called 'a protracted, wearisome, and public debate about how undemocratic rule over alien peoples (accepted before the Wilsonian era as an entirely normal state of affairs) could be justified.' This was the real significance of the mandate system, not as a novel form of imperialism but as a new system of international accountability.[23]

Wilsonianism therefore imposed a significant constraint on Britain's new Middle Eastern Empire, but equally important was growing British concern about global overstretch. When the Armistice was signed the British had 3.5 million troops at their disposal worldwide but this figure fell to 800,000 a year later and 370,000 by November 1920. The mutinies of early 1919 convinced the Cabinet that conscription could not be retained for long in peacetime Britain and so, after a one-year extension, it expired in March 1920. Thereafter the British reverted to the pre-war practice of a volunteer regular army, yet the Cabinet had now taken on commitments vastly larger and more volatile than in 1914. A year after the Armistice Sir Henry Wilson, chief of the Imperial General Staff, fumed that 'we have between 20 and 30 wars raging in different parts of the world', which he blamed on Britain's political leaders who were 'totally unfit and unable to govern'. Wilson's deputy, General Sir Philip Chetwode, warned colourfully that 'the habit of interfering with other people's business, and of making what is euphoniously called "peace" is like "buggery"; once you take to it you cannot stop.'[24]

The Cabinet's penchant for novel military interventions was not the only problem: in 1919 the British also faced serious unrest in heartland colonies. In March a crackdown on nationalist agitators in Egypt sparked strikes, marches and sabotage in which 800 people died. In May the Afghan government seized the opportunity to invade India, starting a border war that lasted most of the summer. All this at a time when Sinn Féin had declared independence and Ireland was sliding into the vortex of terror and counter-terror, tying down some 30,000 British troops by the winter of 1919–20. Henry Wilson, a diehard Irish Unionist who was later gunned down by the IRA, warned that 'surrender to the murder gang in Ireland', an integral part of the UK, would have 'a deplorable and very immediate effect' on nationalist agitators in Egypt and India.[25]

Some British policymakers blamed all these troubles on Woodrow Wilson and his 'impossible doctrine of self-determination'[26] but in reality the causes lay deep in indigenous societies. The 'great acceleration' of global change in the late nineteenth century had already eroded peasant agriculture through the spread of cash crops, urban manufacturing and international markets.[27] Mobilizing the European empires for world war had even more explosive effects, very evident in the Egyptian crisis. Despite British occupation from 1882, Egypt had remained officially a tributary of the Ottoman Empire but after the Ottomans declared war in 1914 Britain imposed martial law and declared Egypt a British 'protectorate'. Wartime British rule penetrated deeper into peasant life through higher taxes and the demand for labour and animals, while tighter controls over food, weapons and transport eroded traditional privileges of the elite. The 1919 crisis culminated in a power struggle between the Sultan's court and dissident notables who used popular unrest and Wilsonian rhetoric as political weapons against the regime.

Although Egyptian nationalists later talked up 1919 as their 'Revolution', a combination of British force and tactical concessions soon defused the worst of the crisis. In February 1922 Britain abandoned the protectorate and recognized Egypt as an 'independent sovereign state', buying off the political elite and separating it from popular discontent – thus breaking the unholy alliance that had been behind the crisis of 1919. The British retained only some 'reserved powers' including trusteeship of foreign interests (such as the Suez Canal), supervision of foreign policy and complete freedom of movement for British troops – but these, of course, were the essentials. 'Why worry about the rind', asked Curzon grandly, 'if we can obtain the fruit?'[28]

The pattern was similar elsewhere. Beleaguered and overextended, the British government tried to pull back after 1919 from the heady ambitions of war imperialism. But this was particularly difficult in the former Ottoman Middle East because of conflicting territorial deals with key allies. In May 1916 diplomats Sir Mark Sykes and François Georges-Picot concluded a secret agreement delineating British and French spheres of influence in most of the old Ottoman Empire: this gave the British control of what is now southern Iraq and the French most of present-day Syria and Lebanon. Meanwhile Sir Henry McMahon, the British high commissioner in Egypt, had been corresponding with Hussein bin-Ali, leader of the Hashemite clan and guardian (Sharif) of the holy places of Mecca. MacMahon made

vague but sweeping promises to Hussein about the post-war 'independence of the Arabs' in order, as he put it, to 'tempt the Arab
people into the right path' and encourage a revolt against Ottoman
rule.[29] When the Bolsheviks published the Allied secret treaties in late
1917, the British and French were seriously embarrassed because the
Sykes–Picot condominium, though phrased in general terms, clearly
conflicted with what had been promised to the Hashemites.

The Hussein–McMahon correspondence was also at odds with the
declaration made by Balfour, as foreign secretary, in November 1917
that the British government supported 'the establishment in Palestine
of a national home for the Jewish people'. Although Balfour also
pledged that 'nothing shall be done which may prejudice the civil and
religious rights of existing non-Jewish communities in Palestine' –
actually 90 per cent of the population – it was clear from the start that
'home' was a euphemism for an eventual Zionist state. *The Times*
printed the Balfour Declaration under an unequivocal headline:
'Palestine for the Jews'.[30]

The British had got themselves into a monumental mess in the
Middle East, signing agreements that, as Balfour later admitted, were
'not consistent with each other' and represented 'no clear-cut policy'.
In part the chaos reflected a chronic lack of co-ordination between
London, Cairo, Delhi and Basra. The High Commission in Cairo
focused on the Arabs, exaggerating their capacity to mount a major
revolt, whereas policymakers in London, lobbied by Zionists, fixated
on the supposed influence of international Jewry in key Allied countries. 'The vast majority of Jews in Russia and America, as, indeed all
over the world, now appear to be favourable to Zionism,' Balfour
assured the Cabinet in October 1917. A pro-Zionist declaration
would therefore be 'extremely useful propaganda both in Russia and
America'.[31]

Yet Britain's diplomatic mess was the result of cynical opportunism
as much as bureaucratic confusion. After Russia's collapse the Middle
East campaign became overwhelmingly British. The French had
barely a thousand troops in the Middle East in November 1918; to
their fury, the armistice with the Turks was concluded unilaterally by
a British admiral. The mood in London became distinctly bullish. The

British had captured three or four Turkish armies, and 'incurred hundreds of thousands of casualties in the war against Turkey,' Lloyd George declared. 'The other Governments had only put in a few nigger policemen to see that we did not steal the Holy Sepulchre.'[32] Unwilling to share the hard-won spoils of victory, for much of 1919 the Cabinet hoped to wriggle out of the Sykes–Picot deal, product of a very different era of the war. It wanted Palestine and possibly even Syria as a buffer zone to protect Egypt. The Cabinet also firmed up MacMahon's pledges to the Arabs: a declaration of November 1918 claimed that Britain and France were fighting for 'the complete and definite emancipation of the peoples so long oppressed by the Turks and the establishment of national governments and administrations deriving their authority from the initiative and free choice of the indigenous people.'[33]

British policy in the Middle East therefore grew out of calculation as much as confusion – in ways that expressed deeper assumptions about nations and empires. 'The weak point of our position', Balfour observed, 'is that in the case of Palestine we deliberately and rightly decline to accept the principle of self-determination.' The word 'rightly' is worth a moment's comment. Balfour, though a particularly passionate Zionist, spoke for most British policymakers who considered the Arabs no more capable of administering themselves than the 'Red Indians', to quote a senior official at the India Office. The Jews, by contrast, were seen (albeit with more than a touch of anti-Semitism) as a people who for centuries had made money and made history – in fact as a nation in embryo. 'Zionism is a purely nationalistic question,' Balfour observed in September 1918, 'just as much as that of Poland, Esthonia or any other of the hundred and one nationalities who now demand our support to secure their self-determination.' Indeed the Zionists built up their contacts with editors and politicians in London in ways similar, say, to Thomas Masaryk and the advocates of Czechoslovakia. But the persuasive power of lobbyists such as Vladimir Jabotinsky and Chaim Weizmann depended on the prior assumption, generally accepted in the Cabinet, that the Jews constituted a nation not a religion.[34] By contrast British leaders regarded the Arabs as an inert, backward mass, unready for nationhood, who should be managed by the old imperial practice of client regimes. And this could be accommodated to the new verities of Wilsonian self-determination and the mandates system. 'We could maintain an Arab façade and yet ensure British paramountcy,' argued Edwin Montagu, secretary of state for India.[35]*

And so a new order gradually emerged in the Middle East in 1919–20, based on earlier deals with the Hashemite clan but also on a new mood of Anglo-French compromise. Sharif Hussein's son Feisal had led the Arab revolt against the Ottomans. Tall, dignified and regal, the Western ideal of an Arab chieftain, he made a powerful impression at the Paris peace conference and was then installed by the British as their client ruler of Syria ('British imperialism with Arab headgear' remarked one French diplomat sourly).[36] But as the manpower crisis bit hard in the autumn of 1919, Lloyd George belatedly decided to honour the Sykes–Picot agreement and let the French have Syria. When Britain pulled out its troops, Feisal was quickly evicted by the French. As a consolation prize for the Hashemites, the British installed Feisal as their client in Mesopotamia, cobbled together from three diverse Ottoman provinces – Basra, Baghdad and Mosul. They also established Hussein's brother Abdullah in Transjordan, invented in 1922–3 in the hope of harmonizing Britain's other set of conflicting promises – to the Arabs and the Jews. The official British mandate in Palestine covered a huge, ragged area, stretching from the Mediterranean far across the Jordan River, in some places three hundred miles into the desert. By establishing another Hashemite client in the larger but sparsely populated region east of the river (Transjordan), while restricting the Jewish Homeland to a narrow but fertile sliver of land running west to the coast (redefined as Palestine), British officials sought to square the dual promise in the Balfour Declaration to both create a Jewish National Home and respect the rights of existing

* Whether Jews constituted a religion or a nation was an issue that divided the two Jewish members of the Cabinet. Herbert Samuel was a staunch Zionist but Montagu, his cousin, insisted that Britain was his 'national home', where his family had lived for generations. Montagu wanted his co-religionists to be treated as 'Jewish Britons': Zionism, he claimed, encouraged the impression that they were 'British Jews' of dubious patriotism.

inhabitants. The two pledges would somehow be embodied in these two states, Palestine and Transjordan, even though neither of them was really viable economically.

France also split its mandate for political convenience, carving a separate Lebanese state out of Syria. As with the British in Palestine, both religious and strategic reasons played a part. Since 1860 Mount Lebanon had been an autonomous province of the Ottoman Empire, with France offering special protection to its Maronite Catholic community. When the French took over Syria in 1920, they acceded to Maronite demands to enlarge their isolated hinterland province westward to the coast, north-east into the fertile Beqaa Valley and eastward almost to Damascus. The French expected this 'Greater Lebanon' to be a valuable client state, totally reliant on French protection, with Beirut and Tripoli as useful naval bases to match the British further south in Haifa and Jaffa. But their state-building created a Palestine-style communal problem because the additional territory was predominantly Muslim, reducing the fragmented Christian community to barely half the population. And the expansion of Lebanon at Syria's expense created abiding irredentist anger in Damascus.

Although the new map of the Middle East followed some Ottoman administrative boundaries, the successor states had largely been invented by the British and French. In some ways this paralleled the cartography of post-Habsburg Europe. But eastern Europe had a pre-history of nations and kingdoms and the war also aroused powerful nationalist movements with influence in London and Paris. In the Middle East, by contrast, the success of Zionism points up the failure of Arab nationalism to take hold at a popular level. Nor were the Middle Eastern mandates, unlike the post-Habsburg states, in any real sense democratic. The French never really tried to develop democracy, ruling Syria and the Lebanon largely by force; the British did establish representative institutions but these were only skin-deep. By 1932 the Mesopotamian mandate had been converted into a nominally independent state, Iraq, but the British still pulled the strings; parliamentary elections masked a spoils system among the Arab elite.

In Palestine, democracy stood no chance in such a divided community. The Arabs refused to accept the existing Jewish presence, let alone further immigration, and in 1922–3 they boycotted plans for an elected legislative council bringing together Muslims, Christians and Jews. Thereafter, Britain ruled Palestine autocratically as a crown colony, restraining the Jews, supposedly an embryo democratic nation, and also denying the Arabs any training in parliamentary politics. In fact, Palestine proved unique in the history of British imperialism. Although essentially a colony of occupation, held for strategic reasons, it was also a colony of settlement, except that the settlers were not British but Jews. But, unlike the rest of Britain's settler colonies, there was never any real prospect of accommodation between settlers and natives.[37]

The British and French were drawing lines in the sand, both literally and metaphorically, yet their inscriptions would mark the region to the present day. In Palestine, where a peaceful transfer of power was impossible, the Zionists gained the upper hand in 1948, driving out many of the Palestinian Arabs. Control of the fertile Jordan valley then became central to the wars between Israel and its neighbours. Further north, the ideal of *Syrie intégrale* hung like an eternal question mark over the independence of Lebanon, as became clear in the conflicts of the 1970s and 1980s. In Iraq, British backing for the minority Sunni Muslims against the Shia majority and the Kurdish north created fault lines that endured long after the Hashemite carpetbaggers were toppled in 1958, as was brutally evident during the dictatorship of Saddam Hussein.[38] Ironically it was Jordan, the least plausible mandate, which proved the most durable. Despite many vicissitudes and a continued democratic deficit, Abdullah's Hashemite descendants survived into the twenty-first century.

In today's Middle East it is therefore easy to discern the Great War's long shadow. Yet the flaws in the post-Ottoman settlement were not immediately evident. Risings in Mesopotamia and Syria had been quelled by the mid-1920s and Palestine remained manageable until the Arab revolt of 1936–9, triggered by rising Jewish immigration from Germany and Austria after Hitler gained power. In all of these states the situation only became really explosive after the Second World War, whereas in eastern Europe the intertwined problems of nation, state and democracy came to a head in the 1930s, proving an important contributory cause of that second war. For much of the interwar era the post-Ottoman Middle East was relatively stable: despite the challenges from Wilsonian rhetoric and nationalist agitation, empire was still a fact of international life.

One other feature of Britain's post-1918 position in the region should be emphasized – oil. Although Europe had gone to war in 1914 by steam train, the fuel that won the war was oil, not coal. The internal combustion engine proved crucial not only for tanks and aircraft but also for trucks to supply the troops, and Britain, France and America were far better endowed with petroleum than the Central Powers. As Curzon put it, the Allies 'floated to victory upon a wave of oil.' The British kept their eyes on this prize. 'Oil in the next war will occupy the place of coal in the present war,' warned Cabinet secretary Maurice Hankey in 1918, and the 'only big potential supply' for Britain lay in Persia and Mesopotamia, which made control of them what he called 'a first-class British war aim'. Balfour entirely agreed but, he added, 'I do not care under what system we keep the oil.' The Mesopotamian mandate proved a convenient alternative to annexation – less costly to maintain and also less offensive to Wilsonian sensitivities. With the British government having a controlling interest in the Anglo-Persian Oil Company and British finance prominent in the Royal Dutch/Shell combine, the country was well placed in the 1920s and 1930s with regard to the one vital natural resource that the British Empire lacked.[39]

Looking beyond the Middle East, we need to examine how the two leading imperial powers, Britain and France, viewed and managed their resurgent empires. Of the two the British Empire was more extensive, ruling at its post-1918 peak nearly a quarter of the earth's land surface and a similar proportion of the global population, whereas France embraced just under a tenth of the earth's landmass and one-twentieth of its population.[40] The French had nothing comparable to the resources of British India or to the settler colonies of Canada, Australia, New Zealand and South Africa. The British also took empire more seriously, developing strategies for managing post-1918 nationalism that seemed more effective and less expensive than those of France. After 1945, of course, both empires were shown to have feet of clay but – and this is a fundamental point of this chapter – Britain adapted surprisingly well to the winds of change in the 1920s and 1930s. This success strengthened London's commitment to empire in ways that endured long after decolonization had taken hold.

Britain's empire had always been decentralized. It originated in commerce and, as Lord Palmerston observed in the Victorian era, 'land is not necessary for trade; we can carry on commerce on ground belonging to other people.' Even though military force and direct rule often proved unavoidable to protect trading interests, formal empire was always costly and burdensome, so British policy was to expand 'informally if possible and formally if necessary'.[41] This was, moreover, an empire of free trade during its halycon century from 1830 to 1932 whereas France, never able to compete with British industry and shipping, maintained a tightly centralized mercantilist regime.

French political traditions were also much more dirigiste. A prime legacy of the revolution was the ideal of a universal rationality: colonies were deemed an extension of *la patrie*, subject to metropolitan laws and tightly controlled from Paris. The ultimate goal was supposedly *assimilation* – the evolution of colonial 'subjects' into French 'citizens' who elected representatives to the Assembly in Paris – but the qualifying criteria (including linguistic skills and the acceptance of Christianity) were demanding and often arbitrary: in 1939, for instance, less than 1 per cent of the natives in French West Africa were citizens. Overwhelmingly France ruled an empire of 'subjects'. In fact there was no functioning parliamentary system in any French colonial territory: their assemblies had limited scrutiny over budgets but no powers to initiate legislation.[42]

The contrast ran deeper still. Far more than the French Empire, let alone those of other European powers, Britain had created an 'empire of settlement', established by British migrants who gradually arrogated to themselves British rights of self-government. By 1914 the numbers were substantial: 8 million in Canada, 5 million in Australia and just over 1 million in New Zealand, plus 1.4 million whites in South Africa. The total settler population, predominantly of British stock, was one-third of the United Kingdom's 46 million people.[43] This was a very different kind of empire from Curzon's India and, to many in Britain, one which was much more acceptable. 'England in the East is not the England we know,' observed the Liberal MP Charles Dilke in 1868: there 'flousy Britannia, with her anchor and ship, becomes a mysterious Oriental despotism.'[44]

The question of whether Britain could sustain liberty at home while building an empire abroad preoccupied many Victorian reformers, mindful of ancient Rome whose republican virtues had supposedly been corrupted by militaristic imperialism. But, it was widely believed, this classical dilemma of *imperium et libertas* could be successfully resolved in the colonies of British settlement that Dilke called 'Greater Britain'. The argument was developed most famously by the Cambridge professor John Seeley in his book *The Expansion of England*, published in 1883 to great acclaim and still selling 11,000 copies in 1919. It did not go out of print until 1956 – the year of the Suez debacle. Seeley regretted the acquisition of India, where the British had no community of 'blood' or even of 'interest', though he saw no easy exit without the subcontinent falling again into anarchy. But he was enthusiastic about the settler colonies, arguing that 'Greater Britain is not in the ordinary sense an Empire at all' but a 'normal extension of the English race into other lands'. Lands, moreover, where 'everything is brand-new. There you have the most progressive race put in the circumstances most favourable to progress. There you have no past and an unbounded future' whereas 'India is all past and, I may almost say, has no future.' Seeley believed Britain was following two radically different policies – 'despotic in Asia and democratic in Australia' – with the second expressing its true values.[45]

Regional groups of settler colonies gradually coalesced, forming the Dominion of Canada in 1867, the Commonwealth of Australia in 1901, the Dominion of New Zealand in 1907 and the Union of South Africa in 1910. In the last case union followed the brutal Boer war of 1899–1902 in which the British conquered the Dutch-speaking colonies of the Transvaal and Orange River but then allowed them provincial self-government within the Union. These settler colonies had their own executives and legislatures but, under the system known as 'dyarchy', some powers, particularly in defence and foreign policy, remained with London. By the 1900s there was much debate about whether the self-governing settler colonies, now collectively called the Dominions, would follow the same course as the American colonies in 1776 and break away from the mother country. From empire to nations: that seemed to be the logic of history.

A small but well-placed coterie of intellectuals proposed an alternative scenario, turning the empire into a federation, inspired by their role in helping to craft federal union in South Africa. This 'Round Table' group, founded in 1910 by the Oxford don Lionel Curtis, was sure that the empire itself could not survive without closer coordination. Curtis personally favoured 'organic union' – an elected imperial parliament and taxation system with control over the empire's armed forces. Most of his colleagues would not go that far but, like Seeley, they argued that the empire faced a stark choice: 'federate or disintegrate'. Federalism was in the air in the 1900s because of the recent evolution of the individual Dominions and the success of the United States in surmounting the crisis of civil war to become an economic giant, and the idea was much debated for the UK during the Home Rule crisis of 1911–14. But although a detailed federal blueprint for the empire was proposed by Sir Joseph Ward, the New Zealand premier, at the Imperial Conference in 1911, it was dismissed by the other Dominions' leaders as 'idiotic' and 'absolutely impractical'.[46]

The wartime experience of the Dominions is often seen as a huge step down the road to independence, but the story is actually more circuitous. Certainly there was pride at national heroics (the Anzacs at Gallipoli in 1915 or the Canadians storming Vimy Ridge in 1917), coupled with mounting indignation about 'British bungling' at the top. A Canadian Cabinet minister remarked that, despite all the talk in London about 'shell shortages', the 'chief shortage was of brains'. Dominion leaders also became incensed at the lack of consultation, especially as their own losses mounted. 'It can hardly be expected that we shall put 400,000 or 500,000 men in the field', complained the Canadian premier Sir Robert Borden, and yet 'willingly accept' being regarded as 'toy automata'. In the autumn of 1918, when the Armistice was negotiated without reference to the Dominions, Billy

Hughes, the Australian premier, fumed about being treated 'like lack-eys'. The issue was especially sensitive for Hughes because, unlike Canada and New Zealand, he had been unable to impose conscription on his countrymen. Australians voted this down, albeit narrowly, in referenda in October 1916 and again in December 1917, splitting Hughes' Labor Party and reviving sectarian tension in a country where Irish Catholics comprised one-fifth of the population.[47]

Yet the supposed new nationalism of the Dominions requires closer scrutiny. In part it reflected an erosion of provincialism – thinking of oneself now as 'Australian' rather than as a 'Victorian' or a 'New South Welshman'. The same was true in the British army as losses and cross-drafting diluted the regionalism of regiments, especially when rubbing shoulders with troops from France, Belgium and other Allied nations. But Haig's army was predominantly English: the UK provided all but ten of the seventy-four British and Dominion divisions in the main theatres of war and over 80 per cent of those UK troops came from England, the mother country of the empire. Little wonder that it was against the English that other troops measured themselves – Scots as well as Dominions (who felt a good deal of affinity with the 'Jocks') – and the English Tommy was usually deemed inferior. This was partly because, paid one shilling a day, he could not afford the beer, coffee and other pleasures available to 'fuckin five bobbers' from Australia and New Zealand, but also, at a deeper level, because of the peculiar English caste system of the British army, whose insistence on spit and polish, petty punishments and rigid separation of the ranks was at odds with the ethos of the Dominion armies and even that of France. The British army was also much less inclined to promote men from the ranks, relying instead on young 'gentlemen' from the public schools. The Aussies, who remained a volunteer army for the duration of the war, were notorious for lack of respect towards officers but it became axiomatic among most Dominion troops that British Tommies, especially the 'little runts' with northern accents, showed an almost bovine lack of initiative and intelligence. An Australian cartoon depicted some Tommies huddled around a brazier at a desolate cross-roads; its solitary lamp post was adorned with a sign 'Lamp Post Corner':

Aussie [passing by]: Ay, Digger, is this Lamp Post Corner?
Tommy: Don't know, Choom. I've only bin 'ere a month.[48]

In 1916 Haig and the British high command regarded the caste system as the only way to manage an army of ill-educated and inexperienced volunteers: the men were trained to do simple tasks unquestioningly, such as walking in a line across no-man's-land behind a creeping barrage. But the victories of 1918, both German and Allied, were won by small groups of officers and men moving fluidly across the battlefield and seizing their opportunities, which placed a premium on initiative not obedience.[49] Given both the chance and proper training, British troops could fight that kind of battle as well as Dominion soldiers but, for much of the war, they were imprisoned by British army discipline. The root problem, one might say, was not differences of 'national character' but the English class system.

Dominion complaints about London's conduct of the war also need to be placed in perspective. Heavy losses early in 1915 and 1916 reflected poor training as much as ineptitude at the top. Dominion commanders, just like Haig and his staff, had much to learn: in this phase of the war, notes Canberra historian Jeffrey Grey, 'Australian generals were as good at killing Australian troops as were British generals.' By the summer of 1918, however, Canada and Australia had each established its own Army Corps under an able national commander – respectively Arthur Currie and John Monash – and their men, now rigorously trained, were in the vanguard at Amiens and other great breakthroughs in the last months of the war, lauded as some of the best shock troops in the Allied armies. These triumphs were tribute not merely to the superior fighting spirit of the 'colonials', as claimed by nationalist writers such as the Australian Charles Bean, but also to the new way of waging war by 1918. Currie and Monash proved masters of the close, integrated use of infantry with tanks, aircraft and especially artillery – but it was the British who provided most of that essential heavy support for Dominion soldiers. And many of the senior staff positions were still held by British officers, now of high quality, who played a large part in the meticulous planning for which Currie and Monash became renowned.[50]

In diplomacy, too, the motto was interdependence not independence. In 1917 Dominion leaders dealt briskly with renewed talk of imperial 'federation' but they appropriated the Round Table term 'Commonwealth' to describe the mixture of autonomy and cooperation now emerging between Britain and the Dominions. General Jan Smuts, the South African representative, became the symbol of that new sense of community, lionized in London society in 1917 not only for his victories in Africa but also because he had been one of the Boer leaders fifteen years before. His career seemed to show the capaciousness of the British imperial tent, compared with the iron cage of Prussianism. For Smuts, the granting of self-government to the defeated Boer provinces in 1906 had been a wondrous sign of Britain's root commitment to the values of liberty; increasingly he romanticized 1906 as 'the greatest experience of my life'. And it was Smuts who gave voice to this vision of the British world as something new under the sun when he told both houses of Parliament, 'We are not an Empire. Germany is an empire, so was Rome, and so is India, but we are a system of nations, a community of States and nations far greater than any empire which has ever existed.' He called it 'the British Commonwealth of nations'.[51]

At Paris the Dominions' leaders got the best of both worlds – separate representation and also membership of the British Empire delegation, what Smuts liked to call 'Independence Plus'. During the 1920s, however, it might seem that the Dominions finally broke away from Britain. In 1926 the Balfour Report clarified their status as 'autonomous' and 'equal' communities who 'freely associated as members of the British Commonwealth'. In 1931 the Statute of Westminster renounced the imperial Parliament's right to legislate for the Dominions. But this was largely a ploy to keep South Africa and Ireland within the Commonwealth; the other Dominions were less concerned and the statute was not even ratified in Australia and New Zealand. That was partly because of continued reliance by the Dominions on Britain for trade and investment (explored more fully in the next chapter) but also because of renewed migration from Britain after the war. Between 1920 and 1929 1.81 million people emigrated from the UK, more than in the boom decade 1900–9 (1.67 million), with 60 per cent of them going to Canada and Australia, whereas the United States had been the main attraction around the turn of the century. All this helped nurture deeper feelings of what was sometimes called 'British race nationalism', a phrase deconstructed by historian John Darwin to mean 'an aggressive sense of cultural superiority as the representatives of a global civilization then at the height of its prestige' because of victory in 1918. Being a Dominion within the British Commonwealth was therefore 'a distinctive blend of national status and Imperial identity'.[52]

So, instead of assuming a classic trajectory from imperial subject to national citizen, we should recognize that many in the Dominions and indeed the UK during the 1920s were comfortable, indeed proud, about their multiple identities. Speaking 'as a Scotsman', Balfour exclaimed in 1926, he was not going to surrender his 'share of Magna Charta and Shakespeare on account of Bannockburn and Flodden.' Likewise Keith Hancock, the Australian historian, declared in 1930 that although 'a country is a jealous mistress' it was 'not impossible for Australians, nourished by a glorious literature and haunted by old memories, to be in love with two soils.' Imperial loyalty was particularly fervent in New Zealand – the most British and Protestant of the Dominions, without the fractious Catholic minorities of French Canada and Irish Australia. William Massey, New Zealand's premier from 1912 to 1925, had been born and raised an Orangeman in Ulster and considered the British to be nothing less than God's Chosen People. He publicly stated that 'the Empire would last to the end of time', that 'London would always be the capital' and that 'nothing but a miracle – nothing but an interposition of Divine Providence – saved us in March 1918'.[53]

Massey's British Israelite philosophy was extreme, not to say eccentric, but it reminds us that we should not breezily project back to the Great War era the nationalism of a post-colonial age. Even after the travails of Australia's war Billy Hughes could still declare in 1919 that 'we are more British than the people of Great Britain', while his successor Stanley Bruce insisted in 1926 that 'the British Empire is one great nation'. Canadian premiers usually spoke in more muted tones, at least when wooing voters in French-speaking Quebec, but their dominant viewpoint was still the same. Rather like John Seeley in the

1880s, the elites and the bulk of the population in Canada, Australia and New Zealand saw themselves in the 1920s as new and better versions of Britain, freed from the encrustations of caste and class, people who had pioneered the secret ballot, universal manhood suffrage and votes for women (in 1893 in New Zealand, a quarter-century before the UK). Their nationalism was conceived in familial terms – children seeking to outstrip a parent, the new British better-ing Old England – rather than as a bipolar reaction of nations to empire, as in much of post-imperial Europe after 1918.[54]

Memorialization of the war was therefore complex. Take the case of Canada for whom, like Australia, 1914–18 has often been depicted as the birth of a nation. Today that idea is understood in the sense of 'Othering' – Canada starting to define itself against Britain – yet at the time emphasis was placed on a new inclusivity. Canada's spectacular National War Memorial was sited at Vimy Ridge, rather than at another more strategically important battlefield, because it was there on Easter Monday 1917 that the four divisions of the Canadian Corps went into action together for the first time. 'The boys at Vimy Ridge represented Canada as a whole,' their commander Field Marshal Julian Byng declared in 1925. 'It was then that all the nine provinces walked up the hill as one, all with the same ideal before them.' Vimy was a symbol of Canada coming together rather than breaking away.[55]

In 1939, when a second great war broke out, the four overseas Dominions once again answered the call of liberty and empire – even South Africa, albeit after a close vote in parliament. Constitutionally, under the Statute of Westminster, they could all have chosen to remain neutral, like Ireland, the other Dominion. Here was the ultimate reminder that the extent, resources and interconnection of Britain's set-tler colonies did indeed make the British Commonwealth something unusual in a world of empires and nations. This sense of Britishness, accentuated and even consecrated by the Great War, would prove an important and abiding legacy of 1918.

But most of the British Empire was not white. In 1903 the black American commentator W.E.B. Du Bois predicted that the 'color line' would be the great problem of the twentieth century and in fact the rhetoric of British imperial liberties was often racially coded. Stanley Bruce, for instance, spoke of Australia as 'the most wonderful unprotected white man's country in the world', meaning that this paradise could only be defended against the Yellow Peril from Japan with British help.[56] As the debates about mandates and Palestine had shown, there was widespread doubt about when and even whether non-whites would be capable of self-government. Forty years on, Seeley's conceptual divide between Britain's colonies of settlement and of conquest remained stark: 'democratic' empire set against 'despotic'. By 1918, India, the big blind spot in Seeley's imperial project, could no longer be ignored. Yet the Indian experience of the Great War and its aftermath does not point us unequivocally along a clear road to the end of the Raj in 1947.

In August 1914 the Indian army, over 150,000 strong, was the British Empire's largest trained force of soldiers. Although its main duty was defending the North-West Frontier of India, it rushed an expeditionary force to France to help stem the crisis on the Western Front. In 1914 and 1915 the Indian Corps fought in several of the battles around Ypres before most of the troops – whose morale plummeted during the wet, cold winters – were moved to the Middle East. The defence of Egypt and the conquest of Mesopotamia and Palestine were achieved mainly by Indian units. The troops were largely from the Punjab, especially Muslims and Sikhs whom the British regarded as 'martial races' in contrast to Hindus. Most were middling peasants, attracted by the secure pay. In other words, contrary to modern impressions of the British Raj, the wartime Indian army was an all-volunteer force. By the end of 1918, India, with a population of some 300 million, had provided 1.27 million soldiers, roughly a tenth of the British Empire's war effort.[57]

In India, as elsewhere, the war stirred up politics and society. Prices more than doubled and shortages of essentials such as kerosene provoked strikes, looting and riots in many provinces. The main political party, the Indian National Congress – hitherto a loose confederation of high-caste politicians centred on Calcutta, Bombay and Madras – began to act more cohesively and to channel popular grievances. The Congress Party also forged links with the main Islamic party, the

Muslim League, an unlikely move but reflecting Muslim anxieties now that Britain was at war with the Ottoman Emperor, guardian of Islam's holy places. In 1916 two Indian 'Home Rule Leagues' were organized, the name deliberately echoing earlier debates in the UK. They used rallies, pamphlets and songs to spread the nationalist message across the subcontinent. 'The war has put the clock ... fifty years forward,' declared the veteran Congress politician Madan Mohan Malaviya in March 1917, expressing the hope that India would achieve 'in the next few years' what might otherwise have been impossible in half a century.[58]

The focal point of Indian protest was Mohandas Gandhi, who would shape Indian history until his assassination in 1948. Trained as a barrister in Victorian London, Gandhi learned his politics during twenty years in South Africa championing the rights of the Indian community. In the process he developed from a dapper, westernized lawyer into a celibate spiritual leader who shaved off his moustache and adopted outcast dress. In South Africa Gandhi also developed techniques of non-violent resistance (*satyagraha*) rooted in spiritual change, being adamant that national self-rule (*swaraj*) must start with personal self-rule. Wilsonianism left him cold, even as a propaganda tool, for his real bogey was materialist industrial society, exemplified by America as much as Britain. In his 1909 manifesto, *Indian Home Rule* (Hind Swaraj), he argued that 'India is being ground down not under the English heel but under that of modern civilisation.' The English 'have not taken India', Gandhi asserted; 'we have given it to them' and 'we keep the English in India for our base self-interest. We like their commerce.' Unless Indians rejected industrialism and state power, independence would simply mean 'English rule without the Englishman'.[59]

In retrospect Gandhi stands out clear and prophetic, a spiritual exemplar for Martin Luther King and many others, but he was also a politician, who struggled initially to find his niche in Indian politics. In the war crisis of 1918 Gandhi insisted it was the 'duty' of members of the Home Rule Leagues to support recruitment for the British forces – a stance that some biographers have found 'bizarre' for an avowed pacifist. In fact, Gandhi's line was not dissimilar to that of John

Redmond and his followers in Ireland – arguing that in this war Britain, for all its faults, was fighting for freedom and that it would concede *swaraj* more readily if Indians balanced their protests at home by loyal service on the battlefields of France, which he hoped to 'crowd' with what he called 'an indomitable army of Home Rulers'. That way Indians would become 'partners in the Empire as are Canada, South Africa and Australia', enjoying 'the rights of Englishmen'. But Gandhi's campaign raised few recruits for the Raj and it infuriated Congress politicians: he was close to a nervous breakdown by the time the Armistice was signed.[60]

In the New Year of 1919 Gandhi changed tack, as the winds of nationalism and democracy swept out from Europe across Asia. The Viceroy of India, Lord Chelmsford, decided to prolong wartime emergency powers in order to deal with 'anarchical and revolutionary movements', pushing the measure through his Legislative Council despite opposition from all the Indian members. Gandhi, claiming he could 'no longer render peaceful obedience to the laws of a power that is capable of such a piece of devilish legislation', mounted a *satyagraha* in protest but he could not control his followers. The worst violence occurred in the Punjab city of Amritsar, where property was looted and several Europeans murdered. On 13 April 1919 troops under General Reginald Dyer dispersed an unarmed crowd of protestors, opening fire without warning in an enclosed square and continuing to shoot even when people were fleeing, so as to produce what Dyer called 'a sufficient moral effect . . . throughout the Punjab.' Even on official estimates 379 people died in what became known as the Amritsar Massacre.[61]

Gandhi immediately halted his campaign, admitting it had been a 'Himalyan miscalculation' to promote *satyagraha* among insufficiently trained people and deploring what he called the 'utter lawlessness bordering almost on Bolshevism' that had resulted in some places. It took him months to regroup and build support among Congress politicians but in 1920 he mounted a new campaign, fuelled by anger at what he called the 'official whitewash' of Dyer's crimes. But although his call for non-cooperation with the British authorities mobilized politics on an unprecedented scale, drawing in the lower castes and people from less developed provinces such as Gujarat and the Punjab, it had minimal effect on the machinery of government while again unleashing local violence that he could not control. In February 1922, after rioters burned a police station and twenty-two officers died, Gandhi suddenly called off his campaign of civil disobedience, asserting that it had 'unconsciously drifted from the right path'. Congress leaders who had supported him were left high and dry. Thanks to Gandhi's 'over-confidence' and 'impulsiveness', lamented Lajpat Rai in his prison cell, 'we are simply routed.'[62]

For the British, the upheavals of 1919–22 in India, as elsewhere, constituted a crisis of war imperialism more than a crisis of empire itself. While the British had no compunction about using force to maintain imperial rule, the Amritsar Massacre (like the conduct of the Black and Tans in Ireland) was an aberration born of the panic about revolution, when the army was given its head rather than being used to back up the police power. Dyer became a convenient scapegoat – denounced even by Churchill, a diehard opponent of Indian self-government, who likened the shootings to Bolshevik 'terrorism' which, he insisted, was 'not the British way of doing business.'[63] Learning its lesson, in 1920–1 the government of India made a point of not allowing Gandhi 'the crown of martyrdom' by imprisonment let alone death, throwing him into jail only after his civil disobedience campaign had collapsed. Ho Chi Minh, the future nationalist leader of Vietnam, observed sagely that agitators such as Gandhi and de Valera 'would have long since entered heaven had they been born in one of the French colonies.'[64]

The dramas of 1919–22 prefigured the dynamics of India's next two decades. Gandhi could bring out the crowds but he was not effective in using street power to leverage political gains. Most Congress politicians allied with him for tactical reasons, because of his ability to mobilize unprecedented popular support in 'backward' regions and among the lower castes. But they worried about the dangers of anarchy and certainly did not share his pastoral vision of India's future. Jawaharlal Nehru, emerging as his heir apparent, believed that India had to become a modern industrial state on socialist lines. Above all Gandhi was never able to sever the complex bonds of collaboration that, as he recognized, made Indians accomplices in empire. Indeed Britain succeeded in weaving new bonds during the 1920s and 1930s.

The crux was whether India could be drawn down the same road taken by Britain's settler empire and this issue became a fundamental divide in British politics. In 1917 Curzon stated that never 'in the wildest of dreams' would India become a Dominion like Australia or Canada. Such a day was '500 years off'. Balfour, the great exponent of self-government for the white settler societies, agreed. 'East is East and West is West,' he observed. 'Even in the West, Parliamentary institutions have rarely been a success, except among English-speaking peoples. In the East, not only have they never been seriously tried, but they have never been desired, except by intellectuals who have come under Western influences.' Balfour encapsulated the Tory perspective on Indian nationalism, as the obsession of an unrepresentative Asian elite.[65]

In the post-war crisis, however, the Lloyd George coalition conceded India the principle of dyarchy applied earlier in the white colonies. The Government of India Act in 1919 kept a firm grip on the centre, as Tories wanted, but transferred some powers, such as agriculture and education, to provincial legislatures. It also widened the tax-based franchise and gave the vote automatically to all ex-soldiers, so that about one-tenth of the adult male population plus a few wealthy women were eligible to vote. Although this was hardly full democracy, the Act transformed the Indian political arena by opening up new avenues for power and patronage in the provinces which Congress and Muslim politicians were keen to exploit. For much of the 1920s, after the collapse of civil disobedience in 1922, politics atrophied at the national level.

The British government was, however, required to review the 1919 Act after ten years. That in itself would have put India's national question back on the agenda but insensitive Tory handling of the matter generated a full-blown crisis. By sending an all-white British commission to India and allowing Indians only to submit comments, the Baldwin government managed to administer nothing less than a racial snub, expressing the underlying belief of many Tories that Indians were incapable of self-government. The commission provided a new focus for politics at the all-India level, rallying the various Congress factions. It also brought Gandhi back into the national arena with his brilliantly conceived Salt March in March 1930. This simple, peaceful protest by a balding old man, wrapped in his dhoti, against a tax on one of life's necessities dramatized the iniquities of imperialism for a world audience and inaugurated a new campaign of civil disobedience in India.

The crisis would, however, have been far worse but for a shift of policy at the top. In October 1929 Lord Irwin, the viceroy, stated explicitly that 'the natural issue of India's constitutional progress' must be 'the attainment of Dominion status'. He also offered Round Table talks in London with representatives of the 'different parties and interests' in India – a clear gesture of equality. Irwin (better known by his later title of Lord Halifax) blamed much of India's unrest on Wilsonian ideas of self-determination which had 'confused and conquered the Western world' and then spread to Asia. But he had no doubt that what he called a 'Mussolini system of government' – arrests, deportations, press censorship and 'a good deal of shooting' – would only 'make our main problem of keeping India within the empire a hundred times more difficult'. His conciliatory approach was supported by MacDonald's new Labour government. Indeed, without this unlikely (and brief) conjunction in 1929–31 of a progressive Tory viceroy and a socialist Cabinet, both the announcement of Dominion status and the convening of a Round Table conference would not have happened.[66]

Tory diehards were appalled. 'We are not dealing with the case of a daughter nation of our own creed and of our own blood,' exclaimed Lord Birkenhead, in a clear reference to the racial issue. They were even angrier when Irwin released Gandhi from jail and met him for direct talks. Yet Gandhi once again failed to cash in his chips, agreeing to end civil disobedience and join in the Round Table talks (where he made little impression) without even securing full abolition of the salt tax in return. Nehru wept at what he considered to be a betrayal of Congress's demand for complete independence. But the symbolism of the Gandhi–Irwin Pact infuriated Tory right-wingers. 'It is alarming and also nauseating', Churchill declared in a memorable caricature, 'to see Mr. Gandhi, a seditious Middle Temple lawyer, now posing as a fakir of a type well-known in the East, striding half-naked up the steps of the Vice-regal palace, while he is still organizing and conducting a defiant campaign of civil disobedience, to parley on equal terms with the representative of the King-Emperor.'[67]

But the diehards did not speak for the party as a whole. Baldwin, as Tory leader, believed that India represented 'the acid, and ultimate test' of Britain's fitness for 'democratic conditions'. By this striking phrase, reflecting his underlying concern about the challenge of democracy, he meant both Labour's readiness to accept the responsibilities of empire and Tory recognition of the need for change. When Baldwin returned to power in 1931 as de facto leader of a National Government, he backed the next stage of constitutional reform. The Government of India Act was approved in 1935 despite a monumental rearguard action by Churchill and Tory diehards, involving 1,951 speeches that filled 4,000 pages of *Hansard* with some 15.5 million words. Churchill predicted the Act would sound 'the knell of the British Empire in the East' but in fact it was intended to continue the strategy of holding India to the empire by adapting the concessions previously made to the white colonies. This time the British sought to combine further devolution to the Indian provinces with the idea of federalism at the centre – in essence the South African gambit of thirty years before.[68]

The all-India federation did not come off: lengthy talks to safeguard princely privileges – revenues, currencies, postage stamps and the like – were still dragging on when war broke out in 1939. But provincial devolution, the other strand of the 1935 Act, did go ahead. From the spring of 1937 Indian ministers, responsible to their electorates, were given full charge of almost all aspects of provincial government. The franchise, though still based on a property qualification, was enlarged again to include some 30 million people – only one-sixth of those who would have been eligible under universal suffrage but still a democratic electorate comparable in size to that of Britain. And Congress, which won nearly half the seats in the provincial elections of 1937, did not boycott the process as feared. Instead its politicians got down to the business of provincial administration, forming majority governments in seven of the eleven provinces in British India. Despite all Gandhi's efforts to bridge the communal divide, Congress was now over-whelmingly a Hindu party.

Looking at 1937 from the vantage point of 1947, it is tempting to discern intimations of things to come – a 'dysfunctional' Raj that should already have conceded independence,[69] a Congress Party eager to dominate the subcontinent, and Hindu–Muslim tensions that portended the bloodbath of partition. Yet hindsight can mislead. The 1935 Act was 'a major experiment in the devolution of power to a non-white part of Britain's empire' – indeed of any European empire. It also 'succeeded as a temporary solution to the problem of govern-ing British India' by giving Indian ministers control over vast areas of provincial government and also the responsibility and opprobrium for maintaining law and order.[70] The situation seemed like a repeat of the mid-1920s, with Congress politicians again becoming immersed in local government as their unity crumbled on a national level. In 1939 Gandhi fought a bitter battle for control of the party against Subhas Chandra Bose, a radical modernizer who flirted with European-style fascism. And despite some heady talk of Pakistan, an Islamic 'land of the pure', Muslim politics were as fragmented as ever.

This late-1930s stalemate was not sustainable in the long term but neither the nature nor the outcome of the next crisis was predeter-mined. In 1933 Sir Malcolm Hailey, who as governor of two Indian provinces had weathered a decade of nationalist turbulence, could seriously envisage British India still existing in the 1980s, albeit with 'an increasing measure of Indianization of the Army.'[71] Against the odds, Britain had held on to its Indian Empire during the two decades after 1918, while gradually – and often brutally – manoeuvring India's volatile politics along the path already blazed by the white Dominions.

What really undermined the Raj was not the Great War but its suc-cessor. Japan's spectacular victories in 1941–2 exposed the nakedness of colonial rule throughout Asia and it was American power, not British, which gradually reversed the Japanese tide. In fact, the most dangerous shadow cast by the Great War over the European empires was not new nationalism but new imperialism.

*

Although France and Britain were beneficiaries of the crisis of empire in Europe and the Near East, the Great War accelerated the emergence of imperial rivals in the Pacific: Japan and the United States. In each case empire and race were tightly entangled – Japan being the only non-white great power while America, though intensely racist, prided itself rather casuistically on not being a colonial empire. Both of them ended the Great War as major naval powers in the Pacific and this created a new challenge for the British.

At the Paris peace conference Japan was treated as one of the Big Five allies, adjudicating the post-war order. All this seemed to vindicate the modernization policy of the past four decades, using Western methods to make Japan a great power with an empire of its own in Manchuria and Korea. Yet, in racial terms, Japan did not feel one of the club, being stigmatized in the West by the growing outcry about the 'Yellow Peril'. The idea, derived from the writings of the French author Arthur de Gobineau, that there were three basic 'races' – white, black and yellow – was widely held around 1900, not least in Japan. In 1908 the intellectual journal *Taiyō* devoted a special issue to 'The Clash of the Yellow and the White Peoples'. Resentment was particularly intense about racial discrimination against Japanese workers in Australia, Canada and the United States. So there seemed an inherent contradiction between 'the treatment of Japan as a first-class power' in the new world order and the treatment of 'the Japanese as second-class citizens in the Anglo-Saxon territories'.[72]

This issue was entangled with the debate in Japan about democracy. In the late nineteenth century the country's principal model had been Bismarck's Germany, whose militarist, oligarchic ethos suited a polity in which power still resided largely with elder statesmen (*Genro*) drawn from a few clans. But Japan also had a minority tradition of Anglophilia, attracted by Britain's free trade and parliamentary politics, and this was institutionalized in the Anglo-Japanese alliance of 1902 – Britain's attempt to break out of its turn-of-the-century sense of isolation. During the Great War Japan's navy, much of it constructed in British shipyards, proved a useful adjunct to British seapower, both in the China Seas and for the defence of India. In the crisis of 1917 two flotillas of Japanese destroyers were sent to the Mediterranean to help protect Britain's trade. In return the British backed Japan's claims to Germany's rights in China and the North Pacific. On Japan's side the alliance had even larger significance as the first acknowledgment by a European great power of Japan's equality of status.[73]

The Japanese debate about German and British models of development intensified during the Great War. September 1918 saw the installation of Japan's first government formed by a political party, as distinct from an oligarchic faction, and Hara Kei, a former journalist and diplomat, became the first commoner to serve as prime minister. This historic moment coincided with imperial Germany's defeat and disintegration and with the craze for Wilsonianism. Pro-democrats in Japan, such as the Tokyo professor Yoshino Sakuzo, predicted that 'the trend of the world' was now 'the perfection of democracy' at home and the establishment of 'egalitarianism' in international relations. Joining the League of Nations became the prime aim of Hara's new government. But many vocal conservatives suspected the League as a device for continued 'Anglo-Saxon' dominance. In response, Japan's delegation at Paris requested that the League's Covenant endorse the principle of 'equal and just treatment' of nationals from all member states, 'making no distinction, either in law or in fact, on account of their race or nationality.'[74]

This principle, which became known as the racial equality clause, reflected long-standing Japanese resentment about immigration restriction but it was intended above all as a test of whether Japan was regarded as an international equal. The term 'racial' equality is actually misleading: there was never any question of ending the oppression of Chinese and Koreans within Japan's empire. Most Japanese had a 'two-tiered' approach to race, seeing themselves as equal to the West but a cut above the rest of Asia. This double standard aside, Japan's démarche put the Paris peacemakers on the spot. The French, true to their universalist ideology, endorsed it as 'an indisputable principle of justice', even though honouring it more in the breach than the observance within their empire. The British wriggled out, claiming that Japan's proposal was mainly about immigration and therefore, constitutionally, a matter for individual Dominions. This allowed Billy Hughes of Australia to turn it into a fundamental challenge to his

'White Australia' policy and a platform to prove his nationalist credentials before the next election. 'Sooner than agree to it,' he ranted, 'I would rather walk into the Seine – or the Folies Bergères – with my clothes off.' So embarrassing was Hughes' demagoguery that even Louis Botha, the South African premier, no advocate of racial equality, told the Japanese delegation, 'strictly between ourselves, I think he is mad.' In the end Wilson blocked the proposal to avoid a damaging public row that might have jeopardized the creation of the League but Western rejection of the racial equality clause was not forgotten in Japan. In 1946 Emperor Hirohito cited it as a prime cause of the Second World War.[75]

A further slight was the US immigration act of 1924, intended to preserve the 'Nordic' character of America's population. Migration from the 'Slavic' countries of southern and eastern Europe was restricted by tight national quotas, but immigrants from Asia were totally prohibited. The act, which remained in force until after the Second World War, was built on long-standing discrimination against 'Orientals', especially in California, ostensibly because their cheap labour threatened American jobs but essentially on racial grounds. 'The Chinese and Japanese ... are not the stuff of which American citizens can be made,' pontificated Senator James Phelan, a leading Californian Democrat. He called them 'a blight on our civilization'.[76]

Phelan's racist views were shared by many Americans and they illustrate the country's complex world-view. As we have seen in Chapter One, the United States had developed an ideology of civic nationalism in which migrants from various countries chose to adopt the values of American liberty. Ethnicity, in other words, would be subsumed in democracy. But liberty had its limits, and they were largely defined by race. Despite the abolition of slavery, most blacks remained second-class citizens, denied civil and voting rights, and similar restrictions had been imposed on the Chinese and Japanese in California. In the racially charged atmosphere of the Great War era, many congressmen wanted to keep the blacks down and the yellow men out. What masked American racism on the international stage was its lack of a colonial empire. The annexation of Hawaii and the conquest of the Philippines during the Spanish–American war of

1898 had been aberrations. A bloody war to control the Philippine archipelago, with atrocities on both sides, soon turned American opinion against further colonial adventures. The United States started to prepare an exit strategy from the Philippines that would safeguard its economic interests through close ties with the conservative, landowning elite, and Wilson liked to cite US 'trusteeship' of the islands as a model for the League mandates system. The American flag 'stands for the rights of mankind,' he declared, 'no matter what the race involved.'[77] The Philippines were accorded internal self-government in 1935, with a commitment to full independence ten years later. In this way, the United States could remain true to an essential element of its civic nationalism – the repudiation of imperialism rooted in the Declaration of Independence in 1776.

Most sensitive and substantive of all for Japan was the new international order of seapower. Naval rivalry before 1914 centred on the race between Britain and Germany to build bigger and better battleships, but by the end of the war, noted the British naval staff, 'the strategical centre of gravity' had 'shifted from the North Sea to the Pacific' because of the destruction of the German fleet and the expansion of the US and Japanese navies. In 1916 Wilson – tired of being intimidated by both German and British seapower and also with an eye to the forthcoming election – committed the United States to building 'incomparably the greatest navy in the world', as he put it in a heady moment. The transcript of his speech was amended by the White House, rather lamely, to read 'incomparably the most adequate navy in the world' but the goal of 'a navy second to none' became a simple, attractive patriotic slogan, eagerly exploited by admirals and defence contractors alike. Although the 1916 programme was not completed – once America entered the war the focus changed from battleship construction to destroyers, submarines and merchant ships because of the U-boat crisis in the Atlantic – it hung like a sword over Britain's historic naval supremacy.[78]

In 1920 the Japanese parliament approved a new naval programme, responding to the growth of the US fleet and also to its move, after the war, from the Atlantic seaboard to California. This was a clear signal that Japan, with the third largest fleet in the world, was now regarded

as America's main potential enemy. In 1917 Wilson had spoken privately of the need to 'keep the white race or part of it strong to meet
the yellow race' and said that, although the idea of Japan successfully
invading California was 'absurd', the possibility of 'an attack on the
Philippines or some other outlying possession' could 'not be over-
looked'. From this perspective the Anglo-Japanese alliance seemed a
major challenge to US interests. Many Americans did not accept
British assurances that the treaty specifically ruled out a war waged by
the two of them against the United States. The US Navy's General
Board was a hotbed of Anglophobes: naval war games in 1916 still
included a British invasion of New England, followed by an assault
along Long Island towards Manhattan.[79]

Given America's economic might, Lloyd George observed in 1920,
if the British decided to enter an arms race with the USA, 'it would
be the biggest decision' since going to war with Germany in 1914 and
'conceivably, greater'. In the event, the threat of another naval race
was defused by growing pressure for disarmament in all three countries in 1920–1 because of the economic slump and anti-war feeling.
Charles Evans Hughes, the US secretary of state, convened a special
naval conference in Washington. In his speech of welcome Hughes,
eschewing the usual rhetoric, proposed a ten-year freeze on naval
building by all the great powers. He offered to abandon America's
1916 programme but, in return, he wanted to set a template for battleship strength, with the USA and Britain equal in tonnage and Japan
at 60 per cent (the 5–5–3 ratio). He went on to list the names of
twenty-three ships that, he said, the Royal Navy must cut up for
scrap. The British delegation was astonished and affronted. One
American journalist likened Admiral Beatty, the First Sea Lord, to 'a
bulldog, sleeping on a sunny doorstep, who had been poked in the
stomach by the impudent foot of an itinerant soap canvasser.'[80]

Despite the initial shock of the Hughes 'bombshell', it suited the
British very well to build down to parity, as it were, rather than start
a ruinous arms build-up to match the 1916 US programme. In any
case they had to scrap 50 per cent less tonnage than the Americans,
almost all of it obsolete warships.[81] In other words, what the United
States really wanted was not a big navy but equality of status with the

British Empire. For Japan, however, the symbolism of the Washington Conference of 1921–2 was deeply hurtful. The 5–5–3 ratio was a clear sign of inferiority – known disparagingly as the 'Rolls-Royce, Rolls-Royce, Ford' formula. In addition, the British terminated the Anglo-Japanese alliance because the Americans made that a condition of any naval agreement. To sweeten the pill, the Japanese were included in two international pacts about peace and stability in the Pacific but, given the importance of the Anglo-Japanese alliance since 1902 in validating Japan's rank as a great power, its termination was widely regarded as a snub. Britain's concurrent decision to start building a major naval base at Singapore was another straw in the wind: clearly this would be required only if the Royal Navy were sent east to fight Japan.

By the end of the decade the 5-5-3 formula had been extended beyond battleships to smaller naval vessels, despite another of Churchill's maverick campaigns. As over India, his language became remarkably intemperate, telling the Cabinet, for instance, in 1927 that although it was doubtless 'quite right in the interests of peace' to keep saying that war with America was 'unthinkable', in fact 'everyone knows this is not true.' However 'foolish and disastrous such a war would be,' Churchill went on, 'we do not wish to put ourselves in the power of the United States. We cannot tell what they might do if at some future date they were in a position to give us orders about our policy, say, in India, or Egypt, or Canada.' Churchill's obduracy served only to provoke another spasm of American naval building. Again, as with Dominion status for India, the issue was resolved by MacDonald's Labour government in 1930, which extended the principle of parity to cover cruisers as well as battleships, whereupon US construction atrophied once more.[82]

So the Royal Navy remained the largest in the world, whatever was said on paper, while Japan's democratic political leaders accepted their country's status as a Ford not a Rolls. Rival imperialisms, like the nationalist challenge in the Dominions and India, seemed to have been contained. And talk of 'pan-Asian' solidarity against white hegemony – like the rhetoric of *négritude* in French Africa – remained the discourse of a minority of intellectuals.[83]

Yet America's bid for naval supremacy was a clear sign that the country was now measuring itself against the world's greatest empire, Great Britain. And that bid was predicated on America's vast financial and industrial resources, which the war had directed outward on to the world stage. The impact of America's globalization on Britain, capitalism and the world economy was far-reaching. Not least it helped precipitate an international depression of unprecedented magnitude, during which the grievances of fringe militarists in Japan and Germany were transformed into basic goals of national policy.

4

CAPITALISM

Scarcely anyone in England now believes in the Treaty of Versailles or in the pre-war Gold Standard or in the Policy of Deflation. These battles have been won – mainly by the irresistible pressure of events . . . But most of us have, as yet, only a vague idea of what we are going to do next . . .

John Maynard Keynes, 1931

In the course of a decade we shall know whether American capitalism or Russian communism yields the better life for the bulk of the people; whichever of these 'cultures' wins, we in Great Britain will have to follow suit.

Beatrice Webb, 1931[1]

In 1914 the gold standard had been the hallmark of international capitalism, guarantor of a global trading system based on fixed exchange rates pegged to gold. The war tore that fabric apart and the gold standard had to be suspended but its reconstruction in the mid-1920s was taken as a sign that things were returning to normal. So when Ramsay MacDonald's government abandoned gold in peacetime in 1931, it seemed, in the words of one New York banker, 'like the end of the world.'[2] The financial crash and the global depression made clear that the clock could not be put back to 1914. They also highlighted the new and problematic role of the United States in global capitalism.

Politically, too, the crisis of 1931 proved a turning point, persuading the Labour Party that socialism would not evolve gradually out of capitalism, as widely expected in the 1920s, but required decisive governmental action of the sort taken from 1915 to galvanize the war effort. The crisis of 1931 helped put the Great War into a new perspective – not as a brief aberration from liberal capitalism but as the precursor of a new political economy whose character theorists such as Keynes struggled to discern. There was also a larger international dimension to Labour's adoption of nationalization and planning. In the 1930s the left in Britain and across Europe was fascinated by the apparent success of Stalin's Russia in modernizing a backward peasant economy. As America's boom turned to bust, intellectuals asked whether Soviet communism was the harbinger of the future.

The crisis of capitalism, both international and domestic, is the theme of this chapter – a crisis rooted in the upheavals of the Great War. But, as we shall see once again, Britain's experience of the postwar era differed significantly from that of the other wartime belligerents, particularly America and Germany.

In 1914–18 the European Allies mobilized resources on a global scale. This helped them win the war but also unbalanced the international economy. Wheat production, for instance, was vastly expanded in America, Argentina, Canada and Australasia and this created excess global capacity when Russia and eastern Europe recovered in the 1920s, resulting in persistently low prices. The same was true for other key commodities such as rubber and sugar. More striking still was the diffusion of industrial production away from Europe, especially to America and Japan but also India and the British Dominions. US manufacturers moved into many of Britain's markets in Latin America, similarly the Japanese in China and South-East Asia. The growth of textile production in Japan and India inflicted a severe blow on the cotton mills of Lancashire but other European countries also suffered from war-induced import substitution. In 1914, for instance, Germany produced four-fifths of world output of dyes; ten years later its share was less than half because all the main Allied states had been forced to develop their own industries. Economically the United States was the biggest beneficiary of the war, replacing Britain as the world's largest exporter by 1929 and surpassing Germany to become the second largest importer after Britain.[3]

The nature of industrial production was also changing, with America again setting the pace. The lead sector in its boom from 1922 to 1929 was consumer durables – automobiles above all but also housing and household appliances such as radios and gramophones. US automobile production soared from 2 million vehicles in 1919 to 4.5 million a decade later, almost one car for every household, with spin-off benefits for cognate industries such as rubber and oil. This consumer-durables revolution was funded on credit ('Buy Now, Pay Later') with easy instalment plans at high rates of interest. Leaving aside mortgages, consumer debt doubled during the 1920s to over 9 per cent of US household income. Seductive advertising spread the gospel of 'progressive obsolescence', with annual changes of colour and style to stimulate new 'needs'. Even Henry Ford succumbed, moving on from his standardized black Model T to a snazzier Model A in 1927. The aim, as one General Motors executive admitted, was 'to keep the customer reasonably dissatisfied with what he has.' Fordist assembly-line methods were admired across the world, even in the Soviet Union, which had its own *Fordizatsia*. Josef Stalin told party workers in 1924, 'The combination of Russian revolutionary sweep and American efficiency is the essence of Leninism.'[4]

Most significant of all was the transformation in global finance. In 1914 the United States was a net international debtor to the tune of $3.7 billion; by 1919 it was a net creditor on almost exactly the same scale. This shift was partly due to Britain's wartime sale of gold stocks and US securities owned by its citizens, such as railroad shares, to generate dollars for essential purchases of munitions, food and raw materials. Britain also borrowed heavily in the United States, initially from private investors via loan syndicates mobilized by J.P. Morgan & Co. and then from the federal government after the USA entered the war. 'We are down on our knees to the Americans,' groaned Lord Northcliffe, head of the British war mission in the USA, in July 1917. The post-war legacy was a debt to the United States of about $4.7 billion and also the emergence of America in global finance, as the federal government relaxed earlier restrictions on US banks and American investors looked outward from their vast domestic market. The USA replaced Britain as the biggest foreign investor in Canada by 1922 and in Latin America by the end of the decade. Although Britain's overall global stake remained larger (about $18 billion in 1930 compared with America's $15 billion), during the 1920s the United States became the world's main source of *new* capital, to the tune of $6.4 billion in 1924–9 – nearly half of it in Europe, especially Germany. 'We are the first empire of the world to establish our sway without legions,' declared the theologian Reinhold Niebuhr. 'Our legions are dollars.'[5]

America's new place in global finance was reflected in the restructured international monetary system. By 1914 most of the major economies had established fixed exchange rates, pegged to the price of gold. Theoretically this gold standard was supposed to be an automatic regulator of the global economy: countries that permitted high inflation would price their goods out of foreign markets, running up a payments deficit and draining gold reserves, thereby forcing a compensatory fall in prices. In reality, however, its operations were far less smooth. Reducing prices only had an effect if costs could also be forced down but wages often proved 'sticky' because of the resistance of labour unions. Nor, if a country accumulated gold, was there an automatic converse pressure towards credit expansion. This depended on the policy of individual central banks. Quite how the system worked remains mysterious. Some analysts have argued that central banks cooperated to maintain stable exchange rates. Others have suggested that, even in the supposedly halcyon age of the gold standard, national rivalry was the norm. What remains clear is the City of London's pivotal role in global trade, investment and financial services such as insurance, combined with Britain's self-interest in the expansion of international commerce. London was the cornerstone of the prodigious yet fragile edifice.[6]

During the Great War governments blocked the convertibility of their currencies into gold in order to prevent massive falls in their reserves. Even so, most currencies were artificially kept close to their pre-war parities, often at considerable expense – the British government spending $2 billion during the war to support the dollar–sterling exchange rate. When wartime controls ended in 1919 most countries allowed their currencies to float but there was a general commitment to return to gold as soon as possible and this was achieved by the mid-1920s. The new gold standard was, however, significantly different from the old. Instead of one dominant financial centre there were now two: London and New York, supplemented by Paris after the French stabilized their currency in 1926. Moreover, America had accumulated about 40 per cent of world gold reserves by the end of the decade; even France, with another 10 per cent, had more than Britain. The new system was in reality a gold-exchange standard, based not merely on gold stocks but on national foreign exchange reserves of sterling, dollars and francs – a further source of strain at times of international crisis when demands could come from several directions simultaneously. In 1923 twenty central banks held sterling, compared with only four in 1914.[7]

Cooperation between the three financial centres was also strained. Both New York and Paris were jealous of London's now shaky pre-eminence: one aim of their accumulation of gold in the late 1920s was to force Britain back on to a true gold standard, rather than a system based partly on sterling. There was particular animosity between Montagu Norman, governor of the Bank of England, and Emile Moreau, his French counterpart. 'He's an imperialist,' Moreau noted bluntly after their first meeting in 1926: 'he wants his country, which he loves passionately, to dominate the world.' For their part, Norman and his colleagues considered Moreau to be 'stupid, obstinate' but also 'formidable'.[8]

Personalities aside, neither the French nor, critically, the Americans had the same stake as Britain in the health and harmony of the global economy. 'Britain's empire is abroad; America's is at home,' a Chicago banker observed in 1921 and the statistics bear him out. Although the United States was now the world's leading exporter, the country's exports amounted to little more than 6 per cent of national income in 1928, compared with over 20 per cent for Britain. The ratio of imports to national income told a similar story: 5 per cent for America and nearly 29 per cent for Britain. In short, there was a new and critical asymmetry in the post-war global economy: whereas in the late nineteenth century Britain had needed the world as much as the world needed Britain, in the 1920s the world needed America far more than America needed the world.[9]

This became clear when the American consumer boom started to subside in 1928. The Federal Reserve, focused on the overheated stock market rather than the real economy, exacerbated the deflationary trend by keeping US interest rates high in 1928–9. Not only was this too late to stop the stock market spiralling out of control, but it also made domestic credit more expensive: so households postponed their purchases of consumer goods, thereby accelerating the downturn. Car production collapsed from 4.5 million vehicles in 1929 to 1.1 million in 1932; steel output, similarly, fell to a quarter of the 1929 figure.[10] The American downturn had global repercussions. US demand for imports contracted, undermining the world's primary producers as prices plummeted. And higher interest rates encouraged US investors to turn inward, fuelling the stock market and choking off foreign lending just when it was needed to counter the global contraction. Central European banks were especially dependent on foreign deposits. After the collapse of Vienna's largest bank, the Credit-Anstalt, in May 1931, the crisis spread to Germany and then Britain. The Bank of England's reserves, already limited in the new international order, had been further squeezed by a 50 per cent fall in Britain's invisible earnings (income from shipping, dividends, insurance and other financial services) in 1930–1, caused by the deepening global depression. Support from Paris and New York was inadequate and Britain was forced to suspend the convertibility of sterling into gold on 21 September 1931.

The crisis exposed the salient feature of the post-war international economy – what has been described as America's 'flawed hegemony'. In recent years revisionist scholars have emphasized the instabilities of the pre-1914 'golden age' and also the contribution of other countries in the origins of the Depression, but this research serves to touch up the picture rather than repaint it. Historian Charles Kindleberger's stark summary remains apt: 'The world economic system was unstable unless some country stabilized it, as Britain had done in the nineteenth century and up to 1913. In 1929, the British couldn't and the United States wouldn't.' In the gap developed the modern world's worst depression.[11]

The claim that the United States wouldn't take on a stabilizing role not only refers to America's lack of self-interest in the world economy but also highlights institutional problems within the United States. Victorian Britain had an unquestioned stake in the global economy and its polity was structured around this. There was a close axis between the City of London and the Treasury, and the executive was normally able, in a parliamentary system, to get its way in the legislature. Across the Atlantic, however, where president and Congress were elected separately and the constitution delineated a separation of powers, the White House had little control over key areas of economic policy. Tariffs, for instance, were set on Capitol Hill, largely by mutual backscratching among congressmen intent on protecting local business interests to ensure re-election. US tariff levels rose sharply in 1930 at a time when, from the global perspective, they should have been cut to help boost global trade. Throughout the 1920s, similarly, any significant reduction in war debts was anathema to Congress, conscious that the cost would otherwise fall on US taxpayers, even though debt reduction might have eased the global payments problem. And, in marked contrast to the ties between the City and Whitehall, there was a fundamental disjunction, even antipathy, between Washington, the political capital, and New York, the financial capital – reflecting old political shibboleths about banks, bankers and Wall Street.

Consequently, the United States did not have a central bank with control of the currency: the Federal Reserve system, established only in November 1914, was a public regulatory structure with limited powers, built around a Board of Governors and twelve regional banks. Although the Federal Reserve Bank of New York emerged as first among feuding equals, its chairman Benjamin Strong was unable to make it the equivalent of the Bank of England. His death in 1928 left a policy vacuum just as America's monetary crisis began. But the root problem was the Federal Reserve system itself, an uneasy compromise between East Coast bankers and their political enemies, which was structurally inadequate for the decisive macroeconomic role it needed to play as boom turned to bust.[12]

Those limitations in turn reflected the inadequacy of the whole US financial system in an era of modern international capitalism. In contrast with Britain, American banking remained local and atomistic – such was the phobia about octopus-like money trusts still entrenched in law and popular culture after the furore about the great monopolies of Rockefeller, Carnegie and other 'robber barons' at the turn of the century. In 1920 the United States had 30,000 separate banks, only 500 of which had branches, and assets averaged less than $2 million per bank. Mostly one-off operations, they had no lender of last resort to sustain them in the dash for cash when the economic downturn took hold. Between 1930 and 1933 the number of banks in operation fell by nearly half, and all the rest experienced heavy losses. The consequences of such a massive and systemic bank failure were profound. It exacerbated America's Depression, which was far worse than anywhere in Europe apart from Germany. In 1933 a quarter of America's workforce was unemployed and GDP had sunk by about a third since 1929. The collapse of faith in financial institutions also reflected a deeper crisis of confidence. 'What we have lost', opined the critic Edmund Wilson, was 'not merely our way in the economic labyrinth but our conviction of the value of what we are doing.'[13]

America's unwillingness and unreadiness to assume economic leadership reminds us that there was no smooth transition from 1917 into what would later be dubbed the 'American century'. The Depression stalked America for most of the 1930s: nearly a fifth of the workforce was still jobless in 1938. But the country's political institutions proved resilient. American democracy survived the Depression but Germany's did not. There, as in America, economic crisis was tied up with financial collapse – both reflecting a failure to come to terms with what had happened in 1918.

The headline story for Germany is rooted in the most notorious legacy of the Great War – reparations. In the Treaty of Versailles the peacemakers established the principle that Germany and its allies were responsible for the damage caused by their war of aggression (article 231) while also acknowledging in article 232 that their resources were not adequate to make 'complete reparation'. Similar statements were inserted in all the treaties with the defeated powers but only the Germans (for propagandistic reasons) turned this into an issue of 'war guilt' – a phrase never used in the Treaty. In 1921 an Allied commission drew up a reparations bill for Germany of 132 billion gold marks, about $33 billion, plus interest, but this draconian figure was largely window dressing to satisfy French and British hardliners. In practice, the real figure was 50 billion marks over thirty-six years, but this was still a huge sum. Removing the burden became the main aim of every German government of the 1920s.

In Britain and America the popular image of reparations is still derived from John Maynard Keynes. Clever and opinionated yet earnestly ethical, Keynes spent the war as a Treasury official, but he shared with his fellow Bloomsbury intellectuals a growing abhorrence of total war. 'I work for a Government I despise for ends I think criminal,' he anguished privately in December 1917; Lloyd George he considered a 'dirty scoundrel'. At Paris Keynes tried to cut the German reparation bill in return for a substantial reduction in debt payments among the Allies, but this proposal was politically impossible in the United States. Deeply depressed by his role as 'accomplice in all this wickedness and folly', Keynes resigned from the Treasury and poured out his anger in *The Economic Consequences of the Peace*, published on 12 December 1919. Within four months it had already sold 18,500 copies in Britain and nearly 70,000 in America, as well as being translated into eleven languages from German to Chinese. Keynes became a global intellectual celebrity.[14]

The impact of *Economic Consequences* was a compound of the book's brevity (some 60,000 words), its polemical urgency and, above all, its devastating character sketches. Clemenceau – impassive and cynical, convinced that 'you must never negotiate with a German or conciliate him; you must dictate to him.' Wilson – a lonely, dogged

'Presbyterian', his mind more 'theological' than 'intellectual' – no match for the feline Celtic wiles of Lloyd George with his 'six or seven senses not available to ordinary men' and his 'telepathic instinct' for the argument 'best suited to the vanity, weakness, or self-interest of his immediate auditor'.* In the cut and thrust of conference bargaining the Gallic nationalist and the Welsh wizard reduced the Presbyterian president to a 'blind and deaf Don Quixote', unable to see that his liberal vision had become a 'Carthaginian Peace', a 'policy of reducing Germany to servitude for a generation' and thereby causing 'the decay of the whole civilised life of Europe'.[15]

Keynes' vivid polemic, for all its contemporary influence, has now been superseded. Viewed historically, the reparations bill was the latest round in a Franco-German game of tit for tat. When French policymakers considered reparations in 1919 they had in mind the provisions of the Treaty of Frankfurt in 1871, which Bismarck imposed on France after its devastating defeat. He, in turn, had looked back to Napoleon's treatment of Prussia in the Treaty of Tilsit in 1806. The 1921 schedule of payments, known in Germany as the London Ultimatum, imposed at most an annual burden of around 8 per cent of German national income: less than the 9–16 per cent France paid annually in reparations after 1871. That had been set in order to pay a smaller total bill over a shorter period (three years) but in the 1870s the French had every incentive to pay up because that would end the occupation of much of northern France by German troops. After 1919, although the Allies were in temporary occupation of the Rhineland, they did not control most of the country: no Allied soldiers paraded in triumph along Unter den Linden, unlike the Prussians down the Champs Elysées in 1871. Indeed the fact that the peace treaties of both 1871 and 1919 were concluded at Versailles is telling: had the French been able to continue the tit-for-tat diplomacy, 1919 should have been a 'Treaty of Potsdam', signed in the Kaiser's palace

---

* The original sketch of Lloyd George was even more candid. 'One catches in his company that flavour of final purposelessness, inner irresponsibility, existence outside or away from our Saxon good and evil, mixed with cunning, remorselessness, love of power ...'

after a peace conference in Berlin. Instead the replay of 1871 in Louis XIV's Hall of Mirrors, though humiliating for Germany, actually revealed the limits of its military defeat. France's struggle over reparations in the 1920s therefore represented a desperate attempt to secure an economic substitute for the decisive victory that the Allies had failed to win on the battlefield in 1918. It was, as one German official put it, 'the continuation of the war by other means.'[16]

In the first round of this battle, Weimar governments used their own currency as a weapon. As with all belligerents, the mark had slipped in value during the war but it was not until 1919, when exchange controls were lifted, that the slide became severe. The economics ministry was happy to let this continue, even intervening *against* the mark in 1920 by buying substantial amounts of foreign currency in an effort to make German exports more competitive. An export boom, according to one key economic adviser, would 'ruin trade with England and America, so that the creditors themselves will come to us to require modification' of the 1921 ultimatum. But the trade war rebounded on Germany: the growth in its exports was offset by a boom in imports because German wage costs remained high and consumption rose sharply. Whereas the Allied powers were now clamping down on post-war inflation, Weimar governments failed to follow suit – a contrast of some importance, as we shall see.[17]

Germany's unbalanced budget was another weapon in its battle against reparations – used, almost flaunted, to show how hard they would be to pay. 'The goal of our entire policy must be the dismantling of the London Ultimatum,' argued the chancellor Joseph Wirth. He warned against imposing a property tax to help balance the budget because that would, in effect, 'declare the Ultimatum to be 80 per cent possible.' The budget deficit reflected domestic political imperatives as well. Germany's new democratic rulers were acutely conscious that their electorate, like those in Allied countries, expected recompense for sacrifices made during the war. In 1921 total public spending in Germany aside from reparations amounted to a third of GNP, compared with under a fifth before the war. In addition to unavoidable items such as war pensions, that bill included higher public-sector pay, unemployment relief, subsidies for food and housing, plus the notorious overmanning of the rail and postal systems. These were in effect 'German reparations to Germans' – politically necessary because the country did not admit its defeat and because of its scary brush with Bolshevism in 1918–19. Covering this budget deficit meant printing money, which fuelled inflation, but tycoon Hugo Stinnes spoke for much of the German elite when he insisted in 1922 that 'the choice had been between inflation and revolution'. It was, he said, 'a question of your money or your life.'[18]

Yet inflation caused revolution of a different sort. From the autumn of 1922 price rises spiralled into hyperinflation, on a scale dwarfing anywhere else in Europe. Germany defaulted on its reparations payments, so in January 1923 the French premier Raymond Poincaré, following the principle of war by other means, sent in troops to occupy the Ruhr, Germany's industrial heartland, and extract reparations in kind. Spontaneous local protests escalated into a campaign of passive resistance by workers and managers, subsidized by the German government, and then spread across the whole country, fomented in places by the communists. By the time a new coalition government led by Gustav Stresemann called off passive resistance (amid cries from the right about another stab in the back, like the Armistice of 1918), the Ruhr was on the verge of famine and the currency had been destroyed. In January 1914 it took 4.2 Reichsmarks to buy $1 US; a decade later the nominal exchange rate was 4.2 trillion Reichsmarks (an addition of twelve zeros). During 1923 daily life became utterly surreal. Employees collected their wages in baskets or wheelbarrows, often using them immediately to pay regular bills and buy non-perishables because the banknotes lost value literally hour by hour. On 24 July Victor Klemperer, a struggling academic, paid 12,000 marks for a cup of coffee and a cake; ten days later coffee and three cakes cost him 104,000 marks. No one who lived through German's hyperinflation ever forgot the experience. This wasn't anarchical violence as in 1918–19 but it was revolution all the same. Klemperer noted in his diary, 'Germany is collapsing in an eerie, step-by-step manner.'[19]

What pulled the country back from the brink was the financial intervention of bankers in London and New York. In 1924 they provided funds to support a new German currency and helped restructure reparations payments at a lower level, backed by an international loan. This package was known as the Dawes Plan, testimony not only to the energetic chairmanship of Charles Dawes, a Chicago banker, but the leading role now of American finance. Under this settlement the Germans got the French out of the Ruhr, while France started to get reparations again from Germany. Above all, American investors became enmeshed in the German economy: the Dawes loan, floated in October 1924 by a nationwide syndicate of 400 banks and 800 bond houses, was oversubscribed six-fold within ten minutes. This triggered a flood of US investment, followed by British and other lenders. Between 1924 and 1930 Germany borrowed nearly three times what it paid in reparations. The rest of the money was invested in German business (Ford and GM both bought up several automobile plants), in shares and also in municipal bonds – issued to pay for apartments, schools and other amenities. In other words, foreign loans were being used in the same way as currency depreciation in the early 1920s – to sidestep the reparations burden and subsidize growth and welfare. By 1929 Germany's share of global industrial output (11.6 per cent) was greater than Britain's (9.4 per cent). But just as depreciation eventually led to disaster, so debt dependence became catastrophic when US loans tailed off from 1928 at the same moment that Germany's economy began to turn down. By 1932 industrial production was only 60 per cent of the 1929 figure; a third of the workforce was unemployed, millions more were on reduced wages and much of the banking system had fallen apart.[20]

As with hyperinflation in 1922–3, the German depression of 1930–2 was rooted in politics as much as economics. Heinrich Brüning, the austere Prussian autocrat who served as chancellor from March 1930 to May 1932, pursued a relentlessly deflationary policy which only exacerbated the crisis. Although Brüning's economic options were limited in a pre-Keynesian era, his top priority was not reducing unemployment but reining in Weimar's welfare spending and especially ending reparations, by now the scapegoat for all Germany's ills. 'Cutting back, again and again, without reparations reform,' he insisted, would 'tear our poor nation to pieces' and he too was ready to exploit the economic malaise in the hope of persuading Germany's creditors to relent. In the summer of 1931, at the height of the banking crisis, President Herbert Hoover orchestrated a one-year moratorium on all payments of reparations and war debts. This proved to be permanent – leaving Germany the biggest beneficiary to the tune of £77 million while America, at the other end, lost £54 million* – but Brüning, unsure that the freeze would last, did not change course.[21] In any case, a counter-cyclical policy of easing credit and expanding the money supply was ruled out by memories of 1923. Germany's leaders were more afraid of renewed inflation than of deepening depression. As a result, the struggle for daily existence became a nightmare for the second time in less than a decade. Little wonder that many Germans were ready to turn to a nationalist messiah. In the election of September 1930 the Nazi Party won 18 per cent of the vote, becoming overnight the second largest party in the Reichstag. 'I'll see to it that prices remain stable,' Hitler asserted bombastically. 'That's what my stormtroopers are for.' There is 'no doubt', observes historian Jürgen von Kruedener, 'that the rise of Hitler would have been unthinkable without the catastrophic effects of the Depression.'[22]

Here again we see the entanglement of economics and politics. Just as the extent of the global depression reflected America's reluctance to assume the role of international leadership that its wartime economic power entailed, so Germany's successive economic crises were exacerbated by political assumptions rooted in the stab-in-the-back myth about 1918. Economic collapse had political consequences as well as causes: in Germany a lurch to the right that paved the way for Hitler's seizure of power, in America a withdrawal into economic and diplomatic isolationism. In both countries, too, the banking crisis generated huge populist anger against bankers and high finance, raising doubts about the survival of capitalism. Against this background, we need to look at the contrasting experience of Britain, where the 1920s were grim and the 1930s much better.

*

* Although further scaled-down payments were made by the Federal Republic of Germany during the Cold War and again in the 1990s, after reunification.

The distinctive feature of the British economy after 1918 was unprecedentedly high and persistent unemployment. In both America and Germany the jobless rates were more severe than Britain's in the early 1930s but the US economy had boomed in the 1920s and Germany's had enjoyed some febrile surges. In Britain, however, the average unemployment rate for 1921–38 was 10.9 per cent, nearly double the average for 1870–1913. More, perhaps, than anything else, the image of men out of work has shaped the stereotype of the 1920s and 1930s, encapsulated in the Hunger Marches to lobby Parliament and in novels such as Walter Greenwood's best-seller *Love on the Dole* (1933).

Two more specific contrasts with pre-war experience also stood out. Before 1914 unemployment followed fairly regular business cycles of boom and recession, whereas the post-war era saw abrupt and shocking rises in the jobless rate – to 12 per cent almost overnight in 1920–1 and up to 17 per cent in 1929–31. The 1921 crisis, now largely forgotten, was one of the most severe recessions in British economic history – 'the greatest setback to real GDP that the country had experienced since the industrial revolution'. Largely as a result, the economy actually contracted between 1913 and 1924, posting a negative growth rate of -0.1 per cent. The other contrast was in the duration of unemployment. Before 1914 most of the registered jobless were out of work for less than three months; by 1933–7 nearly 30 per cent had been out of work for over a year. This dramatic and sustained rise in the number of long-term unemployed generated a pervasive sense of hopelessness. Quite literally, it seemed, capitalism wasn't working.[23]

In this grim new world contemporaries struggled to explain what had happened. As he had on German reparations, Keynes offered an influential first draft of history, following up *The Economic Consequences of the Peace* with his pamphlet entitled *The Economic Consequences of Mr. Churchill* (1925). This lambasted the decision of the chancellor of the exchequer to return to the gold standard at the pre-war parity of $4.86 to £1 which, Keynes argued, had the effect of overvaluing sterling by about 10 per cent, pricing British goods out of export markets unless wages or jobs were slashed to compensate. The workers, he claimed, were 'the victims of the economic Juggernaut. They represent in the flesh the "fundamental adjustments" engineered by the Treasury and the Bank of England to satisfy the impatience of the City fathers.' In fact, Churchill had privately shared some of Keynes' doubts, fearing that this policy would exacerbate the country's high unemployment and sluggish output. 'I would rather see Finance less proud', he noted, 'and Industry more content.' He even invited Keynes to a seminar over dinner with leading officials to debate the issues. But the Treasury was adamant, insisting that the gold standard was a 'knave-proof' automatic regulator and that the hallowed rate of $4.86 was vital to show the world that sterling was once again as good as gold.[24]

After the financial crisis of 1931, the return to gold in 1925 became symbol and scapegoat for the failures of interwar economic management. It was taken to show the folly of focusing on monetary policy and, at a deeper level, of privileging global financial services over the needs of manufacturing industry – the bias of what has been called Britain's 'gentlemanly capitalism'. In the late twentieth century, however, as Keynesianism lost its canonical status, the debate reopened. Although Keynes was probably right about the overvaluation of sterling, this single act of policy, like the reparations burden on Germany, was not decisive: it has to be set within a larger context, one in which politics mattered as much as economics and the immediate post-war era of boom and recession in 1919–21 deserves as much attention as the more celebrated Slump of 1929–31.[25]

The reconstruction boom of 1919–20 was not unique to Britain but its consequences were particularly severe. By the end of the war there was a crying need for investment in many industries because of both wartime neglect and pent-up consumer demand. Under wartime restrictions companies and individuals had also accumulated considerable purchasing power in savings, cash and government bonds. The boom took off in the spring of 1919 and lasted for about a year but supply could not satisfy the huge demand both at home and abroad, so prices rose sharply. Because of the liquidity of the economy, much of the economic activity was speculative in nature: companies were bought and sold, merged and floated, in an orgy of financial activity.

New capital issues on the London money market rose nearly sixfold, from £65 million in 1918 to £384 million in 1920 – a figure not matched again until well after 1945. This artificial boom was already subsiding by April 1920 when the Bank of England raised interest rates suddenly and savagely to 7 per cent, aggravating the economic downturn.[26]

Speculation was most feverish in the buying and selling of shipyards and cotton mills at inflated values, which then proved debt-ridden, uncompetitive victims of the global overcapacity in staple industries. British shipbuilding was a product of the age of steam: international competitors had responded more quickly to the era of oil. Likewise the Lancashire cotton industry lagged behind its rivals in introducing ring spindles for spinning and automatic looms for weaving. Although British steel plants improved efficiency from 30,000 tons per blast furnace in 1913 to 83,000 in 1937, the average by that date in the United States was 210,000 tons and 125,000 tons in Germany. As the 'first industrial nation' Britain would always have been peculiarly vulnerable to eventual catch-up by its economic rivals exploiting more modern technologies. But the combined effect of wartime demand and the post-war boom was to entrench the place of coal, shipbuilding, cotton textiles, iron and steel in the British economy – all with obsolescent technologies – just when diversification and modernization should have occurred.[27]

The effect of the 1919–21 era on labour relations was equally important for Britain's economic future. The government's concessions to head off possible revolution helped entrench the position of labour in a distinctly British form. Legislation for the 8-hour day (or 48-hour week) had an immediate and dramatic effect in 1919, cutting working hours by 13 per cent compared with the pre-war average. This reduction in the working week, implemented during the post-war boom, was not matched by a commensurate reduction in real wages, thereby weakening overall productivity and price competitiveness. Wage levels might have been expected to respond to the severe rise in unemployment in 1921 and the steady fall in living costs for most of the next two decades but such flexibility was constrained by Britain's emerging system of collective bargaining. During

the war the government had created a system of joint industrial councils bringing together employers and unions across many industries to
arbitrate disputes and avert strikes. Perhaps as many as 60 per cent of
British employees were covered by industry-wide pay agreements in
the mid-1920s; a decade later, even after the Slump, the proportion
was still about 40 per cent. These pay deals were hammered out
piecemeal industry by industry, rather than in a more coordinated way
across the whole labour market as was the pattern after 1945. Pay rates
therefore took less account of the overall economic situation and this
retarded wage flexibility during the Slump.[28]

Another concession to labour in 1920–1 also entrenched a distinctive system of unemployment benefits. In 1911 Asquith's Liberal
government had passed a pioneering Unemployment Insurance Act
but this covered only 2¼ million of Britain's 19 million workers, with
limited benefits. New legislation in 1920–1 extended coverage to 12
million workers at a level of about one-third of the national minimum
wage. The 1911 Act assumed a self-financing National Insurance
Fund based on contributions from employers and employees but this
principle was eroded in 1920–1 amid the panic about mass unemployment: the government extended help to those in need, even if
they had not paid contributions, and also made payments to wives and
children. The result was a generalized 'dole' subsidized by the
Treasury from taxation and justified by the unprecedented levels of
unemployment. Attempts to limit the escalating cost through means
tests and other devices were resisted during the 1920s by the two
Labour governments. By 1931 unemployment benefits amounted to
£120 million a year, nearly two-thirds of which were being paid for
by the state.[29]

This bill for these benefits became the central issue of the financial
and political crisis of August 1931. Wall Street refused to support
sterling's increasingly precarious position without confirmation from
the City that Labour was moving towards a balanced budget. The
sticking point in Cabinet was a 10 per cent cut in unemployment
benefit, opposed by Arthur Henderson, several other ministers and
many union leaders. Personal animosity between Henderson and
MacDonald played a part in the battle but the root issue was one of

principle. To quote Ernest Bevin, leader of the transport workers, the 'City must not be saved at the expense of the working class'. Bevin no longer felt the gold standard was worth preserving, whereas MacDonald believed that the City represented the larger national interest in sound finance. Yielding to the unions, he said, would show that Labour was 'ruled by narrow self-interested sections rather than the well-being of the country', thereby undermining all his efforts to make it an accepted national party of government. On the immediate financial issue, Bevin was right: like Keynes, though from instinct more than intellect, he already glimpsed the benefits that would stem from devaluation instead of deflation. MacDonald, by contrast, was wrong on economics, destroying his government in a futile bid to keep Britain on gold, but his political judgment may have been wiser in the longer term. To appreciate this, we need to glance sideways at the 1930s in Germany.[30]

Sociologists of the welfare state often contrast the German and British systems as fundamentally different types – the first rooted in Bismarckian principles of paternalistic social control, the latter in liberal affirmations of basic individual rights. Whatever the divergence in their origins, the two systems were in practice converging during the crisis of mass unemployment in the 1920s: both had to be bailed out by taxpayers, leading to a political confrontation between right and left. The outcomes of that struggle were, however, very different. In Germany it brought down the 'great coalition' in March 1930, ushering in Brüning's relentlessly deflationary government and then Chancellor Franz von Papen's attack on what he called Weimar's 'welfare state' (*Wohlfahrtsstaat*) which, he argued, imposed burdens far beyond the capacity of the government and corroded individual responsibility. In Britain, by contrast, the financial and political crisis of August 1931 paved the way for a broad coalition, the National Government, which imposed the controversial cuts but maintained the basic welfare system. Welfare provision in Britain relied more than the continentals on state funding and also offered general public assistance rather than targeted social insurance. These distinctive features, rooted in the panic measures of 1920–1, would create problems in the long term. On the other hand, the scope and continuity of

Britain's welfare system helped cushion society against the worst economic and political shocks of the depression.[31]

We have seen that Britain's economic malaise in the 1920s owed much to the inevitable catch-up by rivals but it was compounded by specific post-war problems – the structural inertia of staple industries, a commitment to gold-standard orthodoxy and the economic gains made by labour. Yet, as the example of the dole suggests, there was a more positive side to the story. For all its faults, British capitalism and consequently British society survived the Slump better than most of the continent or America. At the heart of this story are some ostensibly boring institutions – taxation, the national debt and the banking system – which present the more positive face of the City and gentlemanly capitalism.

Britain had waged previous wars largely out of taxation – nearly half the cost of fighting France, for instance, in 1792–1815. During the Great War, however, the proportion was only 26 per cent, close to Germany's figure of nearly 17 per cent. In other words, both of these powers waged the war mostly by borrowing and this had serious inflationary potential. Yet, as the world's leading financial power, Britain coped much more effectively. Not only did it have the credit and contacts to raise American loans – responsible for about a quarter of the wartime growth of Britain's national debt – but the London money market was also better able than Berlin to absorb the huge amount of floating debt in the form of short-term Treasury bills. After the war some Labour radicals wanted to 'abolish this hideous war memorial of capitalist finance and financial jugglery' by a capital levy on the rich, but the party leadership soon abandoned that idea in its efforts to secure the middle ground. The Treasury was adamant that the government should return to principles of sound finance: converting the short-term bills into long-term debt, using a sinking fund to reduce the overall debt burden and ensuring that peacetime expenditure was once again met from taxation. 'The present parlous condition of public finance in many European countries', observed Otto Niemeyer of the Treasury in 1923, 'is largely due to the habit of their governments to spend money without covering their expenditure out of ordinary revenue.' Not only did such recklessness fuel inflation, it also undermined government credit which, as Britain's recent experience showed, was essential for borrowing in time of war.[32]

The Treasury's insistence from the spring of 1920 on high interest rates to control speculation and its determination to reduce the national debt (accounting for over 40 per cent of government spending in the late 1920s) undoubtedly had a deflationary effect, exacerbating unemployment. But these policies did help to prevent German-style hyperinflation which, as we have seen, shredded public confidence in both the currency and also the state itself. Despite fears that the British people had reached the limits of their taxable capacity by 1918, thereafter the tax burden remained at double the pre-war level without sparking political revolt. A system of personal allowances for poorer men and for men with wives and children helped ensure general acceptance. By 1930 two-thirds of British government revenue came from direct taxes, in contrast with much greater continental reliance on excise and sales taxes, borne disproportionately by the lower classes. Britain's tax revolution proved profoundly important. In 1913 total public expenditure amounted to 12 per cent of GDP, with less than 4 per cent of GDP spent on social services and 3 per cent on defence. By 1937 total public expenditure had more than doubled to 26 per cent of GDP, with less than 5 per cent of GDP spent on defence and 10.5 per cent on social services. In fact, during the two decades after 1918 British government spending rose more rapidly than at any other time in the twentieth century: not only did this reduce the war debt, thereby maintaining financial stability, but it also funded social welfare on a scale unmatched except in Sweden. This helps to explain why economic dislocation was not translated into political extremism.[33]

Nor should one underestimate the importance of Britain's stable banking system – in dramatic contrast with Germany and the United States where the banking collapse did lasting damage to economic confidence. The late nineteenth century had seen a steady process of concentration in England and Wales, reducing the number of banks from over 400 in 1855 to only 70 in 1913, and this trend accelerated during the Great War. By 1920, when the government started to block further mergers, British banking was dominated by an oligopoly –

Midland, Lloyds, Barclays, Westminster and National Provincial – each with hundreds of local branches: Barclays, for instance, had over 1,700 by 1919. The Big Five controlled 80 per cent of bank deposits and operated as a cartel, agreeing rates for interest on deposits and overdrafts, but the system of a few big banks with multiple branches did ensure a stability that was totally lacking in the United States. There, not only did banks fail in their thousands but bank shares tumbled further and faster than the price of industrial securities. In Britain, by contrast, there were no bank failures during the depression and the prices of bank shares held up well: even in June 1931, at the height of the Austrian and German banking crises, they still stood at 90 per cent of late 1928 levels. Because Britain went off gold the collapse of the gold standard constituted a crisis for the Bank of England but not for British banking as a whole.[34]

What may seem surprising in retrospect about 1931 is that the Bank and the government did not do more to defend the sterling parity in which they had invested so heavily. But Britain's distinctive response to 1931 was shaped by its experiences in the 1920s. On the one hand, the country's persistently high levels of unemployment made it difficult to impose further deflation. Although Britain escaped relatively easily from the General Strike in May 1926, which lasted only nine days, that reinforced anxieties from 1919–20 about worker discontent. The whole issue was peculiarly sensitive in Britain in 1931 because the country was governed by a minority Labour government: this fell over budget cuts that would have seemed trivial to the rightist governments of France or Germany. So the political dangers of staying on gold were huge while, on the other hand, the economic dangers of letting sterling float seemed less alarming than in countries whose currencies had been ravaged by 1920s inflation. In contrast with Brüning's ruinously deflationary policies in Germany, the National Government in Britain was willing to cut its golden anchor and risk the inflationary consequences. And its landslide victory in October 1931 produced what Neville Chamberlain called a 'Parliamentary Dictatorship', able to impose the anti-socialist policies it wanted. But although ruling out public works as both economically unproductive and financially dangerous, the coalition did not seriously tamper with unemployment benefits.[35]

The crisis of 1931 was perhaps the most dramatic of twentieth-century Britain's peacetime history, reducing Montagu Norman, the governor of the Bank of England, to a nervous breakdown. Yet his apocalyptic fears and those of many contemporaries about the collapse of capitalism and democracy were not realized. 'We have fallen over the precipice but we are alive at the bottom,' gasped Norman in January 1932. 'The main point', Keynes remarked more presciently, 'is that we have regained our freedom of choice.' The floating pound, instead of bobbing around violently, settled at a level around $3.50–3.70 – providing a degree of stability while making British exports much more competitive. Britain also gained a comparative advantage by coming off gold much earlier than many of its rivals – nearly two years before America and five years before France. Contrary to Keynesian orthodoxy, fiscal policy was not decisive in Britain's recovery: rather than lower taxes and higher budget deficits, what mattered was the expansion of money and credit now that currency depreciation had removed fears that such expansion would undermine the balance of payments. In short, 1931 finally freed Britain to develop an active domestic monetary policy. America expanded its monetary supply even more than Britain but the benefits were offset by abandoning gold later and by the collapse of the banking system.[36]

The most striking contrast is between Britain and France, which stuck to gold much longer than any of the great powers. France was far less successful than Britain in coping with its post-war short-term debt: governments had to borrow heavily, pushing up prices and undermining confidence in the franc which had collapsed to one-eighth of its 1914 value by the summer of 1926. Matters were not helped by France's acute political instability after 1919: eight ministries came and went during this period. That in turn reflected the deep divisions between right and left, which impeded agreement on balanced budgets, higher taxes and debt stabilization of the sort imposed in Britain by the coalition in 1920–1. Only when a political truce allowed Raymond Poincaré to form a moderate, centrist government in July 1926 was it possible to push through deflationary measures and stabilize the franc at 20 per cent of its 1914 value. This left the franc undervalued, unlike sterling after 1925, and thereby benefited French exports. Having rescued the country from the brink of disaster (inflation was running at 350 per cent in 1926), the French clung on to the new gold standard tenaciously, even after their international rivals had abandoned gold and devalued their currencies. The franc was now seriously overvalued and France's gold hoard, trade surpluses and balanced budgets all disappeared. But in France a policy of deflation was less politically contentious than in Britain: unemployment remained relatively low because industry was generally smaller scale, French workers could shift back to the farms (the agricultural sector being far larger than in Britain) and governments in the early 1930s came mostly from the right and centre right rather than the left. Only with the Popular Front in 1936 – an unholy alliance of socialists, communists and radicals formed in part because of the fate of democracy in Germany – did a French government reverse the deflationary tide in order to support workers and fund rearmament, making devaluation inevitable.[37]

Although the British government never had a clear, coherent policy, the somewhat fortuitous combination of early devaluation, low interest rates and stable banking fostered economic recovery which, in turn, contributed to the political stability described in Chapter Two. In 1929–31 industrial output had dropped by 20 per cent; by 1935, however, it was 20 per cent higher than in 1929 – while in France, and in other countries that stayed on gold, output was still stagnant. British exports showed a modest recovery but the real growth came from domestic demand. In the 1930s Britain experienced its own version of America's 1920s consumer revolution, centred on cars and electrical products – sectors in which the country had hitherto lagged behind but which, like mortgage-funded housing, now benefited from easier credit under the government's freer monetary policy.[38]

In 1938 Britain produced 341,000 cars – double the figure for 1930 and nearly 40 per cent of total car production in Europe. France, the leader in the early 1920s with half of Europe's output, had slumped to less than a quarter, far behind Britain and Germany. Although US manufacturers had established themselves in Britain – Henry Ford's new factory at Dagenham, east of London, being the largest car plant outside the USA – the dominant companies were Morris and Austin, both British family-owned firms building small, mass-produced cars. As in the United States, the benefits for related industries such as steel and rubber were immense. Britain had also lagged behind America and Germany in the use of electrical power, mainly because of historic reliance on coal, but this too changed dramatically during the 1930s. The National Grid, established in 1926, covered virtually all the UK by the mid-1930s, cutting the cost of electricity by half. In 1926 there were only 1.76 million consumers of electricity, in 1938 nearly 9 million – three-quarters of all houses in Britain. This generated spin-off demand for electrical appliances such as radios, irons, cookers and vacuum cleaners. Sales of these goods and also of cars was assisted by the spread of consumer credit, far earlier than in France, through the hire purchase system.[39]

Although cars and the more expensive consumer durables such as fridges and washing machines were largely confined to the middle class in the 1930s, many working-class people did acquire radios and electric irons. They also benefited from the housing boom in private construction and council housing which, in tandem with new roads and electrification, accelerated the suburbanization of England. The resulting ribbon developments of semi-detached houses, often in 'mock Tudor' style to evoke a rural image, appalled aesthetic purists: 'Come friendly bombs and fall on Slough! / It isn't fit for humans now,' exclaimed the poet John Betjeman in 1937. But the combination of a new home with inside lavatory and fitted bath, some basic electrical appliances to ease the daily grind and even a car to open up new leisure opportunities all made the 1930s a turning point for hundreds of thousands of British families.

The impact of these new industries and suburbanization should not be exaggerated because it was regionally specific, being most evident in south-east England and the Midlands. Although about a million men from the depressed north and Wales did move south during the interwar years to find new work, many more stayed put and became long-term unemployed.[40] One could say that Britain survived the crisis of capitalism at the price of impoverishing a significant minority of its population – notably in the old industrial areas of northern England, south Wales and central Scotland where coal, steel, textiles and shipbuilding had collapsed after the war. In 1934 unemployment in St Albans, on the northern fringe of London, was less than 4 per cent; in Jarrow on Tyneside half the men were out of work, in the Welsh steel town of Merthyr Tydfil over two-thirds. Many of these depressed areas were Labour strongholds, yet the party had also been sidelined after its split in 1931 and the creation of the National Government. This marginalization of economic and political discontent served to heighten the sense of relative stability in Britain in contrast with much of the continent in the 1930s.

Stability but at a price: the theme can be amplified. The merger boom of the 1920s accentuated a tendency towards cartels and restrictive practices in British industry. What was called 'rationalization' often meant a low-risk defensive strategy of protecting market shares without implementing radical restructuring. Management, labour and the banks that had invested heavily during the 1920–1 boom all had a vested interest in keeping things ticking over, however unprofitably. This was true not just of coal, cotton and steel but even of new industries such as car manufacturing, where British companies produced a wide variety of products rather than pressing ahead with standardization. In 1938 the Big Six British carmakers produced forty different types of engine and an even larger range of chassis and body types. This helped them sustain niche markets among the middle class but retarded the cost and efficiency savings needed to break into an American-style mass market. Playing safe cushioned the shock of the depression but damaged Britain's long-term competitiveness – as would become evident after 1945.[41]

Probably the biggest comfort blanket of all was a new tariff wall. On and off for thirty years the debate about free trade versus protection had wracked British politics but the economic crisis and the creation of a National Government dominated by Tories allowed Neville Chamberlain, as chancellor of the exchequer, to complete the project his father Joseph had begun. On 4 February 1932, with Joe's widow and children in the gallery of the House of Commons, Neville proudly announced a general tariff of at least 10 per cent on most imports, bringing to an end nearly a century of free trade. That summer the Ottawa economic conference agreed preferential access for goods from the British Empire, in return for some concessions to British exports. In 1930 about 83 per cent of imports were admitted to Britain free of duty; after 1932 the proportion was only 25 per cent. Protection had a limited impact on overall recovery but it did accentuate the shift of Britain's trade from global to imperial markets. Exports to empire countries increased from 43.5 per cent of total British exports in 1930 to nearly 50 per cent in 1938, while imports from the empire rose from 29 per cent to over 40 per cent. Belatedly Britain was following the path taken incrementally by France since the late nineteenth century, using protected imperial markets to shore up domestic industries that could no longer compete globally. Here, too, policies that helped cope with the immediate economic crisis would damage British competitiveness in the long run.[42]

So Britain came through the 1930s much better than most of the developed world. The economy survived, albeit in the form of a new 'insular capitalism' based on devaluation and protectionism to ensure domestic stability.[43] But this is clear only with hindsight. In the early 1930s it seemed debatable that British capitalism would survive the shocks of the Slump and the end of the gold standard. And the ignominious collapse of the second Labour government raised troubling questions for the British left about whether socialism could evolve peacefully out of capitalism. Nor was this debate confined to Britain. 'In 1931,' wrote the historian Arnold Toynbee, 'men and women all over the world were seriously contemplating and frankly discussing the possibility that the Western system of society might break down.'[44]

Meanwhile it seemed that a new society was emerging in Soviet Russia. By the early 1930s the threat of world revolution, so much in the air in 1919, had receded; Russia was now seen as the country of Stalin, not Lenin, a state that had withdrawn from the global stage to enact an epic drama of modernization at home. Precisely what was achieved in Russia in the 1930s remains hard to judge: Soviet statistics were deficient and often deliberately falsified. Yet the broad result is clear: a transformation of the Soviet economy and society that was more revolutionary than the Bolshevik seizure of power. Within a decade from 1929 some 25 million peasant holdings cultivated by horsepower had been combined into 250,000 collective farms, backed by 8,000 machine tractor stations. Opting far more than Britain and western Europe for American mass-production methods, the Soviet Union created major new industries such as manufacture of motor vehicles (700 trucks in 1928, over 180,000 ten years later), machine tools, aircraft and armaments. Stalin, the party name adopted by Josef Vissarionovich Djugashvili, meant 'man of steel' and steel was at the heart of his revolution. 'We are becoming a country of metal, a country of automobiles, a country of tractors,' he proclaimed in 1929. 'And when we have put the U.S.S.R. on an automobile, and the peasant on a tractor, let the worthy capitalists, who boast so much of their "civilisation", try to overtake us!' Even more pressing than national pride was fear of another war. 'We are fifty or a hundred years behind the advanced countries,' Stalin warned in 1931. 'We must make good this distance in ten years. Either we do it or we shall go under.'[45]

The centrepieces of Stalin's revolution were gigantic prestige projects such as the iron and steel complex of Magnitogorsk, the 'magnetic mountain' in the Urals (modelled on US Steel's works at Gary, Indiana) and the vast car plant at Gorky on the Volga (based on Ford's factory at Dearborn, Michigan). Stalin saw them as symbolic proof that the Soviet Union could 'catch and overtake' the capitalists. A demonic image of capitalism became the all-purpose justification for the regime's brutality and inefficiencies – the equivalent on a systemic scale of the West's Bolshevik bogey in 1919. In the 1930s Stalin seemed to have history on his side: as Magnitogorsk burst into production (its manifold faults hushed up), Gary, shining icon of Great War America, seemed to be rusting away. American steel production fell from 60 million tons in 1929 to 15 million in 1932.[46]

Stalin's grand projects and omnicompetent Five Year Plans were lauded by leftist intellectuals in the West as evidence of a society where the dross of selfish individualism had been consumed in the fires of a collective crusade for the good of all. In retrospect some of these fellow-travellers seem unbelievably credulous. Take, for instance, Beatrice and Sidney Webb, the grand old couple of British Fabian socialism.* Although an unlikely pair – Beatrice was a tall, handsome woman, with aquiline nose and fearsome energy; Sidney a fat little Cockney with goatee beard and pince-nez – since the turn of the century they had churned out pioneering works of sociology and political science with the constant refrain that a socialist society could be created gradually and peacefully. But their tune changed in the crisis of 1931. Beatrice now privately doubted the 'inevitability' and even the 'practicability' of gradualness in the transition from 'a capitalist to an equalitarian civilisation'. The collapse of MacDonald's government was, in her view, 'a victory for American and British financiers' and an 'open declaration' of 'capitalist dictatorship', for which the traitor MacDonald now served as the figurehead. 'In the course of the next decade', she reflected in September 1931, 'we shall know whether American capitalism or Russian communism yields the better life for the bulk of the people.' Whichever won, she believed that Britain would 'have to follow suit' because there was no 'third creed' available. Likening the struggle to that between Christianity and Islam for 'the soul of Europe' at the end of the Middle Ages, Beatrice declared that 'without doubt we are on the side of Russia.'[47]

In the summer of 1932 they went, as it were, on pilgrimage to Russia and then wrote *Soviet Communism: A New Civilisation?* – two massive volumes running to 1,100 pages, published in November 1935. When the book was reprinted two years later the Webbs deleted the question mark, confident that the USSR had indeed created a new civilization characterized by 'deliberately planned production for community consumption' and an ideology rooted in science which 'rejects every element of the superstition and magic' still pervading the West. Like all their books, *Soviet Communism* was hard going – biographer Margaret Cole once likened Sidney's prose to 'the slow passing

* Classically educated Fabians took their name from Fabius Maximus Cunctator, the Roman general who advocated a strategy of attrition to wear down Hannibal, rather than a direct assault. Their target was capitalism not Carthage.

of an infinitely long, laden freight train' – but in this case their usual 'heavy artillery of fact' was infiltrated by a 'Fifth Column of palpable untruths and distortions'. The book seemed to take completely at face value the Soviet statistics and statements that were its main sources. It also rested on a contempt for Russian society ('its masses illiterate, superstitious, exceptionally diseased, and in places actually barbarous') which served as recurrent justification for the persistent violence and brutality of the revolution. The Webbs brushed aside talk of mass famine in the Ukraine and assertions that Stalin was a dictator: 'We do not think that the Party is governed by the will of a single person; or that Stalin is the sort of person to claim or desire such a position.'[48] Privately they did have their doubts: in 1937–8 Beatrice studied reports of the purges and show trials, fearing that Stalin and his clique '*may* have lost their heads!' But in public she kept the faith.[49]

The Webbs were not alone. Other fellow-travellers of the 1930s, in what has been called 'a postscript to the Enlightenment', chose to see Stalin's Russia as the embodiment of 'progress', the latest and best hope of a rational, scientific society. And, despite their rationalism, many did so as a leap of faith, born of utter disenchantment with Labour in 1931.[50] Yet few became outright Marxists or abandoned their root commitment to liberal democratic values. Harold Laski, an owlish little politics professor at the LSE but in his day one of Britain's leading public intellectuals, visited Russia in 1934 and declared that there his lifelong 'dream' of socialism had 'become a reality'. But Laski questioned the Webbs' blindness about Stalin's purges and the show trials: in the words of one biography, he 'saw Soviet Russia as the harbinger of a new civilization and its crimes broke his heart.'[51] Alfred Sherman, a young communist in the 1930s who eventually became a guru of Thatcherism, later summed up the mental gymnastics of these fellow-travellers: 'If the Soviet paradise did not exist, it had to be invented to substantiate their socialist faith. It was not so much that they were deceived by Soviet propaganda as that they deceived themselves with the aid of Soviet propaganda.'[52]

The Labour Party carefully distanced itself from communists and fellow-travellers. Some of its leading figures such as Clement Attlee and the union boss Ernest Bevin were vehement anti-communists who watched with alarm as the Communist Party of Great Britain was Stalinized from the late 1920s. Yet, in its own way, Labour was also influenced by Stalin's revolution. During the 1920s Labour 'had broadly conceived of socialism emerging out of a vibrant capitalism, with improved social services, education and international peace paving the way for common ownership.' The electoral debacle of 1931 did not shake Labour's commitment to parliamentary democracy but it did force a fundamental rethink of Fabian gradualism. Instead of grassroots socialism 'enabling' local authorities to administer both essential and social services, the party now championed national solutions, especially government ownership of key industries guided by an overall economic plan. Although insistent that Britain was very different from Russia, Labour ideologues were deeply affected by the perceived success of Soviet planning. They believed that this could and should be adapted to Western liberal norms. In the words of Hugh Dalton, one of the intellectual architects of Labour's new course, after his visit to the USSR in 1932, 'It is my firm conviction that, unless we in this country also adopt the principle of economic planning on Socialist lines, we shall find no solution of our economic troubles. And if the Russians can do it and can make much remarkable progress in so short a time how much more effectively could we in England do it!'[53]

Planning was not just an obsession of the left: it was also taken up by centre-left Tories who shared the widespread doubts about laissez-faire capitalism. They pointed to precedents other than Soviet Russia. In 1927, for instance, Harold Macmillan, Robert Boothby and Oliver Stanley – all up-and-coming Conservative MPs – published *Industry and the State*, in which they noted, 'The tremendous economic movements, arising from a multitude of causes, which periodically surge across the world, cannot be prevented or accurately predicted by the individual, but the history of the war teaches us that they can to a very considerable extent be mastered and controlled by governments. The war period shattered preconceived economic notions, proved possible theoretical impossibilities, removed irremovable barriers, created new and undreamt-of situations.' The MPs had in mind the range of controls in 1914–18, such as nationalization of the railways, shipping and

eventually collieries, the regulation of the stock market and the conscription of manpower. But all of these had been reversed after the
war, so that 'by far the greater part of the legislation which to-day
governs trade and industry dates from before that period.' Was this,
they asked, the best way 'to meet the vastly changed conditions of the
modern economic era'? Surely a Britain that had freed itself from late-
Victorian shibboleths such as the gold standard and free trade should
grow up about the hands-off, laissez-faire state?[54]

Such questions seemed even more pertinent after 1931. Macmillan,
his Teesside constituency ravaged by the Slump, was appalled at the
misery and wastage of mass unemployment. Three decades later, when
writing his memoirs, it was still vivid in his mind: 'I shall never forget
those despairing faces, as the men tramped up and down the High
Street in Stockton.' One consequence of the crisis, he reflected in
1938, was finally to 'liberate men's minds from a continued sub-
servience to the economic orthodoxy of the pre-war world.'
Economic planning became for Macmillan a central feature of what
he called 'the Middle Way' between uncontrolled capitalism and
'totalitarian dictatorship' – which would show that 'freedom and efficiency' could be combined and thereby preserve democracy from
'reaction or revolution'.[55] Like the Tory right, Macmillan and his ilk
were scripting a new historical narrative, with 1931 completing the
destruction of pre-war verities started in 1914, but instead of the
panacea of protection they advocated planning as the progressive
future for modified capitalism. Many Labour supporters of the
National Government also shared Macmillan's faith in a middle way.
The Next Five Years Group, established in 1935, was the brainchild of
Clifford Allen, a National Labour peer. Although its name may have
echoed Stalin's Five Year Plans, its mission was squarely British: what
could be accomplished within the span of a five-year Parliament?
The group's manifesto insisted that the 'historic controversy' between
'the idea of a wholly competitive capitalistic system and one of State
ownership, regulation and control' appeared 'largely beside the mark'
in 1930s Britain. 'For it is clear that our actual system will in any case
be a mixed one for many years to come.'[56]

The strength of this 'middle opinion' was a feature of mid-1930s

Britain.[57] Here is another reason why the country avoided the polarization of right and left so evident on the continent. The concept of
planning attracted moderate Tories, Labour and Liberals, and also
major figures from the business world. The pressure group Political
and Economic Planning (PEP), founded in 1931, included among its
sponsors Sir Basil Blackett, a director of the Bank of England, and
Israel Sieff, vice-chairman of Marks and Spencer. PEP applauded the
early New Deal in the United States, particularly the National
Recovery Act with its emphasis on planning, and in 1935 Lloyd
George called publicly for a 'British New Deal'. Roosevelt's dynamic
leadership became a stick with which to beat MacDonald and his
lethargic colleagues. In 1933 the Liberal Violet Bonham Carter had
asserted that 'action, vision and statesmanship' could save this 'crumbling world', just as 'America is showing us to-day'. But Roosevelt's
America never gripped the British imagination to the extent of Stalin's
Russia. Even the PEP broadsheet *Planning* cited the New Deal for its
bold leadership rather than for specific policies, while the conservative
Daily Telegraph noted loftily that 'most of the salient features of Mr.
Roosevelt's social legislation have been established here for two generations.' During the 1930s the United States did not seem like a
model for the future, let alone the embryo of a 'new civilisation'.[58]

A different critique of capitalism was emerging from Keynes, whose
treatise *The General Theory of Employment, Interest and Money* appeared
in February 1936. Unlike the hard left, Keynes did not see the Slump
as the final crisis of capitalism: 'the Economic Problem', he stated in
November 1931, was 'nothing but a frightful muddle, a transitory and
an *unnecessary* muddle'.[59] Searching for policy remedies, Keynes was
attracted neither by socialism nor by planning. Would-be planners
wanted to replace failed market forces, whereas he 'wanted to supply
the market system with enough demand to maintain full employment.' Although the Slump does not feature in his magnum opus, it
was an essential stimulus to his rethinking of orthodox economics,
shaking his remaining faith in classical remedies for adjustment such as
cuts in wages or interest rates. Yet Keynes' proposals had limited
impact in the 1930s. His complex, rambling book took several years
for economists and politicians to digest and the role he proposed for

the state in closing the gap between the capacity to produce and the failure to consume could only be enacted under conditions of another war.[60]

All these writers shared a deeper sense that the crisis extended far beyond capitalism itself. Keynes was as much a moral philosopher as an economist: he sought new certainties for an age that had lost its religious faith and thereby its anchors for economic and social conduct. No enthusiast for capitalism, he nevertheless believed that it had to be shored up because society and civilization depended on it.[61] Macmillan, likewise, argued that 'economic progress' was vital for the survival of democracy and freedom, which in turn were essential for 'the possibilities of progress in every branch of science, art, and learning.' Clifford Allen for his part lamented that in the twentieth century 'so many nations should be reverting to the political barbarism of the Dark Ages'. Here, it seemed, was the fundamental problem. The Great War had not only dislocated the structure of capitalism, it had also undermined civilization itself.[62]

5

CIVILIZATION

Before art can be human it must learn to be brutal.

John Middleton Murry, 1911

I don't think these shell-shocked war poems will move our grandchildren greatly.

Sir Henry Newbolt, 1924[1]

The medal given to British servicemen and women after victory in 1918 stated that they had fought in 'The Great War for Civilisation'. But the reality of that war seemed like the utter negation of civilized values – human beings reduced to the level of animals in the mud or blown to pieces by those miracles of modernity, the machine gun and heavy artillery. Sixty per cent of British army deaths in the entire war were caused by artillery fire; for the Germans the proportion was even higher. Warfare was not the man-to-man knightly heroics idealized medieval-style on war memorials; it had become an industrial enterprise waged anonymously from afar. *The Times* war correspondent Colonel Charles Repington characterized it as 'the butchery of the unknown by the unseen'.[2]

Even caring for the wounded was an industrial process. The French author Georges Duhamel devoted the final chapter of his prize-winning war memoir *Civilization* (1918) to a mobile ambulance unit. This 'last word in science' was, he said, a 'factory' to repair the 'parts of the military machine that are the worst destroyed'. But those 'parts' were actually human beings, like the *cuirassiers* he could see piled up for treatment – 'the finest men in France' with big chests and powerful limbs now reduced to 'broken statues'. The mobile ambulance, declared Duhamel, was 'civilization's reply to itself, the correction it was giving to its own destructive eruptions'. Yet such a correction could only be superficial: 'you can't climb back up a slope like the one the world is going to roll down from now on.'[3]

How could one talk about civilization in the wake of such barbarism? That was the question for thinking men and women after 1914. And how should this horrific industrialized war be represented in art, architecture and literature? Were traditional cultural forms now irrelevant? Intellectuals and artists in all the belligerent countries grappled with these questions, but the British response was distinctive. In part this was because the modernist movements that had swept the continent hardly touched pre-war Britain, where the pastoral tradition still held sway especially in painting and poetry. Equally important, the British government took a uniquely high-profile role in arts patronage, especially for painting during the war and the architecture of commemoration afterwards. In Britain artistic modernism was very much a product and a phenomenon of the war years. In the field of English literature modernism had more impact, but not until the 1920s. Together works of art, architecture and literature helped eventually to create an image of 1914 as the poignant finale of an age of innocence, a second Fall from which Britain was never really redeemed.

Like all 'isms', modernism is a slippery term whose meaning is elusive. But very generally it is used to signify a 'crisis of representation' in art and literature in the early twentieth century: a crisis about both what could be represented and how it should be represented, thus raising issues of both content and form.[4] In art the products of this crisis were images that challenged the conventional principles of perspective that had been used for centuries to depict three-dimensional 'reality' on paper or canvas. This revolt took various forms, now known as Cubism, Expressionism and Futurism – movements which seem more coherent in retrospect than they did at the time.

'When we invented cubism', recalled Pablo Picasso tongue in cheek in 1935, 'we had no intention whatever of inventing cubism. We simply wanted to express what was in us.'[5] Painters, of course, have a necessarily ambivalent relationship with tradition – even those from the avant-garde. That term dates back to the revolutions of 1848 and conveys the idea that artists and intellectuals form the vanguard of cultural and political change. 'We fight like disorganized "savages" [*Wilde*] against an old, established power,' proclaimed the German Expressionist Franz Marc in 1912. 'The dreaded weapons of the savages are their *new ideas*. New ideas kill better than steel.'[6] On a personal level, artists also have an egotistic interest in exaggerating their novelty to distinguish themselves from both teachers and peers. All of these early-twentieth-century movements were revolts against national artistic establishments, which shaped the art market and controlled the teaching academies. Yet struggling bohemians have to earn a living and, in the absence of an exclusive contract with a dealer, that meant pandering to the conventional tastes of the elite and middle class via the despised world of galleries and salons. 'I am not discouraged by my own powers,' wrote the Italian avant-gardist Umberto Boccioni in 1907, 'but over my financial means, which don't ever seem to increase without the most ignoble self-prostitution.'[7] Much of art history is framed between these competing pressures of heady revolt against tradition and the necessary embrace of patronage.

Cubism, Expressionism and Futurism were all reactions to what was deemed the superficiality of Impressionist art, mesmerized by ephemeral surface appearances. Cubism engaged in novel ways with form and space, breaking them down into fragments: the term 'Cubist' was coined in 1908 after a critic mocked a painting full of 'little cubes'. Its artist was Georges Braque – once regarded, in Gertrude Stein's words, as 'the one who put up the hooks' for Picasso's canvases, but now recognized as his partner in a 'dual effort' of friendly, creative rivalry between 1908 and 1914 that has been described as the 'most phenomenal' relationship in the history of art.[8] Although Picasso's traumatic brothel scene, decorously known to posterity as *Les Demoiselles d'Avignon*, is now dubbed the 'first' Cubist painting, much of the Picasso–Braque oeuvre was not exhibited and sold before the war because the two artists enjoyed secure patronage. The *Demoiselles* achieved cult status only in the late 1930s, after being acquired by the Museum of Modern Art in New York. More celebrated in pre-war Europe was the work of so-called Salon Cubists, such as Albert Gleizes, Jean Metzinger and Henri Le Fauconnier. The latter's *Abundance* has been described as 'perhaps the best-known Cubist painting in Europe before 1914'. Gleizes and Metzinger promoted the Salonists' work as a distinct movement in their influential essay *Du Cubisme* (1912). There was also a nationalist undertone to Cubism's appeal: it could be seen as a reinvention of classical painting that was proudly French, hence the frequent depiction of the Eiffel Tower, pre-eminent symbol in the 1900s of France's modernity.[9]

Expressionist painters presented themselves explicitly as a reaction to French Impressionism. The Austrian critic Hermann Bahr asserted that Impressionism was the 'consummation' of classical art, seeking to 'rule out every inner response to the outer stimulus', to 'leave nothing to man but his retina' whereas the Expressionist 'tears open the mouth of humanity' so as to 'give the spirit's reply.'[10] Bahr was writing during the Great War as part of the nationalist culture war that accompanied the military conflict: theorists sought to reify Expressionism as a radical and distinctively German movement in modern art. Earlier usage of the term Expressionist, by contrast, was more catholic and embraced artists such as Braque and Picasso, all of whom supposedly privileged subjective response over visual impression. That said, Expressionist art was indeed rooted in the Germanic world and included groups such as The Bridge (Die Brücke), which originated in Dresden in 1905, and the more programmatic Blue Rider (Der Blaue Reiter) circle, who exhibited in Munich in 1911–12 and toured continental Europe. Their expressive response was evident most of all in abstracted forms and vivid, non-naturalistic colour to convey emotion, not least a sense of horror at the travails of modernity. Expressionist art romanticized the past and celebrated the natural and erotic: the term 'blue rider' stemmed from Wassily Kandinsky's fascination with medieval knights and Franz Marc's obsession with horses.

Futurism, by contrast, revelled in modernity; it was also the most ideological of these three artistic movements. Its 'Manifeste du Futurisme' of February 1909, authored by the flashy Italian poet Filippo Marinetti, affirmed the 'beauty' of the modern industrialized world, a world of 'speed', of soaring airplanes, 'great-breasted loco-motives' and the 'roaring motor car'. Futurists sought to 'glorify war' as 'the world's only means of keeping itself clean' (*seule hygiène du monde*). Their manifesto of 'ruinous and incendiary violence' was aimed particularly at Italy, with its 'gangrene of professors, archaeol-ogists, tour guides and antiquaries', but it was also a nationalist riposte to Cubism and Expressionism, to prove that Italians could embrace the modern with more ardour than their northern neighbours.[11] Much Futurist art was overtly political. *The Revolt* by Luigi Russolo (1911) depicted a red mass of frenzied but abstract humans driving a series of red arrows into the blue and black forces of tradition. Although on a philosophical level, theorists of Cubism and Futurism each exagger-ated their distinctiveness, in practice Italian and French artists learned enormously from each other – art historians talk, for instance, of 'Cubo-Futurism'.[12] Cubist painters such as Fernand Léger were influ-enced by Futurist abstraction, while Futurists such as Boccioni used the fragmentary techniques of the Cubists to capture the motion of a crowd or a locomotive.

These swirling artistic currents that we now clinically label Cubism, Expressionism and Futurism were all part of an international ferment in European art during the decade before 1914. They were, however, currents that barely touched English shores. Edwardian art was intensely conservative, dominated by traditional portrait painters such as Augustus John and William Orpen, and the big 1905 show of some three hundred French Impressionist paintings was a flop. It was only when the critic Roger Fry mounted two big shows of post-Impressionists in 1910 and 1912 that the British art world became seriously acquainted first with Gauguin, van Gogh and Cézanne and then with Picasso and Matisse. 'The combined effect of both events', observes art historian Frances Spalding, 'meant that a London audience had to catch up, in the space of two years, with artistic developments that had taken place in France over the last thirty.' But the response of critics and the public was generally negative. The author Wilfrid Scawen Blunt found no 'trace of sense or skill or taste' in the paintings, 'nothing but the gross puerility which scrawls indecencies on the walls of a privy.'[13]

When the Futurists hit London, reactions were even more hostile. Marinetti's June 1914 manifesto on 'Vital English Art' – in which he tried to enlist radical young London artists in the Futurist cause – succeeded only in provoking a backlash from the so-called Vorticists, led by Percy Wyndham Lewis, a thirty-two-year-old rebel painter and writer, well versed in continental art. Tall and dashing, with dark eyes and a clipped moustache, Lewis had charisma, brains and a talent for polemic. He turned Marinetti's methods on the master with his own Vorticist manifesto *Blast* (published in lurid pink) which 'blasted' pet cultural and artistic hates in a strident, billboard style. Like the other 'isms' the term Vorticism was contrived and vague – it originated from the poet Ezra Pound who celebrated England as a great Vortex 'from which, and through which, and into which ideas are constantly rushing'. Such vagueness allowed Lewis to embrace aspects of all recent continental movements and attack traditionalist features of English culture ('We must kill John Bull with art') while also claiming Vorticism had a distinctively national ethos – controlled, individualistic and 'Anglo-Saxon' – unlike the emotional 'Latins' with their 'Futuristic gush over machines, aeroplanes, etc.'[14]

Lewis published the Vorticist manifesto in July 1914. Unlike the continental experience, modernist art was only just getting going in Britain before the Great War. But it would find its moment and its subject in the ensuing conflict, again in contrast with the rest of Europe.

The continental avant-garde movements lost much of their force and vitality once war broke out. The art market collapsed in 1914–15 and artistic circles broke apart, as painters joined up in the patriotic fervour. Some did not return: Franz Marc and August Macke among the

German Expressionists, and the Futurists Umberto Boccioni and Antonio Sant'Elia. Georges Braque was shot in the head and only just survived.

In Germany the world of culture had always been tightly censored, with the Kaiser seeing himself as the upholder of traditional artistic values. 'The supreme task of our cultural effort is to foster our ideals,' he declared in 1901. 'That can be done only if art holds out its hands to raise the people up, instead of descending into the gutter.' In wartime, German conservatives mounted a campaign against avant-garde art with a French or Italian taint but, after the carnage of Verdun and the Somme, Expressionists gave vent to their growing disillusion. 'Either you are a painter and you shit on the whole caboodle', wrote Karl Schmidt-Rottluff, 'or you join in and kiss painting goodbye.' In fact he, like many of those who had joined in, fell apart amid the horrors of war and became unable either to fight or to paint. Otto Dix, whose nerves and hand remained steady, was a rare exception, sending home several hundred sketches from the front. After the war Dix, like other German Expressionists such as George Grosz, turned to political art drawing on Dadaist techniques of ridicule to dramatize the revolutionary upheavals of 1918–19. But then Dix returned to his wartime sketches, in *Der Krieg* (The War) (1924), a series of fifty etchings depicting the degradations of the front, where men are reduced to the level of animals (plate 10), and in *Der Schützengraben* (The Trench) – a revolting pile of brains, guts, blood and excrement, with a decaying corpse impaled at the top. This canvas was probably destroyed in the Nazi era, but Dix reworked it for his triptych *Der Krieg* (1932), which has survived. In the post-war art of Dix, Max Beckmann and other disillusioned veterans, the cruelty of war is depicted with an almost obscene candour, unmatched in France or Britain – not just in gross depictions of the dead and dying but also in frequent pictures of war cripples.[15]

In France some 3,000 men and women, many of them professional artists, spent the war in the camouflage division of the army, using Cubist techniques to 'de-form' guns, observation posts and other military objects. Hence Picasso's remark to Gertrude Stein as they watched a camouflaged cannon trundling down the boulevard

Raspail, '*C'est nous qui avons fait ça.*' The jingoistic fervour of wartime also called into question artistic modernism. French conservatives attacked 'Kubisme', insinuating it was a form of 'boche art', so artists reached back to the classical past for a style that suited propaganda claims about France as a bastion of 'Latin' civilization against German barbarism. Thus Picasso – a Spaniard and therefore exempt from French military service though resident in Paris – displayed a new interest in painters such as Ingres and Poussin and in the Harlequin figure of the Italian *commedia dell' arte*. Picasso was already moving on from his pre-war experiments with Cubism, but the 'return to order' demanded by wartime opinion guided the next phase of his artistic odyssey.[16]

Aside from public pressures, artists across continental Europe had a real problem in conveying the visual horrors of the Great War. Images of the front were provided by photographs and film and these were vivid, often shocking, despite government censorship especially of their own country's dead and wounded. Artists struggled to match the effect, or to reveal something strikingly different. Highly abstract techniques were inappropriate to show what war actually did to human bodies and the natural landscape, so even exponents of extreme abstraction such as Kandinsky and Marc Chagall brought recognizable people, buildings and trees into their pictures. Most artists really struggled to find a style that seemed suited to modern war in a photographic age and this was another reason why most of them – with exceptions such as Dix in Germany or Léger in France – shied away from the war as a subject.

In the middle of the conflict most belligerent countries experienced a renaissance in the art market and a surge in museum attendance. But the public turned to paintings not to see vistas of war but to escape from them, craving soothing subjects and conventional styles. One Polish refugee in Russia burst into tears before a beautiful landscape in an exhibition. 'Blood, blood, everywhere,' she cried, '*but here* it is so nice!' If people desired war-related art it was in the form of paintings that helped them to mourn or evoked the mystery of mortality – hence the renewed appeal of religious themes. In Russia Natalia Goncharova, previously an ardent Cubo-Futurist, drew on Byzantine

1. *Statesmen of the Great War*: Sir James Guthrie's theatrical depiction (1924–1930), with Andrew Bonar Law, the Conservative Party leader standing (centre). Seated to the right of Law is Herbert Asquith, Prime Minister until 1916; to the left, leaning forward, is Sir Edward Grey, Foreign Secretary in 1914, then Winston Churchill and, two along, David Lloyd George, Asquith's successor as premier.

PRESIDENT MASARYK:
Budeme vždy spojeni s národem americkým,
spojeni duchem svobody a demokracie.

2. Tomáš Masaryk, father of the new Czechoslovakia, on a postcard celebrating Czech–American solidarity with President Woodrow Wilson, whose calls for national self-determination ignited anti-imperialist feeling across the world.

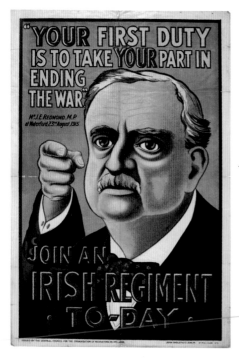

3. On a 1915 recruiting poster John Redmond, leader of moderate Irish nationalism, calls for patriotic Irishmen to fight with the British Army to defeat German militarism and thereby win Irish Home Rule.

4 and 5. Two views of a very different Irish nationalist. Eamon de Valera in Dublin in 1916, under British military arrest after the Easter Rising, and as President of Ireland in 1966, escorted by his own soldiers during commemorations for the fiftieth anniversary of the Rising.

THE MAN OF DESTINY

NO
REASONABLE
OFFER
REFUSED.

NOTHING DOING.

6. The two 'ordinary men' who dominated interwar British politics, Stanley Baldwin (left) and Ramsay MacDonald, turn their backs on the Napoleonic figure of Lloyd George. A Bernard Partridge cartoon for *Punch*, 12 June 1929.

7. The other 'superman' of the era depicted as 'Adolf Churchill' by Will Dyson in the *Daily Herald*, 30 March 1933, two months after Hitler seized power in Germany. Dyson was satirising Churchill's diehard campaign to maintain British rule in India.

8 and 9. In the early 1930s a consumer boom and the availability of cheap mortgages via building societies helped pull southern Britain out of the Slump and head off the appeal of extremist politics that wracked the continent.

10. One of a cycle of 50 prints, *Der Krieg* (1924), by German Expressionist artist and war veteran Otto Dix, which depicted his experiences in almost pornographic gruesomeness – as with this wounded soldier (*Verwundeter*) on the Somme in 1916.

11. But British avant-garde war art remained representational. Richard Nevinson's painting of a French machine-gun crew locked into their gun, *La Mitrailleuse* (1915), was Futurist in style but appealed to critics, civilians and soldiers alike.

12. Paul Nash used Cubist techniques to evoke the blasted landscape of *The Menin Road* (1919) outside Ypres, where thousands of British Empire soldiers met their end – a landscape (and a war) from which there seems to be no exits.

13. John Singer Sargent was a grand old man of British society portraiture. But *Gassed* (1919) captured the pity of war and the dignity of its victims with unique power. His 'realism' was a far cry from that of Otto Dix.

PEACE or WAR?

A National Declaration on the League of Nations and Armaments

NATIONAL DECLARATION COMMITTEE, 15, Grosvenor Crescent, S.W.1.

TO MEN AND WOMEN OVER EIGHTEEN.

Will you please answer overleaf these five questions :—

1. Should Great Britain remain a Member of the League of Nations ?

2. Are you in favour of an all-round reduction of armaments by international agreement ?

3. Are you in favour of the all-round abolition of national military and naval aircraft by international agreement ?

4. Should the manufacture and sale of armaments for private profit be prohibited by international agreement ?

5. Do you consider that if a nation insists on attacking another the other nations should combine to compel it to stop by
   (a) economic and non-military measures ;
   (b) if necessary, military measures ?

These questions are put to you as a means of showing to our Government and to the world where Britain stands as to Peace and the Price of Peace.

We want your answers whether "Yes" or "No," with or without explanation or commentary.

A leaflet will be supplied in which you will find the guiding considerations which, in our view, should be kept in mind when answering the questions.

Kindly hand this Ballot Paper to a collector, who will call in a day or two.

Published by the National Declaration Committee, 15, Grosvenor Crescent, S.W.1, and printed by King & Jarrett, Ltd., Holland St., Blackfriars, S.E.1.

14. The Peace Ballot of 1935 was signed by 11.6 million people, over a third of the UK's population. The results showed strong support for the League of Nations but opinion was split down the middle on the use of force to keep international peace.

15. In October 1939, a few weeks into another great war, the next generation of soldiers set off for Cambridge railway station, paying wary respect to the men who marched away in 1914 – never to return. *Cambridge Daily News,* 21 October 1939.

religious art for her 1914 series of lithographs 'Mystical Images of War', in which angels mingled with airplanes.[17]

Nor did most governments make a big effort to promote war art, perhaps because of their concentration on film, photos and posters. The US army sent eight war artists to Europe in 1918 but most were magazine and book illustrators by background, and that showed. Harvey Dunn, in his youth a burly farmboy from South Dakota, was unusual in producing art that seemed emotionally engaged with the travails of the individual soldier and the horrors of the Western Front. Dunn's output amounted to fewer than thirty finished pieces, each taking a huge emotional toll, but he managed to 'capture the feeling of war with exceptional quality'. Most of the American war art, however, was descriptive rather than evocative, often charcoal or crayon drawings rather than full-size paintings, and they totalled only five hundred pieces.[18]

In France there was a larger art scheme. *Les peintres en mission aux armées* were supposed to 'seize the atmosphere of the front' and 'grasp what is happening with sensitivity, with emotion'. But although eight teams of official artists were at work in 1916 and 1917, the works they produced seemed remote and traditional – formal images of camps and transports, of prisoners, ruins and empty landscapes. There were few close-ups of troops in peril, of explosions and shelling, and little sense of the frenzy of modern conflict because the painters were not allowed near the front line. One critic was reminded of 'those hurried travellers who, guidebook in hand, visit a foreign country without having the time to penetrate it deeply enough to understand it.'[19]

In reality France's supreme artistic memorial to the war was *Les Nymphéas*, eight elongated panels of water lilies which Claude Monet, the great survivor of the Impressionist generation, had laboured on reclusively since 1914 while his son fought at the front. On the day after the Armistice Monet presented the work to the French nation. Clemenceau, an old friend and himself an art critic, arranged for the panels to be displayed in two special rooms in the Orangerie in Paris – what one commentator called 'the Sistine Chapel of Impressionism'. Monet's memorial of peace is perhaps the most eloquent testimony to what French historian Philippe Dagen has called 'the silence of the painters' about the Great War.[20]

In Britain and its empire, however, the story is very different because modern artists did face up to modern war; indeed large numbers were paid to do so by the state. In the 1920s and 1930s the 'most significant and important collection of modern British art in the country' was to be found in the Imperial War Museum, established in 1919, whose holdings were superior to those of the Tate Gallery, founded more than twenty years before. The museum held over 3,000 works of art, many of them commissioned by the government as part of a 'deliberate exercise in creating a public for avant-garde works and managing the avant-garde for public use.'[21]

In Britain, as on the continent, the early months of the conflict had seen a patriotic backlash against the avant-garde. In March 1915 *The Times* damned a recent exhibit of works by Wyndham Lewis, William Roberts and other Vorticists as 'Junkerism in Art'. These paintings, declared the paper's art critic, were essentially 'Prussian' in spirit, executing 'a kind of goose-step' rather than painting 'naturally'. Another critic even hoped that the Vorticists might 'all perish in the war'.[22] Some did indeed perish, including the sculptor Henri Gaudier-Brzeska, while others such as Roberts and David Bomberg joined up under the pressure of patriotic expectations and in order to make a living after the collapse of the art market. Like artistic circles on the continent, the Vorticists were dispersed by war: the second and final issue of *Blast* appeared in July 1915.

What saved the artists was war propaganda – or more exactly the peculiar British conception of war propaganda in 1914–18, formed out of a compromise between War Office secrecy and Liberal openness. Here the key figure was the politician Charles Masterman, who headed Wellington House, the government's clandestine bureau for war propaganda. Easily underestimated because of his boyish looks and sloppy dress, Masterman was actually a brilliant intellect and a superb Whitehall fixer. 'He knew little about art, but he had infinite experience of exploiting the talents of others; official war art in its early stages was entirely a product of his readiness to experiment.'[23]

The British military stood out among the belligerents for its obsessive secrecy. Until mid-1916 there had been no official photographers in France: the few images of the British in France in 1914 and 1915 came from surreptitious snaps by soldiers using their own cameras. Only the need to build up domestic support for the great offensive on the Somme forced Haig's staff to appoint two official photographers for the Western Front – reasoning, in the words of intelligence chief General John Charteris, that 'he who lives by the river must make friends with the crocodile.' During the whole war British official photographers produced only 40,000 negatives, 28,000 of them from the Western Front. By contrast, the French army created a Section photographique as early as April 1915, with a staff of more than a hundred, backed by mobile laboratories, which produced over 150,000 plates during the war. Similarly the German army's Picture and Film Bureau (Bild- und Filmamt) had generated 200,000 slides and 30,000 negatives by 1917.[24]

The War Office and the Admiralty had an equally obstructive attitude to film-makers. Masterman wanted to promote the British war effort both abroad and at home through good motion pictures but the service chiefs were convinced that this would expose vital secrets. Many in Whitehall also viewed the cinema as an even more vulgar version of the music hall. The first film, *Britain Prepared*, was not launched until Christmas 1915, by which time German propaganda was being screened all over the world. 'Wake Up, England', warned one film magazine, claiming that Germany had developed 'a practical monopoly of the cinema as a means of instructing public opinion.'[25]

By early 1916, Britain was lagging behind the enemy in both war photos and film but this visual void was partly filled by the war art programme. Its origins appear to lie in a chance conversation between one of the Wellington House staff and Muirhead Bone, a well-known etcher, who mentioned that he was about to be called up by the army. That seemed a waste of Bone's talents and the issue was brought to Masterman's attention. Not being much interested in art himself, he asked his wife, 'Do you know anything about an artist called Muirhead Bone?' She replied, as she recalled later, 'with some heat', reminding her husband that one of Bone's etchings was hanging on their wall. And so in mid-August 1916 Bone arrived in France as an honorary second lieutenant equipped with chauffeur-driven car and a brief to depict the Western Front. War artists, unlike photographers and film-makers, were part of British army tradition and Bone was a conventional artist: his appointment was approved at the very top by Haig himself. Bone's meticulous but bloodless charcoal drawings, with accompanying text, were reproduced in a series of best-selling pocket books entitled *The Western Front*. This was a sanitized view of the front, a 'travelogue composed by an uninvolved spectator', but Bone paved the way for the appointment of young modernists such as Richard Nevinson and Paul Nash, as well as society portraitists like William Orpen. Crucially these artists were under little constraint. Nevinson once asked whether there was any subject he should avoid. 'No, no,' replied Masterman with a wave of his hand. 'Paint anything you like.'[26]

It is worth dwelling on that remark for a moment because it reflects Masterman's creed as a Liberal. His philosophy for British propaganda was 'the presentation of facts and of general arguments based upon those facts.' Man was assumed to be an essentially rational animal, persuaded by arguments not swayed by emotions. German propaganda, by contrast, was directly controlled by the military, under the draconian 'Law of Siege' which largely overrode the civil power. The army leaders, contemptuous of politicians and suspicious of the masses, displayed what has been called 'a crucial failure to understand or to trust the home front' which contributed to Germany's eventual collapse in 1918.[27] Trusting the home front was, of course, hard for elites in all the belligerent countries: as the war went on a greater degree of compulsion was applied and, like others from his party (for instance on the issue of conscription), Masterman struggled to relate his Liberal values to the exigencies of total war. His answer was partly the conventional one that German barbarism, exemplified by Louvain, Reims and the *Lusitania*, imperilled the ideals of liberty and civilization. But Masterman also wanted the means to reflect those ends, otherwise Britain would have abandoned the very values for which it claimed to be fighting: hence his preference for factually based propaganda and considerable artistic freedom.[28]

Masterman got the war art programme going but its great impresario was the press tycoon Max Aitken, Lord Beaverbrook. 'The Beaver' was a dynamic and unscrupulous Canadian businessman, who moved to Britain in 1910 and rapidly established himself in politics as a close ally of Bonar Law and then Lloyd George. Biographer A.J.P. Taylor reckoned that his character remained 'the one he was born with – a clever restless little boy always up to mischief', as his impish face suggested. In February 1918 Beaverbrook was given charge of a full-scale Ministry of Information, whose priority was to up-to-date news via wireless and cable, plus films and photographs. Traditional modes of propaganda seemed outmoded and the withdrawal of all war artists from France in March 1918 because of the German offensive could easily have heralded the end of the whole scheme. Instead war art flourished as never before in the last months of the conflict – not as liberal propaganda (Masterman's original brief) but because Beaverbrook wanted paintings to record and memorialize the war. He had already pioneered a scheme for the Canadian army and now sought to replicate this on a larger scale. Almost his first act as Minister of Information was to create a British War Memorials Committee (BWMC), which included Masterman and the writer Arnold Bennett. They drew up an ambitious and systematic programme covering eight areas of the war both abroad and at home, including 'Munitions' and 'Clerical and Other Work by Women'. Guided by Muirhead Bone, the BWMC commissioned a wide range of artists, including the Vorticists Lewis and Roberts. Plans were also developed for a grand Hall of Remembrance to epitomize the nation's sacrifice, possibly in Whitehall itself, graced with a special series of large 'superpictures' featuring the Western Front.[29]

The BWMC has been described by its historian Sue Malvern as 'the most ambitious' twentieth-century British programme of 'state patronage to commission modern history paintings'. Certainly it would have been impossible outside the context of total war and the concomitant government direction. Yet to call the scheme 'state patronage' is to slide over the distinctive liberalism of British politics and society – so very different from the militarized statism of the Kaiserreich – which a buccaneering individualist such as Beaverbrook could exploit. His war art schemes for Canada and Britain showed, in the words of Maria Tippett, 'the kind of personal and ad hoc organization that could be assembled by a hard driving entrepreneur of means and connections'. Beaverbrook even created a legally dubious charity to keep the project going after the ministry was wound up, in order to create 'a legacy for posterity'. Unlike the classically heroic battle paintings of the past, executed academically in the studio, the canvases had to be 'based on personal experience', captured while 'emotions and passions and enthusiasms are at their highest', with each artist enjoying the 'fullest liberty to do whatever may best suit his temperament'.[30]

The results of this licensed freedom was war art with a distinctively English character, rooted in earlier traditions of representation and landscapes but infused with the attitudes and techniques of modernism. For many young artists, the war commissions gave them both a subject and a vision that had been lacking before the war.

Wyndham Lewis, for instance, had spent six months as an artillery officer on the Western Front in 1917. Twenty years later he recalled his baptism of fire, 'plunged immediately into the romance of battle', by which he meant its emotional intoxication rather than any inherent beauty. 'Yes, romance is the enemy of beauty. That hag, War, carries it every time over Helen of Troy.' This is why Lewis wrote, sardonically, 'you must not miss a war, if one is going! You cannot afford to miss that experience.' Yet he might not have lived to capture the experience but for the war artists programme, which pulled him away from the guns for the whole of 1918. His technique was now very different from pre-war Vorticist abstraction. As he remarked later, 'The geometrics which had interested me so exclusively before, I now felt were bleak and empty. They wanted *filling*. They were still as much present in my mind as ever, but submerged in the coloured vegetation, the flesh and blood, that is life.' He added that 'those miles of hideous desert known as "the Line" in Flanders and France presented me with a subject-matter so consonant with the austerity of that "abstract" vision I had developed, that it was an easy transition.'[31]

Lewis' abstracted vision of war was expressed in a series of paintings of artillerymen in action, most notably *A Battery Shelled* – a jarring blend of Vorticism and representation. Filling most of the canvas, a team of gunners frenziedly rush to feed their guns. Angular stick men, they seem like robots or even insects, serving the mechanized master. In the left foreground, however, three officers are depicted with sombre realism. One of them watches the frenzy of the gunners, a second looks wearily down, pipe in hand, while a third (resembling Lewis himself) stares fixedly away from the action. How to interpret these onlookers has generated endless debate. Do they represent Lewis' old Vorticist self in the face of a new world? Are they there to point up the tragedy of war, functioning almost as a Greek chorus? Is the divide between officers and men a reflection of the deeper existential rift, as Lewis saw it, between individualists and the crowd? Or, given his interest in Matthew Arnold, is this perhaps an evocation of Culture versus Anarchy, Civilization against Chaos, Reason in the face of Lunacy? For, as he wrote later, 'to obtain this parched, hollow, breathless desert you have to postulate madmen.'[32]

The debate about how to interpret *A Battery Shelled* will never be resolved, but there is no dispute that the romance of war had aroused Lewis to artistic heights that he would never reach again. The same was true of Richard Nevinson, another product of the Slade School of Art in Bloomsbury – well trained in draughtsmanship but seeking a style of his own. In 1914 he came out as a passionate disciple of Marinetti, pitting himself against Lewis in a juvenile confrontation, but several harrowing months with an ambulance unit in France in 1915 marked his coming of age as an artist as he found his subject and his style – like Lewis but in a very different way.

Nevinson's idiosyncratic blend of Cubist simplification and Futurist energy produced several riveting paintings of troops in action, notably *La Mitrailleuse* (plate 11). This rendition of a team of French machine-gunners frenziedly locked in place around their weapon against a sky etched with barbed wire was acclaimed by the poet Laurence Binyon as a haunting illustration of 'a world of men enslaved to a terrible machine of their own making'. Art critics were virtually unanimous in agreement: 'When war is no more,' wrote Lewis Hind, 'this picture will stand, to the astonishment and shame of our descendants, as an example of what civilised man did to civilised man in the first quarter of the twentieth century.' *La Mitrailleuse* was modernist but not too abstract: soldiers on leave queued up for a view because in it they could recognize themselves. Later in the war Nevinson's style shifted towards graphic realism as he closed in on soldiers in their fortitude or suffering, but one of his last war paintings, *The Harvest of Battle*, returned to the theme of troops in action, though this time not as a mechanized mass but as a ragged line of wounded trudging through a blasted quagmire of mud and bodies. Although based on a war photo, Nevinson gave the scene poetic depth by arranging the men in a huge ellipse, from right to left, circling a belching gun – symbol of what they and their generation could not escape.[33]

'Harvest' was also an ironic title for other war paintings, for instance Orpen's brightly coloured depiction of three peasant women, one with a young baby, tending the earth – but earth that was replete with graves and barbed wire. The harvest theme picked up the pastoral landscape tradition, stretching back through Turner to Constable, in which English art was rooted. Its most accomplished practitioner among the war artists was Paul Nash, another Slade graduate who had struggled to find his own style before the war. Nash had long been obsessed by trees – seeing them, he said, 'as tho[ugh] they were human beings' – but the Pre-Raphaelite sentimentalism of his student days was blown to bits in 1917 when he encountered the landscape of the Western Front, initially as an infantry officer and then as a war artist. His first visit was in springtime. Like many painters he was intoxicated by the amazing shapes and colours – 'wondrous ruinous forms ... toast-rackety roofs and halves of houses here and there' among the 'bright trees' and a riot of blooming flowers. 'I believe I am happier in the trenches than anywhere out here,' he wrote home to his wife. 'It sounds absurd, but life has a greater meaning here and a new zest, and beauty is more poignant.' But when Nash returned in November to the rain and mud of Passchendaele, he was transfixed by 'the most frightful nightmare of a country more conceived by Dante or Poe than by nature' with 'no glimmer of God's hand' to be seen anywhere. 'Sunrise and sunset are blasphemies,' he exclaimed; 'they are mock-eries to man.' The scene was gilded with the colours of hell: yellow stinking mud, shellholes filled with green-white water, black dying trees and unceasing shells that churned up the land into a graveyard. 'I am no longer an artist interested and curious,' Nash declared. 'I am a messenger who will bring back word from the men who are fighting to those who want the war to go on for ever. Feeble, inarticulate, will be my message, but it will have a bitter truth, and may it burn their lousy souls.'[34]

On fire for art, Nash ventured into oils and applied to the traditions of landscape the new vocabulary of Cubism and Futurism – 'geometric shapes, staccato movement, and fractured planes'. *The Menin Road* (plate 12), like Nevinson's *Harvest of Battle*, depicted the wasteland of the Western Front, but its focus was on the land not the men. Nash exposed what art historian Paul Gough has called the 'latent violence' filling the 'void of war' – diverse zones of water, mud, pathways and trees from which, on closer inspection, there were no ways of escape.[35] Even starker is *We are Making a New World*, in which a silver sun rises over clouds coloured like dried blood to shed pale light on a lunar landscape of pummelled earth and limbless trees. Today that painting is one of the most iconic images of the Western Front; its title sounds bitingly ironic. Yet it is worth remembering that the picture was a piece of official art and that it first appeared, untitled, as the cover of an issue of *British Artists at the Front* published by *Country Life*. In other words, as art historian Sue Malvern reminds us, what is now assumed to be an 'anti-war image' was promulgated in 1917 as covert propaganda for the Allied cause. What we now see as a universal and abstract image of the horror of war, was offered to British people as graphic evidence of Hunnish aggression in France and Belgium. They would view it knowing that England remained a green and pleasant land, yet also conscious that England could easily be ravaged like the continent but for the blood sacrifice of the Tommies. Understood in this way the picture conveys a more positive meaning, that heroic British soldiers were indeed making a new world.[36]

And so Nash was enabled to 'fuse his early pastoral vision with the forces of modernity', expressing 'the full horror of the Great War.'[37] Nevinson developed in the opposite direction, tempering abstraction with a new sense of humanity, and Lewis followed a similar trajectory at a more intellectualized level. Many of the war artists, of course, did not come from the avant-garde; much of the scheme was conventionally representational, though often of fine quality. But even established artists felt moved to something special. The portrait painter John Singer Sargent was commissioned to produce the central 'super-picture' for the proposed Hall of Remembrance. Being American by birth, he seemed ideal for a canvas depicting transatlantic cooperation but the portly, ageing celebrity from London struggled to find a suitable subject – so completely out of his depth on the front that he even wondered if the troops stopped fighting on Sundays. In the end Sargent came up with one of the most haunting images of the war, based on a scene witnessed near Arras in August 1918. It took him a year to turn his sketches into a 20-foot picture showing a line of gassed and blindfolded soldiers processing from left to right along a road already strewn with men lying in agony on either side (plate 13). Like a classical frieze, the stricken walkers, viewed from slightly below against an ochre sky, seem statuesque, bearing themselves with dignity. Although devoid of modernist touches, *Gassed* is a searing vision of modern war. Yet it evokes not revulsion – one's reaction to the brutalized Expressionism of Dix – but compassion. This was war art that drew you in rather than turning you off.

All this was, however, a brief phase. The Hall of Remembrance, the intended home for *Gassed*, was never built: that lavish project withered away amid peacetime austerity. There was also a backlash against modernist war paintings: when some of them were shown at the Royal Academy in 1919, the popular press screamed about 'Bolshevism in art' and 'heroes made to look like clowns'. A critic for the *Daily Mirror* said he now knew what people meant by 'the horrors of war', adding 'it's the pictures.'[38] In the 1920s many modernists struggled to find a vision once the 'romance of war' had gone. Nevinson toyed with various subjects and styles, more pundit than painter, while Lewis became, in W.H. Auden's words, a 'lonely old volcano of the right' belching pro-fascist eruptions. More successfully Paul Nash went back to scenes pastoral, with mystical depictions of the Kent marshes and the South Downs; his return to landscape was typical of English art and, in some ways, English culture as a whole in the 1920s and 1930s.[39] But the unique British oeuvre of war art – inspired by

Masterman's liberal vision, sustained by Beaverbrook's ego and funded by Britain's warfare state – eventually found its home in the new Imperial War Museum. There it would provide a treasury of images for Britain's changing perspectives on the Great War.

Although government funding for war art was strangled by post-war austerity, the 1920s did see a remarkable official programme of commemorative architecture. All the belligerent countries faced the challenge of coping with mass death on a scale not seen in any previous European wars and the result was a vast network of battlefield cemeteries, especially along the old Western Front. But, as with war art, the British response was distinctive.

The Armistice on 11 November 1918, though widely and often wildly celebrated across Britain, was officially only a ceasefire. Formal celebrations of peace had to await the signature of the Treaty of Versailles the following June, which was marked in Britain by a special Peace Day on 19 July 1919. Its highpoint was a Victory March through London; at Lloyd George's insistence this centred on a 'catafalque' in the middle of Whitehall where troops would salute the memory of the dead. This was put together in a couple of weeks in wood and plaster by the distinguished architect Sir Edwin Lutyens, who proposed the name 'Cenotaph' or empty tomb. To the surprise of the government, the edifice proved a huge success, featured in press photos surrounded by floral wreaths. *The Times* led a chorus that this 'simple, grave and beautiful' design should be 'retained in more permanent form' and by the end of July the Cabinet commissioned Lutyens to recreate it in stone. At this time there was no intention of marking the anniversary of the Armistice on 11 November 1919. It was only on 5 November that the Cabinet agreed to a proposal for a national two-minute silence, based on the South African practice of observing a 'Three Minutes Pause' at noon each day during the war to recall the soldiers, living and dead. The silence on Armistice Day had a huge impact across the country; in London Lutyens' temporary cenotaph, which had been left in place by popular demand, became the focal point for tributes headed by the King.[40]

A year later on 11 November 1920 George V duly unveiled the new stone Cenotaph and stood there for the two-minute Silence. He then proceeded to Westminster Abbey for the formal interment of an 'Unknown Warrior of the Great War', chosen at random from four bodies exhumed on the Western Front, and now reburied with full honours in the nave. Although the remains were probably those of a regular soldier from 1914, they could theoretically have been those of anyone's relative: hence the symbolic appeal of the tomb. Since it represented the dead of the whole empire, the British government resisted demands to build similar memorials in Commonwealth countries.

Britain's memorialization was not unique. France erected its own monument to the Unknown Soldier on Armistice Day 1920; the Americans followed suit in 1921. And the Cenotaph in London was adapted from a temporary catafalque designed for victory celebrations in Paris on *quatorze juillet* in 1919. But the idea never caught on in France, whereas it became absolutely central for the British. The permanent structure was even more popular than the original: within a week 1.25 million people had passed by and the memorial was ten feet deep in flowers.[41] Its appeal was partly testament to the artistry of Lutyens' design – a blend of classical and modernist, reverential yet secular – using the principle of entasis so that apparently straight sides are actually the gentlest of curves. On to its graceful, blank public space millions of men and women could project their own private feelings. But there was a deeper reason for the Cenotaph's popular appeal. Apart from the token grave in Westminster Abbey, Whitehall's empty tomb would be the repository of the nation's grief because Britain's war dead would lie for ever in foreign fields.

The British government had decided early in the war that the soldiers should be buried near where they had fallen: the cost of bringing home all the bodies, even where found and identified, would have been prohibitive. The French government initially adopted a similar position but then relented in 1920 because of popular outcry: eventually about 30 per cent of France's identified war dead (240,000 bodies) were reinterred in family vaults. Most of the remainder, who had died fighting to defend their homeland, were buried on French soil. The

Germans, like the British, were not in a position to bring home most of their dead but, given their political and financial crisis in the early 1920s, architectural memorialization was understated and interment was often in large graves. The dead were honoured as fallen heroes rather than citizen soldiers and buried in dark 'heroes' groves' (*Helden-haine*) surrounded by 'Teutonic' oak trees. The French and Germans did erect commemorative monuments – the grisly Art Deco ossuary at Verdun, for instance, or the Stonehenge-style Tannenberg memorial – but the British were unique in the money, artistry and emotion lavished on the architecture of their war memorials along the Western Front.[42]

The British programme was defined by the vision and energy of Fabian Ware, a former educator and journalist who had also been an administrator in South Africa – so he had both a sense of the public and also a feeling for the empire. Aged forty-five when war broke out and too old to serve, Ware volunteered as an ambulance driver in France, where he was appalled at the random carnage and became determined to register and memorialize soldiers' graves. A fluent French speaker, by mid-1915 he had persuaded the French government to donate land for the burial of Allied soldiers. A couple of years later the British government accepted his proposals for a permanent body – like the War Museum, empire-wide rather than merely British – to tend these graves after the war and the Imperial War Graves Commission (IWGC) received its royal charter in May 1917. It faced challenges unprecedented in the long history of Britain's wars: not only the scale of the killing – by the end of the war the empire's dead exceeded 1 million – but also very different attitudes to the bodies of the war dead in a democratic age.[43]

In Shakespeare's *Henry V*, after the battle of Agincourt is over the French herald asks leave to '... wander o'er this bloody field / To book our dead, and then to bury them' and especially 'To sort our nobles from our common men.' In *Henry VI, Part One*, after the tables have been turned by Joan of Arc, it is an English knight who asks the French

Give me their bodies, that I may bear them hence,
And give them burial as beseems their worth.[44]

This Shakespearean idea of burying according to their 'worth' remained the norm in later wars. After Waterloo in 1815, when 15,000 British soldiers died, most of the officers were transported home for family burial while the corpses of private soldiers were dumped in mass graves. Not until 1890, after a public subscription campaign initiated by Queen Victoria, was a special monument erected at the Evere cemetery in Brussels. Underneath were reinterred the remains of seventeen bodies from the field of Waterloo, most of them senior officers.

A hundred years later, after the Great War, Ware and his colleagues adopted a very different position. They stuck to the government's decision that no bodies should be repatriated, even for the rich who could afford to pay, despite sustained pressure from relatives. 'Many thousands of Mothers and Wives are slowly dying for want of the Grave of their loved ones to visit and tend themselves,' one petition informed the Queen, 'and we feel deeply hurt that the right granted to other countries is denied us.' But the commission decided that each body should have its own grave and that there should be no distinction 'between officers and men lying in the same cemeteries in the form or nature of the memorials.' Otherwise, Ware explained in a press statement, 'costly monuments put up by the well-to-do over their dead would contrast unkindly with those humbler ones which would be all that poorer folk could afford.' Instead 'in death, all, from General to Private, of whatever race or creed, should receive equal honour under a memorial which should be the common symbol of their comradeship and of the cause for which they died.' As to the form of the gravestone, the commission also took a firm line, insisting on a plain and uniform headstone rather than a Christian cross. This suited the empire's religious diversity and would be more durable against the elements. A headstone also allowed extra room for name, rank, regiment and date of death, plus a short inscription supplied by next of kin – though the wording would be checked to avoid allowing 'free scope for the effusions of the mortuary mason, the sentimental versifier, or the crank.'[45]

The commission's 'tyranny' aroused a storm of protest. The sculptor Eric Gill deplored the idea of half a million standardized

headstones as a 'Prussian' imposition, championing 'uniform medi-
ocrity' over individual craftsmanship. One mother expressed horror
that 'tombstones should resemble so many milestones.'[46] Disquiet was
also expressed in the Church of England and in Parliament, led by
senior politicians such as Balfour, Lansdowne and Robert Cecil, who
forced a debate in the Commons on 4 May 1920. Feelings ran high on
both sides. An MP defending the commission quoted a letter from a
bereaved father. 'Our boy was missing at Loos. The ground is of
course battered and mined past all hope of any trace being recovered.
I wish some of the people who are making this trouble realise how
more than fortunate they are to have a name on a headstone in a
named place.' The author of that letter was Rudyard Kipling, the
populist bard of empire, who had banged the drum for volunteering
in 1914 and even pulled strings so that his only son, Jack, was commissioned as an officer despite very poor sight. Kipling's grief and guilt
at Jack's death is perhaps expressed in one of his sardonic *Epitaphs of the
War*: 'If any question why we died / Tell them, because our fathers
lied.' Jack's body was never clearly identified and Kipling sublimated
his personal anguish in national commemoration.[47]

But others were not content to do so. In the Commons debate,
Cecil insisted for the opposition that 'the object of a tombstone is
really a memorial to the individual'. In peacetime those 'nearest and
closest to the deceased' were naturally left to decide; so why, he asked,
should it be any different in war? 'Right through the Graves
Commission', fumed Cecil, 'is the conception of a national monument' which was 'an entirely novel idea. It has never been done
before in the world's history ... It has never been said that the State
has a right to turn the individual memorials to individual persons into
a national memorial against the will and against the desire of their
relatives.'[48]

But Winston Churchill, secretary of state for war, endorsed the
commission's ambition to make the war cemeteries into an enduring
national memorial. 'It is little enough, but that is the least we can do.
We can give these soldiers who have perished in the War memorials
which will last for hundreds of years.' In that way, Churchill declared,
their relatives would find some consolation to know that even 'the

humblest soldier who has fallen' would be remembered by name, regiment and place of death 'through periods so remote that probably all the other memorials of this time will have faded and vanished away'. This was enduring memory of a sort previously possible only for monarchs and aristocrats, immortalized in stone within great cathedrals.[49]

Cecil objected to what he regarded as the statism of the project, overriding the cherished principle of individualism. But what really animated Ware was the spirit of democracy. He and his supporters had grasped the new, democratic mood in both the army and the country, which found expression in the 1918 franchise reform act.[50] The soldiers who survived would now have the right to vote, their opinions weighed equally with those of any gentleman. So the soldiers who did not return should at least share a similar equality, and recognition in death by naming was essential to that dignifica-tion. Hence the immense efforts undertaken to record even the missing. At Ypres thousands of British Empire soldiers had marched east through the Menin Gate, many of them never to return. Like much of the city, it was devastated during the war but inside the arches of the rebuilt gate, opened in 1927, were engraved the names of 55,000 soldiers of the British Empire from the Ypres salient who had no known graves. Again there were critics: Siegfried Sassoon denounced 'these intolerably nameless names' of 'the unheroic Dead' who had simply 'fed the guns'. He called the New Menin Gate nothing less than a 'sepulchre of crime'.[51]

But the commission pressed on. Even more ambitious was its Memorial to the Missing of the Somme on the Thiepval Ridge, where so many soldiers of Britain and the empire had died in 1916. This towering edifice in stone and pink brick, visible for miles around, was dedicated in 1932. It had been designed by Lutyens, like the Cenotaph in a mysterious blend of ancient and modern. And he again employed a complex geometry, this time a network of inter-woven arches on whose inner faces some 72,000 names were carved. Below the memorial, down the hill, was a cemetery containing the remains of 300 French soldiers and 300 British, mostly unidentified soldiers. The joint burial was intended to symbolize the Entente

Cordiale but visually it demonstrated the contrasting forms of national memorialization. French graves were marked with crosses that bore the stark, almost shocking word 'Inconnu', whereas the British head-stones included what details could be gleaned about rank, regiment and date of death, plus the words 'Known unto God'. This phrase for the headstone was proposed by Kipling, who worked indefatigably for the commission, and it was he who also suggested the quotation 'Their Name Liveth for Evermore', from Ecclesiasticus, for the Stone of Remembrance in each cemetery. The Stone was designed by Lutyens in a form suggestive of an altar yet also abstract and non-denominational – another example of the IWGC's evasive engagement with official Christianity.[52]

Attitudes to naming were, however, different for non-white soldiers in Britain's armed forces. On the assumption that most African troops were pagan and had not reached 'the stage of civilisation', they were not usually commemorated through individual graves and naming. This policy was also adopted for the more highly regarded troops of the Indian army, including monotheistic Muslims. A particularly poignant example was the British Empire war memorial at Basra – an elegant colonnade in memory of some 40,000 missing from the Mesopotamia campaign, built on the banks of the Shatt al-Arab waterway.* Basra was no Thiepval. The memorial listed by name some 8,000 British soldiers; likewise the names of 665 Indian officers. But 33,222 Indian 'other ranks' were recorded merely as the number of men lost by each military unit. For the most part, Britain's non-white soldiers from the Great War were memorialized namelessly, 'as beseems their worth', in an age when only whites were generally deemed safe for democracy.[53]

The democratic obsession with names and naming perhaps owes something to the example of the United States. Not so much from 1917–18, because fewer than 30 per cent of America's war dead were interred in foreign fields. Many relatives brought the bodies home; in any case more than half America's 116,000 official service deaths actually occurred from the influenza epidemic that ravaged the United

* Later moved thirty kilometres into the desert by Saddam Hussein, at massive cost.

States in 1918.[54] The real trailblazer for commemorating democratic death was the Civil War of 1861–5, America's Great War. Forty per cent of the Northern dead and a far higher proportion of Confederates perished anonymously – identified only by what the poet Walt Whitman called 'the significant word UNKNOWN'. But later in the war the North made a real effort to collect and dignify some of its dead in National Cemeteries. Of these the most important was Gettysburg, partly because of its size but also because of the intent behind it. Each grave was given equal status, not privileged by army rank or social status, and this principle was affirmed in President Abraham Lincoln's address at the cemetery's formal opening in November 1863. In a mere 272 words, little noted at the time but soon gaining rhetorical immortality, Lincoln ennobled the grisly business of industrialized killing, urging his countrymen to complete the 'unfinished work' that 'these honored dead' had begun so that the 'government of the people, by the people, for the people, shall not perish from the earth.'[55]

Lincoln's example as a war leader, principled yet pragmatic, was much invoked in Britain during the Great War, not least by Lloyd George, and a replica of the famous Saint-Gaudens statue of the President was unveiled in Parliament Square in 1920. The Gettysburg mode of commemoration was also cited with approval: one journalist in 1916, even before the Somme, noted that America had 'made stately pleasances of meditation in some of the scenes of her Civil War – places still haunted by the words of Lincoln's Gettysburg oration, the noblest of all modern valedictories to the undying dead.'[56]

Whatever the direct influence of Gettysburg on the Imperial War Graves Commission, its project was certainly in that mould – seeking to endow democratic death with nobility and meaning – but in the 1920s it did this on a far grander scale, with nearly a thousand architect-designed cemeteries and memorials running like a ribbon through Belgium and France. Some of them, like Tyne Cot, Vimy Ridge and Thiepval, were on a truly lavish scale. The total bill was £8.15 million, roughly double the cost of a single day's shelling in the final weeks of the war. So burying was much cheaper than killing. But, measured against the different fiscal arithmetic of peacetime, the IWGC's work constituted the biggest government construction project of the 1920s, eclipsing the modern stations on the London Underground or the programme of new telephone exchanges. By the early 1930s the cemeteries on the Western Front had become popular sites of what was called 'pilgrimage', including visits by school groups. Lutyens and his fellow architects had created what has been aptly called 'a populist and nationalist art form for a nation that was awestruck by what nationalism had done but which could not, and would not, forget it.'[57]

War art and war cemeteries were great official projects, funded by the British government. By contrast there was no official programme of war poetry and the poets we now revere are known for their deep scepticism about the war and officialdom. The fullest bibliography of individuals from the United Kingdom who published some form of poetry about the Great War in 1914–18 lists 2,225 names. Of these 532 (24 per cent) were female and only 417 (19 per cent) saw service in the armed forces or uniformed organizations.[58] Much of this verse was of indifferent literary quality but, in numerical terms, most of Britain's poets of the war were civilians rather than combatants, with women outnumbering soldiers. Yet we now reserve the term 'war poets' for a few celebrated soldiers such as Siegfried Sassoon and Wilfred Owen. The latter were, moreover, atypical soldiers as well as unrepresentative poets, being young, unmarried officers, sometimes uneasy about homosexual leanings and uncertain about their own courage – who often ended up with a martyr complex. 'For God's sake cheer up and write more optimistically,' Robert Graves rebuked Owen in December 1917; 'the war's not yet ended but a poet should have a spirit above wars.' The fact that Owen, Sassoon and their ilk penned some of the most powerful anti-war poetry in modern literature should not blind us to their atypicality.[59] Later in the book I will examine how these war poets were transmuted into the supreme truth-tellers of the Great War. But this chapter examines what the rich variety of poetry from 1914–18 reveals about how the British understood the meaning of the war experience.

Adopting a Europe-wide perspective we find English poetry, like art, to be something of a backwater in the early twentieth century. The fascination for *vers libre*, evident in France for several decades, had barely touched Britain. One of its great promoters, the 'democratic' American poet Walt Whitman, was little read in England despite being anglophone. English poetry seemed set in a dead husk of nineteenth-century Romanticism. The interaction of man and nature, explored with passionate intensity by Wordsworth and Keats, had been reduced by early-twentieth-century poets such as Stephen Phillips to a cloying sentimentality which one critic likened to 'pouring a pot of treacle over the dinner table'. British debate about poetry took off in the very last years before the war, as part of the general ferment in the arts in continental Europe that belatedly hit Britain. 'Slowly we have emerged from the nineteenth century,' declared the poet and artist Laurence Binyon in 1912. 'We are breathing a different air. We are no longer *fin de siècle*. We are being changed, and the world with us.'[60]

As with painting, the ferment produced various claustrophobic cliques, trying to define themselves against each other via grandiloquent manifestos. The so-called Imagists championed 'hard', direct, unadorned language and also free verse suited to the image that the poet sought to evoke. That seemed far better than shackling ideas to some mechanical metre rather like 'putting a child into armour', to quote the poet-philosopher T.E. Hulme. Much of their writing appeared in the journal *The Egoist*, which published Ezra Pound and T.S. Eliot, as well as serializing James Joyce's *Portrait of the Artist as a Young Man*. By 1914 Pound and Hulme had transferred allegiance to Wyndham Lewis, giving Vorticism in turn a philosophical patina.[61]

The other passionate reaction to Victorian poetry took the form of the Georgians, adopting the title of five volumes of *Georgian Poetry* published between 1912 and 1922. Their editor Edward Marsh, civil servant and patron of the arts, was private secretary to Winston Churchill, which helped give his patronage political clout. In a preface to the first volume Marsh asserted that 'English poetry is now once again putting on a new strength and beauty' and he predicted 'another "Georgian period" which may take rank in due time with the several poetic ages of the past.' The Georgians were hardly a tight-knit school – the first issue of *Georgian Poetry* included Rupert Brooke and D.H. Lawrence – but the Georgian revolt was another facet of the self-conscious reaction against supposedly moribund Victorianism in favour of art that was true to life's raw vitality. 'Before art can be human it must learn to be brutal,' insisted the critic John Middleton Murry, editor of another new journal, *Rhythm*, which advocated painting and writing that was 'the rhythmical echo of the life with which it is in touch'. Ultimately, though, Georgians such as Lascelles Abercrombie were happier with conventional forms, particularly metre, and traditional themes, especially the world of nature: their aim was to revivify the Romantic heritage.[62]

Although an enraged Pound did once challenge Abercrombie to a duel,[63] the divide between Imagists and Georgians should not be exaggerated. As with the 'isms' of art – Cubism, Expressionism and Futurism – they should be understood not as rival schools but as different currents in the same swirling stream. In any case such distinctions were almost overwhelmed in a tidal wave of verse generated by the outbreak of the Great War.

This outpouring was not peculiar to Britain. At least 300 volumes of poetry were published in wartime France; the German book trade catalogue for 1915–19 listed over 1,000 entries under the category 'World War: Poems' including six collections of 'Inscriptions on Railway Carriages, Dug-Outs and the Like' – in other words, literary graffiti. And these collections represented only a fraction of the poems that appeared in the popular press. The explosion of poetry in Britain in 1914 (*The Times* was receiving over a hundred verses a day in August) might have been larger in scale than in Germany but it was certainly not unique.[64]

As in Germany, the bulk of British war poetry was patriotic, indeed propagandist. Today we recall with amusement a few trite utterances, such as Henry Newbolt's public-school injunction to 'play up, play up, and play the game', or Rupert Brooke's sententious sonnet 'Peace', welcoming the coming of war:

Now, God be thanked Who has matched us with His hour,
And caught our youth, and wakened us from sleeping . . .
To turn, as swimmers into cleanness leaping . . .
And the worst friend and enemy is but Death.[65]

Yet in fact, most of the poems published in Britain in 1914 and indeed throughout the war were strongly supportive of the national cause. Instead of 'emotion recollected in tranquillity' – Wordsworth's classic definition of poetry in his *Lyrical Ballads* – this was heat-of-the-moment stuff, mostly penned not by soldiers who had seen battle but by civilians reacting to war news in the daily papers. And that news was shaped by the stereotype of German brutality established in Belgium during the opening weeks of the conflict, so that 'a deliberate campaign to vilify the enemy was quite unnecessary, since the public was already convinced.' Although not invaded like Belgium or France, England was, in the words of one poet, fighting 'for the freedom of less favoured folk' and in order to keep the barbarous foe away from England itself. Although authors in all belligerent countries evoked images of their homeland, English poetry was extreme in its pastoralism, rooted in the heritage of Romanticism, which celebrated the peaceful beauty and seasonal verities of rural life – fields and flowers, hills and vales, sheep and horses, larks and nightingales, dawns and sunsets. The French evoked their homeland through villages, churches and the values of *civilisation*; German writers also focused on their cultural heritage (*Kultur*) but often celebrated their cities and industry. Where English poets were unusual was in defining their country so intensely through its countryside.[66]

'English' and 'England' are definitely the right terms here. Much of this patriotic verse drew not simply on Romantic poets such as Keats and Shelley but also on the newly self-conscious canon of 'English literature'. Responding to the cultural nationalism of late-nineteenth-century France and Germany, anthologies of the 'best' and most typical English poets had been published in the late Victorian era – including Palgrave's *The Golden Treasury of the Best Songs and Lyrical Poems in the English Language* (beginning in 1861) and *The Oxford Book of English Verse* (from 1900) which had sold half a million copies in twenty reprints by 1939. Produced for a newly literate population and widely used in schools, these anthologies helped make literature, to quote Stefan Collini, 'one of the central symbolic expressions of the "imagined community" of the English people.' By 1900 the geographical focus for English writers had shifted from the wild northern mountains of the Lake District, beloved by the Romantics, to the gentle rolling downs of southern England, idealized in the writings of Hardy and Kipling. Here, supposedly, was where the country's quiet quintessence could best be discerned. Across the centuries, of course, some of the most celebrated 'English literature' has been written by non-Englishmen – one thinks of Walter Scott and Robert Louis Stevenson or of Irish writers from Swift to Yeats. But the poetic explosion that fired British patriotism in 1914–18 drew predominantly on images of Englishness. Take, for instance, John Masefield in 'August 1914':

> . . . These homes, this valley spread below me here,
> The rooks, the tilted stacks, the beasts in pen,
> Have been the heartfelt things, past-speaking dear
> To unknown generations of dead men . . .

These were men who had left England and, in Masefield's words, 'died (uncouthly, most) in foreign lands' because they loved the land of home. Masefield was folding the men of 1914 and their soldier ancestors into a unity formed by history and literature.'[67]

This canon defined the idiom of war poetry as much as its imagery. Most writers used four- or eight-line stanzas, rhyming alternately or in couplets, with a regular metre. They favoured an archaic vocabulary full of adjectives like 'bold', 'valiant', 'pure' and 'mighty', extolling a war waged with swords and helmets, flags and drums. And they employed 'elevated' language about the epic of battle, the glory of patriotic death and the immortality of fame, extending this genre now from classical warriors to mass armies. Brooke's war sonnets of 1914 again set the tone – 'Blow out, you bugles, over the rich Dead!' – but he was only the most famous. It is now often said that such 'high diction' was silenced by the Somme but there were plenty of critics earlier in the war, at home more than at the front. In August 1915 the Liberal weekly *The Nation* urged people to dig down 'through all this mud of word-making and worship of phrases, to the bedrock facts of reality' about the war. The decline of patriotic verse from 1916 owes as much to the introduction of conscription as it does to the Somme: in 1914 and 1915 such poems were often intended to inspire volunteers to join up. And the rhetoric of 1914 was heard again in the spring of 1918, when the great German offensives towards the Channel generated a renewed sense of crisis.[68]

Perhaps the most celebrated poet of the war, now totally forgotten, was John Oxenham, pen name of the novelist William Dunkerley, by then in his sixties. His collection of poems *All's Well!*, published in November 1915, had sold more than 200,000 copies by 1918 and his 'Hymn for the Men at the Front' ran to more than 7 million copies as a broadsheet. What made Oxenham so popular, writes critic Martin Stephen, was that he 'does not seek to offer comfort by ignoring the reality of combat, but he offers that comfort despite it.' Oxenham tells readers, for instance, that a soldier 'died unnoticed in the muddy trench' before affirming, 'God was with him, and he did not blench.' Hardly great poetry, but clearly consolation for many. One of the most popular hymns later in the war was a poem by William Cowper, the eighteenth-century pastoralist, affirming the ultimate beneficence of divine providence: 'God moves in a mysterious way / His wonders to perform.'[69]

Nowadays the most celebrated exposé of 'real' war is Wilfred Owen's 1917 poem 'Dulce et Decorum Est'. In it Owen is haunted by the face of a soldier who failed to get his mask on in time: 'He plunges at me, guttering, choking, drowning', as though 'under a green sea'. If you could see that face, Owen tells his reader, if you could hear the blood 'Come gargling from the froth-corrupted lungs,' then

> My friend, you would not tell with such high zest
> To children ardent for some desperate glory,
> The old Lie: Dulce et Decorum est
> Pro patria mori.[70]

Today Owen stands as the archetypal 'war poet' – meaning a soldier poet who was anti-war – but, just as most of Britain's wartime poets were actually civilians who supported the war, so much of Owen's ire was directed against jingoistic rhetoric ('war words'), not the war itself. What's more, like Siegfried Sassoon whose savage satire greatly influenced Owen in the summer of 1917, Owen was not a pacifist but a courageous, sometimes reckless officer who won the Military Cross for killing Germans – a point that his brother Harold later tried to conceal because it did not fit Wilfred's 1960s image as the supreme anti-war poet. Though anguished about the war, Owen concluded that his place was on the battlefield. This was partly from love of his men – 'I came out in order to help these boys,' he wrote his mother not long before being killed in November 1918 – but it also reflected his residual belief in what they were all fighting for.[71]

Consider a couple of examples of this belief. Owen's famous draft preface for a future collection of poems insisted, 'I am not concerned with Poetry. My subject is War, and the pity of War. The Poetry is in the pity.' What he meant was that his book would not be 'about heroes', nor about 'glory, honour, might, majesty' and all the other grand words of the poetic vocabulary. All he could do was to 'be truthful' about war, thereby arousing pity. But in a little-noted coda to the preface Owen expressed the hope that his book 'survives Prussia'. He sometimes used 'Prussia' to signify militarism in London as well as Berlin, but his basic anti-German thrust is clear. One catches it, too, in his poem 'Exposure', finished in France in September 1918 and now usually quoted to illustrate the misery of soldiers stuck in wind, rain and ice. Owen uses pastoral imagery ironically to depict the tribulations of the men ('mad gusts' tugging on 'brambles' of barbed wire, dawn's 'melancholy army' of rain attacking 'in ranks on shivering ranks of grey'). But he also employs it to envision the verdant, peaceful England for which he eventually gave his life:

... Since we believe not otherwise can kind fires burn;
  Nor ever suns smile true on child, or field, or fruit.
  For God's invincible spring our love is made afraid;
  Therefore, not loath, we lie out here ...

'Exposure' suggests that even in the last months of the war Owen believed the struggle still had a point.[72]

Other so-called 'war poets' shared Owen's ambivalence about surface rhetoric and deeper meaning. Edward Thomas, for instance, whose December 1915 poem 'This is no case of petty right or wrong' begins

> ... I hate not Germans, nor grow hot
> With love of Englishmen, to please newspapers.

But eventually he cries

> ... God save England, lest
> We lose what never slaves and cattle blessed.
> The ages made her that made us from the dust:
> She is all we know and live by, and we trust
> She is good and must endure, loving her so:
> And as we love ourselves we hate her foe.

Thomas, a Londoner born and bred, was passionate about the countryside. Although in his late thirties with wife and children, he decided not only to enlist but then to volunteer for overseas duty. Asked what he was fighting for, he bent down, crumbled some earth in his hand and replied, 'Literally, for this.' None of Thomas' 'war poems' dealt directly with war; instead they extol his homeland, its character and continuity, in lines made sharper by his sense of looming death.[73]

For many during the Great War, both in Britain and at the front, the 'civilization' for which they fought therefore boiled down to a profound if nebulous love of home, often expressed in pastoral idiom. This was true for poets like Thomas, just as it was for war artists such as Paul Nash. Man and nature ravaged in Flanders fields; man and nature in harmony in an idealized England – the war's meaning lay somewhere in the gap.

Nature domesticated was also the central motif of British war cemeteries. Planting graves with flowers was strictly forbidden in German cemeteries: that was deemed a mark of sentimental Frenchified *civilisation* whereas facing up to tragedy starkly was what distinguished German *Kultur*. Hence the dark stones and shadowed groves. British war cemeteries, on the other hand, were striking for their profusion of colourful flowers and shrubs, mostly native to England. Roses and pinks, beech and yew – the latter encouraged because of its 'association with our own country churchyards.' An echo here of Brooke's already famous lines:

> If I should die, think only this of me;
> That there's some corner of a foreign field
> That is for ever England ...[74]*

The keenest criticism of the 'Great War for Civilisation' came not from those within the pastoral tradition who wrote in wartime but writers looking back in the 1920s from a very different perspective, shaped by pre-war Imagism. The real divide was not between Owen, a self-confessed Georgian,[75] and Brooke – it is unlikely that the latter could have sustained the tone and form of the 1914 sonnets if he, like Owen, had soldiered on to 1917–18 – but between both of them and the tradition pioneered by Ezra Pound. Pound was an American who lived in London between 1908 and 1920. A would-be poet from an early age, his roots spread far more widely than English pastoralism. Pound knew the Romantics and the classics; he also immersed himself in French Symbolists like Baudelaire and in the Oriental. Indeed few poets have educated themselves so widely in the riches of world poetry. Pound advocated free verse, where rhythm and metre were adapted to the emotion the poem sought to convey rather than the other way round, and also 'permanent metaphor', using 'absolutely no word that does not contribute to the presentation'. The result was a hard, astringent style that proved ideal to express his bleak disillusion about the post-war world, notably in

---

* Brooke was borrowing a conceit already found in Tennyson's 'In Memoriam' (1849) where the roots of the 'Old Yew' are 'wrapt about the bones' in the churchyard and again in Hardy's poem 'Drummer Hodge' (1899), about a young soldier killed on the South African veldt, for whom 'portion of that unknown plain / Will Hodge for ever be'.

Hugh Selwyn Mauberley (1920). Like Owen this attacked the supreme war words *dulce et decorum est pro patria mori* but went on to damn the whole idea of a war for civilization:

> There died a myriad,
> And of the best, among them,
> For an old bitch gone in the teeth,
> For a botched civilization . . .
> For two gross of broken statues,
> For a few thousand battered books.[76]

Pound also served as midwife to the great modernist long poem of the 1920s, T.S. Eliot's *The Waste Land* (1922). Eliot, like Pound, was American and widely read in French poetry. Unlike Pound he settled permanently in Britain, becoming studiously anglicized and increasingly conservative. In contrast with both Pound and the Georgians, his immersion in English literature was Elizabethan and Jacobean rather than pastoral and Romantic. On and off since the start of the war Eliot had written various pieces, full of literary allusions, without finding an overarching unity. When he pulled the material together in the winter of 1921–2, with his nerves and his marriage falling apart, the theme that emerged was the decay of Western civilization caused by mass culture but accelerated by the war. Much of the poem was set in London:

> Unreal City,
> Under the brown fog of a winter dawn,
> A crowd flowed over London Bridge, so many,
> I had not thought death had undone so many.

But the Bolshevik threat also lurked in his mind: 'Who are those hooded hordes' he asks, 'swarming / Over endless plains'? The original version read 'over Polish plains'. Eliot's correspondence around this time shows his concern about the 'fiasco' of Wilson's 'reorganization of the nationalities' and the resulting 'Balkanization' of Europe. That mood is also evident in the poem:

... Cracks and reforms and bursts in the violet air
Falling towers
Jerusalem Athens Alexandria
Vienna London
Unreal[77]

Still uncertain about his sprawling draft, Eliot entrusted it to Pound, who cut away many of the allusions and excursions and brought out the underlying rhythms in a way that conformed to his own terse, hard definition of true poetry. *The Waste Land* remained a work of fragments but, as Stephen Spender observed, this became a virtue rather than a defect because 'the poem is about a fragmented culture'. The recondite allusions to past literature themselves become cultural fragments – Pound's 'broken statues' from the ruins of the past. Eliot's decaying civilization was urban and often sordid – a cityscape of trams and taxis, canals and gasworks, with no vestige of the pastoral. Nature appears mostly in the form of fertility myths and their debasement; suffering is not redeemed in an idealized landscape but endured with words of resignation from the Buddhist scriptures. The published edition of *The Waste Land* was something of a con trick: Eliot, like Pound, was keen to make his mark and the literary allusions were explained in footnotes that Eliot himself later called a 'remarkable exposition of bogus scholarship'. But the sheen of erudition helped attract attention to the work, while Pound's stern pen gave the text an abstract, 'gnomic' quality: rather like Lutyens' Cenotaph, this was a waste land that could be envisioned and inhabited as each reader desired. The poem quickly achieved cult status among young intellectuals.[78]

After 1922 Pound and Eliot went their separate ways – Pound's disillusion drawing him to Italy and fascism, while Eliot stayed in England and eventually embraced what he called 'Christian Civilisation'. But in the early 1920s they both wrote poetry about the Great War that was strikingly different in content as well as style from the Georgians and those who, like Owen and Thomas, were still rooted in that tradition. The poetic form that Eliot and Pound pioneered would define much of twentieth-century English poetry.

The pastoral tradition had come to a dead end, rather like its poets. But in time that fate would enhance its attraction (and theirs) as emblems of a lost age.

Although Eliot and Pound's poems were particularly vivid responses to the chaos after 1918, the future of civilization was intensely debated by intellectuals all through the 1920s. The classic statement was Oswald Spengler's two volumes on *Der Untergang des Abendlandes*, published in 1922–3. A best-seller in 1920s Germany, the work appeared in English as *The Decline of the West*. Sales were not spectacular but the title became popular shorthand for cultural pessimism. The Great War also forced Sigmund Freud to rethink his theory of the self: alongside the drive to procreate (*Eros*) he now postulated a drive to destroy (*Thanatos*). Developing these ideas in a book translated into English as *Civilization and Its Discontents* (1930), Freud concluded that 'the meaning of the evolution of civilization' had always been the struggle between 'the instinct of life and the instinct of destruction'. But now, he warned, men have gained such control over the forces of nature that 'they would have no difficulty in exterminating one another to the last man.' In the next round of the struggle for civilization Eros would again pit itself against Thanatos but, asked Freud ominously, 'who can foresee with what success and with what result?'[79]

British authors struck a similar note. *The Revolutions of Civilisation* by the Egyptologist Flinders Petrie, first published in 1911, familiarized many with the idea that civilizations rise and fall rather than constituting a narrative of sequential progress. The most famous British exemplar of this cyclical view was Arnold Toynbee. His ten-volume *Study of History* did not start to appear until 1934 and gained a wide readership only through an abridged edition after the Second World War, but Toynbee's basic ideas were already widely known. Western civilization, he told radio listeners in 1931, was just another bubble in the stream of world history. 'Isn't it most probable that our bubble will burst like the rest?[80]

In 1928 the art critic Clive Bell published a rather hackneyed essay on *Civilization*. He justified his title on the grounds that 'the story of this word's rise to the highest place amongst British war aims is so curious'.[81] By the late 1920s many sceptics offered a simple explanation – propaganda. Masterman's discreet campaign to promote the British cause through well-placed articles and art and the more direct methods of Northcliffe and Beaverbrook had now become public knowledge through memoirs and exposés. Similar volumes appeared in France, Germany and America, and social scientists began to reflect on the place of propaganda in a democratic world. Perhaps the most influential writer was Harold Lasswell, a precocious twenty-five-year-old professor at Chicago, who reworked his doctoral dissertation as a book entitled *Propaganda Technique in the World War* (1927). For Lasswell propaganda was 'a concession to the rationality of the modern world' but, despite the veneer of civilization, it was really just an updated version of the tom-tom that aroused war lust among primitive tribes. In pithy prose he identified a series of general rules: 'mobilize hatred against the enemy', 'preserve the friendship of allies', 'procure the co-operation of neutrals' and 'demoralize the enemy'. On most scores, he argued, the British were 'amazingly successful' in 1914–18 whereas German propaganda was remarkable only for its 'stupidity' and 'maladroitness'.[82]

For Lasswell propaganda had been the third front of Allied victory, alongside economic blockade and massive armies. And 'the great generalissimo on the propaganda front was Wilson', whose rhetoric 'declared war on autocracies everywhere' while welding the American people, 'sprung from many alien and antagonistic stocks' into 'a fighting whole'. It was Wilson who 'brewed the subtle poison, which industrious men injected into the veins of a staggering people, until the smashing power of the Allied armies knocked them into submission.' And 'the propaganda of disintegration which was directed against the tottering realm of the Hapsburgs bore fruit in disaffection and ultimate secession among the Czechs, Slovaks, Rumanians, Croats, Poles and Italians.' All this was a rather swashbuckling version of the history of 1918 but Lasswell was more concerned to promote propaganda (and himself). Readers were left with the impression that it was words that really won the war. Ten years on, Lasswell had turned Wilson the Idealist into Wilson the Propagandist – whose 'matchless skill' in that role had 'never been equalled in the world's history'.[83]

Lasswell's academic cynicism dealt impassively with all the belligerents of 1914–18. But in practice, most of the late 1920s exposés of propaganda focused on the Allies. One of the most polemical was *Falsehood in War-Time* (1928) by Arthur Ponsonby. 'International war', he exclaimed, was 'a monster born of hypocrisy, fed on falsehood, fattened on humbug' and 'directed to the death and torture of millions'. Although asserting that lying was a universal feature of war, he devoted only a few pages of the final chapter to German transgressions. Nearly all his book was taken up with indictments of the British government – for the web of secret treaties that, he argued, were the real reason for the conflict, for its claims of sole German war guilt, and for the exploitation of neutral Belgium and Germany's alleged atrocities there so as to 'colour the picture with the pigment of falsehood' and 'excite popular indignation'.[84]

Ponsonby was a pacifist, a leader of the anti-war Union of Democratic Control in 1914–18 who continued his campaign against the 'monster' of war in the 1920s. Far from being an objective exposé of propaganda, *Falsehood in War-Time* was itself 'a propaganda lie', argues historian Adrian Gregory, 'fabricated from contentious interpretation and downright invention' by a publicist 'deeply sympathetic to Germany'. Some of the 'atrocities' were indeed unfounded rumour, notably the story of the 'crucified Canadian', but the basic facts about German aggression and brutality in Belgium, accounting for around a quarter of a million deaths during the war, have been substantiated by subsequent research. Yet many people doubted this in the late 1920s.[85]

Ponsonby's 'facts' were often gleaned from material produced by post-war German governments to discredit the 'war guilt' clause of the Treaty of Versailles and justify revision of the peace settlement. This 'massive and successful campaign of disinformation', to quote historian Holger Herwig, was coordinated by a special 'War Guilt Section' of the German Foreign Ministry but fronted by tractable scholars and ostensibly private academic bodies such as the Centre for the Study of the Causes of the War. The result was a forty-volume collection of documents from the German diplomatic archives, cherry-picked to show that Germany went to war in self-defence against mobilization by the despotic Tsarist regime and its French ally.

Published between 1922 and 1927, this oeuvre forced other governments, including Britain, to bring out their own selected documents but the Germans had got in first and in bulk, so that in the 1920s and 1930s most scholars of the origins of the Great War relied heavily on German materials. These served as the basis for the influential works of American revisionist historians such as Sidney B. Fay and Harry Elmer Barnes. The effect was to encourage a general belief, to quote Lloyd George's memoirs, that 'nobody wanted war' in 1914. The July crisis was, he claimed, a gigantic 'muddle': the nations 'slithered over the brink into the boiling cauldron', they blindly 'backed their machines over the precipice'. By the 1930s it seemed hard, even in Britain, to sustain the argument that Germany was straightforwardly guilty for the Great War. Most Germans certainly believed their official line that 1914 had been a defensive war. For them propaganda was something practised by 'the All-lies'.[86]

The late 1920s was in general a moment ripe for reflection, being a decade since the Armistice and Versailles. The books by Lasswell and Ponsonby were part of a rash of novels, memoirs and studies that cast a more sceptical eye over the war for civilization. In Britain the most celebrated was *Good-Bye to All That* (1929) by the poet Robert Graves. Subtitled 'an autobiography' but distinctly cavalier about factual accuracy, Graves' version of wartime life attracted attention because of the breezy, matter-of-fact tone in which the trials of soldiering are related. 'There was no patriotism in the trenches,' he told his readers. From the perspective of ten years on, Graves set wartime in a larger narrative which took him from a starched Victorian childhood to a promiscuous, bohemian present. This sense of a seismic rift in time was evident in other best-sellers such as Siegfried Sassoon's fictionalized *Memoirs of a Fox-Hunting Man* (1928). Most of his book evoked an idyllic pre-war existence playing cricket and riding horses in rural Kent. Near the end, in the 'cloudless' summer of 1914 under the 'spellbound serenity of its hot blue skies', Sassoon simply rides on into the Yeomanry – out of that 'life-learned landscape which, we all felt, was threatened by barbaric invasion' to confront the German soldiers who had 'crucified' Belgian babies. 'Stories of that kind were taken for granted: to have disbelieved them would have been unpatriotic.' By the last pages of

Memoirs of a Fox-Hunting Man, however, Sassoon's best friend is dead, his horse has gone and he is sploshing around in the trenches of Flanders.[87]

Virginia Woolf conveyed the sense of time passing in a different way in her modernist novel *To the Lighthouse* (1927). Its three sections follow the Ramsay family in their summer house on the island of Skye from 1910 to 1920. For most of the book there is no overall narrator: the plot develops through the shifting perspectives of various people, while momentous events occur, literally, in brackets. That is how we learn of the sudden death of Mrs Ramsay; likewise the demise of her son. '[A shell exploded. Twenty or thirty young men were blown up in France, among them Andrew Ramsay, whose death, mercifully, was instantaneous.]' Then the novel (and life) goes on. The war has been 'parenthesized, contained as an interlude', writes critic Vincent Sherry, yet the interlude is horrifically vast and leaves an irreparable sense of loss. Graves, Sassoon and Woolf all portray 1914 as a great divide.[88]

The most influential of these books from ten years on was *Im Westen nichts Neues* by a young German veteran, Erich Maria Remarque, which was published in Germany in January 1929. The title, a formulaic phrase from German military despatches, was translated as *All Quiet on the Western Front*, and that ironic cliché soon entered the English language. Through the eyes of Paul Bäumer the book tells the story of 'a generation of young men who, even though they may have escaped its shells, were destroyed by the war'. With sympathy but not sentiment Remarque describes the small pleasures of a soldier's life such as lice hunts and good latrines, their closeness as comrades and their growing alienation from family and home: 'What is leave? – A pause that only makes everything after it so much worse.' These are men who have become estranged from civilization, from life itself – 'we are dead'. Caught in no-man's-land, Paul frantically knives a French soldier who has fallen into his shell-hole but then has to watch for hours as the man gasps and gurgles his way to death. Overcome with remorse, he talks to the Frenchman and looks at photos and letters from his family. The enemy has become a human being: 'I have killed the printer, Gérard Duval.' Paul vows that, if he survives, he will fight against the war that has struck down both of them: 'I promise you, comrade. It shall never happen again.' But Paul himself is killed a few weeks before the Armistice: 'his face had an expression of calm, as though almost glad the end had come.'[89]

All Quiet on the Western Front became an international best-seller. By May 1930 it had sold 2.5 million copies in twenty languages, including 1 million in Germany and over 300,000 in both Britain and America, plus extensive newspaper serialization. Hollywood naturally jumped on the bandwagon. The movie version made at Universal Studios and directed by Lewis Milestone, began filming, quite deliberately, on Armistice Day 1929 (the head of Universal, Carl Laemmle was a pacifist with a message to preach). When the film was released in April 1930, it made as big an impact as the book. Although banned in Nazi Germany and never screened in the Soviet Union, it proved a box-office hit in America, Britain and most of the world. Lloyd George called it 'the most outstanding war film I have ever seen'. Sydney Carroll in the *Sunday Times* said 'it brought the war back to me as nothing has ever done before since 1918.' The film revealed the basic humanity of the ordinary soldier – the German 'enemy' – and also of his own enemy in that muddy death-pit. Equally important, *All Quiet on the Western Front* was the first major 'talkie' about the war. Not merely did this make it possible for audiences to hear actors speak sequences of moving dialogue rather than read them on the inter-titles, the movie also conveyed the noise of battle in booming sound – hissing bullets, rattling machine guns, thunderous shells and the screams of the wounded.[90]

Here was a cultural shift of signal importance. The tenth-anniversary book boom is often cited as shaping public attitudes but the movies reached a far wider audience and did so with much greater power. Richard Aldington, the Imagist poet and war veteran, observed sagely in 1926, 'Those who have attempted to convey any real war experience sincerely, unsentimentally, avoiding ready-made attitudes (pseudo-heroic or pacifist or quasi-humorous), must have felt the torturing sense of . . . trying to communicate the incommunicable.'[91] Some of the wartime footage started to bridge that gap but sound movies did so with transcendent power. War no longer had to be imagined through words, or glimpsed from afar in still photographs; now it could be seen, heard and almost felt. German and French film-makers also evoked the trench experience. *Westfront 1918* (1930) followed four German lads to their death in what was literally a soldier's-eye view of the war, shot claustrophobically from the trenches with no panoramas of the battlefield. *Les Croix de bois* (1932) lacked some of the intense violence of *All Quiet* and *Westfront* but it also evoked the horrors of battle, the camaraderie of the trenches and the universality of death for French and Germans alike under the ubiquitous wooden crosses of the title. *Les Croix de bois* was a rare exception to what has been called 'the silence of the French cinema' as well as French painters about the tragedy of the Great War. These three classic movies from America, Germany and France helped create an iconography of enduring images used recurrently in later films about the Great War: the subterranean world of the trenches, the night patrol caught in barbed wire, the ravaged landscape and the omnipresent mud. The films also established a narrative pattern in which there are no protagonists let alone heroes, only a few young men fated to die, with the larger meaning of the conflict left unclear.[92]

For Americans the Great War remained a distant conflict, played out 'over there', three thousand miles from home. Just as the New World and the Old World 'fought different wars' in 1917–18, so in remembrance they drew different meanings from the conflict. The United States had no deep-rooted tradition of pastoral poetry, or even a firm poetic canon: *The Oxford Book of American Verse* did not appear till 1950.[93] Much of American literature has explored the country's supposed polarization between the protean west and the cultivated east, with the rugged frontier as the great divide. Europe functioned as a sort of Far East – good or bad depending on one's judgment of the basic east–west polarity. Many of America's war novels fitted this pattern. In Willa Cather's Pulitzer Prize-winning novel *One of Ours* (1922) Claude Wheeler, a farmboy from the lost frontier of Nebraska, finally finds fulfilment on the battlefields of France. *A Son at the Front* (1923) by Edith Wharton, an American exile in Paris, told a heroic story of a young man who finally breaks free of his ageing parents to fight and die in Europe convinced that 'if France went, western civilization went with her.'[94]

Similarly, most American films about the war portrayed it as a great adventure story, with the US army as redressers of European wrongs. The most famous, *Sergeant York*, was not made until 1941 but Gary Cooper's portrayal of Alvin York, who won the Medal of Honor in October 1918 for eliminating a German machine-gun nest and taking 130 prisoners, brought alive a story that had been engraved in American folk memory since the early 1920s. York was a mountain boy from Tennessee, born in a log cabin, straightforward, religious but a brilliant shot, who did his duty and then returned home to marry his true love – in short a classic American hero.[95] The few movies that sounded a more sceptical note addressed the experience of other nations – Germany, France and Britain. America's own involvement and the motives behind it 'went almost unquestioned by the country's motion picture industry', writes historian Michael Isenberg. 'The awful harvest of war, in this view, was reaped legitimately by those nations that had begun the whole thing in 1914.'[96]

One example was *A Farewell to Arms* by Ernest Hemingway, published in 1929 and made into a movie starring Gary Cooper in 1932. Loosely based on Hemingway's own experiences as an ambulance driver on the Italian front, the plot tells the doomed love story of the wounded American Frederic Henry and the British nurse who cares for him and weaves that story into the larger tragedy of brutal war in the foothills of the Alps. 'I was always embarrassed by the words sacred, glorious, and sacrifice,' declares Henry: 'the sacrifices were like the stockyards of Chicago.' In the end 'only the names of places had dignity ... Abstract words such as glory, honor, courage, or hallow were obscene.' The film version brought this home above all through its graphic depiction of the carnage and chaos of the battle of Caporetto. In *Tender is the Night*, the 1934 novel by F. Scott Fitzgerald, a couple of American tourists visit the old trenches on the Somme. Dick Diver tells his wife, 'See that little stream – we could walk to it in two minutes. It took the British a month to walk to it – a whole empire walking very slowly, dying in front and pushing forward behind. And another empire walked very slowly backward a few inches a day, leaving the dead like a million bloody rugs.' Dick concluded his history lesson emphatically: 'No Europeans will ever do that again in this generation.'[97]

Today most of these books and films from ten years on are often interpreted as unequivocally anti-war but that is not how their authors presented them at the time. 'My work', insisted Remarque, 'is not political, neither pacifist nor militarist in intention, but human simply ... I merely wanted to awaken understanding for a generation that more than all others has found it difficult to make its way back from the four years of death, struggle and terror.' Robert Graves professed a similar motive, encapsulated in the title of his memoir, to say 'goodbye to all that' because 'once all this has been settled in my mind and written down and published it need never be thought about again'. Despite his studied cynicism, Graves remained proud of his wartime service and volunteered again in 1939, only to be declared unfit.[98]

A particularly interesting example of authorial ambivalence is the English dramatist R.C. Sherriff, whose play *Journey's End* ran for 593 performances at the Savoy Theatre in 1929–30 and was broadcast over the radio on Armistice Day. Set in a claustrophobic British dugout, the play explores the relentless psychological pressures of war on a group of soldiers and ends with them all being overwhelmed in the great German offensive of 21 March 1918. Today *Journey's End* is seen as an anti-war classic and many reviewers took that line at the time, J.B. Priestley calling it 'the strongest plea for peace I know.' But the word most used by reviewers and audiences was 'realism': the play's evocation of life at the front grabbed both those who had endured the trenches and those who had wondered from afar. Sherriff, who had served as an officer on the Western Front, insisted, 'I have not written this play as a piece of propaganda. And certainly not as propaganda for peace. Neither have I tried to glorify the life of the soldier, nor to point any kind of moral. It is simply the expression of an ideal. I wanted to perpetuate the memory of some of those men.'[99]

There is, of course, nothing definitive about an author's intention. Most significant works of art can be read in various ways; that openness is, indeed, what helps make them significant. Yet Sherriff's assertions remind us of the dangers of translating our attitudes back into the 1920s and 1930s. The bulk of British novels and films about the war in those decades did not preach a clear anti-war message. What they did was to highlight sharply the horrors of war while leaving open its ultimate meaning: readers and audiences judged that meaning according to their own prior convictions. For Arthur Ponsonby the war had been wrong in 1914 and it was still wrong in 1928: he deployed the latest evidence accordingly. For Henry Newbolt the war was unequivocally right in August 1914 and he had not changed his opinion on the tenth anniversary. The 'best' of Wilfred Owen's poems he considered 'terribly good, but of course limited, almost all on one note . . . Owen and the rest of the broken men rail at the Old Men who sent the young to die: they have suffered cruelly, but in the nerves and not the heart.' Newbolt concluded sternly: 'I don't think these shell-shocked war poems will move our grandchildren greatly.'[100] At the time, this seemed a reasonable bet. Although a full edition of Wilfred Owen's poems appeared in 1931, his poetry did not attract real attention until the 1960s.

However tempting it is to generalize, the 'meaning' of the Great War was judged in many different ways by some 40 million British people, of differing ages and political persuasions. Even those who lived through 1914–18 had been 'fighting different wars' – men and women, adults and children, soldiers and civilians, Tommies in the trenches and behind the lines.[101] As time elapsed, with around three-quarters of a million births each year, a significant segment of the British population had no experience or memory of the war at all. That is why it is problematic to write off Britain in the 1920s and 1930s as a 'morbid age', obsessed with 1914–18, or to claim that 'the Myth of the War' had been fixed in the British consciousness by 1930, as a story of young men sent by their elders to senseless slaughter.[102] War was hell – that was axiomatic – but Britain had emerged victorious and few people would go so far as to assert that the Great War had been pointless, if only out of respect for the dead and the bereaved. Ten years after the Armistice the concept of 'sacrifice' remained compelling.[103] So 1914–18 might still be justified if it did indeed prove to be the war to end wars. Ultimately the meaning of the War would depend on the persistence of the Peace.

6

PEACE

We have got all that we want − perhaps more. Our sole object is to keep what we have and live in peace.

British Foreign Office memorandum, 10 April 1926

Cities, I thought, will wait them in the night ...
Poor panic-stricken hordes will hear that hum,
And Fear will be synonymous with Flight.

Siegfried Sassoon, from 'Thoughts in 1932'[1]

On 9 June 1920 George V opened the new Imperial War Museum, temporarily housed in the Crystal Palace in south London − a huge long glasshouse originally built for the Great Exhibition of 1851. 'We cannot say with what eyes posterity will regard this Museum', the King admitted, 'nor what ideas it will arouse in their minds.' But he hoped that 'as a result of what we have done and suffered, they may be able to look back on war, its instruments, and its organisation as belonging to a dead past.' In other words, this was to be a museum not just *of* war but *for* war. Putting war to death, turning it into history, would be the ultimate justification for 1914–18.[2]

'Never again' was a catchphrase of the 1920s and 1930s. But, as we have seen in earlier chapters, violence was still endemic in post-war Europe: the issue was whether it could be contained in order to avoid another great war across the continent. We now know that these hopes were in vain but, by exploring attitudes to peace in the 1920s and 1930s, particularly through rituals of remembrance and the anti-war movements, we learn more about how the Great War was understood across Europe, about the singularities of the British experience and, even more, of the United States. We shall also see that, as war clouds gathered in the late 1930s, 'lessons' from the last war would guide planning for the next.

Ten million soldiers had died in the conflict, 20 million had been severely wounded and 8 million returned home permanently disabled. How to commemorate the dead, solace the bereaved and support the disabled were central issues in the political life of all the belligerent countries, yet attitudes to commemoration differed widely. Consider a few examples.

The death toll in Russia was around 2 million, comparable in numbers to Germany's dead. Yet during the Soviet era (from 1917 to 1991) there were no official monuments to the Great War. The communist regime dismissed 1914–17 as an imperialist conflict, memorable only because it helped trigger the Bolshevik revolution. And for the Russian people 2 million dead was eclipsed by the 9–14 million fatalities over the next five years as a result of the civil war and its concomitant epidemics and famines. It was not, however, inevitable that Russia's war should be entombed in silence. In 1915–16 the Tsarist government developed elaborate plans for a national war museum, church and cemetery on the outskirts of Moscow, under the patronage of the Tsarina's sister, but this grand project was overwhelmed by the revolution. Although the cemetery did survive, it gradually fell into disrepair and became a convenient dumping ground for the victims of Stalin's purges. Eventually in the 1950s the site was cleared to build a movie theatre, 'Leningrad', named for the Hero City of 1941–4. Here was telling evidence of official priorities: although the Soviet regime blotted out any memory of 1914–17, it elevated the Great Patriotic War of 1941–5 into the central myth of the Soviet state.[3]

In Germany the anniversary of the Armistice on 11 November naturally held little attraction: instead remembrance focused on 'the August Days' of 1914. The right seized on Hindenburg's victory over the Tsarist army at Tannenberg in East Prussia, which became the annual occasion for demonstrations against both the Versailles treaty and the Weimar Republic. The left used the anniversary of the start of the war to mount big peace demonstrations with the slogan 'Never again war' (*nie wieder Krieg*). In August 1924 the government tried to channel this mood by turning a tenth-anniversary tribute to the fallen into a non-bellicose celebration of the supposed unity of all Germans in August 1914, hoping thereby to promote the unity of the republic. But the event proved a fiasco: some states, notably Bavaria, refused to participate in a 'defeatist' and 'republican' charade; elsewhere in big cities such as Berlin and Dresden pacifists and communists disrupted the ceremonies with anti-war protests that often led to violent clashes. In 1927 Tannenberg became the site of Germany's principal war memorial, a vast medieval-style fortress centred initially on the bodies of twenty unknown soldiers and then from 1935 featuring the grave of Hindenburg himself. Tannenberg had long been a site of German 'memory', the place where the Teutonic knights had been cut to pieces in 1410. But now it was the name of a great victory, where Hindenburg's armies encircled and destroyed the invading Russians in 1914. The monument dramatized the national myth of the war as self-defence, very different from the British and French perception of Germany as the aggressor in the west. Hindenburg's square rugged face had been a national icon since the early weeks of the war: a decade later the mythology of 1914 was translated to the silver screen in movies such as *The Iron Hindenburg* (1929) and *Tannenberg* (1932) – a nationalist response to Hollywood's *All Quiet on the Western Front*.[4]

Although virtually all Germans repudiated the idea of German 'war guilt' and yearned to overturn the *Diktat* of Versailles, the majority in the 1920s wanted to do so by peaceful means. 'The foolish call "Never again war" finds a widespread echo,' admitted Hans von

Seeckt, chief of the army command, in 1922. 'Certainly there is in the German people a widespread and explicable desire for peace.' In 1927 the former Prussian minister of war noted that war weariness among the people was 'so great' that 'parties have to take account of that at election time.'[5] Although Hitler and the extreme right celebrated the 'front experience' (*Fronterlebnis*) of the trenches, the vast majority of Germany's 11 million veterans settled back into civilian life in the 1920s rather than mounting militaristic protests. No more than 400,000 joined the right-wing Freikorps. The biggest single organization for war victims was the Reichsbund, founded by Social Democrats, which at its peak in 1922 had a membership of over 800,000 veterans, dependants and war disabled. The Reichsbund officially declared itself 'among the opponents of new wars'.[6]

In fact Hitler's famous account of his own war experience in *Mein Kampf* was largely made up. Although he did serve at the front for most of the conflict, 42 months out of 51, he was not a trench fighter but a despatch runner based at regimental headquarters – still a hazardous business but not like the death sentence of a front-line soldier. He was spared most of the battle of the Somme thanks to a leg wound and his second hospitalization in October 1918 – attributed by Hitler to blindness from a British mustard-gas attack – was probably the result of 'war hysteria' or shell shock. Hitler's evocation of the fighting spirit of the trenches was really a later invention in *Mein Kampf*, after the failure of his 1924 putsch. The cult of the trench fighter did not become mainstream ideology until the Nazis gained power, suppressing the socialists, their veterans' associations and the anti-war tradition of remembering 1914–18. Despite a surge after 1929 in nationalist books about the war – partly in reaction to Remarque but also reflecting frustration at the slide into depression – there was little enthusiasm in 1930s Germany for another conflict. The glum public mood was a major reason why Hitler drew back from war during the Czech crisis of 1938.[7]

Germany's conflicted attempts at memorialization focused on the start of the war in 1914 because there was nothing to celebrate about its ending. The victorious Allies, by contrast, naturally featured Germany's concession of defeat in 1918, usually commemorated on

11 November, though the Italians marked it on 4 November when their armistice with the Habsburgs came into effect. The rites of remembrance in Britain, though improvised at the start as we saw in the last chapter, soon gained a set and hallowed form with the Cenotaph and the Silence. In November 1921 the Royal British Legion, newly founded as the country's primary organization for veterans, ordered 1.5 million artificial poppies from France for sale to help ex-servicemen. Once again public enthusiasm caught the authorities by surprise: the Poppy Appeal, under the patronage of Field Marshal Haig, quickly became another national ritual, with the poppies manufactured by disabled veterans and sold mainly by women. By 1928 receipts exceeded £500,000 and the wearing of poppies on Armistice Day had become almost obligatory.[8]

In France and the United States Armistice Day was quickly made into a public holiday, thanks to their veterans' organizations which were bigger and more politicized than the British Legion and also because veterans' affairs were handled by a dedicated ministry or bureau – again in contrast with Britain. In both of these countries, too, 11 November offered the chance for former soldiers to celebrate victory and wartime comradeship. The American Legion's suggested programmes for Armistice Day combined a solemn patriotic service in the morning with sports events in the afternoon and 'fireworks and dancing' in the evening. In Britain, however, the idea of Armistice night dinners and dances was much more sensitive, with a proposed Victory Ball (in aid of servicemen's charities) provoking intense controversy in 1925. The 'really astonishing feature of Armistice Day' the following year, noted the *Daily Express*, was 'its pronounced seriousness. As time passes, the sense of jubilation on this day of memory decreases.' In 1927 the newspaper sponsored the first British Legion Festival of Remembrance at the Royal Albert Hall – with community singing and military parades – and this became an annual fixture, providing what was felt to be a decorous element of celebration. In Britain, therefore, Armistice Day was geared much more to the civilian bereaved than to the surviving veterans.[9]

The relative weakness of the British Legion needs to be underlined. In Germany, by contrast, there was a plethora of veterans' groups, all politically polarized and enjoying mass support. The Reichsbanner, for instance, was linked to the Socialist Party, while the Stahlhelm was identified with the extreme right. Each inflated its numbers for propaganda effect – the Reichsbanner boasted of 3 million members in 1925, whereas its active membership probably never exceeded 1 million – but this was still an impressive figure, probably double the size of the Stahlhelm. In further contrast with Britain, these German organizations were also paramilitary in nature and often vehemently opposed to the Weimar Republic. The Reichsbanner was a partial exception: it did not idolize the figure of the soldier and was formed to defend the republic against the Freikorps, but its existence reflected Weimar's failure to establish a monopoly of armed force. In France political divisions and militaristic tendencies were less intense among veterans' groups than in Germany but, of the two biggest organizations, the Union Fédérale (UF) was distinctly more leftist than the Union nationale des combattants (UNC). The UF advocated links with like-minded German veterans whereas extremists from the UNC were involved in the dramatic street demonstrations of February 1934 that toppled Edouard Daladier's government.[10]

By contrast, the British Legion, formed from four previously rival organizations, was firmly controlled and directed by former officers. Its ethos was therefore conservative but not partisan or militarist. The legion was much stronger in the south and west of England than in the urban north or Wales, drawing its strength mainly from English villages and market towns. The legion's paid-up membership peaked in the 1920s at 312,000 (1929), before falling in the depression, and then recovering to 409,000 in 1938. This meant that it never amounted to more than 10 per cent of the ex-service community, whereas French veterans' associations in the 1930s recorded some 3 million members, roughly half of all surviving ex-soldiers and nearly a quarter of the electorate. 'As a unified, national movement with no overt political affiliations and a low percentage of the total ex-service community within its ranks, the Legion was unique in Europe,' observes historian Niall Barr.[11]

The ineffectiveness of the Legion as a direct veterans' lobby is strikingly illustrated by the fraught issue of war pensions. Since the

Crimean War support for disabled British ex-servicemen had traditionally been left to private philanthropy; this reflected liberal
predilections for a limited state and for a small, balanced budget. In
the Great War the pensions issue was much more problematic – at
least a million British soldiers returned home disabled – yet volunteers and philanthropists again took the lead, as in the Poppy Appeal,
the St Dunstan's homes for the blind and the Roehampton centre
for artificial limbs. In late 1920s Britain war pensions of various
sorts accounted for less than 7 per cent of the government's annual
budget, whereas in Germany the proportion was nearly 20 per cent.
Not only did the Weimar Republic create Europe's 'most comprehensive programs for disabled veterans', it also eliminated almost
all rival private charities in a deliberate effort by the socialists and
the centre parties to strengthen the legitimacy of the contested
state by making it the main social provider. A similar attitude under-
pinned Weimar's generous support for young people, women and
the unemployed. The policy failed in its primary aim – veterans'
organizations simply lobbied for more money – and there was an outcry when welfare payments were cut back in the depression, further
eroding Weimar's authority and strengthening Nazi support. British
veterans, who never expected much from the state, were not disap-
pointed and they never turned against the government, even though
personally paying 'a high price for the country's stability and democratic survival.'[12]

The veterans' lobby was particularly powerful in the United States
thanks to the Civil War of 1861–5, in which 620,000 died. By the
1890s nearly a million ex-soldiers and their dependants were receiving government pensions, accounting for over 40 per cent of the
federal budget. This scheme was based on a very generous definition
both of war service (no more than ninety days in uniform) and of dis-
ablement (from any cause, during or following the war). Building on
this precedent, the American Legion (founded in 1919) successfully
lobbied for similarly generous treatment of the country's 4 million
Great War veterans. With more than 1 million members in 1931,
and 10,000 posts across the country, it could bring intense pressure
to bear on Capitol Hill, which was hard to resist. One lobbyist told

recalcitrant congressmen, 'If you don't support this bill, your successor will.' And so benefits expanded piecemeal in what became known as the 'veterans racket' until, in 1933, spending on veterans accounted for 26 per cent of the federal budget, even though this benefited a mere 1 per cent of the population. Whereas only 500,000 of Britain's 2 million wounded from the Great War received disability allowances in that year, the figure for the United States was 776,000, yet a mere 234,000 Americans had been wounded! It took both the Depression and a strong president to impose significant cuts. Even so the issue was in doubt on Capitol Hill until Franklin Roosevelt judiciously announced that, once Congress had passed the Economy Bill in March 1933, he would ask it to repeal Prohibition – observing with a smile, 'I think this would be a good time for beer.'[13]

The American Legion provides an interesting counterpoint to the veterans' scene both in Britain and on the continent. In 1920 it was one of several rival ex-soldier organizations in the United States. But the radical World War Veterans, who claimed 700,000 members in 1921 and whose demands included the distribution of 'idle acres' to 'the soldiers who are conceded to have saved civilization at $30 a month', was destroyed by the Red Scare of 1919–20. The Veterans of Foreign Wars survived but its membership never exceeded 300,000 in the 1920s or 1930s. Unlike Germany, therefore, the American Legion became the country's predominant veterans' organization and it also achieved its ends through democratic rather than paramilitary means, especially pressure on Congress. In contrast to the British Legion, however, the American Legion had an extensive political and social agenda, not least promoting 'one hundred percent Americanism'. The director of its National Americanism Commission, Henry Ryan, declared in 1921, 'The beginning and end of our work is nationalism, to create a national consciousness.' The legion played a central role in the Red Scare, used by state governments in Illinois, Massachusetts and elsewhere to help confront the radical threat. One of its foes was the American Civil Liberties Union (ACLU), formed during the war to combat patriotic intolerance, and the legion sometimes tied itself in knots over the issue of freedom of speech. 'We don't mind open discussion of forms of government,' a legion spokesman declared when advocating a loyalty oath for teachers, 'but every safeguard must be taken to prevent advertising any form of government except our own.' To advance Americanism at the grass roots, the legion funded school essay competitions, Boy Scout camps and, most successfully, Junior Baseball which involved 500,000 boys in all the states by 1930. The Junior World Series, said one legionnaire from Nebraska, had 'solved the problem of approach to the red-blooded American boy who has no time for preachments or studious appeals to the doctrine of good citizenship.' Across the Atlantic, the British Legion was certainly patriotic but the strenuous inculcation of Britishness was no part of its agenda.[14]

Although the British veterans' lobby was weak compared with other belligerents, in the 1930s the country nurtured the strongest peace movement in the world. As noted in the previous chapter, the flurry of books and films about the war after 1928 reshaped public attitudes. Exposés of the war's origins and conduct had questioned the wisdom of British politicians and generals; revelations about war propaganda and profiteering left a nasty taste. The demoralizing onset of the Slump and the election in 1929 of a Labour government led by prominent wartime pacifists also encouraged debate about the meaning of the conflict. It was now that H.G. Wells' dictum about 'the War that will end War' – originally a 1914 propaganda slogan against Prussian militarism – caught the popular imagination as a statement of faith. The tragedy and loss of the war, its grubbiness and incompetence, could still be justified in the language of sacrifice – at times almost Christ-like in tone. 'The millions of dead speak with one voice,' declared Sir Fabian Ware, head of the Imperial War Graves Commission, in an Armistice Day broadcast in 1932, 'and they say to the statesmen of the world: "You have failed to achieve your ends by other means than war, and we have expiated your failure – fail not again, accept our atonement and give faith and life to the world."' Moments like the two-minute Silence were 'a mockery', claimed the writer Ralph Hale Mottram, unless they led to 'some purification, some definite resolution that such wholesale mechanical slaughter will never happen again.' By the 1930s the war for civilization had been transmuted into a war for peace – and that became the main rationale for remembrance. In November 1933 the cover of the *British Legion Journal* featured a statue of a mother holding the body of her dead son, with the words 'disarm' on the plinth.[15] And so at Thiepval and Ypres, at the Cenotaph in Whitehall and hundreds more memorials across Britain, people enacted an annual ceremony of remembrance that 'managed to remain ambivalent' – a 'death cult which idealised the young "fallen" as patriots but which also underlined the new idealism: "Never again".'[16]

Women were central to the peace movements of the 1920s and 1930s, expressing their activism as newly enfranchised citizens. Although women became a majority of the electorate after 1928, the number of female MPs during these decades never exceeded 15 (out of a total of some 550); in the 1920s there was a backlash against feminism and an assertion of 'domesticity'. Yet women's organizations – even conservative elements such as the half-million-strong Mothers' Union – energetically encouraged women to use their votes and voices by agitating for gender equality (for instance reforms to divorce and property laws) and for the promotion of world peace.[17] They claimed a special interest in disarmament by virtue of their double position as mothers of the fallen and as historic victims of male violence. 'Because women produce children,' observed the pacifist intellectual Vera Brittain in 1934, 'life and the means of living matter to them in a way that these things can never matter to men.' She insisted that 'a civilisation in which military values prevail is always hostile to women's interests' because 'militarism and the oppression of women are both based on force.' In the vanguard of peace agitation was the Women's International League for Peace and Freedom (WIL), formed in 1919 from wartime peace movements and capitalizing on the recent granting of votes for women in Austria, Britain, Canada, Germany, Hungary, Iceland, Poland, Russia and soon the United States. Although the WIL remained a minority organization – by 1926 its membership was only 50,000 women from forty countries – it proved very effective at mobilizing opinion. These efforts peaked during 1931 in advance of the World Disarmament Conference. The WIL secured over 3 million signatures for its disarmament petition, half of them from Britain, soliciting support via a network of women's organizations across the country.[18]

The disarmament conference, six years in the making, finally convened in Geneva in February 1932 with 59 nations represented. Millions of men and women signed pro-peace petitions all over the world. Even in Germany, which was demanding 'equal rights' with the other great powers, more than 600,000 people attended rallies organized by the trade unions in support of the conference. The desire for peace was sharpened by the spiralling costs of armaments at a time of global depression. Over the next year and a half the twists and turns of the Geneva disarmament conference became the focus of international hopes and fears. Every country created problems: what was for one a legitimate means of defence was, for others, a blatant instrument of aggression. In a speech in 1928 Winston Churchill neatly captured this dilemma with his fable of a zoo. The rhino declared that the use of teeth was 'barbarous and horrible and ought to be strictly prohibited', while insisting that horns were entirely defensive weapons. Not surprisingly the buffalo, stag and porcupine supported the rhino but the lion, tiger and the other big cats strenuously disagreed. The bear differed from them all, wanting to ban both teeth and horns: he argued that 'it would be quite enough if animals were allowed to give each other a good hug when they quarrelled' – at which 'the Turkey fell into a perfect panic.' In Churchill's fable the zookeepers were eventually able to calm the animals down but in Geneva the keepers were the animals themselves, each with its own interest; all too easily, the law of the jungle could prevail.[19]

In late 1931 the British Foreign Office succinctly summed up the issues for the conference: 'World recovery (the aim of our policy) depends on European recovery; European recovery on German recovery; German recovery on France's consent; France's consent on security (for all time) against attack.' Germany had invaded France twice in less than half a century and its population was 50 per cent larger, so French leaders would not reduce their armaments before achieving firm guarantees of security, above all from Britain. 'England needs only say "If Germany attacks France I shall be at your side",' the French foreign minister told British diplomats in 1934.[20]

But this was the one thing that successive British governments would not do, after the experiences of 1914–18. Recurrent French demands for a formal alliance were rebuffed; likewise requests to join France's network of security treaties with the new states of eastern Europe – intended as a surrogate for the Franco-Russian alliance that had encircled Germany in 1914. In 1925 Austen Chamberlain, the most Francophile of British foreign secretaries between the wars, did broker the Locarno Treaty, under which France, Germany and Belgium accepted their existing borders and Britain and Italy promised to act against any 'flagrant violations'. But direct commitments to France remained anathema and, by the early 1930s, the mood among politicians and public in Britain had become distinctly isolationist. The idea of a Channel Tunnel, touted in 1929–30, was rejected very firmly by the government: 'So long as there are great military establishments in Europe, the Tunnel, if not adequately defended, becomes a potential danger; if it is properly defended, a military commitment is incurred, in which considerable forces would be locked up and immobilised.' Even Sir Robert Vansittart, the Francophile head of the Foreign Office, remarked in early 1932 that France had 'virtually attained the very thing that we have traditionally sought to avoid in Europe, hegemony, if not dictatorship, political and economic.'[21]

So at the Geneva disarmament conference Germany's demand for equal rights immediately and France's insistence on security before disarmament left matters deadlocked. Once Hitler gained power in 1933 he soon walked out of the conference and also left the League of Nations. With German rearmament now public knowledge, Britain began its own build-up in 1934. This escalating arms race, alarmingly reminiscent of Europe before 1914, turned the British peace movement into a major political force.

At the heart of this movement was the League of Nations Union (LNU). The league had inspired voluntary societies in many member states but none of them matched Britain's LNU in size, scope or political connections. Founded in 1918 with cross-party support, the LNU secured a Royal Charter in 1925 and all subsequent prime ministers accepted the position of honorary president. Its leader was Lord Robert Cecil, scion of one of the country's great political families but also an instinctive reformer, who loved fighting for unlikely causes. Cecil was an early champion of women's suffrage and a long-serving president of the Pedestrians Association, which helped bring in the driving test and a 30 mph speed limit in towns. But a league for international peace became his greatest passion after 1918: he was convinced that the war was 'the greatest catastrophe that has perhaps ever occurred.'[22]

Cecil was the LNU's driving force in the 1920s and 1930s. But the organization's real strength lay in the depth of its membership. At its peak in 1931 the LNU had 407,000 members in over 3,000 branches across Britain, though support was strongest in London, the Midlands and the Home Counties. It also had some 4,400 'corporate affiliates', ranging from trade unions to Boy Scout troops and Women's Institutes, with especially deep penetration of the Protestant churches. By contrast, French supporters of the Société des nations numbered only 127,000 in 1927. The LNU's broad reach reflected its belief that the disaster of the Great War showed the need to abandon narrow nationalism and give citizens more of a say in the making of foreign policy. Hence the priority given to promoting internationalism in schools and universities: 'There is no reason why the "international sense" should not become part of the stock-in-trade of the ordinary man,' observed Professor Alfred Zimmern. 'A hundred years ago, it was regarded as equally inconceivable that the ordinary man should become literate, or capable of reading a map.' The LNU was therefore an expression of the increasingly 'democratized' political culture of Britain after 1918.[23]

Hitler's coming to power encouraged the growth of isolationist sentiment in Britain, both on the right, especially in the Beaverbrook press, and also on the left: the Labour Party conference in October 1933 passed a resolution that Britain should 'take no part in war'. In response Cecil and the LNU organized a national canvass of public opinion in 1934–5, culminating in a triumphant rally in the Royal Albert Hall in London in June 1935. A total of 11.6 million people (38 per cent of the UK population) responded; even more striking, half a million volunteers were mobilized to deliver ballot papers to individual households, with the majority of this 'door-knocker parade' being female.[24] Women often used their place within the local community to secure trust and interest. 'I discovered that the little shop in the neighbourhood was a good place to say exactly what the ballot was for,' recalled one volunteer. Schoolteachers, both male and female, were particularly active proselytizers. A Leeds headmaster wrote to his MP about the importance of the ballot: 'I held my Armistice Service at school this morning. I faced 450 lads who may be involved in the "next war".' That was why, even though the voting age was twenty-one, the ballot was open to anyone over eighteen: the age for conscription.[25]

Although known to posterity as the Peace Ballot, the official title of the survey was the National Declaration on the League of Nations and Armaments. The Beaverbrook press dubbed it the Blood Ballot. Its real object was to combat the isolationists by pushing the government to take an active role in European peacemaking. The result was definitely not a random sample of public opinion: opponents of the LNU were under-represented, because either they did not return a ballot paper or were not asked to do so. Nevertheless the results showed a clear nationwide pattern, with 90 per cent or more affirming Britain's continued membership of the League of Nations and supporting international agreements to reduce armaments and ban the manufacture and sale of arms for private profit. There was also overwhelming support for economic and non-military sanctions against an aggressor nation (87 per cent). But, critically, on the use of force (question 5b), opinion was much more divided: 59 per cent said yes, 20 per cent no, but another 20 per cent offered no answer. The results of the Peace Ballot therefore require careful interpretation. In his memoirs *The Gathering Storm* (1948), Winston Churchill claimed that the responses to question five demonstrated a strong readiness 'to go to war in a righteous cause'. But it would be more accurate to say that the results showed public support for the principle of 'collective security' against the proponents of isolationism, while also suggesting considerable doubts about rearmament and the use of force against the dictators.[26]

The climax of the Peace Ballot coincided with Mussolini's brutal invasion of Abyssinia. Its political impact was evident in the Cabinet's reluctant imposition of economic sanctions on Italy and then the resignation of foreign secretary Sir Samuel Hoare after his secret deal with Italy was exposed. In both cases the government, though keen to buy off Italy because of the greater threats from Germany and Japan, felt obliged to take account of the public mood. But Hitler's annexation of the Rhineland in March 1936 and the onset of the Spanish civil war a few months later exposed the latent tensions within the British 'peace movement', already evident in responses to question 5b, with those willing to use force to maintain collective security separating from overt pacifists who opposed military action in any form. Absolute pacifists found their champion in Revd Dick Sheppard, a charismatic Anglican priest and pioneer 'radio parson', who formally established the Peace Pledge Union (PPU) in May 1936. Previously no overtly pacifist society had secured even 10,000 members in the UK but by the end of 1936 PPU membership had reached 118,000. This was still only one-third of the support for the LNU but the latter's membership was now in decline, falling to under 200,000 by 1939. Despite the adherence of national figures such as Aldous Huxley and Bertrand Russell, much of the PPU's spectacular growth was due to the appeal of the founder, who combined an aristocratic manner with striking intellectual humility: after his death in October 1937 PPU members were likened to 'sheep' without 'a Sheppard'. But the bifurcation of Britain's peace movement from the mid-1930s showed that the growing threat of war posed tough questions about how far people were willing to use force in the interests of collective security. 'Ultimately it is a clash between two religions,' observed the journalist Kingsley Martin in 1938. 'In a crisis people find out what they are.'[27]

On the continent there was nothing comparable to either the LNU or the PPU. The German peace movement (Das Deutsche Friedenskartell) was suppressed by Hitler, but even at its peak in 1928 it boasted at most 100,000 members (probably far fewer), fragmented across 22 different organizations. In France the peace movement was even more 'Balkanized', with some 200 organizations in 1936, and it was also in decline, not growth, during the 1930s. The French equivalent of the PPU, the Ligue internationale des combattants de la paix (LIPC) had fewer than 7,500 members in 1935; the Association de la paix par le droit (APD), an organization of elite intellectuals, only about 5,300. The APD was rooted in a distinctively Gallic approach to peacemaking, through international law and arbitration. 'The Anglo-Saxon', declared politician Pierre Cot in 1919, 'tours the world with his Bible and the Frenchman with his code. We have a conception of peace which is more juridical than mystical.'[28]

Cot was pointing to the distinctively religious roots of British peace movements, going back to seventeenth-century Quakers with their unconditional commitment to non-violence. Such was the strength of this tradition that when the Asquith government introduced conscription in 1916, it affirmed the right to be a conscientious objector (CO) and some 16,000 men were registered as COs during the conflict. This right of conscience was alien to continental countries, where the obligation to military service was deemed central to citizenship: Germany, for instance, had only a few hundred COs in the Great War. Traditional British reliance on a regular army meant that conscription was a momentous innovation in 1916, bringing home to every family the distinction between peace and war. In the mid-1930s the National Government's repeated pledge, for political reasons, not to introduce conscription complicated rearmament until it was abandoned in April 1939 after Hitler devoured all of Czechoslovakia.

The respectability of conscientious objection to war was a major reason for the distinctive strength of the British peace movement. But equally important was Britain's geopolitical position. On the continent, where land borders were porous and ever changing, pacifism was deemed a dangerous political luxury, eroding the country's capacity for self-defence. Britain, by contrast, enjoyed the benefit of a 21-mile-wide 'moat defensive', in Shakespeare's picturesque phrase, between itself and continental enemies. The English Channel was broad enough to foster a sense of security but not so wide as to engender complacency, as invasion crises such as 1588 and 1804 made clear. In consequence Britain felt an historic interest in maintaining the continental balance of power to deter potential aggressors: hence the commitment to France and Belgium in August 1914 to prevent Germany gaining control of the Channel ports. The novel element in the 1930s debate about British security was the threat of bombing by long-range aircraft. 'Since the day of the air,' Stanley Baldwin warned the Commons in July 1934, 'the old frontiers are gone. When you think of the defence of England you no longer think of the chalk cliffs of Dover, you think of the Rhine.' To shouts of 'Hear, hear' from MPs, he continued, 'That is where our frontier lies.'[29]

The problem was not just the enlargement of Britain's security perimeter but the country's new vulnerability. Baldwin offered this morbid diagnosis to the Commons in November 1932. 'What the world suffers from', he asserted, 'is a sense of fear, a want of confidence' and 'there is no greater cause of that fear than the fear of the air' because aerial bombing had made women and children as vulnerable as front-line soldiers. Baldwin continued with chilling candour, 'I think it is well also for the man in the street to realise that there is no power on earth that can protect him from being bombed. Whatever people may tell him, the bomber will always get through.' This was also the view of military planners. In October 1936 the Joint Planning Committee (JPC), representing the three services, warned that, in any future war, Germany would seek a quick victory before Britain's superior economic strength could be brought to bear: 'the concentration, from the first day of the war, of the whole of the German air offensive against Great Britain would be possible. It would be the most promising way of trying to knock this country out.' The JPC noted that 'our civilian population has never been exposed to the horrors of War', unlike the continentals, and the Germans 'may believe that if our people and particularly our women and children were subjected to these horrors ... the majority would insist that surrender was preferable.' There had been some ugly anti-war protests in London during the Gotha raids of 1917–18 and casualties in the next war were likely to be much worse. The planners predicted 20,000 casualties in the initial twenty-four hours of air attack, rising to perhaps 150,000 by the end of the first week.[30]

The JPC report was toned down before circulation in Whitehall but it expressed widely held ideas – a point that should be underlined if we want to understand British attitudes in the 1930s. First, the concept of a 'knockout blow': when policymakers and public spoke of a future war in the 1930s, this was the scenario that they assumed – an immediate and devastating attack on Britain. In fact, the Germans did not try this until after the collapse of France, nearly a year into the conflict. Second, it was assumed that the human losses would be utterly appalling. To put the JPC body count in perspective, we should note that Britain sustained fewer than 150,000 casualties from all forms of aerial bombing during the whole of the Second World War, including the Blitz and the V-weapons. As Harold Macmillan admitted, looking back from the 1960s after being prime minister during the Cuban missile crisis: 'We thought of air warfare in 1938 rather as people think of nuclear warfare today.'[31]

It was an apt comparison. In the mid-1930s the threat from the air was sensationalized in films, novels and political tracts. After only one air raid, predicted the philosopher Bertrand Russell in 1936, London 'will be one vast raving bedlam, the hospitals will be stormed, traffic will cease' and the government 'will be swept away by an avalanche of terror. Then the enemy will dictate its terms.' The following year the architect John Gloag foresaw 'a new age of architecture: future civilizations may call it the Funk-hole Age. It may be the prelude to another Dark Age in which our children and grandchildren and great grandchildren will live amid ruins.' Gloag even suggested building 'special shelter cities' for the survivors to 'enable at least a nucleus of civilization to be preserved in the event of a general breakdown.'[32] Such fears were particularly acute in late September 1938, when it seemed that war with Germany was inevitable. The historian Arnold Toynbee tried to evoke the mood a little later, after the Munich agreement, in a letter to an American friend:

It is probably impossible to convey what the imminent expectation of being intensively bombed feels like in a small and densely populated country like this. I couldn't have conveyed it to myself if I hadn't experienced it in London the week before last (we were expecting 30,000 casualties a night in London, and on the Wednesday morning we believed ourselves, I believe correctly, to be within three hours of the zero hour). It was just like facing the end of the world. In a few minutes the clock was going to stop, and life, as we had known it, was coming to an end. This prospect of the horrible destruction of all that is meant to one by 'England' and 'Europe' was much worse than the mere personal prospect that one's family and oneself would be blown to bits. Seven or eight million people in London went through it.[33]

Of course, the shadow of the bomber hung over all of Europe in the 1930s, obscuring the conventional distinction between soldier and civilian. In France, like Britain (but not Germany), the capital city dominated the country's political, financial, industrial and cultural life and Parisians entertained a similar obsession about bombing. In the words of one journalist, they expected 'towns destroyed in a few hours by a rain of bombs, toxic gas capable of destroying in a few minutes every kind of life in a great city such as Paris, millions of children, women, men slaughtered together.'[34] But for the French in the 1930s the fear of bombing was essentially an intensification of historic anxieties, with the Luftwaffe accentuating the Wehrmacht's threat to northern France, whereas for Britain the bomber created a totally new sense of insecurity. The 1930s air panic was therefore particularly acute in Britain and this helps explain the unprecedented support for anti-war movements such as the Peace Ballot and the Peace Pledge Union.[35]

The bomber also shaped British diplomacy. In March 1933, a few weeks after Hitler gained power, Baldwin told the Cabinet's disarmament committee that two things frightened him most. 'The first was the liability of this country to air raids and the second was the rearming of Germany.' Convinced that 'the air was the first arm which the Germans will start to build up', he insisted that 'we must have a convention prohibiting bombing.' This was Baldwin's main objective during the Geneva disarmament conference, shared by the Foreign Office and indeed senior army and naval officers. 'Only the Air Ministry wants to retain these weapons for use against towns,' fumed one Admiralty memorandum, calling it 'a method of warfare which is revolting and un-English.' Even after the conference collapsed, the Foreign Office pushed hard for an agreement among the Great Powers, but the French would not separate an anti-bombing pact from a general settlement with Germany. For them, as we have seen, the Luftwaffe was one facet of the overall German threat; across the Channel it was the Achilles heel of British security.[36]

Baldwin was seeking a multilateral European agreement but in 1938, as war clouds gathered over Czechoslovakia, Neville Chamberlain decided to deal directly with Hitler. Today Chamberlain is usually stereotyped as a credulous old fool but for most of the 1930s he was seen as the truly dynamic force in the National Government, first as chancellor of the exchequer and then from 1937 as premier. His three visits to Germany over two weeks in September 1938 to negotiate with the Führer were a high-risk bid to avert war over Czechoslovakia. He used a plane not merely to save time but in order to seize the initiative: a meeting in London or on the North Sea 'would not have suited me,' he told his sister, 'for it would have deprived my coup of much of its dramatic effect.' Photos and film of Chamberlain climbing into a small propeller plane for his first real flight, aged sixty-nine, hit the headlines around the world. He was taking to the air to avert the threat from the air, deliberately using the vehicle of mass destruction as an instrument of peace. Neville had lost his cousin and closest friend, Norman, in the Great War; now, as premier, he was haunted by the responsibility of taking Britain into another conflict that could prove to be Armageddon. After his second visit to Hitler he spoke movingly about his feelings as he flew home up the Thames and looked down over the East End of London. According to the Cabinet minutes 'he had imagined a German bomber flying the same course. He had asked himself what degree of protection we could afford to the thousands of homes which he had seen stretched out below him, and he had felt that we were in no position to justify waging a war to-day in order to prevent a war hereafter.'[37]

The climax of Chamberlain's summit diplomacy was his third meeting with Hitler at Munich. There he sacrificed the security and much of the territory of Czechoslovakia, but what counted for most British people was the famous piece of paper signed by the two leaders stating that Britain and Germany would never go to war again. 'Ce n'est pas magnifique,' remarked the pundit Cyril Joad drily, 'mais ce n'est pas la guerre.'[38] The Munich agreement was greeted ecstatically by people in both countries. On 30 September Chamberlain's car was mobbed by Munich crowds before he flew home – evidence, according to one contemporary, of how the Prime Minister had made himself 'the mouthpiece of the horror with which millions of men and women ... regard the brutish devilries of modern war.' In London it took him ninety minutes to drive the nine miles from Heston airfield to Whitehall, so thick was the cheering throng; people jumped on to the running board trying to shake his hand. George VI took the remarkable step of inviting Chamberlain on to the balcony of Buckingham Palace to acknowledge the acclaim. Finally back at 10 Downing Street the Prime Minister, carried away by emotion and exhaustion, waved the piece of paper again and declared, 'I believe it is peace for our time.'[39]

These images from 30 September 1938 would shape public memory in years to come. Any politician soaring so high was clearly riding for a fall, and the collapse of Chamberlain's reputation was truly vertiginous. Munich soon became a synonym for craven surrender, as did the term 'appeasement', which had begun the 1930s as a perfectly respectable diplomatic term signifying the peaceful settlement of grievances. This sad denouement was partly because Chamberlain proved an inept negotiator, failing to understand Hitler's mind or the art of hard bargaining. He also got carried away by the hubris of power, telling his sister that, as premier, 'I have only to raise a finger & the whole face of Europe is changed.' Arrogance aside, however, Chamberlain's high-wire summitry was a direct response to the panic about bombing in 1930s Britain – evoked so movingly in Toynbee's letter. The perceived extremity of the danger elicited a response that was unique in British diplomatic history. Never before or since has a prime minister staked so much of his personal credibility on a bid for peace.[40]

The bomber overshadowed British strategy as well as diplomacy. Once Germany began to rearm it was inevitable that Britain must follow suit, even though still seeking international agreement on arms control. When the Defence Requirements Committee (DRC) was set up in November 1933, it initially proposed a balanced programme of rearmament to remedy deficiencies in all three services in the face of threats from Germany and Japan. It agreed that Germany was the ultimate potential enemy and that the government should be ready, in the event of war, to deploy another British Expeditionary Force (BEF) of five divisions and a tank brigade on the continent. The DRC proposed a five-year programme of some £97 million, with £40 million allocated for the army. But these proposals were radically reshaped by Chamberlain and the Treasury, alarmed at both the cost and the public paranoia about bombing. They proposed cutting the total budget to £69 million, with only £19 million for the army, while the air component was increased from 52 squadrons to 80. Mindful of public memories of the Western Front, Chamberlain warned that the proposed army spending would 'give rise to the most alarmist ideas of future intentions and commitments'. Instead, he argued, rearmament should concentrate on areas 'in which public interest is strongest', namely the RAF proposals for home defence. Britain's best protection, he insisted, 'would be the existence of a deterrent force so powerful as to render success in attack too doubtful to be worthwhile. I submit that this is most likely to be attained by the establishment of an Air Force based on this country of a size and efficiency calculated to inspire respect in the mind of a possible enemy.'[41]

This concept of deterrence lay at the heart of British defence policy throughout the 1930s. As Baldwin argued in 1932 when warning that the 'bomber will always get through', 'the only defence is in offence, which means that you have to kill more women and children more quickly than the enemy if you want to save yourselves.' Although in 1934 Baldwin dissented from the imbalance of Chamberlain's proposals, he did not deny that 'from the political point it was necessary to do something to satisfy the semi-panic conditions which existed now about the air and for obvious reasons.' Hence his reiterated pledge that the National Government would not allow British air-power to be 'inferior to any country within striking distance of our shores'.[42]

The defence debate in 1933–4 established the parameters for subsequent rearmament. Budgets came and went amid the ever-changing international situation but the RAF remained on top, with a future BEF always bottom of the priority list. This reflected the public's other phobia, about a second bloody land war on the continent. No nation 'would stand the losses we went through again for another 100 years,' warned General Sir George Milne; 'civilisation itself would go to pieces if a war similar to the last one were fought.' Mindful of the public mood the Cabinet banned use of the term 'Expeditionary Force' even in secret papers ('Field Force' being used instead) and concluded that 'the time was inopportune for a resounding Declaration of our concern in the integrity of Belgian territory'. Army planners tried to rebut claims that in a future conflict airpower would be decisive and that Britain could adopt a 'limited liability' approach to continental commitments: 'if war with Germany comes again', noted Colonel Henry Pownall in 1936, 'we shall again be fighting for our lives. Our effort *must* be the maximum, by land, sea and air.' But Chamberlain disagreed: 'I believe our resources will be more profitably employed in the air, and on the sea, than in building up great armies.' In December 1937 the Cabinet instructed army planners to assume that Britain would not commit a Field Force to any European war at the start of hostilities.[43]

The RAF reigned supreme in the budget battles all through the 1930s, but with a significant change of emphasis. By late 1938 it no longer seemed inevitable that the bomber would always get through. One reason was the development of fast, monoplane fighters – especially the Hurricane and Spitfire – capable of destroying enemy bombers before they reached their targets. But equally vital was the concomitant development of radar (then known as Radio Direction Finding), thanks in considerable measure to political and financial support secretly provided by Baldwin in 1934–5. In the winter after Munich the government rushed to complete the Chain Home system of radar stations around England's south-east coast, linked by secure command and control phone networks to the headquarters of RAF Fighter Command. The Air Ministry, now with a strong vested interest in the bomber force, continued to insist that 'counter-attack still remains our chief deterrent and defence' but one heavy bomber cost the equivalent of four fighters, so the Treasury threw its weight behind the new concept of home defence. Radar provided a crucial ten-minute warning of enemy attack – just enough time to get the Hurricanes and Spitfires airborne, as would become clear in 1940. With these new electronic eyes, it seemed that the white cliffs of Dover could still serve as rampart to Britain's moat defensive.[44]

Hurricanes, Spitfires and radar are all reminders that, in the two decades after 1918, Britain remained a major military power, often at the cutting edge of new technology. During the 1920s Britain probably had the highest warlike expenditure in the world in absolute terms; by the mid-1930s it was no longer top of the table but this was due to heavy spending by Germany, Japan and other powers rather than to British cuts. 'The Royal Navy out-built all other navies in nearly all periods of the interwar years and in nearly all classes of warships.' Even though its investment in battleships seemed outmoded during the war of 1939–45, the navy was also at the forefront of the vital new weapons system of aircraft carriers. In 1939 Britain had seven carriers, America and Japan six each, and Germany none. British seapower rested on a vast naval-industrial complex embracing the Clyde, Mersey and Tyneside as well as the Royal Dockyards, which also drew on the steel mills of Yorkshire and the machine-tool factories of the Midlands. Although slimmed down after 1918, this complex was sustained through the 1920s and 1930s so that relatively little investment was needed to gear up for war. The aircraft industry, still largely craft-based rather than utilizing mass production, did need substantial funding but this, too, was a major industrial operation at the vanguard of new technologies – notably the Spitfire fighter and the Lancaster bomber. And until the early 1930s Britain was the largest overall arms exporter in the world, often cornering a quarter of the market; thereafter it shared leadership of the international arms trade with France. Contrary, therefore, to the familiar stereotype now of Britain as an emerging 'welfare state' whose liberal values inculcated an anti-militarist ideology, the country in the 1930s can be described in many ways as a 'warfare state' with a military-industrial sector that certainly kept pace with its rivals.[45]

Britain also managed the hazardous economics of rearmament more effectively than its neighbours. For good or ill Chamberlain and the Treasury exerted a controlling hand over the process, establishing priorities within arms spending and restraining the worst interservice rivalry. At a deeper level, they also insisted that rearmament must not undermine the fundamentals of Britain's economy against those, like Churchill, who demanded more rapid rearmament. 'I do not believe that [war] is imminent,' Chamberlain wrote in late 1936. 'By careful diplomacy I believe we can stave it off, perhaps indefinitely, but if we were now to follow Winston's advice and sacrifice our commerce to the manufacture of arms we should inflict a certain injury upon our trade from which it would take generations to recover, we should destroy the [business] confidence which now happily exists, and we should cripple the revenue.' These concerns ruled out increased taxation and also, in a pre-Keynesian age, heavy borrowing. Chamberlain's policy was intended not just to satisfy peacetime exigencies but also as part of future war strategy. It was axiomatic that Britain's financial and economic health was the country's 'fourth arm' – as vital for a future conflict as the three armed services. 'At the present moment', wrote Sir John Simon, Chamberlain's chancellor of the exchequer, in March 1938, 'we are in the position of a runner in a race who wants to reserve his spurt for the right time, but does not know where the finishing tape is. The danger is that we might knock our finances to pieces prematurely.' The Treasury maintained this position until the spring of 1939, after Hitler seized all of Czechoslovakia: Simon was then forced to admit that 'other aspects in this matter now outweigh finance.'[46]

Across the Channel, there was no such coordination of rearmament. In France arms policy became politicized in 1936–8 in the frenzied left–right battle over the Popular Front and its package of social benefits, with one ministry following another in quick succession. It did not help that French rearmament got going seriously in 1936 just as financial crisis and depression began to bite, whereas British rearmament from 1934 coincided with recovery from the Slump. As a result France was still converting its air force to fast monoplane fighters in 1940 as the phoney war came to an end.[47]

Germany's rearmament, driven by Hitler's megalomaniac vision, was even more chaotic, leading by 1936 to acute pressure on the budget and balance of payments. Overriding the efforts of

Reichsbank president Hjalmar Schacht to coordinate the process in a Chamberlainesque manner, Hitler decreed in September 1936 that 'the German army must be operational within four years' and the economy made 'fit for war' within the same time frame. Germany's payments crisis worsened and, by the time of Munich, the shortage of raw materials and food threatened not only continued rearmament but also domestic stability. The Reichsbank frantically warned that Germany was 'already on the threshold of inflation' – dread word from the 1920s – whose consequences 'would be almost as dangerous' as war. But Hitler saw the dilemma differently: with British and French rearmament now gathering pace, it made sense, at least according to his mad logic, to use Germany's army sooner rather than later, in a desperate bid to revise the European balance of power before the external pressures became overwhelming. The Nazi-Soviet pact of August 1939, though making nonsense of earlier ideological pronouncements about mutual hatred, was an inspired act of political opportunism, allowing Hitler to attack in the west without fear of an Eastern Front, but going to war was still an enormous gamble.[48]

In September 1939 the anguish of Chamberlain and millions of British peace activists about the failure of their hopes must be set against the fact that Whitehall was essentially optimistic about Britain's prospects in the coming war. Thanks to Chamberlain and the Treasury, it seemed that the country had managed to rearm without undermining the economy or sterling. Chances of surviving Germany's initial onslaught, the dreaded knockout blow, had vastly improved thanks to the new air defence system. And policymakers assumed that France's army could take care of any attack on the Western Front. In August 1939 Pownall, now the army's senior planner, was confident that if war did come, 'we can't lose it. Last September we might have lost a *short* war. Now we shouldn't, nor a long one either.'[49] Today such confidence seems ludicrous but, as we shall see in the next chapter, the dramatic German victory in May 1940 astounded Berlin as much as London and Paris.

Confident or not, by 1938–9 the British were thinking about war again. Already one can sense a change in basic perceptions. Consider two verbal snapshots. In 1932 Sir Alexander Cadogan, a senior British diplomat, mused about what he considered the 'fundamental question' facing the disarmament conference in Geneva:

> are we to try to keep the present Europe by force, by maintaining the restrictions imposed on Germany by the peace treaty, or are we to bring to an end the 'post war' period, allow Germany to resume her place and rights as a great power on equal footing with the others, and trust that the reluctant removal of her grievances coupled with the security offered by the Covenant of the League will initiate a period of real peace? French policy plainly cannot be maintained for ever ...[50]

In 1932 Cadogan was determined to move on from the 'post-war' years but, like Keynes in 1931 (see p. 127), he was unsure what would replace them. Five years later the future seemed clearer but also more like the past. In 1937 the Welshman David Jones published *In Parenthesis*, an epic prose-poem about an English soldier in France in 1915–16. Jones was, unusually, a war poet writing years after the war – and it showed in the double meaning of his title. First, for young men called up as soldiers 'the war itself was a parenthesis': Jones added, 'how glad we thought we were to step outside its brackets at the end of '18'. Secondly, he wished to convey a feeling that 'our curious type of existence here is altogether in parenthesis.' The word 'here' may have been intended existentially – to signify our life between birth and death – but I think it reveals Jones' looming fear by 1937 that he was living in parenthesis between one great war and another. So we catch here an early intimation of the 1920s and 1930s not as the 'post-war' years but as the 'interwar' era.[51]

The passion for peace was equally intense in 1930s America. What happened there helps put the British story into sharper perspective.

Like Britain, American anti-war movements had their roots in Christian traditions of non-violence, especially among the Quakers and the Mennonites: the American Peace Society was founded as early as 1828. Secular forms of pacifism were a product of the twentieth century, especially the Great War, during which nearly 4,000 men

were registered as 'conscientious objectors', borrowing British terminology.[52] After 1918 peace groups proliferated in America, as in
Britain, with newly enfranchised women playing a leading role. 'War
is in the blood of men; they can't help it,' declared the veteran suffra-
gette leader Carrie Chapman Catt. 'They have been fighting ever
since the days of the cavemen.' The New York branch of the Women's
International League for Peace and Freedom (WIL) declared in 1919
that 'by aiding men to release themselves from bondage to violence and
bloodshed, we shall also free ourselves, for women can never know true
liberty in a society dominated by force.'[53] Influenced by the ideology
of the progressive era, many peace activists in the 1920s hoped that the
carnage of 1914–18 and the advance of democracy would persuade
nations to 'outlaw war'. The Kellogg–Briand Pact of 1928 was partly
a product of this agitation. Concluded initially between America and
France, who both formally renounced war as an instrument of national
policy, the treaty was eventually signed by over fifty nations, including
Britain, Germany, Japan and the Soviet Union – in fact most of the
countries who would be at each other's throats a decade later. The pact
was, actually, a shrewd tactical move by the State Department to deflect
French pressure for a real security treaty while appeasing America's
peace movement. This balancing act reflected the basic dilemma of
American policy after 1918: a commitment to peace in principle but
not to any mechanisms for its enforcement.

Because the US Senate had refused to join the League of Nations in
1919–20, the country was left outside the main international structure
for peace and this had important consequences for the American peace
movement. In Britain, as we have seen, the League of Nations Union
enjoyed mass support and was closely intertwined with the political
elite. By contrast the League of Nations Association (LNA) in the
United States, though rooted in the Eastern Establishment and having
close ties to Washington, remained small-scale (peaking at 19,000
members in 1931). The lack of popular appeal was partly because it
concentrated, like the French APD, on legal issues but the root problem was simply that the LNA's main objective, American membership
of the League of Nations, was politically a non-starter after 1920. By
contrast the pacifist element of the peace movement was stronger in

America than in Britain, coordinated by the National Council for the Prevention of War (NCPW). Peace groups under its umbrella proved very effective both in mobilizing mass support and in influencing congressmen. In 1931 they led the petitioning for the world disarmament conference; their Emergency Peace Campaign of 1936–7 has been described as 'the greatest unified effort made by peace advocates until at least the Vietnam war'. It began in April 1936 with half a million high-school and college students going on strike from their classrooms to attend demonstrations.[54]

Pacifists were also in the vanguard of America's very distinctive witch-hunt against the 'merchants of death'. A key figure here was Dorothy Detzer, the dynamic executive secretary of the WIL. A Midwesterner with only a high-school diploma, her background was very different from that of traditional women's leaders like Catt – mostly college graduates from wealthy East Coast families. She became a committed pacifist after her beloved twin brother died from poison gas in the war. In 1932–3, following the failure of the Geneva disarmament conference, Detzer toured Capitol Hill pressing for an inquiry into the international arms trade. Eventually Senator Gerald P. Nye, an austere progressive Republican from North Dakota, sponsored a resolution. Its passage was assisted by lobbying from peace groups and by publication in the spring of 1934 of several sensational indictments of the 'blood brotherhood' of arms manufacturers. Their creed, according to an article in *Fortune* magazine, was 'when there are wars, prolong them; when there is peace, disturb it.'[55]

Chaired by Senator Nye, the Special Committee on Investigation of the Munitions Industry was dominated by progressives and isolationists, deeply suspicious of the Eastern Establishment and of Great Britain. Nye himself had not been outside the United States or even east of Chicago until entering the Senate in 1926, and he never visited Europe.[56] Under his crusading leadership the committee's ninety-three hearings between September 1934 and February 1936 ranged far beyond the arms trade to scrutinize America's whole involvement in the Great War. Such is the authority of congressional committees that titans of business such as the banker J.P. Morgan felt obliged to testify, under the glare of intense media scrutiny (plate 17).

Although the Nye Committee found extensive evidence of bribery and insider dealing, it failed to substantiate its big claims about an international arms ring that was bent on fomenting wars. But the sensational headlines seemed to confirm the late 1920s revisionism about the Great War. 'It is almost a truism', noted journalist Raymond Gram Swing in 1935, 'that the United States went into the World War in part to save from ruin the bankers who had strained themselves to the utmost to supply Great Britain with munitions and credits.'[57]

Intent on applying the 'lessons of history' to shape the future, the Nye Committee was a prime mover of the Neutrality Act of August 1935. In any future war the president would be obliged to impose a mandatory embargo on the sale of munitions to any of the belligerents and also prohibit the carriage of munitions on American ships. The following February, after Italy's war in Abyssinia, new legislation added a ban on American loans to belligerent countries and in May 1937 a third Neutrality Act banned American citizens from travelling on passenger vessels owned by belligerent countries. Critics joked that these laws were a belated attempt to stop America entering the war of 1914–18. Considered more broadly, they were also a reversal of the traditional American policy of freely trading with all belligerent countries in time of war so that, as Thomas Jefferson memorably put it, the New World could 'fatten on the follies of the Old.'[58] America's commercial and financial reach, seen in the 1920s as a mark of international influence, was now deemed a source of vulnerability. 'In my view,' declared Senator Arthur Vandenberg, a member of the Nye Committee, 'we want an American neutrality which quarantines us against the wars of others to the last possible practicable and realistic extent. It cannot be done under the old rules which subordinate peace to commerce.' In his view, 'the loss of incidental commerce is infinitely less important than a maintenance of American peace.'[59] The attitudes that shaped the Neutrality Acts were a product of the Depression, emblematic of a nation that had lost confidence in its ability to shape world events. 'Of the hell broth that is brewing in Europe we have no need to drink,' wrote novelist Ernest Hemingway. 'We were fools to be sucked in once in a European war, and we shall never be sucked in again.'[60]

Similar words emanated from the White House. 'I have seen war,' declared President Franklin D. Roosevelt (FDR) in August 1936. 'I have seen war on land and sea. I have seen blood running from the wounded. I have seen men coughing out their gassed lungs. I have seen the dead in the mud. I have seen cities destroyed . . . I hate war. I have passed unnumbered hours, I shall pass unnumbered hours, thinking and planning how war may be kept from this Nation.'[61] Roosevelt's lurid language, though partly electioneering, shows how far even internationalist Americans had moved since 1919. Despite serving as Assistant Secretary of the Navy during the Great War, FDR was never a whole-hearted supporter of Wilson's agenda. He believed that the United States should play an active role in world affairs but considered Wilson's conception of the League of Nations too rigid for American interests. He also learned profound lessons from the President's failure to persuade political and public opinion. 'It is a terrible thing to look over your shoulder when you are trying to lead', he once observed, 'and to find no one there.' Aide Robert Sherwood reckoned that 'the tragedy of Wilson was always within the rim of his consciousness.' Wilson's stroke, brought on by his frenetic tour of the country in 1919, left him an invalid for the rest of his life. This drama of personal and political paralysis was particularly vivid for Roosevelt, unable to walk unaided after contracting polio in 1921.[62]

In 1935 it was actually FDR who encouraged the Nye Committee to consider neutrality legislation, possibly hoping to divert them from more muckraking about the munitions industry. But Roosevelt also shared the belief that America's emotional and economic entanglements with the Allies from 1914 had limited Wilson's freedom of action and helped suck the United States into the war.[63] He wanted to avoid another outcry reminiscent of the sinking of the *Lusitania* in 1915, when 128 Americans were lost after a U-boat torpedoed a British passenger liner that was secretly carrying munitions. Once Nye got the bit between his teeth, however, the result was legislation that went far beyond what FDR had desired and would shape US diplomacy for the rest of the decade.

To understand what was at stake we need to distinguish between two sets of legal matrices. First, arms embargoes and other bans could be either universal or discriminatory in scope; in other words, applying to all belligerents or only against aggressor states. Secondly, they could be either mandatory or discretionary in application, depending on whether the president had leeway about when and how to invoke the law. Roosevelt wanted legislation that was discriminatory and discretionary, allowing him the freedom to apply it against aggressor states. The peace movement, backed by isolationists deeply suspicious of the President, sought mandatory, universal legislation that would insulate the United States from all sparks of war, and they got their way in 1935. But the 1937 Act gave Roosevelt more of what he wanted. Although including mandatory and universal bans on arms, loans, shipping and travel, the President now had discretion to allow non-arms trade with belligerent countries if he believed this necessary for the peace and security of the United States and if that trade was on a 'cash and carry' basis. This phrase was popularized by Bernard Baruch, former chairman of Wilson's War Industries Board: 'We will sell to any belligerent anything except lethal weapons, but the terms are "*cash on the barrel-head and come and get it*."' Cash and carry would preserve the profits of neutral trade while minimizing the risk of involvement in war. Yet it would also benefit nations with large financial reserves and merchant fleets, pre-eminently Britain. In this way, Roosevelt hoped, the United States could assist in the containment of Hitler without being dragged into another war. He spoke publicly in October 1937 of the need to 'quarantine the aggressors' – not, like Vandenberg and his ilk, quarantining America from the contagion of war. 'We don't call them economic sanctions,' he told his Cabinet later, 'we call them quarantines. We want to develop a technique which will not lead to war.'[64]

America's contorted debate in 1935–7 over the Neutrality Acts replicated the split that opened up in the British peace movement after the Peace Ballot of 1935 between proponents of collective security, willing to use sanctions to enforce peace, and those intent on avoiding war at all costs. But there were significant national differences because the United States was outside the League of Nations and because of the intensity of American revisionism about the Great War. American revelations about the 'merchants of death' did stimulate British agitation for a similar inquiry into the activities of Vickers and other British arms manufacturers but the government managed to avoid a Nye-style witch-hunt. It created a Royal Commission – a familiar way to bury a controversial issue by taking minutes and spending years. Although over 2 million Britons submitted views and opinions to the commission in 1935–6, the whole process was a sop to the public outcry about the arms trade and served to divert attention from national rearmament – whereas the Nye Committee led directly to legislation that cramped US government policy.[65]

American fear of war was intense yet abstract: three thousand miles from Europe, there was no equivalent of the British panic about bombing. But FDR was ahead of his countrymen in thinking about the implications of air warfare. During October 1938 he mulled over the lessons of the Czech crisis, absorbing reports from his ambassadors in Europe. This helped the President to understand the gut-wrenching fear of massive airborne destruction that had gripped Paris and London during the crisis. Helping them redress the air balance, in the long-term interests of American security, became his preoccupation during the winter of 1938–9. He told his military advisers that 'the recrudescence of German power at Munich had completely reoriented our own international relations' and that America must therefore immediately create 'a huge air force so that we do not need to have a huge army to follow that air force.' He considered that 'sending a large army abroad was undesirable and politically out of the question.' FDR also saw rearmament as a form of diplomatic leverage: 'when I write to foreign countries I must have something to back up my words. Had we had this summer 5,000 planes with the capacity immediately to produce 10,000 per year, even though I might have had to ask Congress for authority to sell or lend them to the countries in Europe, Hitler would not have dared to take the stand he did.'[66]*

Roosevelt's conception of air rearmament in 1938–9 was similar to Chamberlain's in the mid-1930s – an alternative to a large army and an instrument of diplomacy. He told leading senators privately that Hitler was a 'nut', that Germany, Italy and Japan were developing 'a

* The comment about selling or lending planes to Europe strikingly prefigured Lend-Lease in 1941.

policy of world domination' and that the Congress must now recognize that 'the first line of defense in the United States' was 'the continued independent existence' of key nations in Europe, particularly Britain and France. But, he warned, their chances of defeating Germany and Italy in a future war were only 'fifty-fifty' because of the Luftwaffe's air supremacy. Once dominant in Europe, Hitler could apply economic and political pressure on Argentina, Brazil and other Latin American countries, building up air bases that could threaten American interests. Miami was less than three hours' flying time from Venezuela; planes based in Colombia could attack the Panama Canal in less than an hour. In essence, Roosevelt was arguing that to keep America at peace in the air age meant keeping the peace in Europe.[67]

This remarkable outburst by the President was full of exaggerations – especially about German air strength and the vulnerability of Latin America – but it reflected his genuine belief that America's cherished conception of a separate and defensible western hemisphere formed by North and South America was no longer tenable. Air-power called into question not only the insuperability of the English Channel, as Baldwin had warned, but even the vast wastes of the Atlantic. Once war broke out in Europe the changed international situation gave FDR the necessary leverage to push through a new Neutrality Act in November 1939. This retained the mandatory bans on loans, travel and shipping but placed all trade with belligerents, including armaments, on a cash and carry basis. The administration insisted that this was a 'peace' measure, Roosevelt even arguing that 'by the repeal of the arms embargo the United States will more probably remain at peace than if the law remains as it stands today.' His critics saw through the doubletalk. 'I hate Hitlerism and Naziism [sic] and Communism as completely as any person living,' Senator Vandenberg wrote in his diary. 'But I decline to embrace the opportunist idea – so convenient and so popular at the moment – that *we* can stop these things in *Europe* without entering the conflict with everything at our command, including men and money. There is no middle ground. We are either *all the way in* or *all the way out*.'[68]

Vandenberg's critique was apt. Roosevelt's bid to shape the war

while remaining at peace would soon prove untenable. But his casuistry pushed the peace lobby further into the hands of conservative
isolationists, led by the America First Committee who urged a
Fortress America policy of 'Hemisphere Defense'. Whereas FDR's
tortuous efforts at collective security gradually sucked the United
States into war, his opponents ended up advocating peace at any price.

The peace movement was hugely influential in both Britain and
America in the 1930s – far more than on the continent of Europe –
but the contrasts between these two countries are also important. What
mattered for Britain, it has been argued, was the country's 'moderately
secure strategic position and its moderately liberal political culture' –
with 'moderately' the operative word.[69] A feeling of extreme insecurity, normal on the continent in the 1930s, encouraged the idea that
peace movements were inherently traitorous. Conversely a strong sense
of security, evident among most Americans in the 1930s, fostered the
feeling that, if necessary, the country could insulate itself from world
war. America's oceanic barrier was three thousand miles wide, whereas
Britain's was barely twenty: this generated some sense of security for
the British but not enough in the air age to foster escapism – hence
both the Peace Ballot and also Chamberlain's frantic appeasement.

Britain's 'moderately liberal political culture' reinforced the effects
of geopolitics. Continental countries had a rooted tradition of military
service and were intolerant of conscientious objection. This was evident in Germany and also in France where the Catholic and
republican traditions alike encouraged a keen sense of national con-
formity. By contrast, the Protestant dissenting tradition was central to
Anglo-American liberalism and to its peace movements. But
America's lack of political pluralism, especially the weakness of socialism, and the strength of its patriotic creed as the New World at odds
with the Old often served to channel American liberalism into a crusading idealism, as happened during the Great War and the Red Scare.
In Britain, however, the strong conservative tradition, on the one
hand, and the rise of the Labour Party on the other fostered a more
diverse political culture in which peace movements could flourish,
especially in the 1930s.

*

In the spring of 1939 the director of the Imperial War Museum in London submitted his annual report. Leslie Bradley was a war veteran, wounded at Ypres, and he alluded with feeling to George V's words when opening the museum in 1920 about turning weapons of war into relics from the past. Although 1938–9 had been the museum's best-ever year, with over 450,000 visitors, many of them had actually been seeking lessons from the last war about how to face a future conflict. Their very practical concerns included the construction of trenches and air-raid shelters, defence against gas attacks and methods of effective camouflage. These, declared Bradley indignantly, were 'not the functions which the Museum was founded to perform'. It was established, he insisted, to 'show the futility of war' – to 'make an historical record of the war "that was to end war"' rather than to record 'the first of a series of world wars, each more terrible than the last.'[70]

The director of the Imperial War Museum submitted his report on April Fool's Day 1939. Exactly five months later Hitler invaded Poland.

PART TWO

REFRACTIONS

7

AGAIN

Geography costs – why does the map of Europe never stay put?

Carl Sandburg, 1940

Let us therefore brace ourselves to our duties, and so bear ourselves that if the British Empire and its Commonwealth last for a thousand years, men will still say: 'This was their finest hour.'

Winston Churchill, 18 June 1940[1]

'One could hardly keep from crying', a volunteer nurse E.M. Selby noted on Armistice Day 1918, 'when one thought of all the boys who would never be coming home.' That was the last entry in her diary of the Great War. She took up her pen again on 7 June 1940, just after the evacuation from Dunkirk, with the laconic entry: 'Another war. Same enemy.'[2]

Those four words speak volumes. 'Never again' had been the watchword of the 1930s. Now the second German war within a generation transformed British perspectives on 1914–18. The 'Great War' would become the 'First World War', an inconclusive prelude to a

'Second World War' of even greater magnitude and horror. The pattern of the conflict was also very different: this time Germany was decisively defeated, unlike 1918, but along the way Britain came close to invasion and defeat. The summer of 1940 – immortalized in Churchill's phrase as Britain's 'finest hour' – became a defining moment against which to judge not only the experience of 1914–18 but also, in due course, the rest of the twentieth century.

For all the countries involved, the First World War would be refracted through the prism of the Second, as we shall see throughout Part Two of this book. But in France and Germany, indeed across continental Europe and even for the victorious Soviet Union, the second war posed serious problems for memorialization. In Britain, however, and also the United States, the conflict against Hitler created an unequivocally positive narrative, which put the Great War into a very different perspective.

At 11.15 on Sunday 3 September 1939 Neville Chamberlain announced over BBC radio that Britain and Germany were now at war. Speaking more in sorrow than in anger he lamented the 'bitter blow' that his 'long struggle to win peace has failed'. Hardly had Chamberlain finished speaking when the air-raid sirens sounded across London. 'I was playing the piano in the front room,' recalled one student teacher in Romford, Essex, 'when suddenly my mother burst in, shouting: "stop that noise!" and then flung open the windows, letting in the scream of the air-raid siren . . . Immediately, my father assumed the role of the administrative head-of-the-house, issuing commands and advice: "All get your gas masks! Steady, no panicking! Every man for himself!"' Some people did panic. A mother out for a Sunday walk rushed to a ditch by the road and pulled up handfuls of grass, somehow thinking 'I would push the children down there and hide them.' Others put on a brave face but one man in Chelsea – heart pounding, bowels churning – spoke for many: 'I am a coward from the neck down.'[3]

The terror about air war, evident throughout the 1930s, drove government policy as the new conflict loomed. Assuming deadly mass air raids on London and other industrial centres, with possibly 600,000

deaths in the first sixty days, the government had developed plans for
the mass evacuation of 4 million civilians, especially mothers and children but also key civil servants, to Wales, the West Country and other
rural areas. The Ministry of Health scoured the country to find
300,000 hospital beds for the first month's predicted casualties; the
Home Office planned mass graves and the burning of bodies in quick-
lime because it could not afford an estimated 20 million square feet of
seasoned timber every month to make coffins. Love as well as death
was on people's minds: in the months of July, August and September
1939 the marriage rate in Britain hit what was then an all-time high
of 29.3 per thousand people. The peak during the Great War had
been 22.5 marriages per thousand at the end of 1915.[4]

In the first three days of September 1939 1.5 million people were
evacuated under official programmes; probably another 2 million
made their own arrangements and fled from target areas. Of course,
we now know that there was no Armageddon: both sides refrained
from bombing each other's homeland that autumn and many of the
British evacuees had trickled home by Christmas. But the reality of
the Bore War (as 1939–40 was often known in Britain) should not
obscure a fundamental difference between this war and the last. In
August 1914 the crisis had unfolded across the Channel, with the
British army in the front line, as the Germans drove through Belgium.
In September 1939 the home front had already become the war front,
as Britain faced the dreaded knockout blow from the air. Taking
account of the 3.5 million people who moved, the family members
left behind and the homes where evacuees were billeted, it has been
calculated that between a quarter and a third of the British population
had their daily lives fundamentally disrupted by the outbreak of war in
1939.[5]

In other respects, however, the second war was seen as a continuation of the first. By early 1940 British policymakers now admitted, at
least privately, that they had been naïve in the 1920s and 1930s about
the threat from Germany. Determined not to repeat such a mistake
again after the current conflict was over, they envisaged a peacetime
alliance with France of the sort that leaders in Paris had sought in vain
after 1918. Sir Orme Sargent, a senior official at the Foreign Office,

suggested in February 1940 that the only alternative to France trying to impose an even more punitive peace than Versailles would be to show the French that they could 'count on such a system of close and permanent cooperation between France and Great Britain – political, military and economic – as will for all international purposes make of the two countries a single unit in post-war Europe.' By this remarkable phrase Sargent signified close intergovernmental cooperation rather than any federal structure, but even that would require a revolution in British thinking. He therefore proposed a major propaganda and education campaign for the public at large. 'I entirely agree,' noted Chamberlain. On 28 March 1940 the two countries publicly pledged that 'after the conclusion of peace' they would maintain 'a community of action in all spheres for as long as may be necessary to safeguard their security and to effect the reconstruction, with the assistance of other nations, of an international order which will ensure the liberty of people, respect for law, and the maintenance of peace in Europe.' Behind the scenes an interdepartmental Whitehall committee was established to identify areas of administration in which the experiment of Anglo-French union could be tried. And the Board of Education set up special committees to promote greater understanding of France in primary and secondary schools, liaising with the BBC about appropriate radio talks.[6]

For British diplomats, therefore, the second German war was seen in 1939–40 as a continuation of or, more exactly, an improvement on the first – learning from the errors of the interwar years. British strategy was also shaped by Great War precedents, envisaging another long conflict in which Britain's superior wealth, seapower and global resources would eventually wear Germany down. It was assumed that the Germans would stake all on an early knockout blow, by air on London and by land on the Western Front. But the general expectation was that in this war, as in 1914–18, defensive firepower would dominate the battlefield itself – a conviction held even by former exponents of tank warfare. The military pundit Basil Liddell Hart penned a series of articles for *The Times* in October 1937 entitled 'Defence or Attack?' which came down firmly on the side of the defensive. Privately he noted, 'There is no sign of any development in military technique so potent as to promise an attacking army a reasonable prospect of breaking through the front of a defending army of more or less equal strength.' Liddell Hart judged that 'the only serious chance of French resistance collapsing completely is as a sequel to a rash offensive on their part, and the crippling of their forces in it, as happened in 1914.' Similarly Winston Churchill, although extolling the 'glorious' contribution made by tanks in the victory of 1918, expressed doubt twenty years later that they would 'play as decisive a part in the next war ... Nowadays, the anti-tank rifle and the anti-tank gun have made such great strides that the poor tank cannot carry a thick enough skin to stand up to them.' And although renowned for apocalyptic warnings about strategic bombing, Churchill was complacent about *tactical* airpower. 'So far as fighting troops are concerned,' he wrote in January 1939 citing the Spanish civil war, 'it would seem that aircraft are an additional complication rather than a decisive weapon.'[7]

Not everyone in Whitehall was so confident but nobody predicted the astonishing debacle of May and June 1940. In four weeks a jumped-up Austrian corporal did what the Kaiser's best generals had failed to do in four years – knocking France out of the conflict. In consequence the war of 1939–45 would be fundamentally different from 1914–18 because the Western Front had ceased to exist. It would have to be recreated – a Herculean task entailing an amphibious landing far more hazardous than Gallipoli – as the platform for any Allied victory. This did not happen until June 1944, four years after the fall of France. And Britain could only do it by the closest possible alliance with the United States, creating a level of dependence not seen in even the darkest days of the Great War.

May 1940 was also a turning point for Britain's home front. The German offensive began on the same day, 10 May, as Chamberlain, the dominant figure of British politics throughout the 1930s, was evicted from Number 10. The timing was purely accidental – Chamberlain was toppled by a parliamentary revolt over the shambolic campaign in Norway – but the coincidence of events certainly proved providential for Churchill. Chamberlain had brought him into government at the start of war after a decade in the political 'wilderness'.

This was done reluctantly because Chamberlain, like Baldwin, feared Winston's impetuous and domineering manner; indeed Churchill, as he himself privately admitted, was more to blame than Chamberlain for the Norway debacle, which could easily have been marked up against him as another Gallipoli.[8] But with Chamberlain now discredited by the evident failure of appeasement and Lord Halifax, the only alternative for the premiership, almost physically sick at the prospect of acting as warlord, Churchill – despite having no real party base – was catapulted into the job he had always craved.

Equally important, Churchill formed a war coalition that included senior figures from the Labour Party, who would not serve with the hated Chamberlain. Particularly crucial was the elevation as Minister of Labour of Ernest Bevin, a bluff, earthy, ex-union boss who proved essential in persuading British workers to accept the demands of total war. Ever since 1931 Labour had been on the margins of British politics: the so-called National Government of the 1930s included only renegade Labour figures such as Ramsay MacDonald. Labour was now a vital part of a real coalition. The importance of 10 May 1940 was therefore fundamental in domestic as well as foreign policy: the disaster in France protected Churchill from criticism in his first six months, when Chamberlain was still Tory Party leader, and it also gave Labour a place at the heart of government which became a springboard for outright power in 1945. All very different from the piecemeal coalition building during the Great War – hesitantly in May 1915 and for real in December 1916.

The disaster in France was partly the result of Allied failure to anticipate Germany's innovative use of armoured spearheads and tactical airpower to punch right through the enemy's lines. But luck was as important as design. Had the Wehrmacht attacked as originally intended across Belgium – repeating the Schlieffen Plan of August 1914 – then it would have crashed into the bulk of the French army, plus the British Expeditionary Force, including most of the Allies' armoured and motorized forces. Instead, postponement of the offensive until the spring of 1940 and French capture of Germany's original plans prompted a radical rethink in Berlin. The new plan, pressed by General Erich von Manstein and strongly supported by Hitler, treated the invasion of Belgium as a feint. The real centre of gravity (*Schwerpunkt*) would now be further south: a thrust through the Ardennes, across the Meuse River (guarded by two weak French armies) and then north-west up to the Channel to cut off the Allied forces advancing into Belgium. In other words, not a right hook as in 1914, but a left hook – or sickle-cut (*Sichelschnitt*), as the plan was known. Informed intelligence reports and imaginative war-gaming persuaded the German High Command that the French were locked into their Belgium plan and that their command and control system would be too rigid to react quickly. These assumptions proved absolutely right. It took four days for Paris and London (where Churchill was preoccupied with forming his new government) to grasp how completely they had been deceived. By then the Germans were across the Meuse at Sedan and driving towards the Channel, reaching it on 20 May, only ten days after the campaign began.[9]

However logical and brilliant the plan may seem in retrospect, it was an incredible gamble at the time. No German military leader was hopeful of success – Franz Halder, the army chief of staff, reckoned the odds were at least ten to one against – and even Hitler, who had mystical faith in Germany and its army, called the news from Sedan 'a miracle'.[10] The German High Command committed most of its fighters to ensure initial air superiority: by the end of May, 30 per cent of Germany's air strength had been written off. Seven of Hitler's nine armoured divisions had been thrown into the Ardennes and there was no armoured reserve. The main thrust had to be mounted along only four narrow forest roads; columns of vehicles stretched back 300–400 kilometres – creating massive traffic jams that should have been sitting targets for Allied bombers. And, since surprise and speed were all important, most of Germany's stocks of petrol, sufficient for just five months of mobile warfare, were earmarked for the assault. Tank drivers received large doses of amphetamines (colloquially known as *Panzerschokolade*) so they could keep going round the clock for the critical first seventy-two hours.[11]

Afterwards Allied analysts such as Liddell Hart, trying to cover their embarrassment, explained the German victory as the result of a brilliant and coherent strategy of 'Blitzkrieg warfare' for which the

Nazi economy had been designed. This was a fiction, but a convenient one since it distracted from the military incompetence of France
and Britain. The Third Reich, on the other hand, did not credit its
triumph to technology and strategy – Hitler himself called the term
Blitzkrieg 'a completely idiotic word' (*ein ganz blödsinniges Wort*) and it
was practically never used officially by the Wehrmacht. Instead Nazi
propaganda argued that victory in the west proved the superiority of
the Aryan race and above all the genius of the Führer, now billed as
the 'Greatest Military Leader of All Time'. This claim was even more
fallacious – and far more dangerous because the Manstein plan was not
an all-purpose strategic blueprint. It worked in France thanks to skil-
ful planning, breathtaking audacity, Allied ineptitude, massive luck and
the proximity of the Ardennes to the Channel. It would not succeed
in 1941–2 across the vast expanse of Russia, against an enemy with
huge human and material resources. But after the triumph of June
1940 Hitler's generals stopped contesting his judgment. The Führer
had apparently rewritten the military textbooks, so the 'lessons' of the
last war no longer seemed relevant. Such hubris would prove fatal.[12]

During the Great War, of course, there had been moments of acute
crisis on the Western Front. In August 1914 the French commander-
in-chief, General Joseph Joffre, fixated on liberating Alsace and
Lorraine, was slow to appreciate the magnitude of the German thrust
through Belgium. A vivid passage in Churchill's Great War memoirs
records the moment when the penny dropped for him, on 24 August,
as he read a telegram from the BEF. 'Namur fallen! Namur taken in a
single day ... The foundations of thought were quaking ... Where
would it stop? What of the naked Channel ports? Dunkirk, Calais,
Boulogne!' The commander of the BEF, Sir John French, wanted to
pull back his battered troops and refit nearer the safety of the coast.
Only after direct orders from the Cabinet, acutely sensitive about the
Anglo-French alliance, did he commit his troops to Joffre's counter-
attack, where they played a small but vital part in the 'Miracle on the
Marne' which saved Paris in September 1914.[13]

The other great moment of Anglo-French crisis in the Great War
occurred in April 1918, during Ludendorff's massive spring offensives.
Haig, the British commander-in-chief, had left the southern part of

his sector relatively weak: there, faced by eight-to-one German superiority in Operation Michael on 21 March, his Fifth Army collapsed
and his Third Army began to crumble. The Germans were driving a
wedge between the British and French forces. Then Ludendorff's
second offensive, codenamed Georgette, mounted along the Flanders
coast, threatened the Channel ports. By the evening of 12 April 1918
the Germans were within six miles of the key railway junction of
Hazebrouck: if that fell, Dunkirk would probably follow, jeopardizing
British control of the Channel. Haig was not given to grand rhetoric
but on 11 April he issued what has been called 'one of the most
melodramatic (and thus memorable) orders of the day in British military history.' Its peroration ran as follows: 'Every position must be
held to the last: there must be no retirement. With our backs to the
wall and believing in the justice of our cause each one of us must fight
on to the end. The safety of our homes and the Freedom of mankind
alike depend upon the conduct of each one of us at the critical
moment.' Haig's 'Backs to the wall' order made a vivid impact on
civilians as much as soldiers. Vera Brittain never forgot the moment in
1918 when, as an exhausted nurse just behind the front, she read
those words on the hospital noticeboard. Despite subsequent attacks
on Haig, she wrote in 1933, 'I have never been able to visualise Lord
Haig as the colossal blunderer, the self-deceived optimist, of the
Somme massacre of 1916. I can think of him only as the author of that
Special Order, for after I had read it I knew that I should go on,
whether I could or not.'[14]

On 18 April 1918, a week after Haig's order, Churchill submitted
a memo to the Cabinet coyly entitled 'A Note on Certain Hypothetical Contingencies'. The looming question, he warned, was
'whether we should let go our left hand or our right.' By this he
meant either losing touch with the Channel ports or becoming
detached from the French army. Churchill had no doubt that Haig
must keep in contact with the French, retiring together as in 1914, in
order to continue the common cause against an exhausted enemy.
Keeping a grip on the Channel ports in the hope of preserving the
BEF's line of retreat would be futile, he warned, because this would
make it easier for the Germans to defeat France and then drive the

British into the sea. Churchill's judgment about these 'Hypothetical Contingencies' was also the consensus in Whitehall but for a few days the outcome on the Western Front was in the balance until Germany did indeed run out of steam.[15]

August 1914 and April 1918 were therefore two decisive moments in the Great War when, to use Churchill's image, the British hung on with their right hand to the French rather than grasping with their left for the Channel ports. But May 1940 was totally different. This time the German left hook eliminated the line of retreat to Paris, forcing the BEF and much of the French army against the coast. The 'miracle' occurred not on the Marne, as in 1914, but at Dunkirk – and that saved Britain rather than France. Had Hitler not called off his exhausted Panzers, to allow them to refit and to prepare for a possible French counter-attack, the British and French units could easily have been destroyed on the beaches. Fortunately neither the German infantry nor the Luftwaffe could finish off the job. Instead of saving 50,000 troops – Whitehall's best hope when the Dunkirk evacuation began – the eventual total was 335,000. Roughly one-third of these were French, most of whom returned to France and ended up in German prisoner-of-war camps, but the British soldiers, mostly regulars and territorials, became the nucleus of a viable defence against possible invasion. Without them, suggestions at the end of May 1940 about using Italy to sound out possible Axis peace terms would have been much harder for Churchill to resist.[16]

Even though, after the great escape at Dunkirk, the War Cabinet was united in the policy of fighting on, Hitler's conquest of western Europe forced a radical rethink of 1914–18 scenarios. On 25 May the Chiefs of Staff submitted a memo entitled 'British Strategy in a Certain Eventuality'. This subliminal echo of Churchill's paper of April 1918 was Whitehall's euphemism for the possible fall of France. The Chiefs' central assumption for continuing the war was that the United States would be 'willing to give us full economic and financial support, *without which we do not think we could continue this war with any chance of success.*' This became the basic axiom of British foreign policy, for the war and beyond. As early as July 1940 Halifax, still foreign secretary, noted, 'It may well be that instead of studying closer union with France, we shall find ourselves contemplating some sort of special association with the U.S.A.'[17]

Equally important, the fall of France had global ramifications. Hitler was now free to move east in search of living space years earlier than he had expected. At the end of July 1940 he ordered military planners to prepare to invade Russia the following spring. Operation Barbarossa on 22 June 1941 signalled the opening of what became the crucial struggle of the war. The collapse of France also transformed Italian foreign policy. Previously the opposition of the king and the general staff, mindful of the country's military weakness relative to Britain and France, had restrained Mussolini from entering the war. But the dramatic success of *Sichelschnitt* transformed debate. 'Internal resistance to war in Italy is melting,' noted General Halder on 17 May. 'Mussolini has a free hand.' On 11 June Italy declared war on Britain and France, opening up a battlefront in North Africa that would add another novel geographical dimension to this war. Events in Europe also had a knock-on effect in Asia. With the French and the Dutch under Germany's thumb and Britain fighting for survival, none of these European empires were in a position to resist Japanese expansion. In September 1940 Tokyo joined the Rome–Berlin Axis; the following summer, once the Soviet Union was locked in war with Germany, the Japanese seized their opportunity to move south into Indochina. Only the United States fleet at Pearl Harbor in the Hawaiian Islands constituted a significant deterrent: attacking that in December 1941 was the prelude to Japan's lightning conquest of South-East Asia. By the spring of 1942 the Axis controlled over a third of the population and mineral resources of the world. So the fall of France turned a limited European conflict into a truly world war, radically different from 1914–18.[18]

The summer of 1940 endowed Britain's war with a luminous centre point that was totally lacking in 1914–18. This emerged very quickly at the time and was little dimmed or tarnished thereafter, again unlike the tangled and messy revisionism about the Great War. The British grand narrative of 1940 comprises three dramatic moments – Dunkirk, the Battle of Britain and the Blitz – each of which blended heroic, historic and populist elements that were largely absent from the discourse about the Great War.[19]

Churchill, the great speechmaker, helped frame this narrative, not just in his famous sound bites but also through instant historical analysis. On 18 June, for instance, he crafted those enduring labels 'the Battle of France' and 'the Battle of Britain', as well as predicting that 1940 would be seen as Britain's 'finest hour'. His address on 20 August not only coined the phrase 'The Few' about the RAF, it also sought to distinguish this war from its predecessor – less destructive of life but more decisive in impact, and involving 'the whole of the warring nations, not just soldiers, but the entire population, men, women and children . . . The front line runs through factories.'[20]

But Churchill's contribution to myth-making was only a part, because pundits, commentators and the newsreels also shaped the saga at the same time. The first ingredient, in contrast with the now established narrative of 1914–18, was a sense of the heroic. The classical language of heroism had been a feature of 1914, most famously in the poems of Rupert Brooke, and it never disappeared from the daily poetry offerings in *The Times* during the Great War. But heroism was not the refrain of Sassoon or Owen, nor was it part of the revisionist discourse about the war in the late 1920s. In 1940, by contrast, heroes were back with a vengeance and they were not in the trenches. The most purple passage in Churchill's 4 June speech was devoted to the fighter pilots who drove the Luftwaffe from the beaches: 'The Knights of the Round Table, the Crusaders, all fall back into the past: not only distant but prosaic.' The 'knights of the sky' were not entirely new, having been lionized during the Great War, but then they were marginal to the war story, whereas in 1940 the fighter pilots were absolutely central. What's more they were jousting not over the blackened wasteland of the Western Front but above England's 'green and pleasant land' – which, like the knights, became a feature of media depictions of the Battle of Britain.[21]

The place of 'The Few' in history was confirmed by a special thirty-page pamphlet on the Battle of Britain which the Air Ministry published in March 1941. It was expected to sell about 50,000 copies;

instead, within the first month, sales had exceeded 1 million and orders for the illustrated edition had reached half a million; the pamphlet was also translated into many languages. The story recounted was not of an earthbound combat, vintage 1916 – shells, smoke, noise and 'avalanches of earth' – but 'a duel with rapiers' thousands of feet up in the air, 'fought by masters of the art of fence'. The Battle of Britain was also represented as a struggle of epic importance: 'Future historians may compare it with Marathon, Trafalgar and the Marne.' (The reference to Trafalgar was omitted from the pamphlet when it was translated into French!) 'More than anything else,' writes historian Richard Overy, this widely read pamphlet 'gave the conflict the legendary dimensions it has borne ever since.'[22]

As its epigraph, the pamphlet quoted Churchill's words of 20 August: 'Never in the field of human conflict was so much owed by so many to so few.' But in that speech Churchill actually devoted less than a sentence to the fighter pilots 'whose brilliant actions we see with our own eyes day after day', whereas he spent two long paragraphs extolling the bomber squadrons flying night after night over Germany: 'On no part of the Royal Air Force does the weight of the war fall more heavily.' A fortnight later Churchill told the Cabinet that 'the Fighters are our salvation,' as protection for the British Isles, 'but the Bombers alone provide the means of victory' because 'in no other way at present visible can we hope to overcome the immense military power of Germany.'[23] In 1940–2 the British government gave Bomber Command its head and avoided asking just how precise so-called 'strategic bombing' really was. Churchill's faith in strategic bombing would ebb later in the war, after the vast manpower and resources of Russia and America had been deployed against the Axis and by 1945 the bomb crews had been almost written out of the grand narrative of Britain's war because they muddied a clear morality play about knightly courage to protect British women and children against foreign aggression. The Blitz (a contraction of *Blitzkrieg* that quickly caught on in Britain in the autumn of 1940) was a story of Hunnish barbarism against British innocence and children – reworking, one might say, the atrocity stories of 1914. It is worth noting how, right to the present day, 'the British prefer to use a German word for such a

"German" act, as if there could not be an English word to cover the stunning and brutal destructive power of air attack.' Yet the total UK death toll from German bombing in the Second World War amounted to 61,000. By contrast, British and American bombers killed more civilians in France – 67,000. The death toll they inflicted on Germany was at least 400,000 and even more in Japan.[24]

Reinforcing the heroic was a sense of the historic. Again this emerged very quickly: on 25 May *The Times* coupled the struggle for the Channel ports with epic moments of English history – Agincourt, the Armada, Waterloo and also the battle fought by 'Haig's men' in March 1918. After the Dunkirk evacuation, Churchill told the Commons, 'We are told that Herr Hitler has a plan for invading the British Isles,' before adding that 'this has often been thought of before' – most recently by Napoleon. In his peroration Churchill declared himself fully confident that 'we shall prove ourselves once again able to defend our island home, to ride out the storm of war, and to outlive the menace of tyranny, if necessary for years, if necessary alone.' That last word became something of a catchphrase in the summer of 1940. 'Very Well, Alone', David Low's now celebrated cartoon of 18 June after the fall of France, depicted a Tommy, fist in the air, defying the storm-tossed seas. Low captured a common feeling. 'Now we know where we are!' shouted the skipper of a Thames tugboat. 'No more bloody allies!' George VI made the same point more decorously, telling his mother, 'Personally, I feel happier now that we have no allies to be polite to & to pamper.'[25] T.S. Eliot declared that 'History is now and England' – capturing the incandescence of the moment in his poem 'Little Gidding', drafted in 1941 while fire-watching in the Blitz. Eliot's line would have been inconceivable during the Great War – more likely in September 1914 'History is now and Belgium' – and the contrast with 1914–18 was made explicit by the Scottish poet Hugh MacDiarmid:

> At last! Now is the time with due intensity
> To hew to what really matters – not
> 'Making the world safe for democracy',
> 'Saving civilization', or any such rot.[26]

'What really matters': 1940 was clearly a struggle for survival, which set it apart from the British experience of 1914–18. And, in further contrast, it was a struggle involving all the people: they were integral to the heroism and the history. This populist inclusivity of the national narrative constitutes the third big contrast with the Great War, illustrated in different ways by Dunkirk, the Battle of Britain and the Blitz. In his BBC radio 'Postscript' on 5 June 1940, the author J.B. Priestley singled out the part played in the improvised evacuation by 'little pleasure steamers' such as the *Gracie Fields*, which he recalled affectionately as a pre-war ferry shuttling between the mainland and the Isle of Wight. She and many of 'her brave and battered sisters' were now gone for ever, sunk by German bombs, but, concluded Priestley, 'our great-grandchildren, when they learn how we began this War by snatching glory out of defeat, and then swept on to victory, may also learn how the little holiday steamers made an excursion to hell and came back glorious.' In reality, the paddle steamers, fishing boats and other 'little ships' played a minor part in the evacuation but Priestley's picaresque vignette, invoking in his mellow Yorkshire accent the name of one of the country's best-loved popular singers, was a masterstroke and it set the tone for how Dunkirk has been remembered. A leading article in *The Times* the next day, 6 June 1940, was already encouraging readers to draw inspiration from 'the spirit of Dunkirk'.[27]

The populist theme was also evident in the Battle of Britain. Despite their fascination with the fighter pilots, the media lauded the part played on the ground by men and women in the factories and by the new Home Guard, which had enlisted 1.5 million people by the end of June. With the Labour Party a full partner in Churchill's coalition, Bevin captured the popular imagination as Minister of Labour, imposing conscription on the home front while supporting the rights of working people. Lord Beaverbrook's campaign in July for pots and pans to turn into fighter planes aroused mass support, even though there was actually no shortage of aluminium, and by the spring of 1941 almost every town in Britain had its own Spitfire Fund. One pound would pay for the thermometer in a Merlin engine; one penny covered the cost of a rivet. The £13 million raised thereby 'contributed virtually nothing' to the total cost of armaments but these campaigns were 'a significant means of including the "many" with the "few".'[28]

The 'people's war' (a term spread by leftist veterans of 1930s Spain) was embodied most of all in the Blitz, when the front-line heroes were civilians. Until late 1942, after the desert victory at Alamein, more British women and children had been killed by the enemy than British soldiers – a remarkable contrast with 1914–18. The trenches of this war were not etched in the mud of the Somme or Flanders Fields but carved from the ruins of city streets in London or Manchester. The Blitz's enduring images, already featured on the newsreels and in journals such as *Picture Post*, were of a fireman, high on his ladder, courageously playing his hose into a burning building, or families dossing down for the night on the platform of an Underground station. As with the 'little ships', image did not match reality – peak use of the Tube, by 177,000 people sheltering on 27 September 1940, involved only 5 per cent of those left in London – but it was the image that endured. The Blitz became 'a key moment in the war' – the moment when 'the people' were incorporated into 'the nation'.[29]

This vivid instant history of 1940 – heroic, historic and populist – also cast the decades since 1918 in a new and sombre light. The tone was set by *Guilty Men* – a ferocious polemic published only two weeks after France had surrendered under the pseudonym 'Cato' by three left-wing journalists – including Michael Foot, a future leader of the Labour Party. Starting on the beaches of Dunkirk, it told 'the story of an Army doomed *before* they took the field' and tracked back over the 1930s to find the culprits. The indictment was stark: 'MacDonald and Baldwin took over a great empire, supreme in arms and secure in liberty' and then 'conducted it to the edge of national annihilation', abetted by the 'umbrella man' Neville Chamberlain. Their blindness about Hitler and their failure to rearm, argued Cato, had left Britain criminally unprepared for the Blitzkrieg unleashed in May 1940. *Guilty Men* was an immediate best-seller, selling 50,000 copies in a few days and 200,000 by the end of 1940. It set the agenda for subsequent debates about appeasement, rather as Keynes' *Economic Consequences of the Peace* in 1919 shaped perceptions of the Treaty of Versailles. *Guilty Men* nailed Chamberlain's reputation into a coffin from which it has

AGAIN   263

still not escaped and it served as cue for a series of broader critiques of the 1930s directed by the left against the right.[30]

In these accounts, appeasement and the Slump were both used to indict the Tory and National governments of the era and to argue that 'the Thirties were everything that the postwar world should not be.' *Love on the Dole*, the 1941 film version of Walter Greenwood's best-selling novel, was couched in this vein. One caption quoted A.V. Alexander, a Labour member of the wartime coalition: 'Our working men and women have responded magnificently to any and every call made upon them in this war. Their reward must be a New Britain. Never again must the unemployed become the forgotten men of the peace.' The phrase 'never again' had been a cliché of Armistice Day remembrance in the 1920s and 1930s but now it was being used for a different purpose. At the end of 1942 the Beveridge Report, calling for a comprehensive system of social security 'from the cradle to the grave', caught the public imagination, selling 635,000 copies – an utterly unprecedented figure for an official publication. Opinion polls indicated nearly 90 per cent support. Under the surface, there was cynicism about the report being implemented – 'I don't forget the Land fit for Heroes of the last war,' remarked one old soldier – but the Ministry of Information found it 'difficult to exaggerate the growing force of the demand for guarantees that "privilege" be not allowed to lose the next peace, as it is generally felt to have lost the last one'.[31]

In the election of 1945, when Labour won a landslide victory, its election manifesto set out a clear radical narrative linking the two world wars, with 1940 at the centre. 'So far as Britain's contribution is concerned', it argued, 'this war will have been won by its people.' Much the same had been true of the last war but afterwards the people had allowed 'the hard-faced men who had done well out of the war' to craft 'the kind of peace that suited themselves.' They con-trolled the government and the economy, not just in Britain but across the industrialized world, and the great interwar slumps were the direct result of leaving 'too much economic power in the hands of too few men.' Similar forces were at work in 1945, Labour warned. 'The problems and pressure of the post-war world threaten our security and progress as surely as – though less dramatically than –

the Germans threatened them in 1940. We need the spirit of Dunkirk and of the Blitz sustained over a period of years.' On election morning the pro-Labour *Daily Mirror* told readers, 'Vote on behalf of the men who won the victory for you. You failed to do so in 1918. The result is known to all.' The paper devoted most of its front page to reprinting a Zec cartoon first published on VE Day (plate 16). This showed a weary, battered soldier holding out the laurel wreath of 'Victory and Peace in Europe'. The caption read: 'Here you are – don't lose it again!'[32]

So 1940 became central to a new national myth. Not, like Gallipoli for the Australians, a myth of national 'discovery' but a story of 'rediscovery', when a country that had lost its way after the lost peace regained its identity and purpose in the furnace of the people's war. In Charles Mowat's mammoth history of *Britain Between the Wars, 1918–1940*, published in 1955, the final section was headed simply 'Alone'. In the summer of 1940, Mowat asserted, as the British people awaited the Battle of Britain, 'they found themselves again, after twenty years of indecision. They turned from past regrets and faced the future unafraid.' The contrast between the supposedly dark, wasted decade of the 1930s, on the one hand, and the shining achievements of 1939–45, on the other, represents an interesting inversion of popular mythology about the Great War era. In that case the shading was exactly the opposite – a dark war (whether tragic or futile) set against a golden Edwardian era evoked nostalgically in the 1920s writings of Sassoon and Graves. In both cases, of course, the pre-war was a caricature – ignoring the bitter conflicts before 1914 over labour rights, women's suffrage and the Irish question and, equally, the stability and prosperity of Britain in the 1930s when compared with continental Europe. But, unlike the Edwardian age, the pre-war era of the 1930s could now be understood as the inter-war era – a 'parenthesis' already glimpsed by poet David Jones in 1937. Having to wage the struggle all over again set the whole period since 1914 in a totally different light.[33]

In the United States, too, 1940–1 proved a turning point – as in Britain, putting both the 1930s and the earlier war into a new perspective.

The American media were now offering a much more positive view of the British. In contrast with the suspicions of the 1930s, their new focus was on the values that the two countries had in common. As in Britain, Dunkirk was a turning point. Columnist Dorothy Thompson called it 'almost an allegory for a strange sort of social revolution' as 'the little men of England' took command of the nation's destiny from the historic 'hierarchy of title and wealth'. During the summer the threat of invasion unleashed more purple prose. On 24 July 1940 the *New York Times* editorialized: 'It is twelve o'clock in London. ... Is the tongue of Chaucer, of Shakespeare, of Milton, of the King James translation of the Scriptures, of Keats and Shelley, to be hereafter, in the British Isles, the dialect of an enslaved race? ... It is twelve o'clock in England. Not twelve o'clock for empire – there is no empire any more ... Twelve o'clock for the common people of England out of whom England's greatest souls have always come.'[34]

Americans were deeply moved by the Battle of Britain and the Blitz, by vivid stories about Londoners, rich and poor, carrying on their daily business despite Hitler's bombs in terraced houses and air-raid shelters, or asleep on the platforms of Underground stations. The major US radio networks sent some of their best correspondents to London – the most celebrated being Edward R. Murrow of CBS, whose live broadcasts of air raids brought the sounds of modern war into American living rooms. Murrow's gravelly voice narrated events, matter-of-factly, against the wail of air-raid sirens, the crash of exploding bombs and the clatter of anti-aircraft guns. 'You burned the city of London in our houses, and we felt the flames,' wrote the poet Archibald MacLeish in tribute. The British Ministry of Information gave Murrow and colleagues such as Eric Sevareid full cooperation, waiving their normally strict censorship requirements. Given Americans' residual phobia about British propaganda, a legacy of 1920s revisionism, it was clear that raw American voices would sound far more credible in heartland America than clipped, snooty English accents.[35]

The moving accounts of the Blitz and the evocations of shared Anglo-American values had a profound effect in the United States. The majority of the population had never been emotionally neutral between the Axis and the Allies but most Americans were not persuaded that their antipathy to Nazism required more than stout defence of the western hemisphere. That changed in the summer and fall of 1940, even though an overwhelming majority still hoped to keep out of the war. In late June, just after the fall of France, 64 per cent of those questioned believed it was more important to keep out of the war than to help England. By mid-November 60 per cent felt it was more important to help England, even at risk of the United States getting into the war.[36]

This change in public mood gave Roosevelt more room for manoeuvre. In 1938–9 he had dressed up his policy of bolstering Britain under the cloak of neutrality. After the fall of France he came off the fence. Not only did he now run for and win an unprecedented third term as president, he also spoke openly of Britain as America's front line of defence and in a bruising two-month battle on Capitol Hill in early 1941 he enshrined this principle in law. The Lend-Lease Act allowed the President to loan or lease weapons and materiel to countries whose survival he deemed vital for the defence of the United States. Lend-Lease would play a vital part in winning the war and FDR's justification for it set out many of the themes of American policy during the Cold War.

Take, for instance, his radio address to the nation on 29 December 1940. 'This is not a fireside chat on war,' he began. 'It is a talk on national security.' This was an early use of a term that would become central to the American diplomatic lexicon – one that was suitably elastic about how the country's interests should be defined. Quoting Hitler's recent statement that there were 'two worlds that stand opposed to each other', FDR insisted that 'the Axis not merely admits but proclaims that there can be no ultimate peace between their philosophy of government and our philosophy of government.' This image of a world divided between good and evil prefigured the Truman Doctrine of 1947. FDR also mocked those who still talked in terms of a defensible western hemisphere, arguing that 'if Great Britain goes down, the Axis powers will control the continents of Europe, Asia, Africa, Australasia, and the high seas – and they will be in a position to bring enormous military and naval resources against this hemisphere.' He even argued that celebrated acts of American self-assertion in the past, such as the Monroe Doctrine of 1824, warning off reactionary European powers from the western hemisphere, had been policed with the aid of the British: 'we stood on guard in the Atlantic, with the British as neighbors. There was no treaty. There was no "unwritten agreement"' – just natural cooperation between like-minded freedom-loving peoples. 'Does anyone seriously believe', he asked, 'that we need to fear attack anywhere in the Americas while a free Britain remains our most powerful naval neighbor in the Atlantic?'[37]

Underlying Roosevelt's perspective on the Atlantic was a fundamental reinterpretation of America's war in 1917–18. He did not admit this lest it encouraged critics who warned he was covertly taking the country into war again but pro-Allied publicists made the point explicitly. The most influential was the journalist Walter Lippmann, an adviser to Woodrow Wilson in 1919 who then became deeply critical of the President's rigidity as a peacemaker. In February 1917 arguing the case for American entry into the war, Lippmann had coined the term 'Atlantic community' to describe the 'highways' and values that connected America with western Europe. In April 1941 he returned to this concept in an article for Henry Luce's widely read *Life* magazine, entitled 'The Atlantic and America'. Lippmann's explicit aim was to reinterpret US entry into the war in 1917. It was not, he said, an exercise in misguided idealism but a hard-headed attempt to preserve the security of the Atlantic, in which the United States had a vital interest. This theme was developed later in 1941 by the journalist Forrest Davis. His book *The Atlantic System* sought to trace an Anglo-American community of interest back via the Monroe Doctrine to the Founding Fathers. The chapter on US belligerency in 1917 was entitled 'The First Battle of the Atlantic'.[38]

During the course of 1941 the President extended the range of naval operations further into the Atlantic, to protect Lend-Lease supplies to Britain, claiming that he was simply enlarging the boundaries of the western hemisphere to take account of the new realities of national security. In the Pacific, similarly, he kept the main US fleet at Pearl Harbor, two thousand miles from its normal bases in California, as a deterrent pressure on Japan. In the end the fleet served to provoke rather than deter, becoming the main target of Japan's bid to gain a Pacific empire while the West was on the defensive – long-desired revenge for the humiliations of Paris 1919. But although America's main war in 1942 was against Japan in the Philippines, the Coral Sea and Midway, the geopolitical centre of American policy remained the Atlantic. Capstone of the new Atlanticist ideology outlined by Roosevelt in 1940 was Lippmann's book *U.S. Foreign Policy: Shield of the Republic*, published in April 1943. A slim volume, less than two hundred pages long, this quickly became a best-seller, notching up nearly half a million copies and being serialized in journals such as *Reader's Digest* as well as being distributed in a 25-cent paperback for American troops. Its central theme was that the Atlantic Ocean was 'not the frontier between Europe and the Americas. It is the inland sea of a community of nations allied with one another by geography, history, and vital necessity.' Lippmann's sense of community was capacious, including continental allies such as France, and he also urged a continued alliance in peacetime with the Soviet Union. But his community centred on the Anglo-American axis and his conception of Atlanticism as the heart of American foreign policy would define the country's diplomacy for the rest of the century.[39]

So the crisis of 1940–1 proved a turning point for both Britain and America in how they viewed the Great War. Its effects were consolidated by what happened between 1941 and 1945. The outcome, this time, was total victory – brought about for Britain by novel and, as it proved, lasting dependence upon America which, unlike the post-1918 era, now assumed a permanent leadership role in global affairs.

The fall of France was again crucial because it removed the Western Front that had been central to the Great War. Although the British narrative of the war highlights Britain fighting on 'alone' in 1940–1, the eventual defeat of the Third Reich occurred largely on the Eastern Front, which had been the Allies' weakest link in 1914–18. After Hitler turned east to mount Operation Barbarossa, for the rest of the war at least two-thirds of the Wehrmacht was engaged against the Red Army. Between June 1941 and D-Day in June 1944, 90 per cent of

German army battle casualties (killed, wounded, missing and prisoners) were inflicted by the Soviets.[40] If Stalin beat Hitler (and that was
a big 'if' until late 1942), then the Soviet Union would inevitably end
the war deep in eastern Europe, making it a major factor in the post-
war world.

As soon as Barbarossa began, Stalin kept demanding that the
British mount a 'Second Front' in France. He was not deceived by
Churchill's encouraging noises, quickly recognizing the deep British
reluctance to cross the Channel, and even taunted the Prime Minister
to his face that the British army was scared to fight the Germans.
Churchill was furious, but the accusation was essentially true. Stalin,
a brutal dictator ruling over a country with huge reserves of population, had no compunction about using hundreds of thousands of
troops as cannon fodder; Churchill, leading a small democracy still
haunted by the Somme, shunned going head to head with the
Wehrmacht. He told Stalin repeatedly, 'I would never authorise any
cross-Channel attack which I believed would lead to only useless
massacre.' Even in mid-1942, with Russia and America as allies, he
still felt that 'upon the whole, our best chance of winning the war is
with the big Bombers. It will certainly be several years before British
and American land forces will be capable of beating the Germans on
even terms in the open field.' Although Churchill wrote detailed
memoranda about invading the continent, his preference was for a
series of landings around the coast of occupied Europe by 'armies of
liberation' spearheaded by British and American 'armoured and
mechanised forces' that were 'strong enough to enable the conquered
populations to revolt.' He envisaged the invasion as 'a knock-out
blow' when the Reich was on its last legs. All this was a far cry from
the hazardous, concentrated assault mounted on Normandy in June
1944.[41]

Churchill's peripheral strategy also reflected deep doubts about his
army. After the heady days of 1940, the next two years saw a succession of British defeats – Greece, Crete, Singapore and Tobruk. The
term BEF was no longer taboo but people joked that it meant 'Back
Every Friday'. Churchill experienced the fall of Tobruk in June 1942
as 'one of the heaviest blows' of the whole war. A total of 33,000

British Empire troops surrendered to a German and Italian force half their size. As he wrote later, 'Defeat is one thing; disgrace is another.' Churchill placed much of the blame on his generals. Undoubtedly they were slow to master the combined arms tactics – using tanks, infantry and artillery – that the Germans had displayed so successfully in 1940. But, more deeply, this was an army still scarred by the Great War. Sir Alan Brooke, chief of the Imperial General Staff, wrote in his diary in March 1942, 'Half our Corps and Divisional Commanders are totally unfit for their appointments, and yet if I were to sack them I could find no better! They lack character, imagination, drive and power of leadership. The reason for this state of affairs is to be found in the losses we sustained in the last war of all our best officers, who should now be our senior commanders.' Of course, the German High Command could have uttered a similar lament, having borne even heavier losses in 1914–18, but it drew very different lessons. Mindful of the Great War, Brooke and his colleagues were also sure that they could not push their troops very far. Units were given carefully defined tasks and told to consolidate their gains rather than push on opportunistically: the initiative allowed to junior commanders in the German army was foreign to British thinking. Fearful of brittle morale and conscious of Britain's limited manpower reserves, battlefield doctrine concentrated on heavy firepower to undermine enemy resistance. 'We have got to try and do this business with the smallest possible casualties,' General Bernard Montgomery remarked in March 1944.[42]

Monty – the supreme exponent of careful, set-piece battles – became a celebrity after defeating Rommel's German-Italian army at Alamein in the Egyptian desert in November 1942 and then driving it back to eventual surrender in Tunis. Alamein featured concentrated firepower, in a battle plan that had distinct echoes of Haig's victories of 1918. The irony is that Haig's sixty-division army was the biggest that the British Empire ever put into the field, yet its achievements were largely forgotten by the 1940s and remain so today, despite the efforts of revisionist military historians. By contrast Monty, whose Eighth Army was roughly a quarter of the size, made Alamein a household name across Britain. This was partly because of the immense political importance of the victory in Britain after two years of morale-sapping defeats that had raised questions about Churchill's continued leadership. Twice in six months he had faced votes of no confidence in the House of Commons and his symbols of defiance in 1940 now seemed less impressive: 'If only he'd keep those great gross cigars out of his face,' noted one peeved diarist. Little wonder that, after Alamein, the Prime Minister ordered the ringing of church bells, silent since the Battle of Britain. As in 1940, Churchill the wordsmith gave instant historical shape to the molten mess of war, describing what he dubbed the 'Battle of Egypt' as not 'the end' or 'even the beginning of the end' but 'perhaps, the end of the beginning.' Propaganda aside, the Haig–Monty contrast also reflected the confused narrative of Britain's Great War compared with that of 1939–45. Alamein was an unequivocal victory occurring at the midpoint of the conflict, whereas Haig's 'Hundred Days' of surging advance came near the end of the Great War and were obscured by the breathtaking internal collapse of the Kaiser's Germany. The midpoint of the Great War was the battle of the Somme. Although there is now much evidence that this four-month slaughter gravely sapped the strength and morale of the German army, this was not evident at the time. In 1916 the Allies advanced no more than seven miles. Much more obvious were the massive British casualties, totalling 420,000 killed, wounded and missing. The Somme could not be spun as a success, whereas Alamein was plausibly hyped as one of the decisive moments of the Second World War.[*43]

The attrition strategy of Churchill and Brooke was intended to wear the enemy down at minimal cost in British lives by targeting the Mediterranean as the 'soft underbelly' of the Axis. After victory in North Africa, they invaded Italy in September 1943, hopeful of a rapid collapse that would drop most of the peninsula into Allied hands. But the Germans decided to fight for Italy and the Apennine range provided ideal cover for the defence: battles such as the four-month struggle to take the mountain-top Benedictine monastery of

---

* Even though the 5,000 or so death toll at Alamein pales into insignificance against the half-million men that the Germans and the Russians each lost during the Stalingrad campaign.

Cassino were reminiscent of trench warfare in 1914–18. Surveying the devastated landscape, the German commander at Cassino was carried back to visions of the Somme nearly thirty years before. Similarly, in the bloody battle to break out of the Normandy beachhead in June–July 1944, the Allies' daily casualty rate exceeded that of Passchendaele in 1917. In fact, the mobile warfare of France in May 1940, Russia in the summer of 1941 or the North African desert in early 1942 were exceptional: much of the 1939–45 war was fought by infantrymen in trenches and foxholes, making incremental gains. Yet the British Tommy of the second war seems to have clung stubbornly to the belief that, however bad things were, his father's generation had it far worse in 1914–18. And the statistics bear him out. In 1939–45 total British army casualties (killed, missing and wounded) amounted to 366,000; for the Western Front alone in 1914–18 the figure was at least 2.5 million.[44] And the second war climaxed in May 1945 with Germany's unconditional surrender and the death of its Führer – a marked contrast with 1918 when the war ended with the German army still on foreign soil and the Kaiser slipping away into his Dutch exile. Little wonder that Churchill ordered that the end of hostilities in Europe should be called 'Victory Day' not 'Armistice Day' or 'Cease Fire Day'.[45]

Back in 1927 officers at the Army Staff College were reminded that 'war is not an end in itself but a means to an end, namely, an economical victory which will secure a prosperous and contented peace.' Unlike 1918, 1945 was for the British both a clear victory and an economical one – thanks largely to Britain's allies. The Soviet Union bore the brunt of the land war against Germany, with a death toll of at least 27 million; American losses were even smaller than Britain's but US manpower and materiel, supplies and finance provided aid for the British on a scale that dwarfed the contribution of France in 1914–18. Lend-Lease, for instance, covered more than half of Britain's balance of payments deficit for the whole war.[46]

It was Stalin and Roosevelt at Teheran in November 1943 who finally pinned Churchill down to a cross-Channel attack the following spring. But the Prime Minister kept complaining that 'this battle has been forced upon us by the Russians and by the United States military authorities' and the night before D-Day, heavy with fore-boding, he told his wife, 'Do you realise that by the time you wake up in the morning twenty thousand men may have been killed?' In fact, the casualties on 6 June were 'only' 11,000 and, although the battle of Normandy took time, the breakout from the beachhead was spectac-ularly fast. By mid-September, with France and Belgium liberated, Eisenhower's armies were in positions that Allied planners had not expected to reach until late May 1945. One of the now forgotten war-winning weapons was the 2½-ton truck – vital in 1944–5 for supplying Eisenhower's armies along grossly extended lines of com-munication. Churchill, still thinking literally in terms of 'foot soldiers', confessed himself hugely impressed with the 'admirable speed and flexibility' of the American war machine. But he also recognized the implications for British diplomacy. 'Our armies are only about one-half the size of the American and will soon be little more than one-third,' he lamented in December 1944; 'it is not so easy as it used to be for me to get things done.'[47]

Whereas British military doctrine was indelibly shaped by 'lessons' drawn from the Great War, American involvement in that struggle had been too brief to obscure the lasting legacies of that country's great-est war in 1861–5. Afterwards the North's strategy for victory over the Confederacy was generalized by the American military into 'the appropriate strategy for all major, full-scale wars'. That meant apply-ing overwhelming superior power to destroy the enemy's armed forces, his economic resources and his will to fight – the emblematic figure being General Ulysses S. Grant, the North's ruthless com-mander. In the war against Hitler the US army's decisive edge was not in combat manpower: it raised only 90 divisions in 1941–5 – 'not an altogether impressive performance for a superpower' when compared with the Red Army's 400 in 1945 or the 300 divisions mobilized by Nazi Germany. America's winning weapon was firepower. This meant artillery in numbers and accuracy ('on time, on target') of which the British could only dream. And also combat aircraft: in 1944 America produced 74,000 planes, a third more than both Britain and Russia put together. To destroy the enemy's home base and will to fight, America had the resources to truly 'blitz' the enemy's homelands, culminating, at the cost of $2 billion, in the atomic bomb. By 1944 America's GDP was equivalent to those of Britain, Russia, Germany and Japan combined.[48]

Britain's more limited resources, plus the mental constraints of the Great War, made a war of annihilation inconceivable – hence Churchill's indirect strategy – whereas the United States had not only the capacity but also the intent. Reading 1914–18 differently from the British and, like the US military, in the light of the American Civil War, Roosevelt proclaimed in January 1943 that the 'elimination' of German 'war power' required nothing less than the enemy's 'unconditional surrender' – explicitly adopting the phrase popularized by Grant in 1862. In using it FDR was, in part, seeking to address Russian suspicions that the British and American failure to mount a Second Front in France in 1942 reflected a readiness to sign a separate peace with Germany. But the President's deeper motive in issuing the 'unconditional surrender' statement was to avoid a repetition of the 'stab in the back' legends peddled by Hitler and extreme German nationalists after 1918. This time Germany had to be totally and unequivocally defeated. Roosevelt had developed an *idée fixe* about innate German militarism and aggression. 'There are two schools of thought,' he wrote in 1944: 'those who would be altruistic in regard to the Germans' (a view exemplified, he believed, in Keynes' *Economic Consequences of the Peace*) and 'those who would adopt a much "tougher" attitude', as advocated at the time by Clemenceau and his own relative Teddy Roosevelt. 'Most decidedly', FDR went on, 'I belong to the latter school.' In his view 'unconditional surrender' was only the first step to a full and lasting 'elimination' of German 'war power'. He flirted with the idea of erasing German industry, fundamental to war-making power, and he certainly wanted the country dismembered into a number of smaller states, as in the days before Bismarck. The important thing, he insisted, was 'not to leave in the German mind the concept of the Reich' – that word 'should be stricken from the language'.[49]

The other big lesson Roosevelt drew from the previous war was the need to ensure a more effective peace. Never, as we have seen, a wholehearted supporter of Wilson's conception of the League of

Nations, he concluded that the league had become 'nothing more than a debating society' and, he added, 'a poor one at that'. As early as 1923 FDR proposed an 'Executive Council' of the league, with a mix of permanent and rotating members, to give weight and direction to the assembly's deliberations, and this was the idea he developed during the war.[50] When he and Churchill drafted the Atlantic Charter in August 1941, it was the Prime Minister who wanted to include a clear commitment to an 'effective international organization' to placate what he called 'extreme internationalists' back home. The President was completely against such wording because of the 'suspicions and opposition' that would be aroused in America. In any case he felt that 'nothing could be more futile than the reconstitution of a body such as the Assembly of the League of Nations'. Effective peace-keeping after the war would depend on what he quaintly called 'the policemen' – initially envisaged as America and Britain but gradually expanded during the war to include the Soviet Union, China and France. Smaller Allied powers such as Norway or the Netherlands could, he conceded, be allowed an 'ostensible' role in global policing but nothing more than that because none of these nations 'would have the practical means of taking any effective or, at least, considerable part in the task involved.' Roosevelt's conception of international security was embodied in the structure of the eventual United Nations in 1945, with the General Assembly balanced by a Security Council in which the Big Five were permanent members – echoing, as FDR liked to point out, his proposal of 1923.[51]

In 1944–5 the US State Department made a huge effort, working with internationalist groups, to promote the United Nations to the American public as the country's 'Second Chance'. 'Today in 1944, we are living through experiences that parallel 1918,' wrote Charlotte B. Mahon, director of the Woodrow Wilson Foundation. 'Never before has one generation had the privilege of looking back and profiting by its own tragic mistakes. We are that generation.' The Wilson Foundation, almost moribund in the 1930s, was rejuvenated by the war, doubling its staff in 1944. And the Great War president was now resurrected as the self-sacrificial pioneer of American internationalism – canonized in a series of simplistic biographies and especially in the Twentieth Century Fox movie *Wilson*, which premiered in August 1944 (plate18).[52]

Wilson was the obsession of producer Darryl F. Zanuck, who specialized in biographical epics such as *Young Mr. Lincoln* and now wanted to bring to the big screen what he called 'the tragic story of one man who literally gave his life to the cause of world peace.' With lavish sets and massive casts, production costs alone were an unprecedented $5.2 million – $1 million more than even *Gone with the Wind* – but box office returns, especially in America's hinterland, were not good and the studio ended up making a massive $2.2 million loss. Zanuck's refusal to cast a matinee idol such as William Powell or Ronald Colman as Wilson – rather than an unknown Canadian lookalike Alexander Knox – was cited as one reason for the financial disaster. Another was Zanuck's obstinate insistence on *Wilson* as the title, rather than more evocative alternatives such as *In Time to Come* or *Goodbye Dolly Gray* (the 1914–18 marching song). But the root problem was probably the personality of Wilson himself who, despite strenuous efforts to play him up as a family man who loved sport and songs, was always going to come over as an earnest professor and preacher – certainly not the sort of guy with whom the average American would want to spend a Saturday evening. 'Why should they pay seventy-five cents to see Wilson on the screen', asked Zanuck's old family doctor in Nebraska, 'when they wouldn't pay ten cents to see him alive?'[53]

Yet the fact that *Wilson* was a commercial flop should not obscure its political impact. By February 1945 an estimated 10 million Americans had seen the film at premium rates, even before its release at normal prices to second-run cinemas. Although some Republican papers denounced the movie as 'fourth term propaganda' for 'Franklin Delano Wilson', the response of critics was highly positive. *Life* magazine called *Wilson* 'one of the best pictures Hollywood ever made'; another review was headlined 'The Movie to Prevent World War Three'. The film's message was stark, even melodramatic, with Wilson as the goody and his Republican opponent, Henry Cabot Lodge, as the baddy, frustrating the President's great crusade for his own narrow political ends. At the end Wilson, invalided by his stroke and no longer president, tells his former Cabinet that the ideal of the League of Nations will never die and that 'it may come about in a better way than we proposed'. Then, taking his wife's arm, he walks out of the room and into history. The message was not lost on audiences. Wilson's Navy Secretary Josephus Daniels felt those at the New York premiere left the cinema feeling 'that this generation must repair the errors which made possible the present holocaust'.[54] Interest in Wilson and his writings rose dramatically and in July 1945 Americans ranked him fifth among the greatest men in the nation's history. Little wonder that FDR considered the film 'excellent' and predicted it would 'have a splendid effect' – even though muttering to his physician as Wilson collapsed with his stroke, 'By God, that's not going to happen to me.'[55]

Ironic words, of course. By the time the United Nations Organization was inaugurated in April 1945, Roosevelt had been dead for two weeks – taken by a massive cerebral haemorrhage – and friction with Stalin over Poland was already straining the inner circle of great powers that he had laboured so hard to create. Roosevelt never envisaged a permanent American military presence in Europe: at Yalta he warned that Congress would oblige him to bring all GIs home within two years. Some in the British Foreign Office feared a repeat of 1919–20, with the United States swinging away from international cooperation into 'an expansionist isolationism of a highly inconvenient character'.[56] This was why Churchill bent all his efforts during and after the war to forging a permanent alliance with the United States, making the term 'special relationship' one of his catchphrases. His famous 'Iron Curtain' speech at Fulton, Missouri, in March 1946, often seen as an anti-Soviet clarion call, was actually as much about building a 'fraternal association' with America, involving military cooperation, shared bases and even common citizenship. Churchill was talking up the Cold War to justify the special relationship.[57]

Within four years of victory over Germany, the confrontation with the Soviet Union had drawn the United States into a permanent Atlantic alliance. A decade after the end of the Third Reich, West Germany was a member of NATO. None of that was imaginable in

1945. But even though America's future world role was still nebulous on Victory Day, no one could doubt American power. 'The Great Republic has come into its own,' exulted the *New York Herald Tribune*: 'it stands first among the peoples of the earth.'[58] Despite the tensions underlying the war effort, such as fraught race relations and an acute housing shortage, one can already discern an overwhelmingly positive narrative about 1941–5. This also put the war effort of 1917–18 into a more favourable light, while highlighting the 'mistakes' of the League of Nations fight in 1919. The war had not only ended with the total defeat of Germany, as FDR had envisaged, it had also served to pull the United States out of the worst depression in its history, which many blamed on the legacies of the Great War. In 1933 unemployment stood at 25 per cent and the figure was still 14 per cent in 1940, but by 1944 it was barely 1 per cent. Much of the growth in the labour force was due to the Draft but, for many young Americans, the armed forces offered not only their first secure job but also other novelties such as three square meals a day and decent medical care. Uniquely among the belligerents, the United States produced massive armaments without suppressing civilian living standards – on the contrary between 1939 and 1945 output of alcoholic drinks rose by 50 per cent and that of processed food by 40 per cent. The job half done in 1917–20 had now been finished triumphantly by a country producing both guns and butter on a scale that powered it to the peak of world affairs. War was hell but 'for millions of Americans on the booming home front, World War II was also a hell of a war'.[59]

What, then, to call this epic struggle? Roosevelt toyed with various titles, trying to convey the idea that it was 'a war for the preservation of smaller peoples and the Democracies of the world'. At a press conference in April 1942 he even asked the American public for help: over the next couple of weeks, 15,000 letters and cards poured in with suggestions such as 'The War for Civilization', 'The War against Enslavement' and 'The People's War'. But none of these came to replace the terminology he himself had suggested back in the spring of 1941, months before Pearl Harbor, when he spoke on several occasions about the 'first world war' and the 'second world war'.[60] Americans had always referred to 1917–18 as 'the world war', as

distinct from the largely European conflict of 1914–17 before the
United States, China and Brazil joined the Allies. The Germans also
consistently described 1914–18 as a world war (*Weltkrieg*), on the
grounds that it was fought for world power (*Weltmacht*) against
Britain's world empire (*Weltimperium*). The British label, however,
was almost always the 'Great War', echoing the twenty-year struggle
against France in the era of Napoleon. A very rare exception was *The
First World War (1914–1918)* published in 1920 by journalist Charles
Repington, but that title was an eye-catching sales pitch largely unre-
lated to the text itself. After September 1939 the predominant British
label for the new conflict was simply 'the War' but in 1944 the publishers Macmillan asked for an official guidance, noting that many
American publications were using the terms 'First World War' and
'Second World War'. The Cabinet Secretary Sir Edward Bridges
admitted that '"Great War" certainly seems pretty inappropriate now'
but no official decision was made until January 1948, when the
Cabinet Office was asked to confirm a title for the impending series
of official histories of the war. Eschewing alternatives such as the 'Six
Years' War', it was decided to follow the American convention, which
Churchill was also adopting for his war memoirs. Clement Attlee, the
prime minister, gave his approval and so the British government finally
decided, two and a half years after the guns fell silent, that it had been
fighting the Second World War.[61]

The point here is not one of semantic trivia. The term 'Great War'
had placed 1914–18 on a pinnacle of its own: the struggle of
1792–1815, its implicit comparator, had occurred a century before.
But to say that 1914–18 was simply the First World War, a quarter-
century before the next, suggested a very different narrative arc, which
put that conflict in the shade. The journalist E.H. Carr's phrase about
a 'twenty years' crisis' from 1919 to 1939[62] was developed by other
writers, particularly Churchill. In the preface to his first volume of war
memoirs, published in 1948, the former prime minister introduced
them 'as a continuation of the story of the First World War' which
he had set out in six earlier tomes. Taken together, he stated, 'they will
cover an account of another Thirty Years War.' In this volume, surveying the period from 1919 to 1939 and entitled *The Gathering*

Storm, his theme was 'how the English-speaking peoples, through their unwisdom, carelessness and good nature, allowed the wicked to rearm.' Linking 1914–18 and 1939–45 in an overarching 'Thirty Years War' would be a trope much favoured by subsequent pundits and historians.[63]

'Never again' had been proved true but in ways that few had anticipated in 1939, let alone 1940. By 1945 the Second World War had turned out very differently from the First. It finished the job apparently botched in 1918 by imposing the unconditional surrender of the Third Reich, the death of its leader and Germany's occupation by Allied troops. The drama of 1940 also engendered a real sense of British achievement, so clearly absent the last time. And this war had far greater impact on the home front through mass evacuation and sustained bombing. Even though the worst of the Blitz was over in May 1941, the V-bomb attacks from June 1944 caused another surge of evacuees (over a million) and another 11,700 civilian dead.[64] And the conflict, played out visually on the newsreels, came over as far more varied than 1914–18 – with fighting in the deserts of North Africa and the steppes of Russia, through the mountains of Italy and the hedgerows of Normandy, across the plains of Germany and in the jungles of Asia. All this was a real contrast with the film material from the Great War and subsequent movies about it, which disproportionately featured the trenches.

There was another important contrast. This was also a war which exposed human evil in forms that put the 1914–18 debates about 'Atrocities' and 'Civilisation' into a new perspective. That is the theme of the next chapter.

8

EVIL

Made skeptical by World War I 'atrocity propaganda', many people refused to put much faith in stories about the inhuman Nazi treatment of prisoners. Last week Americans could no longer doubt . . .

Life magazine, 7 May 1945

. . . the problem of evil will be the fundamental problem of postwar intellectual life in Europe – as death became the fundamental problem after the last war.

Hannah Arendt, 1945[1]

'I have never seen British soldiers so moved to cold fury as the men who opened the Belsen camp this week,' BBC reporter Richard Dimbleby told radio listeners on 19 April 1945. 'I picked my way over corpse after corpse in the gloom, until I heard one voice raised above the gentle undulating moaning. I found a girl, she was a living skeleton, impossible to gauge her age for she had practically no hair left, and her face was only a yellow parchment sheet with two holes in it for eyes . . . And beyond her down the passage and in the hut there were the convulsive movements of dying people too weak to raise themselves from the floor.'[2]

Such stories are now commonplace. In the twenty-first century we have become almost inured to images of the Nazi Holocaust and of other atrocities against civilians in later wars from Cambodia to Bosnia. So we need to understand why Dimbleby, a seasoned war reporter, was so appalled by his first glimpse of a Nazi camp – breaking down five times while recording his despatch and telling a colleague Wynford Vaughan-Thomas, 'You must go and see it, but you'll never wash the smell of it off your hands, never get the filth of it out of your mind.' Thomas could not remember him so outraged: 'here was a new Dimbleby, a fundamentally decent man who had seen something really evil'.[3]

Images of Belsen were novel and genuinely shocking in 1945. They helped give the Second World War a moral clarity that the conflict of 1914–18 had lost in the 1920s and never thereafter regained. Film and photos of the camp were shown at the Nuremberg war trials which, again in contrast with the aftermath of 1914–18, pinned unequivocal guilt on Germany's leaders for appalling war crimes. And in Asia the war was terminated in 1945 by a new weapon of mass destruction far more terrible than poison gas or high-explosive shells. The Bomb posed the ultimate question of whether a third world war would destroy the whole human race. In due course the stark morality of evil and good, Axis versus Allies, would become blurred, but for a generation after 1945 this black-and-white Manichean divide would define perceptions of the Second World War – consigning its morally more ambiguous predecessor to grey obscurity.

To appreciate the impact of evil at the end of the Second World War we must go back to the opening weeks of the Great War. In August and September 1914 the analogue of Belsen was Louvain. As we saw in Chapter One, the sacking by German troops of this Belgian city became one of the ideological benchmarks of the Great War for British opinion – gruesome evidence of Hunnish barbarity that justified a 'war for civilisation'. Research in the 1990s has confirmed that around 6,500 Belgian and French civilians (mostly adult males) were massacred by the Kaiser's troops between August and October 1914: contemporary German claims that they were guerrillas engaged in a people's war (*Volkskrieg*) lacked almost any foundation. In all probability panicky and ill-trained German soldiers were projecting on to a confused situation their deeply ingrained folk-memories of the *francstireurs* (free-shooters) who harassed the Prussian army in France during the war of 1870. Persuaded that the Belgians were doing the same in 1914, they lashed out frenziedly in Louvain, Dinant and elsewhere, shooting civilians indiscriminately and even using some as human shields.[4]

The Germans stuck tenaciously to the claim that they had simply been taking 'legitimate reprisals' against the terrorists of 1914. Their official 'White Book' of justification was entitled 'Human Rights Breaches in the Conduct of the Belgian People's War' – with the breaches made entirely by the other side. The White Book was highly selective in its use of evidence but the Entente powers weakened their own case by exaggeration. The British official report, presented by a committee headed by Lord Bryce in May 1915, concluded from the mass of Belgian and French testimony that 'these excesses were committed – in some cases ordered, in others allowed – on a system and in pursuance of a purpose. The purpose was to strike terror into the civilian population.' The report continued: 'In the minds of Prussian officers War seems to have become a sort of sacred mission, one of the highest functions of the omnipotent State.' On the popular level in Britain and France the stereotype of ruthless Prussianism was pushed even further. Essentially true accounts of German conduct became embroidered into a fantastical tapestry of myths, including stories about how the Huns had crucified soldiers, cut off children's hands and built factories to turn corpses into margarine.[5]

Atrocity stories were also disseminated across the Atlantic in the battle for American opinion in 1914–15: fortunately for Britain the Bryce report appeared a week after 128 Americans had died on the *Lusitania*. And German atrocities were featured in 1917–18 by the US government's Committee on Public Information (CPI) to help mobilize support for a faraway war in which Americans seemed to have little direct interest. By this time atrocity stories had lost their shock value among people in Britain and France, sobered by Verdun and the Somme. But in 1918 they were pedalled crudely by CPI director George Creel in his 'fight for the *minds* of men, for the conquest of their convictions' via poster campaigns enjoining Americans to 'Remember Belgium' and films such as *The Prussian Cur* and *The Kaiser, The Beast of Berlin*.[6]

Not surprisingly, therefore, it was in the United States that the reaction against such 'atrocity propaganda' became most intense, as we saw in Chapter Five, fuelling the revisionist arguments of the late 1920s about the moral equivalence of the two sides in 1914–18 and strengthening the isolationist backlash of the 1930s against entanglement in another European war. British opinion became equally wary of atrocity stories, as shown by responses to the British government's report on Nazi concentration camps published in October 1939 under the sober title 'Papers concerning the treatment of German nationals in Germany, 1938–1939'. Most people did not seriously question the content of the document, which served to strengthen distaste for Hitler's regime, but this was undercut by widespread scepticism about the government's motives for publication. 'All these details were known last September', observed one man sourly, 'and yet we signed at Munich.' Another asked, 'How come the atrocity stories?', to which his sister replied that 'people were not being sufficiently enthusiastic about the war, so the Government had to whip up some hate.'[7]

Mindful of the public allergy to propaganda and of an undercurrent of anti-Semitism, Britain's Ministry of Information (MOI) shied away from circulating 'horror stories' about what was happening in occupied Europe, noting in a memo of July 1941 that 'the effect of the Bryce report in the last war should never be forgotten.' The MOI felt that 'a certain amount of horror is needed, but it must be used very sparingly and must deal always with treatment of indisputably innocent people. Not with violent political opponents. And not with Jews.' The backlash about Great War propaganda even made some senior British officials hesitate in accepting the mounting evidence about Nazi extermination camps. Victor Cavendish-Bentinck, chairman of the Cabinet's Joint Intelligence Committee, had no doubt by August 1943 that 'the Germans are out to destroy the Jews of any age unless they are fit for manual labour' but 'as regards putting Poles to death in gas chambers', he wrote, 'I do not believe there is any evidence that this has been done.' Cavendish-Bentinck felt 'we weaken our case against the Germans by publicly giving credence to atrocity stories for which we have no evidence. These mass executions in gas chambers remind me of the story of employment of human corpses during the last war for the manufacture of fat, which was a grotesque lie and led to true stories of German enormities being brushed aside as being mere propaganda.'[8]

The atrocity phobia persisted for much of the war. In March 1944 George Orwell, already a keen student of propaganda, remarked on how the 1920s reaction against a four-year 'orgy of lying and hatred' had vitiated attempts in the 1930s to arouse public opinion about the horrors of fascism. '"Atrocities" had come to be looked on as synonymous with "lies",' Orwell noted. 'But the stories about the German concentration camps were atrocity stories: therefore they were lies – so reasoned the average man.' In April 1945, likewise, the initial reaction of incredulous BBC staff was to embargo Dimbleby's sensational account of Belsen until it had been verified by newspaper reports. Only his threat of resignation forced them to broadcast a highly edited but still deeply moving version, which was probably heard by 10–15 million people in Britain.[9]

Visual evidence from Belsen proved even more compelling. The 33 rolls of film and over 200 photographs taken by members of the British Army Film and Photographic Unit (AFPU) have been described as 'arguably the most influential of any record or artefact documenting the Nazi concentration camps'. The images were shown repeatedly in 1945 newsreels and in subsequent films and television documentaries. 'No other camp was filmed so comprehensively and over such a long period', for nearly two months after its liberation on 15 April. Belsen contained over 40,000 people, most of them suffering from acute malnutrition, typhus and other diseases, together with some 10,000 decomposing corpses littered around the excrement-filled compounds. The AFPU painstakingly filmed these horrors and the ensuing clean-up, including the mass graves and the 'human laundry' where survivors were washed and then dusted with DDT. Adding to the power of such imagery was the contrast between the emaciated victims and the well-fed SS guards – male and female – whose arrogant, impassive faces were often captured on camera, together with shots of local Germans enjoying themselves in the surrounding countryside. The cameramen took particular care technically to counter possible accusations that these 'atrocity pictures' had been faked – for instance taking long and wide establishing shots of the camp before gradually moving in to close-ups of particular scenes. They understood that their work would provide what one called 'pictorial evidence of the brutality and callousness of the "Master Race"'.[10]

Although the grisly images were heavily edited for public consumption, their effect when shown in Britain was overwhelming. 'Everybody everywhere, in the tram, in the office,' according to one diarist, was 'talking about the German atrocities now being uncovered and really, our wildest imaginings couldn't have pictured things as bad as they are.' Another noted, 'I'm always hearing bits of conversation in shops and buses: "it must be true, because I've seen the pictures."' Photographs were also printed in newspapers and magazines, often with the headline 'Lest We Forget' – adapting the liturgy of the interwar Armistice Day services. The *Daily Express* mounted an exhibition in Trafalgar Square of twenty-two particularly graphic photographs from Belsen and other camps entitled 'SEEING IS BELIEVING'. The larger moral was underlined by 'Horror in Our Time' – a newsreel distributed by Gaumont British News in April 1945 – which interspersed footage from the camps with shots of 1940 while the commentator observed, 'Never forget, but for the Battle of Britain this might have been you.'[11]

An opinion survey on 18 April 1945 suggested that 81 per cent of the British population would answer 'yes' to the question 'Do you think the atrocity stories are true?', whereas in December 1944 the proportion had been only 37 per cent.[12] Over half a century later the playwright Alan Bennett could recall dozens of films from his youth but only one of the newsreels that preceded them. This was 'the discovery of Belsen with the living corpses, the mass graves and the line-up of the sullen guards. There were cries of horror in the cinema, though my recollection is that Mam and Dad were much more upset than my brother and me. Still, Belsen was not a name one ever forgot and became a place of horror long before Auschwitz.'[13]

That last sentence deserves a moment's reflection. It is often said that the revelations of April 1945 exposed the British people to the Holocaust, but that claim is misleading. The most striking feature to us now of the 1945 revelations in Britain is the relative lack of emphasis on the Jewishness of many of the victims in the overall coverage, whose main aim was to show the bestiality of the Nazi regime in general through the gruesome but anonymized depiction of mass victimhood. This was partly a continuance of wartime policies about how to present Nazi 'atrocities' but it also reflected the fact that all the Nazi camps liberated by the British and US armies lay within Germany. They were therefore 'concentration camps' of the sort already familiar through the British official report of 1939, which housed not only Jews but also communists, homosexuals and other 'deviants' – overwhelmingly of German extraction. Belsen, Buchenwald and Dachau were therefore very different from the 'extermination camps' in Poland, notably Auschwitz where at least 1.3 million were done to death (overwhelmingly Jews).

These camps, the true killing fields of Nazidom, had been liberated by the Red Army and Soviet reports had much less impact in the West. Shadowy references did appear occasionally in the 1945 British commentary – for instance a delegation of British MPs who reported on Buchenwald often heard prisoners saying that the camps further east were 'far worse' and that the 'worst camp of all was said by many to be Auschwitz' – but such comments did not really penetrate public consciousness. A popular *Victory Book* produced by Odhams Press in the summer of 1945 made vague allusion to 'a Silesian death camp' before stating, 'It was, however, within the frontiers of Germany itself that the most horrific sights were discovered' at the 'great Nazi concentration camps of Buchenwald, Dachau, Belsen and the like.'[14]

American reaction to the camps was similar to that in Britain. Buchenwald and Dachau had both been liberated by the US army and the images from there caused outrage in the United States. Edward R. Murrow, the gravelly voiced CBS radio commentator, was a household name across America after his 'This is London' reports during the Blitz. But his broadcast from Buchenwald on 15 April 1945, prefaced with the warning that it would not be 'pleasant listening', became even more celebrated. Murrow described being surrounded by an 'evil-smelling horde' of starving survivors: 'Death had already marked many of them, but they were smiling with their eyes.' Looking over this 'mass of men' he could see 'green fields beyond where well-fed Germans were ploughing.' General Dwight Eisenhower, the Supreme Allied Commander in Western Europe, was appalled by the 'indescribable horror' he saw at Buchenwald. In one room were 'piled up twenty or thirty naked men, killed by star-vation.' George Patton, macho commander of the US Third Army, 'would not even enter', Ike added: 'He said he would be sick if he did so.' Eisenhower steeled himself to tour the camp in order, as he told the Pentagon, 'to be in a position to give *first-hand* evidence of these things if ever, in the future, there develops a tendency to charge these allegations merely to "propaganda".' Eisenhower insisted that local Germans must visit the camps themselves and he also arranged special visits by congressmen and editors. *Life*, the best-selling American weekly, published a searing set of pictures under the head-line 'ATROCITIES'. 'Made skeptical by World War I "atrocity propaganda",' the magazine's editors noted, many people during the 1930s had 'refused to put much faith in stories about the inhuman Nazi treatment of prisoners.' But now 'Americans could no longer doubt stories of Nazi cruelty. For the first time there was irrefutable evidence as the advancing Allied armies captured camps filled with political prisoners and slave laborers.'[15]

That last phrase is worth noting. As in Britain, American com-mentary, derived from concentration camps within Germany, did not foreground the Jewish tragedy. The most common term for camp survivors was the anonymous 'Displaced Persons' or DPs. The concept of the Holocaust only became common currency in the United States from the 1960s – after the trial of Adolf Eichmann and the Arab-Israeli wars of 1967 and especially 1973.[16] What 1945 exposed for most Americans, as in Britain, was a clear-cut justifica-tion for the Second World War that had been lacking for the First. An opinion poll in May 1945 recorded 84 per cent of Americans believing that the Germans had murdered 'many people in concentration camps'. As *Life* put it, 'Capture of the German concentration camps piles up evidence of barbarism that reaches the lowest point of human degradation.'[17]

Positive proof of evil deeds raised the question of punishment. 'War guilt' had been an issue after 1914–18 but, as with the debate about atrocities, the denouement in 1945 was very different. Indeed the victors of the Second World War took careful note – albeit in different ways – of the lessons from the First.

Today the term 'war guilt' is entwined with Article 231 of the Versailles treaty. But Article 231 never used the term 'guilt', speaking only of the 'responsibility of Germany and its allies' for war damage to the Allies in 'the war imposed on them by the aggression of Germany and her allies'. The terms 'responsibility' and 'aggression' were primarily intended as a statement of legal liability, to help justify Allied claims for reparations, but their ambiguity was exploited by German apologists in the 1920s who portrayed Article 231 as an attempt by the Allies to assert Germany's exclusive 'guilt' for starting the war.[18]

In fact articles 227 to 230 attracted more immediate anger in Germany in 1919. Article 227 stated that the victor powers would establish a 'special tribunal' to try the ex-Kaiser for 'a supreme offence against international morality and the sanctity of treaties' while in articles 228 to 230 the German government recognized the right of the victors to 'bring before military tribunals persons accused of having committed acts in violation of the laws and customs of war' and promised to hand over accused people and provide all relevant documentation. To contemporaries articles 227 to 231 were seen all together as the 'responsibilities clauses' of the treaty; Germans called them the 'shame paragraphs' (*Schmachparagraphen*) and considered the question of Germany's conduct during the war to be as explosive as that of its 'guilt' in causing the war. Men whom Germans regarded as war heroes, from Hindenburg downward, were, it seemed, to be handed over to foreign courts in a humiliating derogation of national sovereignty. Only the most adroit political manoeuvring by Matthias Erzberger, chairman of Germany's Armistice Commission, ensured acceptance of these articles on 23 June 1919 – just minutes before expiry of the Allied ultimatum to sign the Versailles treaty or face invasion.[19]

The idea of trying the Kaiser was a peculiarly British obsession. To some extent it was a product of the election campaign of December 1918 when demands for 'hanging the Kaiser' and 'making Germany pay' were staples of hustings rhetoric. Lloyd George's exploitation of this public mood was castigated by Keynes in *The Economic Consequences of the Peace*. But the Prime Minister was not alone: most candidates, even Labour and Asquith Liberals, wanted to try Wilhelm II. Feeling among both the public and MPs had been inflamed anew by reports in the last weeks of the war about German mistreatment of British prisoners of war (POW). The German POW camps, many of them little more than forced-labour installations, had been simply overwhelmed by the haul of prisoners from their spring 1918 victories, leading to a collapse of food and hygiene. Photos of the 'moving skeletons' finally liberated by the Allies in November, infested with vermin and crazed with hunger, caused deep anger in Britain, and the trial of war 'criminals' became a central British peace aim.[20]

Lloyd George was passionate about trying the Kaiser. 'Kings have been tried and executed for offences which are not comparable,' he told the Imperial War Cabinet (IWC) on 20 November 1918. Lloyd George's radical roots seem to have been stirred by imagining the German monarch arraigned in Westminster Hall like Charles I in 1649 – a prospect that, of course, appalled the Kaiser's cousin, George V, in Buckingham Palace. Curzon agreed that the Kaiser was 'the arch-criminal' but most Cabinet colleagues were sceptical about a trial. Billy Hughes of Australia pointed out that going to war had been the prerogative of every sovereign through the ages. Churchill warned that an impartial tribunal might not convict the Kaiser for starting the war in 1914 because there was 'a great deal to be said about Russia in this matter, if you unfolded the question'. Some in the IWC favoured the precedent established with Bonaparte in 1815, exiling the Kaiser to some far-flung part of the South Atlantic such as Saint Helena or the Falklands. But that, too, had its danger: Austen Chamberlain warned lest the Allies 'create a Hohenzollern legend like the

Napoleonic legend'. Yet the IWC eventually gave reluctant consent, after a committee of lawyers advising on war crimes trials stated that, unless the Kaiser was himself tried, 'vindication of the principles of International Law' would remain 'incomplete'. As head of Germany's armed forces, they argued, he could be charged with ordering or sanctioning violations of the laws of war set out in the Hague Convention of 1899, including unrestricted U-boat warfare and the mistreatment of prisoners. Four of the seven members of the committee even recommended an indictment for 'having provoked or brought about an aggressive and unjust war'.[21]

Such comments take us back to the very particular grounds on which the British had gone to war with Germany in the first place. Britain's preoccupation with German 'atrocities' (from Belgian nuns in 1914 to British POWs in 1918) reflected the lack of a tangible justification for belligerency in terms of strict national interest because, unlike Belgium or France, British soil had not been invaded. Belgium in 1914 was, if you like, the original sin: Hunnish atrocities there were not only intrinsically appalling, they were also expressions of that ultimate atrocity – the violation of Belgian neutrality, ordered as a deliberate act of state. Hence the importance of holding to account Germany's head of state and supreme commander of its armed forces.[22]

Britain's allies did not share this passion for trying the Kaiser. France was not afflicted with election fever at the end of 1918 and public opinion seemed less aroused than in Britain about punishment. The idea that Saint Helena was the appropriate place for a war criminal sounded rather different in Paris than in London! Eventually Clemenceau did support Lloyd George's demand that the Kaiser be put on trial, perhaps to help establish German responsibility for the war and thereby strengthen France's claim for reparations.[23] But the Americans strongly opposed all war crimes trials. Their position is worth particular attention in view of the almost diametrically opposite arguments they advanced in 1945.

On 18 January 1919, at the very beginning of the Paris peace conference, the Allies set up a 'Commission on the Responsibility of the Authors of the War and the Enforcement of Penalties', chaired by the US secretary of state Robert Lansing, an international lawyer by background. Although Lansing was now disenchanted with Wilson, on the issue of war crimes the two men saw eye to eye, determined to safeguard full American autonomy. Lansing insisted that 'the essence of sovereignty was the absence of responsibility': a state could not be deemed sovereign if it were accountable to some higher authority. The Americans therefore rejected any reference to the 'laws of humanity' and also the creation of an international court before which, 'under circumstances which could not be foreseen', a US president might be 'haled as an ordinary individual'. The idea of charging the Kaiser with starting an 'unjust war' or a 'war of aggression' was also dismissed – to Lloyd George's regret. 'In my view,' he remarked, 'if important personalities who unleash such calamities could be rendered responsible for this, the greatest of all crimes, there would be less danger of war in the future.' Wilson reminded him that although 'Charles I was a contemptible character and the greatest liar in history,' he was 'transformed into a martyr by his execution.'[24]

Lloyd George, harping on August 1914, insisted that 'aggression without provocation' was 'an indisputable crime' and eventually Wilson agreed to try the Kaiser in order to win British support for a clause in the treaty safeguarding the Monroe Doctrine. But on the same day, 8 April, the President insisted on two points that undercut his concession. The charge against the Kaiser would not be that of violating criminal law but, more vaguely, of 'a supreme offence against international morality and the sanctity of treaties'. And the Kaiser, together with all those accused of violating the laws of war, would be tried before 'special tribunals' from the victor powers rather than an international court. These points were embodied in articles 227 and 228 of the Treaty of Versailles.[25]

Over the next couple of years the attempt to hold Germany accountable for war crimes degenerated into farce. The Kaiser had fled to the Netherlands amid the German revolution of November 1918 and the Dutch, following their tradition of giving refuge to the defeated, refused to hand him over to the Allies. The charges in Article 227 were not covered in any extradition treaty and the peacemakers, divided on the whole idea, refused to apply political pressure on the Dutch government. So the Kaiser lived out his days until 1941 on a country estate near Utrecht – in the words of one New York paper, 'unwept, unhonored, and unhung' – chopping wood, writing his memoirs and fulminating about how the Jews had deceived the German people into betraying him. 'Jews and mosquitoes', he told one correspondent in 1925, were 'a nuisance that humankind must get rid of some way or other', adding, 'I believe the best thing would be gas!'[26]

The quest to punish other 'war criminals' also ran out of steam. The Germans, government and people, remained adamantly opposed to handing over accused persons. Rightists demanded a 'counter-list' (Gegenliste) of Allied war criminals, including those who mounted the blockade and starvation of German women and children. The Allies were warned that a continued hard line could provoke civil war in Germany, undermining its fragile new democracy, and facilitate either a military coup or a Bolshevik revolution. 'O my God, where are we being driven to?' Gustav Noske, the German defence minister, asked a British official in Berlin with calculated emotion in December 1919. 'If we refuse to hand these officers over, the Entente will act, and the Government will have to go ... Leave me the means of maintaining order. Don't ask for these officers.'[27]

In a reversal of the punitive mood of a year before, the Allies decided to let the Germans try the accused and also cut the list down drastically to some 800 'flagrant cases'. Lord Birkenhead, the British attorney general, said that they wanted to vindicate 'the moral law of the world' by punishing a token few. 'If even twenty were shot', Lloyd George added, 'it would be an example.' The process of emasculation continued. To ensure that France did not indict generals such as Hindenburg and Ludendorff, still heroes for millions of Germans, Britain deleted all the admirals, thereby undermining any credible case against unrestricted U-boat warfare. And Sir Hugh Trenchard, Chief of the Air Staff, threatened to testify in defence of any German prosecuted for bombing London, which ensured that no German airmen were on the British list. Trenchard was an advocate of the 'air control' of colonial insurgencies and also pioneered the concept of strategic bombing: he could see that war crimes tribunals might be a double-edged sword. Others agreed. 'We who own so vast a portion of the world will have to be very careful,' warned the journalist Austin Harrison in February 1920, 'with Ireland on our conscience . . . and the abominations of Amritsar to atone for.'[28]

Eliminating from the list of war criminals all the leaders of the German armed forces made the prosecution of their subordinates seem both pointless and unjust. But the Allies continued to insist on at least some token trials, though it required their threat in May 1921 of imminent occupation of the Ruhr valley to prod the Germans into action. The proceedings took place before the Imperial Court of Justice (Reichsgericht) in Leipzig, prosecuted by German state attorneys using evidence furnished by the Allies. Of the four British cases, one was acquitted and the other three led to prison sentences of between six and ten months. Britain's solicitor-general told Parliament that the guilty verdicts offset the light sentences – 'For the first time in the history of the world, we have made a vanquished country try some of its own criminals' – but few British commentators were impressed. The French and Belgians, who had targeted more senior Germans and made little use of corroborative German evidence, secured only one conviction out of five, leading to a wave of anger back home, especially over the acquittal of General Karl Stenger – regarded by the French as one of the leading butchers of August 1914 but, in German minds, a war hero who had lost one leg to a French shell. Once the process ended, the French and Belgians tried war criminals in absentia, while the Reichsgericht methodically overturned the convictions. Little wonder that the Leipzig war trials were widely described as a 'farce'. In London *The Times* decried 'a scandalous failure of justice'; its counterpart in New York spoke of a 'great moral show' in which the German Supreme Court was 'making of a few privates and minor officers scapegoats for the army and the nation'.[29]

Leipzig was 'victors' justice' but it was 'delivered on the terms of the vanquished.'[30] The process had failed as a war crimes trial; it also had not resolved the historical questions of responsibility for the war: indeed the assiduous German campaign of historical revisionism left most people by the 1930s convinced that all the European powers had been responsible.

So, in the Second World War the Allies were determined to deal decisively with both war 'crimes' and war 'guilt': failure to convict German war criminals in 1919, a 1943 report stated, 'had undoubtedly sowed the seeds for ruthless disregard by the Nazis, two decades later, of accepted principles of international law governing the conduct of war.' A similar mistake must not be made again, which was a central reason for the policy of unconditional surrender. By invading and occupying the whole of Germany, the Allies were able to capture both the Nazi leaders and their documentation in a way that had been impossible after the Armistice of 1918.[31]

Although Hitler, Goebbels and Himmler committed suicide, most of the German leadership were rounded up and fifty-two of them were held at a hotel in Bad Mondorf in Luxembourg (known as Camp Ashcan). There they were subjected to periodic inspection by the world's press, who commented exhaustively on their foibles – Ribbentrop's chaotic room, Keitel's obsessive tidiness and Doenitz's taste in pink underwear. All this helped to undermine their credibility at home and abroad. 'Who'd have thought that we were fighting in this war against a bunch of jerks?' remarked one American guard. In the autumn of 1945 the Allies put twenty-two of the leading war criminals on trial before an International Military Tribunal in Nuremberg. Equally important, in 1945 German bureaucrats ignored orders from Berlin to destroy the archives, already dispersed because of Allied bombing. The Foreign Ministry records were found in the Harz Mountains, the navy's archives in Coburg, and both were sent to London, while the German army files were shipped across the Atlantic to the suburbs of Washington. The military documents alone comprised some 1,500 tons of paper – much of it worthless for historical research but including some 60,000 files 'of the greatest importance'. Over the next decade the captured documents formed the basis of a major publishing project intended to serve scholarship but also to document Nazi responsibility for the war. Indeed there was considerable opposition to handing the archives back to Germany. 'So long as these German archives are in the hands of the Western Allies', observed British historian Elizabeth Wiskemann, 'there need be no fear of the manipulation of texts such as those which have been discovered to have taken place in Germany after the other war.' These documents proved essential for the Nuremberg trials.[32]

But the idea of trying the German leadership was not axiomatic: in fact it was the subject of intense Anglo-American debate, based on divergent readings of the lessons from the previous war. In a complete reversal of 1918–19, the British government was totally opposed to any judicial process. Citing what he called 'the experience of that ill-starred enterprise at the end of the last War', foreign secretary Anthony Eden told the War Cabinet, 'I am convinced that we should avoid commitments to "try the war criminals" and "hang the Kaiser (*alias* Hitler)".' Churchill himself told the Cabinet in July 1942 that 'if Hitler falls into our hands we shall certainly put him to death.' He was 'not a Sovereign who c[oul]d be said to be in [the] hands of Ministers, like the Kaiser. This man is the mainspring of evil.' With macabre humour Churchill suggested that the instrument of execution should be the 'electric chair' – as used for 'gangsters' in America. 'No doubt', he said, it would be 'available on Lease-Lend'.[33]

John Simon, who as lord chancellor was the government's chief legal officer, agreed that 'trying' Hitler was a ludicrous idea. He argued that the treatment of 'notorious ringleaders' such as Hitler, Goering and Goebbels was 'a political, not a judicial, question', which should be decided by the Allied leadership. Simon was 'very worried by the prospect of a trial which might be drawn out almost indefinitely, in which all sort of things might be raised and discussed – whether legal or historical – leading to controversy and debate in the world at large, with a reaction which we can hardly calculate.' Rather than open such a can of worms, it would be better to deal with the leading Nazi war criminals by summary execution. This was the settled opinion of Churchill's government: the leading criminals should be captured, identified, notified of their crimes, convicted and executed by firing squad. The Foreign Office reckoned that each case could be dealt with in less than six hours.[34]

In Washington the treasury secretary Henry Morgenthau also favoured summary execution but he was in a minority. Unlike 1919 it was the US government that demanded a full-scale international trial. The lead was taken by Henry Stimson, the secretary of war, who as a young New York lawyer had been enthused with the idea of using international law to control relations between states. Stimson was a figure of considerable authority within the Roosevelt administration, a former Republican secretary of state (1929–33) who had been brought back to Washington by FDR in 1940 to head the War Department as a bipartisan symbol amid global crisis. By that time Stimson was a venerable seventy-three years old and needed to husband his energies but he assembled an able team of aides, allowing him to influence areas of policy far beyond his strict domain.[35]

Stimson still championed the Kellogg–Briand Pact of 1928 'outlawing' war, to which over sixty nations (including Germany) had signed up by 1939. The pact had been widely dismissed in Europe as a paper pledge, without clear definitions or means of enforcement, but Stimson and US army lawyers argued that it constituted a legal revolution: 'whatever may have been the law at the time of the Versailles conference [sic], the law of today condemns aggressive war as an international crime, triable and punishable as such.' At American insistence the launching of aggressive war (renamed 'crimes against the peace') became central to the Nuremberg indictment, backed by presidents Roosevelt and Truman and championed by the chief American prosecutor, Robert Jackson. The Europeans, he declared, were 'less obsessed than Americans with the ambition to reform the world and have less confidence in their ability to do so. Hence there is more disposition to accept future wars as natural.' On this issue Jackson displayed a crusading zeal.[36]

The launching of aggressive war, which Britain had tried and failed to pin on the Kaiser in 1919, was one pillar of the Allied case at Nuremberg. The other was 'crimes against humanity' – also brushed aside by the Americans in Paris but now central to their indictment of the Nazis. Stimson believed that a full-scale trial would have a 'greater effect on posterity' than summary execution, affording 'the most effective way of making a record of the Nazi system of terrorism'. After the evidence had been set out meticulously in court, the Germans would 'not again be able to claim, as they have been claiming with regard to the Versailles Treaty, that an admission of war guilt was extracted from them under duress.' The Nuremberg indictment included statements that Jews were victims of a 'deliberate and systematic genocide' and that 'millions of Jews from Germany and the occupied Western countries were sent to the Eastern countries for extermination'. The trial firmly established a figure of 5.7 million Jews as the death toll.[37]

Yet Nuremberg did not prove definitive as Stimson and his colleagues had hoped. The Cold War put paid to hopes of a full-scale international criminal court: this was set up only in 2002, after the bloodbaths in Bosnia and Rwanda. The concept of aggressive war did not become an established norm of international law and Nuremberg, for all its significance, did not really expose the scale and horror of the Nazi extermination programme. Auschwitz, Sobibor, Treblinka and the other death camps outside Germany were again neglected: ironically Rudolf Hoess, the brutal commandant of Auschwitz, was called only as a defence witness. And although two senior army officers were among those put to death, the American emphasis on criminal conspiracy at the very top reinforced the myth that the Wehrmacht had nothing to do with Nazi genocide. It also served to exempt the population at large even though between 15 and 18 million Germans served in the armed forces during the Nazi era.[38]

But after eleven months and 50 million typed pages, the trial of twenty-two of Hitler's leading accomplices, ten of whom were hanged, served to establish Germany's war guilt for the outside world. In 1919–22 the British had been unable to hold Germany to account for wartime atrocities and for the ultimate atrocity of war itself. In 1945–6 the Americans were much more successful on both counts. The Nazi regime was, of course, in a different league from the Kaiserreich – making the case for war crimes and war guilt much easier to establish – but Nuremberg was another reason why the Second World War helped put the First into the shadows for a generation.

At the heart of Stimson's case for outlawing wars of aggression was the horrific expansion of weapons of mass destruction. 'A fair scrutiny of the last two World Wars', he argued, 'makes clear the steady intensification in the inhumanity of the weapons and methods employed by both the aggressors and the victims,' so that 'a continuance of war will in all probability end with the destruction of our civilization.' Stimson acknowledged that the United States had been caught up in this spiral of brutality. In the Pacific the US navy had waged 'unrestricted submarine warfare not unlike that which 25 years ago was the proximate cause of our entry into World War I'. He also admitted that Allied strategic bombing had taken 'the lives of hundreds of thousands of civilians' in Germany and Japan. Similar warnings about the destructive power and moral corrosion of modern weaponry had been uttered after the Great War but Stimson had in mind a new weapon that shifted the debate on to a completely new level – the atomic bomb.[39]

Consider, for a moment, the most notorious weapon pioneered in the Great War – poison gas. The human toll from gas was relatively low on the Western Front: fewer than 20,000 dead and half a million casualties, around 3 per cent of the total casualties from the war. The Russians were the main victims of gas and their losses are a matter of guesswork but most casualties of gas attacks in east and west were back in action within a few weeks. Nevertheless, front-line soldiers seem to have been more terrified of gas than artillery and this was also conveyed in some of the most celebrated war writing and art. Wilfred Owen's classic poem 'Dulce et Decorum Est' centres on the nightmare of watching a soldier who had failed to put on his gas mask in time 'guttering, choking, drowning', as if 'under a green sea'. John Singer Sargent's painting *Gassed* with its helpless line of blinded soldiers stumbling along, hand on the shoulder of the man in front, became one of the most familiar and widely reproduced images of the war in mid-1930s Britain. The idea of a man slowly being suffocated or blinded seemed somehow more dreadful than his body suddenly being blown to bits by a high-explosive shell – the fate of most of those killed in the Great War.[40]

All the Great Powers used gas in 1915–18 but Germany was the biggest producer, manufacturing more chlorine and mustard gas than Britain, France and America combined. And it was also the first country to use the new weapon, at Ypres on 22 April 1915: although the British and French quickly followed suit, this was another propaganda own-goal by the Kaiserreich, evidence of the Hun's 'cynical and bar-barous disregard of the well-known usages of civilised war' – as Field Marshal Sir John French put it with apparently unconscious irony. Germany's gas supremo was the chemist Fritz Haber: his wife, also a chemist, was outraged at what she saw as this debasement of science. Unable to persuade her husband, who insisted that death was death whatever the means, she took her own life. Like most wartime scien-tists, Haber was proud of his service for his country; being Jewish made him even keener to prove his patriotism. But in 1919, fearful he would be tried by the Allies as a war criminal, Haber fled to neutral Switzerland for some months, growing a beard to help conceal his identity. Meanwhile colleagues in his lab went on to develop the gas Zyklon B, at the time a useful insecticide but later the main killing agent in the Nazi death camps. Some of Haber's relatives would be among its victims.[41]

In 1925 a protocol to the Third Geneva Convention banned the use of biological and chemical weapons (though not their production and storage). Britain, France, Germany and America were all among the signatories, though the protocol was never formally ratified by the US Senate. During the Second World War all the belligerents stock-piled large quantities of poison gas but never used it on any scale. The United States, in particular, made renunciation into a major issue of principle. 'Use of such weapons has been outlawed by the general opinion of civilized mankind,' Roosevelt declared in June 1943. 'I state categorically that we shall under no circumstances resort to the use of such weapons unless they are first used by our enemies.' In May 1945 General George C. Marshall, the US army Chief of Staff, did propose the use of mustard gas in an invasion of Japan, arguing that it was 'no less inhumane than phosphorus and flame throwers and need not be used against dense populations or civilians' but merely against 'last pockets of resistance which had to be wiped out'. Roosevelt's ban, however, held firm: Admiral William Leahy, the White House Chief of Staff, insisted that the unprovoked use of gas 'would violate every Christian ethic I have ever heard of and all of the known laws of war. It would be an attack on the noncombatant population of the enemy.' By contrast, the administration felt little moral compunction about using the far greater and more controlled power of the atom bomb against overwhelmingly civilian targets – the cities of Hiroshima and Nagasaki. That seemed simply the logicial continuation of the 'strategic' bombing inflicted on other Japanese cities, often using incendiaries to start a deliberate inferno. In the fire-bombing of Tokyo on the night of 9 March 1945, between 80,000 and 90,000 people died – more than the death toll at Nagasaki.[42]

This American debate in 1945 about the ethics of atomic versus chemical weapons may strike us today as casuistical but it testified to the residual hold of the Great War over the moral imagination. On 6 August 1945, however, all thoughts of mustard gas simply disappeared in the mushroom cloud at Hiroshima and in another, three days later, consuming Nagasaki. There was immediate recognition that weapons of mass destruction had been revolutionized and the world was now a different place. *Life* magazine – devoting most of its 20 August issue to the story, illustrated with graphic 'before' and 'after' pictures – spoke of Hiroshima being 'obliterated' and Nagasaki being 'disemboweled'. *Time*, which had been planning a lavish cover story featuring radar as the weapon that won the war, relegated all that to page 78 in order to describe what it called 'an event so much more enormous that, relative to it, the war itself shrank to minor significance'. These issues of *Life* and *Time* appeared just as the Japanese surrendered: as *Life* observed, parodying T.S. Eliot, the war had ended with a 'bang' not a 'whimper'. Subsequently historians have debated whether the Soviet declaration of war on Japan (8 August) and the Red Army's invasion of Manchuria played a significant part in Japan's capitulation, but for most Americans in 1945 the causal chain was clear: the Bomb had ended the War. Hence the statement in *Life* and many other publications that a new era in world history had dawned: 'the atomic age'.[43]

Two weeks after Hiroshima a Gallup poll indicated that 85 per cent of Americans endorsed the dropping of the Bomb. Two months later, over half still approved of what had been done, 'without reservation'. But undercurrents of fear swirled close to the surface. 'For all we know, we have created a Frankenstein monster,' declared veteran radio commentator H.V. Kaltenborn on the very evening of

Hiroshima. 'Whatever elation there is in the world today is severely tempered by fear,' Norman Cousins editorialized in the *Saturday Review*, 'a primitive fear, the fear of the unknown, the fear of forces man can neither channel nor comprehend'. By 1946 polls showed that at least half the American public believed another world war was either certain or possible during the next quarter-century, including atomic bombs dropped on the United States.[44]

This feeling that the Bomb, though ending the Second World War, might also trigger the Third World War, grew during 1946. Twenty-two American intellectuals openly questioned the decision to use it as 'morally indefensible', including leading Protestant clergy such as Reinhold Niebuhr. The US Strategic Bombing Survey added fuel to the flames by concluding that Japan would probably have surrendered anyway by the end of 1945, without atomic bombs or invasion. And the *New Yorker* magazine devoted an entire issue to journalist John Hersey's quietly devastating description of the aftermath of Hiroshima from the perspectives of six survivors. Widely serialized in newspapers around the world, republished as a best-seller book and broadcast on ABC in America and the BBC in Britain, Hersey's *Hiroshima* exposed the stark human reality of nuclear victimhood. Cousins, in an editorial praising Hersey's account, called the bombings quite simply a 'crime'.[45]

Concerned at the negative drift of American opinion, Henry Stimson delivered an authoritative response in an article entitled 'The Decision to Use the Atomic Bomb'. He was persuaded to do so by James Conant, president of Harvard and one of the architects of the Bomb project, who warned Stimson that 'we are in danger of repeating the fallacy which occurred after World War I'. In the 1920s, Conant recalled, 'it became accepted doctrine among a group of so-called intellectuals who taught in our schools and colleges that the United States had made a great error in entering World War I, and that the error was brought about largely by the interest of powerful groups.' This revisionism became one of the intellectual foundations for isolationism in the 1930s and was, said Conant, an example of how 'a small minority' of well-placed people could effect 'a distortion of history' with grave consequences. In 1946 he did not want similar criticism of the Bomb decision to undermine America's power in the post-war world and maybe lead to another bout of appeasement – in other words revisionism about World War Two helping cause World War Three.[46]

Stimson agreed. His article, ghostwritten by the young Harvard scholar McGeorge Bundy using War Department papers, set out a clear narrative of the process of decision-making. Acknowledging that the Bomb had caused over 100,000 Japanese deaths, Stimson argued that 'this deliberate, premeditated destruction was our least abhorrent choice'. He stated that the Japanese army had already cost the Americans 300,000 casualties and still 'had the strength to cost us a million more'. The moral he drew from all this, as in his article about Nuremberg, was that 'the face of war is the face of death ... The bombs dropped on Hiroshima and Nagasaki ended a war. They also made it clear that we must never have another war' because, 'with the release of atomic energy, man's ability to destroy himself is very nearly complete.'[47]

Stimson's article, published in *Harper's Magazine* in February 1947 and widely circulated around the world, 'would stand for at least two decades as the definitive explanation of the decision to use the atomic bomb', glossing over the effect of Russian entry into the Asian war and the question of whether Japan was ready to surrender. At its heart was the widely quoted statement that killing 100,000 Japanese saved 'a million lives'. Stimson's alchemy of evils turned upon this calculus of death, yet it was creative arithmetic. As Bundy later admitted, he and Stimson did not have any official casualty estimates before them: they simply used a million as 'a nice round figure'.[48] In fact, the War Department had predicted 46,000 American dead if it were decided to invade the Japanese home islands – sobering indeed for an administration anxious to save American lives, and reason enough at the time for Hiroshima. But that was before the magnitude of the mushroom cloud became clear and in the ensuing controversy a much larger figure must have seemed tempting. Stimson's million became widely quoted and served as the benchmark for later commentary. Truman's memoirs, published in 1955, claimed that 'General Marshall told me that it might cost half a million lives to force the enemy's surrender on his home grounds' – another nice round figure raised in draft from 300,000 to avoid seeming too much at odds with Stimson's account. In his memoirs Churchill, likewise, stated in 1954 that to 'conquer the country yard by yard might well require the loss of a million American lives and half that number of British'. Whatever the precise arithmetic, big figures clearly seemed essential to justify a big, if necessary, evil.[49]

In time Americans learned to live with the Bomb through what commentator Raymond Gram Swing called 'the corrosion of familiarity'. One farmer in Arkansas who wanted to blow out some tree trunks asked the US Atomic Energy Commission in all seriousness, 'Have you got any atomic bombs the right size for the job?' Lethal drinks became known as 'Atomic Cocktails' and after the 1946 atomic test on a Pacific atoll a new two-piece women's bathing suit was named the 'Bikini' because of its explosive potential. Journalists and policymakers also hyped up the positive possibilities of the atomic age. 'Instead of filling the gasoline tank of your automobile two or three times a week,' predicted science editor David Dietz, 'you will travel for a year on a pellet of atomic energy the size of a vitamin pill.' *Collier's Magazine*'s feature on the 'Medical Dividend' included a recovered paraplegic emerging wreathed in smiles from a mushroom cloud, with his wheelchair abandoned in the background.[50]

But the underlying anxiety could not be dispelled. The Bikini tests, screened on television worldwide, drew attention not only to the power of the Bomb but also to the appalling side effects of radiation. David Bradley, a doctor who attended the tests and then published a best-selling exposé in 1949, *No Place to Hide*, warned that there was 'no real defence against atomic weapons' or any effective means of decontamination. Nuclear fallout 'may affect the land and its wealth – and therefore its people – for centuries through the persistence of radioactivity.'[51] To cap it all, in 1949, years earlier than expected, the Soviet Union tested its own atomic device. Truman responded by authorizing the hydrogen bomb project, thereby ratcheting up the arms race to a new level, and also started civil defence programmes for American cities. The debate about the Bomb peaked on both sides of the Atlantic in the 1960s, after the Cuban missile crisis, but from the dawn of the atomic age there was no doubt of the weapon's phenomenal power. In America and Britain most people in the 1940s probably accepted that its use had been necessary but there was also little doubt that, as a result of the way in which the Second World War had ended, the human race now lived in the shadow of an evil that put Belgian atrocities or poison gas into the shade.

Hannah Arendt was therefore essentially correct when she wrote that mass death – the horrifying legacy of the Great War for that generation – had been eclipsed in 1945 by the problem of evil.[52] The camps, the war trials and the atomic bomb all served to raise vast moral questions about whether human nature itself was the greatest threat to civilization. As we have seen, these questions were double-edged: in time the victors could not escape debate about their acquiescence in the Holocaust, the ethics of 'strategic bombing' and the decision to drop the atomic bombs. But, on the whole in the 1940s and 1950s, war crimes seemed overwhelmingly the domain of Germany and Japan: those countries were the original Axis of Evil. As we shall see in the rest of this chapter, the Soviet Union, the United States and Great Britain used this perception, albeit in different ways, to celebrate themselves as the 'goodies' of the Second World War. Victory was therefore sanctified by morality – further sharpening the contrast with the equivocal ending and moral ambiguity of the Great War.

Of the 'Big Three' victors in 1945 the Soviet Union suffered by far the most, with perhaps 27 million 'premature deaths'. The population figure at the start of the war in 1941, 200 million, was not reached again until 1956. Western regions of the USSR had been a battlefield twice over, as the Wehrmacht drove east to Moscow and Stalingrad and then the Red Army pushed back west to Berlin: total capital losses amounted to 30 per cent of national wealth. The Soviet Union also faced the most severe problems of post-war adjustment. The collective farm system had collapsed and famine in 1946–7 took another 2 million lives, many of them in the Ukraine, which had been decimated in 1932–3.[53] Twelve million demobilized soldiers, though lauded as heroes, were given little assistance by the regime whose goal was 'to unmake veterans as a social group as quickly as possible'. Soldiers

returning to Leningrad, where maybe a million citizens were home-
less after the city's epic nine-hundred-day siege, had to struggle
through a maze of form-filling for food, jobs, housing, clothes and
pensions, which they blamed bitterly on a corrupt bureaucracy run by
'rear-line rats'.[54]

Stalin had little incentive to focus on wartime because his own
crimes were so glaring – the failure, for instance, to foresee the
German attack in June 1941, the orders to shoot soldiers who dared
to retreat and the mass deportation of ethnic groups such as Chechens
and Tartars. So the Soviet leader quickly drew a veil over 1941–5. It
was officially stated that 7.5 million Soviet citizens had died in the
conflict – another nice round figure, large enough to be sobering but
not so high as to raise difficult questions. Fearful of 'Bonapartism',
Stalin marginalized the generals who had led the country to victory:
barely a year after conquering Berlin, Marshal Georgy Zhukov was
found guilty of 'unworthy and harmful conduct' and packed off to the
Crimea. In 1947 Stalin demoted Victory Day (9 May) from a state
holiday to an ordinary working day and crippled veterans begging for
alms were swept off the streets to live out their days in special colonies
in the far north. Given the sensitivities of the war, Soviet film-makers
tended to avoid the subject: the few war films that were made all
observed the cult of Stalin as heroic, omniscient leader – notably
Mikhail Chiaureli's *The Fall of Berlin* (1949), a seventieth birthday
present to the dictator, which ended with him descending in his plane
from the clouds, dressed in a white uniform, into the rubble of Hitler's
Reich.[55]

Stalin finally died in 1953. His successor, Nikita Khrushchev, began
to admit some of Stalin's crimes, such as the purges of the 1930s and
the shambles of June 1941. 'Stalin was devoted to the cause of socialism, but by barbaric means,' he told colleagues. 'He wiped out
everything sacred in people.' Khrushchev upped the official death toll
for the war to 20 million and credited victory not to Stalin but to 'the
magnificent and heroic deeds' of the Soviet people: 'these are the ones
who assured victory in the Great Patriotic War'. During Khrushchev's
'Thaw' the Soviet film industry produced dozens of films about
1941–5, many of them home-front romantic melodramas but also

classics such as *The Cranes are Flying* (1957) with complex characters and ambiguous meanings, suggesting that, although the war itself was heroic, not all Russians were heroes. A few movies in the 1950s did touch on 1914–18, such as the film adaptation of Mikhail Sholokhov's epic novel *The Quiet Don*, but this was usually to present 'the First Imperialist War' as a backdrop to the revolution of 1917 and the ensuing civil war – a popular topic because of the fortieth anniversary in 1957. Whereas the first edition of the *Great Soviet Encyclopedia* in 1939 had devoted over 125 pages to the causes, course and effects of the Great War, the second edition in 1958 dealt with the entire story in a mere five pages. Only the author Alexander Solzhenitsyn took that war seriously in itself but *August 1914* (1971), the opening novel of his four-volume cycle *The Red Wheel*, was first published in Paris and the work did not appear in Russia until the 1990s.[56]

The campaign of destalinization opened up a Pandora's box: were these horrors the fault of one man or a product of the whole system? After Khrushchev was toppled in 1964, Leonid Brezhnev tried to put the lid back on again. A cult of Stalin was now impossible, so instead the regime elevated the Great Patriotic War to cult status. May 1965, the twentieth anniversary, was a turning point, with Victory Day re-established as a national holiday and major museum displays opening in Moscow and other Hero Cities such as Leningrad and Volgograd (the new name for Stalingrad). In 1967 a Tomb of the Unknown Soldier was dedicated under the Kremlin Wall, nearly half a century after its Great War predecessors in Western Europe. Visiting the tomb became an integral part of the wedding-day ritual for young Muscovites, to acknowledge their debts to parents and grandparents before stepping out into the future, and the practice was emulated at war memorials across the country. Pride in the Great Patriotic War served as the cement of the crumbling Soviet system – the tragic good that justified or cloaked necessary evils. Official histories presented Stalin's frenzied Five Year Plans in the 1930s as the essential basis of heroic victory against the fascist aggressor. Many Russians still believe this in the twenty-first century.[57]

In the United States, too, 1941–5 assumed a sacred place in the nation's social memory. Three and a half years of fighting had left many more families bereaved than in the six-month campaign of 1918, with some 300,000 combat dead and another 1 million wounded. A harrowing example was the little town of Bedford, Virginia, sixteen of whose sons died on Omaha Beach on D-Day. (The shock mirrored that of some British towns in 1916 whose locally recruited Pals battalions had been mown down on the first day of the Somme.) One grieving father said he wanted to 'blow Franklin D. Roosevelt's brains out'. When the town erected a memorial ten years later, the local paper did not link the dead of the Second World War to those of the First but to the Confederates of 1861–5, America's great war, claiming the Bedford boys as 'lineal descendants of the men in gray who had followed Lee, Jackson and Stuart'.[58]

America's survivors got their rewards, unlike Soviet veterans. Sixteen million men and women had served in the armed forces, an eighth of the US population, which gave the American Legion even greater leverage than it had exerted in the 1920s. Mindful of the bonus controversy after the Great War, President Roosevelt did not want to confer special benefits on soldiers. He advocated a general package to ensure economic security for the whole nation, warning, 'People who are hungry, people who are out of a job, are the stuff of which dictatorships are made.' The remedy, he said, was a 'Second Bill of Rights' to complement the political rights guaranteed in 1791. But, cleverly picking up his slogan, the legion demanded a 'G.I. Bill of Rights' privileging veterans; it lobbied Congress assiduously, backed by the Hearst press and a petition with 1 million signatures. The GI Bill became law in June 1944: over the next decade 3.7 million veterans secured guaranteed home loans at tiny rates of interest and 7.8 million received grants for education and training.[59]

Like the Soviet Union, and much more quickly, 1941–5 was fitted by Americans into a sequential, soaring narrative. This moved from America's first crusade in 1917–18 and Wilson's tragedy through the follies of appeasement and America's 'Second Chance' to climax in total victory and the status of global 'superpower' – a word coined in 1944. Might was also right: for the *Chicago Tribune*, 'the good fortune of the world is that power and unquestionable intentions go together.' The nation's iconic war monument was not, as in the 1920s, the

Tomb of the Unknown Soldier in Arlington National Cemetery but the Iwo Jima Memorial outside the cemetery walls, erected in 1954 to honour the dead of the US Marine Corps, a third of whose losses were incurred in taking that Pacific island in 1944. Modelled on Joe Rosenthal's famous picture of marines finally raising the Stars and Stripes on top of Iwo Jima's body-strewn peak, this was a monument to hard-won triumph not poignant loss.[60]

There was, in fact, no pacifist or anti-war backlash as in the 1920s and 1930s. Lewis Milestone, director of the mood-changing 1930 classic *All Quiet on the Western Front* did not follow the same course after the Second World War. His movie *Halls of Montezuma* (1951), for instance, celebrated the heroism of marines in the Pacific against the wicked and treacherous Japanese. The definitive American war film of the post-war decades was *The Longest Day* (1962) about D-Day – masterminded by Darryl Zanuck who, as when making *Wilson*, wanted to convey a clear-cut message of good versus evil. To do so he assembled a star-studied international cast, including John Wayne, Robert Mitchum and Richard Todd.* Given substantial assistance from the American, British and French governments and filmed in black and white to enhance 'authenticity', *The Longest Day* celebrated the victors and their rightness, with few questions asked and relatively little blood or guts. Released at the height of the Cold War, just weeks before the Cuban missile crisis, it made no reference to the even more titanic struggles of the Red Army. The phrase 'The Good War' was coined by journalist Studs Terkel in the 1980s, when the Second World War looked even better against the defeat and shame of Vietnam, but this was essentially the judgment of Americans right from the summer of 1945.[61]

Of the Big Three victors, the British were somewhere in between the Soviet Union and the United States in their attitudes to the conflict. As with America the war seemed essentially positive, but the British viewed it with more nostalgia and rewarded the people even more generously. As in the Soviet Union, the myth of the war became

---

* Alexander Knox (President Wilson in Zanuck's 1944 movie) had a cameo role as Eisenhower's chief of staff.

basic to the sense of national identity, but this happened much more quickly and unequivocally. Above all, explicit contrasts with 1914–18 were central to the British perception of 1939–45.

Reflecting twenty years later on the reasons for Labour's landslide victory of 1945, Clement Attlee offered a simple contrast: 'We were looking towards the future. The Tories were looking towards the past.' Actually, the Tory manifesto contained many policies that were similar to Labour's – 'the maintenance of a high and stable level of employment', a crash programme of house-building, implementation of the Beveridge plan for national insurance and the creation of 'a comprehensive health service ... available to all citizens'. All these were recognized, especially by younger progressive Tories such as R.A. Butler, as part of the essential pay-off for the people after enduring the evils of a second great war in a generation. But the two parties differed fundamentally on the speed of implementation and the extent of state control – the Tories wishing to proceed slowly, as the economy allowed, and especially to avoid extensive nationalization. Churchill asserted on 4 June 1945 that 'no socialist system can be established without a political police' and that Labour 'would have to fall back on some form of Gestapo, no doubt very humanely directed in the first instance'. This crass piece of electioneering, just weeks after images of Belsen had filled the papers and newsreels, was a remarkable political blunder. Attlee deftly exploited it as evidence that 'the great leader in war of a united nation' was coming down to earth as 'the Party Leader of the Conservatives'. And he reminded listeners of what had happened to the country after 1918 in the hands of 'a huge reactionary majority' elected 'at the instance of the War Leader, Lloyd George'. This became a key theme of much Labour electioneering – how Lloyd George's election victory in 1918 had been followed by broken promises, industrial strife and economic slump.[62]

Labour's 1945 election manifesto, though entitled 'Let Us Face the Future', was inspired by the desire to right past wrongs and help the victims of interwar stability. State ownership of the coal mines, for instance, was depicted as the last battle in a long war that stretched back to the great strikes of 1913, 1919 and 1926. There was real emotion behind the official sign posted outside every pit on New

Year's Day 1947: 'This colliery is now managed by the National Coal Board on behalf of the People.' Similarly, nationalization of the Bank of England was partly a response to the financial crisis of 1931 which had brought down the second Labour government. In fact the party saw itself as using its massive Commons majority to deliver at last on an agenda frustrated in 1924 and again in 1929–31 by being an embattled minority government. Although Labour's reforms were not all as radical as they seemed – the new National Health Service, for instance, had to allow doctors to continue their own private practices – the whole package marked the biggest change in Britain's political landscape during the twentieth century. Equally significant, when the Tories returned to power in 1951 they accepted a good deal of Labour's nationalization, including coal, railways and the NHS, together with the Keynesian economics on which the whole programme rested. Only in the 1980s under Margaret Thatcher was this post-war consensus seriously challenged. To quote Ralf Dahrendorf, an observer of both post-war Britain and Germany, what Attlee's government did was to 'complete the interwar policies of redistribution rather than prepare the ground for a new period of growth' – making 1945–51 'a postscript to the interwar period'. Labour's agenda, he argued, was 'right in social terms, wrong in economic terms.' Some said as much at the time, questioning for instance the cost of a universal health service, but after 1939–45, especially when seen against the bitter legacies of 1918, doing what was socially 'right' seemed politically necessary.[63]

By the 1950s it was commonplace to describe Britain as a 'welfare state'. The Nazis had used the term *Wohlfahrtsstaat* to denigrate the Weimar Republic but it was picked up in Britain during the 1930s and the war as the antonym of the tyrannical 'warfare state' obsessed with power: a limited state based on democracy, consensus and concern for the public good. Only in the late 1940s, under Labour, did 'welfare state' connote centralized direction and high public spending to advance the public good. This became standard usage, though by the Thatcher era often negative rather than positive in tone.[64]

Yet Labour and their Tory successors also kept Britain going as a 'warfare state', maintaining conscription until 1960 and continuing

Britain's global role. In May 1947 Ernest Bevin, Labour's foreign secretary, rejected claims that Britain had 'ceased to be a great Power',
insisting that 'we regard ourselves as one of the Powers most vital to
the peace of the world'. He and Attlee were also sure that Britain
needed its own atomic bomb, for security and also status. 'We have
got to have this thing over here whatever it costs,' Bevin told sceptical ministers. 'We've got to have the bloody Union Jack flying on top
of it.' The high-profile retreats from empire, notably India and
Palestine in 1947–8, should therefore not distract from the basic commitment of both parties to maintaining Britain's position in Africa, the
Middle East and key South-East Asian countries such as Malaya. All
this entailed a massive financial commitment. In 1953 defence consumed 9.3 per cent of national income and social services only 5.6 per
cent. Admittedly this was at the end of the Korean War but only in the
1990s did defence spending as a proportion of national income return
to pre-1914 levels.[65]

A central justification for large armed forces was the global Cold
War. In the early 1920s a combination of relative peace and domestic
protest had spurred a rapid retreat from the excesses of war imperialism (as we have seen in Chapter Four), whereas this seemed
imprudent after 1945 in the face of Soviet and Chinese expansion.
Britain's dual commitment to both the welfare state and the warfare
state also reflected confidence about the country's capacity to pay. This
was not entirely unwarranted – in 1951 the figures for Britain's industrial production and its exports were both comparable to those for
France and West Germany *combined* – but, as we shall see in the next
chapter, by the 1960s rapidly changing economic realities would force
a radical rethink in Whitehall. In the 1950s, however, victory in the
world war confirmed underlying assumptions about Britain as a world
power.[66]

The sense of achievement shines through most of all in the caval-
cade of films about the war produced by British studios. The total
number was remarkable: roughly one hundred between 1946 and
1965. In the late 1940s some 30 million people went to the cinema
every week, at a time when the population of Britain totalled 51
million. By 1959 attendance figures had fallen below 15 million, but

this still almost matched the circulation of all national daily newspapers and many of the movies enjoyed a new lease of life when recycled on television in the 1960s and 1970s, often reaching much larger audiences. The films were striking in the essential uniformity of their message. Unlike the interwar period there was no questioning of the validity of the war; nor were soldiers on both sides depicted as essentially ordinary men led as victims to the slaughter. In most movies the Germans and Japanese were clearly 'baddies', with Nazism treated not as a special evil but essentially a continuation of the militaristic tradition that had long poisoned Germany. Because the underlying theme was the essential madness of war, so abhorrent to ordinary Britons, a few of these movies, such as *The Bridge on the River Kwai* (1957) did explore the distortions and even insanities that were necessary to make an effective soldier. But the majority were straightforward in approach and overwhelmingly positive in tone. The films were mostly about men and masculine virtues; their heroes – stars such as Jack Hawkins and Richard Todd – were generally tough and reserved, stereotypically English. Apart from occasional Australians, the contributions of the empire to victory did not figure much, nor those of allies such as the Americans, let alone the Russians. And there was not much about the home front and civilians, especially women. These movies conveyed a largely heroic narrative about the war centred on white British masculinity. Of course, people watched them mostly for action-packed entertainment – escapes from prisoner-of-war camps being particularly popular. But, at a subliminal level, the films served to reinforce the 1940 narrative of Britain Alone and they had a lasting impact on a sense of national identity.[67]

In these two chapters I have shown how British views of the Second World War redefined perceptions of the First. The end of the war in 1945 was seen as a decisive victory against demonstrable evil with Britain playing a heroic role – all very different from the experience of 1918. For two decades after 1945 the British lived, more or less contentedly, in the reflected glory of the Second World War. Only when that light began to lose its lustre did attitudes to 1939–45 begin to change. In the process 1914–18 would emerge from the shadows.

9

GENERATIONS

My generation did not fight in the Second World War. To many of us the First is as remote as the Crimean, its causes and its personnel obscure and disreputable.

Alan Clark, *The Donkeys* (1961)

I was born in that war . . . the story of us – the victims, the people, the unprivileged – has not been told before . . . we know about the sacrifices of the people who supported the system . . . But what about our fathers, who went as their dupes?

Joan Littlewood on *Oh What a Lovely War* (1963)[1]

Anniversaries matter. In private life, of course – especially those birthdays with a zero at the end – but also in the lives of nations. We have seen (in Chapters Five and Six) that the tenth anniversary of the Armistice in 1928 prompted numerous reflections on the meaning of the war, many of them nuanced and sometimes overtly sceptical. The next big wave of anniversaries, a quarter-century on, was overshadowed by an even greater conflict, which started just one month after the twenty-fifth anniversary of the outbreak of the Great

War and cast the meaning of 1914–18 in a totally new light (Chapters Seven and Eight). By the 1960s, however, the Second World War was receding into the past, with national narratives taking on a settled form. Most of the former belligerent countries used the fiftieth anniversary of the Great War between 1964 and 1968 to take a long look at that half-forgotten conflict, viewing it in the light of contemporary concerns but also with keen awareness that the generation of 1914 was passing on and that the Great War was sliding from 'memory' into 'history'.

In recent years the concept of 'cultural memory' has become central to historical writing; on a popular level the so-called 'memory boom' has fed a huge and profitable heritage industry. The pioneer in this field was the French sociologist Maurice Halbwachs in the 1920s: he argued that personal memories are not the product of solitary reflection but are formed by talk and action within the groups to which we belong – be they family, workplace, country, and so on. To convey this point he coined the term 'collective memory'. Although Halbwachs insisted that it was 'individuals as group members who remember',[2] the term 'memory' is problematic when transposed from the individual to culture and society. 'Collective memory' implies some kind of metaphysical group-mind and this led some scholars to suggest terms such as 'collected memories' or even 'collective remembrance' in order to retain a sense of personal agency without abandoning Halbwachs' emphasis on social context.[3] 'Remembrance' rather than 'memory' is the word I shall generally use in this book. A more recent influence on the field is the German Egyptologist Jan Assmann, who distinguished between 'communicative' and 'cultural' forms of social remembrance. The former is transmitted personally through conversation and other 'everyday' modes of direct communication, whereas cultural remembrance is conveyed through writings, monuments and cultural artefacts, thereby outlasting the shift of generations.[4]

Why does this memory theory matter? First, because the 1960s marked a transitional moment in the remembrance of the Great War from communicative to cultural memory. The participants were beginning to die off and this prompted vigorous efforts to 'collect' their memories before it was too late – hence the vogue for oral and family history that will be explored in the next chapter. This same awareness of being on the generational cusp also stimulated efforts at cultural remembrance, not just in print but, more influentially, through the newer media of film and television. But this memorialization of the Great War was not simply an act of 'memory', of capturing the past before it was lost for ever. As Halbwachs and his successors insisted, the effort involved an act of social construction, shaped by the circumstances, perceptions and politics of the present. As we shall see, that act of construction varied markedly from country to country, reflecting not just domestic changes in society and culture but also new patterns of international relations, including the escalating nuclear arms race and the efflorescence of the European Community. In Britain this social reconstruction of the Great War around its fiftieth anniversary served to drive 1914–18 firmly into the trenches and into poetry. Across the Irish Sea the 1966 commemorations of 1916 – the year of the Easter Rising and the first day of the Somme – helped spark civil strife in Northern Ireland that would last thirty years. And in America, 1914–18 was revisited via the country's engagement with the global Cold War.

In October 1962 humanity seemed to teeter on the brink of a third world war. As the White House and the Kremlin squared off over Soviet nuclear missiles in Cuba, there was a chilling sense that, if this war did break out, it would indeed be the war to end wars. John F. Kennedy and Nikita Khrushchev had stumbled ineptly into the missile crisis but the American president desperately wanted to avoid further miscalculations and end the face-off peacefully. He was very struck by a book published that spring by the American journalist and popular historian Barbara Tuchman, entitled *The Guns of August*. As an account of July and August 1914, Tuchman's book left much to be desired: the assassination in Sarajevo and the Habsburg ultimatum to Serbia were written off in one page as evidence of 'the bellicose frivolity of senile empires'. She focused overwhelmingly on western Europe, on the pretext that 'the inexhaustible problem of the Balkans divides itself naturally from the rest of the war' and therefore could be ignored. Tuchman began with a caricature of the world before 1914 as an age of innocence, depicting the funeral of Edward VII in London in May 1910 as a last reunion of the crowned heads of Europe: 'the sun of the old world was setting in a dying blaze of splendour never to be seen again.' Most of her book was devoted to the opening few weeks of battles in France and Belgium, with a brief 'Afterwards' insisting that 'the deadlock, fixed by the failures of the first month, determined the future course of the war, the terms of the peace, the shape of the inter-war period and the conditions of the Second Round.' By entangling 'the nations of both hemispheres in a pattern of world conflict', Tuchman declared, the whole globe was caught in a trap 'from which there was, and has been, no exit.'[5]

Tuchman's 'Afterwards' reads like an afterthought, added to satisfy a publisher's demand for 'relevance'. The precise causal chain that took her breathlessly from 1914 to 1962, from Great War to Cold War, is obscure – to put it mildly. But President Kennedy was deeply affected by the book. In an era when the Pentagon was awash with spurious business-speak rationality, he seems to have been genuinely shocked by the concatenation of accident, misunderstanding, ego and plain stupidity in 1914 as national leaders 'somehow seemed to tumble into war' rather than embarking on it as a considered act of policy. Musing about *The Guns of August* during the Cuban missile crisis, the President told his brother, 'The great danger and risk in all this is a miscalculation – a mistake in judgment.' JFK instructed that all US officers should read the book and copies were duly placed in the day room of every military base around the world.[6]

Kennedy's warnings about miscalculation now seem ironic in view of the trajectory of American foreign policy during the 1960s. In 1963 he was clearly fearful of generals once again commandeering policy as he considered his options in South Vietnam, pressed by Pentagon analysts to introduce US combat troops in order to resist communist subversion. 'They say it's necessary in order to restore confidence and maintain morale,' he told an aide wryly. But 'the troops will march in; the bands will play; the crowds will cheer; and in four days everyone will have forgotten. Then we will be told we have to send in more troops. It's like taking a drink. The effect wears off, and you have to take another.' So he sent in more 'military advisers' to take over direction of South Vietnam's war against the guerrillas, without committing combat troops. By the time of his assassination in November 1963 there were 16,000 such advisers in South Vietnam: despite his intentions Kennedy had staked out a position in Indochina that would make it harder for his successor Lyndon Baines Johnson to avoid escalation as the crisis deepened.[7] In 1965, justifying his decision to commit US combat troops, LBJ invoked not the lessons of miscalculation from the First World War but those of appeasement before the Second. 'If we are driven from the field in Viet-Nam, then no nation can ever again have the same confidence in American promises, or in American protection,' he declared in July 1965. 'Nor would surrender in Viet-Nam bring peace, because we learned from Hitler at Munich that success only feeds the appetite of aggression. The battle would be renewed in one country and then another country, bringing with it perhaps even larger and crueler conflict, as we have learned from the lessons of history.'[8]

American foreign policy in the 1960s was dominated by Cuba, a communist outpost only ninety miles from Florida, and the deepening war in Vietnam which, between 1964 and 1973, would cost 47,000 combat deaths. This was fewer than the 53,000 combat losses during America's much shorter participation in the Great War in 1917–18 but Vietnam was the first war that Americans could watch nightly on television in their own living rooms.[9] Cuba and Vietnam were seen as part of the global struggle against communism and this helped push public attention back to 1917 and the primal Bolshevik revolution. Those critical of the trajectory of US Cold War diplomacy were inspired by *The Tragedy of American Diplomacy* (1959) by the Wisconsin historian William Appleman Williams. A native of the small-town Midwest who had served in the US navy at the end of the Second World War, Bill Williams took up earlier criticisms by progressive historians in the 1920s, insisting that American foreign policy had been intended not just to promote 'freedom' and 'self-determination' abroad but also to foster an informal American 'empire' based on free trade, which would allow the innate power of the American economy to dominate global markets. At the centre of his indictment was Woodrow Wilson – understood as a 'capitalist' as much as a 'Calvinist'. Equally central was the Bolshevik revolution because Williams saw the Cold War as rooted not in American fears of Soviet military power (which was demonstrably inferior to that of the United States until at least the late 1950s) but in what he called a 'myopic and self-defeating preoccupation' with communist revolution and its threat to the established order, going back to the Red Scare of 1919. Williams' book, reissued in expanded form in 1962, became a set text for the so-called 'New Left' historians of the 1960s, its arguments widely disseminated on campuses across the country.[10]

Other historians picked up the refrain. The paperback edition of Arno Mayer's study of *The Political Origins of the New Diplomacy, 1917–18* (1959) appeared in 1964 under the catchier title *Wilson vs Lenin*. Here, it seemed, were the roots of the Cold War. In *Woodrow Wilson and World Politics* (1968) N. Gordon Levin constructed his account of 1917–19 not as the story of a tragically unfulfilled internationalism – the theme of the Wilson revival in 1944 – but around the conjunction of 'America's entrance into World War I and the Bolshevik Revolution in Russia, the two seminal events with whose endless consequences the foreign relations of the United States have since been largely concerned.' For Levin Wilson was not a 'liberal' but a 'liberal-capitalist'. He argued that, although 'losing the battle over the League of Nations', the President 'eventually triumphed in the more long-term struggle over the ultimate definition of the nature of twentieth-century American foreign policy', establishing its 'main drift toward an American liberal globalism, hostile both to traditional imperialism and to revolutionary-socialism.' Such interpretations of Wilson were much disputed but they set the parameters for Cold War debate about the meaning of America's First World War.[11]

The 1960s also stimulated debate in West Germany about 1914–18, though in very different ways. After 1945 Germans faced the most demanding task of coming to terms with their past (*Vergangenheitsbewältigung*). Although the enormity of the Holocaust was still emerging in the 1940s, there was no denying the culpability of Nazi Germany for waging war and perpetrating atrocities on a gargantuan scale. In the east the German Democratic Republic (GDR), led by communists who had always opposed Nazism, proclaimed itself as a new and authentically anti-fascist state. It was the Federal Republic of Germany (FRG) in the west whose leaders engaged in a massive and contorted struggle with the Nazi past. The venerable chancellor, Konrad Adenauer, had been an interwar opponent of the Nazis, but much of the FRG's elite in post-war politics and business were complicit in some measure with Hitler's regime. The official line was one of 'public penance' but also 'strictly limited liability' – acknowledging the appalling crimes of 1933–45 but blaming them on a small criminal clique while absolving the 'desk perpetrators' (*Schreibtischtäter*) in the bureaucracy and the armed forces, who supposedly had simply been obeying orders. Adenauer's 1951 statement of reconciliation and restitution with Israel and world Jewry made this point clearly: 'The vast majority of the German people rejected the crimes which were committed against the Jews and did not participate in them,' the chancellor asserted. 'But in the name of the German people unspeakable crimes were committed, which impose on us the duty of moral and material compensation.' In effect, Adenauer was saying, stuff happened, regrettably in Germany's name, but decent Germans would make amends. And so the Nazi era was portrayed as an exception to the course of German history. To quote the ponderous formulation of the historian Friedrich Meinecke, 'Singular therefore was the personality and singular the constellation of circumstances under which alone the party could succeed in coming to power and in compelling the German people for a limited period to follow a false path.'[12]

The idea of the Nazi era as a temporary aberration – a glitch in the works (*Betriebsunfall*)[13] – also helped to preserve remembrance of 1914–18 intact through the 1950s as essentially a good war, waged for national defence. This position, fundamental to German self-esteem, was eventually undermined in the 1960s by Fritz Fischer, a professor at Hamburg, in his book *Griff nach der Weltmacht* (1961) about Germany's grab for world power in 1914. Fischer focused on domestic pressure groups and politicians close to the policymaking elite who, he argued, had imperialist designs on eastern Europe and colonial Africa for which they were ready to risk war. Apart from rewriting 1914, he saw his book more broadly as 'a contribution to the problem of continuity in German history from the First to the Second World War'. Fischer's 900-page tome was a complex work, based on masses of new documentation from the Kaiserreich era, much of it recently returned by the Soviets to East Germany and available in Potsdam, but it was this comment about continuity that outraged the German establishment. Gerhard Ritter, dean of German historians, led the charge – attacking Fischer for manipulating evidence in order to advance 'a renewal of the war guilt clause of Versailles'.[14] Ritter, born in 1888 and so twenty years Fischer's senior, was a Great War veteran, a National Conservative and a practitioner of traditional politico-military history, whereas Fischer and acolytes such as Imanuel Geiss and Hans-Ulrich Wehler were leftists who promoted social and economic history. Ritter versus Fischer therefore represented a clash between generations, classes and historical styles which, most unusually for an academic debate, resonated in the mass media through the pages of *Die Zeit* and *Der Spiegel*. In the process both sides became ever more extreme, with Ritter persuading the German government to block travel funds for Fischer's lecture tour of the United States and Fischer eventually stating baldly in *Krieg der Illusionen* (1969) that in 1914 German leaders not merely risked a great war but wanted it and actively prepared for it.

What became known as the 'Fischer Thesis' suggested that Hitlerite expansionism was no singular aberration but part of the dynamic of German history since at least Bismarck and that it was also the responsibility of the whole people rather than just a criminal few. Here was a direct assault on the basic fictions of Adenauer's Germany and it coincided with new revelations of war crimes provided by the televised trial of Adolf Eichmann in Jerusalem in 1961 and by a series of trials of lower-level functionaries in Frankfurt in 1963–5. Together these helped make Auschwitz into the global synonym for Nazi genocide. The Fischer debate also reflected the leftward lurch of West Germany during the decade, as radical students protested against the 'silent generation' of their parents and the country eventually elected a Social Democrat-led government in 1969.

In France, as well, the two world wars were central to public debate

GENERATIONS   323

during the 1960s, but in different ways from West Germany. The French had ended up on the winning side in 1945 but the country's humiliating defeat in 1940 and the complicity of the Vichy regime with the Third Reich posed huge moral problems. When Churchill's memoirs appeared in French, his Paris publishers faithfully translated all the titles of his six volumes except for one: volume two about 1940, entitled *Their Finest Hour*, became *L'Heure tragique*. With nearly 850,000 *anciens combattants* of 1914–18 still alive in 1948, the French found it easier and more comfortable in the 1950s to commemorate La Grande Guerre rather than *les années sombres* – the dark years of 1940–4.[15] Yet the two wars were painfully entangled, not least in the person of Marshal Philippe Pétain – heroic defender of Verdun in 1916, acclaimed saviour of France in 1940 from total German occupation but vilified by the end of the war as leader of the Vichy government. In 1945 Pétain was tried and sentenced to death: this was commuted to life imprisonment and he died in exile in 1951, still a hugely controversial figure.

It was Charles de Gaulle, leader of the Free French in London during the war and president of the new Fifth Republic from 1958 to 1969, who constructed the dominant French narrative of 1939–45. In his war memoirs written during the 1950s and in his actions as head of state, de Gaulle presented a distinctive version of history with himself as the embodiment of the national will and as the defender of France against not only the German foe but also British and American allies who sought to 'vassalize' the country. His monopolistic claims were contested strenuously by the communists, who had played a major role in the Resistance movement within France and who regularly won a fifth or more of the vote in post-war elections. But in 1964 de Gaulle arranged for the remains of Jean Moulin, his emissary to the Resistance who had been tortured to death by the Nazis, to be interred in the Panthéon in Paris – mausoleum for France's *grands hommes*. The speech given there by culture minister André Malraux summed up the Gaullian version of the war: 'the Resistance equals de Gaulle; de Gaulle equals France; hence the Resistance equals France.'[16]

During the 1960s de Gaulle's rendition of history managed to paper over the ugly cracks. First, by highlighting the Resistance it sought to obscure the extent to which French people had collaborated with the Nazi occupiers. Rather like the Adenauer-era treatment of Nazism as an aberration from German history, the Vichy regime was marginalized in de Gaulle's France as the actions of a misguided few. Second, by glossing over 1940, the Gaullian narrative linked Resistance and Liberation with the heroic deeds of 1914–18. Seeking to take ideology out of the war (Vichy had espoused a version of fascism, so the theme of an anti-fascist war would have been problematic) de Gaulle depicted the struggle against Hitler as part of a Thirty Years War dating back to 1914. As early as 1941 he insisted 'the world has been at war for thirty years, for or against the universal domination of Germanism.'[17]

By the 1970s, however, what has been called 'the glacier of official memory' in France began to break up.[18] As in West Germany, the student revolt posed a challenge to established authority in history as well as politics, because both the Gaullists and communists had based their legitimacy on the pedestal of wartime. And the film *Le chagrin et la pitié* (1969) contested most of the national myths about the war. This was a four-hour account of daily life in the town of Clermont-Ferrand under German occupation, an account in which the General was conspicuous by his absence. Built around extended interviews, the film suggested that many citizens collaborated or sat on the fence and also hinted at the extent of French anti-Semitism. Although shown across Western Europe and America as *The Sorrow and the Pity*, Marcel Ophüls' film was banned for years by French television on the grounds that it 'destroys myths that the people of France still need'. It was eventually screened in a couple of Paris cinemas in 1971 and seen by some 600,000 people. Not until 1981 did French television relent but long before that *The Sorrow and the Pity* – seen or heard of – had become a *cause célèbre* in France, opening up the debate on Vichy's complicity in the deportation of the Jews and underlining the extent to which the Second World War had been a civil war in France.[19]

And so, by the late 1960s, in West Germany both wars had become profoundly negative; in France, despite the Gaullian narrative, the

dark shadows of the Second tended to obscure the continuing lustre
of the First. All very different from the situation in Britain where the
Second World War was seen as a heroic triumph. But France and West
Germany found a way to dig themselves out of the entrenched narrative of two world wars – through a process that was denied to Britain,
or more exactly the British denied to themselves. This was European
integration.

As the French socialist and Resistance leader Christian Pineau
observed, a couple of years in a Gestapo cell and Buchenwald concentration camp could inspire either a passion for revenge on Germany or
a determination that there would be no more camps.[20] Vengeance had
been the fuel of the Thirty Years War – for France in 1914 the recovery
of Alsace and Lorraine, lost in 1870, for Germany in the 1930s the
annulment of the *Diktat* of Versailles and the achievement of 'living
space' in Europe. Although no formal peace conference was held after
1945 because of the Cold War, the Treaty of Rome which Pineau
signed for France in 1957 was effectively a peace settlement for Western
Europe.

The idea of France and Germany as founder members of the
European Economic Community would have seemed totally incredible a decade before. In 1945, when de Gaulle headed France's
provisional government, French foreign policy seemed like a repeat of
1919. 'Consider this,' the General declared at a press conference: 'that
we are neighbours of Germany, that we have been invaded three
times by Germany in a single lifetime, and you will conclude that we
want no more of the Reich.' His government blocked the creation of
any central German government and, as in the 1920s, tried to hive off
the Ruhr and the Rhineland. Mindful of their 'betrayal' after 1919,
the French placed little faith in the 'Anglo-Saxons' – 'You are far away
and your soldiers will not stay long in Europe,' de Gaulle told the US
ambassador. He considered the British to be 'worn out' so that France
could expect 'nothing from them in the way of facing the Russo-
German combination'. In fact de Gaulle talked ominously in 1945
about being once again 'between two wars'.[21]

In the mid-1940s de Gaulle's successors continued the policy of
war by other means, seeking to keep Germany down, but as the

decade neared its end, the international situation changed dramatically. The Marshall Plan of 1947 and the North Atlantic Treaty in 1949 showed that America would, this time, be a reliable ally for Western Europe, while France was unable to stop America and Britain from rebuilding West German industry and creating a new government in Bonn. So French diplomats and policymakers reached back into the alternative history of the 1920s, to the ideas of technocrats such as Jacques Seydoux for Franco-German cooperation built around the synergy of German coal and French steel. In the 1920s such cooperation had been essentially private, through cartels of key manufacturers in the two countries; a quarter-century later the approach was institutionalized at the governmental level. A key mover behind the scenes was the economic planner Jean Monnet but the public face of the new policy was France's foreign minister Robert Schuman – whose life perfectly embodies the tangled story of Franco-German relations in the era of the two world wars.

Born in 1886, Schuman grew up in Luxembourg but was educated at German universities and practised law in Metz, in Lorraine, then under German control. When war broke out in 1914 he was conscripted into the German army: only medical problems ensured a desk job and saved him from having to fight against the French. After 1918, when France recovered Alsace and Lorraine, Schuman became active in French politics and he also served in the French Resistance during the next war, but his earlier life in the ever-changing Franco-German borderlands highlighted for him the pointlessness of hard-line nationalism. Equally formative in Schuman's outlook was his Catholic background and membership of the post-war Mouvement républicain populaire (MRP), which for a few critical years around 1950 acted as the cornerstone of French politics. The MRP was a Christian Democratic party: its leaders like Schuman and Georges Bidault had much in common with their Christian Democrat counterparts in Germany and Italy, Konrad Adenauer and Alcide De Gasperi. Adenaeur, a Rhinelander, was keenly aware of the historically shifting frontiers of France and Germany, and of the blood that had been shed every time they moved. De Gasperi had started his political life in 1911 as a deputy in the Austrian parliament: in those days his homeland, the Tyrol, was part of the Habsburg Empire. After the Great War, however, it was transferred to Italy and De Gasperi resumed his political career in Rome, opposing first Mussolini's fascists and then the post-war communists. Schuman, Adenauer and De Gasperi all shared a historic sense of Catholic Europe, of a Holy Roman Empire going back to Charlemagne. It was from this perspective that Schuman approached European integration. 'If one does not want to fall back [*retomber*] into the old errors in dealing with the German problem,' he insisted, 'there is only one solution and that is the European solution.' In other words, if you can't beat them, join them: that was essentially Schuman's message in May 1950 when he proposed a European Coal and Steel Community (ECSC) as 'a first step in the federation of Europe'.[22]

Coal and steel were double-edged – essential for industrial growth but also for waging war. Surrendering national control over these key assets seemed imperative for prosperity and for peace. As the French foreign ministry put it, 'We have to abandon a part of our sovereignty to a democratic European organisation which would render a new Franco-German conflict economically and politically impossible.'[23] The European Coal and Steel Community (ECSC) came into operation in 1952 with six members: France, West Germany, Italy, Belgium, Netherlands and Luxembourg. The latter three countries, which had already formed their own Benelux customs union in 1948, constituted the vanguard of Western European integration – not surprisingly given their geopolitical position, trapped, as it were, in the jaws of the Franco-German antagonism. When those jaws closed in war, Belgium, Luxembourg and the Netherlands were gobbled up.

The onward march to the Treaty of Rome and the European Economic Community (EEC) was slow and erratic. The essential deals were hammered out by France and Germany, with Adenauer insisting against his economics minister Ludwig Erhard that forging a new relationship with France was more important than the specific details. The French were therefore able to set their own terms, not least the protectionist bias of the new Common Market and preferential treatment for agriculture (an especially important sector in France). The terms would have lasting consequences for the EEC but what mattered in 1957 was doing a deal at all. 'The era of wars by West European people against one another has finally come to an end,' Adenauer proclaimed in delight. De Gaulle became president in May 1958, five months after the EEC had come into existence, and he had to accept it as a fait accompli. But he quickly forged a close rapport with the German chancellor – somewhat against expectations since de Gaulle had spent half of the Great War in German prisoner-of-war camps while Adenauer's first visit to Paris had been just before the German delegation signed the Treaty of Versailles. In a richly symbolic moment in July 1962 the two leaders received the Sacrament together at the High Altar in Reims Cathedral – sacred coronation place of French kings but also site of one of Germany's most notorious cultural 'atrocities' of 1914. Later, at the Elysée Palace, de Gaulle spoke movingly about how the long rivalry between France and Germany had led only to a cycle of victories and defeats marked by countless graves. But now, he predicted, their two countries would finally be able to realize 'the dream of unity' that had 'haunted the souls of our Continent for twenty centuries' back through Charlemagne to imperial Rome. The Franco-German treaty of 1963 featured grass-roots cooperation, such as town-twinning, youth exchanges and mutual language-learning to help promote less nationalistic attitudes among the next generation.[24]

And so, despite the difficulties both France and West Germany faced in coming to terms with the past, they were now clearly moving on. European integration promised a new and more hopeful future, transcending the animosities of two world wars. Across the Channel, British governments of the 1950s, both Labour and Conservative, were taken aback by the speed and intensity of European integration. They stood aloof from the ECSC and EEC, convinced that Britain's economic interests lay in its global trading networks with the United States and the Commonwealth rather than a tight, protectionist continental bloc. Indeed there was an underlying doubt that the 'Europeans' would really get their act together, especially given the history of the last half-century. Once the Six was up and running, however, there was a real danger of Britain being marginalized. Aside from 'the economic damage which we will suffer

Daily Mirror

FORWARD WITH THE PEOPLE

No. 12,960   ONE PENNY
Registered at G.P.O. as a Newspaper.

THUR
JULY 5
1945

DON'T LOSE IT AGAIN

Vote for them

WE reproduce on this page Zec's famous VE-Day cartoon. We do so because it expresses more poignantly than words could do the issues which face the people of this country today.

As you, the electors, with whom the destiny of the nation rests, go to the poll, there will be a gap in your ranks. The men who fought and died that their homeland and yours might live will not be there. You must vote for THEM. Others, happily spared, are unable for various reasons to have their rightful say in this election. You must represent them.

Vote on behalf of the men who won the victory for you. You failed to do so in 1918. The result is known to all. The land "fit for heroes" did not come into existence. The dole did. Short-lived prosperity gave way to long, tragic years of poverty and unemployment. Make sure that history does not repeat itself. Your vote gives you the power. Use it. Let no one turn your gaze to the past. March forward to new and happier times. The call of the men who have gone comes to you. Pay heed to it. Vote for THEM.

Remember the issues. They are national not personal. Your own interest, the future of your children, the welfare of the whole country demand that today you do your duty and

VOTE

"Here you are—don't lose it again!"

(Reproduced from our VE-Day issue without apology.)

16. Zec's cartoon for Victory Day on 8 May 1945 was reprinted by the pro-Labour *Daily Mirror* for the General Election on 5 July 1945. This warning – that the people had won the war of 1914–18 but lost the peace – was fundamental to Labour's manifesto and its post-war programme.

17. By the mid–1930s most Americans regarded their entry into the Great War as a disaster. Here banker J.P. Morgan (right) confronts Senator Gerald P. Nye of North Dakota during Nye's inquiry into how the 'merchants of death' in Wall Street and the arms industry had supposedly dragged America into Britain's war.

18. But after Pearl Harbor, Woodrow Wilson's war was gradually rehabilitated. The 1944 movie *Wilson* depicted the president (played by Alexander Knox) as an internationalist visionary, tragically frustrated by parochial pigmies on Capitol Hill.

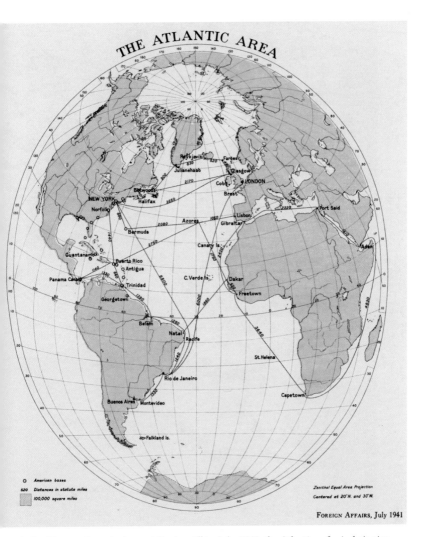

THE ATLANTIC AREA

Reykjavik
Faroes
Julianehaab
Glasgow
Cobh LONDON
Brest
Bermuda
Halifax
NEW YORK
Norfolk
Port Said
Lisbon
Azores
Gibraltar
Bermuda
Canary Is.
Aden
Guantanamo
Puerto Rico
Antigua
Panama Canal
Trinidad
C.Verde Is.
Dakar
Freetown
Georgetown
Belem
Natal Recife
St.Helena
Rio de Janeiro
Capetown
Buenos Aires Montevideo
Falkland Is.

○ American bases
620 Distances in statute miles
▨ 100,000 square miles

Zenithal Equal Area Projection
Centered at 20°N. and 30°W.

FOREIGN AFFAIRS, July 1941

19. In this map from the journal *Foreign Affairs*, July 1941, the Atlantic – for isolationists
an oceanic barrier against aggressors – becomes a lake linking the countries of Western
Civilization. This points towards the 'North Atlantic Treaty' of 1949.

Opening captions from the BBC TV series *The Great War* (1964), which helped reshape British attitudes fifty years on. The descent into the hell of the trenches (20, above) and (21, below) the haunted face of a solitary survivor.

with the voices of
SIR MICHAEL REDGRAVE
as
Narrator

SIR RALPH RICHARDSON
as
Douglas Haig

22. In fact the lone soldier had been cropped from a group photo of Royal Irish Riflemen on the Somme in 1916, but the image has become perhaps the most familiar face of a Great War Tommy – used here (23) for the cover of a book to accompany the Imperial War Museum's 2002 exhibition about 1914–18 war poets.

ANTHEM
FOR
DOOMED
YOUTH

Twelve Soldier Poets
of the First World War

JON STALLWORTHY

24. Edmund Blunden, one of the soldier poets who survived 1918, helped shape our sense of 'true' Great War poetry through his introductions to anthologies and his editing of Wilfred Owen's poems.

25. The Central London Recruiting Depot, August 1914. Men queuing for war, it seemed to Philip Larkin, like crowds to watch a cricket match. This picture inspired his poem 'MCMXIV' (published 1964), which evoked an idyllic pre-war world.

By the late 1990s Northern Ireland was finally moving out of The Troubles. The Island of Ireland Peace Tower (26, top left), near Mesen/Messines in Belgium, commemorated the men of the whole of Ireland who fought in the British Army in 1914–18. It was dedicated by Mary McAleese, the Irish president, and Queen Elizabeth II on 11 November 1998 (27, top right). Three tablets (28, below) record the dead from the Ulster division and two Irish divisions who fought alongside each other in 1917.

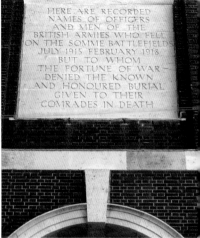

Sir Edwin Lutyens' great arch at Thiepval (29, left) is a 'Memorial to the Missing of the Somme' (30, above). In front are the graves of 300 French soldiers (crosses) and 300 British soldiers (headstones).

Headstones for unidentified British soldiers bore the legend 'Known Unto God' (31, above). On the arches (32, right) are etched the names of some 72,000 British soldiers whose remains were never found.

from the consolidation of the Six,' a Whitehall committee warned, 'if we try to remain aloof from them ... we shall run the risk of losing political influence and of ceasing to be able to exercise any claim to be a world Power.'[25]

Two considerations gave point to this warning. First, the British Empire was contracting suddenly and sharply. Seventeen British colonies gained their independence in 1960–4, compared with only three in the period 1948–60. Secondly, the United States enthusiastically backed the process of integration, welcoming this sign that the ever-feuding Europeans were finally burying the hatchet. Britain could not afford to remain outside Europe's new magic circle if it wanted to retain credibility in Washington. Britain's impotence during the Cuban missile crisis, despite being a nuclear power, added to the sense of marginality. When former US secretary of state Dean Acheson declared in December 1962 that 'Great Britain has lost an Empire and has not yet found a role' he struck a very raw nerve in London. Prime Minister Harold Macmillan issued a lofty rebuke, claiming that Acheson had 'fallen into an error which has been made by quite a lot of people in the course of the last four hundred years', from Philip II of Spain and Napoleon to the Kaiser and Hitler. But this missed the point: a heroic saga of past victories cut little ice in the New Europe and the post-colonial world.[26]

Acheson's warning proved apt when, in 1963 and again in 1967, de Gaulle vetoed Britain's application to join the EEC on the grounds that the country was not truly 'European' and would act as a 'Trojan horse' for American influence. The French President still smarted at his position of inferiority when exiled in Britain between 1940 and 1944. He had not forgotten Churchill's warning on the eve of D-Day that the transatlantic alliance would always be Britain's first principle of foreign policy: 'each time we must choose between Europe and the open sea, we shall always choose the open sea.' The dramatic events of 1940 had indeed proved a great divide between Britain and France and, more generally, Britain and the continent. By the time de Gaulle's successor, Georges Pompidou, relented and the British were finally able to join the EEC in 1973, the community had been in operation for a decade and a half. The original deal-making among the Six had set firm, requiring Britain to accept arrangements that did not really fit its economic interests.[27]

As the New Europe rose and the British Empire crumbled, Britain's heroic narrative about the Second World War began to look less compelling. Our 'finest hour' remained sacrosanct but doubts grew about what victory had really achieved. Churchill's death in January 1965, almost twenty years after V-E Day, was taken by many to mark the end of 'the post-war era' – so powerful had been his hold on national life and thought. On his ninetieth birthday, the year before, Churchill had received 300,000 cards; a similar number of people filed past his coffin as it lay for three days in Westminster Hall. The state funeral, modelled on those of Wellington and Gladstone but watched by 25 million Britons on television and by maybe half a billion around the world, was superbly choreographed and movingly elegiac. Labour politician Richard Crossman called it 'a day of orgiastic self-condolence on the end of our imperial destiny'. With Churchill's death, observed *The Economist*, 'an era, even the memory of an era, fades into the past. We participate today in a great recessional, and at a time to start afresh.' Most sharply John Grigg, in *The Guardian*, commented that Churchill had won 'a delusive victory for Britain' in 1945 because the country's power was shattered in the process. His death relieved the British of 'a well-loved presence' but also of 'a psychological burden'. Now, said Grigg, 'we can take stock ... face contemporary facts unblinkingly and shape our policies accordingly.'[28]

Whether 1960s Britain faced the future unblinkingly is debatable. But Churchill's funeral, the passing of the post-war era and the apparently endless Cold War all helped the British look back beyond 1939–45 to discover a new past – the Great War.

A taste of things to come was a book entitled *The Donkeys* (1961) by Alan Clark about the battle of Loos in 1915, during which Britain's 'old professional army' was destroyed. Clark, the son of art historian Kenneth Clark, was a maverick on the make who had no scruples about cutting corners. He ascribed his title to an exchange between Ludendorff and his chief of staff Max Hoffmann (whose name Clark misspelled) which was sourced to Falkenhayn's memoirs.

| *Ludendorff*: | The English soldiers fight like lions. |
| *Hoffman* [sic]: | True. But don't we know that they are lions led by donkeys. |

Years later, however, Clark admitted to having made up the exchange – adapting for his own ends a phrase used in several earlier wars. His book was a sustained indictment of Britain's generals, notably Sir John French ('a weak-willed man' of 'very secondary mental calibre') and Sir Douglas Haig (whose progress 'owed more to influential connections than to natural ability'), for remorselessly driving brave men into 'hopeless offensives'. Clark was mostly reworking criticisms from the 1930s, but these were unfamiliar to a new generation and made a considerable impact. Above all, Clark saw the value of a catchy title: thanks to him and despite the efforts of later military historians, the tag 'lions led by donkeys' has become the accepted shorthand for the story of the British army in the Great War.[29]

To understand quite why this happened we need to explore further the revisiting of Britain's Great War during the 1960s. From the flood of anniversary offerings a play, a book and a television series left indelible impressions on British attitudes.

Oh What a Lovely War, a product of Joan Littlewood's Theatre Workshop, opened in East London in March 1963 but proved such a hit that it quickly moved to the West End. Deliberately untheatrical in style, it blended the techniques of Brecht and other continental modernists with the older British traditions of the music hall – drawing the audience into the action. This was workers' theatre, a bottom-up, lower-class view of the war. In Littlewood's view, the stories of the politicians and commanders were well known but not those of 'the victims, the people, the unprivileged ... what about our fathers, who went as their dupes?' The cast, attired as pierrots to suggest the sad clowns who were sent to war, sang soldier songs (one of which became the title) and acted out scenes caricaturing the story of lions led by donkeys. Alan Clark secured damages for unacknowledged use of material from his book and the play was popularly assumed to be based on his work.[30]

In fact *Oh What a Lovely War* drew on a potpourri of sources, often using quotations out of context to skewer the generals.

Haig:	We must break through.
British General:	Regardless of loss, sir?
Haig:	The loss of, say, another 300,000 men may lead to really great results.[31]

The drama was played out in front of a screen on which were projected photographs from the war and a news panel displaying headline points about the battles. For instance: 'November ... Somme Battle Ends ... Total Loss 1,332,000 Men ... Gain Nil.' The camaraderie between the donkeys on both sides is depicted in a long scene about the Christmas truce in 1914. These men, British and Germans, are the victims of a war that is without point:

British Admiral:	Have you got a plan?
British General:	Of course.
Slide 5:	*A blank*

And without values:

America:	My president is deeply grieved by this war ...
Britain:	I understand he's a very sick man.
America	Yes, he's an idealist.

By the end of the play all the belligerents are predicting victory (aka *Sieg*) in nineteen-eighteen, or nineteen, or twenty, or twenty-five, and so on – 'any advance on sixty-four? Plenty more numbers where they came from.' Slides of exhausted soldiers lead into a final reprise of the title song.[32]

Oh What a Lovely War led from lost innocence in Act One to war without end in Act Two. Significantly it had nothing to say about how and why the war did end in 1918, simply announcing on the news panel that 'the war to end wars ... killed ten million'. The ending became more poignant when the play was turned into a movie in 1969, directed by Richard Attenborough (now with an exclamation mark added after the *Oh*). The cast-list boasted most of the luminaries of British stage and screen – from Laurence Olivier to John Mills, from Vanessa Redgrave to Maggie Smith. The line-up was as stellar as *The Longest Day*, except that this was a film to satirize war rather than celebrate it. The pierrots disappeared but the air of frivolity was enhanced by setting the war show on Brighton Pier. All those who pay to enter/join up come from the Smith family. At the end the last Smith is transported from the trenches via the red tape of the peace conference back to the Sussex Downs, where his dead comrades and their white-clad womenfolk gradually dissolve into an infinitude of white crosses. One reviewer described the movie as 'the most pacifist statement since *All Quiet on the Western Front*' and this comparison was apt. There had, in fact, been no British film directly about the trenches since 1931: the Great War films that were made concentrated instead on less sensitive themes such as spies – Hitchcock's *Secret Agent* (1936) being a classic. *Oh! What a Lovely War* was also the first British film to discuss the causes of the war, dismissing it as a family quarrel among the crowned heads of Europe.[33]

To some, this was all propaganda masquerading as history. Oliver Lyttelton, Viscount Chandos – an Old Etonian Guards officer from the Great War – remarked plaintively that 'we, by which I mean both officers and men . . . thought we were fighting in a worthy cause, and had no idea that our efforts would one day appear to Miss Littlewood as merely absurd.' But what audiences actually made of *Oh What a Lovely War* is an open question. Many recognized the caricature of history but were moved by the songs, which older people often found particularly evocative. 'For those of us who fought in that war and were lucky to survive it,' wrote one reviewer, 'this show conjures up memories that are not all painful. To hear the songs we sang – even though the younger generation doesn't know how to sing them – is to catch again the whiff of that wry, disillusioned resignation with which our armies faced trench life.' It was entertainment and nostalgia, rather than the potency of political theatre, which drew many people to the play and ensured its move to the West End.[34] The film, perhaps, had a more subliminal effect. Its sustained satire of the military elite and its powerful ending, far more didactic than in the play, preached a clear anti-war message. Above all, the young, without any memories or knowledge of the war, were offered no explanation of what happened in 1914–18 – just a sense of meandering pointlessness, teetering between tragedy and farce.

The lack of a meaningful narrative about the Great War was highlighted by the success of A.J.P. Taylor's *The First World War: An Illustrated History*, published in 1963 a few months after the opening of *Oh What a Lovely War*. This has been described as 'almost certainly the most widely read historical work on the war as a whole in the English language' – selling 250,000 copies in its first quarter-century.[35] The volume was originally intended as a coffee-table book, for which Alan Taylor was enlisted simply to help choose two hundred unusual photographs and add some accompanying text. But Taylor, then in his mid-fifties, was at the height of his powers as both a historian and a controversialist – renowned for his opinionated newspaper columns and for his virtuoso television lectures, delivered live, to time and without a note. His iconoclastic book *The Origins of the Second World War* had caused a storm in 1961 and he was keen to turn his fire on to the Great War. The particular impact of his illustrated history stemmed from two distinctive features. First, its breezy, ironic tone, totally lacking in deference and often verging on farce (revealingly Taylor dedicated the book to Joan Littlewood). The captions were particularly impish. Sir John French, scurrying through London in top hat and tails, is described as being 'in training for the retreat from Mons'. As for Field Marshal Haig, 'He relied on the divine help, became an earl and received £100,000 from parliament.' Another picture is captioned 'President Wilson and his Cabinet prepare to rule the world', while a photo of the British Prime Minister, a notorious womanizer, carries the legend 'Lloyd George casts an expert eye over munitions girls'. Taylor's 'palpable lack of deference' marked 'a departure from previous historical representations of the war.'[36]

In another way, too, Taylor broke new ground: his book was the first short and incisive overview of the whole conflict, offering a clear

and compelling argument. The instant histories that had appeared
after 1918 were mostly long, plodding chronologies of battles, lacking
interpretative power. The most famous, published by the novelist
John Buchan in 1922, was a four-volume reworking of his magazine
articles during the war – heavy on narrative, light on analysis and necessarily striking a cautiously positive note about the future. No one
struggling through these volumes would gain much sense of what the
war had been about. They might have done so from Basil Liddell
Hart's *The Real War* (1930), but he offered a very partial and partisan
view of the conflict. Liddell Hart focused on strategy and operations
with little discussion of diplomacy or (despite the book's title) the
experience of soldiers. He was preoccupied with the Western Front
and also deliberately raced over the climactic battles in France in 1918
to ram home his *idée fixe* that the naval blockade not Haig's army had
been 'the decisive agency' in winning the war. *A History of the Great
War* (1934) by the Oxford historian and war veteran Charles Cruttwell
was less openly opinionated and had more to say on soldierly experience but it was even more narrowly a history of military operations
than Liddell Hart's volume.[37]

In other words, by the time the Great War was overtaken by instant
histories of the Second World War, there existed no clear and compelling popular narrative of 1914–18. Certainly nothing compared to
Churchill's speech-bites during the war and book titles from his memoirs which were already inscribing the British narrative of 1939–45.
This was the gap that Taylor triumphantly filled almost fifty years on
with his succinct, barbed and highly readable illustrated history.

From start to finish Taylor depicted the war as a succession of
accidents, the product of human error. Contrary to the assumption
that great events have great causes, he found it hard to discover any
'profound forces' at work behind the outbreak of the conflict: quite
simply 'statesmen miscalculated' in July 1914. 'The deterrent on
which they relied failed to deter,' Taylor wrote pointedly, just a few
months after the Cuban missile crisis. Once mobilization began, the
process developed a momentum of its own because of the need to get
troops to the right places before it was too late. War, declared Taylor
tendentiously, was 'imposed on the statesmen of Europe by railway

timetables. It was an unexpected climax to the railway age.' Picking up
Alan Clark's epigraph he claimed that the 'lions led by donkeys' were
not merely British: 'all the peoples were in the same boat. The war
was beyond the capacity of generals and statesmen alike.' This theme
ran right through his book – from Gallipoli in 1915 to the equally
bumbling German and Allied offensives in 1918. 'No one asked what
the war was about' and 'there were no clear war aims.' Joffre's calm
confidence, asserted Taylor, was based on the belief that 'one of these
days all the Germans would be killed, even if far more British and
Frenchmen were killed in the process.' The war eventually ended, as
it had begun, with miscalculation. Ludendorff's 'rather childish cunning' in asking for an armistice that he intended to manage actually set
in motion a complete collapse of the German home front and a revolution in Berlin. Taylor rounded things off by implying that 'there
was nothing to choose between the two sides and that the only fault
of the Germans was to have lost.'[38]

Here was a very different account of the war's origins and meaning
from the revisionism being developed by Fritz Fischer in Germany.
Instead of overriding German responsibility, which Taylor himself
had emphasized only a few years before in *The Struggle for Mastery of
Europe*,[39] he was now pushing to almost perverse extremes the 1930s
idea that the nations had 'slithered' into war and then bumbled their
way through it. His irreverent tone added to the feeling of utter irra-
tionality. 'Verdun was the most senseless episode in a war not
distinguished for sense anywhere.' Passchendaele was 'the blindest
slaughter of a blind war ... Even the generals at last realized that
something had gone wrong.' Taylor reserved his harshest words for the
first days of the Somme in July 1916, glossing over the rest of the
battle. 'Idealism perished on the Somme ... The war ceased to have
a purpose. It went on for its own sake, as a contest in endurance ...
The Somme set a picture by which future generations saw the First
World War: brave helpless soldiers; blundering obstinate generals;
nothing achieved. After the Somme men decided that the war would
go on for ever.'[40] Previously Passchendaele had featured in British
memory as the archetype of tragic sacrifice but Taylor helped set the
Somme on its own as a spectacle of futility – further strengthening the

contrast (noted in Chapter Seven) with Alamein as the triumphant turning point of Britain's Second World War.[41]

Writing from the depths of the Cold War, Taylor also placed 1914–18 within a new narrative of the twentieth century. Although addressing some of the familiar legacies of Versailles, his main interest was not in the German question or the linkages between 1919 and 1939. 'The great failure of the peacemakers', Taylor asserted, 'was that their work stopped short in eastern Europe, at the frontiers of Soviet Russia.' Although most of the world eventually extended diplomatic recognition to the Bolshevik regime, 'in a deeper sense,' he wrote, 'the non-Communist world has not "recognized" Soviet Russia to the present day. This was the most important legacy of 1919 ... Two worlds had come into existence. Hence all our troubles at the present day.' In the early 1960s Taylor was an outspoken supporter of the Campaign for Nuclear Disarmament (CND) and his version of the Great War was in part a tract for the times. Out of the mindless slaughter of European war, he was saying, there emerged an ideological divide that, fifty years on, had trapped the whole world on the brink of possible nuclear annihilation.[42]

The third distinctive British reinterpretation of 1914–18, apart from Littlewood's play and Taylor's book, was the BBC television series *The Great War*. This aired in twenty-six episodes from 30 May to 22 November 1964, as the centrepiece of the BBC's commemoration of the fiftieth anniversary of the outbreak of the war and it also served to launch the new BBC2 channel. Replayed on BBC1 over the autumn and winter of 1964–5, it reached on average around 8 million people, almost one-fifth of the total viewing population, which put it on a par with some of the most popular contemporary television, such as the police series *Z Cars* and *The Dick Emery Show*. But the audience reaction index averaged about twenty points higher than these household favourites, at well over eighty, which was comparable to an FA Cup Final or a royal wedding. How to explain such impact remains a matter of debate. In part it is attributable to the scope and novelty of the series – masses of unknown silent archive film enhanced with sound effects, interviews with veterans and specially composed music, plus the voices of some of the greatest British actors of the era headed by Sir Michael Redgrave as the sonorous narrator. The footage also looked extremely realistic, having been 'stretch-printed' at considerable expense from the original sixteen frames a second to the modern twenty-four frames, thereby eliminating the intrinsic jerkiness of old films. Seeing and hearing 1914–18 as a real war came as a revelation to a generation reared on movies of 1939–45. Many viewers approached the series with personal and familial interests: here was a chance to find out what dad or granddad had done in the war. And many veterans, now in their seventies, found the series a cathartic opportunity to excavate a buried past, as if the BBC had created 'a safe space in which memories could be retold'.[43]

The Great War was intended to offer a robust defence of the British army and its generals against the likes of Alan Clark and A.J.P. Taylor. This was particularly the aim of military historian John Terraine, the principal scriptwriter, who had recently published a highly commendatory study of Haig as commander-in-chief subtitled *The Educated Soldier*, and Tony Essex, the lead producer of the series. 'The Second World War was won by vast battles of attrition on the Eastern Front,' Essex noted: 'is it not true that in the First World War the same type of battles were fought on the Western Front and that there, in the last analysis, Germany was defeated?' His core idea for the series was that 'there is no cheap, easy or quick way to win *any* war.' This was also Terraine's view, developed most of all in his script for the battle of the Somme, episode thirteen and therefore exactly at the midpoint of the series. Terraine did not flinch from the enormity of the first of July: 'Night fell on a disaster never equalled in the British Army's history ... This was mere massacre.' But he moved on to the rest of the five-month battle, stressing how the raw soldiers of Kitchener's New Army were beginning to 'learn' – a recurrent word – as they grew 'old and wise in battle'. Terraine highlighted the damage they were inflicting on the German army which was gradually 'bleeding to death' on the Somme under the 'mighty material superiority' of the Allies. In the nightmare artillery barrage on the German trenches 'even the rats became hysterical'.[44]

Here was a powerful and sustained reading of the Somme as a successful war of attrition – prefiguring, as we shall see, a whole school of revisionist military historians. But it was also a selective reading, glossing over evidence of Haig's persistent belief that he was on the verge of a war-winning victory: hence his repeated orders for just one more push. Liddell Hart's anger at Terraine's 'wearing out' thesis and at the implication that it was only the soldiers, not the high command, who needed to learn, prompted his highly publicized resignation from *The Great War*'s team of historians. In any case, for much of the audience, the visuals overcame the words; what lingered in the mind was not Terraine's script but the images of mud and destruction, and also fragments from some of the interviews: according to one Australian veteran, 'we were living like wild animals and in fact we became wild animals.' Although Terraine aimed to show that the cost had a purpose, millions of viewers came away with a sense of futility and waste. The episode's very title 'The Devil is Coming' seemed to evoke the ubiquitous descent into hell – yet it was revealed near the end as a German soldier's comment about the first British tanks. This 'disjunction between intention and reaction' was much like that between the writing and reception of R.C. Sherriff's play *Journey's End* in 1928–9 (discussed in Chapter Five).[45]

Tony Essex's own agenda was in fact somewhat schizophrenic. Although keen to educate viewers about there being no cheap victories, he also yearned to make a tragic epic. This is evident in the striking opening title sequence, which has been described as both 'an elegy and an overture', built around a montage of three different photos from the Western Front. First a helmeted soldier stands silhouetted against the sky, gazing down at a rough wooden cross inscribed 'In Memory'. Then, in Essex's directions, 'as the music is sizzling and growing in stridency and volume', the camera begins to slide ever faster into a trench – 'tilting down into almost blackness (like Alice falling down the rabbit-hole to wonderland – only this time it's to horror).' At the bottom of the trench the camera lingers on the second key image – 'a ghastly uniformed shattered skeleton' – hollow eyes leering out, left hand clutching at its throat. Then, with the music 'strong, melodic, passionate, tragic', Essex instructed, 'pan across derelict trench to another part where two dead bodies lie. Over them tired, exhausted, with uncomprehending eyes a British soldier leans against the trench wall. He looks at camera with a strange tired appeal' as the lens tracks slowly into his face.[46]

Of the three stark images in this remarkable opening sequence, it was the staring soldier who captured the nation's imagination. He became such a cult figure that the BBC, breaking its rule about not providing prints of film footage because it did not hold the copyright, sent out hundreds of postcards. By April 1965 the *Radio Times* could reasonably claim him as 'the most famous unknown soldier in the world'. At first the Tommy was identified as Private Joseph Bailey of the 12th Yorkshire and Lancashire Regiment, who was killed on the Somme a few hours later. Subsequent research suggests that this was not his name and that the man probably served in an Irish regiment, but the Bailey story added to the poignancy of the image – a doomed, romantic hero who became a pin-up for many teenagers. One wrote, 'I am 13 and agree entirely with the girl who said "he means more to me than the Beatles."' In fact the image in the film was a fabrication: the original photograph showed the soldier not in a dark hole with corpses in the background but in an open trench surrounded by comrades. Essex had deliberately 'designed the titles as a montage of images that resonated with ideas about the war already embedded in British modern memory' (plates 20-23).[47]

It is instructive at this point to go back to the showing of the 1916 film *Battle of the Somme* in British cinemas in August and September of that year. In the Great War era the cinema held a place in popular culture that television had acquired by the mid-1960s. Twenty million cinema tickets were sold each week, overwhelmingly to people who wanted entertainment. 'All that changed, however, and changed dramatically with the release of *Battle of the Somme* in August 1916.' A black-and-white silent movie, shot in five sections with inter-titles as brief explanation, this 75-minute film seems extraordinarily crude to modern eyes. Yet it had formidable impact when first screened, playing to packed houses across the country: some 20 million people saw it in the first six weeks. Shown again and again during 1916, it was probably eventually seen by a majority of the British population. Reviews and comments repeatedly noted the film's realism – 'the real thing at last', commented the *Manchester*

Guardian. 'Crowded audiences', *The Times* reported, 'were interested and thrilled to have the realities of war brought so vividly before them, and if women had sometimes to shut their eyes to escape for a moment from the tragedy of the toll of battle which the film presents, opinion seemed to be general that it was wise that the people at home should have this glimpse of what our soldiers are doing and daring and suffering in Picardy.' When the Dean of Durham protested against 'an entertainment which wounds the heart and violates the very sanctities of bereavement', he aroused passionate letters to the press. 'I have lost two near relatives,' one person wrote, 'yet I never understood their sacrifice until I had seen this film.' The brother of Frances Stevenson, Lloyd George's secretary, had been killed on the Western Front. 'I have often tried to imagine myself what he went through,' she wrote in her diary after seeing the film, 'but now I *know*, and I shall never forget.'[48]

This 'realism' was somewhat contrived: the only footage of battle, as soldiers climbed out of a trench into no-man's-land, was probably filmed afterwards behind the lines, yet the image of a wounded man slipping back into the trench was recalled endlessly by viewers as one of the most graphic moments in the film. Other scenes, such as the (silent) artillery barrage, the explosion of a massive mine, the recovery of wounded soldiers and shots of ruined villages, all conveyed destruction on a scale apparently far beyond people's imagination hitherto. What, in a larger sense, they made of it is less clear. For some reviewers, echoing the government's object in showing the film, it was expected to galvanize civilian support for the war effort. James Douglas, in *The Star*, claimed that *Battle of the Somme* was 'the only substitute for invasion', demonstrating 'the power of the moving picture to carry the war to British soil.' James Cooper in *The Times* drew a different lesson, arguing that 'no better means could be found of making English men and women determined to stop the repetition of such a war'. Yet the frightful images did not prompt demands for an immediate negotiated peace. Fairly typical were lines from the *London Evening News* used in many advertisements: 'In this picture the world will obtain some idea of what it costs in human suffering to put down the devil's domination.'[49]

In 1916, whatever people's private doubts, the devil was the enemy, not the war itself. The fighting was still going on and, as during any conflict, criticism was widely felt to be unpatriotic and unsupportive of 'our lads'. But fifty years on *The Great War* evoked very different reactions, with the negative suppressing the positive. By the 1960s the war was ancient history and the bereaved were dying off – removing the constraints of propriety. What's more, the Second World War had cast the First in a new light. Tony Essex captured and yet missed the point when he noted that Germany had to be defeated by massive battles of attrition on the Eastern Front in 1941–5, so we should acknowledge the same process at work on the Western Front in 1914–18. Crucially, he had reversed the chronological sequence. It was precisely because of the costly attrition in the West against the Kaiser that this way of war could not be repeated against Hitler. In the wake of 1914–18 Monty could not be a Haig; it would have needed a Stalin rather than a Churchill to make the British fight another Somme or Passchendaele. The Soviet leader's promiscuous disregard for human life and ruthless control over Russian society were essential for sustaining attritional warfare 1940s-style. To reprise the Somme for a 1960s television audience was bound to evoke different reactions from those of cinema-goers in 1916.

Not least because of the war poets. Even Tony Essex, despite his robust revisionism, was in their thrall. Wilfred Owen and other war writers figure in most episodes of *The Great War* and lines of poetry provided titles for many of the episodes. Essex even thought of asking Siegfried Sassoon to write a special poem for the opening title sequence.[50]

The 1960s was, in fact, the decade when the Great War poets became iconic, which is rather ironic when one considers that the most extensive bibliography of poetry from both world wars identifies 2,225 'English poets' from 1914–18 and 2,679 from 1939–45.[51] So, in terms of output, the Second World War was no less 'poetic' than the First yet, with a few exceptions such as Keith Douglas and Sidney Keyes, its 'anti-war' poets are little celebrated. This was partly because, between Dunkirk and D-Day, 'patriotic poetry was not seen as a contradiction in terms', while the war's near incomprehensible ending – Belsen and the Bomb – seemed to defy poetic expression.[52] But many writers also found the literary burden of the Great War too heavy. 'Almost all that a modern poet on active service is inspired to write, would be tautological,' Douglas argued in 1943: 'hell cannot be let loose twice'.[53]

Although a few poets of the Great War were published in individual volumes, much of the legacy of 1914–18 was handed down in anthologies – rather like the Romantic corpus of pastoral poetry in which writers like Wilfred Owen and Edward Thomas were steeped had been transmitted to their generation via canonical collections such as *The Oxford Book of English Verse*. Anthologies of poems about the Great War started to appear in the autumn of 1914. Most were collated by older men of a literary background who were overage for fighting but wanted to contribute to the cause. The tone of these collections was highly patriotic: it would have been almost unthinkable in 1914 and 1915 to include anti-war poems. But the introduction of conscription in 1916 'put an end to recruiting verse and helped to silence the "old men".' Fewer anthologies were published but, in those that did appear, the bulk of the poems now came from serving soldiers, mostly junior officers. In July 1918 Bertram Lloyd's *Poems Written during the Great War* represented the first anthology to target 'the cant and idealization and false glamour' with which the war had been marketed. Although patriotic collections still appeared in the early 1920s, the public quickly lost its appetite for war poetry of any sort and in the flurry of 'war books' around the tenth anniversary of the Armistice there was only one anthology of verse.[54]

This volume was, however, of considerable significance. Frederick Brereton's *An Anthology of War Poems* (1930) was eclectic in range, including civilians such as Hardy and Kipling, but soldiers critical of the war predominated – with seven offerings by Sassoon, five from Owen and three by Robert Graves. Although the poems were printed in the alphabetical order of their authors' names, the anthology was defined by a twelve-page preface by Edmund Blunden. He was a war poet and veteran, winner of the Military Cross, who had survived the Somme and Passchendaele remarkably unscathed in body, if not in mind. Small, birdlike and modest – passionate mostly about cricket and the Kent countryside – Blunden did not make a huge impact as a person and his poetry is much less celebrated than that of Owen, Sassoon or Graves. But 'as critic, editor and academic', the literary scholar Dominic Hibberd has observed, Blunden 'probably had more influence than anyone on the modern view of 1914–18 verse'.[55]

In 1928 Blunden published a little volume called *Undertones of War*, a reminiscence of 1914–18 with a selection of his own war poems. This quickly established itself as one of the classic war memoirs, along with those of Sassoon and Graves. It also revealed an obsession with his war experience that, as we have seen, was not true of all veterans. 'I must go over the ground again,' Blunden wrote in the preface. 'A voice, perhaps not my own, answers within me. You will be going over the ground again, it says, until that hour when agony's clawed face softens into the smilingness of a young spring day.' The 'voice' was right: more, perhaps, than any of the poetic survivors of Britain's Great War – even than his increasingly self-absorbed friend Sassoon – Blunden trod the Menin Road and the Ancre Valley for the rest of his life, leaving an indelible mark on our understanding of what constitutes 'war poetry'.[56]*

Blunden's preface to Brereton's 1930 anthology was tellingly entitled 'The Soldier Poets of 1914–18'. Of the 2,225 poets of 1914–18, less than one-fifth saw active service – the rest being civilians – and nearly a quarter of the total were female. But, as Blunden's title suggests, he privileged the 'soldier poets' above the rest. More particularly his 'soldiers' were junior officers, mostly from public schools. Five of these young men were given special mention in Blunden's essay, arranged chronologically to create a narrative arc. First came Rupert Brooke, the poet of 'chivalrous obligation', who 'perfected' the patriotic theme of 1914. Then Charles Sorley who, like Brooke, died early but nevertheless 'began to feel the futility of the argument, the doom of the best of men', before his demise at Loos in 1915. By 1916, amid the 'relentless crowding of men into the Golgotha', the

---

* One of his wartime nightmares was being sentenced by an angel for a petty misdemeanour. The order read: 'Menin Road; Front Line; For All Eternity.'

war had become 'a recognized error'– captured by Robert Graves. In 1917–18 it was Sassoon who mounted 'the attack on war' on 'a large scale' in his collections *The Old Huntsman* and *Counter-Attack*. Finally there was Owen, his creativity catalyzed by Sassoon, who was 'probably the greatest of the poets that were killed.' Blunden enjoined readers not to 'blame too earnestly' the young soldier poets of 1914–15 whose 'delicate and unreflecting stanzas failed to present war as it is' – they were 'not experienced' and at that time 'the country needed their sweetness'. What mattered was that amid the 'prehistoric' horrors of the Somme and Passchendaele there 'arose two poets of unshakable resolution, whose protests will not be surpassed for poetic intensity and plan or for selflessness in fighting this world's battles.' No reference here to 1918, to the war's end, or to victory because the idea of 'victory' in such a war was meaningless. For Blunden the task of war poetry was to make 'effectual and eager complaints against the survival of that false gross idol, War'. In his view the best men for that 'crusade' were those who had fought.[57]

Blunden's short introduction traced what might be called a kind of poetic 'learning curve' – one that the soldier poets of 1914–18 had painfully followed in order to gain their literary victory. His edition of *The Poems of Wilfred Owen* (1931) was largely responsible for keeping Owen's poetry alive during the 1930s. Blunden's long biographical essay in that volume also 'created what Owen had never had – a poetic character of his own'[58] as the self-sacrificial victim of a war whose immoral nature he abhorred but whose moral demands he could not escape. In 1954 another collection prepared by Blunden rescued from oblivion the verse of the poet-composer Ivor Gurney. Here were markers for the future. During the Second World War a few selections of patriotic verse from 1914–18 were published as a patriotic venture, but it was not until the fiftieth anniversary of 1914–18 that Great War anthologies became fashionable again, and now Blunden's interpretative framework came into its own.

He was asked to provide the foreword to the most durable of those anthologies, Brian Gardner's *Up the Line to Death* (1964). In this Blunden described how the poetic voice of 'idealism' in 1914 had turned into 'a cry' by 1917 and he praised Gardner for bringing the

writings of 'the Brooke, Sassoon, Owen generation' to a 'new generation', fifty years on. Gardner, a popular historian rather than a literary
scholar, penned his own Blundenesque introduction, insisting that
the 'experiences, and thus many of the emotions, of the poets were no
different from those of the rest of the generation' and laying particular emphasis on the first day of the Somme: 'After July, 1916, the poets
differed only in that they were more articulate than their comrades.'
Gardner divided up the poems in thematic sections, among them 'To
Unknown Lands' and 'Home Front', but most of his sections focused
on the trench experience which was traced along a narrative arc from
innocence ('Happy is England Now') via agony ('O, Jesus, Make it
Stop') to the 'dirge of victory ('At Last, At Last!'). The book title itself
comes from one of Sassoon's most savage satires on staff officers, 'Base
Details':

> If I were fierce, and bald, and short of breath,
> I'd live with scarlet Majors at the Base,
> And speed glum heroes up the line to death.[59]

Gardner's volume was the best known of the fiftieth-anniversary
anthologies – a staple of the school curriculum that is still in print
today – but others were equally didactic. A year later I.M. Parsons
published a collection entitled *Men Who March Away* (1965). Like
Gardner, he arranged the poems in sections, 'each representative of a
mood or a subject connected with the war'. Again Blunden's schema
shines through. After 'Visions of Glory' (evoking 'the mood of optimistic exhilaration' in 1914), we move 'from the vision to the reality'
(a section entitled 'The Bitter Truth'). Then follow 'No More Jokes'
and 'The Pity of War' (titles taken from Sassoon and Owen respectively) before sections on 'The Wounded', 'The Dead' and 'The
Aftermath' round off the anthology. Going even further, Maurice
Hussey, in his collection *Poetry of the First World War* (1967), asserted
that the poems he had chosen, though 'the work of many hands,
may for a moment be approached as that of one composite writer, the
English war poet'. His 'mind', Hussey argued, 'can be seen developing as the conduct of the war makes certain ideas less and less tenable.'

Thus the war poet moves from a mood of 'patriotic prompting' to 'a more meditative position' and then, in 1916 or 1917, either to angry protest against both the conflict and romantic poetry or else to an acceptance of war as 'the inevitable condition against which the individual's struggle is fruitless.' These three phases were expressed in sections entitled 'Before Marching' (a title from Ivor Gurney), 'Marching' (containing the bulk of the poems) and finally 'After Marching' – each with a short introduction aimed at a secondary school audience. These anthologies by Gardner, Parsons and Hussey were bought in large quantities by schools and then recycled year after year by teachers to justify the original investment.[60]

The fiftieth-anniversary anthologies sanctified Blunden's canon of Great War poetry: the verse of junior officers steeped in Romantic literature who moved from patriotic innocence to horrified candour and eventually a recognition, in Owen's now clichéd words, of 'the pity of War' rather than its glory. It was in the 1960s that Owen became the pre-eminent symbol of war poetry for British popular culture. This status was partly thanks to the efforts of Sassoon and Blunden in keeping Owen's verse in print: a fuller edition of *The Collected Poems* appeared in 1963, incorporating Blunden's 1931 memoir. Owen's war story also had a moving simplicity, dying at the head of his men in one of the last battles of the war so that the news reached his parents in Shrewsbury just as church bells announced the Armistice. And many of his poems were not rooted in the trenches, giving them a ubiquitous relevance to war in general. In 1962 Benjamin Britten used Owen's poetry in his *War Requiem*, composed for the consecration of the new Coventry Cathedral, twenty-two years after the original church had been destroyed by the Luftwaffe. Britten, a pacifist in 1939–45, had originally conceived the piece after the incineration of Hiroshima; in 1962 his setting of poems such as 'Anthem for Doomed Youth' and 'Strange Meeting' was intended to convey the universal enormity of war. Because Owen's poems spoke so much of suffering and victimhood, they fitted the British experience of the Second World War and 1960s attitudes to war in general better than poetry that focused on the moral ambiguities of fighting and killing. Thus Owen became what historian Daniel

Todman aptly calls the 'Known Poet' to set alongside the 'Unknown Warrior'.[61]

But the canon of war poetry had become increasingly detached from the trajectory of English poetry as a whole – a divergence already prefigured in the 1920s with the emergence of modernist writers such as Ezra Pound and T.S. Eliot. As Eliot became lauded as 'the greatest living English poet', recipient of the Order of Merit, Blunden remarked (to Sassoon's approval) that 'if we are to have Tom as our bard we may as well hand over the Empire to the U.S.A. – for my feeling is that to this day T.S.E. is an American and his verse is not part of our natural production'.[62] For Blunden that 'natural production' was rooted in a romanticized English landscape, celebrated by Wordsworth, Keats and other nineteenth-century pastoralists, and then savagely inverted by the war poets in their depictions of the trenches of Flanders and Picardy. Yet as the war poets became isolated from the broad flow of English and American literature, so they became for many people the true chroniclers of Great War history.

The afterlife of the war art from 1914–18 followed a rather different course from that of war poetry. During the Second World War the government again sponsored an official scheme of war art – larger and more centralized than in the Great War. The War Artists Advisory Committee (WAAC) commissioned or purchased over 5,000 works of art, of which over half ended up in the Imperial War Museum. More than 400 artists were involved, including 52 women. Yet this vast effort had relatively little cultural impact: even Kenneth Clark, chairman of the WAAC, admitted that much of the work was rather tame.[63]

Part of the reason was stylistic. Whereas the official programme in the Great War had caught artists such as Richard Nevinson and Paul Nash just as they discovered continental modernism, thereby combining the shock of a new war with the shock of a new style, the art of 1939–45 was doubly familiar. Its style was firmly rooted in the English landscape tradition – nostalgically Romantic in the work of John Piper, darkly Gothic as rendered by Graham Sutherland. In the 1940s this was a style that seemed appropriate to depict the ravages of wartime, especially bombed and ruined cities, and many war artists adopted it, but the result was hardly innovative art. In any case modern industrialized warfare, for artists as for poets, was no longer surprising, as it had been for the artists of 1914–18. The most vividly depicted human beings in the war art of 1939–45 were civilians not soldiers, continental rather than British – revealed in all their pathos as the camps were opened in 1945. Both visually and morally, rather as Hannah Arendt had predicted, mere death had lost its sting for this generation. It had real impact only when bedevilled by evil.[64]

The 'Englishness' of much of this war art was self-conscious. It seemed appropriate at a time when the country was celebrating its separation from the horrors on the continent and seeking cultural roots for its own sense of distinctive identity and values. As supremo, Clark certainly pushed the idea, inveighing against theoretical approaches to art as 'essentially German' and arguing that 'the influence of international "French" painting, for twenty years a necessary tonic, is now declining, and national virtues are free to reassert themselves.' Clark felt that 'English painting cannot be grand and external as the Latin schools can; it must grow out of deep intimacy' – intimacy, for instance, with 'the countryside and the weather'.[65]

But the national mood, like the English weather, soon changed. When a thousand examples of the WAAC's war art went on display at the Royal Academy in October 1945, critical reaction was muted. 'This has been a war of many phases,' observed *The Times*, in contrast with 'the long period of static trench warfare' that 'came to typify for the public the war of 1914–18.' And artists were no exception. 'No single phase has burnt deep enough into their minds and emotions to impress itself upon their work as the mud and blasted trees of no-man's-land impressed themselves on the work of the brothers NASH, of MR. ERIC KENNINGTON and MR. C.R.W. NEVINSON thirty years ago. It is perhaps for this reason that the current war pictures, admirable as many of them are, seem to lack something in depth of feeling.' Ironically Paul Nash was again an official artist, likewise the veteran Muirhead Bone, but neither had much new to say. One of the few war artists singled out by *The Times* for 'strong penetrating emotion' was Henry Moore, for his 'half sculptural, half mummified' sleepers in the London Underground during the Blitz. Here was a modernist rendering of war, abstract yet recognizable, reminiscent of the best work of Nevinson and Nash during the Great War: something that moved beyond mere representation to hint at the universal.[66]

This autumn of British war art was eclipsed by a winter of Picasso and Matisse. Over ten weeks at the Victoria and Albert Museum this exhibition, largely funded by the French government, attracted 220,000 visitors, plus another 150,000 when on tour in Glasgow and Manchester in early 1946 – far outstripping the 20,000 in six weeks who paid to see British war art. The Picasso and Matisse exhibit 'effectively put an end to the inward-looking melancholy and nostalgia that had characterised neo-romanticism' during the war.[67] Although Picasso's work remained controversial – Winston Churchill and the President of the Royal Academy being in rare agreement in 1949 that he needed a kick up the backside – a major solo exhibition in the summer of 1960 proved a definitive turning point. Over ten weeks it was seen by nearly half a million people in a ferment of what the press called 'Picasso-mania'. Some reviewers even presented the artist as a closet Anglophile, citing as evidence his predilection for bowler hats.[68]

The 1960 exhibition was staged at the Tate Gallery, which was now fully independent of the National Gallery and had become a major collector of modernist art since the Second World War. The Tate presented these works in a cosmopolitan way, narrating modernism as a progressive history of art's 'emancipation into the universal', the redemption of culture from narrow nationalism. After 1965 the Tate also stopped hanging 'Modern British Art' separately from 'Modern Foreign Art' because 'the art of the present is indivisible and it is no service to British artists to consider them in isolation'.[69]

As modernist British art was swept up into the continental mainstream, much of the representational and landscape art from the two wars seemed increasingly marginal. By contrast, the best realist-modernist art of the Great War assumed a new stature, fulfilling the criteria of what was now deemed to constitute the artistic canon, while being recognizable and also English. This apotheosis was slower and less dramatic than the consecration of the war poets, not really evident until the 1980s. The Imperial War Museum only featured its major pieces of Great War art in a separate gallery after a big renovation in the early 1990s. But gradually the paintings of Nevinson, Nash, Sargent and Wyndham Lewis achieved public recognition, often as apt images to complement the words of Owen and his fellow war poets about lost souls, gassed soldiers and tortured landscapes. This was done systematically in a major five-month exhibition at the Imperial War Museum in 2002–3, 'Anthem for Doomed Youth: Twelve Soldier Poets of the First World War' (plate 23). And so, in an ironic symbiosis, modernist war art became the illuminator of war poetry that was anything but modernist – another very British construction.[70]

And so from the 1960s the British rediscovered the Great War with a vengeance. More exactly, they reconstructed it, in forms that accorded with contemporary social attitudes and with perceptions of how 1914–18 and 1939–45 fitted into the trajectory of modern British history. Across the Irish Sea, however, the Great War had never been forgotten – the Easter Rising and the first day of the Somme had been the founding myths of the Irish Republic and Northern Ireland – but the fiftieth anniversary of 1916 provided an opportunity to reinvent them for a new generation, with grave consequences for peace and civil harmony.

The 1960s were a time of profound change in the Irish Republic. Ever since he became Irish premier (Taoiseach) in 1932, Éamon de Valera had towered both literally and metaphorically over the country's politics – in power continuously until 1948 and then back for two more spells in the 1950s. De Valera remained a pragmatist: although Ireland was officially neutral during the Second World War, his government quietly tilted to the Allies, for instance returning American and British aircrew who had landed by mistake in the South while German offenders were interned. Yet in public, to assert Irish sovereignty, de Valera maintained a punctilious even-handedness, notoriously conveying his sympathies to the US government on the death of Roosevelt on 12 April 1945 and then three weeks later visiting the German legation in Dublin to express condolences on the death of Hitler. Morally de Valera's gesture, just as news of the death camps was hitting the headlines, was 'both senseless and deeply wounding to the millions who had suffered in the war', observes historian Robert Fisk. 'But symbolically, it could not be misunderstood: Eire had not accepted the values of the warring nations and did not intend to do so in the future.'[71]

De Valera's sense of Irish values remained rooted in the precarious early days of independence: a rural economy, as self-sufficient as possible, directed by the Catholic Church and smothered in Gaelic language and culture to insulate itself from Protestant, modernizing England. By the 1950s, however, such policies had become a recipe for economic suicide: during this baby-boom decade across Europe the Irish population actually fell by 400,000, many of them moving to Britain where per capita income was almost double the Irish average. In 1957 de Valera, now seventy-five and virtually blind, was returned to power yet again. As the only surviving senior commander from the Easter Rising, he retained an extraordinary hold over both his country and his party, Fianna Fáil. It took an energetic young civil servant heading the Department of Finance, T.K. Whitaker, to push through a change of policy. Born in 1916 and an economist by training, Ken Whitaker offered a very different vision in a paper for the Cabinet provocatively entitled 'Has Ireland a Future?' His answer was industrial development based on foreign investment and free trade, looking to eventual Irish membership of the EEC. As the Whitaker plan gained acceptance within Fianna Fáil, de Valera was finally persuaded to move out or at least sideways: in 1959 he became Ireland's elected president.[72]

His successor as Taoiseach, Sean Lemass, though also a veteran of the Easter Rising, was much more attuned to the mood of the Sixties and he threw himself into the modernization programme. Lemass wanted to wrest the saga of 1916 away from the old guard of the IRA, mired in nostalgia and still bitter about partition. Quoting the dictum of Padraig Pearse, leader of the original rebels, that 'every generation has its task', Lemass claimed that the men of 1916 would now 'accept that the historic task of this generation is to consolidate the economic foundations which support our political institutions'. He envisaged April 1966 as not just an opportunity to reflect on the 'historical significance' of 1916 but also 'a time of national stocktaking ... for trying to look ahead into the mists of the future'. True to that spirit, he announced his own retirement later in the year: 'The 1916 celebrations marked the ending of a chapter in our history and a new chapter has now to begin. As one of the 1916 generation this marked the end of the road for me also.'[73]

But instead of moving Ireland out of its past, the week of what were indeed 'celebrations' brought Easter 1916 alive for a new generation. Not so much through the traditional marches, parades and commemorative services, though some were very moving – notably dedication of a Garden of Remembrance by the blind de Valera surrounded by aged veterans, a few even on stretchers. Much more influential was the new medium of television, little more than four years old in Ireland. The state broadcaster Raidió Teilifís Éireann (RTE) devoted over fifty hours to coverage of the week's events. Particularly potent was the historical epic *Insurrection*. Unlike the BBC's *Great War* this was not a documentary but a historical drama, imagining how the events of the Rising would have been covered as hot news if television had been around in 1916. So the series mixed archive footage (the opening was newsreel of Verdun) with invented reportage from news crews and a studio anchorman (including a studio 'interview' with the commander of the British forces) and re-enactments of the fighting in the centre of Dublin. *Insurrection* was a hugely expensive enterprise, involving 93 speaking roles and 200 extras, plus the services of 300 members of the Irish defence forces. 'Before it is all over', quipped one journalist, 'I swear there'll be more people involved in recreating 1916 than there were in the original affair.' The series aired nightly at 9.15 pm in eight half-hour episodes from 10 to 17 April 1966, drawing some of the highest viewing figures of the week. It was shown again in its entirety the following month, as well as being broadcast in Britain on BBC2.[74]

Although some found *Insurrection* contrived and overhyped, the series did have a powerful impact. One member of the IRA later recalled seeing it as a child of eight in his grandmother's border farmhouse: 'Each evening we would be sitting riveted to granny's television watching what was going on. Then we were straight out the following morning and, instead of playing Cowboys and Indians or Cops and Robbers, we would immediately engage in our own version of Easter Week, which entailed storming our grandmother's hay shed and taking it over. It represented the GPO and here we were, a glorious little band of Irish rebels, holding out against the British Imperial hordes, armed with stick rifles and tin-can grenades.'[75] Of course, many children indulge in such fantasies without going on to a career of homicidal crime. But *Insurrection* did grab the imagination of the young and not-so-young. It turned the heroes of 1916 from fading icons on living-room walls into 'real people' on the television. It also transformed an ancient saga into a living drama whose outcome was both known to viewers yet also in doubt on the screen. And although the intention was to show how 1916 had paved the way for modern progressive Ireland, images of which brought the series to an end, *Insurrection* raised many unresolved questions from the past. The BBC's *Great War* had also brought to life events fifty years before, especially the experience of the Tommies, yet without rekindling Anglo-German animosities. But *Insurrection* was a drama of 'goodies' and 'baddies' and, to hardline nationalists, the 'baddies' were still winning because Ireland remained divided.

Nowhere was this message from 1916 more important than for Catholics in Northern Ireland, whose second-class status was quietly ignored by the Lemass government in its efforts to move Ireland on from the past. So in Ulster nationalists and republicans were determined to make maximum political capital out of the 1916 commemoration. Their precise object varied: the Gaelic Athletic Association, for instance, wanted to promote Irish language, sports and culture, whereas Sinn Féin, after its failed campaign of border shootings in the late 1950s, was moving to a new civic activism, using 1966 to build up support in trade unions, leftist organizations and community groups. Nationalist plans posed a real problem for the Unionist government led by Terence O'Neill. His aim was similar to that of Lemass, namely to shift Ireland, north and south, out of the entrenched mindsets of 1916. O'Neill was particularly concerned about attitudes in Britain, which bankrolled the Ulster state, ruled since 1964 by a Labour government sceptical of Unionist domination. Most of his 'reforms' were symbolic rather than substantial – he did nothing to reduce discrimination against the Catholic minority in jobs and housing or to erode Protestant domination of the police – and therefore gained little support among Catholics. But his token gestures, such as visiting Catholic schools and meeting with Lemass, were played up by hardline Protestants, notably Revd Ian Paisley, the demagogic founder of a breakaway evangelical church, as betrayals of the faith and of the Union.

The commemorative events in April 1966 therefore caught O'Neill between a rock and a hard place. Worried about reaction in London and possible IRA violence, he decided to let the marches go ahead. The most significant was a parade along the Falls Road said to be two miles long and involving 70,000 people. The form was deliberately provocative: a colour party carried the Irish tricolour, followed by large, sheet-like banners with etchings of the executed leaders of 1916. Paisley responded with a counter-march of some 5,000 people and what he called a 'thanksgiving' service in the Ulster Hall for the defeat of the 1916 'Papal plot to stab England in the back'. Denouncing O'Neill's 'appeasement', he declared that 'Ulster people are definitely not going to bow to IRA thugs.' Paisley was skilfully using the confrontation to question the Unionist credentials of O'Neill, Eton-educated scion of a landed Anglo-Irish family, by mobilizing the growing disenchantment of the Protestant working class. O'Neill, for his part, likened Paisley's movement to the threat posed by fascism in the 1930s, seeing both Paisleyism and republicanism as bent on destroying Northern Ireland's new prospects by stirring up community strife. O'Neill asked Ulster Protestants to make a 'positive' display of loyalty on 1 July when, he said, Northern Ireland would engage in 'a great national festival of remembrance for the men of the Ulster Division who fell at the Somme.' Despite his reformist agenda, O'Neill made no effort to include Catholic veterans in this commemoration, which therefore served to confirm Unionist entrenchment in their own blood sacrifice of 1916. But none of this helped head off the emboldened Paisley, who took his supporters out on to the streets in July. Clashes flared with Catholics and nationalists and by the end of the month Paisley was inside Crumlin Road jail, having refused to pay fines for public order offences. A martyr's imprisonment proved the perfect way to attract publicity and gain support. In the period 1951 to 1966 Paisley's Free Presbyterian Church had formed only thirteen congregations; in just eighteen months after July 1966 it added twelve more.[76]

Officially, the 'Troubles' in Northern Ireland are dated from October 1968 when police and civil rights marchers clashed in Derry, but O'Neill later claimed, 'It was 1966 which made 1968 inevitable.' Similar views were expressed in the Republic. During the 'great commemorative year' of 1966, declared Conor Cruise O'Brien, 'ghosts were bound to walk, both North and South.'[77] To be more precise, the ghosts were summoned and dressed up in new clothes by politicians who had their own agenda – Lemass to assist his modernization campaign, nationalists in the north to remind him of their existence, O'Neill to demonstrate 'positive' loyalism and Paisley as a way to undermine O'Neill. All of them had used and abused 'history' for their own ends.

The Troubles, of course, had many causes, especially the systemic discrimination against Catholics in Ulster. The protestors also drew on many models, not least the Civil Rights Movement in 1960s America. But the competing re-enactments of 1916 for new generations, north and south, in the television age were significant catalysts. By the 1970s Ireland seemed almost to be back in the 1916 era, with the British army on the streets and a tit-for-tat cycle of violence. Over the next thirty years some 3,500 people would be killed. As we shall see in Chapter Eleven, when the Troubles ended 1916 would be revisited anew but this time very differently.

No other countries commemorated the Great War with such passion on its fiftieth anniversary. The Soviet regime's obsession with the twentieth anniversary of victory over Nazi Germany (Chapter Eight) ensured that 1914–17 remained in the shadows, except as an 'imperialist war' that triggered the revolution. It was only in the troubled border republics of the USSR that Great War anniversaries had resonance. In April 1965 the fiftieth anniversary of the Armenian genocide by the Turks brought thousands on to the streets of the Armenian capital, Yerevan. Two years later a monument to the victims was unveiled by the Armenian communist leadership in an effort to appease popular feeling.[78]

The French experience of Great War remembrance in the 1960s was somewhat closer to that of Britain. There too a second state television channel was launched in 1964 and the government invited three historians to present long programmes on the Great War, the interwar period and the Second World War. The one about 1914–18 was produced by Marc Ferro, distinguished both as a historian and a film-maker, and it proved a landmark in its own way, being a joint Franco-German production that was aired simultaneously in both countries and later distributed by Pathé to cinemas. Eschewing interviews with survivors or with scholars, Ferro concentrated on hitherto-unseen footage from film archives all over Europe, much of it extremely compelling. Yet one 150-minute film did not compare in sustained impact with the twenty-six hours of *The Great War* on the BBC. And Ferro's subsequent book *La Grande Guerre* (1969) enjoyed nothing like the attention and sales of Taylor's illustrated history, which became 'a fundamental point of departure for all subsequent studies in the Anglo-Saxon world'.[79]

Nor did the British cult of the anti-war officer poets have any parallel on the continent. In France, only the war poetry of Guillaume Apollinaire has been taken really seriously and few general verse anthologies were published. In the 1960s the limited interest in Great War poetry centred on the *Unanimistes* circle around Jules Romains including Georges Duhamel and René Arcos. Interwar Germany saw more anthologies but, as befitted the mood of national resentment against Versailles, these were mostly collections of patriotic verse. After the demise of the Third Reich it was not until the 1980s that interest in German poetry of 1914–18 began to revive, and then mostly for Expressionist writers.[80]

This peculiar British preoccupation with the Great War via poetry rather than history became dominant during the 1960s. It reinforced another contemporary trend, emphasizing the experiences of individual soldiers rather than the big-picture issues of strategy and diplomacy, finance and production. This trend was evident elsewhere in Europe in the 1960s and 1970s but, as we shall see in the next chapter, once again the British pattern was unusual.

10

TOMMIES*

. . . there __is__ something Treblinka-like about almost all accounts of 1 July, about those long docile lines of young men . . . numbered about their necks, plodding forward across a featureless landscape to their own extermination inside the barbed wire.

John Keegan, 1976

Those long uneven lines
Standing as patiently
As if they were stretched outside
The Oval or Villa Park . . .

Philip Larkin, 1964[1]

I n this poem Philip Larkin was responding to a photograph of young men in August 1914 waiting to volunteer for Kitchener's New Armies, almost as if they were queuing to watch a game of cricket or

* 'Tommy' was the ubiquitous term for Great War soldiers, a contraction of 'Thomas Atkins' who had figured in War Office form-filling since 1815 as the specimen British private.

football (plate 25). Some 2.5 million volunteers enlisted in 1914–15, making up nearly half the total of 5.7 million soldiers who served in the British army during the Great War. Larkin's response to the photograph was wistfully romantic, investing it with images that were becoming fashionable in the 1960s about the innocent Edwardian era. A bygone age of 'moustached archaic faces' and 'farthings and sovereigns', of 'dark-clothed children' and 'pubs / Wide open all day', and of 'differently dressed servants / With tiny rooms in huge houses'. (Not surprisingly Larkin was one of the few modern poets admired by Blunden and Sassoon.) At the end he could only sigh:

Never such innocence,
Never before or since ...
Never such innocence again.[2]

Larkin's evocation of August 1914 fifty years on was entitled, with deliberate archaism, 'MCMXIV'. Here was one generation seeing another through its own eyes and imaginings. What made those 'long uneven lines' of men so poignant was what was coming to them – as we know but they did not. During the 1970s a new kind of military history sought to bring alive their war story, through books composed around the recollections of ordinary soldiers rather than the papers of generals and politicians. The object of this new history was to convey the mud, blood and trauma of battle. In the process the meaning of Britain's Great War was gradually whittled down to one sacred day, the First of July 1916 – understood as a holocaust moment.

The 1960s had seen several books about the battle of the Somme. Brian Gardner, compiler of the anthology of war poetry *Up the Line to Death*, published a short, sceptical account of the battle in 1961. He prefaced it with a deadpan quotation from the semi-official history of *Haig's Command*: 'The battle of the Somme was a great triumph for the genius of British military leadership.' For the fiftieth anniversary in 1966 the novelist John Harris brought out *The Somme: Death of a Generation*, which characterized the five-month struggle as 'a wanton pointless carnage' but also 'an epic of heroism'. Harris claimed that no battle affected the history of the world more than the Somme 'because of its far-reaching effect on the political history of the next generation', especially fostering an 'obsession with peace at any price' that paved the way to another world war.[3]

The most authoritative and balanced 1960s volume on the Somme was authored by Anthony Farrar-Hockley, a serving officer, decorated in the Second World War and Korea, but also a military historian. At the end of his book, evaluating the various controversies, he stated that 'two facts are incontrovertible': first, Haig 'did not succeed in breaking out' but, secondly, 'he weakened the German Army in the west in much the same way as the Russian Army weakened Hitler's at Stalingrad.' Farrar-Hockley estimated the casualties on each side at 600,000. 'Decades later,' he reflected, 'the sum of anguish which these figures represent horrifies us, as once it horrified Lloyd George.' But he ducked the question of blame, arguing that 'the Somme battle, as indeed the whole of the Great War, was ultimately the responsibility of the peoples of Europe and the United States, who permitted conditions to come to such a pass.'[4]

Each of these volumes dealt with the whole battle of the Somme, mostly using official histories and the memoirs of officers and politicians. Martin Middlebrook's *The First Day on the Somme*, published on 1 July 1971, was very different, and the reasons for this are worth a moment's attention. In 1966 the British government, operating what was then a fifty-year rule for the closure of official archives, opened the bulk of its documentation about the 1914–18 war. Middlebrook was an early beneficiary of this mass of material in the Public Record Office. And he was also the first to talk extensively to ordinary soldiers from the Great War, most now in their seventies – recently retired from work, with time on their hands and an inclination to ponder anew those traumatic days of their youth. Middlebrook interwove the evidence from unit records with the recollections of ex-soldiers – 526 British and 20 Germans – interviewed directly or via questionnaires. This was a very personal quest for understanding by a man who was not a professional historian. Middlebrook, born in 1932, had built up a prosperous business as a poultry farmer in

Lincolnshire. But he had always been fascinated by the Great War, not least because two soldier uncles had been among its victims and he was deeply affected by touring the Somme in 1967 – especially the sight of so many gravestones bearing the date 1 July 1916. Back home, he treated some dried Somme mud from his boots 'almost as a religious relic'.[5]

The final spur to authorship for Middlebrook was *Covenant with Death*, a 1961 novel about the Somme by John Harris, who had gone on to write the short popular history published in 1966. Harris was best known for the Inspector Pel series of crime novels (written under the pseudonym Mark Hebden) but, before becoming a freelance writer, he had been a reporter on the *Sheffield Telegraph* and got interested in the Somme from talking with survivors from the city's Pals battalion. His novel narrated the story of a fictional group of friends, from joining up, wearing their best suits, in August 1914 to being literally blown to bits on the morning of 1 July 1916 near the village of Serre. The book's title came from a verse in the book of Isaiah – 'We have made a covenant with death, and with hell are we in agreement' – which the narrator opened by chance on the day he enlisted. The 450-page novel is overly long and often lacks pace but its last sixty pages, about 1 July, are riveting, and the barbs at the end particularly telling: 'There never was an enquiry into the Somme ... After Gallipoli, many people got the sack ... But after the Somme, it went on just as it had gone on before.' The novel's final words became totemic for many former Pals: 'Two years in the making. Ten minutes in the destroying. That was our history.'[6]

After rereading *Covenant with Death* in April 1968, Martin Middlebrook told his wife, 'I'm going to write a book about the Somme, through the eyes of the ordinary soldiers.' Whereas Harris had created vivid fiction about one battalion, Middlebrook intended to write factually about all the British units on 1 July 1916. But the element of imagination was as essential to the whole creative process as the documents and the interviews: Middlebrook *knew* the Somme, but he also *felt* it; this new emotionalism was a feature of 1970s writing about Great War soldiers.[7]

Initially Middlebrook had intended to do the research and get a friend, who taught in a higher-education college, to do the writing. But that partnership did not work and eventually Middlebrook set out, with trepidation, to write the book himself despite, on his own admission, having 'written nothing longer than a business letter' for over twenty years since leaving school aged seventeen. He faced a steep learning curve – one friendly reader asked, 'Have you never heard of semi-colons?' – and the literary agent he approached needed a good deal of persuasion. But the publishers Penguin recognized the merits of his sample chapters and gave him a contract. Gradually a distinctive style evolved. Instead of laboriously turning each soldier's recollections into dry third-person prose, Middlebrook suddenly decided, 'Why not let him speak directly to the reader?' Henceforth quotations were worked into the narrative, with author and unit identified in brackets. To 'keep alive the spirit' of Kitchener's New Army, Middlebrook also retained the original Pals titles of the volunteer battalions rather than using the official names bestowed on them by the army. Thus he referred to the 15th West Yorks as 'The Leeds Pals', the 14th Royal Irish Rifles were 'The Belfast Young Citizens', and so on. In fact, dozens of regular and Territorial battalions also fought on 1 July, many of which were also decimated but, by highlighting the poignant stories of these local units, Middlebrook helped foster what has become an enduring cult of the Pals.[8]

The resultant book reads like a Greek tragedy. We know the outcome but can only watch as the men move inexorably to their fate. Middlebrook's vivid detail adds to the tension of those last hours. Here are a few examples:

The divisional commander's cheery words as they marched up to the front line: 'Good luck, men. There is not a German left in their trenches, our guns have blown them all to Hell.'

A glimpse of cavalry ready to exploit the breakthrough ... Sweat-soaked artillerymen, stripped to the waist, some with ears bleeding after days manning the deafening guns ... And freshly dug, extra-wide trenches – ready for mass burials.

'I have a lasting memory of the man who was closest to me as I marched. I was only eighteen at the time, having joined the army under age, and he was some years older than I ... "Don't worry, Bill," he said. "We'll be all right." And he spoke as gently as a mother trying to soothe a frightened child.'

A night standing in the assault trenches, too crowded to lie down ... Maybe dozing a bit, propped up against the sandbags ... Petrol tins of hot coffee for the lucky ones, with the inevitable lashing of rum. 'As we were standing in water-logged trenches ... who minded the flavour of petrol anyway?'

A midsummer dawn, very early, soon after four ... A last, massive British bombardment ... Some Tommies kneel and pray; others stare at family photos, or pull out their paybook, to fill in the will at the back ... Suddenly orders to fix bayonets.

At 7.30 am the British guns fall silent. 'It was eerie; the sun was shining out of a cloudless sky, birds hovered and swooped over the trenches, singing clearly.' And then ...[9]

After the soldiers go over the top at seven thirty, Middlebrook takes us along the front, following the battalions in turn through a narrative constructed from official war diaries and the recollections of survivors. By Chapter Eight ('Review at 8.30 A.M.') the denouement is not in doubt: 'probably half of the 66,000 British soldiers who had attacked were already casualties – 30,000 infantrymen killed or wounded in just sixty minutes!' But still the attacks go on as Middlebrook narrates what he calls 'the holocaust' through to the fall of that midsummer night.[10]

His final chapters are more reflective and analytical. With regret Middlebrook saw no alternative to mounting the attack, because of the need to support the French at Verdun, but he was severely critical of the battle plan. Principal target, following John Terraine's biography of Haig, was the Fourth Army commander, General Sir Henry Rawlinson, especially his confidence that the artillery barrage would destroy the Germans and his related refusal to follow standard infantry tactics and send in 'bombing parties' as quickly as possible to seize the enemy trenches. Instead the long lines of Tommies, often walking slowly across no-man's-land, became sitting ducks for German machine-gunners. For Middlebrook, 1 July 1916 was, therefore, both a necessary operation and also an avoidable tragedy. He acknowledged briefly that the battle of the Somme continued through the autumn and that it was there that 'the Germans lost the core of their battle-hardened army'. Yet his focus remained on the First of July as 'a separate battle in its own right'. Its final casualty list (19,240 dead and 35,493 wounded) represented the bloodiest day in the history of the British army, with losses far exceeding those in the Crimea, the Boer War and Korea combined. Middlebrook also suggested that, 'for the British at least, it was the turning point of the First World War.' Eighty per cent of the country's 2.7 million war casualties occurred after 1 July 1916, mostly on the Western Front. Having 'invested so much prestige and blood on this one day', Middlebrook asserted, Britain 'could not pull out without getting what she considered the only just return for that investment – a total victory.'[11]

In 1976 another book, *The Face of Battle*, illuminated the British experience of 1 July 1916 with comparable intensity though in a very different way. Like Middlebrook, John Keegan was a child of the interwar period (born in 1934) and therefore fought in neither of the world wars. But, as a teacher of military history at the Royal Military Academy at Sandhurst, he became increasingly dissatisfied with the 'de-sensitized treatment of war' that he and his colleagues disseminated in its 'studiedly unmilitary' setting – an 'English ducal mansion' amid serene parkland – which helped to foster a 'country-house illusion' of warfare, shaped by thought not action, words rather than blood, maps instead of mud. 'The compilers of the *British Official History of the First World War*', he observed dryly, 'have achieved the remarkable feat of writing an exhaustive account of one of the world's greatest tragedies without the display of any emotion at all.' Keegan's question, as a classroom warrior, was 'How would *I* behave in battle?' and he set out to answer it through case studies of three great English battles – Agincourt, Waterloo and the Somme – each from a very different era of military technology. By looking at how soldiers 'control their fears, staunch their wounds, go to their death', he hoped to 'catch a glimpse of the face of battle.'[12]

In his case study of 1916 Keegan discussed only the first day of the Somme. He paid tribute to Middlebrook's 'remarkable achievement', likening his book to William Siborne's classic history of Waterloo, also constructed from soldiers' recollections. Keegan did not undertake new research, either through interviews or in archives: he used the existing sources to analyse the technological encounters, especially in this case between infantry and machine guns. Like Middlebrook he mourned the Pals – 'perhaps no story of the First World War is as poignant' – but was less fulsome about their skill as soldiers, arguing that the 'stark simplicity' of the tactics (shelling and walking) were the Fourth Army staff's understandable response to the volunteers' 'lack of experience'. The first day of the Somme was not, he admitted, 'a complete military failure' but 'it had been a human tragedy' which, like Middlebrook, he described in the language of the Holocaust, asserting that there was 'something Treblinka-like' about most accounts of the First of July – 'those long docile lines of young men, shoddily uniformed, heavily burdened, numbered about their necks, plodding forward across a featureless landscape to their own extermination inside the barbed wire.' Again like Middlebrook, he saw 1 July 1916 as 'the opening of a crucial phase' of the Western Front experience, as industrialized warfare really hit home. Keegan ended his account of the Somme with the protest literature of Blunden, Graves, Sassoon and their ilk, contrasting what he called the 'eternal quality' of the best writing of the First World War with the paucity of such offerings from the Second. By way of explanation he discerned a recognition after 1914–18 that 'some limit of what human beings could and could not stand on the battlefield had at last been reached', so that 'the voice from the trenches spoke for every soldier of the industrial age'.[13]

The efforts of Middlebrook and Keegan to evoke the experience of the Great War were frowned on by traditional military historians. Correlli Barnett wrote a damning report for Penguin on Middlebrook's sample chapters, complaining that the interviewees were spouting 'pretty familiar stuff', reminiscent of Sassoon, that Middlebrook tended to 'repeat all the old bromides about the high command' and that the writing itself was 'flat and boring'. Barnett never changed his view of the book, which was also condemned by Haig's champion, Terraine.[14] Other historians complained that Middlebrook and Keegan had strengthened 'the tyrannical hold which July 1916 is now beginning to exert on British First World War studies': by focusing on the

British army's 'worst day of the whole war' they fortified 'the myth of incompetence and pointless slaughter which is all too often applied to the whole Somme campaign, and indeed to Western Front operations throughout.'[15]

A divide was now opening up between orthodox military historians who still focused on strategy, command and operations and a new breed of writers, fascinated by the soldier's experience of war. This 'new' military history was often written by self-trained amateurs like Middlebrook, building on the growing vogue for family history. A huge stimulus for that came from *Roots: The Saga of an American Family* (1976) by the African-American writer Alex Haley, which traced his family's story over the first century after Kunta Kinte arrived in Maryland in 1767 to be sold as a slave. The book and the television mini-series encouraged people worldwide to investigate their own roots. In Britain a Federation of Family History Societies was formed in 1974, helping to foster interest via publications and twice-yearly conferences, and the BBC broadcast the first of many television series on 'family history' in 1979. Specialist magazines also fostered the process. One of the earliest was *Family History Tree*, started in November 1984 by Michael and Mary Armstrong, using a portable typewriter on their dining-room table in the Cambridgeshire village of Ramsey. They were family history enthusiasts who saw a niche for such a magazine but could not attract a commercial publisher so, rather like Middlebrook, they took the plunge themselves. The Great War proved particularly fertile terrain for family historians because otherwise shadowy ancestors left a brief but clear paper trail in the official archives while serving in the armed forces. Although many documents were destroyed during the Blitz in 1940, service records for 2.75 million soldiers survived and became one of the main attractions at Britain's National Archives when the files were gradually opened from 1996.[16]

It was the new military history, rooted in this growing passion with ancestors, which attracted readers. Middlebrook's *First Day on the Somme* sold 40,000 copies in its first five years and topped 130,000 by 2005.[17] In 1986, following a series of articles in the *Barnsley Chronicle*, local author Jon Cooksey published *Pals* – the saga of the two volunteer battalions that were raised by the town and fought on the Somme in July 1916 – relying heavily on stories from survivors. This spawned a series of books on various Pals battalions, at least a dozen to date, from Accrington and Durham to Liverpool and Swansea. Most concentrate on 1914–16, especially the first days of the Somme, and say relatively little about the units during the rest of the war. In other words they conform to a now familiar narrative, established by Harris and Middlebrook, about how local history became national tragedy. It is worth noting that most of the books published during and after the Great War about Kitchener's volunteer New Armies did not single out the Pals. Their identification, almost consecration, has been a legacy of the 1970s.[18]

Like Middlebrook, Lyn Macdonald, a BBC radio producer, was drawn to the Great War after visiting the battlefields in 1972 with a group of veterans. She went freelance and began interviewing ex-soldiers for a book about the third battle of Ypres in 1917, *They Called It Passchendaele*, which was published in 1978. 'If this book reads like a novel, or even a horror story, please do not blame me,' she told readers. 'It is all true, or rather it is compiled from more than 600 true stories and eyewitness accounts of men and women who were in the blood-bath of Ypres.' The writing, she explained, 'was a straightforward task of compiling and interpreting their experiences in the light of the events that took place as the campaign unrolled.' Over the next two decades Macdonald accumulated a huge database of interviews and produced six more best-selling books on various phases of the war, including Gallipoli, the Somme and the spring of 1918, but their format remained essentially the same – built around lengthy quotations from interviews with veterans so that we can 'stand in their boots' and 'see things through their eyes'. Her narrative was essentially a framework in which to lay out, almost reverentially, the testimony of veterans.[19]

This is, however, a problematic approach to the writing of history. Although the recollections of ordinary participants can often provide fascinating and important historical detail that is not recorded in official archives, scholars cannot treat such 'testimony' as intrinsically more reliable than any other source. Consider an example from Lyn Macdonald's book about the battle of the Somme – the recollections of Lieutenant F.W. Beadle, an artillery officer, about a British cavalry charge on 14 July 1916:

> It was an incredible sight, an unbelievable sight, they galloped up with their lances and with pennants flying, up the slope to High Wood and straight into it. Of course they were falling all the way ... horses and men dropping on the ground, with no hope against the machine-guns, because the Germans up on the ridge were firing down into the valley where the soldiers were. It was an absolute rout. A magnificent sight. Tragic.[20]

Military historian Richard Holmes has dealt clinically with this vivid piece of apparently eyewitness testimony. First, as photographic evidence from 1916 makes clear, British cavalry units had dispensed with frills such as pennants. Second, a cavalry charge right into a wood that was full of summer foliage and had been heavily shelled would have been virtually impossible: High Wood on 14 July was hard enough for the infantry to get through. Finally, the war diaries of the units in question show they incurred very light casualties on that day, while inflicting considerable damage on German machine-gunners. The cavalry had been used, in effect, as mounted infantry, rapidly moving against German emplacements before dismounting and digging in. In short, High Wood was 'not the Charge of the Light Brigade', even though that was how, a half-century later, Lieutenant Beadle saw it in his mind's eye.* In Holmes' words, Beadle 'tells us precisely what we expect to hear', given our assumptions about the archaic futility of the Somme, but 'it is something that did not actually take place.'[21]

'Memory' is therefore not a quasi-photographic record of the past, more or less sharp, but rather, for all of us, an ever-changing process of construction involving past and present. Shakespeare's Henry V captured the point beautifully in his oration before the battle of Agincourt:

---

* It is probably not irrelevant that *The Charge of the Light Brigade*, Tony Richardson's movie about the notorious Crimean fiasco of 1854, had appeared in 1968 – another product of the anti-war mood of the Vietnam era.

Old men forget: yet all shall be forgot,
But he'll remember with advantages
What feats he did that day . . .[22]

'Remembering with advantages' – in other words gilding the lily, embroidering the story. This theme has been explored by Alistair Thomson in *Anzac Memories* (1987), a subtle analysis of how Australian veterans of the Great War spoke about their experiences at various points in the 1980s. To describe this process he preferred the term 'composure', using it in two senses: we compose memories 'using the public languages or meanings of our culture' and we also do so in ways that 'help us feel relatively comfortable with our lives and identities, that give us a feeling of composure'. Thomson's extended interviews showed one soldier, a natural raconteur, had an oft-used repertoire of personal anecdotes that actually mirrored almost exactly passages from his battalion's official history. Another veteran, who experienced a difficult post-war transition both psychologically and economically, took on the full 'Digger' identity – boozy, matey and irreverent – to make himself acceptable as an embodiment of Australian masculinity. A third veteran, whose nerves disintegrated under shellfire at Fromelles in 1916, was driven into silent alienation from the cult of Anzac Day on 25 April: his later conversion into a labour activist gave him a new and articulate identity as a working-class victim of imperialist folly. Yet, in retirement in the 1970s, he was finally able to address his war experiences, talking about them publicly and positively without sacrificing his anti-war principles.[23]

Reflecting on these three contrasting examples Thomson noted that oral history – in origin a justified reaction to academic fetishism about documents being the only proper source – needed to be self-critical about its own methods. What soldiers said fifty years on was not automatically 'the truth': historians had to reflect sensitively about the way such testimony was 'articulated in relation to public narratives and personal identities', both of which were in constant flux.[24]

Thomson's criticisms, applicable to the general cult of soldier 'voices' from the Great War, had particular relevance in Australia because it was in the 1970s and 1980s that the Anzac saga took a real hold on the public imagination there. In 1965 the fiftieth anniversary of the Gallipoli landings had been a somewhat muted event in Australia. Its ceremonies were dominated by ex-servicemen of the Returned and Services League (RSL), against a background of left-wing sniping that the morning service served to glorify war and excuse an afternoon of booze and gambling. For many schoolchildren Anzac Day rituals were 'solemn occasions marked by puzzling words intoned with an earnestness we could only dimly understand ... We were forever warned lest we forget. But it was far from clear what we might forget.' Some newspapers wondered whether the whole thing would simply fade away: the Sydney *Mirror* asked, 'Will Anzac Day be as meaningless to future generations as Trafalgar and Waterloo?'[25] Over the subsequent quarter-century from 1965, however, the saga of the Diggers entrenched itself in Australian public life even more deeply than that of the Tommies in Britain. Along lines that Alistair Thomson described, this reflected a new engagement between present and past.

Although Australia's 1915 baptism of fire at Gallipoli on 25 April became established during the 1920s as Australia's national day, the commemoration still featured what one celebrant called the 'crimson thread of kinship' with the 'British race'. The city of Melbourne's great Shrine of Remembrance, completed in 1934, declares on the east wall that it honours 'the men and women of Victoria who served the Empire in the war of 1914–1918'. When Australia went to war a second time in 1939, its soldiers took on the mantle of their revered predecessors as the '2nd Australian Imperial Force'.[26] Although there was a temptation in Australia during the Second World War, as in the First, to blame wartime setbacks on London's ineptitude, especially the surrender of Singapore in early 1942, it is too simple to suggest that this was the moment when Australia suddenly turned away from Britain towards America or to a policy of independent self-assertion. 'First and foremost, Australia is a Pacific power', declared the Liberal politician Percy Spender in 1944 but, he insisted, that did not 'in the slightest degree lessen her ties of kinship with Great Britain.' A continued sense of being part of a British world was particularly intense for Robert Menzies and the Liberals during their long tenure in office from 1949 to 1972 but it was also true of their Labor opponents such as Arthur Calwell and Ben Chifley.[27]

Post-war Australia was certainly strengthening its ties with America and its interactions with the countries of the Pacific – as became dramatically evident during the country's deep and controversial involvement from 1965 in America's Vietnam War, from which Britain stood aloof. But the catalyst for clear-cut policy change was not so much burgeoning Australian nationalism as declining British imperialism. Britain's decision in 1961 to apply for membership of the European Economic Community pointed up in stark symbolic terms a fundamental shift of British attention from the empire to Europe. This forced Australians, both politicians and public, to address explicitly the readjustments in the country's position that had been going on gradually for some years. Australia then moved rapidly to assert much greater independence – pushed on by Labor leaders eager to attack Menzies and his conservative colleagues for their 'forelock-tugging' towards London. In the blunt words of Paul Keating, Britain had simply 'walked out on us and joined the Common Market'.[28]

At this time when Australia's present and future seemed uncertain, a few writers aroused new interest in the country's Great War past. Ken Inglis drew attention to the now neglected war histories of C.E.W. Bean, leading popularizer of the Anzac myth. Charles Bean had been the Australian official historian for the Great War but his output was very different from the emotionless, top-down British tomes castigated by John Keegan. Bean practised bottom-up history long before it was developed in Britain by Martin Middlebrook, making extensive use in the 1920s of personal diaries, soldiers' letters and oral history. From all this he distilled the image of the Australian soldier (or Digger) as a uniquely outstanding fighter because he was a rugged product of the 'bush' and of a classless society defined above all by a deep loyalty to one's 'mates'. This latent identity was made real in war: at Gallipoli, declared Bean in 1924, nothing less than 'the consciousness of Australian nationhood was born.'[29] Bean's definition of Australian identity, resurrected by Inglis and others around the fiftieth anniversary of Gallipoli, became the template for new studies of the

Diggers of the Great War. Bill Gammage's emotionally charged *The Broken Years* (1974) drew inspiration from Bean, whose work he described as 'among the greatest contributions yet made to the history of Australia'. His book was based on extensive quotation from the diaries and letters of roughly a thousand soldiers, including 272 with whom he personally talked and corresponded. Gammage's stated aim was simply to show 'what some Australian soldiers thought and felt during the war' but, in consequence, he conveyed little sense of strategy or tactics: soldiers were essentially victims of the high command. In fact Gammage, unlike Bean, saw the Digger's war as irredeemably tragic. 'There never was a greater tragedy than World War,' he insisted. 'It engulfed an age, and conditioned the times that followed. It contaminated every ideal for which it was waged, it threw up waste and horror worse than all the evils it sought to avert.' Gammage featured 'nationhood, brotherhood and sacrifice' at Gallipoli but he also emphasized the far greater losses experienced by Australian soldiers on the Somme – over 5,000 casualties in a supposedly 'feint' attack at Fromelles on 19–20 July ('Australians had never experienced a more calamitous or tragic night') and another 23,000 at Pozières – 'a monstrous sacrifice' over several weeks in July and August to 'win a few yards of ground'.[30]

His Diggers were ordinary men caught up in this 'maelstrom', yet 'their spirits were rarely broken' and Gammage celebrated many acts of courage and tenacity. What broke, he argued, was the old pre-1914 world-view. This was not simply because 'an upsurge of Australian nationalism', glorified by Anzac heroes, displaced the old imperial sentiment: there was also a political rupture. Writing from the left in the early 1970s when the Australian Labor Party (ALP) was finally back in power, Gammage asserted that 'Australians in 1914 had wanted a paradise for the majority', cleansed from 'Old World evils' and characterized by democracy and egalitarianism. But the strident war nationalism and the bitter 1916 debate over conscription sundered the ALP, so that 'the general majority which in 1914 had sought to create a social paradise in Australia was both split and made leaderless by the war', while 'the conservatives had joined with those who had fought in the war to take firm possession of the spirit of Anzac, and to maintain an influence in Australian life which is only now diminishing.' Gammage's depiction of the Digger's war had much in common with the saga of the Tommy's hellish journey out of Edwardian innocence. Although 'the boundless eagerness of August 1914 is a world removed from our time,' he concluded, 'what began to happen on Gallipoli nine months later is with us yet.'[31]

Building on Gammage, the popular author Patsy Adam-Smith produced *The Anzacs* (1978), a heavily illustrated book in short and readable chapters, based on the testimony from an even larger number of veterans. 'War *is* hell,' Adam-Smith declared in the preface. 'But in our attempts to denigrate it, to outlaw it, we must not castigate the victims of war – and every man who fights is a victim.' Although victims, the soldiers chronicled were no saints. She addressed taboo subjects such as brothels and venereal disease and also demythologized John Simpson, the fabled Australian hero of Gallipoli who carried the wounded down 'Shrapnel Valley' to the beach on a donkey from morning till night for three weeks until he was finally killed on 18 May 1915. Simpson, she reminded readers, was born and raised in Britain, on Tyneside, until he set off around the world as a merchant seaman, aged seventeen. He was also 'a boozer, a brawler' who 'enjoyed a good punch-up' rather than 'the delicate, aesthetic visionary the artists and eulogists have recorded.' Adam-Smith deliberately did not write about strategy or generals. Playing war games miles from the battlefields, she said, commanders 'could sacrifice as many men as they liked without the sight of the gobbets of flesh on tangled barbed wire to trouble them.' Her heroes, warts and all, were the Diggers, to whom she effusively dedicated her book. 'When time has removed this age to a distance, our descendants will speak of you as we now speak of the three hundred at Thermopylae – but I have had the rare, and peerless, privilege of knowing you.'[32]

Gammage and Adam-Smith stimulated a new wave of interest in the Aussies of 1914–18. By 1981 *The Broken Years* had sold 17,000 copies and *The Anzacs* 30,000, even before it went into paperback that year.[33] Also important was the rejuvenation of the Australian War Memorial in Canberra. This was another of Bean's creations – an internationally unique mixture of shrine, museum and archive that opened in 1941. By the early 1970s it had a 'rather fusty image', to quote Labor prime minister Gough Whitlam, with conservative staff, dated exhibits and poor facilities, but then substantial government investment, especially in education and outreach, transformed its profile. The number of visitors doubled between 1965 and 1982 to over a million a year, most of whom were under forty with no personal knowledge of the Great War.[34]

As in Britain, it was above all on the screen that the Anzac saga was conveyed to new generations. In Australia the equivalent of *Oh! What a Lovely War* was Peter Weir's 1981 feature film *Gallipoli*, for which Gammage acted as historical adviser. The film's publicity poster – 'From a place you have never heard of ... A story you'll never forget' – said a lot about where the Anzac saga had been in the 1970s and equally where it would be going. A vivid story of two young Aussies, *Gallipoli* did a huge amount to revive popular interest in 1915, bringing to life the soldiers as youthful adventurers rather than grizzled veterans, and spawning several imitative television series. The movie has been described as 'pure Bean, complete with traditional stereotypes of the bushman–digger and incompetent British commanders'.[35]

Australia's obsession with their Great War heroes was also promoted officially, after the country's acrimonious bicentenary celebrations in 1988. Aboriginal groups and their supporters dubbed Australia Day on 26 January (which commemorated the arrival of the First Fleet of British settler ships in Botany Bay) as 'Invasion Day', protesting that 'White Australia has a Black History'. With this debate rumbling on, Anzac Day seemed to offer a more consensual focus for national identity. In 1990, the seventy-fifth anniversary of the Anzac landings, Bob Hawke became the first Australian prime minister to attend the Dawn Service at Gallipoli. His successor, Paul Keating, presided over the campaign to have Australia's own Unknown Soldier finally interred in the memorial in Canberra on 11 November 1993, the seventy-fifth anniversary of the end of the Great War. The grave in Westminster Abbey, intended in 1920 to symbolize the missing from all the British Empire, was no longer acceptable. As the country's ties with Britain loosened, the Anzac legend 'could now be refashioned as the Bastille

Day or Fourth of July Australia never had, the day which cut Australia adrift from its Imperial past'.[36]

Although New Zealand was Australia's full partner in the original Australia New Zealand Army Corps (ANZAC), the Kiwis never achieved the cult status of the Diggers. This is ironic given New Zealand's losses in 1914–18 – its 18,000 dead represented 8 per cent of men of military age, a higher proportion than for any country in the empire except Britain. And the culture of Kiwi soldiers was similar to that of the Diggers – boozy and matey, contemptuous of officers and especially of the English. But there was no New Zealand equivalent of Charles Bean to turn folk culture into national myth, and New Zealand remained a particularly Anglophile part of the Commonwealth. There was no Australian-style revisiting of Gallipoli for the fiftieth anniversary and it was only after Christopher Pugsley's pioneering account of the New Zealanders at Gallipoli in 1984, a decade after Bill Gammage, that interest in the men of 1914–18 began to revive. Not until 2004 was an Unknown Warrior disinterred from the Western Front and reburied in front of the National War Memorial in Wellington. New Zealand rediscovered its Great War soldiers more slowly and less stridently than its Anzac partner.[37]

So it was the British and the Australians who pioneered this new and passionate interest in the soldiers of the Great War. But there were also revealing national contrasts. First, Australians made the anniversary of a botched battle into virtually the country's national day. In Britain, by contrast, Remembrance Sunday in November – though far more esteemed than the Queen's Official Birthday, let alone St George's Day – never made any connection with national identity. Here is another sign, I think, of how the world wars, while emotionally important in Britain, have been detached from any clear narrative structure of meaning.

This contrast raises a second point: Remembrance Sunday in Britain recalls the end of hostilities, whereas Anzac Day marks their start for Australia, both as the Australian Imperial Force's baptism of fire and, in a larger sense, Australia's birth as a nation. So the act of commemoration is coupled with a celebration of Australian virtues. For the British, on the other hand, Remembrance Day is entirely a moment to honour the war dead, sombre in tone and tapping into a rich vein of poetry with Wilfred Owen at its heart.

This raises a third and fundamental difference between the two countries. Australian literature about the Great War, both during it and afterwards, was 'based on one fundamental premiss: that the Australians excel, even revel, in battle.' Nor was this a passing phase: throughout the twentieth century 'every mode of Australian war prose' has functioned 'either overtly or covertly as publicity for the Australian soldier and twentieth-century embodiment of classical heroic virtue.'[38] In short, there was nothing comparable to the corpus of anti-war poetry and prose so evident in Britain. And in the 1970s that writing was revivified and sanctified for a new generation by Paul Fussell.

Born in 1924, so roughly a decade older than Middlebrook and Keegan, Fussell fought in the US Army in France and Germany at the end of the Second World War and then became a university professor. His early work explored eighteenth-century English literature but it was The Great War and Modern Memory (1975) that made his name. 'This book is about the British experience on the Western Front from 1914 to 1918,' he explained, and also about 'some of the literary means by which it has been remembered, conventionalized, and mythologized.' Fussell selected features of what he took to be a standardized trench experience, illustrating each with reference to a classic anti-war poet or memoirist – for instance, Edmund Blunden's use of pastoral imagery to indict with quiet irony the gross destructiveness of modern war. This analysis was not of mere antiquarian interest: Fussell argued 'that there seems to be one dominating form of modern understanding; that it is essentially ironic; and that it originates largely in the application of mind and memory to the events of the Great War.' Irony, he stated, 'is the attendant of hope, and the fuel of hope is innocence.' Using Larkin's line from the poem 'MCMXIV' 'Never such innocence again' and the photograph of volunteers in August 1914 that inspired it, he summoned up 'those sweet, generous people who pressed forward and all but solicited their own destruction'. He claimed that 'the innocent army fully attained the knowledge of good and evil at the Somme on July 1, 1916.'[39]

As these quotations suggest, Fussell did not believe in understatement. His book is full of tendentious generalizations and its mode of argument is highly selective. Most chapters posit a theme and then develop this with reference to a Great War writer, whose vision is validated as typical by a few snippets from soldiers' letters and diaries, before Fussell fast-forwards to some extracts from war literature later in the twentieth century, usually by Norman Mailer, Joseph Heller or Thomas Pynchon. So, for example, the 'binary vision' of Siegfried Sassoon is used to illuminate the 'gross dichotomizing' – us and them, friend and foe – which Fussell asserted to be 'a persisting imaginative habit of modern times, traceable, it would seem, to the actualities of the Great War ... Paranoid trench warfare, whether enacted or remembered, fosters paranoid melodrama, which I take to be a primary mode in modern writing.'[40]

Central for Fussell was his belief in the primacy of experience. He brought to bear on the writings of Britain's 1914–18 generation his own time as a bloodied American veteran from 1944–5. *The Great War and Modern Memory* is dedicated to the memory of a fellow GI 'killed beside me in France, March 15, 1945'. To be more explicit, as he admitted later, his buddy was blown to bits all over him by German shellfire. Anger at such war experiences festered beneath the surface of Fussell's post-war academic life – resentment about how ordinary soldiers were manipulated by the men at the top and about the lofty ideas and sly euphemisms with which they justified mass killing. What brought all this into the open was his anger at the same pattern being repeated once again. 'In 1975,' he reflected later, 'my American readers had also experienced in Vietnam their own terrible and apparently pointless war of attrition, which made *body counts* a household phrase.' Here was yet another war 'dichotomized' between good and evil. Fussell hoped that his book might persuade American readers 'that even Gooks had feelings, that even they hated to die, and like us called for help or God or Mother when their agony became unbearable.'[41]

Fussell's Great War was set entirely in the 'troglodyte world' of the Western Front. 'Correctly or not,' he explained, 'the current idea of "the Great War" derives primarily from images of the trenches in

France and Belgium. I have thus stayed there with the British infantry, largely disregarding events in Mesopotamia, Turkey, Africa, and Ireland, and largely ignoring air and naval warfare.' Of the massive war effort on Britain's home front, there was virtually no mention. Yet, as historians critical of Fussell pointed out, 'these major aspects of the war are not tragic or ironic or self-evidently futile. Even more, they rescued the Western Front from being these things, if only after an abysmal three years of waiting and enduring.' In other words, Fussell presents the Great War with 1918 left out – apart from a cursory half-page in Chapter One – because, he insists, the war 'still goes on', pervading the rest of the century, especially in Britain: 'The whole texture of British daily life could be said to commemorate the war still', from pub-closing hours to 'the current economic bankruptcy of Britain' and the 'Americanization of Europe'. Even when depicting the Western Front, Fussell was on shaky ground: men usually spent only three weeks in the forward trenches before being rotated back to rest and training areas and then working their way through the rear trenches to the front line once again. So, even for combat soldiers, much of the Great War was uneventful: 'the war's atrociousness' lay not so much in its longevity but in the horrors that 'could be compressed into a few hours or days' at the front.[42]

Twenty-five years later in 2000 Fussell, a famously combative figure, was unusually defensive about *The Great War and Modern Memory*, admitting many of its limitations with plaintive excuses: 'After all, I was writing not a history, only an elegiac commentary ... a book in which historical data was called on to enhance the elegiac effect ... the work of an essayist, not, at the time, that of a scholar.' This was, perhaps, a natural response after being savaged by military historians, but it also reflected the fate of any book that attracts voracious attention and in the process has been picked to the bone. Whatever Fussell said he intended, the book *has* been taken as history – its account of experience at the front through the eyes of anti-war poets and memoirists reinforcing the 1970s fascination with ordinary soldiers. Like Middlebrook and Keegan, Fussell felt a deeply emotional reaction to evidence he discussed – derived, in contrast to them, from his own experience of combat – and this gave his writing at times a passionate intensity. On specific authors he could be strikingly innovative – about the homoerotic element in Owen's poetry, for instance, or on the 'caricature' theatricality of Graves' *Good-Bye to All That*. But, rather than breaking new historical ground, one might say that his book dug up the old mud in a provocative way, telling readers 'a great deal that at some level they already knew about very well-established characteristics of war writing in general and the Great War in particular.'[43]

Fussell gave canonical form to the story of soldiers as victims, immured in the trenches, their tragic experience interpreted by poets. By 2012 his book had sold over 100,000 copies, exerting a powerful influence on academic thinking across the English-speaking world. Fussell saw 1914–18 as the defining event of Britain's twentieth century. And, across the Atlantic, his picture of a civilization coming to terms with a disaster for which it was totally unprepared appealed to intellectuals struggling with America's own supposed loss of idealistic innocence in Vietnam.[44]

It should be admitted that this rediscovery of the ordinary soldier was not just a British or anglophone phenomenon. In fact, it was pioneered in France. Yet the story there, and in West Germany, both serve to point up the peculiarities of Britain.

The *poilu* – France's equivalent of the Tommy – had been written out of interwar histories of the Great War. There had been a few attempted counter-attacks, such as Jean Norton Cru's *Témoins* (1929) – a critical analysis of soldiers' novels, memoirs and letters – and Jacques Péricard's *Verdun* (1933), based, rather like Middlebrook, on soldiers' accounts which he solicited through the newspapers. But these were very much the exceptions. The accepted form for Great War history in France was set in 1934 by *La crise européenne et la Grande Guerre (1904–1918)* by Pierre Renouvin, professor at the Sorbonne for thirty years, who dominated French history-writing about 1914–18 in a way that has no equivalent in Britain or Germany. Renouvin's classic text went through five editions, two of them published during the 1960s. This was a vast study of diplomatic, political and military history, with virtually no reference to the home front, workers' strikes or even soldiers' mutinies, let alone what Renouvin dismissed as 'the atmosphere of battle'. His strict definition of war history is all the more striking because Renouvin was a gravely wounded veteran of La Grande Guerre (losing his left arm and the use of his right hand on the Chemin des Dames in 1917) but in his scholarly writing he never mentioned the war he had personally endured. For Renouvin, history required objectivity, the exclusion of self, whereas Cru believed that personal experience was central.[45]

It was not until the twilight of Renouvin's career that his grip on French historiography began to weaken. The year 1959 saw publication of *Vie et mort des français 1914–1918* – an account of the conflict built around extracts from the writings of ordinary people: soldiers but also civilians, women as well as men. The three authors – André Ducasse, Jacques Meyer and Gabriel Perreux – were not scholars but they had written works of popular history and were all veterans of 1914–18. Indeed Ducasse had published an anthology of writings from the front in 1932. Following the success of *Vie et mort des français*, which was republished with extensive illustrations in 1963 (the same year as A.J.P. Taylor's illustrated history of the war), in 1966 Meyer and Perreux brought out parallel volumes looking in more detail at the daily life of, respectively, soldiers and civilians, again composed largely from contemporary writings. Although Meyer spent about half his book in the trenches, he was at pains to stress the variety of the war experience, getting away from the familiar set-piece battles. Verdun, for instance, took up only 33 of his 370 pages; the 90-page chapter entitled '*Sensations et Sentiments*' explored courage and fear, faith and fatalism, attitudes to allies and the enemy. Throughout Meyer emphasized the varieties of soldiering (artillerymen lived different lives from riflemen), the profound contrasts between the front line, the rear trenches and the leave areas, and the vast diversity of place and time along a front that extended for 'eight hundred kilometres' during a war that lasted 'nearly sixteen hundred days'. All very different from the narrowing British gaze into the abyss of 1 July 1916.[46]

Perreux's counterpart volume on daily civilian life was equally capacious, including sections about 'women without men', restrictions (rationing, health and food shortages) and changing social fortunes (the new poor and the new rich). Like Meyer, its tone was descriptive and unsentimental, stressing the fundamental social changes wrought by the war, whether recognized or not: 'in four years, one had quite frankly changed centuries'.[47] There were similarities here in intent, if not style, with Arthur Marwick's *The Deluge* (1965), which gained a wide readership as a set-text for Britain's new Open University. This book was a breezy, broad-brush study of how British society (though not the state) was transformed during the war and many of Marwick's conclusions have been modified by later research, for instance on the transformed position of women or the irresistible rise of 'collectivist' economics. But *The Deluge* was significant as a determined assault on the Western Front and its hold on the British conception of the Great War. Fifty years on, argued Marwick, 'without denying the validity of the bitterness, or forgetting the futile horror which gave rise to it', one should recognize that 'on the whole Britain in the inter-war years was a better place to live in than it had been in 1914' – which did not imply, he hastened to add, that the war itself had been 'a good thing'.[48]

Marwick was, however, a relatively lone voice amid the British dirge about the trenches. There was nothing comparable in 1970s Britain to the major works of archive-based scholarship that started to appear in France, such as Jean-Jacques Becker's critique of the myth of war enthusiasm in August 1914 or Antoine Prost's exhaustive examination of the role of veterans in post-war French social and political life – both published in 1977. Conversely, there has never been a French edition of Fussell's book, and none of the poetry of which he wrote was translated into French until late in the twentieth century – Sassoon in 1987 and Owen in 1995.[49] The stated aim of the *Association Wilfred Owen France* (founded in 2005) is to 'make radiant' (*faire rayonner*) the life and work of a man who is the most studied author in Britain after Shakespeare, while being 'almost totally unknown to the public outside the borders of his native land'.[50]

In West Germany during the 1970s and 1980s, where historical and national debate still revolved around the Nazi era, there was even less interest in the social history of Great War soldiers. The Fritz Fischer controversy rumbled on, fanning the flames of the old debate about 'war guilt', and although there was some significant research about the German home front, notably by Jürgen Kocka, this concentrated on explaining the 1918 revolution. Kocka and other leading historians from the so-called Bielefeld school formulated a highly ideological approach to social history based on Weberian sociology and 'modernization' theory which privileged socio-economic structures over the ideas and actions of individuals. The 1980s did see a reaction against such 'structuralist' social history in the form of the history of daily life (*Alltagsgeschichte*). This featured the experiences of ordinary people using unconventional sources such as photographs and oral history, but its main foci were labour history and the Nazi era, where it proved revealing on the complex personal and local accommodations 'ordinary' Germans made with the Third Reich. Attempts to apply *Alltagsgeschichte* to 1914–18 had limited success until after the end of the Cold War.[51]

Yet in one important, albeit circuitous way Germany did help reinforce this new preoccupation with men at the front. George Mosse's book, *Fallen Soldiers*, published in 1990 but the result of research he began in the late 1970s, reworked the discourse about the 'front experience' (*Fronterlebnis*) that was central to right-wing German writing in the 1920s and 1930s, not least Hitler's *Mein Kampf*. Mosse had been born in 1918 into a wealthy Berlin Jewish family but after 1933 he was educated first in Britain and then America, where he spent his professional academic life. He was particularly concerned with the part played by what he called 'the Myth of the War Experience' – celebrating aggressive, comradely masculinity and 'an acceptance of war' – in the 'brutalization' of post-1918 politics in Germany. But, Mosse insisted, 'no nation after the war could completely escape the process of brutalization ... To many all over Europe it seemed as if the First World War had never ended but was being continued during the interwar years.' His argument was garnished with a few examples from England, a country which, he argued, 'also underwent such a process of brutalization, even if the more courteous and respectful prewar political discourse remained intact.' The Myth was in part political fabrication but, Mosse insisted, it was 'not entirely fictitious', being distilled from 'the reality of the war experience' in 'the little world of the trenches'. In his view 'trench warfare determined not only the perception of war of those who passed through it, but also how the war was understood by future generations.' Mosse's book proved very influential among historians, especially its 'brutalization' thesis, and his postulate that there was a uniform 'front experience' defined by the trenches helped to confirm the image of the Great War conveyed by Middlebrook, Keegan and Fussell.[52]

Fallen Soldiers was subtitled *Reshaping the Memory of the World Wars*. Its discussion of the 'cult of the fallen soldier' and its examination of the design of war memorials reflected a growing interest in the processes of war remembrance. This memory boom forms the subject of my last chapter.

11

REMEMBRANCE

Now all roads lead to France
And heavy is the tread
Of the living; but the dead
Returning lightly dance

Edward Thomas, 1916

If poetry could truly tell it backwards,
then it would.

Carol Ann Duffy, 2009[1]

Maya Lin would probably have had little chance if the competition hadn't been 'blind', judged by number not name. As a student at Yale – only twenty-one, female, from a Chinese-American family – the cards would have been stacked against her in an open contest with the big boys of the architectural profession. And she received abuse in plenty when it became known that her design was the unanimous choice of the judges assessing over 1,400 proposals for a Vietnam Veterans Memorial in Washington, DC – intended for the heart of the nation's sacred space, between the Washington Monument and the Lincoln Memorial.

Lin's proposal diverged sharply from the heroic statuary of previous American war commemoration, such as the Iwo Jima Memorial of 1954 (discussed in Chapter Eight). To appease traditionalists one of the runner-up entries was later erected nearby – a life-size bronze of three soldiers, clearly distinguishable as a white, a black and a Hispanic, all battle-weary but heavily armed and still ready for combat. By contrast Lin offered a stark, non-representational memorial – two long walls gradually gouging into the earth to meet in an elongated V, ten feet high at its apex. Along the walls are listed in chronological order the names of all the US servicemen and women who had died during the Vietnam War. The walls are constructed of black granite, highly reflective, so that the visitor sees his or her face when tracing the name of a buddy or loved one. The result is at once intensely abstract and yet deeply personal, the encounter of the living with the dead through the mystery of names – a memorial which, unlike heroic statuary, does not seek to direct one's response. Although modernist in spirit, Lin's conception had echoes of the past, evoking the vast walls naming the missing from Britain's Great War on the Menin Gate at Ypres and the Thiepval Memorial on the Somme. Lutyens' design for Thiepval was, in fact, a major influence on Lin.[2]

Despite the initial controversy, since its inauguration in November 1982 the Vietnam Veterans Memorial has become one of Washington's most popular spaces, attracting more than 3 million visitors a year. It is now one of America's 'sites of memory' – to render in English the untranslatable neologism *les lieux de mémoire* coined by the French scholar Pierre Nora to entitle his herculean seven-volume project published between 1984 and 1992. Nora's use of the word 'memory' was problematic, suggesting an autonomous almost metaphysical force which he romanticized as living national spirit, in contrast with what he considered the arid science of 'history'. Nora believed that in 1980s France national memory had been overshadowed by scientific history: hence his project, assisted by over 120 authors, to document the monuments, rituals, texts and images that evoke what, he claimed, his countrymen understood by 'France'. Although Nora's *idée fixe* was in many ways inscrutably French, his work, translated into English by the end of the twentieth century, popularized the term 'sites of memory'. Not only did this became almost a cliché for cultural historians, it also fitted the broader public fascination with places and artefacts that, like Maya Lin's wall, left them scope for private remembrance.[3]

Internationally, memorialization of the Great War became much more intense after the end of the Cold War. The fall of the Berlin Wall and the other revolutions of 1989 redrew the map of Eastern Europe, ending the de facto settlement since the demise of the Third Reich that had entrenched Soviet power across half the continent. Germany, divided since 1945, was united again in November 1990; at the end of 1991 the Soviet Union fell apart, leaving a ring of fractious national states around the periphery of the new Russian republic. These dramatic events in 1989–91 reopened many issues from 1917–18 – that earlier era of imperial collapse and popular revolutions – and also prompted a new interest in the First World War, now finally emerging from the long shadow of 1939–45. This chapter will explore how 1914–18 was memorialized in the post-Cold War era – some forms being bitterly divisive, others aimed at reconciliation – with national narratives often brought to life through family history, an escalating hobby in the internet age. In all this we shall also see the persistence of British patterns of remembrance set out in the previous two chapters. Despite the efforts of revisionist military historians, in Britain the Great War has remained a saga of personal tragedies, illuminated by poetry not history, a subject for remembrance rather than understanding.

The dramatic denouement of the Cold War ended the division of Germany but it also reopened the historic question of Germany's place in Europe. Although publicly committed to eventual German unification after 1945, the Western Allies had actually been quite content with the solidification of the Federal Republic of Germany (FRG) and the German Democratic Republic (GDR), especially once the flashpoint of Berlin had been defused by construction of the Wall in 1961. 'I love Germany so much that I am glad there are two of them,' quipped French intellectual François Mauriac. In 1990 the newly unified Germany finally accepted *de jure* the existence of Poland and

renounced all territorial claims in Eastern Europe, ending a revisionist project that had characterized German foreign policy in various
forms since the Treaty of Versailles. But the highly controversial decision to move the capital from Bonn to Berlin, passed in 1991 in the
Bundestag by a mere seventeen votes, opened up old controversies.
Critics argued that Bonn and the Rhineland symbolized the country's
new start in 1945 as a Western democracy, whereas Berlin bore the
indelible stigma of Germany's disastrous 'Prussian', militaristic heritage. Claims that Germany could now become a 'normal' sovereign
state seemed utopian: 'our neighbours and partners will not look at us
as a normal country', warned state secretary Wolfgang Ischinger, 'due
to our particular German history'.[4]

Many commentators saw worrying parallels between the end of the
twentieth century and its beginning: Germany as an independent
nation-state was too strong for Europe's balance of power yet too
weak to exert stable continental leadership.[5] The interface between
Germany's power and weakness had lain at the heart of thirty years of
instability and conflict from 1914 to 1945. But optimists within
Germany and outside pointed to the European Union as a novel
framework that had been lacking after 1918. 'Germany is our fatherland, Europe is our future,' insisted Chancellor Helmut Kohl. His
foreign minister Hans-Dietrich Genscher echoed the aphorism of
Thomas Mann: 'We do not aspire to a German Europe but want to
live in a European Germany.' An amendment to the country's constitution was passed, requiring the Federal Republic to seek a European
Union that was 'bound to democratic, legal, social and federal principles' – in other words not a centralized super-state.[6]

In 1989 Germany's neighbours were not initially persuaded by such
integrationist rhetoric. French president François Mitterrand warned
of a return to the Europe of 1913, with Britain, France and Russia
aligned against the German menace. When Mikhail Gorbachev
failed to resist Kohl, the French leader talked darkly of another
Munich – with France and Britain, as in 1938, lacking the means to
defy Germany. But once Kohl secured American support and the
momentum for unification became unstoppable, Mitterrand revived
the post-1950 French strategy, declaring that 'the German problem

will be regulated by the magnetic force of Europe.'[7] As a condition for accepting rapid German reunification, he obliged Kohl to accept European monetary union to contain the burgeoning economic power of a bigger Germany. This meant an end to the cherished Deutschmark, talisman for many Germans of the FRG's post-war prosperity. The Maastricht Treaty of December 1991 paved the way for a single currency, the Euro, from January 2002.

In this whole process Britain took a negative and increasingly isolated line. Although the fall of the Berlin Wall was welcomed as a sign of freedom, some British commentators soon talked of an impending 'Fourth Reich'. Monetary union, fumed Cabinet minister Nicholas Ridley, was 'a German racket designed to take over the whole of Europe'. As for handing over sovereignty to the European Community, he exclaimed, 'you might as well give it to Adolf Hitler'.[8] After such a tirade Ridley had to be sacked but Prime Minister Margaret Thatcher privately shared his views. Her opposition to German unification, though reflecting sensitivity for Gorbachev's increasingly shaky position in Moscow, really derived from her reading of history as a child of the 1920s nurtured by a staunchly anti-continental father. As she made clear in her memoirs, Thatcher was sure that countries had distinct national characters. 'Since the unification of Germany under Bismarck – perhaps partly because national unification came so late – Germany has veered unpredictably between aggression and self-doubt.' She doubted that 1945 had marked a fundamental change in the national character and dismissed the idea that German volatility could be contained within a European framework: a reunited Germany was 'simply too big and powerful to be just another player within Europe'. The only answer, she argued, was a European balance of power based on a close Anglo-French accord backed by the United States. In other words a Europe based on the Atlantic alliance rather than the European Union. To this end she turned all her persuasive powers on Mitterrand and President George H.W. Bush, often pulling out of her notorious handbag a map showing the various configurations of Germany in the past which, she said, were 'not altogether reassuring about the future'. But Bush (whose Second World War service was not in Europe but the Pacific) did not share her historical hang-ups about Germany, while Mitterrand – like his predecessors – eventually opted for the European answer to the German question. The end result of Thatcher's opposition to unification, reported the British ambassador, was that 'Britain's public standing in Germany is at its lowest for years.' In 1992 her successor John Major, though less of a Eurosceptic, secured a British opt-out from the Maastricht Treaty and monetary union.[9]

Thatcher and Major demonstrated the enduring grip of the essential British narrative about the two world wars – established, as we have seen, in the 1940s. Bush and most of his countrymen took a much more positive view of 1989–91, viewing the lifting of the Iron Curtain and the collapse of the Soviet Union as triumphant vindication of American power and values. The pundit Francis Fukuyama asserted that the end of the Cold War marked nothing less than 'the end of history as such'. Although 'events' would continue to happen, he argued that we had now seen 'the end point of mankind's ideological evolution and the universalization of Western liberal democracy as the final form of human government.'[10]

One expression of this triumphalism was a new interest in what Americans saw as the origins of the Cold War – the 1917 clash of ideologies between Wilson and Lenin. Books and essays on Wilsonianism proliferated in America after 1991: studies about the 'Wilsonian century', 'impulse', 'moment' or 'persuasion'. Their authors discerned in Wilson's inchoate ideas for replacing power politics with a liberal international order the fundamentals of American foreign policy for much of the twentieth century, which had guided Cold War diplomacy and even the shaping of German reunification. It was claimed that Wilsonianism 'launched the transformation of the norms and standards of international relations' that led eventually to global decolonization; even that the President's ideas had been the main instrument of the march of freedom, so that by the 1990s 'the world has been made, if not fully democratic, then safe for democracy.'[11]

According to historian Frank Ninkovich in 1999, the 'Wilsonian century' was over: 'the post-cold-war world' was not another opportunity to 'institutionalize Wilsonian policies' but rather 'the occasion for dispensing with them altogether.'[12] Some older neo-conservatives agreed with Ninkovich. 'It is not within the United States' power to democratize the world,' declared former Reagan adviser Jeane Kirkpatrick. 'With a return to "normal times," we can again become a normal nation.' But Wilsonianism was given a new lease of life in Washington by the advent of the George W. Bush administration in 2001. Younger neoconservatives such as Charles Krauthammer insisted that the promotion of democracy must be 'the touchstone of a new ideological American foreign policy' – a policy of what he grandiloquently called 'universal dominion' in a 'unipolar world'. Some neocons, such as Max Boot, described themselves as 'hard Wilsonians', meaning advocates of American power to enforce liberal values. Their favoured target was the Middle East. 'I think there is a potential civic culture in Arab countries that can lead to demo-cratic institutions', Richard Perle asserted in March 2001, 'and I think that Iraq is probably the best place to put that proposition to the test.' Neocons exploited the Al-Qaeda attacks on America on 11 September 2001 as pretext for an operation to topple Saddam Hussein. 'In word, if not yet in deed, Bush is becoming the most Wilsonian president since Wilson himself,' declared Lawrence F. Kaplan on the eve of the Iraq war, urging the President to 'complete the job Wilson began.' But the botched campaign in Iraq, predicated on simplistic assumptions that removing a 'tyrant' would produce 'free-dom' and 'democracy', was a painful reminder that 'hard Wilsonianism' did not bring about easy solutions. By the twilight of his presi-dency Bush was being denounced as 'Woodrow Wilson on steroids, a grotesquely exaggerated and pridefully assertive version of the original'.[13]

While 1991 strengthened the Wilsonian grip on the discourse of American foreign policy, it finally loosened the stranglehold of Lenin over historical memory in Russia and across Eastern Europe. As we have seen, in contrast to the commemoration of the Great Patriotic War of 1941–5, Russia's First World War remained in the shade. There had been no Soviet equivalent of the Cenotaph in London, the Douamont Ossuary at Verdun, the Australian War Memorial in Canberra or even the Neue Wache in Berlin, even though the Russian death toll from 1914–17 was roughly 2 million. Nor were there memorials to the war dead in towns and villages, again in marked contrast with France, Britain and the countries of the British Empire, especially Australia where roughly 1,500 public memorials were erected to express a 'distant grief' for the bodies of loved ones interred in far-off foreign fields. For the Russians, however, 1914–17 was no distant conflict but a brutal struggle on home soil yet, for the bereaved, their grief was as 'distant' as for Australians – perhaps more so given the chilling official silence.[14]

But the demise of the Soviet Union made it possible for Russian and Western historians to research the war of 1914–17 – both in and for itself and as part of 'Russia's continuum of crisis' from 1914 to 1921, with the revolutions of 1917 as 'fulcrum'. This research often followed themes from recent Western scholarship, such as the extent of 'war enthusiasm' in 1914 or the mobilization of ethnic nationalism.[15] Russians were also finally able to memorialize the conflict in public. On the site of the projected All-Russian War Cemetery of 1915 (see Chapter Six) there now stands a Memorial Park Complex of the Heroes of the First World War. Much of its iconography is religious, with numerous Russian Orthodox symbols and a small chapel of the Transfiguration where the original cemetery church had been. Prominent, too, are national symbols, particularly the double-headed eagle of the Russian federation. The park was formally opened on 1 August 2004, the ninetieth anniversary of the outbreak of war. But this has been a highly contested site, with continuing arguments about how far to commemorate 'all the defenders of Russia who fell during wars for the Fatherland' including 'Whites' who fought against the Reds in the civil war. This reflected the underlying controversy in post-Soviet Russia about the Bolshevik revolution as a triumph or a disaster.[16]

In parts of Eastern Europe, the 1990s also saw the collapse of the post-1918 settlement. Yugoslavia, the contorted South Slav state forged by the Serbs after the Great War, had been held together as a federal polity during the Cold War largely by the will and skill of Josef Broz Tito, half Croat and half Slovene. But economic and ethnic strains intensified after his death in 1980 and the end of communist rule in 1989 precipitated total dissolution. Slovenia seceded quickly in

REMEMBRANCE393

1991 and Croatia the following year, but the struggles in Bosnia-Herzegovina (1992–5) and Kosovo (1998–9) saw ethnic violence comparable to Eastern Europe after the Great War. Sarajevo, infamous as trigger of the July crisis in 1914, gained new notoriety for one of the longest sieges in modern history during the Bosnian war. Czechoslovakia, fabricated by Tomáš Masaryk in 1918, was another casualty of the end of the communist era. Tensions between the Czech lands and Slovakia had been recurrent during the country's troubled history and they reached crisis point after communist rule collapsed. Czechoslovakia ceased to exist on New Year's Eve 1992. Its break-up was far from harmonious, but compared with the horrors of Yugoslavia this was aptly described as a 'velvet divorce' to follow the country's 'velvet revolution' in 1989.

Along the Soviet borderlands, however, the 1990s dynamic was rather different – a return to the post-1918 order rather than its rejection. The Baltic states of Estonia, Latvia and Lithuania had a particularly chequered twentieth-century history. Although under Russian control since the eighteenth century, the Great War was their 'freedom moment': each gained independence in 1920 after savage battles with both Germans and Russians. But then they were gobbled up again in 1940 by the Soviet Union under the Nazi-Soviet pact, before being conquered by Nazi Germany in 1941 and then recaptured in 1944 by the Red Army. During this 'double occupation' local people fought for both sides, and some collaborated in the Nazi extermination of the Jews. When anti-Soviet protest escalated in the late 1980s, Estonia, Latvia and Lithuania took the lead – the human chain across all three states to mark the fiftieth anniversary of the Nazi-Soviet pact in August 1989 being a graphic example. In 1991 the Ukraine also gained its independence from the USSR but, unlike the Baltics, it had never enjoyed freedom between the world wars. The short-lived Ukrainian People's Republic had desperately sought international recognition at the Paris peace conference, only to be partitioned by Poland and the Soviet Union in 1921. During the Second World War thousands of Ukrainian partisans fought alongside the Germans against the Red Army before the region was again brought under Soviet control in 1943.

As Western historians began to recognize in the 1990s, the Baltic states and the Ukraine had been the 'shatter zones' of twentieth-century Europe, where Germany and Russia kept colliding. They were the 'bloodlands' where ethnic conflict, political brutalization and paramilitary violence had been especially ferocious during and after the two world wars.[17]

Coming to terms with such tangled and painful histories all across Eastern Europe was not going to be easy. In the West, especially America, it seemed that the thawing of communist repression had simply revived historic nationalisms frozen during the Cold War – confirming a rather Wilsonian sense of the perpetually feuding Old World. Popular books gave the impression that, especially in the Balkans, ancient 'Ghosts' were emerging from the historical closet, from 'a time-capsule world', a 'dim stage upon which people raged, spilled blood, experienced visions and ecstasies'. It was claimed that we were witnessing a 'Rebirth of History' across Eastern Europe: 'it has emerged dramatically from its artificial hibernation after forty years, and it has much to catch up on.'[18] But 'history' was not an autonomous force: it was being exploited by contemporary politicians for their own ends. The most egregious example was Slodoban Milošević in Yugoslavia. Seeking a new patriotic legitimation for his leadership when communism collapsed, Milošević revived old Serbian folk-memories, especially of the battle of Kosovo Polje against the Muslim Turks in 1389 – parading the coffin of the defeated hero, Prince Lazar, through every town and village in Serbia to arouse feeling ahead of the six-hundredth anniversary in 1989. Just as in the era of Masaryk and Piłsudski nationalism was being whipped up by nationalists, as much as the other way round.

The so-called 'memory wars' across former communist Europe were an extension of this process, as political groups used rival versions of the past to critique the present and shape the future. In the Baltic states, public monuments became particularly contentious. The Bronze Soldier in the centre of Tallinn, erected in 1947 to honour the Soviet 'liberators' of Estonia from Nazi rule, was a focus for riots in 2007, prompting the government to move it to a military cemetery on the outskirts of the city. To mark the 'true' liberation of the country, a War of Independence Victory Column was raised in Tallinn's Freedom Square in 2009, to honour the 4,000 Estonian dead from the struggle against Russia in 1918–20. This finally realized a project planned in 1919 and started in the mid-1930s but then suppressed during the Soviet years. Yet such assertions of a nationalist narrative going back to the First World War are deeply contentious. Estonia's Russian community, a quarter of the population, see the 'war of monuments' as an identity issue about their place in society – marginalizing them in a newly nationalist state. This is a pattern that recurs right across the ethnically diverse states of post-Soviet Eastern Europe and recalls the struggles of the 1920s and 1930s described in Chapter One.[19]

Nationalist insistence across Eastern Europe that the Soviet regime was on a par with that of the Nazis has also proved contentious because it questions the centrality of the Holocaust for Western European memorialization of the twentieth century: 'Whoever says memory, says Shoah', to quote the aphorism of Pierre Nora.[20] For the EU by the new millennium the Holocaust had become a vital element of 'being European' in an era when fear of communism was no longer a unifying force. The Jewish genocide was represented 'as an absolute moral evil against which to define those values – tolerance and diversity – that were seen as essential characteristics of modern western civilization.' During the 1990s the EU encouraged member states to adopt the anniversary of the liberation of Auschwitz, 27 January, as Holocaust Memorial Day. Endorsing the proposal in Britain in 1999, Prime Minister Tony Blair avowed his determination to 'ensure that the horrendous crimes against humanity committed during the Holocaust are never forgotten' – citing the recent wave of 'ethnic cleansing' in Kosovo as 'a stark example of the need for vigilance.'[21]

In America the 'universalization' of the Holocaust was fostered by *Schindler's List* – a blockbuster 1993 movie from Steven Spielberg which won seven Academy Awards. This reduced the tangled complexities to a morality play of good versus evil, embodied in two men – a German Nazi who helps Jews to escape and a sadistic SS camp commandant. Even more important was the opening that same year of the Holocaust Museum in Washington, DC. This project had been a long-standing goal of Jewish organizations but its realization involved a deliberate 'Americanization' of the Holocaust which 'allocated the Jews a privileged role as victims', while giving Americans 'a privileged role as witness by emphasizing the moral failures of passive by-standerdom' on the part of Europeans. The success of this pioneering venture in the nation's capital spawned similar museums or memorials in most major American cities. And so the Holocaust came to be regarded in the West as 'unique with reference to the past and universal for the future' – in other words 'the Holocaust past is something that happened predominantly to the Jews, while the Holocaust future might happen to anyone.'[22]

The putative uniqueness of the historical Holocaust was, however, rejected by many in post-Soviet Eastern Europe, who asserted the moral equivalence of Nazi and Soviet terror. They questioned the distinction made in 2002 by one American historian of Jewish descent between the 'hot' memory of fascist crimes, still a burning issue, and what he considered the increasingly 'cold' memory of communist iniquities, whose embers were dying down as the Soviet era receded into history.[23] Instead, the 2008 Prague Declaration on European Conscience and Communism, promoted by the Czechs but widely supported across Eastern Europe, demanded 'recognition that many crimes committed in the name of Communism should be assessed as crimes against humanity serving as a warning for future generations, in the same way Nazi crimes were assessed by the Nuremberg Tribunal.' This call was taken up by the European parliament. It was, however, denounced by Russia and various Jewish groups, who pointed out that many nationalists in the Ukraine and the Baltics had collaborated in Nazi killings of the Jews – a story rarely commemorated in the new national museums. This fraught debate served to direct renewed attention on the legacies of the Great War in the 'bloodlands' of Eastern Europe, where perhaps 'fourteen million people were deliberately murdered by two regimes over twelve years' between 1933 and 1945, at least a third by the Soviets through starvation and shootings. Belatedly recognizing this crime and remembering its victims was a major demand in twenty-first-century Eastern Europe, which Holocaust memorialization was not allowed to overshadow. As the Polish scholar Maria Janion said when her country joined the EU: 'To Europe, yes, but with our dead.'[24]

In Eastern Europe, as in Russia, the end of the Soviet repression had finally unleashed real historical debate. And this was a region with many skeletons in the cupboard – relics from being the prime battlefield in two world wars, from the double Nazi-Soviet occupation and from the Holocaust, right back to the bloody tangle of nationalism and revolution in 1917–18. After 1989 the cupboard was ransacked and its contents appropriated selectively by rival political and ethnic groups. The bitter, chaotic 'memory wars' that ensued were a far cry from the steady, layered process of reflection and then refraction that had characterized Great War remembrance in Britain since 1918.

Beyond the Russo-German borderlands, in areas where the Great War was not so contentious for current politics, the post-Cold War era allowed opportunities to move beyond narrow nationalistic history into reconciliation. A few are particularly striking.

A moving example in east-central Europe is the First World War museum at Kobarid, better known in Britain and America as Caporetto, scene of the great rout of the Italian army in October 1917. The battlefield now lies in Slovenia, an ironic commentary on the twelve futile battles along the Isonzo River in which hundreds of thousands of Italians died. The Alpine foothills are still littered with the debris of the Great War and this museum began in 1990 as a project by enthusiastic local collectors. Slovenia's early entry into the EU enabled them to secure European money to develop a small but significant international museum, with text in four languages (Slovenian, Italian, English and German). The declared intent is not to score national points but to document the suffering of the soldiers on all sides during twenty-nine months of fighting, paying special attention in displays and film to the climactic battle in October 1917. Kobarid 'is not a museum about victory and glory ... about conquest and revenge, about revanchism and national pride,' the guidebook explains. 'It is men that are at the forefront, the men who – aloud or silently to themselves, for themselves or for their fellow sufferers – in various languages of the world endlessly shouted: "Damn all war!"'[25]

The most sophisticated of these projects of transnational memorialization was the Historial de la Grande Guerre at Péronne – a joint French, German and British commemoration of the Somme in a new purpose-built museum next to the medieval castle used by the Germans as their headquarters during the battle. The Historial had complicated origins. It was in part a product of the 1980s passion for family history, brainchild of Max Lejeune, a powerful regional politician, whose father had fought on the Somme in 1916. The latter returned home a broken man and a difficult parent and by the 1980s Lejeune wished to come to terms in a practical way with the shadow cast over his own life by the Somme. His political clout secured government funding: at Péronne, like Kobarid, the prospect of battlefield tourism rejuvenating an economically depressed area was an added incentive.

So Lejeune's idea for a museum 'originated in family history, his family history', observes Professor Jay Winter, one of the academics who helped establish Péronne, but Lejeune's particular vision was 'seeing that such a museum was a way of turning national narratives into family narratives, resonant to a very wide public of several nationalities.' His conception caught the mood of European cooperation in the late 1980s, especially after Germany was reunified: Péronne opened in 1992, the year of the Maastricht Treaty. By stressing the French role in the battle of the Somme as well as the extent of the British losses, the museum challenged the rooted national paradigms for 1916 – the French transfixed by Verdun, the British mired in the Somme. The neologism Historial was intended to convey a blend of history and memorial and, at Winter's insistence, the museum included a research centre to promote scholarship and conferences. So the project reflected the growing transnational cooperation among scholars of the Great War.[26]

The museum's internal design set precedents in many ways. It was a genuinely trinational presentation, taking equally seriously the French, British and German stories, with text in all three languages. The way the objects were displayed was also distinctive, largely in the form of *fosses* or shallow rectangular pits in the floor to evoke the trenches inhabited by all three troglodyte armies. But the exhibits

paid as much attention to civilians as to soldiers, again breaking new
ground. Visitors move from a room depicting pre-war origins,
through the deepening war of 1914–16 and then into total war in
1916–18. Yet there is a strange, gaping hole at the centre of the
museum – the battle of the Somme itself. Quite deliberately no
attempt was made to explain or even chronicle it as a historical event,
unlike the extensive examination of the build-up to the July crisis.
Instead a blank white wall between the 1914–16 and 1916–18 rooms
was intended to convey 'the impossibility of representing battle in a
direct, figurative manner' or of 'conveying the physical and moral suffering of the soldiers': all this, we are told, is 'the realm of the
ineffable'. Accepting the 'invisibility' of the battle's reality, a specially made film screens a montage of contemporary images,
documents and sounds, often using a medieval triptych form. Most of
the material comes from soldiers, though interspersed periodically by
official communiqués such as Haig's despatch of 23 December 1916
stating that the aims of the battle had been achieved. The overall
intention was to convey how the Somme 'was perceived by those
involved in it', leaving the viewer to respond, but the impression
strongly conveyed is one of an indescribable human tragedy. That
impression is prefigured earlier in the museum by extensive use of
Otto Dix etchings to summon up the bestiality of war and then
underlined by the final room which seeks to 'show that the First
World War was the great catastrophe determining the flow of the
entire century.' So, although Historial was innovative in both form
and presentation, its content conveyed what had become familiar
themes about 1914–18 as the modern *Urkatastrophe* expressed, in this
case almost metaphysically, by the Somme.[27]

Moving outside Europe, the evolution of Anzac Day in Australia
since the 1990s has been a striking hybrid of nationalism and reconciliation. Successive governments have continued to foster public
interest, with the efforts of Labor leaders Bob Hawke and Paul
Keating in the late 1980s and early 1990s (Chapter Ten) given new
momentum by John Howard, leader of the Liberal-National government from 1996 to 2007. For Howard Anzac Day was about
celebration as much as commemoration – as he put it in 2003, 'the

celebration of some wonderful values, of courage, of valour, of mate-
ship, of decency, of a willingness as a nation to do the right thing,
whatever the cost.' Such Australian values, he argued, were as essential in the War on Terror after 9/11 as they had been in past struggles
against dictators.[28] Howard's government provided generous funding
for the Department of Veterans' Affairs (DVA) to develop its educational section and promote Anzac Day through resource packs for
schools. In collaboration with the Australian War Memorial, the DVA
financed completion of the Nominal Rolls of all Australians who
served in war, making them available online. These databases, with the
records of some 300,000 personnel from 1914–18 and over a million
from 1939–45, are an invaluable resource for scholars and genealogists.
But critics argue that this encourages a 'militarization' of family history, because records of Australians in peacetime are far less accessible,
and indeed the 'militarization' of Australian history as a whole, featuring twentieth-century foreign wars as the making of the nation in
order to distract from the first century of white settlement and native
dispossession.[29]

More than for New Zealanders, partners in the original Australia
New Zealand Army Corps, 25 April became Australia's national day.
Attendance at the Dawn Service at the war memorial in Canberra
rose from a mere 2,000 in 1977 and 6,000 in 1989 to 12,000 the following year, the seventy-fifth anniversary of the Gallipoli landings,
when the venue had to be moved from the forecourt to the more spa-
cious esplanade. By 2007 the total was estimated at 28,000.[30] There
was also a surge in 'pilgrimages' to the Dardanelles, amounting now to
over 60,000 Australians a year. Some critics have decried the pilgrimages as 'sentimental nationalism', arguing that if Aussies find Gallipoli
'charged with meanings' it is because those meanings were 'made in
Australia and unpacked in Turkey' rather than being embedded in the
local landscape: 'pilgrims carry the sacred with them' rather than dis-
covering it at their destination.[31]

Yet, despite the strident and sometimes crass patriotism, there is
now a genuinely transnational dimension to Australian remembrance.
Following Prime Minister Bob Hawke's pioneering visit in 1990,
every Anzac Day service at Gallipoli involves Turkish government

participation. Australian memorialization now recognizes the importance of the campaign for the Turks who were, after all, fighting to repel invaders. What they call the battle of Çanakkale (the town on the southern side of the Dardanelles) is celebrated as a great victory, which also helped make the Ottoman commander Mustafa Kemal into Atatürk ('Father of the Turks') and architect of modern Turkey. In the words of one recent transnational history, 'For the British, French, Canadians, Indians and Germans, the Gallipoli campaign is remembered as just another name in a long, tragic list of World War I battles. For Turks, Australians and New Zealanders, Gallipoli is something apart – a significant event in the self-development of their individual nations.'[32]

This more inclusive view of Gallipoli owed a good deal to domestic pressure from Australia's Turkish community – a tiny fraction of the post-1945 Turkish diaspora compared to their presence in West Germany but still politically significant in cities such as Melbourne. Arriving in growing numbers from 1968 under Australia's assisted migration scheme, Turks often bristled at a national commemoration that cast them as primal enemy. Their first attempts to join the Melbourne Anzac Day parade were resisted by veterans' leaders, one of whom warned, 'Anyone that was shooting at us doesn't get in.' But attitudes gradually changed and Turks now march every year in most of the major parades on 25 April. In 1985 the Turkish government renamed Ari Burnu beach, where Kemal commanded, as Anzac Cove; in response an Atatürk Memorial Garden was created in Canberra, just across the road from the Australian War Memorial – all signs of a new approach to remembrance as reconciliation.[33]

Where do the 'British Isles' fit into this story? How far have Britain and Ireland been affected by post-Cold War reconfigurations of the Great War and of twentieth-century history? In terms of national identity, the effect has been very profound, as the huge forces of attraction and division generated in 1914–18 finally began to weaken.

In the summer of 1914 the United Kingdom seemed close to disintegration – on the verge of civil war in Ireland but also challenged by campaigns for Home Rule in Scotland and for disestablishment of the Anglican Church in Wales. Yet, as we saw in Chapter One, the Great War kindled a new feeling of Britishness in England, Scotland and Wales, but it split Ireland into two rival states – one reliant on Britain to safeguard its Protestant identity, the other winning independence only after a brutal war against the British and an even more savage internecine conflict. The events of 1914–18 redefined both the United Kingdom and Ireland for most of the twentieth century and it was only in the 1990s that what we might call the Great War settlement finally came apart.

It may seem ironic that while Scots and Welsh regiments were 'fighting for the rights of small nations, the cause of Home Rule was one of the casualties of the First World War.'[34] But general pride at Britain's victory in the Great War coupled with numerous memorials to its human cost fostered a new acceptance of British identity. Although Plaid Cymru and the Scottish Nationalist Party (SNP) were both founded in the interwar years, they had limited impact and the sense of Britishness was reinvigorated by the Second World War. The Scots and the Welsh shared in the national narrative about Britain's 'finest hour', perpetuated in films through the 1950s. This was a period of strong economic growth, in contrast to the interwar Slump which had hit Scotland and Wales especially hard. The interventionist economics of both Labour and Conservative governments for a quarter-century after 1945 also made the Union seem directly beneficial through a nexus of state subsidies, welfare benefits and public housing. A third of the Scottish workforce was employed in local or central government as late as the 1980s. Even rural areas benefited: by the 1950s the Forestry Commission had become Scotland's largest landowner. Not until the 1960s and 1970s, when Britain's defeated rivals Germany and Japan bounced back economically, did the war dividend run out both economically and psychologically. The Scottish and Welsh economies – dependent on heavy industries such as coal, steel and shipbuilding that had been sustained by Attlee's nationalization – became seriously uncompetitive. In this harsher climate nationalist politics had more appeal: in 1967–8 the SNP finally won a seat in Westminster and Plaid Cymru dramatically cut Labour majorities in hitherto safe constituencies.[35]

The nationalist resurgence took different forms in the two countries, however. In Wales the dominant theme was culture, especially the survival of the Welsh language. In 1900 over half the population spoke Welsh, by the 1960s barely a quarter, but the Language Act of 1967 gave Welsh equal official status with English. Nationalist feeling in Wales was mainly concerned with 'the preservation of a disappearing way of life', whereas Scottish nationalism was more aggressively about 'building on to recognized institutions new ways of asserting distinctiveness from England.' The separate systems of law and education that had survived from 1707 were important foundations.[36]

It was in Scotland that pressures for devolution became particularly insistent, aided by the rapid demise of the British Empire in which the Scottish contribution in manpower, finance and trade had been hugely disproportionate to the country's size and population. The tartan-clad Scottish regiments, now being steadily disbanded, had enjoyed 'unchallenged prominence in Scottish society as symbols of national self-image.'[37] Anxious to head off the SNP, in 1979 a weak Labour government arranged a referendum on devolution in Scotland and Wales, which failed to win the necessary majorities. But the Thatcher government of the 1980s, with its centralizing tendencies, sale of nationalized industries and drastic cuts in public spending, persuaded many Scots that the Union as currently constituted was no longer working to their advantage. Her manner did not help: in the words of one Scottish Tory, 'the problem that Margaret had was that she was a woman; an English woman and a bossy English woman.' Thatcher's reform of local taxation (the notorious 'Poll Tax') was the last straw: Tory support north of the border collapsed from 22 seats in 1979 to none by 1997. On a broader plane the changing international scene by the 1990s also affected attitudes. With not only two world wars but now the Cold War receding into history, the UK had lost a clear Other, an external enemy to 'help to sustain British national identity against a common foe.'[38]

When the Labour government of Tony Blair offered new referenda on devolution in 1997, Scots voted decisively in favour while Welsh nationalists won only a bare majority. Nevertheless the new executives and elected assemblies established in Edinburgh and Cardiff in 1999 gradually acquired more and more devolved powers from Westminster. In Scotland the SNP, in office from 2007, manoeuvred its way to holding a full-scale referendum on independence in 2014. This was a year with special resonance for Scottish nationalists – exactly seven centuries since the great victory over the English at Bannockburn. But 2014 also marked the centenary of the outbreak of the Great War. The recent devolution-independence debate is a reminder of how 1914 helped to freeze British constitutional development for much of the twentieth century.

If Britain has been revisiting debates from before the Great War, Ireland in the 1990s finally began to move beyond its great divide of 1916. This had become more deeply entrenched in 1966 by rival fiftieth-anniversary commemorations of the Easter Rising and the first day of the Somme, which were catalysts for the Troubles (Chapter Nine). For Irish nationalists in the north and most people in the Irish Republic, the Great War as a whole had become a closed book – the service of Irish Catholic soldiers largely forgotten. The 1914–18 Memorial at Islandbridge, on the edge of Dublin, was closed during most of the Troubles for fear of violence. And in 1987 the IRA deliberately chose Remembrance Sunday to blow up the war memorial at Enniskillen, in Northern Ireland, killing eleven people.

But attitudes changed dramatically during the 1990s. The new post-Cold War interest in the Great War as 'the seminal event in the cycle of violence and ideological extremism that marked the twentieth century' directed attention on Ireland's place in that larger story.[39] Even more important, the intense efforts of John Major and Tony Blair to promote the peace process in Northern Ireland and involve the Irish government gradually paid off, culminating in the Good Friday agreement of 1998. Not only did this ease communal tensions and provide a framework for loyalists and republicans to work together in a new devolved government, it also removed British troops from the streets of Ulster, allowing the past involvement of Irishmen in Britain's wars to re-emerge less contentiously. Some community leaders in Belfast, recognizing that rival versions of history had been a root cause of the sectarian divide, tried to retrieve the Western Front as a common site of memory. The growing passion for family history often provided a point of entry: meetings to discuss photos and memorabilia from an ancestor's war service helped develop contacts and networks that would have been unimaginable during the Troubles. The Connaught Rangers proved particularly useful for this purpose because the regiment, lacking the word 'Royal' in its title, was less problematic for Catholics and nationalists.[40]

This theme of remembrance as reconciliation was picked up officially in the Island of Ireland Peace Tower in Belgium. The chosen site was near Mesen/Messines, where the 36th (Ulster) Division and the 16th (Irish) Division went into battle almost alongside each other in June 1917. The 110-foot tower was a public acknowledgment that Protestants and Catholics, loyalists and nationalists, had fought together as volunteers in the British army in 1914–18 – over 210,000 in all, of whom some 25,000 lost their lives.[41] Previous monuments, notably the 1921 Ulster Tower on the Somme, had been effectively loyalist memorials. The Peace Tower was dedicated by President Mary McAleese and Queen Elizabeth on 11 November 1998 after an 11 am Remembrance service. This was the first time the two heads of state of Ireland and the United Kingdom had appeared together in a public ceremony (plates 26–8).

The tower and surrounding Peace Park were initiated as a project in community reconciliation by Paddy Harte, an Irish Fine Gael politician, and Glenn Barr, a former loyalist paramilitary from Belfast. The Peace Pledge on a stone in the park declared: 'From this sacred shrine of remembrance, where soldiers of all nationalities, creeds and political allegiances were united in death, we appeal to all people in Ireland to help build a peaceful and tolerant society. Let us remember the solidarity and trust that developed between Protestant and Catholic soldiers when they served together in these trenches.' This new emphasis on 'equality of sacrifice' was somewhat contrived. Although some Irishmen who fought in the war, such as Tom Kettle, did hope that common service in the trenches might bridge the sectarian divide, historian John Horne observes that probably 'most Irish soldiers could not have cared one way or the other.' But their intentions no longer mattered. 'The Irish dead of the conflict have today been conscripted (as the living Irish of the war years never were) to serve in a very political, if well-meaning, project of mutual communal understanding and reconciliation.'[42]

Although the United Kingdom was moving on in complex ways from the Great War settlement, British images of the war itself continued to be those established in the 1960s and 1970s. Much to the dismay, that is, of some military historians who complained that there were virtually two Western Fronts – the literary and the historical – each self-contained, with the former still dominating the public imagination. These historians countered that the Western Front, although 'a place of horror and violence', was also 'a place of learning and technological advance'. They also counter the cultural turn by 'moving the conduct of battle to its central place within the war'.[43]

The most significant of these revisionist works, *Forgotten Victory* by Gary Sheffield published in 2001, asserted that 'the First World War was a tragic conflict, but it was neither futile nor meaningless. Just as in the struggles against Napoleon and, later, Hitler, it was a war that Britain had to fight and had to win,' another round in 'a long struggle to prevent one continental state from dominating the rest'. As for the cliché that the British army were 'lions led by donkeys', Sheffield argued that, 'against a background of revolutionary changes in the nature of war, the British army underwent a bloody learning curve and emerged as a formidable fighting force.' Situating the first day of the Somme within that process as 'an important point' on the 'learning curve', he highlighted the improvement in operational effectiveness, built around a precise and effective creeping barrage, flexible infantry tactics and all-arms cooperation, which reached its apogee in the last 'Hundred Days' of 1918. That phrase, redolent of 1815, was intended to shift attention from clichéd moments of 1918 such as the near rout on 21 March or Wilfred Owen's death a week before the Armistice. Sheffield insisted that in the autumn of 1918 Haig's army – the largest ever deployed in battle by the British Empire – achieved 'by far the greatest victory in British military history'. Although the psychological impact of fresh American troops was immense, Sheffield questioned their effect on the battles of 1918 and blamed their heavy losses on crude gung-ho infantry tactics reminiscent of the British on the Somme in 1916. In other words, the Doughboys of 1918 were way back on the learning curve.[44]

The thesis of *Forgotten Victory* was echoed by other military historians, for instance William Philpott in his massive study of the Somme, pointedly entitled *Bloody Victory* (2009), which surveyed the five-month battle in its entirety and from the perspective of the Germans as much as the British and French. For Philpott the attrition of Germany on the Somme was 'the military turning-point of the war', even though the denouement came only two years later. This battle was, he argued, the equivalent of Stalingrad in the Second World War, where the appalling human cost has never been used to deny the fact of victory. Why, then, British resistance to a similar proposition about the Somme? Partly because at Stalingrad the Germans were clearly defeated, indeed humiliated, whereas nothing so dramatic was evident by the time the Somme battle petered out. Also because the dead of 1942–3 were Russians, whereas in 1916 they were British, from a nation totally unused to attritional war on that scale. The term 'learning curve', borrowed from business psychology, sticks in the gullet of many people in Britain because the curve was lubricated so plentifully with soldiers' blood. The intent of historians such as Sheffield and Philpott was to rescue the British army from the mud, both literally and metaphorically. They downplayed the contrary argument, propounded decades earlier by Basil Liddell Hart, that it was the maritime blockade that starved Germany into submission, on the Western Front and the home front. They also had difficulty addressing the fact that the eventual 'victory' was far less clear-cut in 1918 than in 1945. The best Sheffield could claim was that the Great War produced 'negative gains' – in other words stopping something worse from happening, namely German domination of the continent, even though there had to be a second round, at greater human cost, in 1939–45.[45]

The revisionists shifted the terms of debate among specialists but they did not alter public perceptions of the Great War. This is evident from three best-selling histories of the war, published around the eightieth anniversary.

John Keegan had certainly not changed his mind since writing *The Face of Battle* in 1976. In *The First World War* (1998) he caustically dismissed the 'learning curve' as 'an argument akin to the thought that Dunkirk was a valuable rehearsal in amphibious operations for D-Day'. For Keegan the technology of warfare in 1914–18, however much generals refined the tactics, simply added up to mass slaughter. 'Only a very different technology' based on tanks and aircraft, which was not available till a generation later, could have averted such an outcome. Keegan regarded the First World War as 'a tragic and unnecessary conflict' – unnecessary because better diplomacy could have arrested the slide to war in 1914, and tragic because of the 10 million dead and the poisonous legacies which led to a Second World War that was 'the direct outcome of the First'. By the final page of his book Keegan had moved beyond the realm of historical explanation, asserting that the First World War was 'a mystery', both in its origins and its course. 'Why', he asked almost imploringly, 'did a prosperous continent, at the height of its success ... choose to risk all it had won for itself and all it offered to the world on the lottery of a vicious and local internecine conflict?' The only positive Keegan could discern was another 'mystery' – the tenacious courage of the ordinary soldiers and the comradeship forged in what he called 'the earthwork cities of the Western and Eastern Fronts'.[46]

Here was the now familiar post-1960s British narrative repackaged for the latest anniversary. Keegan's book was not a work of original research and many of its sources were somewhat dated. By contrast Niall Ferguson based his eightieth-anniversary offering, *The Pity of War* (1998), on substantial research by a team of assistants in British and German archives and on a wide range of recent books and journal articles. The result was a 600-page tome, detailed and analytical yet highly readable and full of provocative arguments. An economic historian by training, Ferguson calculated that despite their substantial superiority in resources, Britain, America and France waged war far less effectively than their enemies. In accountancy terms it cost the Allies $36,485 to kill an enemy soldier, over three times the per capita cost for the Central Powers, who also 'killed at least 35 per cent more men than they lost.' So the learning curve was appallingly expensive in cash as well as corpses. Intrigued by counter-factual history and viewing 1914–18 from the 1990s vantage point of German reunification and the impending Euro, Ferguson also offered the tendentious opinion that, if the British had not gone to war in 1914, Germany would have won but both Britain and Europe would have been better off: 'it would have been infinitely preferable if Germany could have achieved its hegemonic position on the continent without two world wars.' The Kaiser's Reich, he insisted, was not like Hitler's: it was driven by insecurity and weakness rather than the lust for power depicted by Fritz Fischer. Had Britain stood aside in 1914, exclaimed Ferguson, his imagination surging into overdrive, 'Hitler could have eked out his living as a mediocre postcard painter' and 'Lenin could have carried on his splenetic scribbling in Zurich'. Meanwhile continental Europe could have been 'transformed into something not wholly unlike the European Union we know today – but without the massive contraction in British overseas power entailed by fighting two world wars.'[47]

Most of this was pure speculation but, like A.J.P. Taylor, Ferguson liked to stir things up: this was the Great War recooked in a hot sauce to offend traditional British palates. But for all its piquant novelties, at root *The Pity of War* was a conventional view of the conflict, pivoting around the Western Front and informed by its poetry. The title came from Wilfred Owen, with whom the book began and ended. For Ferguson the war was indeed 'piteous' but he would not invoke the oft-used term 'tragedy' because that had Shakespearean undertones of inevitability. No, he concluded, it was 'nothing less than the greatest *error* of modern history.'[48]

The third major anniversary offering was *1914–18: The Great War and the Shaping of the Twentieth Century* (1996) by Jay Winter and Blaine Baggett – a book but also a major television series, shown in America and Britain. Thirty years on this was a very different spectacle from the BBC's *Great War* of 1964. Winter viewed the conflict as 'cultural history': he wanted to explore how leaders and led 'made sense of the war and its consequences' via images, language and artistic forms. Baggett, a television producer, had been inspired by reading Paul Fussell's *Great War and Modern Memory* just as the Cold War ended – what interested him, like Winter, were legacies as much as 1914–18 itself. Personal factors also played a part in shaping the series: both authors were Americans whose attitudes to war and its futility were coloured by Vietnam, while Winter was a descendant of survivors from the Nazi death camps. For him, studying 'what contemporaries of the time called the Great War' was 'as close to the great horror of the twentieth century' – the Holocaust – as he could 'bear to stand'. In the interpretation of Winter and Baggett the First World War started 'a descent into darkness' which 'normalized collective violence' as the 'signature' of the twentieth century from Sarajevo in 1914 to Sarajevo in 1994. It was also the progenitor of 'an industrial killing machine' that reached hellish perfection at Auschwitz.[49]

The television series was a co-production between the Public Broadcasting System (PBS) in America and the BBC in Britain. Reactions to it in the two countries were strikingly different. In America, where PBS is very much a minority channel, the response was huge and overwhelmingly positive – watched by about 5 million households, extensively reviewed in major newspapers and periodicals and winning coveted Emmy and Peabody awards. For many Americans – whose interest in their own Civil War had been kindled by Ken Burns' immensely successful PBS series in 1990–1 – this was their first serious exposure to Europe's 'civil war' of 1914–18. But in Britain, although audiences were relatively large (averaging 2.5 million), the response was more mixed. Not only was this for the British an unfamiliar take on the Great War, with much continental material and a cultural bias, but its relentless sense of futility offended military historians such as John Terraine, Haig's great apologist. Winter had to fight very hard to keep the title 'Slaughter' for the film about the Somme, Verdun and Passchendaele. Cautious figures in the BBC urged 'Sacrifice' but he was insistent: 'Sacrifices redeem; slaughter does not' and 'the loss of life of three quarters of a million men had no redemptive "meaning"'. Correlli Barnett, like Terraine a consultant for the BBC's *Great War*, was particularly incensed. In an article entitled 'Oh What a Whingeing War' he lamented the spotty discussion of strategy and politics without which, he argued, the fighting was bound to lack meaning. Barnett became so irritated by Jay Winter 'honking away in academic's American' and by 'the cocksureness of his expression and pronouncements' that he finally declared, 'I longed to hang one on his hooter.'[50]

These big new histories of the war – presenting it as tragic 'mystery', supreme 'error' or horrific 'slaughter' – served to confirm the familiar British narrative and attracted far more attention than the revisionist views of military historians. But the main way the conflict came alive for a general audience was still through literature. And in the 1990s the war poets were enfolded for the first time into popular fiction.

Novelist Pat Barker wrote a trilogy – *Regeneration* (1991), *The Eye in the Door* (1993) and *The Ghost Road* (1995) – around the story of Siegfried Sassoon and Wilfred Owen being treated for 'shell-shock' in the Craiglockhart Hospital in Edinburgh. The first novel opens with the public declaration of protest in July 1917 by Sassoon, a veteran who has won the Military Cross, against a conflict 'which I entered as a war of defence and liberation' but which 'has now become a war of aggression and conquest . . . deliberately prolonged by those who have the power to end it.' Her protagonist is the neurologist Dr William Rivers, whose task is to 'cure' shell-shocked men so that they can get back to the front. The trilogy revolves around the themes of madness – who exactly is sane in this situation of nightmare war? – and comradeship, not least the friendship between Sassoon and Owen that transforms the stuttering talents of the latter into a major poetic voice able to articulate for all time war's insanity. Although Sassoon, Owen and Rivers are historical characters, Barker creates Billy Prior, a rather anachronistic bisexual working-class junior officer, through whom she explores the issues of wartime homosexuality and the class structure of Britain and its army.[51]

Prior's exploits in London in 1917–18 take centre stage in the second novel but *The Ghost Road* returns to the war during its final months. The novel's title comes from lines by the poet Edward Thomas, quoted in the epigraph to this chapter, about the living soldiers treading heavily along the road to France, while 'the dead / Returning lightly dance'. Prior has been sent back to the front and is serving in the 2nd Manchester Regiment, the same unit as Owen, whom he fancies. Both men are now inured to death and killing – to machine-gunning Germans 'like killing fish in a bucket' and being splattered with the blood and brains of comrades. 'We are Craiglockhart's success stories,' Prior scribbles sardonically in his diary on 6 October 1918. 'By any civilized standards (but what does *that* mean *now*?) we are objects of horror. But our nerves are completely steady and we are still alive.'[52]

Only for a few more weeks, however. Although armistice negotiations have become common knowledge ('nobody here sees the point of going on now'), the 2nd Manchesters are thrown into a canal crossing, over sodden, open ground covered by enemy machine guns. 'The whole operation's *insane*,' one decorated officer exclaims. 'The chances of success are *zero*.' But they are 'told flatly, a simple, unsupported assertion, that the weight of the artillery would overcome all opposition.' Just in case the allusion is not clear, Barker has Prior note in his diary, 'I think those words sent a chill down the spine of every man there who remembered the Somme.' (No learning curve here.) As Prior and Owen breathe their last on the Sambre Canal, at a hospital back in London Rivers endures the final moments of one of their comrades, a young officer who has had half his face blown away. '*Shotvarfet*' the lad keeps crying. 'What's he saying?' asks his anguished father, a retired officer and till now a staunch, unthinking patriot. Suddenly Rivers realizes: 'It's not worth it.' Just as he does so, the cry is picked up around the ward, 'a wordless murmur from damaged brains and drooping mouths. *Shotvarfet. Shotvarfet.*' This, fumed military historian Brian Bond, 'is the authentic whingeing note of the 1990s transposed unconvincingly to 1918.'[53]

The other best-selling Great War novel of the 1990s was Sebastian Faulks' *Birdsong* (1993). The war had been rubbing away at the back of his mind for years: on 11 November 1965 as a twelve-year-old, growing hoarse while reading out the almost endless list of names of 'old boys' from his school who had died in two world wars; and in November 1988 as a journalist covering a tour organized by Lyn Macdonald along the Western Front when old men talked of lost friends at their graves in immaculate English-garden cemeteries.

Faulks began to feel that 'the experience of this war had somehow slipped from public understanding', overshadowed by 'a second frenzy' twenty years later, 'one aspect of which had been so well memorialized at the insistence of its victims that it seemed to leave no room in the public memory for earlier holocausts.'[54]

Birdsong tells the story of Stephen Wraysford, a battle-hardened junior officer who has become, like Owen and Prior in the 'Regeneration' trilogy, almost addicted to the war that he hates. The centrepiece of the novel's war narrative is what Faulks calls 'the most infamous day in British military history', 1 July 1916. His thirty-page account, which drew on Middlebrook's *First Day on the Somme*, is told with familiar tropes such as the 'comic opera' colonel assuring the men that 'the enemy will be utterly demoralized' by the artillery barrage and that 'only a handful of shots will be fired at you'. But also with vividly imaginative writing, such as Faulks' evocation of darkness finally descending upon the battlefield: 'The earth began to move. . . . It was like a resurrection in a cemetery twelve miles long' as the 'bent, agonized shapes' of the wounded crawled back into their trenches 'to reclaim their life'.[55]

Our sense of the soldiers' troglodyte existence is accentuated by Faulks' subplot about the 'sewer rats' who tunnel below no-man's-land to explode mines under the enemy trenches, while the Germans try to do the same to them. Tunnelling, declares Faulks, constituted 'a hell within a hell' and he captures vividly its claustrophobia. Near the end of the book, set in the closing hours of the war, Stephen is freed from incarceration in a ruined tunnel, only to see his rescuer clothed in *feldgrau*, 'the colour of his darkest dreams'. Wild-eyed, he raises his arms, ready to fight, and so does the German. But then the two men fall on each other's shoulders weeping at what Faulks calls 'the bitter strangeness of their human lives.' Here, for cognoscenti, was an echo of one of Owen's most haunting poems, 'Strange Meeting', in which the poet dreams he has died and slipped 'down some profound dull tunnel' into Hell, where one of the 'encumbered sleepers' springs up with 'piteous recognition' in his eyes. 'I am the enemy you killed, my friend.' But that was yesterday. 'Let us sleep now . . .' Here, in *Birdsong*, life was imitating art, all within the realm of fiction.[56]

Around Stephen's war story Faulks spins two other narratives. The first is Stephen's passionate affair in 1910 with a married French woman in Amiens from which, unknown to him, a child is born. This prelude also enables Faulks to create ironic anticipations of things to come. There is, for instance, talk of a fishing trip on the river Ancre. 'You *must* come,' Stephen is told: 'They have famous "English teas" at Thiepval.' But in order to address the reader's anticipated query, 'What has all this remote horror to do with my modern life?', Faulks invented a more contemporary character to 'pose just such questions'. This is Stephen's granddaughter Elizabeth who, in the late 1970s, tries to find out about him – gradually deciphering his diary, discovered in the family attic, and meeting frail survivors of his forgotten war. Here, woven into the novel, is another thread of 1990s remembrance, the passion for family history. Elizabeth's interest takes hold as she faces the prospect, aged thirty-eight and single, that she might die childless. 'In the absence of her own children she had started to look back and wonder at the fate of a different generation', feeling 'almost maternal to them', especially to the man who had been 'her own flesh and blood'.[57]

Unlike the dark, savage conclusion of The Ghost Road, Faulks offers redemption from the past. Emulating Stephen's 'strange meeting' with the enemy at the end of his war, Elizabeth finally does find a partner and she gives birth to a new generation. Honouring a promise she now knows that her grandfather had made to Jack Firebrace, a 'sewer rat' who once saved his life, the child is named John – in memory of Jack's son who had died of diphtheria. Thus, the past is somehow redeemed in the present. This was what Faulks aspired to do through his book and, he hoped, his readers to do as well – making what he called 'gestures of love and redemption towards the past'.[58]

In different, sometimes contrived ways both Pat Barker and Sebastian Faulks drew on 1990s patterns of British remembrance – the axiomatic futility of the Great War, the cruciform centrality of the Somme and the dominant voice of poets such as Thomas and Owen. Their novels became best-sellers – The Ghost Road winning the Booker Prize, Britain's highest award for fiction – and clearly left many people with a vivid and enduring impression of the Great War.

'People should read this book', one fan of *Birdsong* commented, 'to be aware, without reading a dull, factual history book, how dreadful things were in the Great War.' Another described *Birdsong* as 'the book that brought me an understanding of a time in history that before I couldn't identify with.' Fiction, in other words, seems truer than fact. The influence of the novels was further enlarged via the screen. Barker's trilogy was condensed into a film, *Regeneration* (1997), distributed in the United States under the title *Behind the Lines*, while *Birdsong* was finally adapted into a two-part television series in 2012 by the BBC and PBS in America (though removing the Elizabeth sub-plot entirely). In Britain the two episodes attracted viewing figures of 7 million and 6 million respectively – attention on a scale that no history book could match. The American exposure was also significant. When Faulks first hawked his typescript fruitlessly around Manhattan in 1993, one editor advised him to set the story 'in a more recent conflict'. But by the 2000s, thanks to film and television as well as novels, the British narrative of the Great War was becoming entrenched on the other side of the Atlantic.[59]

For these novelists, sites of memory are central to the plots, inspiring some of their most lyrical writing. In Faulks' *Birdsong* Elizabeth's quest turns into an obsession after visiting Lutyens' vast war memorial at Thiepval on the Somme – its multiple, soaring arches chiselled with 73,000 British names 'as though the surface of the sky had been papered in footnotes.' Are these 'men who died in this battle?' she asks. 'No,' a custodian replies. 'The lost, the ones they did not find. The others are in the cemeteries.' So these are 'just the ... unfound', she gasps. 'From the whole war?' The man shakes his head: 'Just these fields.' Elizabeth slumps on the steps of the monument. 'My God, nobody told me.' In this personal encounter with a site of memory – her 'strange meeting' one might say – the past suddenly becomes present. In *Another World* (1998), Pat Barker's grisly exploration of the haunted mind of a Somme veteran, Thiepval seems truly repulsive to Nick, the old man's grandson. It reminded him of 'a warrior's helmet with no head inside. No, worse than that: Golgotha, the place of a skull.' Thiepval is a place of 'annihilating abstractions' – not 'a triumph *over* death but the triumph *of* death' – all very different from what

Lutyens and Kipling intended in 1932 when raising the arches and etching into the stone 'Their Name Liveth for Evermore'. In other words, sites of memory are also *sights* of memory – dependent on the eyes of the beholder.[60]

All of these novels revolved around individual soldiers, explored both in body and in mind, in ways that sum up the British identification of the Great War with the experience of the Tommies. This obsession became yet more marked during the 1990s. The British Legion mounted a determined campaign to revive the two-minute silence on 11 November itself, rather than simply on the nearest Remembrance Sunday. This reversion to the practice of the 1920s and 1930s became established from 1995, the fiftieth anniversary of the ending of the Second World War. In the new millennium the development of the internet gave further impetus to family history of the Great War, as soldiers' records became available online. This made it easier to undertake research from the comfort of home rather than by visiting the National Archives in south-west London.

Public fascination with the Tommies reached a peak early in the new millennium, as the last surviving veterans gradually passed away. This elegiac moment was not narrowly British but transnational. In all the former belligerent countries the surviving veterans were officially identified and their final years observed by officialdom and the media with almost macabre anticipation. Australia, for instance, witnessed what has been called 'an increasingly hysterical countdown' to the death of the last Anzac in 2002.[61] This man was Alec Campbell from Tasmania, who had served for a couple of months at Gallipoli as an ammunition carrier when only sixteen. By the end of his life he was lauded by politicians and the media as an 'Australian Legend' and the country's 'last living link' with Gallipoli. After his death, aged 103, Campbell was accorded a state funeral. In the United States 'The Last Doughboy' from 1917–18, Frank W. Buckles, died in February 2011, aged 110, and was interred in Arlington National Cemetery. Spry and articulate almost to the end, he had become the figurehead of a campaign to establish a formal National World War I Memorial on the Mall in Washington. In France 'le dernier poilu' was identified as Lazare Ponticelli who, somewhat inconveniently, had fought in both

the French and Italian armies during the Great War. He resisted official demands that he be interred among the nation's great and good
in the Panthéon, preferring to rest in the family grave in the Paris
suburbs. But Ponticelli did consent to a state funeral which, after his
death at the age of 110, was duly held in the Invalides in March 2008,
attended by President Nicolas Sarkozy, who then unveiled a plaque
near the tomb of Marshal Foch to all who had fought. This declared:
'La France conserve précieusement le souvenir de ceux qui restent
dans l'histoire comme les poilus de la Grande Guerre.'[62]

From these examples one can discern common threads. Awe at
people who live to such a great age – their present frailties contrasted
visually with photographs of them in full manhood in 1914–18.
Ordinary men made extraordinary by their longevity. Repeated invo-
cation of their status as 'heroes', or at least representatives of a heroic
generation. And a feeling that the last frail threads of 'communicative
memory' back to the Great War were being severed.

All of these sentiments and more were evident at the 'Service to
Mark the Passing of the World War One Generation' at Westminster
Abbey on 11 November 2009. Its cue was the death of the three
remaining British veterans of 1914–18 earlier that year. The man officially designated as 'The Last Tommy', Harry Patch, born two
centuries earlier in 1898, had fought and killed at Passchendaele in
1917. After 1918 he lived an active life, becoming a plumber in peacetime and a volunteer fireman during the Second World War, and
enjoyed a long retirement. Only in the twenty-first century did he
start speaking about the Great War, returning to Passchendaele in
2005, and then being memorialized in a film, a book and a poem.[63]

During the November 2009 service to mark 'the passing of this
remarkable generation', the war poets were very audible. The choir
sang the setting of Wilfred Owen's poem 'Agnus Dei' from Benjamin
Britten's War Requiem and the actor Jeremy Irons, standing by the
memorial in Poets Corner to the First World War poets, read modern
verses composed by the poet laureate Carol Ann Duffy. Her 'Last
Post' starts with the famous lines from Owen's 'Dulce et Decorum
Est', his nightmare vision of a soldier too slow in putting on his gas
mask and now floundering 'as under a green sea':

In all my dreams, before my helpless sight,
He plunges at me, guttering, choking, drowning.

But Duffy's dying soldier is the victim of shrapnel, not gas. She imagines the poet telling his story backwards, willing him to rewrite the past so we watch the Tommy rise up, amazed, from the 'stinking mud' as blood spurts back into his body – and into thousands more men as 'lines and lines of British boys rewind / back to their trenches'. And back further, dropping their guns, back into the town square for coffee and 'warm French bread', and out of the war itself, 'released / from History' with 'several million lives still possible' – lives full of love and hope instead of 'entering the story now / to die and die and die' in muddy oblivion. Then, says Duffy:

You see the poet tuck away his pocket-book and smile.
If poetry could truly tell it backwards,
then it would.[64]

'Last Post' is a quick but sharp piece of writing, playing off a poetic classic from 1917 and using the familiar tropes of mud and death, yet mingling them with images from the contemporary world, such as pressing the rewind button and breakfasting in a French patisserie. Duffy is imaginatively pitting Poetry against History, longing to reverse the horrors and redeem the past – also Faulks' aspiration in *Birdsong*. Yet the poignancy of 'Last Post' derives from the fact that she knows, as do we, that poetry cannot 'tell it backwards'.

History can do that, however – if we understand 'history' to be a process of interpretation and reinterpretation rather than the recitation of immutable facts. Even if historians write forwards, telling a sequential narrative, they *think* backwards from the present into the past. Such a dialogue between past and present has been the dynamic pivot of this book. In the concluding chapter I shall try to 'tell it backwards' – setting the complex legacies of 1914–18 against the current, constricted British view of the Great War and asking, 'Why?'

CONCLUSION

LONG SHADOW

*The dead were and are not. Their place knows them no
more and is ours to-day. Yet they were once as real as we,
and we shall to-morrow be shadows like them.*

G.M. Trevelyan, 1927

'Europe in danger – her liberties imperilled.'
So the statesmen cried.
Stern, stupid Englishmen, foolishly believing them,
Marched and fought and died.

W.N. Ewer, November 1914[1]

W.N. Ewer's '1814–1914' was an anti-war poem written in
November 1914, yet a poem composed around the past as
much as the present. The left-wing journalist was a vehement critic of
Britain's involvement in the Great War but in the stanza quoted above
he was evoking the mood a century before. His poem recalled the
patriotic rhetoric of an earlier age when England also 'fought for
freedom', in that case under Pitt and Castlereagh against the tyranny
of Napoleon. And what happened 'when the Corsican was broke'?,
asked Ewer grimly. France got 'her Bourbons back' while in England

Waterloo was followed by Peterloo.* Now in 1914, warned Ewer, 'stern, stupid Englishmen' once again 'march cheerfully away' – heedless of the broken promises and the bitter fruit from their forefathers' 'War for Freedom'.[2]

Ewer was reflecting on poetry as well as history, evoking Thomas Hardy's verse epic about the Napoleonic Wars, 'The Dynasts', and jousting against Hardy's famous patriotic poem of September 1914, 'Men Who March Away'. '1814 – 1914' was certainly not the only way to comprehend the legacies of the Napoleonic Wars – by the 1920s Ewer had become a covert Bolshevik[3] – yet the poem reminds us that in 1914, but for the Sarajevo surprise, Britain would have been preparing to mark the hundredth anniversary of Waterloo. Instead the British people were suddenly plunged into another 'Great War' which precluded any serious reflection about the significance of June 1815, about the 'long peace' that followed and about its relationship with the country's subsequent industrial growth and imperial prosperity. Today, a century on from Ewer, we are at a similar chronological distance in relation to the Great War of 1914–18. All the veterans and most of their bereaved relatives are dead: the task a hundred years on is not so much remembrance as understanding.

This book has traced the long shadow cast by the Great War over the twentieth century. But it has also shown how the twentieth century kept reshaping the Great War in its own light, with different nations and eras persistently reinterpreting the conflict through their own preoccupations. The historical dynamic between the Great War and the twentieth century is therefore two-way: hence the book's bipartite structure of legacies and refractions. In Part One I outlined some of the diverse and momentous ways in which the war had an impact on the 1920s and 1930s, both positive as well as negative. It is helpful to conceive of these decades as the 'post-war' years – the perspective of contemporaries after 1918 – rather than writing them off with hindsight as the 'interwar' years whose obvious failures would soon be

---

* Peterloo was the infamous 'massacre' at St Peter's Field in Manchester in 1819 when troops charged a large crowd demanding parliamentary reform.

exposed. After 1939, however, the events of 1914–18 did look different when refracted through a new conflict, when the 'Great War'
became the 'First World War'. For most of the nations involved the
two world wars became symbiotic, with each understood in the light
of the other. Only with the end of the Cold War – which had been
the long 'post-war' to the conflict of 1939–45 – has it been possible to
gain some detachment from that entanglement. The centenaries of the
Great War from 2014 to 2018 offer opportunities for fresh reflections
on the conflict's meaning and significance.

Although *The Long Shadow* has ranged across the major belligerent
countries of 1914–18, it has placed the United Kingdom in the foreground of the story. The British, I have argued, were distinctive in
their experience both of the war and of its post-war impacts. Britain
also stands out in the way that it has remembered the conflict in
public culture. All this contrasts with the broad patterns of experience
and memorialization on the continent. The United States was, of
course, even more detached than Britain from the conflict but there
both the cost and the impact were much less, particularly when compared with America's own Great War in 1861–5 and the country's
involvement in the Second World War in 1941–5. For the British,
1914–18 has become a problem that will not go away. Its vexed
interpretation is wrapped up with many ongoing debates, including
the United Kingdom's troubled relationship with the European
Union.

So what is distinctive about the British story? What, in essence, has
been the argument of this book? First, that in 1914 the United
Kingdom was not fighting directly for the homeland, either to protect
it from invasion or add to its territory. By contrast the Belgians, the
French and the Serbs were resisting invasion; the French were also
trying to recover Alsace and Lorraine; while Germany, Russia and the
Habsburg Empire all justified aggression as an act of pre-emptive
defence. Despite Foreign Office concerns about the long-term balance of power in Europe, Germany's warmaking posed no direct
territorial threat in August 1914. It was the Kaiser's violation of
Belgian neutrality, which Britain had pledged to protect, that provided
the *casus belli*, and public anger was accentuated by reports of German

'atrocities' against Belgian civilians. Germany's air raids on London and other centres would later inject an element of territorial jeopardy but, in large measure, these attacks on civilian homes were seen as additions to the list of Hunnish atrocities. Essentially Britain's public case for war was grounded more in morality than self-interest: this was seen as a war to defend the principles of freedom and civilization.

The other principal contrast between Britain and the continent in 1914 was the remarkable phenomenon of volunteering. France, Germany, Russia and the other belligerents required adult males to undertake military service: although conscription was applied patchily, the combination of conscripts and reservists meant that Germany and France could each field armies of around 2 million men on the Western Front in August 1914, whereas the British Expeditionary Force (BEF) amounted to fewer than 100,000 regulars and reservists (even smaller than the Belgian army).[4] As the BEF was destroyed in the frantic fighting of 1914, Britain began to raise a mass army, but it did not impose conscription until 1916. The 2.5 million men who chose to enlist (43 per cent of all who served in the British army in 1914–18) constituted the second-largest volunteer army in history.[*5] The surge of volunteering in the first half of the war set Britain apart from the continental belligerents and also the United States, which enacted conscription within six weeks of entering the conflict in 1917. This adds special poignancy to the death of so many men from Britain's New Armies on the Somme in 1916. Likewise to the losses among the British Dominions, whose forces were also volunteers for at least the first half of the war, and for the whole duration in the case of Australia.

Freely fighting for the freedom of others – that is what made the British feel distinctive. It also suggests the unique questions that would be raised when the taste of victory turned sour. Yet this book has argued that this disenchantment did not occur immediately. Despite all the problems of the post-war era, Britain's experience of the 1920s and 1930s was in fundamental ways more positive than those of the continental belligerents. For instance, as a result of the war that

* The largest, it is interesting to note, was the Indian army of 1939–45.

smashed several great empires, the British Empire actually grew to its largest extent, acquiring remnants of the old Ottoman Empire, including Mesopotamia, Palestine and Transjordan, as well as former German colonies in Africa and the Pacific. The war effort of the 'White Dominions', though in the long run part of a process of gradual independence, served in the medium term to reinforce a sense of shared identity within the British family of nations. Even the strains that the war imposed on British rule in India remained manageable during the 1920s and 1930s.

Within the United Kingdom itself the pattern was more complex but still distinctive. The continental empires of the Romanovs and Habsburgs fell apart at the end of the war as a consequence of war mobilization. Nationalist movements seized their chance but success often came after wars of independence lasting several years, in the process spawning civil wars and paramilitary violence – as in Poland and the Baltic states. Viewing the United Kingdom as an imperial polity, a little English empire within the 'British Isles', one can say that the dynamic was exactly opposite to that in eastern Europe. The UK's crisis of empire peaked before the war, not at its end: in the summer of 1914 Ireland teetered on the brink of civil war, Home Rule for Scotland was debated in Westminster, while the Welsh demanded disestablishment of the Anglican Church. But the outbreak of war took the heat out of Scottish and Welsh protests, and the ensuing conflict generated a new sense of Britishness. The Second World War had a similar effect. Nationalism in both countries did not really revive until the last third of the twentieth century.

Ireland, however, proved the continental-style exception to the British story. Parliament's approval in principle in September 1914 of Irish Home Rule defused the immediate crisis and 210,000 Irishmen volunteered to fight in the British army during the war. The majority were Catholics and nationalists,[6] initially persuaded that the Home Rule Act and the battle for Belgium were two sides of the same coin, showing that the British Empire was finally championing the freedom of small nations. As the war dragged on, however, Britain's failure to implement Home Rule and its brutal suppression of the quixotic Easter Rising in April 1916 changed the mood across much of Ireland.

Simultaneously the losses of the Ulster Division on the first day of the Somme fostered an Ulster Protestant loyalist backlash against the nationalists' stab in the back. These two 'blood sacrifices' in 1916 became enduring markers for nationalist and Unionist opinion respectively. Ireland's bloody war of independence was followed by an even more brutal civil war over whether to accept the partial independence conceded by London: six Ulster counties stayed within the UK and Eire agreed to remain within the British Empire. Both of these wars were characterized by paramilitary violence akin to that in eastern Europe, often waged by brutalized veterans from Britain's wartime army.

Britain's democratic transition was also distinctive. Mass democracy exploded across Europe in the wake of the war, inspired in very different ways by Lenin and Wilson. But its destabilizing effects were soon being channelled by new political elites – the Bolshevik concept of a vanguard supposedly preparing the way for eventual proleterian control, the fascist response in the form of a 'superman' leader directing a dominant party. By the mid-1930s much of continental Europe was polarized between left and right, even in Britain's co-victor France. The United States, uniquely, withstood the appeal of Marxism but the backlash was in its own way destabilizing. Wartime '100% Americanism' and the post-war Red Scare, though a brief spasm, laid the basis for a Manichean ideology of hyper-patriotism and vehement anti-communism that would eventually define America's foreign policy in the second half of the century. In Britain, by contrast, the sudden tripling of the electorate in 1918 was successfully absorbed within parliamentary politics. The threat of an utterly crippling general strike never materialized. Under Ramsay MacDonald the Labour Party was desperate to prove it did not pose a threat to the constitution, the empire or the pound. The party's ideology drew less on continental Marxism than on indigenous traditions of nineteenth-century radicalism and nonconformist religion. At the same time the Tories, led by Stanley Baldwin and Neville Chamberlain, won the support of many of the newly enfranchised women and skilled workers, attracted by policies such as a 'property-owning democracy'. In Britain fascist elements like Mosley remained marginal, and potential 'supermen' leaders, such as Lloyd George and Churchill, were excluded from office.

Global capitalism was also radically transformed by the war – not just through disruption to trade and finance but also through the emergence of new international actors, especially the United States, which unhinged the formerly London-centred global economy. For ordinary Germans the 1920s and early 1930s were truly devastating: first hyperinflation destroyed the value of the currency – turning the daily business of earning a living and finding food and shelter into a nightmare – and then, within a few years, ruinous deflation left nearly a third of the workforce unemployed. This double whammy in one decade inevitably undermined faith in Germany's new and fragile republican democracy, paving the way for Hitler's accession to power. For most ordinary Americans, by contrast, the 1920s were a decade of heady prosperity but, as the financial sector overheated and consumer demand was satiated, the ensuing economic downturn turned into the country's worst Depression – with 25 per cent unemployment in 1933 and the near collapse of the country's banking system. Britain, however, managed to maintain the value of its currency and the stability of its banks. It avoided financial collapse in 1931, going off the gold standard early (unlike France) and pulling out of the Slump relatively quickly, with steady growth in the south and Midlands. The story was much bleaker along the industrial periphery – in the Scottish Lowlands, northern England and south Wales, where the old staples of coal, textiles and shipbuilding were becoming less competitive in global markets. These areas, Labour heartlands, suffered high and sustained unemployment throughout the 1920s and 1930s and their experience generated a different narrative about the period, a story of poverty and betrayal, which became widely accepted after Labour gained power in 1945. But that has obscured the fact that, in terms of broad national comparisons, Britain got through the economic crises of the 1920s and 1930s more successfully than the continent, with beneficial consequences for political stability.

Seeing the post-war decades in themselves rather than through the lens of 1939–45, and setting the British experience in international context have been themes of the early chapters of this book. The result of doing so is a more positive perception of the legacies of the Great War for Britain. But what about the losses – also unique compared with all other British wars? What about the 720,000 dead and the several million who came home maimed in body and mind? Veterans such as the composer-poet Ivor Gurney, who spent his last fifteen years in a mental asylum, convinced by the end that he was Shakespeare.[7]

Seeking to cope with the trauma of the Great War, the British, like most belligerents except the Soviet Union, memorialized war deaths as 'sacrifice'. But they did so in forms which again were distinctive. The Cenotaph, the Silence and the Poppies. The necklace of war cemeteries gracing the scar-torn Western Front. The Names chiselled on the Memorials to the Missing at Ypres and Thiepval. In time these would all become highly charged sites of memory, expressions of Britain's peculiarly statist-democratic project of remembrance, honouring the dead as individuals but in standardized forms. The British government also embarked on a unique programme of war art, commissioning more than a hundred artists yet giving them remarkable artistic freedom. In the very different canvases of Paul Nash, Richard Nevinson and Wyndham Lewis avant-garde techniques, to which British artists came late, were dramatically applied to the subject of war, yet with much more humanity than in the nihilistic Expressionism of Germans such as Otto Dix. Also unusual was Britain's war poetry as it developed from the Europe-wide patriotic rhetoric of 1914. In the stanzas of Owen, Thomas and Gurney war poetry became an encounter between bookish soldiers rooted in the English pastoral tradition and the grotesque violations of nature inflicted by industrialized warfare – also a theme of Nash's ravaged landscapes. Britain's memorials, art and poetry created vivid markers of the war for posterity.

In the 1920s, however, the cultural reading of the Great War in Britain was not fundamentally negative. Even though the tenth anniversary of the Armistice in 1928 stirred up renewed debate, the more open discussion of the horrors and follies of warmaking did not result in wholesale condemnation of the war itself. The suffering of the soldiers might still be justified if 1914–18 did indeed prove to be 'the war to end wars'. Here was a very different interpretation of the conflict from the one being pedalled by the rightist veterans in Germany – about a lost victory that could only be redeemed through another war. In the 1920s Great Britain had the least significant veterans' movement of all the main belligerents – France, Germany and the United States – but by the 1930s it boasted the biggest and most committed peace movement in the world, as shown by the Peace Ballot of 1934–5. Most of those involved were not pacifists but peace activists, hoping to mobilize the League of Nations to deter future aggression. But as the threat grew of another war and with it fear of massive airborne destruction, the peace movement became increasingly passive, even pacifist. Under Chamberlain 'appeasement' was no longer a project to pacify Europe but a desperate bid to keep Britain out of war – peace at almost any price.

And it failed. The twenty-fifth anniversary of the outbreak of the Great War, rather like the centenary of Waterloo, was overshadowed by a new conflict. Here was the fateful coupling: the Great War took on a different aspect once it became the First World War, always to be contrasted with the Second. Consider some of the contrasts. Britain went to war in September 1939 after a 'gathering storm', in Churchill's phrase, that had been brewing for years, rather than 'out of the blue' as in the July crisis of 1914. The pros and cons of resisting Hitler had been the subject of long and intense public debate since 1933. Another contrast: this time there was no volunteer army. Conscription was enacted in April 1939 before the Second World War began. And although the immediate *casus belli* was again Britain's guarantee of a small country – in this case Poland – the issue became one of self-defence once the British Isles were blitzed in 1940 and threatened with invasion. The theme of Britain alone in its 'finest hour' offered a heroic saga at odds with anything in 1914–18. Fighting them on the beaches in defence of hearth and home seemed far more meaningful and impressive than fighting them in the trenches for the freedom of an ally who folded so dismally in 1940. The midpoint of the Second World War was a clear-cut victory for the British Empire at Alamein, unlike its costly and at best equivocal counterpart from

1914–18 – the Somme. And by 1945 the utter bestiality of the Nazi regime became evident when the camps were opened – all very different from the atrocity stories of 1914 that had, for most people, been debunked during the 1920s. Here, in short, was a good war, with Britain and its people playing a heroic role, at the end of which the enemy was totally defeated with roughly half the losses incurred by Britain in 1914–18.

All the belligerents had to engage with this fateful coupling of two world wars, and they responded in different ways. In France the shame of defeat and collaboration in 1940–4 tended to obscure what was still regarded as the noble sacrifice to liberate *la patrie* in 1914–18. The Soviet Union, like Britain, turned its war against Hitler into a national myth, but it did so while relegating 1914–17 to ideological oblivion. In the United States, 1917–18, dismissed in the 1930s as a grave error, became a stepping stone to 1941–5 – a conflict that allowed Americans a 'second chance' to realize the Wilsonian vision. The British were unique in treating the First World War as an almost totally negative experience by which to accentuate the positives of the Second.

But the construction of new narratives did not stop in the 1940s. For both the French and the Germans 1939–45 posed huge political and moral problems, but they managed over the next decade to bury the hatchet and forge the European Economic Community. This was an astounding development, whose historical significance is often ignored in Britain today. The integration process was predicated on a new narrative in which the French and German peoples had finally moved on from the cycle of tit-for-tat wars into a cooperative relationship that could serve as the engine of Europe's future peace and prosperity. By the 1960s in Britain, by contrast, the gloss had worn off 'our finest hour', the British Empire had fallen apart and Britain was sitting importunately outside the booming EEC. So what had the two world wars achieved? Were both conflicts only pyrrhic victories, serving to accelerate Britain's decline?

It was in this mood that the British marked the fiftieth anniversary of the Great War in the mid-1960s, having given the conflict little sustained public attention for a quarter of a century. In a decade when television came of age the BBC series *The Great War* conveyed 1914–18 vividly to a new generation. British views of that war became stuck in the trenches, assisted by the growing cult of a few 'anti-war' poets such as Owen and a vogue for social and family history which shifted attention from generals to ordinary soldiers. In Ireland the fallout from the fiftieth anniversary of the war was positively toxic. The television series *Insurrection*, patterned on the goodies-versus-baddies dramas of American Westerns, brought the Easter Rising to life for young viewers. This was part of a process in which rival commemorations of 1916 in 1966, nationalist and loyalist, helped to rekindle sectarian animosity and spark the Troubles.

In many countries the end of the Cold War was a moment for reassessing the Great War. The collapse of the Soviet bloc and the reunification of Germany redrew the map of Europe. Yugoslavia and Czechoslovakia, both post-1918 creations, fell apart, Ukraine finally gained its independence and the Baltic states regained the freedom they had enjoyed in the 1920s and 1930s. Yet dynamics from the more recent past were also important, particularly European integration, which spread eastwards to embrace much of the former Soviet bloc and also deepened in intensity through full monetary union. All this aggravated the UK's sense of alienation from 'Europe'. The imperatives of integration and reconciliation also informed war commemoration across Europe, notably in the new museum at Péronne on the Somme, which brought together French, German and British perspectives on the war. For Ireland the 1990s were especially important. The waning of the Troubles encouraged new efforts at bridge-building across the past as well as in the present, notably in the Island of Ireland Peace Tower near Ypres. Here was belated acknowledgment that Irishmen from Catholic as well as Protestant families had fought and died in Britain's Great War.

Britain itself was also in flux: as the cohesive effects of two world wars wore off, Wales and particularly Scotland reasserted their own identities. Yet British conceptions of the Great War remained largely set in the mould formed after the fiftieth anniversary – as a human tragedy, bogged down in the trenches and illuminated only by poetry – even though academic study of 1914–18 has advanced hugely in the last two decades. Through writers such as Paul Fussell, Pat Barker and Sebastian Faulks, Americans have come to share in this image of the war. But whereas the British usually look back from the trenches to a lost Edwardian Eden, Americans are still tempted to reach forward towards a tantalizing Wilsonian future. As Scott Fitzgerald said in 1925 at the end of *The Great Gatsby*, 'Gatsby believed in the green light, the orgastic future that year by year recedes before us. It eluded us then, but that's no matter – tomorrow we will run faster, stretch out our arms farther ... And one fine morning – So we beat on, boats against the current, borne back ceaselessly into the past.'[8]

What are we missing? What new vistas might open up for those willing to clamber out of the trenches? First, an appreciation of the whole diverse war from 1914 to 1918. The drama of those opening weeks as German armies nearly made it to Paris, while the French thrust frantically into Alsace and Lorraine. At the other end the renewed war of movement in 1918, when the Germans nearly split the British and French armies and then the Allies, now reinforced by the Americans, pushed back against the exhausted enemy. Only a third of the British troops on the Western Front were infantry; the rest were in support units such as artillery and engineers or served in supply, medical and other non-combatant units. Even in the 'trench era' of 1915–17, offensives were 'the exceptions rather than the rule' and 'it was perfectly possible for an infantryman to spend two years on the Western Front without actually going over the top at all' because battalions were rotated between front-line, support and reserve trenches. The First of July 1916 was very unusual in a war that lasted 1,561 days.[9]

We are also overlooking the fact that this was a war in which the home front mattered almost as much as the battle front. Mobilizing the whole economy was crucial for modern warfare. That meant striking a manpower balance between the armed forces, manufacturing industry and food production, and also making effective use of womanpower in factories, transport, farming and clerical work.

Persuading people to sustain this effort also meant satisfying their material needs, especially for food, and their political demands: Britain and France were far more successful in doing all this than Russia, Germany or the Habsburg Empire. So the 'war experience' covers a multitude of human beings, not just front-line soldiers; in particular the reactions of women to the conflict are still a hugely neglected area. The whole population of the United Kingdom of Great Britain and Ireland in 1914 was about 46 million. The Great War was their story, not just that of the 720,000 men who marched away for ever to foreign fields.[10]

We also need to think more critically about the now iconic 'war poets'. Certainly they are remarkable both as men and as writers – fascinating in their complicated, often contorted, responses to the experience of modern war and how it should be represented in poetry. Yet these men were typical neither of the British Tommy in general nor of the writers (a quarter of them women) who published poems in 1914–18. Their verse should not be used as historical description of the soldier's experience, as suggested by the still influential anthologies from the 1960s.[11] Most Tommies were not hypersensitively reflective about their own manhood, sexuality or even suffering. And much of the war poetry remained unashamedly patriotic, seeking to motivate volunteers to enlist in 1914–15 or sustaining national morale in the great crisis of spring 1918. It is also surely bizarre that more words have been written about a score of war poets than about the 4 million non-white troops who fought for the Allies during the Great War.[12]

This reminds us that horizons should be broadened geographically. Yugoslavia's Great War memorial, the Monument to the Unknown Hero, on a hill above Belgrade, bears the dates 1912 to 1918. The idea that 1914 was actually the Third Balkan War, following on from earlier rounds in 1912 and 1913, has been debated by Western historians for more than forty years but British views of the conflict are still framed by the Western Front and rooted in the country's historical complexes about France and Germany – a mentality that continues to dominate much of the British debate about 'Europe' in the twenty-first century. Understanding the Balkan roots of this conflict is important not just to comprehend 1914 but also to appreciate the war's enduring impact across eastern and south-eastern Europe – from Sarajevo 1914 to Sarajevo 1994, from the Bolshevik revolution to the Soviet collapse. Although the Great War was won by the Allies on the Western Front, Germany's defeat of Russia in 1917–18 unhinged the whole of eastern Europe for the rest of the twentieth century. Yet, despite recent research in Germany and Russia, the Eastern Front remains little known in the West – even in Germany it is *die vergessene Front* – much as in 1931 when Winston Churchill thought of calling his book about it 'The Unknown War'.[13]

Churchill's six-volume series of memoir-history was entitled *The World Crisis* – a reminder that we should also raise our sights beyond Europe. This was not a world war in the full extent of 1939–45 but its repercussions were truly global. The war transformed relationships across the British Empire, it reshaped the Middle East, particularly Palestine and Iraq, and shifted the balance of power in Africa and East Asia. All of these global themes deserve greater study. In Asia Japan was the main beneficiary, seizing former German holdings in China in the first months of the conflict and hanging on to them at the Paris peace conference despite the fury of China. The surge of populist Chinese nationalism unleashed in 1919 by the Versailles treaty (the May Fourth Movement) became a persistent if plastic 'site of memory' throughout the twentieth century – used in 1989 as a democratic symbol by protesting students in Tiananmen Square and more recently by the government as a fount of Chinese nationalism. It is not much of an exaggeration to see 4 May 1919 as the Chinese analogue to 1 July 1916 in Britain. Yet the Chinese dimension of the Great War rarely figures in British-centred narratives despite its importance for understanding our own day.[14]

Changing technologies of communication also affect historical understanding. The fiftieth anniversary of the Great War coincided with the heyday of television: as we have seen television series were particularly significant in Britain and Ireland in the mid-1960s. But we are now in the internet age. Data previously accessible only by a personal visit to archives – for instance the Commonwealth War Graves Commission lists of soldiers who died in the Great War or the service records of veterans at the British National Archives – is now available online and in keyword-searchable form. Official war museums from London to Canberra have established detailed educational websites; private bodies such as firstworldwar.com offer a multimedia history of the battles and the fronts, while most of the war poets have their own association websites. More informally, blogs and message boards facilitate rapid sharing of information and opinion. Yet the effect of this technological revolution is hard to gauge. Potentially the internet is a 'borderless reservoir of information': will it encourage people to surf across the barriers of national memory cultures and gain a broader sense of the conflict? Or will the digital age serve mainly to deepen the conventional channels of British war remembrance, drawing new generations into engagement with the tragedies of individual soldiers?[15]

Death is surely the fundamental issue, especially the unique scale of it in 1914–18 for a country otherwise relatively insulated from the battles and the holocausts of Europe's twentieth century. War, as Wellington said of Waterloo, is 'hard slogging' – with male bodies doing the slogging and being slogged to bits. The first day of the Somme was a horrific glimpse into the continental experience of the whole first half of the twentieth century, a horror sharpened by awareness that these were men who had chosen to fight. Yet the memory of most wars fades as its participants die off. The Great War endures because of the continued human presence of the past, which helps the dead seem 'as real as we' – in the words of historian George Macaulay Trevelyan.

Soldiers' letters, for instance – still found in family attics as well as preserved in scores of archives. The Great War was Britain's first truly literate war, when the ordinary soldier had been taught in school to write, and the missives he sent home – moving or trite – bring alive the hopes and fears, the boredom and the comradeship of army life. Also photographs – sepia-tinted, often stiffly posed portraits. Taken so that wives and children could remember the 'Men Who March Away' and to help soldiers bridge the gulf between the front and the hearth. Ivor Gurney caught something of their import in his 1917 poem 'Photographs':

> ... Though in a picture only, a common cheap
> Ill-taken card ... calling
> Delight across the miles of land and sea,
> That not the dread of barrage suddenly falling
> Could quite blot out – not mud nor lethargy ...[16]

Photos snapped in order to hold a family close. A century later they exert a very different power, giving faces to people who are dead, faces now endowed with what Susan Sontag called the 'posthumous irony' of the photographic image.[17]

Letters, photos – and also stones. At the other end of the spectrum of remembrance is that massive project of national commemoration directed by Fabian Ware and beautified by Lutyens and Kipling, which is now known as the Commonwealth War Graves Commission. Here, too, the past is present but this time on a gigantic scale, fusing the pity of war for individual human beings with the epic of war in the arena of nations. The uniform memorialization that so infuriated critics in 1919–20, especially the standardized headstones, now gives those sites a special solemnity. Without these meticulously tended graves, the borderlands of France and Belgium would have become simply a 'Dead Man's Dump', the title of one of Isaac Rosenberg's most powerful poems – mass graves (as after Waterloo) or random burials that quickly decomposed into oblivion. In the garden cemeteries along the Western Front and on the Memorials to the Missing at Ypres and Thiepval, the dead were religiously named for perpetuity; likewise on local war memorials in British towns and villages. Even today these 'nameless names' exert their own power over the living, stirring our imagination to call back the men from the shadows.

Perhaps the British will lift their eyes beyond the Western Front to the broader canvas of the Great War as the country moves beyond the centenary. After all the Tommies of 1914–18 are now as far away from us as Wellington's redcoats of 1815 were from them. Or perhaps the stones will defy the shadows. Maybe those sites of memory will continue to mesmerize, as their grand designers intended when – inspired by awe, grief, horror, guilt or some tortured combination – they embarked on their unique nationalist, democratic project of remembrance. To quote some remarkable words from 1920 by Winston Churchill who, more than any other politician, hovers over Britain's twentieth century:

> there is no reason at all why, in periods as remote from our own as we ourselves are from the Tudors, the graveyards in France of this Great War shall not remain an abiding and supreme memorial ... We know the mutability of human arrangements, but even if our language, our institutions, and our Empire all have faded from the memory of man, these great stones will still preserve the memory of a common purpose pursued by a great nation in the remote past, and will undoubtedly excite the wonder and the reverence of a future age.[18]

NOTES

Abbreviations

AHR	*American Historical Review*
CAC	Churchill Archives Centre, Churchill College, Cambridge
EHR	*English Historical Review*
EcHR	*Economic History Review*
FRUS	US Department of State, *Foreign Relations of the United States* (multi-volumes, Washington DC, 1861–)
HC Debs	House of Commons, *Debates*
HJ	*Historical Journal*
HZ	*Historische Zeitschrift*
IWM	Imperial War Museum, London
JAH	*Journal of American History*
JBS	*Journal of British Studies*
JCH	*Journal of Contemporary History*
JICH	*Journal of Imperial and Commonwealth History*
JMH	*Journal of Modern History*
MAS	*Modern Asian Studies*
TCBH	*Twentieth Century British History*
TNA	The National Archives, Kew, Surrey
TRHS	*Transactions of the Royal Historical Society*

Epigraphs

From 'The Fourth of August', in Laurence Binyon, *Collected Poems of Laurence Binyon: Lyrical Poems* (London, 1931), p. 205; from 'Simplify Me When I'm Dead', in Keith Douglas, *The Complete Poems*, ed. Desmond Graham (3rd edn, Oxford, 1998), p. 74; from 'MCMXIV', in Philip Larkin, *Collected Poems*, ed. Anthony Thwaite (London, 1988), p. 127; Jay Winter and Antoine Prost, *The Great War in History: Debates and Controversies, 1914 to the Present* (Cambridge, 2005), p. 193.

Introduction

1 Draft preface in Jon Stallworthy, ed., *Wilfred Owen: The Complete Poems and Fragments* (2 vols, London, 1983), 2:535.

2 Jay Winter, *Sites of Memory, Sites of Mourning: The Great War in European Cultural History* (Cambridge, 1995); Annette Becker, *War and Faith: The Religious Imagination in France, 1914–1930* (Oxford, 1998); Stefan Goebel, *The Great War and Medieval Memory: War, Remembrance and Medievalism in Britain and Germany, 1914–1940* (Cambridge, 2007).

3 George Creel, *The War, the World, and Wilson* (New York, 1920), p. 1.

4 Cf. Stéphane Audoin-Rouzeau and Annette Becker, *1914–18: Understanding the Great War* (London, 2002), p. 225, and Richard Overy, *The Morbid Age: Britain Between the Wars* (London, 2009), p. xiii. For a broader approach to the various historiographies of the war see Jay Winter and Antoine Prost, *The Great War in History: Debates and Controversies, 1914 to the Present* (Cambridge, 2005).

5 Niall Ferguson, *The War of the World: History's Age of Hatred* (London, 2006).

6 For suggestive international comparisons see the essays in Stéphane Audoin-Rouzeau and Christophe Prochasson, eds, *Sortir de la Grande Guerre: Le Monde et L'Après-1918* (Paris, 2008), and in 'Aftershocks: Violence in Dissolving Empires after the First World War', *Contemporary European History*, 19/3 (2010), pp. 183–284. For the new Irish interest see John Horne, ed., *Our War: Ireland and the Great War* (Dublin, 2008).

7 As emphasized by Hew Strachan, *The First World War, vol. I, To Arms* (Oxford, 2001) and Daniel Marc Segesser, *Der Erste Weltkrieg: in globaler Perspektive* (Wiesbaden, 2012) and in many of the essays in Hugh Cecil and Peter Liddle, eds, *Facing Armageddon: The First World War Experience* (London, 1996).

8 Figures from J.M. Winter, *The Great War and the British People* (London, 1985), p. 75.

9 Building on my essay 'The Origins of the Two "World Wars": Historical Discourse and International Politics', *JCH*, 38 (2003), pp. 29–44. I have also benefited from two insightful analyses of the British experience by Dan Todman, *The Great War: Myth and Memory* (London, 2005), and Adrian Gregory, *The Last Great War: British Society and the First World War* (Cambridge, 2008).

10 I have adapted the framework in the superb analytical overview by David Stevenson, *1914–1918: The History of the First World War* (London, 2004). Other major recent studies in English include Hew Strachan, *The First World War: A New Illustrated History* (London, 2003) and Ian F.W. Beckett, *The Great War* (2nd edn, London, 2007).

11 Stéphane Audoin-Rousseau and Jean-Jacques Becker, eds, *Encyclopédie de la Grande Guerre, 1914–1918* (Paris, 2004), p. 245. The French death toll during the four days 20–23 August 1914 was 40,000.

12 Hein E. Goemans, *War and Punishment: The Causes of War Termination and the First World War* (Princeton, 2000), p. 85.

13 For the debate about casualty figures see William Philpott, *Bloody Victory: The Sacrifice on the Somme* (London, 2009), pp. 600–3.

14 Lansdowne, memorandum, 13 Nov. 1916, War Cabinet papers, CAB 37/159, doc. 32 (TNA).

15 Gary Sheffield, *Forgotten Victory. The First World War: Myths and Realities* (London, 2001); see also Brian Bond, *The Unquiet Western Front: Britain's Role in Literature and History* (Cambridge, 2002).

16 Josef Redlich, in Holger H. Herwig, *The First World War: Germany and Austria-Hungary, 1914–18* (London, 1997), p. 439.

1: Nations

1 'Empire's Honour', *Times*, 21 Sept. 1914, p. 12; Arthur S. Link et al., eds, *The Papers of Woodrow Wilson* (69 vols, Princeton, 1966–94), 46:323.

2 'President to Occupy Murat Home in Paris', *New York Times*, 25 Nov. 1918; Edith Wilson, *Memoirs of Mrs Woodrow Wilson* (London, 1939), pp. 268–9.

3 Mark Mazower, *Dark Continent: Europe's Twentieth Century* (London, 1998), pp. 1–2.

4 On the theme of brutalization see three recent sets of essays 'Violence and Society in Europe after the First World War', *Journal of Modern European History*, 1 (2003), pp. 11–149; 'Aftershocks: Violence in Dissolving Empires after the First World War', *Contemporary European History*, 19/3 supplement (2010), pp. 183–284; and Robert Gerwarth and John Horne, eds, *War in Peace: Paramilitary Violence in Europe after the Great War* (Oxford, 2012).

5 See, for instance, Eric Hobsbawm, *Nations and Nationalism since 1780: Programmes, Myth, Reality* (Cambridge, 1990); Anthony D. Smith, *Nationalism and Modernism: A Critical Survey of Recent Theories of Nations and Nationalism* (London, 1998); Paul Lawrence, *Nationalism: History and Theory* (London, 2005).

6 Jörn Leonhard, 'Nation-States and Wars', in Timothy Baycroft and Mark Hewitson, eds, *What Is a Nation? Europe 1789–1914* (Oxford, 2006), p. 235.

7 'Am Amfang war Napoleon.' Thomas Nipperdey, *Deutsche Geschichte, 1800–1866: Bürgerwelt und starker Staat* (München, 1983), p. 1.

8 The essays in Baycroft and Hewitson, eds, *What Is a Nation?* constitute a sustained attack on the civic-ethnic schema; see esp. chs 4 and 8.

9 Miroslav Hroch, *Social Preconditions of National Revival in Europe*, transl. Ben Fowkes (Cambridge, 1985), esp. pp. 22–4.

10 Jean-Paul Bled, *Franz Joseph*, transl. Teresa Bridgeman (Oxford, 1992), p. 152. For a succinct analysis of the Habsburg predicament see Dominic Lieven, *Empire: The Russian Empire and Its Rivals from the Sixteenth Century to the Present* (London, 2002), ch. 5; a revealing case study is provided by Mark Cornwall, 'The Struggle on the Czech–German Language Border, 1880–1940', *EHR*, 109 (1994), pp. 914–51.

11 On the Serbian mythscape see Christopher Clark, *The Sleepwalkers: How Europe Went to War in 1914* (London, 2012), pp. 20–7.

12 See Béla K. Király & Nándor F. Dreisiger, eds, *East Central European Society in World War I* (Boulder, 1985), esp. pp. 305–6, 358, and more generally Jonathan

E. Gumz, *The Resurrection and Collapse of Empire in Habsburg Serbia, 1914–1918* (Cambridge, 2009).

13 Peter Gatrell, *Russia's First World War: A Social and Economic History* (London, 2005), pp. 3, 21–2, 188–90. For a good general discussion see Ronald Grigor Suny, 'The Empire Strikes Out: Imperial Russia, "National Identity", and the Theories of Empire', in Suny and Terry Martin, eds, *A State of Nations: Empire and Nation-making in the Age of Lenin and Stalin* (Oxford, 2001), pp. 23–66.

14 Quotations from Gatrell, *Russia's First World War*, p. 64; and Orlando Figes, *A People's Tragedy: The Russian Revolution 1891–1924* (London, 1996), pp. 75–6.

15 Mark von Hagen, 'The Great War and the Mobilization of Ethnicity in the Russian Empire', in Barnett R. Rubin and Jack L. Snyder, eds, *Post-Soviet Political Order: Conflict and State Building* (London, 1998), pp. 34–57; Nancy M. Wingfield, 'The Battle of Zborov and the Politics of Commemoration in Czechoslovakia', *East European Politics and Societies*, 17 (2003), pp. 654–81.

16 *FRUS 1918: The World War* (2 vols, Washington D.C., 1933), 1:15–16, points 10 and 13; Erez Manela, *The Wilsonian Moment: Self-Determination and the International Origins of Anticolonial Nationalism* (New York, 2007), pp. 37–43.

17 Zbyněk Zeman, *The Masaryks: The Making of Czechoslovakia* (London, 1976), chs 1–3, quoting p. 115; Victor S. Mametey, *The United States and East Central Europe, 1914–1918: A Study in Wilsonian Diplomacy and Propaganda* (Princeton, 1957), pp. 342–3.

18 See Ian Bremner and Ray Taras, eds., *New States, New Politics: Building the Post-Soviet Nations* (Cambridge, 1997), p. 240.

19 Viscount D'Abernon, *The Eighteenth Decisive Battle of the World: Warsaw, 1920* (London, 1931), p. 39.

20 Quoted in Mark Mazower, 'Minorities and the League of Nations in Interwar Europe', *Daedalus*, 126/2 (spring 1997), p. 50

21 Quoted in Adam Zamoyski, *Warsaw 1920: Lenin's Failed Conquest of Europe* (London, 2008), p. 67.

22 See David Kirby, *A Concise History of Finland* (Cambridge, 2006), esp. pp. 174–81, 198–9, 216, 218, 271.

23 Theodor Schieder, 'Typologie und Erscheinungsformen des Nationalstaats in Europa', *Historische Zeitschrift*, 202/1 (Feb. 1966), pp. 58–81.

24 Robert Howard Lord, 'Poland', in Edward M. House and Charles Seymour, eds, *What Really Happened at Paris: The Story of the Peace Conference by American Delegates* (London, 1921), pp. 82–3; on the dispute see H.M.V. Temperley, ed., *A History of the Peace Conference of Paris* (6 vols, London, 1920–4), 4:348–63.

25 Alan Sharp, *The Versailles Settlement: Peacemaking in Paris, 1919* (London, 1991), p. 127.

26 See table in M.C. Kaser and E.A. Radice, eds, *The Economic History of Eastern Europe, 1919–1975, vol. 1* (London, 1985), p. 25. For a good recent overview see Alexander V. Prusin, *The Lands Between: Conflict in the East European Borderlands, 1870–1992* (Oxford, 2010), chs 1–4.

27 Mark Cornwall '"National Reparation"? The Czech Land Reform and the

Sudeten Germans 1918–38', *Slavonic and East European Review*, 75 (1997), p. 280.

28 Zara Steiner, *The Lights that Failed: European International History, 1919–1933* (Oxford, 2005), p. 84.

29 See the discussion in Glenda Sluga, *The Nation, Psychology, and International Politics, 1870–1919* (London, 2006), esp. chs 2–3.

30 Cf. John Elliott, 'A Europe of Composite Monarchies', *Past and Present*, 137 (1992), pp. 48–71.

31 On Ireland as a version of 'proconsular despotism', see C.A. Bayly, *Imperial Meridian: The British Empire and the World, 1780–1830* (London, 1989), pp. 193, 196–7. See more generally Alvin Jackson, *The Two Unions: Ireland, Scotland, and the Survival of the United Kingdom, 1707–2007* (Oxford, 2012).

32 Quotations from Linda Colley, *Britons: Forging the Nation, 1707–1837* (New Haven, 1992), p. 368.

33 Robert Colls, *Identity of England* (Oxford, 2002), p. 49.

34 Quoted in F.S.L. Lyons, *Culture and Anarchy in Ireland, 1890–1939* (Oxford, 1982), p. 42.

35 See generally Patricia Jalland, 'United Kingdom Devolution 1910–1914: Political Panacea or Tactical Diversion?', *EHR,* 94 (1979), pp. 757–85.

36 Quotations from T.M. Devine, *The Scottish Nation 1700–2007* (London, 2009), p. 308; House of Commons Debates, 53:481–2, 30 May 1913 [William Cowan].

37 Speeches by Law (27 July 1912) and Churchill (14 March 1914) in Randolph S. Churchill, *Winston S. Churchill, vol. II* (London, 1967), pp. 469–70, 489.

38 David Powell, *The Edwardian Crisis: Britain 1901–1914* (London, 1996), ch. 5, quoting p. 149. On Ulster Catholics see A.C. Hepburn, 'Irish Nationalism in Ulster, 1885–1921', in D. George Boyce & Alan O'Day, eds, *The Ulster Crisis, 1885–1921* (London, 2006), esp. pp. 105–11.

39 Winston S. Churchill, *The World Crisis, 1911–1914* (London, 1923), pp. 192–3.

40 A theme developed in Kenneth O. Morgan, *Consensus and Disunity: The Lloyd George Coalition Government, 1918–1922* (Oxford, 1986), ch. 1.

41 John Horne and Alan Kramer, *German Atrocities, 1914: A History of Denial* (New Haven, 2001), p. 419.

42 Alan Kramer, *Dynamic of Destruction: Culture and Mass Killing in the First World War* (Oxford, 2007), ch.1, quoting p. 13 (Louvain); Adrian Gregory, *The Last Great War: British Society and the First World War* (Cambridge, 2008), ch. 2, quoting p. 57 ('baby killers').

43 Jalland, 'United Kingdom Devolution', p. 759; Richard Toye, *Lloyd George and Churchill: Rivals for Greatness* (London, 2007), p. 22; John Grigg, *Lloyd George: From Peace to War, 1912–1916* (London, 1997), p. 144.

44 Grigg, *Lloyd George*, pp. 162, 164–6; *The Times*, 21 Sept. 1914, p. 12.

45 Kenneth O. Morgan, *Rebirth of a Nation: Wales, 1880–1980* (Oxford, 1982), ch. 6, quoting p. 163.

46 Trevor Royle, *The Flowers of the Forest: Scotland and the First World War* (Edinburgh, 2007), p. 195.

47 Gregory, *Last Great War*, esp. pp. 81–7, 120–1, 228.

48 Jack Brand, *The National Movement in Scotland* (London, 1978), ch. 4, quoting p. 49; see also Atsuko Ichijo, 'Civic or Ethnic? The Evolution of Britishness and Scottishness', in Helen Brocklehurst and Robert Phillips, eds, *History, Nationhood and the Question of Britain* (London, 2004), p. 119, and Catriona MacDonald and E.W. McFarland, eds, *Scotland and the Great War* (Edinburgh, 1999), chs 1–2.

49 Joseph P. Finnan, *John Redmond and Irish Unity, 1912–1918* (Syracuse, NY, 2004), pp. 86, 88–9, 141.

50 Charles Townshend, *Easter 1916: The Irish Rebellion* (London, 2005), p. 72.

51 Townshend, *Easter 1916*, pp. 90, 309.

52 Keith Jeffrey, *Ireland and the Great War* (Cambridge, 2000), p. 51.

53 A point made by Adrian Gregory and Senia Pašeta, eds, *Ireland and the Great War: 'A War to Unite Us All'?* (Manchester, 2002), p. 3.

54 Thomas Hennessey, *Dividing Ireland: World War I and Partition* (London, 1998), p. 142.

55 Townshend, *Easter 1916*, pp. 310–14; Grigg, *Lloyd George, 1912–1916*, pp. 349–55.

56 J.B. Lyons, *The Enigma of Tom Kettle: Irish Patriot, Essayist, Poet, British Soldier* (Dublin, 1983), p. 293.

57 See Gregory and Pašeta, eds, *Ireland and the Great War*, ch. 6, quoting p. 119.

58 Bill Kissane, *The Politics of the Irish Civil War* (Oxford, 2005), pp. 51–2.

59 Peter Hart, *The IRA and Its Enemies: Violence and Community in Cork, 1916–1923* (Oxford, 1998), p. 82. See also Anne Dolan, 'The British Culture of Paramilitary Violence in the Irish War of Independence', in Gerwarth and Horne, eds, *War in Peace*, ch. 12.

60 A.D. Harvey, 'Who Were the Auxiliaries?', *Historical Journal*, 35 (1992), pp. 667, 669.

61 Tom Barry, *Guerilla Days in Ireland* (Dublin, 1949), p. 2; Hart, *IRA and Its Enemies*, pp. 36–7, 50.

62 Martin Gilbert, *Winston S. Churchill, vol. 4* (London, 1975), p. 471.

63 Adrian Gregory, 'Peculiarities of the English? War, Violence and Politics: 1900–1939', *Journal of Modern European History*, 1 (2003), pp. 53–4; Colls, *Identity of England*, p. 93, note 1. For other continental comparisons see Julia Eichenberg, 'The Dark Side of Independence: Paramilitary Violence in Ireland and Poland after the First World War', *Contemporary European History*, 19 (2010), pp. 231–48.

64 Quotations from Roy Foster, *Modern Ireland, 1600–1972* (London, 1988), pp. 506, 511; see also Kissane, *Politics of the Irish Civil War*, ch. 4; Anne Dolan, *Commemorating the Irish Civil War: History and Memory, 1923–2000* (Cambridge, 2003), p. 6.

65 See J. Jorstad, 'Nations Once Again – Ireland's Civil War in European Context', in David Fitzpatrick, ed., *Revolution? Ireland 1917–1923* (Dublin, 1990), pp. 159–73. Nigeria after 1960 and Bosnia post-1991 are other examples.

66 Patrick Buckland, *The Factory of Grievances: Devolved Government in Northern*

Ireland, 1921–1939 (Dublin, 1979), ch. 10; Northern Ireland Parliamentary Debates, vol. 16, col. 1095, 24 April 1934.

67 Jeffrey, *Ireland and the Great War*, p. 2.

68 J.M. Winter, *The Great War and the British People* (London, 1985), pp. 71–2, 75; Basil Collier, *The Defence of the United Kingdom* (London, 1957), p. 528.

69 Steven Casey, *When Soldiers Fall: How Americans Have Confronted Combat Losses from World War I to Afghanistan* (Oxford, 2013), pp. 13–43.

70 Winter, *Great War*, p. 75; Robert H. Zieger, *America's Great War: World War I and the American Experience* (Lanham, Maryland, 2000), p. 108. See also Congressional Research Service, report RL32492 'American War and Military Operations Casualties: Lists and Statistics', 26 February 2010, p. 2, available at www.crs.gov

71 David M. Kennedy, *Over Here: The First World War and American Society* (Oxford, 1980), p. 46.

72 Cf. John Breuilly, *Nationalism and the State* (2nd edn, Chicago, 1994), p. 5.

73 Hobsbawm, *Nations and Nationalism*, p. 88.

74 See David Reynolds, *America, Empire of Liberty: A New History* (London, 2009), pp. 204–5.

75 'An Appeal to the American People', 18 Aug. 1914, in Wilson, *Papers*, vol. 30, pp. 393–4. See also John A. Thompson, *Woodrow Wilson* (London, 2002), pp. 111, 128.

76 Address to a Joint Session of Congress, 2 April 1917, in Link et al., eds, *Papers of Woodrow Wilson*, 41:519–27.

77 Sluga, *Nation, Psychology and International Politics*, p. 35.

78 Lloyd E. Ambrosius, *Woodrow Wilson and the American Diplomatic Tradition: The Treaty Fight in Perspective* (Cambridge, 1987), pp. 11, 14.

79 Robert Lansing, *The Peace Negotiations: A Personal Narrative* (New York, 1921), p. 97; Temperley, ed., *A History of the Peace Conference*, 4:429.

80 Remarks to foreign correspondents, 8 April 1918, in Wilson, *Papers*, 47:288.

81 For discussion see George W. Egerton, *Great Britain and the Creation of the League of Nations: Strategy, Politics, and International Organization, 1914–1919* (Chapel Hill, North Carolina, 1979); Peter Yearwood, '"On the Safe and Right Lines": The Lloyd George Government and the Origins of the League of Nations', *Historical Journal*, 32 (1989), pp. 131–55.

82 Daniel Smith, *The Great Departure: The United States and World War I, 1914–1920* (New York, 1965), p. 185.

2: Democracy

1 Wilson, war message, 2 April 1917, in Arthur S. Link et al., eds, *The Papers of Woodrow Wilson* (69 vols, Princeton, 1966–94), 41:525; speech to Junior Imperial League, 10 March 1928, in Stanley Baldwin, *This Torch of Freedom: Speeches and Addresses* (London, 1935), p. 308.

2 H.G. Wells, *The Shape of Things to Come: The Ultimate Revolution* (London, 1933), p. 96.

3 Dr Cary Grayson, diary, 27 Dec. 1918, in Wilson, *Papers*, 53:521; David Lloyd George, *The Truth About the Peace Treaties, vol. 1* (London, 1938), pp. 180–1; Lloyd C. Gardner, *Safe for Democracy: The Anglo-American Response to Revolution, 1913–1923* (New York, 1984), pp. 2–3; Erez Manela, *The Wilsonian Moment: Self-Determination and the International Origins of Anticolonial Nationalism* (Oxford, 2007).

4 Orlando Figes, *A People's Tragedy: The Russian Revolution, 1891–1924* (London, 1996), respectively pp. 385, 351.

5 S.A. Smith, *Red Petrograd: Revolution in the Factories, 1917–1918* (Cambridge, 1983), pp. 5–14.

6 Quoted in Richard Pipes, *The Russian Revolution 1899–1919* (London, 1990), p. 278. On the garrison strength see Allan K. Wildman, *The End of the Russian Imperial Army* (2 vols, Princeton, 1980–7), 1:123–4.

7 Figes, *People's Tragedy*, p. 813. Cf. Eric Hobsbawm, *Age of Extremes: The Short Twentieth Century, 1914–1991* (London, 1994), p. 61: 'Contrary to Cold War mythology, which saw Lenin as the organizer of coups, the only real asset he and the Bolsheviks had was the ability to recognize what the masses wanted; to, as it were, lead by knowing how to follow' – a splendid piece of Marxist casuistry.

8 Chris Wrigley, ed., *Challenges of Labour: Central and Western Europe, 1917–1920* (London, 1993), ch. 1. See also Leopold Haimson and Giulio Sapelli, eds, *Strikes, Social Conflict and the First World War* (Milan, 1992), pp. 13–21, 587–98.

9 A point emphasized in David Stevenson, *1914–1918: The History of the First World War* (London, 2004), p. 491.

10 Thomas Mann, *Diaries 1919–1939*, transl. Richard and Clare Winston (London, 1983), p. 44, entry for 7 April 1919.

11 Harold Nicolson, *Peacemaking 1919* (London, 1933), p. 298, diary entry for 4 April 1919.

12 Donald Sassoon, *One Hundred Years of Socialism: The West European Left in the Twentieth Century* (London, 1987), pp. 36–41; Robert Gildea, *The Past in French History* (New Haven, 1994), pp. 52–3.

13 As discussed by MacGregor Knox, *To the Threshold of Power, 1922/33: Origins and Dynamics of the Fascist and National Socialist Dictatorships, vol. 1* (Cambridge, 2007), pp. 243–53.

14 Mark Thompson, *The White War: Life and Death on the Italian Front, 1915–1919* (London, 2008), p. 44.

15 Knox, *To the Threshold of Power*, p. 222.

16 Philip Morgan, *Italian Fascism, 1919–1945* (London, 1995), p. 51.

17 'Sie sollen die Suppe jetzt essen, die sie uns eingebrockt haben!' Albrecht von Thaer, *Generalstabsdienst an der Front und in der O.H.L.: Aus Briefen und Tagebuchaufzeichnungen 1915–1919,* ed. Siegfried A. Kaehler (Göttingen, 1956), pp. 234–5, entry for 1 Oct. 1918.

18 Wilhelm Deist et al., *Germany and the Second World War, vol. 1* (Oxford, 2000), pp. 27 [Stahlhelm], 375–6, 555–9; C.J. Elliott, 'The Kriegsvereine and the Weimar Republic', *JCH*, 10 (1975), esp. pp. 118–19.

19 Quotations from Jeremy Noakes and Geoffrey Pridham, eds, *Nazism, 1919–1945* (4 vols, Exeter, 1983–98), 1:121, and Richard J. Evans, *The Coming of the Third Reich* (London, 2003), p. 307.

20 See generally Steven A. Aschheim, *The Nietzsche Legacy in Germany, 1890–1990* (Berkeley, 1992).

21 Quotations from *The Will to Power* (1899–1902), para. 128, and Walter Kaufmann, *Nietzsche: Philosopher, Psychologist, Antichrist* (New York, 1956), p. 268. Kaufmann was trying to rescue Nietzsche from the Nazis by giving him an excessively aesthetic, apolitical reading. Cf. Ruth Abbey & Fredrick Appel, 'Nietzsche and the Will to Politics', *Review of Politics*, 60 (1998), pp. 83–114.

22 Denis Mack Smith, *Mussolini* (London, 1983), esp. pp. 15, 118, 142–4, 193–4; Piero Melograni, 'The Cult of the Duce in Mussolini's Italy', *JCH*, 11 (1976), pp. 221–37.

23 Ian Kershaw, *The 'Hitler Myth': Image and Reality in the Third Reich* (Oxford, 1989), chs 1–2, quoting pp. 21–2, 69–70.

24 Aschheim, *Nietzsche Legacy*, pp. 160–1, 239; Jacob Golomb and Robert S. Wistrich, eds, *Nietzsche: Godfather of Fascism? On the Uses and Abuses of a Philosophy* (Princeton, 2002), esp. pp. 1–16. The nazification of Nietzsche meant, among other things, suppressing all reference to his cultural francophilia, advocacy of racial mixing and opposition to anti-Semitism.

25 Recent interpretations in English include Roger Griffin, *The Nature of Fascism* (London, 1991), Stanley G. Payne, *A History of Fascism, 1914–1945* (London, 1997), and Robert O. Paxton, *The Anatomy of Fascism* (London, 2004).

26 Payne, *History of Fascism*, esp. pp. 129, 141, 312, 324.

27 Cf. Zara Steiner, *The Lights that Failed: European International History, 1919–1933* (Cambridge, 2005), appendix B, pp. 828–9.

28 Philippe Bernard and Henri Dubief, *The Decline of the Third Republic, 1914–1958* (Cambridge, 1985), p. 290.

29 Anthony Adamthwaite, *Grandeur and Misery: France's Bid for Power in Europe, 1914–1940* (London, 1995), p. 172.

30 Raymond Carr, *Modern Spain, 1875–1980* (Oxford, 1980), p. 96.

31 Payne, *History of Fascism*, p. 264.

32 Ronald Fraser, *Blood of Spain: The Experience of Civil War, 1936–1939* (London, 1981), p. 322. On the neglected revolutionary side of Republicanism, see George Esenwein and Adrian Shubert, *Spain at War: The Spanish Civil War in Context, 1931–1939* (London, 1995), ch. 7.

33 Charles Tilly, 'Conclusions', in Haimson and Sapelli, eds, *Strikes*, p. 591.

34 John Turner, *British Politics and the Great War: Coalition and Conflict, 1915–1918* (New Haven, 1992), p. 1.

35 Adrian Gregory, *The Last Great War: British Society and the First World War* (Cambridge, 2008), p. 205; David Lloyd George, *War Memoirs* (6 vols, London, 1933–8), 5:2614–15.

36 Gregory, *Last Great War*, pp. 241–8.

37 Harold Nicolson, *King George V: His Life and Reign* (London, 1952),

pp. 307–10, quoting p. 308 ['alien']; Kenneth Rose, *King George V* (London, 1983), pp. 170–5, 208–18; John W. Wheeler-Bennett, *King George VI: His Life and Reign* (London, 1958), pp. 159–60 [Esher].

38 Martin Pugh, *Electoral Reform in War and Peace, 1906–1918* (London, 1978), pp. 87 (Bryce), 173–4; Ross McKibbin, *The Evolution of the Labour Party, 1910–1924* (Oxford, 1974), p. 111.

39 Richard Holmes, *Tommy: The British Soldier on the Western Front, 1914–1918* (London, 2004), p. 89; Nigel Keohane, *The Party of Patriotism: The Conservative Party and the First World War* (London, 2010), p. 41 [Selborne, May 1915]; HC *Debs*, 84:1049 and 85:1460, 19 July and 14 Aug. 1916 [Carson].

40 Alexandra Woollacott, *On Her Their Lives Depend: Munitions Workers in the Great War* (Berkeley, 1994), esp. pp. 7, 24 [Lawrence], 31, 81, 189; HC *Debs*, 5s. 92:469–70, 28 March 1917 [Asquith].

41 Nicoletta F. Gullace, *'The Blood of Our Sons': Men, Women, and the Renegotiation of British Citizenship during the Great War* (New York, 2002), ch. 8, quoting pp. 191–2; Peter Clarke, *Hope and Glory: Britain 1900–2000* (London, 2004), p. 98 ['housewife suffrage']. Strictly, the 1918 Act conceded the vote to women over 30 who were either local-government electors or the wives of local-government electors: this was effectively a householder franchise.

42 Chris Wrigley, *Lloyd George and the Challenge of Labour: The Post-War Coalition, 1918–1922* (London, 1990), quoting pp. 27–8, 160, 299.

43 Wrigley, ed., *Challenges of Labour*, p. 270; James E. Cronin, 'Industry, Locality and the State: Patterns of Mobilization in the Postwar Strike Wave in Britain', in Haimson and Sapelli, eds, *Strikes*, pp. 93 ['more workers'] and 100.

44 Points emphasized by Gregory, *Last Great War*, pp. 205–7, 294; cf. Niall Ferguson, *The Pity of War* (London, 1998), p. 275.

45 Wrigley, *Lloyd George*, pp. 80–2, 91 [quotation], 249.

46 See Ross McKibbin's essay 'Why was there no Marxism in Great Britain', in McKibbin, *The Ideologies of Class: Social Relations in Britain, 1880–1950* (Oxford, 1990), ch. 1. Stefan Berger, *The British Labour Party and the German Social Democrats, 1900–1931* (Oxford, 1994) has blurred some of the detail but not the overall contrast.

47 Trevor Royle, *The Flowers of the Forest: Scotland and the First World War* (Edinburgh, 2006), pp. 187–8, 308; see also the insightful essay by John Foster, 'Working Class Mobilization on the Clyde, 1917–1920', in Wrigley, ed., *Challenges of Labour*, pp. 147–75.

48 J.M. Winter, 'Arthur Henderson, The Russian Revolution, and the Reconstruction of the Labour Party', *HJ*, 15 (1972), pp. 770–2; Kenneth O. Morgan, *Consensus and Disunity: The Lloyd George Coalition Government, 1918–1922* (Oxford, 1979), p. 78 [Hodge]; J.R. Clynes, *Memoirs* (2 vols, London, 1937), 2:19.

49 On the PR issues see Pugh, *Electoral Reform*, esp. ch. 11.

50 Duncan Tanner, 'Class Voting and Radical Politics: The Liberal and Labour Parties, 1910–1931' in Jon Lawrence and Miles Taylor, eds, *Party, State and*

Society: Electoral Behaviour in Britain since 1830 (London, 1997), pp. 106–30.

51 Nicolson, *King George V*, p. 384.

52 David Marquand, *Ramsay MacDonald* (London, 1977), p. 297; Nicolson, *King George V*, pp. 385–6; Maurice Cowling, *The Impact of Labour, 1920–1924: The Beginning of Modern British Politics* (Cambridge, 1971), p. 359.

53 Wrigley, *Lloyd George*, pp. 301 [Riddell]; Martin Pugh, 'The Rise of Labour and the Political Culture of Conservatism, 1890–1945', *History,* 87 (2002), esp. pp. 523–4.

54 Marquand, *MacDonald*, pp. 90, 458–9, 793–4.

55 John Ramsden, *The Age of Balfour and Baldwin 1902–1940* (London, 1978), pp. 122–3 [including quote]; McKibbin, *Ideologies of Class*, pp. 259–60.

56 Philip Williamson, *Stanley Baldwin: Conservative Leadership and National Values* (Cambridge, 1999), p. 146; Keith Middlemas and John Barnes, *Baldwin: A Biography* (London, 1969), pp. 502–3.

57 Williamson, *Baldwin*, p. 241; Middlemas and Barnes, *Baldwin*, pp. 412, 448–53.

58 Williamson, *Baldwin*, pp. 181–2. See also David Jarvis, 'British Conservatism and Class Politics in the 1920s', *EHR*, 111 (1996), pp. 59–84.

59 The only continental parallel was Belgium – another country that industrialized early and feared proletarian unrest. Denmark and Sweden had similar proportions of owner-occupancy, but this was largely in rural areas. Colin G. Pooley, ed., *Housing Strategies in Europe, 1880–1930* (Leicester, 1992), esp. pp. 73–104, 127–8, 217, 330; see also M.J. Daunton, 'Housing', in F.M.L. Thompson, ed., *The Cambridge Social History of Britain, vol. 2* (Cambridge, 1990), ch. 4, esp. pp. 231–47. The phrase 'silent revolution' comes from Martin Boddy, *The Building Societies* (London, 1980), p. 12.

60 Mark Swenarton and Sandra Taylor, 'The Scale and Nature of the Growth of Owner-Occupation in Britain between the Wars', *EcHR* 38 (1985), esp. pp. 391–2; McKibbin, *Ideologies of Class*, pp. 297–9.

61 David Jarvis, 'The Conservative Party and the Politics of Gender, 1900–1939', in Martin Francis and Ina Zweiniger-Bargielowska, eds, *The Conservatives and British Society, 1880–1930* (Cardiff, 1996), pp. 172–93, quoting p. 175 [J.H. Bottomley advice to canvassers in 1912]; Williamson, *Baldwin*, pp. 240–1; Adrian Bingham, '"Stop the Flapper Vote Folly": Lord Rothermere, the *Daily Mail*, and the Equalization of the Franchise, 1927–28', *Twentieth Century British History*, 13 (2002), pp. 17–27, quoting pp. 19–20, 25.

62 Helen L. Boak, '"Our Last Hope": Women's Votes for Hitler – A Reappraisal', *German Studies Review*, 12 (1989), pp. 289–310, quoting p. 304.

63 Rose, *King George V*, pp. 376–7; Marquand, *MacDonald*, p. 636. Philip Williamson, though playing down the King's role, credits him with influencing Baldwin: see *National Crisis and National Government: British Politics, the Economy and Empire, 1926–1932* (Cambridge, 1992), pp. 341–2.

64 Williamson, *National Crisis*, quoting pp. 427, 455.

65 A point noted by Martin Pugh, *We Danced All Night: A Social History of Britain Between the Wars* (London, 2009), p. xi.

66 Thomas Jones, *A Diary with Letters, 1931–1950* (London, 1954), 28 Oct. 1931, p. 20.

67 Richard Lamb, *Mussolini and the British* (London, 1997), p. 67.

68 Martin Pugh, *'Hurrah for the Blackshirts': Fascists and Fascism in Britain between the Wars* (London, 2006), p. 112; Robert Skidelsky, *Oswald Mosley* (London, 1990), 285 [Mussolini]. See also Simon Ball, 'Mosley and the Tories in 1930: The Problem of Generations', *Contemporary British History*, 23 (2009), pp. 445–59.

69 Quoted in Tom Jeffrey and Keith McClelland, '"A World Fit to Live In": The *Daily Mail* and the Middle Classes, 1918–39', in James Curran et al., eds, *Impacts and Influences: Essays on Media Power in the Twentieth Century* (London, 1987), p. 49.

70 Pugh, *'Hurrah for the Blackshirts'*, pp. 196–7, 315–16.

71 David S. Thatcher, *Nietzsche in England, 1890–1914: The Growth of a Reputation* (Toronto, 1970), ch. 7, quoting p. 197; Richard Toye, *Lloyd George and Churchill: Rivals for Greatness* (London, 2007), p. 236; Middlemas and Barnes, *Baldwin*, p. 123.

72 David Carlton, *Churchill and the Soviet Union* (Manchester, 2000), pp. 15, 18, 20, 32, 37; Middlemas and Barnes, *Baldwin*, p. 411.

73 Roland Quinault, 'Churchill and Democracy', in David Cannadine and Roland Quinault, eds, *Winston Churchill in the Twenty-First Century* (Cambridge, 2004), pp. 33, 36, 38; Carlton, *Churchill and the Soviet Union*, pp. 51, 57.

74 Middlemas and Barnes, *Baldwin*, p. 712.

75 Martin Gilbert, *Winston S. Churchill, vol. 5* (London, 1976), pp. 687, 741.

76 Charles F. G. Masterman, *England after the War, A Study* (London, 1922), p. 32; David Cannadine, *The Decline and Fall of the British Aristocracy* (New Haven, 1990), pp. 81–3, 96–7.

77 Phillip Hall, *Royal Fortune: Tax, Money and Monarchy* (London, 1992), chs 2–5.

78 Harold Nicolson, *Diaries and Letters, 1945–1962* (London, 1968), p. 174; Wheeler-Bennett, *King George VI*, p. 160.

79 John M. Regan, *The Irish Counter-Revolution, 1921–1936: Treatyite Politics and Settlement in Independent Ireland* (Dublin, 1999), p. 374.

80 Anthony J. Jordan, *W.T. Cosgrave, 1880–1965: Founder of Modern Ireland* (Dublin, 2006), p. 73.

81 Tim Pat Coogan, *De Valera: Long Fellow, Long Shadow* (London, 1995), pp. 404–5.

82 *New York Times*, 19 Aug. 1928, p. 32; Richard Dunphy, *The Making of Fianna Fáil Power in Ireland, 1923–1948* (Oxford, 1995), p. 143; Conor Cruise O'Brien, *States of Ireland* (London, 1972), p. 118; Coogan, *De Valera*, p. 426.

83 Dunphy, *Making of Fianna Fáil Power*, p. 150.

84 Coogan, *De Valera*, esp. pp. 3, 36, 495–6; John Bowman, *De Valera and the Irish Question, 1917–1973* (Oxford, 1982), p. 128 [MacDermot].

85 Ferghal McGarry, *Eoin O'Duffy: A Self-Made Hero* (Oxford, 2005), pp. 200, 275; Mike Cronin, *The Blueshirts and Irish Politics* (Dublin, 1997), pp. 115–16, 135–61.

86 McGarry, *O'Duffy*, pp. 268–9; Regan, *Irish Counter-Revolution*, pp. 382–3.

87 Speech of 22 Nov. 1895, reprinted in Eugene V. Debs, *Debs: His Life, Writings, and Speeches* (Chicago, 1908), pp. 327–44.

88 Harold C. Livesay, *Samuel Gompers and Organized Labor in America* (Boston, 1978), p. 112; Robert H. Zieger, *America's Great War: World War I and the American Experience* (Lanham, Maryland, 2000), p. 122.

89 Werner Sombart, *Why Is There No Socialism in the United States?* [1906], transl. Patricia M. Hocking and C.T. Husbands (London, 1976), pp. 105–6; also Jerome Karabel, 'The Failure of American Socialism Reconsidered', *The Socialist Register*, 16 (1979), pp. 204–27.

90 Maldwyn Allen Jones, *American Immigration* (Chicago, 1960), pp. 177–9; Jacob A. Riis, *How the Other Half Lives: Studies Among the Tenements of New York* [1901] (New York, 1971), p. 19.

91 David M. Kennedy, *Over Here: The First World War and American Society* (New York, 1980), pp. 270–9, 287–92.

92 Colby note, published 11 Aug. 1920, in Arthur Link et al., eds, *The Papers of Woodrow Wilson, vol. 66* (Princeton, 1992), p. 23. Roosevelt told the map story to Stalin at Yalta in 1945 – see US Department of State, *Foreign Relations of the United States: The Conferences at Malta and Yalta 1945* (Washington, DC, 1955), p. 921.

3: Empire

1 Keith Jeffery, *The British Army and the Crisis of Empire, 1918–1922* (Manchester, 1984), p. 1; W.E. Burghardt Du Bois, *The Souls of Black Folk: Essays and Sketchers* (New York, 1961 edn), p. 23.

2 Erez Manela, *The Wilsonian Moment: Self-Determination and the International Origins of Anticolonial Nationalism* (Oxford, 2007), p. 221.

3 John Darwin, *The Empire Project: The Rise and Fall of the British World-System, 1830–1970* (Cambridge, 2009), p. 308.

4 See Catherine Hall and Sonya Rose, eds, *At Home with the Empire: Metropolitan Culture and the Imperial World* (Cambridge, 2006), esp. pp. 2–3, 20.

5 P.J. Cain and A.G. Hopkins, *British Imperialism: Crisis and Deconstruction* (London, 1993), p. 3.

6 Christopher M. Andrew and A.S. Kanya-Forstner, *France Overseas: The Great War and the Climax of French Imperial Expansion* (London, 1981), pp. 14–15.

7 Robert Holland, 'The British Empire and the Great War, 1914–1918', in Judith M. Brown and Wm. Roger Louis, eds, *The Oxford History of the British Empire, vol. 4* (Oxford, 1999), esp. pp. 114 [War Office] and 136 [1918 deployments]. For troop statistics (notoriously problematic) see also Gregory W. Martin, 'Financial and Manpower Aspects of the Dominions' and India's Contribution to the British War Effort, 1914–1919' (Cambridge University PhD, 1987), p. 360 and appendices.

8 Hew Strachan, *The First World War, vol. I* (Oxford, 2001), p. 455.

9 I.H. Nish, 'Japan and China, 1914–1916', in F.H. Hinsley, ed., *British Foreign Policy under Sir Edward Grey* (Cambridge, 1977), p. 459.

10 For a full discussion see Strachan, *First World War, vol. I*, ch. 7.

11 Justin McCarthy, *The Ottoman Peoples and the End of Empire* (London, 2001), p. 3.

12 As emphasized by e.g. Nadine Méouchy and Peter Sluglett, eds, *The British and French Mandates in Comparative Perspective* (Leiden, 2004), p. 6, and D.K. Fieldhouse, *Western Imperialism in the Middle East, 1914–1958* (Oxford, 2006), pp. 3–20.

13 M. Sükrü Hanioğlu, *A Brief History of the Late Ottoman Empire* (Princeton, 2006), pp. 187–8.

14 Hanioğlu, *A Brief History of the Late Ottoman Empire*, pp. 180–1.

15 Eitan Bar-Yosef, 'The Last Crusade? British Propaganda and the Palestine Campaign, 1917–18', *JCH*, 36 (2001), pp. 87–109, quoting Lloyd George on p. 105.

16 John Darwin, *Britain, Egypt and the Middle East: Imperial Policy in the Aftermath of War, 1918–1922* (London, 1981), p. 149.

17 David Gilmour, *Curzon* (London, 1994), p. 30 [Asquith]; David Dilks, *Curzon in India* (2 vols, London, 1969–70), 1:113; Darwin, *Britain, Egypt and the Middle East*, pp. 153, 160.

18 Andrew and Kanya-Forstner, *France Overseas*, pp. 172, 194, 197–8.

19 Manela, *Wilsonian Moment*, pp. 55, 65–6.

20 Manela, *Wilsonian Moment*, esp. pp. 60–1, 145–7, 166, 183, and N. Gordon Levin, Jr, *Woodrow Wilson and World Politics: America's Response to War and Revolution* (Oxford, 1973), p. 243. See also Rana Mitter, *A Bitter Revolution: China's Struggle with the Modern World* (Oxford, 2004).

21 George Creel, *The War, The World and Wilson* (New York, 1920), pp. 162–3; Manela, *Wilsonian Moment*, pp. 137, 149, 195–6.

22 *FRUS, 1919: Paris*, vol. 3, pp. 720–2 [Hughes] and 765–6 [Wilson]; David Hunter Miller, *The Drafting of the Covenant, vol. 2* (New York, 1928), p. 28.

23 Susan Pedersen, 'The Meaning of the Mandates System: An Argument', *Geschichte und Gesellschaft*, 32 (2006), p. 571.

24 Keith Jeffery, ed., *The Military Correspondence of Field Marshal Sir Henry Wilson, 1918–1922* (London, 1985), p. 133; Keith Jeffery, *The British Army and the Crisis of Empire, 1918–1922* (Manchester, 1984), pp. 13–15, 36 [Chetwode].

25 Jeffery, ed., *Military Correspondence*, pp. 288–9; see generally John Gallagher, 'Nationalisms and the Crisis of Empire, 1919–1922', *Modern Asian Studies*, 15 (1981), pp. 355–68.

26 Maurice Hankey, the Cabinet Secretary, quoted in Jeffery, *The British Army*, p. 161.

27 C.A. Bayly, *The Birth of the Modern World, 1780–1914* (Oxford, 2004), ch. 13.

28 Darwin, *Britain, Egypt and the Middle East*, chs 3–5, quoting p. 115.

29 Gudrun Krämer, *A History of Palestine: From the Ottoman Conquest to the Founding of the State of Israel* (Princeton, 2008), p. 146.

30 *The Times*, 9 Nov. 1917, p. 7.

31 Michael L. Dockrill and J. Douglas Goold, *Peace Without Promise: Britain and the Peace Conferences, 1919–23* (London, 1981), pp. 141–3; James Renton, *The Zionist Masquerade: The Birth of the Anglo-Zionist Alliance, 1914–1918* (London, 2007), p. 69.

32 Supreme War Council minutes, 30 Oct. 1918, quoted in David Lloyd George, *War Memoirs, vol. 6* (London, 1936), p. 3314.

33 Gudrun Krämer, *A History of Palestine: From the Ottoman Conquest to the Founding of the State of Israel* (Princeton, 2008), p.153.

34 Dockrill and Goold, *Peace without Promise*, pp. 140, 159; Renton, *Zionist Masquerade*, p. 16.

35 Darwin, *Britain, Egypt and the Middle East*, p. 156.

36 Margaret MacMillan, *Peacemakers: The Paris Peace Conference of 1919 and Its Attempt to End War* (London, 2001), p. 401.

37 Points stressed in Fieldhouse, *Western Imperialism in the Middle East*, pp. 117, 219. On the larger issues see Abbas Kelidar, 'States without Foundations: The Political Evolution of State and Society in the Arab East', *JCH*, 28 (1993), pp. 315–39.

38 Pierre-Jean Luizard, 'Le mandat britannique en Irak: une rencontre entre plusieurs projets politiques', in Méouchy and Sluglett, eds, *The British and French Mandates in Comparative Perspective*, esp. pp. 383–4.

39 Daniel Yergin, *The Prize: The Epic Conquest for Oil, Money, and Power* (New York, 1991), p. 183; V.H. Rothwell, 'Mesopotamia in British War Aims, 1914–1918', *HJ*, 13 (1970), pp. 289–90.

40 D.K. Fieldhouse, *The Colonial Empires: A Comparative Survey from the Eighteenth Century* (2nd edn, London, 1982), pp. 242, 303.

41 Ronald Hyam, *Britain's Imperial Century, 1815–1914: A Study of Empire and Expansion* (London, 1976), p. 158 [Palmerston]; John Gallagher and Ronald Robinson, 'The Imperialism of Free Trade', *EcHR*, 6 (1953), p. 13.

42 Fieldhouse, *Colonial Empires*, p. 305; Martin Thomas, *The French Empire Between the Wars: Imperialism, Politics and Society* (Manchester, 2005), p. 57.

43 Robert Holland, 'The British Empire and the Great War, 1914–1918', in Brown and Louis, eds, *Oxford History of the British Empire*, 4:117.

44 Miles Taylor, 'Imperium et Libertas? Rethinking the Radical Critique of Imperialism During the Ninetenth Century', *JICH*, 19 (1993), p. 12.

45 J.R. Seeley, *The Expansion of England* (London, 1883), pp. 176–7, 179, 185; cf. Deborah Wormell, *Sir John Seeley and the Uses of History* (Cambridge, 1979), pp. 154–5.

46 W. David McIntyre, *Historians and the Making of the British Commonwealth of Nations, 1907–1948* (London, 2009), p. 116. On Curtis and the rest see John E. Kendle, *The Round Table Movement and Imperial Union* (Toronto, 1975), pp. 67–8, 302.

47 E.M. Andrews, *The Anzac Illusion: Anglo-Australian Relations during World War I* (Cambridge, 1993), pp. 100, 202–3; Canadian quotations from Martin Thornton, *Sir Robert Borden* (London, 2010), p. 46.

48 J.G. Fuller, *Troop Morale and Popular Culture in the British and Dominion Armies, 1914–1918* (Oxford, 1990), chs 5 and 10, cartoon on pp. 167–8; Andrews, *Anzac Illusion*, pp 170–3.

49 See John Keegan, *The Face of Battle* (Harmondsworth, 1978), pp. 223–30, though a few units on the Somme did adopt more fluid 'infiltration' tactics: see Gary Sheffield, *Forgotten Victory – The First World War: Myths and Realities* (London, 2002), pp. 166–7.

50 Jeffrey Grey, *A Military History of Australia* (3rd edn, Cambridge, 2008), pp. 103–4; Desmond Morton, '"Junior but Sovereign Allies": The Transformation of the Canadian Expeditionary Force, 1914–18', *JICH*, 8 (1979), pp. 63–4.

51 W.K. Hancock, *Smuts* (2 vols, Cambridge, 1962–8), 1: 215–16; W.K. Hancock, ed., *Selections from the Smuts Papers* (7 vols, Cambridge, 1966–73), 3:510–11 and 4:16. On the 'myth' of British magnanimity in 1906 see Ronald Hyam and Peter Henshaw, *The Lion and the Springbok: Britain and South Africa since the Boer War* (Cambridge, 2003), ch. 3.

52 Brown and Louis, eds, *Oxford History of the British Empire*, 4: 71–2 [Darwin] and 165–7 [emigration].

53 Denis Judd, *Balfour and the British Empire: A Study in Imperial Evolution* (London, 1968), p. 375; W.K. Hancock, *Australia* (London, 1930), p. 68; James Weston, *W.F. Massey* (London, 2010), pp. 70–1.

54 Darwin, *Empire Project*, p. 401, and generally Carl Bridge and Kent Fedorowich, eds, *The British World: Diaspora, Culture and Identity* (London, 2003), esp. pp. 1–15, building on the historiographical concept of 'neo-Britain' developed by J.G.A. Pocock – see his *The Discovery of Islands: Essays in British History* (Cambridge, 2005), esp. ch. 11.

55 Jonathan F. Vance, *Death So Noble: Memory, Meaning, and the First World War* (Vancouver, 1997), pp. 66–7, 233.

56 Darwin, *Empire Project*, p. 400, quoting Bruce in 1924.

57 David Omissi, ed, *Indian Voices of the Great War: Soldiers' Letters, 1914–18* (London, 1999), pp. 1–4.

58 Judith M. Brown, *Modern India: The Origins of an Asian Democracy* (Oxford, 1985), p. 191.

59 Hancock, *Smuts*, 1:345; M.K. Gandhi, *Hind Swaraj and Other Writings*, ed. Anthony J. Parel (Cambridge, 1997), pp. 28, 39, 41, 42.

60 David Arnold, *Gandhi*, (London, 2001), p. 108; *The Collected Works of Mahatma Gandhi, vol. 14* (Delhi, 1965), pp. 440, 489.

61 Judith M. Brown, *Gandhi's Rise to Power: Indian Politics, 1915–1922* (Cambridge, 1972), pp. 162–3 and 242 note 2.

62 Brown, *Gandhi's Rise to Power*, pp. 175–6, 307–8, 328, 343.

63 Commons Debates, 8 July 1920, vol. 131, cols 1725, 1729, 1730.

64 D.A. Low, *Britain and Indian Nationalism: The Imprint of Ambiguity, 1929–1942* (Cambridge, 1997), p. 1, quoting Ho in May 1922.

65 Carl Bridge, *Holding Britain to the Empire: The British Conservative Party and the 1935 Constitution* (London, 1986), pp. 5–6; Judd, *Balfour and the British Empire*, pp. 261–2.

66 The Earl of Halifax, *Fulness of Days* (London, 1957), pp. 114, 117; Low, *Britain and Indian Nationalism*, p. 72; Nicholas Owen, *The British Left and India: Metropolitan Anti-Imperialism, 1885–1947* (Oxford, 2007), pp. 172–3, 181.

67 R.J. Moore, *The Crisis of Indian Unity, 1917–1940* (Oxford, 1974), p. 94; Judith M. Brown, *Gandhi and Civil Disobedience: The Mahatma in Indian Politics, 1928–1934* (Cambridge, 1977), p. 188; Martin Gilbert, *Winston S. Churchill, vol. 5* (London, 1976), pp. 390, 397.

68 Philip Williamson, *Stanley Baldwin: Conservative Leadership and National Values* (Cambridge, 1999), p. 267; Graham Stewart, *Burying Caesar: Churchill, Chamberlain and the Battle for the Tory Party* (London, 2000), p. 195; Bridge, *Holding Britain*, p. 158.

69 Ronald Hyam, *Britain's Declining Empire: The Road to Decolonization, 1918–1968* (Cambridge, 2006), p. 65.

70 Brown, *Modern India*, pp. 284, 286.

71 Sir Malcolm Hailey, 'India – 1983', *The Asiatic Review*, 29 (1933), p. 631.

72 Naoko Shimazu, *Japan, Race and Equality: The Racial Equality Proposal of 1919* (London, 1998), pp. 80, 96.

73 Ian Nish, *Alliance in Decline: A Study of Anglo-Japanese Relations, 1908–1923* (London, 1972), chs 8–14.

74 Frederick R. Dickinson, *War and National Reinvention: Japan in the Great War, 1914–1919* (Cambridge, Massachusetts, 1999), p. 235; Shimazu, *Japan, Race and Equality*, p. 20.

75 Shimazu, *Japan, Race and Equality*, pp. 27, 166, 181–4; Macmillan, *Peacemakers*, p. 328 [Hughes].

76 Roger Daniels, *The Politics of Prejudice: The Anti-Japanese Movement in California and the Struggle for Japanese Racial Exclusion* (Berkeley, California, 1977), pp. 21, 55.

77 Manela, *Wilsonian Moment*, pp. 31–2.

78 W. David McIntyre, *The Rise and Fall of the Singapore Naval Base, 1919–1942* (London, 1979), p. 20; Roger Dingman, *Power in the Pacific: The Origins of Naval Arms Limitation, 1914–1922* (Chicago, 1976), p. 34.

79 David Trask, *Captains and Cabinets: Anglo-American Naval Relations, 1917–1918* (Columbia, Missouri, 1972), pp. 112, 120; Phillips P. O'Brien, *British and American Naval Power: Politics and Policy, 1900–1936* (Westport, Connecticut, 1998), pp. 119–21.

80 O'Brien, *British and American Naval Power*, p. 154 [Lloyd George]; Marian C. McKenna, *Borah* (Ann Arbor, Michigan, 1961), p. 176; Thomas H. Buckley, *The United States and the Washington Naval Conference, 1921–22* (Knoxville, Tennessee, 1970), p. 72 quoting journalist Mark Sullivan.

81 As emphasized by O'Brien, *British and American Naval Power*, p. 171.

82 Churchill, Cabinet memo, 20 July 1927, in Martin Gilbert, *Winston S. Churchill, vol. 5, companion part 1* (London, 1979), p. 1033; O'Brien, *British and American*

Naval Power, pp. 154, 172, 188, 195–7; Christopher Hall, Britain, America and Arms Control, 1921–37 (London, 1987), p. 32.

83 Michael Adas, 'Contesting Hegemony: The Great War and the Afro-Asian Assault on the Civilizing Mission Ideology', Journal of World History, 15 (2004), esp. pp. 42, 62.

4: Capitalism

1 John Maynard Keynes, Essays in Persuasion (London, 1931), p. ix, preface dated 8 Nov. 1931; Norman and Jeanne Mackenzie, The Diary of Beatrice Webb, vol. 4 (London, 1985), p. 258, entry for 19 Sept. 1931.

2 Jackson E. Reynolds, President of the First National Bank of New York, in Diane B. Kunz, The Battle for Britain's Gold Standard in 1931 (London, 1987), p. 113.

3 By 1929 the USA accounted for 16 per cent of the world's exports as against 11.8 per cent for Britain, and 12.4 per cent of global imports, compared with Britain's 16.3 per cent. Derek Aldcroft, From Versailles to Wall Street, 1919–1929 (London, 1977), pp. 36–49, 223–31; Frank Costigliola, Awkward Dominion: American Political, Economic, and Cultural Relations with Europe, 1919–1933 (Ithaca, NY, 1984), p. 142.

4 Martha A. Olney, Buy Now, Pay Later: Advertising Credit, and Consumer Durables in the 1920s (Chapel Hill, North Carolina, 1991), pp. 86–91; Maury Klein, Rainbow's End: The Crash of 1929 (Oxford, 2001), p. 255; Hans Rogger, 'Amerikanizm and the Economic Development of Russia', Comparative Studies in Society and History, 23 (1981), p. 385.

5 Mira Wilkins, The Maturing of Multinational Enterprise: American Business Abroad from 1914 to 1970 (Cambridge, Massachussetts, 1974), esp. pp. 29–30, 155–6. Kathleen Burk, 'Great Britain in the United States, 1917–1918: The Turning Point', International History Review, 1 (1979), p. 228; Charles Kindleberger, The World in Depression, 1929–1939 (Berkeley, 1973), p. 56; Reinhold Niebuhr, 'Awkward Imperialists', Atlantic Monthly, May 1930, p. 670.

6 The theme of cooperation is emphasized by Barry Eichengreen, Golden Fetters: The Gold Standard and the Great Depression, 1919–1939 (New York, 1995), pp. 4–12; but see also Marc Flandreau, 'Central Bank Cooperation in Historical Perspective: A Sceptical View', EcHR, 50 (1997), pp. 735–63.

7 Eichengreen, Golden Fetters, p. 192; P.J. Cain and A.G. Hopkins, British Imperialism: Crisis and Deconstruction, 1914–1990 (London, 1993), pp. 66–7.

8 Andrew Boyle, Montagu Norman: A Biography (London, 1967), pp. 198–9; Kenneth Mouré, The Gold Standard Illusion: France, the Bank of France, and the International Gold Standard (Oxford, 2002), p. 156.

9 David M. Kennedy, Over Here: The First World War and American Society (Oxford, 1980), p. 345, quoting banker C.H. Crennan; statistics from John Braeman, 'The New Left and American Foreign Policy during the Age of Normalcy: A Re-examination', Business History Review, 57 (1983), pp. 82–6.

10 Jim Potter, *The American Economy Between the Wars* (London, 1974), p. 95.

11 Kindleberger, *World in Depression*, p. 292; cf. Adam Tooze, *The Wages of Destruction: The Making and Breaking of the Nazi Economy* (London, 2005), pp. 691–2. For analyses of the changing debate see two articles by Barry Eichengreen, 'The Origins and Nature of the Great Slump Revisited', *EcHR*, 45 (1992), pp. 213–39, and 'Understanding the Great Depression', *Canadian Journal of Economics*, 37 (2004), pp. 1–27.

12 See John H. Wood, *A History of Central Banking in Great Britain and the United States* (Cambridge, 2005), pp. 169–73, 210–11; also Allan H. Meltzer, *A History of the Federal Reserve, vol. I: 1913–1951* (Chicago, 2003), pp. 411–13.

13 Potter, *American Economy*, pp. 24, 95; Ben S. Bernanke, *Essays on the Great Depression* (Princeton, 2000), pp. 44–5; Charles C. Alexander, *Nationalism in American Thought, 1930–1945* (Chicago, 1969), p. 2, quoting Wilson.

14 Robert Skidelsky, *John Maynard Keynes* (3 vols, London, 1983–2000), vol. 2, esp. pp. 345–6, 371, 394.

15 John Maynard Keynes, *The Economic Consequences of the Peace* (London, 1920), pp. 29, 37–8, 209; Skidelsky, *Keynes*, vol. 2, p. 389.

16 Niall Ferguson, *The Pity of War* (London, 1998), pp. 414–15, 419; Sally Marks, 'Smoke and Mirrors: In Smoke-Filled Rooms and the Galerie des Glaces', in Manfred F. Boemeke, Gerald D. Feldman and Elisabeth Glaser, eds, *The Treaty of Versailles: A Reassessment After 75 Years* (Cambridge, 1998), pp. 338 [quotation], 347–9; Albrecht Ritschl, 'The Pity of Peace: Germany's Economy at War, 1914–1918 and beyond', in Broadberry and Harrison, eds, *Economics of World War I*, esp. pp. 67–8.

17 Ferguson, *Pity of War*, ch. 14, quoting p. 411.

18 Ferguson, *Pity of War*, esp. pp. 412, 420, 424.

19 Gerald D. Feldman, *The Great Disorder: Politics, Economics, and Society in the German Inflation, 1914–1924* (New York, 1997), pp. vii, 5, 704–6; Richard J. Evans, *The Coming of the Third Reich* (London, 2003), pp. 105–7.

20 Aldcroft, *From Versailles to Wall Street,* pp 85, 300; Costigliola, *Awkward Dominion*, p. 124, Harold James, *The German Slump: Politics and Economics, 1924–1936* (Oxford, 1986), pp. 135–8.

21 William L. Patch, Jr, *Heinrich Brüning and the Dissolution of the Weimar Republic* (Cambridge, 1998), p. 150; Eichengreen, *Golden Fetters*, p. 278.

22 Feldman, *Great Disorder*, p. 855; Jürgen von Kruedener, *Economic Crisis and Political Collapse: The Weimar Republic, 1924–1933* (New York, 1990), p. xiii.

23 Timothy J. Hatton, 'Unemployment and the Labour Market, 1870–1939', in Roderick Floud and Paul Johnson, eds, *The Cambridge Economic History of Modern Britain, vol. 2: Economic Maturity, 1860–1939* (Cambridge, 2004), pp. 348, 353–5; R.C.O. Matthews, C.H. Feinstein and J. Odling-Smee, *British Economic Growth, 1856–1973* (Oxford, 1982), pp. 6 [quotation], 497–8.

24 Keynes, 'The Economic Consequences of Mr Churchill' in *Essays in Persuasion,* pp. 244–71, quoting p. 261; Martin Gilbert, *Winston S. Churchill, vol. 5* (London, 1976), ch. 5, quoting p. 98.

25 D.E. Moggridge, *British Monetary Policy, 1924–1931: The Norman Conquest of $4.86* (Cambridge, 1972) developed Keynes' critique; see also G.C. Peden, ed., *Keynes and His Critics: Treasury Responses to the Keynesian Revolution, 1925–1946* (Oxford, 2004), ch.1. On 'gentlemanly capitalism', see more generally P.J. Cain and A.G. Hopkins, *British Imperialism: Innovation and Expansion, 1688–1914* (London, 1993), ch. 1.

26 Derek H. Aldcroft, *The Inter-War Economy: Britain, 1919–1939* (London, 1970), pp. 31–7; A.J. Arnold, 'Profitability and Capital Accumulation in British Industry during the Transwar Period, 1913–1924', *EcHR*, 52 (1999), pp. 45–68.

27 Aldcroft, *Inter-War Economy*, ch. 5, esp. pp. 157, 167, 173.

28 J.A. Dowie, '1919–20 Is in Need of Attention', *EcHR*, 28 (1975), pp. 439–41; Hatton, 'Unemployment and the Labour Market', pp. 360–9.

29 John Stevenson, *British Society, 1914–1945* (London, 1984), pp. 297–9; Hatton, 'Unemployment and the Labour Market', pp. 360, 372.

30 Philip Williamson, *National Crisis and National Government: British Politics, the Economy and the Empire, 1926–1932* (Cambridge, 1992), pp. 268, 312, 315; see also David Marquand, *Ramsay MacDonald* (London, 1977), chs 25–26, especially pp. 610–11, 625, 633–41.

31 Gaston V. Rimlinger, 'American Social Security in a European Perspective', in William G. Bowen et al., eds, *The American System of Social Insurance: Its Philosophy, Impact, and Future Development* (New York, 1968), pp. 214–17; Peter Flora and Arnold J. Heidenheimer, eds, *The Development of Welfare States in Europe and America* (New Brunswick, NJ, 1981), p. 19, quoting Papen; Jose Harris, 'Enterprise and Welfare States: A Comparative Perspective', *TRHS*, 40 (1990), pp. 182–4, 188.

32 T. Balderston, 'War Finance and Inflation in Britain and Germany, 1914–1918', *EcHR*, 42 (1989), esp. pp. 228, 237–8, 241–2; Martin Daunton, *Just Taxes: The Politics of Taxation in Britain, 1914–1979* (Cambridge, 2002), chs 1–4, quoting pp. 60 [Hugh Dalton] and 88 [Niemeyer].

33 Daunton, *Just Taxes*, chs 1–4, esp. pp. 3, 12–14, 58, 96–9. Standard rate of income tax rose from 5.8 per cent in 1913 to 30 per cent in 1919–22, and remained above 20 per cent for the rest of the interwar era.

34 Mark Thomas, 'The Service Sector' in Floud and Johnson, eds, *Cambridge Economic History*, pp. 118–19; Eichengreen, *Golden Fetters*, p. 279.

35 Barry Eichengreen, 'The British Economy between the Wars' in Floud and Johnson, eds, *Cambridge Economic History*, pp. 332–3; Williamson, *National Crisis*, pp. 480, 494–5.

36 Williamson, *National Crisis*, p. 498; Keynes, *Essays in Persuasion*, p. ix; Eichengreen, 'Origins and Nature of the Great Slump', pp. 232–5; Martin Daunton, 'Britain and Globalisation since 1850: II, The Rise of Insular Capitalism, 1914–1939', *TRHS*, 17 (2007), pp. 3–5.

37 Mouré, *Gold Standard Illusion*, esp. pp. 72, 102, 273; also L.D. Schwarz, 'Searching for Recovery: Unbalanced Budgets, Deflation and Rearmament in

France during the 1930s', in W.R. Garside, ed., *Capitalism in Crisis: International Responses to the Great Depression* (London, 1993), pp. 96–113.

38 Eichengreen, 'British Economy', pp. 330–7.

39 Aldcroft, *The Inter-War Economy*, pp. 177–98; S.M. Bowden, 'Demand and Supply Constraints in the Inter-War UK Car Industry: Did the Manufacturers Get It Right?' *Business History*, 33 (1991), esp. pp. 244, 257–8.

40 Sue Bowden and David M. Higgins. 'British Industry in the Interwar Years', in Floud and Johnson, eds, *Cambridge Economic History*, p, 377; Martin Pugh, *We Danced All Night: A Social History of Britain Between the Wars* (London, 2009), pp. 97–9.

41 S.N. Broadberry and N.F.R. Crafts, 'The Impact of the Depression of the 1930s on Productive Potential in the United Kingdom', *European Economic Review*, 34 (1990), esp. pp. 602–4; Bowden, 'Demand and Supply Constraints in the Inter-War UK Car Industry', pp. 260–4.

42 Aldcroft, *The Inter-War Economy*, pp. 285–94; Eichengreen, 'British Economy', pp. 337–42; cf. Jacques Marseille, *Empire Colonial et Capitalisme Français: Histoire d'un divorce* (Paris, 1984), ch. 2, and Martin Thomas, *The French Empire Between the Wars: Imperialism, Politics and Society* (Manchester, 2005), ch. 3.

43 As argued by Daunton, 'Britain and Globalisation since 1850', pp. 4–5.

44 Quoted in Zara Steiner, *The Lights that Failed: European International History, 1919–1933* (Oxford, 2005), p. 636.

45 Statistics from R.W. Davies et al., eds, *The Economic Transformation of the Soviet Union, 1913–1945* (Cambridge, 1994), pp. 18, 148; quotations from Stalin, *Works* (13 vols, Moscow, 1952–5), vol. 12, p. 141, and vol. 13, pp. 40–1.

46 Stephen Kotkin, *Magnetic Mountain: Stalinism as Civilization* (Berkeley, 1995), esp. pp. 18, 42–5, 71, 363–6.

47 Norman and Jeanne MacKenzie, eds, *The Diary of Beatrice Webb, vol. 4* (London, 1985), pp. 237, 255, 258.

48 Sidney and Beatrice Webb, *Soviet Communism: A New Civilisation* (London: 1937), pp. 431–2, 807, 1213–15; Kevin Morgan, *Bolshevism and the British Left: Part Two, The Webbs and Soviet Communism* (London, 2006), pp. 11–12.

49 Morgan, *Bolshevism and the British Left*, p. 242.

50 On which see David Caute, *The Fellow-Travellers: Intellectual Friends of Communism* (2nd edn, New Haven, 1988), chs 5–7, quoting p. 264.

51 Isaac Kramnick and Barry Sheerman, *Harold Laski: A Life on the Left* (London, 1993), pp. 384–9, 590.

52 Ruth Dudley Edwards, *Victor Gollancz: A Biography* (London, 1967), pp. 253–5. See also Ludmilla Stern, *Western Intellectuals and the Soviet Union, 1920–1940: From Red Square to the Left Bank* (London, 2007) and John McIlroy, 'The Establishment of Intellectual Orthodoxy and the Stalinization of British Communism, 1928–1933', *Past and Present*, 192 (Aug. 2006), pp. 187–230.

53 Matthew Worley, *Labour Inside the Gate: A History of the British Labour Party Between the Wars* (London, 2005), ch. 3, quoting p. 152; Ben Pimlott, *Hugh Dalton* (London, 1985), ch. 14, quoting p. 211.

54 Robert Boothby et al., *Industry and the State: A Conservative Viewpoint* (London, 1929), pp. 35–6.

55 Harold Macmillan, *Winds of Change, 1914–1939* (London, 1966), p. 285; Harold Macmillan, *The Middle Way: A Study of the Problem of Economic and Social Progress in a Free and Democratic Society* (London, 1938), pp. 8, 374–5.

56 Martin Gilbert, *Plough My Own Furrow: The Story of Lord Allen of Hurtwood as told through his writings and correspondence* (London, 1965), pp. 308–9.

57 Still useful here is Arthur Marwick, 'Middle Opinion in the Thirties: Planning, Progress and Political "Agreement"', *EHR*, 79 (1964), pp. 285–98.

58 John Dizikes, *Britain, Roosevelt and the New Deal: British Opinion, 1932–1938* (New York, 1979), quoting pp. 128, 219; *Planning*, 2 July 1935, p. 15. See also R.H. Pear, 'The Impact of the New Deal on British Economic and Political Ideas', *Bulletin of the British Association for American Studies*, 4 (Aug. 1962), pp. 17–28; Barbara C. Malament, 'British Labour and Roosevelt's New Deal: The Response of the Left and the Unions', *Journal of British Studies*, 17 (1978), pp. 136–67.

59 Keynes, *Essays in Persuasion*, p. vii.

60 Skidelsky, *Keynes*, vol. 2, esp. pp. 20, 438, 541.

61 Skidelsky, *Keynes*, vol. 1: 26, 133, and vol. 2: xv, 18; D.E. Moggridge, *Keynes* (London, 1976), pp. 43–5.

62 Quotations from Macmillan, *Middle Way*, pp. 375–6; Allen, *Britain's Political Future* (1934) in Gilbert, *Plough My Own Furrow*, pp. 295–6; see also Sidney and Beatrice Webb, *The Decay of Capitalist Civilisation* (London, 1923), p. 1.

5: Civilization

1 John Middleton Murry, 'Aims and Ideals', *Rhythm*, 1/4 (spring 1912), p. 36; Margaret Newbolt, ed., *The Later Life and Letters of Sir Henry Newbolt* (London, 1942), p. 315.

2 'Changing Warfare', *The Times*, 24 Nov. 1914, p. 5; Alan Kramer, *Dynamic of Destruction: Culture and Mass Killing in the First World War* (Oxford, 2007), pp. 251–2. The German army medical corps calculated that 85 per cent of injuries down to July 1918 were caused by artillery fire.

3 Georges Duhamel, *Civilisation, 1914–1917*, transl. E.S. Brooks (New York, 1919), ch. 16.

4 As for example in Pericles Lewis, *The Cambridge Introduction to Modernism* (Cambridge, 2007), p. 2.

5 John Richardson, *A Life of Picasso, vol. 2* (London, 2009), p. 105.

6 Franz Marc, 'The "Savages" of Germany', in Wassily Kandinsky and Franz Marc, eds, The Blaue Reiter *Almanac* (London, 1974), p. 61. *Wilde* can also be translated as 'loners'.

7 Joan Shapiro, *Painters and Politics: The European Avant-Garde and Society, 1900–1925* (New York, 1976), p. 76.

8 Alex Danchev, *Georges Braque: A Life* (London, 2007), pp. 48–50.

9 See David Cottington, *Cubism in the Shadow of War: The Avant-Garde and Politics in Paris, 1905–1914* (New Haven, 1998), quoting p. 87.

10 Charles Harrison and Paul Wood, eds, *Art in Theory, 1900–2000: An Anthology of Changing Ideas* (2nd edn, Oxford, 2003), pp. 119–20.

11 Published in *Le Figaro*, 20 Feb. 1909, p. 1.

12 Didier Ottinger, ed., *Futurism* (London, 2009), pp. 20–41.

13 Frances Spalding, *British Art Since 1900* (London, 1986), ch. 2, quoting pp. 37–9; John Ferguson, *The Arts in Britain in World War I* (Southampton, 1980), pp. 9–10 (Blunt).

14 Ezra Pound, 'Vorticism', *Fortnightly Review*, 96:573, Sept. 1914, p. 469; *Blast: Review of the Great English Vortex*, no. 1 (1914), p. 41; Paul Gough, *A Terrible Beauty: British Artists in the First World War* (Bristol, 2010), p. 215.

15 Joan Weinstein, *The End of Expressionism: Art and the November Revolution in Germany, 1918–19* (Chicago, 1990), pp. 1–2, 19; Linda F. McGreevy, *Bitter Witness: Otto Dix and the Great War* (New York, 2001), chs 6–8; Peter Paret, 'Betrachtungen über deutsche Kunst und Künstler im Ersten Weltkrieg', in Wolfgang Mommsen et al., eds, *Kultur und Krieg: Die Rolle der Intellektuellen, Künstler und Schriftsteller im Ersten Weltkrieg* (München, 1996), esp. p. 162.

16 Elizabeth Louise Kahn, *The Neglected Majority: 'Les Camoufleurs', Art History, and World War I* (Lanham, Maryland, 1984), pp. 1, 11; Kenneth E. Silver, *Esprit de Corps: The Art of the Parisian Avant-Garde and the First World War, 1914–1925* (London, 1989), esp. chs 2–4.

17 Aaron J. Cohen, *Imagining the Unimaginable: World War, Modern Art, and the Politics of Public Culture in Russia, 1914–1917* (Lincoln, Nebraska, 2008), ch. 3, quoting p. 111; Richard Cork, *A Bitter Truth: Avant-Garde Art and the Great War* (New Haven, 1994), pp. 9–10, 48–51.

18 Alfred Emile Cornebise, *Art from the Trenches: America's Uniformed Artists in World War I* (College Station, Texas, 1991), pp. 12, 35–6, 58; Peter Krass, *Portrait of War: The U.S. Army's First Combat Artists and the Doughboys' Experience in World War I* (New York, 2007), pp. 231–2 [quotations].

19 Kahn, *Neglected Majority*, pp. 92–5.

20 Ségolène Le Men, *Monet* (Paris, 2010), pp. 398–40; Philippe Dagen, *Le Silence des Peintres: Les Artistes face à la Grande Guerre* (Paris, 1996), pp. 15–17, 321–2.

21 Quotations from Sue Malvern, 'War, Memory and Museums: Art and Artefact in the Imperial War Museum', *History Workshop Journal*, 49 (spring 2000), pp. 188–9.

22 'Junkerism in Art', *The Times*, 10 March 1915, p. 8; Gough, *Terrible Beauty*, p. 17.

23 Meirion and Susie Harries, *The War Artists: British Official War Art and the Twentieth Century* (London, 1983), p. 8. See also the essay on Masterman in Gary S. Messenger, *British Propaganda and the State in the First World War* (Manchester, 1992), ch. 3.

24 William Philpott, *Bloody Victory: The Sacrifice on the Somme* (London, 2009), p. 293; Sue Malvern, *Modern Art, Britain and the Great War: Witnessing, Testimony and Remembrance* (New Haven, 2004), p. 48; Jane Carmichael, *First World War Photographers* (London, 1989), pp. 48, 141–2.

25 Nicholas Reeves, 'Film Propaganda and Its Audience: The Example of Britain's Official Films During the First World War', *Journal of Contemporary History*, 18 (1983), esp. pp. 463–6; David Welch, *Germany, Propaganda and Total War, 1914–1918: The Sins of Omission* (London, 2000), p. 53, quoting *The Cinema*.

26 Lucy Masterman, *C.F.G. Masterman: A Biography* (London, 1939), pp. 286–7; Malvern, *Modern Art*, p. 24.

27 Nicholas Reeves, *Official British Film Propaganda During the First World War* (London, 1986), pp. 10–11; Welch, *Germany, Propaganda and Total War*, pp. 21, 51.

28 Malvern, *Modern Art*, pp. 21–4; Gough, *Terrible Beauty*, p. 25. See more generally Matthew Johnson, 'The Liberal War Committee and the Liberal Advocacy of Conscription in Britain, 1914–1916', *Historical Journal*, 51 (2008), pp. 399–420.

29 A.J.P. Taylor, *Beaverbrook* (London, 1974), p. 27; see generally Harries and Harries, *The War Artists*, pp. 82–108.

30 Malvern, *Modern Art*, pp. 69, 75–6; Maria Tippett, *Art in the Service of War: Canada, Art, and the Great War* (Toronto, 1984), p. 111.

31 Wyndham Lewis, *Blasting and Bombardiering* [1937] (2nd edn, London, 1967), pp. 114–15; Wyndham Lewis, *Rude Assignment: A Narrative of My Career Up-to-date* (London, 1950), pp. 128–9.

32 For these different interpretations see Cork, *Bitter Truth*, pp. 226–7; Paul Edwards, *Wyndham Lewis: Art and War* (London, 1992), pp. 39–41; David Peters Corbett, ed., *Wyndham Lewis and the Art of Modern War* (Cambridge, 1998), pp. 51–3 and 71–3. The 'madmen' quote comes from Lewis.

33 Gough, *Terrible Beauty*, pp. 101, 122–5; David Boyd Haycock, *A Crisis of Brilliance: Five Young British Artists and the Great War* (London, 2009), pp. 259–60 (Hind).

34 Cork, *Bitter Truth*, p. 202; Paul Nash, *Outline: An Autobiography and Other Writings*, ed. Herbert Read (London, 1949), pp. 188–9, 210–11.

35 Gough, *Terrible Beauty*, pp. 153–63.

36 See the discussion in Malvern, *Modern Art*, ch. 1, esp. pp. 21, 35.

37 James King, *Interior Landscapes: A Life of Paul Nash* (London, 1987), p. 88.

38 Harries and Harries, *The War Artists*, p. 152.

39 Gough, *Terrible Beauty*, pp. 314–16. See also Spalding, *British Art Since 1900*, ch. 3, and Alexandra Harris, *Romantic Moderns: English Writers, Artists and the Imagination from Virginia Woolf to John Piper* (London, 2011).

40 *The Times*, 26 July 1919, p. 13. This paragraph and the next draw on Adrian Gregory, *The Silence of Memory: Armistice Day 1919–1946* (Oxford, 1994), ch. 1, and David W. Lloyd, *Battlefield Tourism: Pilgrimage and the Commemoration of the Great War in Britain, Australia and Canada* (Oxford, 1998), ch. 2.

41 Tim Skelton and Gerald Gliddon, *Lutyens and the Great War* (London, 2008), p. 47; see also Jay Winter, *Sites of Memory, Sites of Mourning: The Great War in European Cultural History* (Cambridge, 1995), pp. 103–5.

42 Leonard V. Smith, Stéphane Audoin-Rouzeau and Annette Becker, *France and*

the Great War 1914–1918 (Cambridge, 2003), p. 73. See also Ulrich Schlie, *German Memorials: In Search of a Difficult Past. Nation and National Monuments in 19th and 20th Century German History* (Bonn, 2000), and Stefan Goebel, *The Great War and Medieval Memory: War, Remembrance and Medievalism in Britain and Germany, 1914–1940* (Cambridge, 2007).

43 On which see generally Thomas W. Laquer, 'Memory and Naming in the Great War', in John R. Gillis, ed., *Commemorations: The Politics of National Identity* (Princeton, 1994), pp. 150–67.

44 *Henry V*, Act 4, Scene 7, lines 72–4; *Henry VI Part I*, Act 4, Scene 7, lines 85–6.

45 Richard van Emden, *The Quick and the Dead: Fallen Soldiers and their Families in the Great War* (London, 2011), p. 276; Philip Longworth, *The Unending Vigil: A History of the Commonwealth War Graves Commission, 1917–1984* (2nd edn, London, 1985), pp. 33–4.

46 Eric Gill, 'War Graves', *The Burlington Magazine for Connoisseurs*, 34/193 (April 1919), pp. 158–60; Longworth, *Unending Vigil*, p. 53.

47 HC *Debs*, 4 May 1920, vol. 128, col. 1935; see also Charles Carrington, *Rudyard Kipling: His Life and Work* (London, 1970), pp. 497–514.

48 HC *Debs*, 4 May 1920, vol. 128, cols 1960–3; Laqueur, 'Memory and Naming', p. 161.

49 HC *Debs*, 128: 1969–70.

50 Longworth, *Unending Vigil*, p. 13.

51 'On Passing the New Menin Gate' in Siegfried Sassoon, *Collected Poems 1908–1956* (London, 1984), p. 188.

52 Skelton and Gliddon, *Lutyens and the Great War*, pp. 134–9; see also Gavin Stamp, *The Memorial to the Missing of the Somme* (London, 2006).

53 Michèle Barrett, 'Death and the Afterlife: Britain's Colonies and Dominions', in Santanu Das, ed., *Race, Empire and First World War Writing* (Cambridge, 2011), pp. 302–12.

54 See G. Kurt Piehler, 'The War Dead and the Gold Star: American Commemoration of the First World War', in Gillis, ed., *Commemorations*, pp. 168–74, and also the World War I section of the website of the American Battle Monuments Commission http://www.abmc.gov/search/wwi.php

55 Drew Gilpin Faust, *This Republic of Suffering: Death and the American Civil War* (New York, 2009), pp. 99–103; Gary Wills, *Lincoln at Gettysburg: The Words that Remade America* (New York, 1992), p. 261.

56 Richard Carwardine and Jay Sexton, eds, *The Global Lincoln* (Oxford, 2011), pp. 130, 146–52; Lloyd, *Battlefield Tourism*, p. 27.

57 Skelton and Gliddon, *Lutyens and the Great* War, p. 139; Stamp, *Memorial to the Missing*, p. 99; Lloyd, *Battlefield Tourism*, ch. 3.

58 Catherine W. Reilly, *English Poetry of the First World War: A Bibliography* (London, 1978), pp. xiii, xix.

59 *Wilfred Owen, Collected Letters*, ed. Harold Owen and John Bell (London, 1967), p. 596. See generally Martin Stephen, *The Price of Pity: Poetry, History and Myth in the Great War* (London, 1996), ch. 7, esp. pp. 185–93.

60 T.E. Hulme quoted in Ross, *The Georgian Revolt: Rise and Fall of a Poetic Ideal,*
    1910–22 (London, 1967), p. 41 ['treacle']; Laurence Binyon, 'The Return to
    Poetry', *Rhythm*, 1/4 (spring 1912), p. 1.

61 'A Lecture on Modern Poetry' (1908), in Michael Roberts, *T.E. Hulme*
    (London, 1938), p. 266.

62 *Georgian Poetry, 1911–1912* (London, 1912), prefatory note; 'Aims and Ideals',
    in *Rhythm*, 1/1 (spring 1911), p. 36 – Murry's aphorism was adapted from a
    remark by the Irish playwright J.M. Synge.

63 Matthew Hollis, *Now All Roads Lead to France: The Last Years of Edward Thomas*
    (London, 2011), pp. 141–2.

64 Elizabeth A. Marsland, *The Nation's Cause: French, English and German Poetry of*
    the First World War (London, 1991), pp. 1–2; *The Times*, 6 Aug. 1915, p. 7.

65 *The Poetical Works of Rupert Brooke*, ed., Geoffery Keynes (London, 1970), p. 19.

66 Marsland, *The Nation's Cause*, ch. 2–3, esp. pp. 44–5, 50–4; see also Frank
    Field, *British and French Writers of the First World War* (Cambridge, 1991),
    pp. 112–13.

67 Stefan Collini, *Public Moralists: Political Thought and Intellectual Life in Britain*
    (Oxford, 1991), ch. 9, esp. pp. 354–5, 362; Krishan Kumar, *The Making of*
    English National Identity (Cambridge, 2003), pp. 202–25; Samuel Hynes, *A War*
    Imagined: The First World War and English Culture (London, 1990), p. 31; from
    'August 1914', in *The Collected Poems of John Masefield* (London, 1924), p. 375.
    See also David Goldie, 'Was There a Scottish War Literature? Scotland, Poetry,
    and the First World War', in Tim Kendall, ed., *The Oxford Handbook of British*
    and Irish War Poetry (Oxford, 2007), pp. 155–73.

68 Ted Bogacz, '"A Tyranny of Words": Language, Poetry, and Antimodernism in
    England in the First World War', *Journal of Modern History*, 58 (1986), p. 666;
    Dominic Hibberd and John Onions, eds, *The Winter of the World: Poems of the*
    First World War (London, 2007), pp. xv–xxi, xxvii.

69 Stephen, *Price of Pity*, pp. 138–42; Paul Fussell, *The Great War and Modern*
    Memory (New York, 1975), p. 168.

70 Jon Stallworthy, ed., *Wilfred Owen: The Complete Poems and Fragments* (2 vols,
    London, 1983), vol. 1, p. 140. See also Marsland, *The Nation's Cause*, chs 4–5.

71 The official citation in 1919 stated that Owen, using a captured German
    machine gun, 'inflicted considerable losses on the enemy'. A typed copy in
    Harold's papers does not contain that phrase but states that he 'took a number
    of prisoners'. This wording was printed in Harold's published edition of
    Wilfred's letters. See Dominic Hibberd, *Wilfred Owen: A New Biography*
    (Chicago, 2003), pp. 348–50, 376–7; Harold Owen and John Bell, eds, *Wilfred*
    Owen: Collected Letters (London, 1967), p. 580.

72 Stallworthy, ed., *Owen: Complete Poems and Fragments*, vol. 1, 185–7, vol. 2,
    pp. 535–6.

73 *The Collected Poems of Edward Thomas*, ed. R. George Thomas (Oxford, 1978),
    p. 257; W. Cooke, *Edward Thomas: A Critical Biography, 1878–1917* (London,
    1970), chs 5 and 9, quoting p. 93.

74 George L. Mosse, *Fallen Soldiers: Reshaping the Memory of the World Wars* (New York, 1990), pp. 82–90; Longworth, *Unending Vigil*, p. 73; Brooke, *Poetical Works*, p. 23.

75 Cf. Dominic Hibberd, 'Wilfred Owen and the Georgians', *Review of English Studies*, 30 (1979), pp. 28–40.

76 William Pratt, *Ezra Pound and the Making of Modernism* (New York, 2007), p. 10; Ezra Pound, *Selected Poems, 1908–1969* (London, 1977), p.101.

77 'The Waste Land', in *The Complete Poems and Plays of T.S. Eliot* (London, 1969), pp. 61–80, quoting lines 60–3, 368–9 and 372–6; cf. T.S. Eliot, *The Waste Land: A Facsimile and Transcript of the Original Drafts*, ed. Valerie Eliot (London, 1971), pp. 72–5. For Eliot's concerns about contemporary Europe see Stan Smith, *The Origins of Modernism: Eliot, Pound, Yeats and the Rhetorics of Renewal* (London, 1994), pp. 25–6, 144–51.

78 Stephen Spender, *T.S. Eliot* (London, 1975), p. 106; Peter Ackroyd, *T.S. Eliot* (London, 1985), ch. 6, quoting p. 120; T.S. Eliot, 'The Frontiers of Criticism' in *On Poetry and Poets* (London, 1957), p. 109.

79 Sigmund Freud, *Civilization and Its Discontents*, transl. James Strachey (New York, 1962), pp. 69, 92.

80 Richard Overy, *The Morbid Age: Britain Between the Wars* (London, 2009), ch. 1, quoting p. 37.

81 Clive Bell, *Civilization: An Essay* (London, 1928), p. 1.

82 Harold Lasswell, *Propaganda Technique in the World War* (London, 1927), pp. 195–8, 221–2.

83 Lasswell, *Propaganda Technique*, pp. 214–18.

84 Arthur Ponsonby, *Falsehood in War-Time: Containing an Assortment of Lies Circulated Throughout the Nations During the Great War* (London, 1928), pp. 56, 192.

85 Adrian Gregory, *The Last Great War: British Society and the First World War* (Cambridge, 2008), ch. 2, quoting p. 41.

86 Keith Wilson, ed., *Forging the Collective Memory: Governments and International Historians Through the Two World Wars* (Oxford, 1996), chs 3–5, quoting p. 88; David Lloyd George, *War Memoirs* (6 vols, London, 1933–6), 1:52, 55.

87 Robert Graves, *Good-Bye to All That: An Autobiography* (London, 1929), p. 240; Siegfried Sassoon, *Memoirs of a Fox-Hunting Man* (London, 1975 edn), part 9, pp. 247–8.

88 Virginia Woolf, *To the Lighthouse* (London, 1930 edn), pp. 200, 207; Vincent Sherry, *The Great War and the Language of Modernism* (Oxford, 2003), p. 294; Sharon Ouditt, *Fighting Forces, Writing Women: Identity and Ideology in the First World War* (London, 1994), p. 200.

89 Erich Maria Remarque, *All Quiet on the Western Front,* transl. A.W. Wheen (London, 1929), quoting dedication and pp. 107, 155, 193, 248.

90 This paragraph follows Andrew Kelly, *All Quiet on the Western Front: The Story of a Film* (London, 1998), esp. pp. 42–3, 83–8, 126–7, 113, 131, 163.

91 Hynes, *A War Imagined*, p. 424.

92 See the essays by Pierre Sorlin, 'Cinema and the Memory of the Great War' and 'France: The Silent Memory', in Michael Paris, ed., *The First World War and Popular Cinema: 1914 to the Present* (Edinburgh, 1999), esp. pp. 17–22, 118, 129–32.

93 David M. Kennedy, *Over Here: The First World War and American Society* (New York, 1980), p. 366; Paul Fussell, *The Great War and Modern Memory* (New York, 1975), p. 160.

94 Edith Wharton, *A Son at the Front* (London, 1923), p. 314.

95 See David D. Lee, *Sergeant York: An American Hero* (Lexington, Kentucky, 1985).

96 Michael T. Isenberg, *War on Film: The American Cinema and World War I, 1914–1941* (London, 1981), pp. 140–1.

97 Ernest Hemingway, *A Farewell to Arms* (London, 2005 edn), ch. 27, p. 165; F. Scott Fitzgerald, *Tender Is the Night* (New York, 1934), p. 67.

98 Kelly, *All Quiet*, pp. 48, 52; Graves, *Good-bye*, p. 1; Brian Bond, *The Unquiet Western Front: Britain's Role in Literature and History* (Cambridge, 2002), pp. 33–4.

99 Rosa Maria Bracco, *Merchants of Hope: British Middlebrow Writers and the First World War, 1919–1939* (Oxford, 1993), ch. 5, quoting pp. 152–3, 178.

100 Letter of 2 Aug. 1914 in Margaret Newbolt, ed., *The Later Life and Letters of Sir Henry Newbolt* (London, 1942), pp. 314–15.

101 Janet S.K. Watson, *Fighting Different Wars: Experience, Memory, and the First World War in Britain* (Cambridge, 2004).

102 Cf. Overy, *The Morbid Age*, pp. 2–3; Hynes, *A War Imagined*, pp. xi–xii, 459–60.

103 Gregory, *Last Great War*, pp. 273, 292; Watson, *Fighting Different Wars*, pp. 307–8.

6: Peace

1 W.N. Medlicott, et al., eds, *Documents on British Foreign Policy, 1919–1939, series 1A, vol. I* (London, 1966), p. 846; Siegfried Sassoon, *Collected Poems, 1908–1956* (London, 1984), pp. 231–2.

2 3rd Annual Report of the Imperial War Museum, 1919–20, p. 4 (IWM).

3 Catherine Merridale, *Night of Stone: Death and Memory in Russia* (London, 2000), pp. 122–9, 452; Melissa Stockdale, 'United in Gratitude: Honoring Soldiers and Defining the Nation in Russia's Great War', *Kritika*, 7 (2006), pp. 465–8, 482; Daniel Orlovsky, 'Velikaia voina i rossiiskaia pamiat', in N.N. Smirnov, ed., *Rossiia i pervaia mirovaia voina: Materialy mezhdunarodnogo nauchnogo kollokviuma* (St Petersburg, 1999), esp. p. 50.

4 Jeffrey Verhey, *The Spirit of 1914: Militarism, Myth and Mobilization in Germany* (Cambridge, 2000), pp. 207–13; Stefan Goebel, *The Great War and Medieval Memory: War, Remembrance and Medievalism in Britain and Germany, 1914–1940* (Cambridge, 2007), pp. 127–45; Anna von der Goltz, *Hindenburg: Power, Myth, and the Rise of the Nazis* (Cambridge, 2009), pp. 104–9.

5 Alan Kramer, 'The First World War and German Memory', in Heather Jones et al., eds, *Untold War: New Perspectives in First World War Studies* (Leiden, 2008), pp. 390–1.

6 Richard Bessel, *Germany After the First World War* (Oxford, 1993), p. 258; see

also Richard Weldon Whalen, *Bitter Wounds: German Victims of the Great War, 1914–1939* (Ithaca, NY, 1984), pp. 121–9.

7 Thomas Weber, *Hitler's First War: Adolf Hitler, The List Regiment, and the First World War* (Oxford, 2010), esp. pp. 220–2, 345–7; Kramer, 'The First World War and German Memory', pp. 393–4; Benjamin Ziemann, *War Experiences in Rural Germany, 1914–1923* (Oxford, 2007), pp. 274–5; Wilhelm Deist et al., *Germany and the Second World War, vol. I* (Oxford, 1990), pp. 77–82.

8 Gregory, *Silence of Memory*, pp. 99, 102.

9 Gregory, *Silence of Memory*, ch. 2, quoting p. 78; A.P. Sanford and Robert Haven Schauffer, eds, *Armistice Day* (New York, 1927), pp. 447, 455–7.

10 Karl Rohe, *Das Reichsbanner Schwarz Rot Gold: Ein Beitrag zur Geschichte und Struktur der politischen Kampfverbände der Weimarer Republik* (Düsseldorf, 1966), pp. 73, 115–16; James M. Diehl, *Paramilitary Politics in Weimar Germany* (Bloomington, Indiana, 1977), pp. 293–5; Antoine Prost, *In the Wake of War: 'Les Anciens Combattants' and French Society* (Oxford, 1992), ch. 2, esp. p. 44.

11 Niall Barr, *The Lion and the Poppy: British Veterans, Politics, and Society, 1921–1939* (Westport, Connecticut, 2005), chs 1–3, esp. pp. 1, 57–8.

12 Deborah Cohen, 'The War's Returns: Disabled Veterans in Britain and Germany, 1914–1939', in Roger Chickering and Stig Förster, eds, *The Shadows of Total War: Europe, East Asia, and the United States, 1919–1939* (Cambridge, 2003), ch. 6, quoting pp. 114–15, 119; also Whalen, *Bitter Wounds*, esp. ch. 12.

13 Maris A. Vinovskis, ed., *Toward a Social History of the American Civil War: Exploratory Essays* (Cambridge, 1990), pp. 21–3, 172; Frank Freidel, *FDR: Launching the New Deal* (Boston, 1973), pp. 239–47.

14 William Pencak, *For God and Country: The American Legion, 1919–1941* (Boston, 1989), esp. pp. 50–1, 156–7, 266, 285.

15 Gregory, *Silence of Memory*, pp. 123, 126.

16 Malcolm Smith, 'The War and British Culture', in Stephen Constantine, Maurice W. Kirby and Mary B. Rose, eds, *The First World War in British History* (London, 1995), p. 171.

17 See Catriona Beaumont, 'Citizens not Feminists: The Boundary Negotiated Between Citizenship and Feminism by Mainstream Women's Organizations in England, 1928–39', *Women's History Review*, 9 (2000), pp. 411–29; Patricia M. Thane, 'What Difference Did the Vote Make? Women in Public and Private Life in Britain Since 1918', *Historical Research*, 76, no. 192 (May 2003), pp. 269–85; 'Adrian Bingham, "An Era of Domesticity"? Histories of Women and Gender in Interwar Britain', *Cultural and Social History*, 1 (2004), pp. 224–33.

18 Josephine Eglin, 'Women Pacifists in Interwar Britain', in Peter Brock and Thomas P. Socknat, eds, *Challenge to Mars: Essays on Pacifism from 1918 to 1935* (Toronto, 1999), pp. 159–60 [Brittain]; Gertrude Bussey and Margaret Tims, *Pioneers for Peace: Women's International League for Peace and Freedom, 1915–1965* (London, 1980), pp. 32, 76, 96. On the development of post-war internationalism in general see Daniel Gorman, *The Emergence of International Society in the 1920s* (Cambridge, 2012).

19 Speech of 25 Oct. 1928 in Winston S. Churchill, *Arms and the Covenant* (London, 1938), p. 17.

20 Quoting Zara Steiner, *The Lights that Failed: European International History 1919–1933* (Oxford, 2005), p. 775, and Steiner, *The Triumph of the Dark: European International History 1933–1939* (Oxford, 2011), p. 54.

21 Cmd 3591, 'The Channel Tunnel: Statement of Policy', 4 June 1930; see also 'A Brief Historical Survey of the Channel Tunnel Project, 1802–1929', CTUN 5/1 (CAC); Vansittart memo in CP 4 (32), CAB 24/227 (TNA).

22 Cecil to Wiseman, 19 Aug. 1918, in Viscount Cecil of Chelwood, *All the Way* (London, 1949), p. 142.

23 Helen McCarthy, *The British People and the League of Nations: Democracy, Citizenship and Internationalism* (Manchester, 2011), esp. pp. 4, 103.

24 The principal studies are Martin Ceadel, 'The First British Referendum: The Peace Ballot, 1934–5', *EHR*, 95 (Oct. 1980), pp. 810–39; Helen McCarthy, 'Democratizing British Foreign Policy: Rethinking the Peace Ballot, 1934–1935', *Journal of British Studies*, 49 (2010), pp. 358–87. Both draw heavily on Adelaide Livingstone, *The Peace Ballot: The Official History* (London, 1935).

25 Donald S. Birn, *The League of Nations Union 1918–1945* (Oxford, 1981), pp. 146, 150; McCarthy, *British People*, p. 201; Ceadel, 'First British Referendum', p. 824.

26 Winston S. Churchill, *The Second World War, vol. 1* (London, 1948), pp. 132–3; Ceadel, 'First British Referendum', pp. 832–3.

27 Martin Ceadel, *Pacifism in Britain, 1914–1945: The Defining of a Faith* (Oxford, 1980), esp. pp. 249, 262, 266; Richard Overy, *The Morbid Age: Britain Between the Wars* (London, 2009), p. 250 [Martin].

28 Reinhold Lütgemeier-Davin, *Pazifismus zwischen Kooperation und Konfrontation: Das Deutsche Friedenskartell in der Weimarer Republik* (Köln, 1982), p. 92; Norman Ingram, *The Politics of Dissent: Pacifism in France, 1919–1939* (Oxford, 1991), esp. pp 2, 24, 38, 142.

29 HC *Debs*, 5s, 292: 2339, 30 July 1934.

30 HC *Debs*, 5s, 270:631–2, 10 Nov. 1932; Uri Bialer, *The Shadow of the Bomber: The Fear of Air Attack and British Politics, 1932–1939* (London, 1980), pp. 129–30.

31 Harold Macmillan, *Winds of Change* (London, 1966), p. 575. The official history by Basil Collier, *The Defence of the United Kingdom* (London, 1957), p. 528, lists the total casualties as 146,777, including 60,595 dead.

32 Bialer, *Shadow of the Bomber*, pp. 12 [Gloag], 47 [Russell].

33 Arnold Toynbee to Quincy Wright, 14 Oct. 1938, in Roger S. Greene papers, folder 747 (Houghton Library, Harvard University).

34 Gugliermo Ferrero (1931), quoted in Ladislas Mysyrowicz, *Autopsie d'une Défaite: Origines de l'effondrement militaire français de 1940* (Lausanne, 1973), p. 319.

35 As emphasized by Bialer, *Shadow of the Bomber*, pp. 12–13, and Brett Holman, 'The Air Panic of 1935: British Press Opinion Between Disarmament and Rearmament', *JCH*, 46 (2011), pp. 292–3.

36 Bialer, *Shadow of the Bomber*, pp. 20–1, 24 and 76–100.

37 Neville to Ida, 19 Sept. 1938, Neville Chamberlain papers, NC 18/1/1069 (Birmingham University Library); Cabinet minutes, 24 Sept. 1938, CAB 23/95, folio 180 (TNA).

38 James Hinton, *Protests and Visions: Peace Politics in Twentieth-Century Britain* (London, 1989), p. 111.

39 See the insightful study of his changing reputation by David Dutton, *Neville Chamberlain* (London, 2001), quoting pp. 52–3.

40 Neville Chamberlain to Ida, 18 Aug. 1937, NC 18/1/1015; see also David Reynolds, *Summits: Six Meetings that Shaped the Twentieth Century* (London, 2007), ch. 2.

41 Robert Paul Shay, Jr, *British Rearmament in the 1930s: Politics and Profits* (Princeton, 1977), p. 39; Michael Howard, *The Continental Commitment: The Dilemma of British Defence Policy in the Era of the Two World Wars* (London, 1974), p. 110.

42 Bialer, *Shadow of the Bomber*, pp. 50–1.

43 David French, *Raising Churchill's Army: The British Army and the War Against Germany, 1919–1945* (Oxford, 2000), p. 14; Brian Bond, *British Military Policy Between the Two World Wars* (Oxford, 1980), pp. 208, 218; Norman Gibbs, *Grand Strategy, vol. 1, Rearmament Policy* (London, 1976), p. 113; Keith Feiling, *The Life of Neville Chamberlain* (London, 1946), p. 314.

44 Shay, *British Rearmament*, pp. 172–3; Peden, *British Rearmament*, p. 134; Alexander Rose, 'Radar and Air Defence in the 1930s', *TCBH*, 9 (1998), pp. 219–45.

45 David Edgerton, *Warfare State: Britain, 1920–1970* (Cambridge, 2006), ch. 1, esp. pp. 23, 30–2, 46.

46 George Peden, *The Treasury and British Rearmament, 1932–1938* (Edinburgh, 1979), pp. 66, 148.

47 Contrasts brought out well in Joe Maiolo, *Cry Havoc: The Arms Race and the Second World War, 1931–1941* (London, 2010), esp. chs 5, 8, 10.

48 Following the argument of Adam Tooze, *The Wages of Destruction: The Making and Breaking of the Nazi Economy* (London, 2006), chs 7–9, esp. pp. 222, 287, 317, 322–5.

49 Brian Bond, ed., *Chief of Staff: The Diaries of Lieutenant-General Sir Henry Pownall* (2 vols, London, 1972–4), vol. 1, p. 221. See generally Zara Steiner, 'Views of War: Britain Before the "Great War" – and After', *International Relations*, 17 (2003), pp. 7–33.

50 Bialer, *Shadow of the Bomber*, p. 10.

51 David Jones, *In Parenthesis* (London 1963), p. xv.

52 Charles Chatfield, *For Peace and Justice: Pacifism in America, 1914–1941* (Boston, 1973), pp. 68–9.

53 Harriet Hyman Alonso, *Peace as a Women's Issue: A History of the U.S. Movement for World Peace and Women's Rights* (Syracuse, NY, 1993), p. 86.

54 Chatfield, *For Peace and Justice*, pp. 256, 272. On the Anglo-American contrasts see Cecilia Lynch, *Beyond Appeasement: Interpreting Interwar Peace Movements in World Politics* (Ithaca, NY, 1999), pp. 30–8.

55 Robert A. Divine, *The Illusion of Neutrality: Franklin D. Roosevelt and the Struggle over the Arms Embargo* (New York, 1962), p. 65.

56 Wayne S. Cole, *Senator Gerald P. Nye and American Foreign Relations* (Minneapolis, Minnesota, 1962), pp. 81–2.

57 Raymond Gram Swing, 'Morgan's Nerves Begin to Jump', *The Nation*, vol. 140, 1 May 1935, p. 504.

58 Merrill D. Peterson, *Thomas Jefferson and the New Nation* (New York, 1970), p. 398.

59 Divine, *Illusion of Neutrality*, p. 167; C. David Tompkins, *Senator Arthur H. Vandenberg: The Evolution of a Modern Republican, 1884–1945* (East Lansing, Michigan, 1970), p. 125.

60 Cushing Strout, *The American Image of the Old World* (New York, 1963), p. 205.

61 Speech of 14 Aug. 1936, American Presidency Project website, http://www.presidency.ucsb.edu

62 Samuel I. Rosenman, *Working with Roosevelt* (New York, 1952), p. 167; Robert E. Sherwood, *Roosevelt and Hopkins: An Intimate History* (New York, 1948), p. 227. See more generally Graham Cross, *The Diplomatic Education of Franklin D. Roosevelt, 1822–1933* (New York, 2012).

63 Divine, *Illusion of Neutrality*, pp. 86–8.

64 David Reynolds, *From Munich to Pearl Harbor: Roosevelt's America and the Origins of the Second World War* (Chicago, 2001), pp. 32, 37–8.

65 David G. Anderson, 'British Rearmament and the "Merchants of Death": The 1935–36 Royal Commission on the Manufacture and Trade in Armaments', *JCH*, 29 (1994), pp. 5–37, quoting p. 30.

66 Henry Morgenthau diary, vol. 150, pp. 337–8 (Franklin D. Roosevelt Library, Hyde Park, NY).

67 Transcript of conference with Senate Military Affairs Committee, 31 Jan. 1939, in Donald B. Schewe, ed., *Franklin D. Roosevelt and Foreign Affairs, 2nd series, vol. 13* (New York, 1969), doc. 1565.

68 Roosevelt, address of 21 Sept. 1939, American Presidency Project website; Wayne S. Cole, *Roosevelt and the Isolationists, 1932–1945* (Lincoln, Nebraska, 1983), p. 328.

69 I follow here the argument of Martin Ceadel, 'A Legitimate Peace Movement: The Case of Britain, 1918–1945', in Brock and Socknat, eds, *Challenge to Mars*, pp. 143–6.

70 21st Annual Report of the Director, 1 April 1939, pp. 1–2 (IWM); 'Obituary, Mr L.R. Bradley', *The Times*, 30 Jan. 1968, p. 8.

7: Again

1 'Turn of the Wheel', in Carl Sandburg, *Complete Poems* (New York, 1950), p. 645; HC *Debs*, vol. 362, columns 60–1, 18 June 1940.

2 Quoted in Adrian Gregory, *The Last Great War: British Society and the First World War* (Cambridge, 2008), p. 275.

3 Tom Harrisson, *Living Through the Blitz* (London, 1990), p. 47.

4 Richard M. Titmuss, *Problems of Social Policy* (London, 1950), esp. pp. 13, 64 and 91.

5 Titmuss, *Problems*, pp. 101–2, 137.

6 Minutes by Sargent, 28 Feb. 1940, and Chamberlain, 1 March 1940, FO 371/24298, C4444/9/17 (TNA); 'Schools in Wartime' memo no. 18, 'France and Ourselves', April 1940, Board of Education papers, ED 138/27 (TNA); House of Commons Debates, 2 April 1940, vol. 359, cols 40–1.

7 J.P. Harris, *Men, Ideas and Tanks: British Military Thought and Armoured Forces, 1903–1939* (Manchester, 1995), pp. 291–2; Michael Wolff, ed., *The Collected Essays of Sir Winston Churchill* (4 vols, London, 1976), vol. 1, pp. 394–5, 424–5.

8 Drafting his war memoirs (published in 1948), Churchill and his wife were painfully aware of the Gallipoli analogy. In a passage eventually omitted, Churchill wrote of the Norway campaign 'it was a marvel – I really do not know how – I survived and maintained my position in public esteem while all the blame was thrown on poor Mr Chamberlain.' CHUR 4/109, folios 42–3 (CAC).

9 See the insightful analysis by Ernest R. May, *Strange Victory: Hitler's Conquest of France* (New York, 2000).

10 May, *Strange Victory*, pp. 287–8, 414.

11 Adam Tooze, *The Wages of Destruction: The Making and Breaking of the Nazi Economy* (London, 2006), pp. 377–9.

12 On the Blitzkrieg see the comments in Tooze, *Wages of Destruction*, pp. 370–5 and the detailed analysis by Karl-Heinz Frieser, *Blitzkrieg-Legende: Der Westfeldzug 1940* (Munich, 1996), here quoting from pp. 5–6.

13 Winston S. Churchill, *The World Crisis, 1911–1914* (London, 1923), pp. 268–9; Hew Strachan, *The First World War, vol. 1, To Arms* (Oxford, 2001), pp. 249–50.

14 David Stevenson, *With Our Backs to the Wall: Victory and Defeat in 1918* (London, 2011), pp. 68–73; J.P. Harris, *Douglas Haig and the First World War* (Cambridge, 2008), pp. 447–8, 469 ['melodramatic']; Vera Brittain, *Testament of Youth* (London, 1933), pp. 419–20.

15 Winston S. Churchill, *The World Crisis, 1916–1918* (London, 1927), pp. 441–3.

16 On this see David Reynolds, 'Churchill and the British "Decision" to Fight on in 1940: Right Policy, Wrong Reasons', in Reynolds, *From World War to Cold War: Churchill, Roosevelt and the International History of the 1940s* (Oxford, 2006), ch. 2.

17 Memo of 25 May 1940, para. I, CAB 66/7, WP (40) 168; Halifax to Hankey, 15 July 1940, FO 371/25206, W8602/8602/49 (TNA).

18 For fuller discussion see David Reynolds, '1940: Fulcrum of the Twentieth Century?' in *From World War to Cold War*, pp. 23–48, quoting Halder on p. 38.

19 For studies of these themes see Angus Calder, *The Myth of the Blitz* (London, 1991); Malcolm Smith, *Britain and 1940: History, Myth and Popular Memory* (London, 2000); Mark Connelly, *We Can Take It! Britain and the Memory of the Second World War* (London, 2004). See also Sonya Rose, *Which People's War? National Identity and Citizenship in Britain, 1939–1945* (Oxford, 2003), and the

chapter on Great Britain in Patrick Finney, *Remembering the Road to World War Two: International History, National Identity, Collective Memory* (London, 2011), pp. 188–225.

20 HC *Debs*, 362:60–1 and 364:1159–60, 1167, 18 June and 20 Aug. 1940.

21 HC *Debs*, 361:792, 4 June 1940; Connelly, *We Can Take It!*, ch. 3, esp. pp. 97, 115.

22 'The Battle of Britain: An Air Ministry Account of the Great Days from 8th August – 31st October 1940' (London, 1941), pp. 4–5, 35; Peck to Peirse, 6 April 1941, AIR 19/258 (TNA); Richard Overy, *The Battle* (London, 2000), pp. 130–1.

23 Churchill, *Into Battle*, p. 259, speech of 20 Aug. 1940 cited in note 20; Churchill memo, 3 Sept. 1940, WP (40) 352, CAB 66/11 (TNA).

24 Smith, *Britain and 1940*, pp. 70–1 ('Blitz'); Claudia Baldoli, Andrew Knapp and Richard Overy, eds, *Bombing, States and Peoples in Western Europe, 1940–1945* (London, 2011), pp. 1, 18; see also Overy, *The Bombing War* (London, 2013).

25 *The Times,* 25 May 1940, p. 7; HC *Debs*, 361:792, 795, 4 June 1940; Connelly, *We Can Take It!*, p. 66 (Low); Angus Calder, *The People's War: Britain, 1939–1945* (2nd edn, London, 1971), p. 130.

26 'Little Gidding' in *The Collected Poems and Plays of T.S. Eliot* (London, 1969), p.197; Peter Ackroyd, *T.S. Eliot* (London, 1985, pp. 263–4; 'Verses written during the Second World War' in Hugh MacDiarmid, *Complete Poems*, ed. Michael Grieve and W.R. Aitken (Manchester, 1993–4), vol. 1, p. 603.

27 J.B. Priestley, *Postscripts* (London, 1940), p. 4; *The Times*, 6 June 1940, p. 7. See also Siân Nicholas, '"Sly Demagogues" and Wartime Radio: J.B. Priestley and the BBC', *Twentieth Century British History*, 6 (1995), pp. 247–66.

28 Smith, *Britain and 1940*, p. 58.

29 Titmuss, *Problems of Social Policy*, pp. 335–6; Connelly, *Britain Can Take It!*, p. 142; Lucy Noakes, *War and the British: Gender, Memory and National Identity* (London, 1998), pp. 26, 29.

30 'Cato', *Guilty Men*, ed. John Stevenson (London, 1998), pp. xv, 17, 45, 111; Paul Addison, *The Road to 1945: British Politics and the Second World War* (London, 1975), p. 133. See also David Dutton, *Neville Chamberlain* (London, 2001), ch. 3.

31 John Baxendale and Chris Pawling, *Narrating the Thirties: A Decade in the Making: 1930 to the Present* (London, 1996), ch. 5, quoting p. 137; Smith, *Myth of 1940*, pp. 101–2 [Alexander]; Ian McLaine, *Ministry of Morale: Home Front Morale and the Ministry of Information in World War II* (London, 1979), pp. 180, 182.

32 Labour Party, *Let Us Face the Future* (1945) – http://www.labour-party.org.uk/manifestos; *Daily Mirror*, 5 July 1945, p. 1.

33 Calder, *Myth of the Blitz*, p. 7; Charles Loch Mowat, *Britain Between the Wars, 1918–1940* (London, 1955), pp. 656–7; Baxendale and Pawling, *Narrating the Thirties*, pp. 116–17.

34 Nicholas John Cull, *Selling War: The British Propaganda Campaign Against*

American 'Neutrality' in World War II (Oxford, 1995), p. 100; *New York Times*, 24 July 1940, p. 18.

35 Cull, *Selling War*, ch. 4, quoting p. 109.

36 Hadley Cantril, ed., *Public Opinion, 1935–1946* (Princeton, 1951), p. 973. The poll specifically used the word England.

37 Fireside chat, 29 Dec. 1940, American Presidency Project website, http://www.presidency.ucsb.edu

38 Walter Lippmann, 'The Defense of the Atlantic World', *New Republic*, 17 Feb. 1917, p. 61, and 'The Atlantic and America', *Life*, 7 April 1941, pp. 84–8; Forrest Davis, *The Atlantic System* (New York, 1941).

39 Walter Lippmann, *U.S. Foreign Policy: Shield of the Republic* (Boston, 1943), p. 135; Ronald Steel, *Walter Lippmann and the American Century* (New York, 1981), pp. 405–6.

40 Jonathan Adelman, *Prelude to the Cold War: The Tsarist, Soviet, and US Armies in the Two World Wars* (London, 1988), p. 128.

41 Churchill to Stalin, 19 June 1943, PREM 3/402 (TNA); Churchill memos of 21 July 1942, WP (42) 311, CAB 66/26 and 26 Nov. 1943, WP (43) 586, CAB 66/44 (TNA). See also Reynolds, *From World War to Cold War*, chs 5–6.

42 Winston S. Churchill, *The Second World War* (London, 1948–54), pp. 343–4; Lord Alanbrooke, *War Diaries, 1939–1945*, eds Alex Danchev and Daniel Todman (London, 2001), p. 244; David French, *Raising Churchill's Army: The British Army and the War against Germany, 1919–1945* (London, 2000), esp. pp. 242–6, 274–85.

43 J.P. Harris, *Douglas Haig and the First World War* (Cambridge, 2008), pp. 270–3; Max Hastings, *Finest Years: Churchill as Warlord 1940–1945* (London, 2009), p. 302 [cigars]; Niall Barr, *Pendulum of War: The Three Battles of Alamein* (London, 2004), pp. xxxvii, 404–7.

44 John Ellis, *Cassino: The Hollow Victory* (London, pbk edn, 2003), p. 222; John Ellis, *World War II: The Sharp End* (London, 1980), p. 156 [casualties]; G.D. Sheffield, 'The Shadow of the Somme: The Influence of the First World War on British Soldiers' Perceptions and Behaviour in the Second World War', in Paul Addison and Angus Calder, eds, *Time to Kill: The Soldier's Experience of War in the West, 1939–1945* (London, 1997), pp. 29–39.

45 A point made clear in the Cabinet Secretary's notes of the meeting on 9 April 1945, WM 41 (45) 6, CAB 195/3, pp. 85–6 (TNA).

46 French, *Raising Churchill's Army*, p. 14 (1927 lecture); R.S. Sayers, *Financial Policy, 1939–1945* (London, 1956), p. 498.

47 Reynolds, *From World War to Cold War*, ch. 6, esp. pp. 123, 130–1; Mary Soames, ed., *Speaking for Themselves: The Personal Letters of Winston and Clementine Churchill* (London, 1998), p. 497.

48 Russell Weigley, *Eisenhower's Lieutenants: The Campaigns of France and Germany, 1944–1945* (London, 1981), pp. 3–4, 13–14, 28; Mark Harrison, ed., *The Economics of World War II: Six Great Powers in International Comparison* (Cambridge, 1998), pp. 10, 15.

49 John L. Harper, *American Visions of Europe: Franklin D. Roosevelt, George F. Kennan, and Dean G. Acheson* (Cambridge, 1994), pp. 13–18, 36, 91–3, 105–6.

50 Graham Cross, *The Diplomatic Education of Franklin D. Roosevelt, 1882–1933* (New York, 2012), pp. 114–15; Robert A. Divine, *Roosevelt and World War II* (Baltimore, 1970), p. 57.

51 US Department of State, *Foreign Relations of the United States* (Washington, 1862–), 1941, vol. 1, pp. 355, 363, 366.

52 Robert A. Divine, *Second Chance: The Triumph of Internationalism in America During World War II* (New York, 1967), pp. 167–8.

53 Thomas J. Knock, '"History with Lightning": The Forgotten Film *Wilson*', *American Quarterly*, 28 (1976), pp. 523–43, esp. pp. 529, 541; Leonard J. Leff and Jerold Simmons, '*Wilson*: Hollywood Propaganda for World Peace', *Historical Journal of Film, Radio and Television*, 3 (1983), pp. 3–18, esp. pp. 3, 8, 12–14.

54 Knock, '"History with Lightning"', esp. pp. 524, 531, 533, 536, 538.

55 Leff and Simmons, '*Wilson*', pp. 12–13; Knock, '"History with Lightning"', p. 538; Robert H. Ferrell, *The Dying President: Franklin D. Roosevelt, 1944–1945* (Columbia, Missouri, 1998), pp. 84–5.

56 U.S. Department of State, *Foreign Relations of the United States: The Conferences at Malta and Yalta 1945* (Washington, DC, 1955), p. 628; Christopher Thorne, *Allies of a Kind: The United States, Britain, and the War Against Japan, 1941–1945* (London, 1978), p. 502, quoting Richard Law.

57 Reynolds, *From World War to Cold War*, ch. 14, 'Churchill, Stalin and the "Iron Curtain"', esp. pp. 258–60.

58 Thorne, *Allies of a Kind*, p. 503.

59 Harrison, ed., *The Economics of World War II*, p. 101; Peter Fearon, *War, Prosperity and Depression: The U.S. Economy 1917–45* (London, 1987), p. 274; Mark H. Leff, 'The Politics of Sacrifice on the American Home Front in World War II', *JAH*, 77 (1991), p. 1296.

60 President's Official File OF 4675-D (Franklin D. Roosevelt Library, Hyde Park, NY); Reynolds, *From World War to Cold War*, pp. 19–22.

61 CAB 103/286 (TNA), quoting Bridges to Martin, 24 June 1944, and CAB 134/105 (TNA), meeting of 21 Jan. 1948, minute 7, and Attlee's endorsement, 27 Jan. 1948; Reynolds, *From World War to Cold War*, pp. 10–11, 16–17.

62 Carr's book, originally published in 1939 and revised after the war, was actually a critique of liberal utopian internationalism: the title was proposed by his publishers, Macmillan, and was hardly developed in the text itself. Edward Hallett Carr, *The Twenty Years' Crisis 1919–1939: An Introduction to the Study of International Relations* (2nd edn, London, 1946), p. 224; Jonathan Haslam, *The Vices of Integrity: E.H. Carr, 1892–1982* (London, 1999), pp. 68–9.

63 Winston S. Churchill, *The Second World War* (6 vols, London, 1948–54), vol. 1, pp. vii, ix; he had already used the term in his speech about Yalta to the Commons on 27 Feb. 1945 – Winston S. Churchill, *Victory* (London, 1946), pp. 52–3. See also P.M.H. Bell, *The Origins of the Second World War in Europe*

(London, 1986), chs 2–4, and Michael Howard, 'A Thirty Years War? The Two World Wars in Historical Perspective', *TRHS*, 6th series, 3 (1993), pp. 171–84.

64 Titmuss, *Problems of Social Policy*, pp. 559, 562.

8: Evil

1 *Life*, 7 May 1945, p. 33; 'Nightmare and Flight' in Hannah Arendt, *Essays in Understanding, 1930–1954*, ed. Jerome Kohn (New York, 1994), p. 134.

2 Broadcast of 19 April 1945, in Leonard Miall, ed., *Richard Dimbleby, Broadcaster* (London, 1966), p. 44.

3 Wynford Vaughan-Thomas in ed. Miall, *Dimbleby*, pp. 42–3. No sound recordings survive: as to which parts of Dimbleby's script were actually broadcast by the BBC see Judith Petersen, 'Belsen and a British Broadcasting Icon', *Holocaust Studies*, 13 (2007), pp. 19–43.

4 John Horne and Alan Kramer, *German Atrocities, 1914: A History of Denial* (New Haven, 2001), chs 1–2, esp. pp. 74–5.

5 Horne and Kramer, *German Atrocities*, pp. 207–13, 237, 240.

6 Horne and Kramer, *German Atrocities*, pp. 250–5, 317, 321–5; David Kennedy, *Over Here: The First World War and American Society* (New York, 1980), pp. 61–2.

7 Tony Kushner, *The Holocaust and the Liberal Imagination* (Oxford, 1994), pp. 123–7.

8 Ian McLaine, *Ministry of Morale: Home Front Morale and the Ministry of Information in World War II* (London, 1979), p. 166; Richard J. Evans, *Lying About Hitler: History, Holocaust, and the David Irving Trial* (New York, 2001), p. 130.

9 Sonia Orwell and Ian Angus, eds, *The Collected Essays, Journalism and Letters of George Orwell, vol. 3* (London, 1968), p. 117; Petersen, 'Belsen', pp. 22, 26.

10 Toby Haggith, 'The Filming of the Liberation of Bergen-Belsen and Its Impact on the Understanding of the Holocaust' in Suzanne Bardgett and David Caesarani, eds, *Belsen 1945: New Historical Perspectives* (London, 2006), pp. 89–122, quoting pp. 89, 101. See also Hannah Caven, 'Horror in Our Time: Images of the Concentration Camps in the British Media, 1945', *Historical Journal of Film, Radio and Television*, 21 (2001), pp. 205–53, and Joanne Reilly, *Belsen: The Liberation of a Concentration Camp* (London, 1998), pp. 50–77.

11 Kushner, *Holocaust*, pp. 210–11; Caven, 'Horror in Our Time', pp. 231–2; Haggith, 'Filming', p. 110.

12 Reilly, *Belsen*, pp. 64–5. These were Mass-Observation surveys rather than 'scientific' opinion polls but the broad contrast is striking.

13 Alan Bennett, 'Seeing Stars', *London Review of Books*, 3 Jan. 2002, pp. 12–16.

14 Kushner, *Holocaust*, pp. 208, 215, whose ch. 7 examines these issues at length. See also Samuel Moyn, 'In the Aftermath of the Camps' in Frank Biess and Robert G. Moeller, eds, *Histories of the Aftermath: The Legacies of the Second World War in Europe* (New York, 2010), pp. 49–64.

15 Edward Bliss, Jr, ed., *In Search of Light: The Broadcasts of Edward R. Murrow, 1938–1961* (London, 1968), pp. 90–1; Alfred D. Chandler, ed., *The Papers of Dwight David Eisenhower, vol. 4* (Baltimore, 1970), pp. 2615–16, 2613; *Life*, 7 May 1945, pp. 32–7, quoting p. 33.

16 Peter Novick, *The Holocaust in American Memory* (Boston, 1999), pp. 63–6. Similarly Deborah E. Lipstadt, 'America and the Memory of the Holocaust, 1950–1965', *Modern Judaism*, 16 (1996), pp. 195–214. Lawrence Baron, 'The Holocaust and American Public Memory, 1945–1960', *Holocaust and Genocide Studies*, 17 (2003), pp. 62–88, qualifies this argument on points of detail but without really blunting its essential thrust.

17 *Life*, 7 May 1945, p. 33; David Wyman, *The Abandonment of the Jews: America and the Holocaust, 1941–1945* (New York, 1984), p. 326.

18 Robert C. Binkley, 'The "Guilt" Clause in the Treaty of Versailles', *Current History*, 30/2 (May 1929), p. 294.

19 Horne and Kramer, *German Atrocities*, p. 329; James F. Willis, *Prologue to Nuremberg: The Politics and Diplomacy of Punishing War Criminals of the First World War* (Westport, Connecticut, 1982), pp. 82–5.

20 Heather Jones, *Violence Against Prisoners of War in the First World War: Britain, France and Germany, 1914–1920* (Cambridge, 2011), pp. 210–17.

21 IWC 37, 20 Nov. 1918, CAB 23/43 (TNA); Willis, *Prologue to Nuremberg*, pp. 56–9, 102–4.

22 This argument develops Trevor Wilson's judgment on the Bryce report: see Wilson, *Myriad Faces of War*, p. 191.

23 Willis, *Prologue to Nuremberg*, pp. 62–3.

24 Willis, *Prologue to Nuremberg*, ch. 5, esp. pp. 69–70, 73–4; Jürgen Matthäus, 'The Lessons of Leipzig: Punishing German War Criminals After the First World War', in Patricia Heberer and Jürgen Matthäus, eds, *Atrocities on Trial: Historical Perspectives on the Politics of Prosecuting War Crimes* (Lincoln, Nebraska, 2008), p. 6; Margaret MacMillan, *Peacemakers: The Paris Peace Conference of 1919 and Its Attempt to End War* (London, 2001), p. 174.

25 Willis, *Prologue*, pp. 79–80.

26 Thomas A. Bailey, *Woodrow Wilson and the Lost Peace* (New York, 1944), p. 38; Christopher Clark, *Kaiser Wilhelm II: A Life in Power* (London, 2009), p. 350.

27 Willis, *Prologue*, pp. 118–19.

28 Willis, *Prologue*, pp. 119–20, 124, 128; Austin Harrison, 'The Punishment of War Guilt', *The English Review*, 30 (Feb. 1920), p. 166.

29 Horne and Kramer, *German Atrocities*, pp. 345–55, quoting p. 358; Willis, *Prologue*, ch. 8, quoting p. 139; Matthäus, 'Lessons of Leipzig', esp. pp. 9–10, 19–20.

30 Horne and Kramer, *German Atrocities*, p. 351.

31 Horne and Kramer, *German Atrocities*, p. 411.

32 Ann and John Tusa, *The Nuremberg Trials* (London, 1983), pp. 42–8, 94–105, quoting p. 46; *Times Literary Supplement*, 31 July 1953, p. 490; Jeffrey Grey, in Grey, ed., *The Last Word: Essays on Official History in the United States and the*

British Commonwealth (Westport, Connecticut, 2003), pp. 118–19. On the saga of the German archives see Astrid M. Eckert, *Kampf um die Akten: Die Westallierten und die Rückgabe von deutschen Archivgut nach dem Weltkrieg* (Stuttgart, 2004), esp. ch. 1.

33 Eden memo, 5 Oct. 1941, WP (41) 233, CAB 66/19; Cabinet Secretary's notes of WM (42) 86th meeting, 6 [sic] July 1942, CAB 195/1, pp. 67–8 (TNA).

34 Simon, memos of 4 Sept. 1944 and 6 April 1945, in Bradley F. Smith, ed., *The American Road to Nuremberg: The Documentary Record* (Stanford, 1982), pp. 32, 151–2; Tusa and Tusa, *Nuremberg Trial*, p. 25.

35 See Walter Isaacson and Evan Thomas, *The Wise Men: Six Friends and the World They Made* (New York, 1986), chs 6–7.

36 Smith, ed., *American Road*, p. 97; Tusa and Tusa, *Nuremberg Trial*, p. 89.

37 Smith, ed., *American Road*, pp. 31, 43; Baron, 'Holocaust and American Public Memory', p. 66; Michael Marrus, 'The Holocaust at Nuremberg', *Yad Vashem Studies*, 26 (1998), pp. 5–41.

38 On these limitations of Nuremberg, see Donald Bloxham, *Genocide on Trial: War Crimes Trials and the Formation of Holocaust History and Memory* (Oxford, 2001), esp. pp. 124–33.

39 Henry L. Stimson, 'The Nuremberg Trial: Landmark in Law', *Foreign Affairs*, 25/2 (Jan. 1947), p. 189.

40 L.F. Haber, *The Poisonous Cloud: Chemical Warfare in the First World War* (Oxford, 1986), pp. 230–45; Andrew L. Rotter, *Hiroshima: The World's Bomb* (Oxford, 2008), pp. 14–22; Sue Malvern, 'War, Memory and Museums: Art and Artefact in the Imperial War Museum', *History Workshop Journal*, 49 (spring 2000), pp. 191–2.

41 Haber, *Poisonous Cloud*, pp. 169–70; Daniel Charles, *Between Genius and Genocide: The Tragedy of Fritz Haber, Father of Chemical Warfare* (London, 2006), pp. 165–9, 189, 245–6.

42 Barton Bernstein, 'Why We Didn't Use Poison Gas in World War II', *American Heritage*, 36/5 (Aug.–Sept. 1985), pp. 40–5; Rotter, *Hiroshima*, pp. 145, 174–6, 222.

43 *Life*, 20 Aug. 1945, pp. 26, 27, 32; *Time*, 20 Aug. 1945, pp. 1, 78. On the debate see Tsuyoshi Hasegawa, *Racing the Enemy: Stalin, Truman, and the Surrender of Japan* (Cambridge, Massachussetts, 2005).

44 Paul Boyer, *By the Dawn's Early Light: American Thoughts and Culture at the Dawn of the Atomic Age* (New York, 1985), ch. 1 esp. 7–8, 23; Allan M. Winkler, *Life Under a Cloud: American Anxiety about the Atom* (New York, 1993), pp. 29–30.

45 James G. Hershberg, *James B. Conant: Harvard to Hiroshima and the Making of the Nuclear Age* (New York, 1993), ch. 16, esp. pp. 284–5, 292–3.

46 Hershberg, *Conant*, pp. 293–4. See also Barton J. Bernstein, 'Seizing the Contested Terrain of Early Nuclear History: Stimson, Conant, and their Allies Explain the Decision to Use the Atomic Bomb', *Diplomatic History*, 17 (1993), pp. 35–72.

47 Henry L. Stimson, 'The Decision to Use the Atomic Bomb', *Harper's Magazine*, Feb. 1947, quoting pp. 106–7.

48 Kai Bird, *The Color of Truth: McGeorge Bundy and William Bundy: Brothers in Arms* (New York, 1998), pp. 92–3.

49 Bernstein, 'Seizing the Contested Terrain', p. 48; Harry S. Truman, *1945: Year of Decisions* (New York, 1965 pbk edn), p. 460; Hershberg, *Conant*, p. 301; Winston S. Churchill, *The Second World War* (London, 1954), p. 552. In this case Churchill was embroidering the account he gave to the House of Commons only a week after Nagasaki, when he said that the alternative was for the Allies to have 'sacrificed a million American, and a quarter of a million British lives'. See Churchill, *Victory: War Speeches, 1945*, ed. Charles Eade (London, 1946), 16 Aug. 1945, p. 229.

50 Winkler, *Life Under the Cloud*, pp. 27–8, 137; Boyer, *By the Bomb's Early Light*, pp. 156, 291.

51 David Bradley, *No Place to Hide* (London, 1949), p. 176.

52 See note 1.

53 Stephen Lovell, *The Shadow of War: Russia and the USSR, 1941 to the Present* (Oxford, 2010), p. 2; Elena Zubkova, *Russia After the War: Hopes, Illusions, and Disappointments, 1945–1957* (Armonk, NY, 1998), p. 47.

54 Mark Edele, *Soviet Veterans of the Second World War: A Popular Movement in an Authoritarian Society, 1941–1991* (Oxford, 2008), p. 11; Robert Dale, 'Rats and Resentment: The Demobilization of the Red Army in Postwar Leningrad', *JCH*, 45 (2010), pp. 123–4.

55 Dmitri Volkogonov, *Stalin: Triumph and Tragedy*, transl. Harold Shukman (London, 1991), p. 505; Geoffrey Roberts, *Stalin's General: The Life of Georgy Zhukov* (London, 2012), pp. 244–6; Denise J. Youngblood, *Russian War Films: On the Cinema Front, 1914–2005* (Lawrence, Kansas, 2007), ch. 4, esp. pp. 97–102.

56 Lovell, *Shadow of War*, p. 40; Richard Overy, *Russia's War* (London, 1998), p. 323; Youngblood, *Russian War Films*, ch. 5; Karen Petrone, *The Great War in Russian History* (Bloomington, Indiana, 2011), pp. 282–9.

57 Nina Tumarkin, *The Living and the Dead: The Rise and Fall of the Cult of World War II in Russia* (New York, 1994), ch. 6, esp. pp. 133–6, 144.

58 John Bodnar, *The 'Good War' in American Memory* (Baltimore, 2010), pp. 111–13. The parallel with a Pals battalion is, in fact, quite exact because the Bedford boys were all part of a National Guard regiment raised in the Blue Ridge Mountains of Virginia.

59 Davis R.B. Ross, *Preparing for Ulysses: Politics and Veterans During World War II* (New York, 1969), esp. pp. 49–50, 121–2, 124.

60 Christopher Thorne, *Allies of a Kind: The United States, Britain, and the War Against Japan, 1941–1945* (London, 1978), p. 503; Bodnar, *'Good War'*, pp. 87–8.

61 Bodnar, *'Good War'*, esp. pp. 95, 143–4; see also Ann Douglas, 'War Envy and Amnesia: Cold War Rewrites of Russia's War', in Joel Isaac and Duncan Bell, *Uncertain Empire: American History and the Idea of the Cold War* (Oxford, 2012), pp. 115–39.

62 Peter Hennessy, *Never Again: Britain, 1945–1951* (London, 1993), p. 67; Kenneth Harris, *Attlee* (London, 1982), pp. 256–7. See also Kevin Jefferys, *The Churchill Coalition and Wartime Politics, 1940–1945* (Manchester, 1995), ch. 8.

63 Hennessy, *Never Again*, pp. 184, 424–5. On the fraught issue of 'consensus' see Harriet Jones and Michael Kandiah, eds, *The Myth of Consensus: New Views on British History, 1945–64* (Basingstoke, 1996); Brian Harrison, 'The Rise and Fall of Political Consensus in Britain since 1940', *History*, 84 (1999), pp. 301–24; Richard Toye, 'From "Consensus" to "Common Ground": The Rhetoric of the Postwar Settlement and Its Collapse', *JCH*, 48 (2013), pp. 3–23.

64 Rodney Lowe, *The Welfare States in Britain since 1945* (3rd edn, London, 2005), p. 13; David Edgerton, *Warfare State: Britain, 1920–1970* (Cambridge, 2006), pp. 59–60.

65 David Reynolds, *Britannia Overruled: British Policy and World Power in the Twentieth Century* (2nd edn, London, 2000), pp. 148, 152; Edgerton, *Warfare State*, p. 68.

66 Alec Cairncross, *Years of Recovery: British Economic Policy, 1945–1951* (London, 1985), p. 278.

67 Nicholas Pronay, 'The British Post-Bellum Cinema: A Survey of the Films Relating to World War II Made in Britain Between 1945 and 1960', *Historical Journal of Film, Radio and Television*, 8 (1988), esp. pp. 39–41; John Ramsden, 'Refocusing "The People's War": British War Films of the 1950s', *JCH*, 33 (1998), esp. pp. 36–8, 45; Sonya O. Rose, 'From the "New Jerusalem" to the "Decline" of the "New Elizabethan Age": National Identity and Citizenship in Britain, 1945–56', in Biess and Moeller, eds, *Histories of the Aftermath*, p. 238; Wendy Webster, *Englishness and Empire, 1939–1965* (Oxford, 2005), ch. 3, esp. p. 91.

9: Generations

1 Alan Clark, *The Donkeys* (London, 1961), p. 11; Joan Littlewood, *Tribune*, vol. 26, no. 16, 19 April 1963, p. 9.

2 Maurice Halbwachs, *The Collective Memory*, ed. Mary Douglas (New York, 1950), p. 48; see also *Maurice Halbwachs on Collective Memory*, ed. Lewis A. Coser (Chicago, 1957).

3 James E. Young, *The Texture of Memory: Holocaust Memorials and Meaning* (New Haven, 1993), pp. xi–xii; Jay Winter, *Remembering War: The Great War Between Memory and History in the Twentieth Century* (New Haven, 2006), pp. 3–5.

4 Jan Assmann, 'Collective Memory and Cultural Identity', *New German Critique*, 65 (spring–summer 1995), pp. 125–33. See also Alan Confino, 'Collective Memory and Cultural History: Problems of Method', *American Historical Review*, 102 (1997), pp. 1386–1403, and the succinct theoretical discussion in Meike Wulf, *Shadowlands: Generating History in Post-Cold War Estonia* (Oxford, 2014), ch. 1. Major essay collections include Jay Winter and Emmanuel Sivan, eds, *War and Remembrance in the Twentieth Century* (Cambridge, 1999); T.G. Ashplant,

Graham Dawson and Michael Roper, eds, *The Politics of War Memory and Commemoration* (London, 2000), and Karen Tilmans, Frank van Vree and Jay Winter, eds, *Performing the Past: Memory, History and Identity in Modern Europe* (Amsterdam, 2010).

5 Barbara Tuchman, *August 1914* (London, 1962), pp. 7, 13, 78, 426. This was the title of the British edition.

6 Robert F. Kennedy, *Thirteen Days: The Cuban Missile Crisis* (London, 1969), p. 65; Richard Reeves, *President Kennedy: Profile of Power* (New York, 1993), p. 306.

7 Arthur M. Schlesinger, Jr, *A Thousand Days: John F. Kennedy in the White House* (New York: Fawcett, 1971), pp. 505, 909–10.

8 Lyndon B. Johnson, press conference, 28 July 1965, American Presidency Project website, http://www.presidency.ucsb.edu/ Accessed 12 Dec. 2012.

9 Congressional Research Service report RL32492, 'American War and Military Operations Casualties: Lists and Statistics', 26 Feb. 2010, pp. 2–3, http://www.fas.org/sgp/crs/natsec/RL32492.pdf Accessed 13 Dec. 2012.

10 William Appleman Williams, *The Tragedy of American Diplomacy* (2nd edn, New York, 1962), pp. 64–5, 82–3, 99–101.

11 N. Gordon Levin, Jr., *Woodrow Wilson and World Politics: America's Response to War and Revolution* (New York, 1968), pp. 64–5, 99–101, 260.

12 Mary Fulbrook, *German National Identity After the Holocaust* (Cambridge, 1999), pp. 59–60, 66; Friedrich Meinecke, *A German Catastrophe*, transl. Sidney B. Fay (Boston, 1950), p. 96.

13 In origin a mocking caricature by Munich historian Helmut Krausnick – see Astrid Eckert, 'The Transnational Beginnings of West German *Zeitgeschichte* in the 1950s', *Central European History*, 40 (2007), p. 86.

14 Fritz Fischer, *Griff nach der Weltmacht: die Kriegszielpolitik des kaiserlichen Deutschland, 1914/18* (Düsseldorf, 1961), p. 12; Gerhard Ritter, 'Eine neue Kriegsschuldthese? Zu Fritz Fischer's Buch "Griff nach der Weltmacht"', *HZ*, 194/3 (1962), p. 667. See also *JCH* 48/2 (2013), special issue on Fischer.

15 There were still 700,000 alive in 1973. Olivier Wieviorka, *La Mémoire Désunie: Le souvenir politique des années sombres, de la Libération à nos jours* (Paris, 2010), pp. 75–8. See also David Reynolds, *In Command of History: Churchill Fighting and Writing the Second World War* (London, 2004), p. 204.

16 Malraux as encapsulated by Henry Rousso, *The Vichy Syndrome: History and Memory in France Since 1944*, transl. Arthur Goldhammer (Cambridge, Massachussetts, 1991), p. 90.

17 Sudhir Hazareesingh, *In the Shadow of the General: Modern France and the Myth of de Gaulle* (Oxford, 2012), p. 20.

18 Julian Jackson, *France: The Dark Years, 1940–1944* (Oxford, 2001), p. 613.

19 Rousso, *Vichy Syndrome*, pp. 110–11.

20 Wieviorka, *La Mémoire Désunie*, pp. 134–5.

21 John W. Young, *France, the Cold War and the Western Alliance, 1944–1949* (Leicester, 1990), pp. 76, 84.

22 Raymond Poidevin, ed., *Histoire des Debuts de la Construction européenne, mars 1948 – mai 1950* (Brussels, 1986), p. 326.

23 Young, *France*, p. 209.

24 Hans-Peter Schwarz, *Adenauer: Der Staatsmann, 1952–1967* (Munich, 1994), pp. 297, 759–60.

25 N. Piers Ludlow, *Dealing with Britain: The Six and the First UK Application to the EEC* (Cambridge, 1997), p. 32.

26 David Reynolds, *Britannia Overruled: British Policy and World Power in the Twentieth Century* (2nd edn, London, 2000), pp. 208, 212; Harold Macmillan, *At the End of the Day, 1961–1963* (London, Macmillan, 1973), p. 339.

27 *The Complete War Memoirs of Charles de Gaulle* (New York, 1998), p. 557.

28 John Ramsden, *Man of the Century: Winston Churchill and His Legend Since 1945* (London, 2002), pp. 4, 17, 18, 20–1.

29 Alan Clark, *The Donkeys* (London, 1961), pp. 6, 21–2, 182, 186; Ion Trewin, *Alan Clark: The Biography* (London, 2009), pp. 176, 181–2, 188–9.

30 Joan Littlewood, *Tribune,* vol. 27, no. 16, 19 April 1963, p. 9; Trewin, *Clark*, pp. 182–8; see also Derek Paget, 'Remembrance Play: *Oh What a Lovely War* and History', in Tony Howard and John Stokes, ed., *Acts of War: The Representation of Military Conflict on the British Stage and Television Since 1945* (Aldershot, 1996), pp. 82–97.

31 The actual entries in Haig's diary for 1 Aug. 1916 run as follows: '1. "*The Powers that be*" are beginning to get a little uneasy in regard to the situation. 2. Whether the loss of say 300,000 men will lead to really great results, because if not, we ought to be content with something less than we are doing … I replied … Our losses in July's fighting totalled about 120,000 more than they would have been, had we not attacked. They cannot be regarded as sufficient to justify any anxiety as to our ability to continue the offensive.' Gary Sheffield and John Bourne, eds, *Douglas Haig: War Diaries and Letters 1914–1918* (London, 2005), pp. 213–14.

32 Theatre Workshop, *Oh What a Lovely War*, revised and restored edition by Joan Littlewood (London, 2000), pp. 6, 44, 60, 70, 74, 85.

33 *Oh What a Lovely War*, p. 87; Michael Paris, 'Enduring Heroes: British Feature Films and the First World War', in Paris, ed., *The First World War and Popular Cinema: 1914 to the Present* (Edinburgh, 1999), pp. 63, 68; Brian Bond, *The Unquiet Western Front: Britain's Role in Literature and History* (Cambridge, 2002), pp. 65–7.

34 Simon Ball, *The Guardsmen: Harold Macmillan, Three Friends, and the World They Made* (London, 2004), p. 393; Daniel Todman, *The Great War: Myth and Memory* (London, 2005), pp. 108–11.

35 Alex Danchev, '"Bunking" and "Debunking": The Controversies of the 1960s', in Brian Bond, ed., *The First World War and British Military History* (Oxford, 1991), p. 263.

36 A.J.P. Taylor, *The First World War: An Illustrated History* (London, 1966 edn), pp. 28, 85, 108, 238; Todman, *Great War*, p. 138.

37 B.H. Liddell Hart, *The Real War, 1914–1918* (London, 1930), p. 503. See also the discussion by Hew Strachan, '"The Real War": Liddell Hart, Cruttwell, and Falls', in Bond, ed., *First World War*, pp. 41–67.

38 Taylor, *First World War*, pp. 11, 16, 20, 62, 99–100, 230–3, 236, 255, 287.

39 A.J.P. Taylor, *The Struggle for Mastery of Europe, 1848–1918* (London, 1954), pp. 526–7, where he places the main responsibility firmly on Austria-Hungary and Germany.

40 Taylor, *First World War*, pp. 123, 140, 194.

41 Bond, *Unquiet Western Front*, p. 63, perhaps underplays the importance of Taylor in this shift of attention from Passchendaele to the Somme.

42 Taylor, *The First World War*, pp. 276–7; Adam Sisman, *A.J.P. Taylor: A Biography* (London, 1994), pp. 288–9, 307–9.

43 Dan Todman, 'The Reception of *The Great War* in the 1960s', *Historical Journal of Film, Radio and Television*, 22 (2002), pp. 29–36, quoting p. 35.

44 J.A. Ramsden, '*The Great War*: The Making of the Series', *Historical Journal of Film, Radio and Television*, 22 (2002), p. 10; *The Great War*, episode 13, 'The Devil is Coming'.

45 M.L. Connelly, '*The Great War*, Part 13: The Devil is Coming', *Historical Journal of Film, Radio and Television*, 22 (2002), pp. 21–8; Ramsden, '*The Great War*', p. 17 (quote).

46 Emma Hanna, *The Great War on the Small Screen: Representing the First World War in Contemporary Britain* (Edinburgh, 2009), pp. 38–9.

47 Hanna, *The Great War on the Small Screen*, pp. 39–41, 46.

48 Nicholas Reeves, 'Through the Eye of the Camera: Contemporary Audiences and their "Experience" of War in the Film *Battle of the Somme*', in Hugh Cecil and Peter H. Liddle, eds, *Facing Armageddon: The First World War Experience* (London, 1996), ch. 55, quoting pp. 782, 786–90; 'War's Realities on the Cinema', *The Times*, 22 Aug. 1916, p. 3.

49 Reeves, 'Through the Eye of the Camera', pp. 785, 791–2.

50 Hanna, *The Great War on the Small Screen*, p. 36.

51 Catherine W. Reilly, *English Poetry of the First World War: A Bibliography* (London, 1978), p. xix and *English Poetry of the Second World War: A Biobibliography* (London, 1986), pp. vii–viii. 'English poets' comprise those writing in English from England, Scotland, Wales and Ireland.

52 Helen Goethals, 'The Muse That Failed: Poetry and Patriotism During the Second World War', in Tim Kendall, ed., *The Oxford Handbook of British and Irish War Poetry* (Oxford, 2007), ch. 19, esp. pp. 367, 372.

53 Keith Douglas, 'Poets in This War', in Keith Douglas, *The Letters*, ed. Desmond Graham (Manchester, 2000), p. 352.

54 Dominic Hibberd, 'Anthologies of Great War Verse: Mirrors of Changes', in Michael Howard, ed., *A Part of History: Aspects of the British Experience of the First World War* (London, 2009), ch. 13, quoting pp. 110, 111.

55 Hibberd, 'Anthologies', p. 112.

56 Edmund Blunden, *Undertones of War* [1928] (London, 2000), p. xii. The

nightmare comes from Barry Webb, *Edmund Blunden: A Biography* (London, 1990), pp. 80–1.

57 Edmund Blunden, 'The Soldier Poets of 1914–1918' in Frederick Brereton, ed., *An Anthology of War Poems* (London, 1930), pp. 13–24; cf. Reilly, *English Poetry of the First World War*, p. xix.

58 Samuel Hynes, *A War Imagined: The First World War and English Culture* (London, 1990), p. 437.

59 Brian Gardner, ed., *Up the Line to Death: The War Poets, 1914–1918* (London, 1964), pp. vii–viii, xix, 114.

60 I.M. Parsons, ed., *Men Who March Away: Poems of the First World War* (London, 1965), esp. pp. 13–14, 16, 18; Maurice Hussey, ed., *Poetry of the First World War* (London, 1967), esp. p. xv; see also http://greatwarfiction.wordpress.com/2010/10/10/up-the-line-to-death/ Accessed 5 Nov. 2012.

61 This paragraph follows the perceptive discussion of Owen in Todman, *Great War*, ch. 5, quoting p. 161.

62 Blunden to Sassoon, 30 Sept. 1940, in Carol Z. Rothkopf, ed., *Selected Letters of Siegfried Sassoon and Edmund Blunden, 1919–1967* (3 vols, London, 2012), vol. 2, p. 265.

63 Kenneth Clark, *The Other Half: A Self-Portrait* (London, 1977), pp. 22–4; see generally Brian Foss, *War Paint: Art, War, State and Identity in Britain, 1939–1945* (New Haven, 2007).

64 See generally Frances Spalding, *British Art Since 1900* (London, 1986), ch. 6.

65 Foss, *War Paint*, pp. 164–5, 186.

66 'Pictures of the War', *The Times*, 13 Oct. 1945, p. 5.

67 Foss, *War Paint*, pp. 188–9, 192; Spalding, *British Art*, p. 152.

68 James Beechey and Chris Stephens, eds, *Picasso and Modern British Art* (London, 2012), pp. 34, 185, 227.

69 Sue Malvern, 'War, Memory and Museums: Art and Artefact in the Imperial War Museum', *History Workshop Journal*, 49 (spring 2000), pp. 195, 202.

70 Cf. Jon Stallworthy, *Anthem for Doomed Youth: Twelve Soldier Poets of the First World War* (London, 2002).

71 Robert Fisk, *In Time of War: Ireland, Ulster and the Price of Neutrality, 1939–1945* (London, 1985), p. 537.

72 Roy Foster, *Modern Ireland, 1600–1972* (London, 1988), pp. 578–80; Tim Pat Coogan, *De Valera: Long Fellow, Long Shadow* (London, 1993), pp. 670–7.

73 Mary E. Daly and Margaret O'Callaghan, eds, *1916 in 1966: Commemorating the Easter Rising* (Dublin, 2007), pp. 30, 180; Roisín Higgins, *Transforming 1916: Meaning, Memory and the Fiftieth Anniversary of the Easter Rising* (Cork, 2012), p. 115.

74 Higgins, *Transforming 1916*, pp. 121, 124–31, quoting 125; see also Cathal Brennan, 'A TV Pageant – The Golden Jubilee Commemorations of the 1916 Rising', *The Irish Story*, 18 Nov. 2010, http://www.theirishstory.com/2010/11/18/a-tv-pageant-%e2%80%93-the-golden-jubilee-commemorations-of-the-1916-rising/ Accessed 17 Dec. 2012.

75 Peter Wilson, *Provos: The IRA and Sinn Fein* (London, 1997), p. 6.

76 Catherine O'Donnell, 'Pragmatism versus Unity: The Stormont Government and the 1966 Easter Celebration', in Daly and O'Callaghan, eds, *1916 in 1966*, ch. 7, quoting pp. 248–9, 259, 260; Steve Bruce, *Paisley: Religion and Politics in Northern Ireland* (Oxford, 2007), ch. 3, quoting pp. 81, 89; James Loughlin, 'Mobilising the Sacred Dead: Ulster Unionism, the Great War and the Politics of Remembrance', in Adrian Gregory and Senia Pašeta, eds, *Ireland and the Great War: 'A War to Unite Us All'?* (Manchester, 2002), p. 147.

77 *The Autobiography of Terence O'Neill* (London, 1972), p. 87; Conor Cruise O'Brien, *States of Ireland* (London, 1972), pp. 149–50.

78 Karen Petrone, *The Great War in Russian Memory* (Bloomington, Indiana, 2011), pp. 288–9.

79 Jay Winter and Antoine Prost, *The Great War in History: Debates and Controversies, 1914 to the Present* (Cambridge, 2005), pp. 20–1.

80 Elizabeth A. Marsland, *The Nation's Cause: French, English and German Poetry of the First World War* (London, 1991), pp. 11–15.

10: Tommies

1 John Keegan, *The Face of Battle: A Study of Agincourt, Waterloo and the Somme* (London, 1978 pbk edn), p. 260; 'MCMXIV', from Philip Larkin, *Collected Poems*, ed. Anthony Thwaite (London, 1988), pp. 127–8.

2 'MCMXIV', from Philip Larkin, *Collected Poems*, ed. Anthony Thwaite (London, 1988), pp. 127–8; Richard Holmes, *Tommy: The British Soldier on the Western Front, 1914–1918* (London, 2004), p. 138.

3 Brian Gardner, *The Big Push: A Portrait of the Battle of the Somme* (London, 1961), p. x; John Harris, *The Somme: Death of a Generation* (London, 1975 edn), pp. 79, 143–4.

4 A.H. Farrar-Hockley, *The Somme* (London, 1964), pp. 5, 211–12.

5 Martin Middlebrook, *The First Day on the Somme: 1 July 1916* (London: Book Club edn, 1971), p. 353; Martin Middlebrook, 'The Writing of *The First Day on the Somme*', Dec. 2004, p. 6. http://www.fylde.demon.co.uk/middle-brook2.htm Accessed 19 Nov. 2012.

6 John Harris, *Covenant with Death* (London: 1973 edn), pp. 7, 15, 445, 448.

7 Middlebrook, 'Writing of *The First Day*', p. 7.

8 Middlebrook, 'Writing of *The First Day*', pp. 15, 18–19.

9 Middlebrook, *First Day*, pp. 106–22.

10 Middlebrook, *First Day*, pp. 148, 241.

11 Middlebrook, *First Day*, pp. 244, 263–5, 275–80, 290; cf. John Terraine, *Haig: The Educated Soldier* (London, 1963), pp. 200–4.

12 John Keegan, *The Face of Battle*, pp. 16–18, 29, 77.

13 Keegan, *The Face of Battle*, pp. 221, 229, 259–60, 262, 286–9.

14 Middlebrook, 'Writing of *The First Day*', pp. 18, 22, 24.

15 Peter Simkins, 'Everyman at War: Recent Interpretations of the Front Line

Experience' in Brian Bond, ed., *The First World War and British Military History* (London, 1991), pp. 304–5; Brian Bond, *The Unquiet Western Front: Britain's Role in Literature and History* (Cambridge, 2002), pp. 93–4, 120.

16 Entry on 'family history' in David Hey, ed., *The Oxford Companion to Family and Local History* (2nd edn, Oxford, 2008); http://www.abmpublishing.co.uk/About.html Accessed 29 Nov. 2012; Simon Fowler, William Spencer and Stuart Tamblin, *Army Service Records of the First World War* (London, 1996).

17 Middlebrook, 'Writing of *The First Day*', pp. 32–3.

18 A point established by Joanna Costin in her unpublished Cambridge BA dissertation on the Accrington Pals (2013), ch. 6.

19 Lyn Macdonald, *They Called It Passchendaele: The Story of the Third Battle of Ypres and of the Men Who Fought It* (London, 1978), p. xiii; Lyn Macdonald, *To the Last Man: Spring 1918* (London, 1998), pp. xvi–xvii. See also Dan Todman, *The Great War: Myth and Memory* (London, 2005), pp. 206–8.

20 Lyn Macdonald, *Somme* (London, 1983), pp. 137–8.

21 Holmes, *Tommy*, pp. 440–1; William Philpott, *Bloody Victory: The Sacrifice on the Somme* (London, 2009), pp. 239–41.

22 *Henry V*, act 4, scene 3, lines 52–4.

23 Alistair Thomson, *Anzac Memories: Living with the Legend* (Melbourne, 1994), pp. 8–11, 161–71, 205–15.

24 Thomson, *Anzac Memories*, pp. 218, 228.

25 Jenny Macleod, 'The Fall and Rise of Anzac Day: 1965 and 1990 Compared', *War and Society*, 20 (2002), pp. 150–1, 157–8.

26 Graham Seal, *Inventing Anzac: The Digger and National Mythology* (St Lucia, Queensland, 2004), pp. 123, 133–4; Bart Ziino, *A Distant Grief: Australians, War Graves and the Great War* (Crawley, Western Australia, 2007), pp. 158–62.

27 David Lowe, *Australia Between Two Empires: The Life of Percy Spender* (London, 2010), p. 97; Stuart Ward, *Australia and the British Embrace: The Demise of the Imperial Ideal* (Melbourne, 2001), p. 21.

28 Ward, *Australia and the British Embrace*, p. 2.

29 C.E.W. Bean, *The Official History of Australia in the War of 1914–1918, vol. II* (11th edn, Sydney, 1941), p. 910; see also Joan Beaumont, 'Gallipoli and Australian National Identity', in Neil Garnham and Keith Jeffery, eds, *Culture, Place and Identity* (Dublin, 2005), pp. 138–51.

30 Bill Gammage, *The Broken Years: Australian Soldiers in the Great War* (Canberra, 1974), pp. vi, xiii, xvii, 159, 169.

31 Gammage, *Broken Years*, pp. xvii, 1–3, 276–9.

32 Patsy Adam-Smith, *The Anzacs* (London, 1978), pp. vii–viii, 122–7.

33 Thomson, *Anzac Memories*, p. 193.

34 Michael McKernan, *Here Is Their Spirit: A History of the Australian War Memorial, 1917–1990* (St Lucia, Queensland, 1991), p. 272; Macleod, 'Fall and Rise of Anzac Day', p. 159.

35 Beaumont, 'Gallipoli and Australian National Identity', p. 145.

36 Mark McKenna, 'Anzac Day: How did it become Australia's national day?' in

Marilyn Lake and Henry Reynolds, eds, *What's Wrong With Anzac: The Militarisation of Australian History* (Sydney, 2010), ch. 5, quoting p. 122.

37 Jock Phillips, 'The Quiet Western Front: The First World War and New Zealand Memory', in Santanu Das, ed., *Race, Empire and First World War Writing* (Cambridge, 2011), pp. 231–48.

38 Robin Gerstler, *Big-Noting: The Heroic Theme in Australian War Writing* (Melbourne, 1987), pp. 2, 5.

39 Paul Fussell, *The Great War and Modern Memory* (New York, 2000 edn), pp. ix, 18–19, 29, 35.

40 Fussell, *Great War*, pp. 75–6.

41 Fussell, *Great War*, p. 341; see also the profile by Susanna Rustin, 'Hello to All That', *Guardian*, 31 July 2004.

42 Fussell, *Great War*, pp. ix, 18, 36, 315–19; Robin Prior, 'Paul Fussell at War', *War and History*, 1 (1994), pp. 63–80, quoting p. 67.

43 Fussell, *Great War*, p. 338; Leonard V. Smith, 'Paul Fussell's *The Great War and Modern Memory*: Twenty-Five Years Later', *History and Theory*, 40 (2001), pp. 241–60, quotations from p. 247.

44 Frank Field, *British and French Writers of the First World War: Comparative Studies in Cultural History* (Cambridge, 1991), p. 247; sales figures in e-mail of 3 Dec. 2012 from Christian Purdy, Director of Publicity, OUP New York.

45 Jay Winter and Antoine Prost, *The Great War in History: Debates and Controversies, 1914 to the Present* (Cambridge, 2005), pp. 9–11, 13–15, 82–8; Kelly Boyd, ed., *Encyclopedia of Historians and Historical Writing* (2 vols, Chicago, 1999), 2:995.

46 Jacques Meyer, *La vie quotidienne de soldats pendant la grande guerre* (Paris, 1966), quoting p. 12.

47 Gabriel Perreux, *La vie quotidienne des civils en France pendant la grande guerre* (Paris, 1966), quoting p. 346.

48 Arthur Marwick, *The Deluge: British Society and the First World War* (London, 1965), pp. 10, 12.

49 Originally theses, it should be acknowledged, that were directed by Renouvin.

50 Jay Winter, *Remembering War: The Great War Between Memory and History in the Twentieth Century* (New Haven, 2006), pp. 118–19; http://www.wilfredowen.fr/ Accessed 28 Nov. 2012.

51 Gerd Krumeich, 'Kriegsgeschichte in Wandel', in Gerhard Hirchfeld and Gerd Krumeich, eds, *Keiner fühlt sich hier mehr als Mensch . . . Erlebnis und Wirkung des Ersten Weltkriegs* (Essen, 1993), pp. 11–14; see also David F. Crew, '*Alltagsgeschichte*: A New Social History "From Below"?' *Central European History*, 22 (1989), pp. 394–407.

52 George L. Mosse, *Fallen Soldiers: Reshaping the Memory of the World Wars* (New York, 1990), pp. 3–5, 7, 159–60, 174.

11: Remembrance

1 Edward Thomas, 'Roads', *The Collected Poems of Edward Thomas*, ed. R. George Thomas (Oxford, 1978), p. 267; Carol Ann Duffy, 'Last Post', in *The Bees* (London, 2011), p. 4.

2 Maya Lin, 'Making the Memorial,' *New York Review of Books*, 2 Nov. 2000.

3 Pierre Nora, ed., *Rethinking France: Les Lieux de Mémoire, vol. 1* (Chicago, 2001), Nora's general introduction, pp. vii–xxii.

4 Konrad H. Jarausch, *After Hitler: Recivilizing Germans, 1945–1955* (New York, 1994), pp. 267–8; Kristina Spohr Readman, *Germany and the Baltic Problem after the Cold War: The Development of a New Ostpolitik, 1989–2000* (London, 2004), p. 76.

5 Thomas Nipperdey, *Nachdenken über die deutschen Geschichte* (Munich, 1986), pp. 213–14.

6 Timothy Garton Ash, *In Europe's Name: Germany and the Divided Continent* (London, 1993), pp. 384–8.

7 Jacques Attali, *Verbatim: Tome 3, Chronique des années 1988–1991* (Paris, 1995), pp. 331, 363, 369.

8 Werner Weidenfeld, *Aussenpolitik für die deutsche Einheit: Die Entscheidungsjahre, 1989/90* (Stuttgart, 1998), p. 73; *The Spectator*, 14 July 1990, pp. 8–10.

9 Margaret Thatcher, *The Downing Street Years* (London, 1995), pp. 790–9; Patrick Salmon et al., eds, *Documents on British Policy Overseas, series III, vol. VII: German Unification, 1989–1990* (London, 2010), p. 151.

10 Francis Fukuyama, 'The End of History?' *The National Interest*, summer 1989, pp. 3–4.

11 Mary N. Hampton, *The Wilsonian Persuasion: U.S. Foreign Policy, the Alliance, and German Unification* (Westport, Connecticut, 1996); Erez Manela, *The Wilsonian Moment: Self-Determination and the International Origins of Anticolonial Nationalism* (Oxford, 2007), p. 5: Matthew C. Price, *The Wilsonian Persuasion in American Foreign Policy* (Youngstown, NY, 2007), p. 3.

12 Frank Ninkovich, *The Wilsonian Century: U.S. Foreign Policy Since 1900* (Chicago, 1999), p. 289.

13 Stefan Halper and Jonathan Clarke, *America Alone: The Neo-Conservatives and the Global Order* (Cambridge, 2004), pp. 18, 74–9, 146–54; John A. Thompson, 'Wilsonianism: The Dynamics of a Conflicted Concept', *International Affairs*, 86 (2010), p. 27, quoting Kaplan and historian David Kennedy.

14 Catherine Merridale, *Night of Stone: Death and Memory in Russia* (London, 2000), pp. 122–4, 452; Bart Ziino, *A Distant Grief: Australians, War Graves and the Great War* (Crawley, Western Australia, 2007), pp. 1–7. Ken Inglis, *Sacred Places: War Memorials in the Australian Landscape* (3rd edn, Melbourne, 2008), p. 471, gives a figure of 1,455 Australian memorials to the First War World.

15 Peter Holquist, *Making War, Forging Revolution: Russia's Continuum of Crisis, 1914–1921* (Cambridge, Massachussetts, 2002), pp. 1–2. For a synthesis of recent work see Peter Gatrell, *Russia's First World War: A Social and Economic History* (Harlow, 2005).

16 Karen Petrone, *The Great War in Russian History* (Bloomington, Indiana, 2010), pp. 292–300.

17 E.g. 'Violence and Society after the First World War', *Journal of Modern European History*, 1 (2003), pp. 7–149; Alexander V. Prusin, *The Lands Between: Conflict in the East European Borderlands, 1870–1992* (Oxford, 2010); Timothy J. Snyder, *Bloodlands: Europe Between Hitler and Stalin* (New York, 2010); Robert Gerwarth and John Horne, eds, *War in Peace: Paramilitary Violence in Europe After the Great War* (Oxford, 2012).

18 Robert D. Kaplan, *Balkan Ghosts: A Journey Through History* (New York, 1993), pp. xxi–xxii; Misha Glenny, *The Rebirth of History: East Europe in the Age of Democracy* (London, 1990), p. 236.

19 David J. Smith, '"Woe from Stones": Commemoration, Identity Politics and Estonia's "War of Monuments"', *Journal of Baltic Studies*, 39 (2008), pp. 419–430; Aro Velmet, 'Occupied Identities: National Narratives in Baltic Museums of Occupations', *Journal of Baltic Studies*, 42 (2011), pp. 189–211. quoting p. 191; see also Meike Wulf, *Shadowlands: Framing the Past in Post-Soviet Estonia* (Oxford, 2014).

20 Jan-Werner Müller, ed., *Memory and Power in Post-War Europe: Studies in the Presence of the Past* (Cambridge, 2002), introduction, p. 14.

21 James Mark, *The Unfinished Revolution: Making Sense of the Communist Past in Central-Eastern Europe* (New Haven, 2010), p. 95; HC *Debs*, 11 June 1999, vol. 332, col. 408.

22 Daniel Levy and Natan Sznaider, 'Memory Unbound: The Holocaust and the Formation of Cosmopolitan Memory', *European Journal of Social Theory*, 5 (2002), pp. 96–9.

23 Charles S. Maier, 'Hot Memory ... Cold Memory: On the Political Half-Life of Fascist and Communist Memories', *Transit*, 22 (winter 2001–2), pp. 153–65.

24 Snyder, *Bloodlands*, pp. x, 406.

25 http://www.kobariski-muzej.si/exhibitions/permanent/ Accessed on 10 Dec. 2012.

26 Jay Winter, *Remembering War: The Great War between Memory and History in the Twentieth Century* (New Haven, 2006), pp. 41–2, 222–37; Gerd Krumeich, 'Der Erste Weltkrieg im Museum: Das *Historial de la Grande Guerre* in Péronne und neuere Entwicklungen in der musealen Präsentation des Ersten Weltkriegs', in Barbara Korte, et al., eds, *Der Erste Weltkrieg in der populären Erinnerungskultur* (Essen, 2008), pp. 59–71.

27 Caroline Fontaine, et al., eds, *The Collections of the Historial of the Great War* (Paris, 2008), pp. 38, 117–19, 150.

28 Speech of 25 April 2003, accessed on 26 April 2011 from John Howard prime ministerial website at http://pandora.nla.gov.au/pan/10052/20031121–0000/www.pm.gov.au/news/speeches/speech94.html

29 On the DVA see Marilyn Lake, 'How do schoolchildren learn about the spirit of Anzac?' in Marilyn Lake and Henry Reynolds, eds, *What's Wrong With Anzac? The Militarisation of Australian History* (Sydney, 2010), ch. 6.

30 K.S. Inglis, *Sacred Places: War Memorials in the Australian Landscape* (3rd edn, Melbourne, 2008), pp. 411–12, 547.

31 Mark McKenna and Stuart Ward, '"It Was Really Moving, Mate": The Gallipoli Pilgrimage and Sentimental Nationalism in Australia', *Australian Historical Studies*, 38 (2007), p. 146.

32 Kevin Fewster, Vecihi Başarin and Hatice Hürmüz Başarin, *Gallipoli: The Turkish Story* (2nd edn, Crows Nest, New South Wales, 2003), p. 7.

33 Fewster et al., *Gallipoli*, ch. 1, quoting p. 18.

34 Trevor Royle, *The Flowers of the Forest: Scotland and the First World War* (Edinburgh, 2007), p. 329.

35 Alvin Jackson, *The Two Unions: Ireland, Scotland, and the Survival of the United Kingdom, 1707–2007* (Oxford, 2012), esp. pp. 172–7.

36 Kenneth O. Morgan, *Rebirth of a Nation: Wales, 1880–1980* (Oxford, 1981), pp. 367–8, 384, 414–15.

37 Stuart Allan and Allan Carswell, *The Thin Red Line: War, Empire and Visions of Scotland* (Edinburgh, 2004), p. 40.

38 Jackson, *Two Unions*, pp. 265–8, 278; T.M. Devine, *The Scottish Nation, 1700–2007* (2nd edn, London, 2006), p. 662.

39 John Horne, ed., *Our War: Ireland and the Great War* (Dublin, 2008), introduction, p. ix.

40 Richard S. Grayson, *Belfast Boys: How Unionists and Nationalists Fought and Died Together in the First World War* (2nd, edn, London, 2010), pp. 181–4.

41 Keith Jeffrey, *Ireland and the Great War* (Cambridge, 2000), pp. 6, 35, 138–43. The figures are for Irishmen born and enlisting in Ireland; if men born in Ireland who served in the Canadian or American forces are included the death toll rises to perhaps 35,000.

42 Horne, ed., *Our War*, pp. 273–4.

43 S.D. Badsey, 'The Great War since *The Great War*', *Historical Journal of Film, Radio and Television,* 22/1 (2002), p. 44. See also Brian Bond, *The Unquiet Western Front: Britain's Role in Literature and History* (Cambridge, 2002), ch. 4.

44 Gary Sheffield, *Forgotten Victory. The First World War: Myths and Realities* (London, 2001), pp. xvii, 48, 169, 253–4, 263.

45 William Philpott, *Bloody Victory: The Sacrifice of the Somme* (London, 2009), pp. 626–9; Sheffield, *Forgotten Victory*, pp. 92–3, 280.

46 John Keegan, *The First World War* (London, 1998), pp. 3, 315–16, 456.

47 Niall Ferguson, *The Pity of War* (London, 1998), pp. 445, 460–1.

48 Ferguson, *Pity of War*, pp. 447, 462.

49 Jay Winter and Blaine Baggett, *1914–18: The Great War and the Shaping of the Twentieth Century* (London, 1996), pp. 6, 10–11, 361, 392, 398, 402; see also Winter, *Remembering War*, pp. 207–8.

50 Winter, *Remembering War*, pp. 214–15; Bond, *Unquiet Western Front*, pp. 80–2; Todman, *Great War*, pp. 147–51; 'Oh What a Whingeing War!', *The Spectator*, 18 Jan. 1997, pp. 18–19.

51 Pat Barker, *The Regeneration Trilogy* (London, 1998), p. 5.

52 Barker, *Regeneration Trilogy*, pp. 427, 544–5, 559.

53 Barker, *Regeneration Trilogy*, pp. 544–5, 559, 576–7, 588–9; Bond, *The Unquiet Western Front* (Cambridge, 2002), p. 77.

54 Sebastian Faulks, *Birdsong* (London, 2007 edn), quoting introduction (2004), pp. ix–xi.

55 Faulks, *Birdsong*, pp. xvi, 215, 236, 238–9.

56 Faulks, *Birdsong*, pp. x, 482–3; C. Day Lewis, ed., *The Collected Poems of Wilfred Owen* (London, 1963), pp. 35–6.

57 Faulks, *Birdsong*, pp.xii, 65, 261–2, 266–7.

58 Faulks, *Birdsong*, p. xv.

59 Faulks, *Birdsong*, p. xvii; Daniel Todman, *The Great War: Myth and Memory* (London, 2005), pp. 175–6. Viewing figures from http://en.wikipedia.org/wiki/Birdsong_(TV_miniseries) Accessed 19 Dec. 2012.

60 Faulks, *Birdsong*, pp. 263–4; Pat Barker, *Another World* (London, 1998), pp. 72–4; see also Virginie Renard, 'Reaching Out to the Past: Memory in Contemporary British First World War Narratives', in Jessica Meyer, ed., *British Popular Culture and the First World War* (Leiden, 2008), pp. 292–5.

61 Joan Beaumont, 'Gallipoli and Australian National Identity', in Neil Graham and Keith Jeffrey, eds, *Culture, Place and Identity* (Dublin, 2005), p. 145.

62 'L'hommage à Ponticelli honore tous les poilus', *Le Figaro*, 17 March 2008.

63 Obituary, 'Harry Patch', *Guardian*, 27 July 2009, p. 30; 'A Service to Mark the Passing of the World War One Generation', Westminster Abbey, 11 Nov. 2009.

64 'Last Post', reprinted in Carol Ann Duffy, *The Bees* (London, 2011), pp. 4–5.

Conclusion: Long Shadow

1 G.M. Trevelyan, 'The Present Position of History' in *Clio, A Muse, and Other Essays* (2nd, edn, London, 1930), p. 196; W.N. Ewer, '1814–1914', reprinted in Dominic Hibberd and John Onions, eds, *The Winter of the World: Poems of the First World War* (London, 2007), p. 28.

2 Ewer, '1814–1914', in Hibberd and Onions, eds, *Winter of the World*, p. 28.

3 Christopher Andrew, *The Defence of the Realm: The Authorized History of MI5* (London, 2009), pp. 145, 152–9.

4 David Stevenson, *1914–1918: The History of the First World War* (London, 2004), pp. 47–8.

5 Richard Holmes, *Tommy: The British Soldier on the Western Front 1914–1918* (London, 2004), p. 89.

6 John Horne, ed., *Our War: Ireland and the Great War* (Dublin, 2008), pp. 5, 133.

7 John Lee, 'Shakespeare and the Great War', in Tim Kendall, ed., *The Oxford Handbook of British and Irish War Poetry* (Oxford, 2007), pp. 138, 145–6.

8 F. Scott Fitzgerald, *The Great Gatsby* [1925] (London, 1974), p. 188.

9 Richard Holmes, *Tommy: The British Soldier on the Western Front 1914–1918* (London, 2004), pp. 273–6.

10 Important studies include Stephen Constantine, Maurice W. Kirby and Mary B.

Rose, eds, *The First World War in British History* (London, 1995); Sharon Ouditt, *Fighting Forces, Writing Women: Identity and Ideology in the First World War* (London, 1994); Gail Braybon, ed., *Evidence, History and the Great War: Historians and the Impact of 1914–18* (Oxford, 2003); Janet S.K. Watson, *Fighting Different Wars: Experience, Memory, and the First World War in Britain* (Cambridge, 2004); and Adrian Gregory, *The Last Great War: British Society and the First World War* (Cambridge, 2008).

11 For examples of anthologies that break the mould see Catherine Reilly, ed., *Scars Upon My Heart: Women's Poetry and Verse of the First World War* (London, 1981) and Dominic Hibberd and John Onions, eds, *Winter of the World: Poems of the First World War* (London, 2007).

12 Santanu Das, 'Introduction', in Das, ed., *Race, Empire and First World War Writing* (Cambridge, 2011), pp. 4, 7.

13 Joachim Remak, '1914: The Third Balkan War: Origins Reconsidered', *JMH*, 43 (1971), pp. 353–66; Christopher Clark, *The Sleepwalkers: How Europe Went to War in 1914* (London, 2012), pp. xxvi–xxvii; Barbara Korte, et al., eds, *Der erste Weltkrieg in der populären Erinnerungskultur* (Essen, 2008), p. 9; Winston S. Churchill, *The World Crisis: The Eastern Front* (London, 1931), p. 7; Gerhard P. Gross, ed., *Die vergessene Front. Der Osten 1914/15: Ereignis, Wirkung, Nachwirkung* (Paderborn, 2006). A pioneering exception to this neglect in English was Norman Stone, *The Eastern Front* (London, 1975).

14 Hew Strachan, *The First World War, vol. I, To Arms* (Oxford, 2001), p. xvi; Daniel Marc Segesser, *Der Erste Weltkrieg in globaler Perspektive* (Wiesbaden, 2012); Rana Mitter, *A Bitter Revolution: China's Struggle with the Modern World* (Oxford, 2004); Xu Guoqi, *China and the Great War* (Cambridge, 2005).

15 Dan Todman, 'The First World War in Contemporary British Culture', in Heather Jones, Jennifer O'Brien and Christopher Schmidt-Supprian, eds, *Untold War: New Perspectives on First World War Studies* (Leiden, 2008), pp. 434–5, 439; Gundula Bavendamm, 'Der Erste Weltkrieg im Internet', in Gross, ed., *Die vergessene Front*, quoting p. 389.

16 'Photographs (To Two Scots Lads)' in P.J. Kavanagh, ed., *Collected Poems of Ivor Gurney* (Oxford, 1982), pp. 46–7.

17 Susan Sontag, *On Photography* (New York, 1977), p. 70. I follow here the insightful discussion in Catherine Moriarty, '"Though in a Picture Only": Photography and the Commemoration of the First World War', in Braybon, ed., *Evidence, History and the Great War*, pp. 36–9.

18 HC *Debs*, 4 May 1920, vol. 128, cols 1970–1.

PERMISSIONS

INDEX

abdication crisis 73, 76, 78
Abdullah I of Jordan 100
Abercrombie, Lascelles 189
Abyssinia, invasion of 222–3
Acheson, Dean 329
Action française 54
Adam-Smith, Patsy, *The Anzacs* 374
Adenauer, Konrad 321, 326, 327, 328
Afghanistan 96
Africa
  British Africa 87
  see also individual countries
aggressive war, concept of 297, 298
air warfare
  anti-bombing pact proposal 227–8
  death tolls 260
  fear of 225–7, 241, 248–9, 427
  Second World War 226, 273
  strategic bombing 251, 259, 293, 299
aircraft carriers 232
aircraft industry 232
Al-Qaeda 391
Alamein 270–1, 337, 427
Aldington, Richard 203
Alexander III, Tsar 8
All Quiet on the Western Front (film) 203, 309

Allen, Clifford 158, 160
Allenby, General Sir Edmund 91
Alsace and Lorraine 14, 34, 254, 325
'American century' 134
American Civil Liberties Union (ACLU) 216
American Federation of Labor (AFL) 80
American Legion 213, 215–17, 308
American Peace Society 235
Amiens 108
Amritsar Massacre 114, 115
Anglo-American community of interest 265, 267
Anglo-Irish Treaty 31
Anglo-Persian Oil Company 103
Anschluss 14
anti-Semitism 72, 99, 324
anti-war movement *see* peace movement
Anzac Day 371, 375, 376, 399–401
Apollinaire, Guillaume 357
appeasement xvii, 229, 243, 263, 303, 427
Arabs 99–100
  Arab revolt 98, 100, 102
  Arab–Israeli wars 288
  nationalism 101

architecture
    memorials 173, 179–80, 181, 385–7
    war cemeteries 179, 180–5, 186–7,
        194–5, 434–5
Arcos, René 357
Ardennes 253, 254
Arendt, Hannah 281, 305, 349
Argentina 87
Armenian massacre 90, 356–7
Armistice 93, 106, 179, 213
    anniversaries of 211, 315, 426
arms embargoes 238, 239–40
arms race 124, 220, 304, 317
arms trade 232, 237–8, 239–41
Armstrong, Michael and Mary 367
Army Film and Photographic Unit
        (AFPU) 285
art
    art market collapse 166
    Cubism 163–4, 165, 167, 168, 177
    Edwardian conservatism 165
    'Englishness' 348, 349
    Expressionism 163, 164–5, 167, 178
    Futurism 163, 165, 166, 167, 177
    Impressionism 163, 165
    war art 168–9, 171–2, 173–9,
        348–51, 426
    see also entries for individual artists
arts
    modernism 162–3, 176, 348, 349–51
    patronage 162
    propaganda 170
    see also architecture; art; film-
        making; literature;
        photography; poetry
Asquith, Herbert Henry 20, 21, 27, 59,
        63, 70
Asquith, Margot 92
Assmann, Jan 316
Association de la paix par le droit
        (APD) 223–4, 236
Atlantic Charter 275
Atlanticist ideology 267–8, 275, 277,
        389

atomic bomb 274, 282, 299, 301–5,
        312, 343
    'corrosion of familiarity' 304
    justification of use of 303–4
    nuclear fallout 304
    Soviet tests 304
atrocities 172, 200, 201, 281–305, 428
    accepted as true 200, 286, 288–9
    atrocity phobia 285
    biological and chemical weapons
        299–300
    propaganda value 284
    weapons of mass destruction 298–9
    White Book of justification 283
    see also atomic bomb; concentration
        camps; extermination camps;
        Holocaust; war crimes trials
Attenborough, Richard 333
Attlee, Clement 156–7, 279, 310, 312
Auden, W.H. 178
Auschwitz 287, 298, 322, 395, 410
Australia 87, 104, 105, 107, 110, 111,
        112, 120
    Anzacs 106, 370, 371, 376
    Australian identity formation 372–3
    Digger's War 373–4
    Great War 88, 89, 95, 106–7, 108,
        371
    heroic narrative 377
    nationalism 372, 373
    remembrance of war 371, 392,
        399–401
    Second World War 371
    veterans 370
    and Vietnam War 372
    war literature 372–3, 377
    'White Australia' policy 122
Australian Labor Party (ALP) 373
Australian War Memorial 374–5, 401
Austria 10, 53
Austria-Hungary 9, 21
    see also Habsburg Empire
Axis of Evil 305
Azerbaijan 92

Baggett, Blaine, *1914–18: The Great War and the Shaping of the Twentieth Century* 409–11
Baghdad 100
Bahr, Hermann 164
Bailey, Private Joseph 340
Baku 91
Baldwin, Stanley
  and abdication crisis 73, 76
  and air defence 225, 227, 230, 231
  and Churchill 72–3, 74
  and democracy 41, 65–7, 68, 83, 424
  and India 118
  and Lloyd George 72
  and National Government 69, 70
  reputation of 262
Balfour, A.J. 92, 98, 99, 103, 110, 116, 183
Balfour Declaration 98, 100
Balfour Report 109
Baltic states 12, 14, 31, 394, 429
  see also Estonia, Latvia, Lithuania
bank failures 134, 147, 148
Bank of England, nationalization of 311
Barker, Pat
  Another World 415–16
  The Eye in the Door 411
  The Ghost Road 411–12, 414
  Regeneration 411
Barnes, Harry Elmer 201
Barnett, Correlli 366, 410–11
Barr, Glen 405
Barry, Tom 30
Baruch, Bernard 240
Basra 100, 185
Battle of the Boyne 28
Battle of Britain 257, 258–9, 261, 265
Battle of France 258
Battle of the Somme (film) 340–1
Bavarian republic 45, 211
BBC 250
  1914–18: The Great War and the Shaping of the Twentieth Century 409–11, 429
  Belsen broadcast 285
  Birdsong 415
  'family history' series 367
  The Great War TV series 337–40, 342, 354
Bean, C.E.W. 372–3, 374
Beatty, Admiral 124
Beaverbrook, Lord 173–4, 199, 261
Becker, Jean-Jacques 382
Beckmann, Max 167
Bedford, Virginia 308
Belgium
  Benelux 327
  German atrocities 22, 200, 201, 282–3, 291, 421–2
  German invasion of 22, 23, 253, 421
  liberation of 273
  neutrality xix, 22
Bell, Clive 198–9
Belsen 281–2, 285–7, 310, 343
Benelux customs union 327
Beneš, Eduard 15
Bennett, Alan 286–7
Bennett, Arnold 173
Berlin Wall, fall of 387, 389
Betjeman, John 151
Beveridge Report 263, 310
Bevin, Ernest 145, 156–7, 252, 261, 312
Bidault, Georges 326
Bikini atomic tests 304
Binyon, Laurence 175, 188
biological and chemical weapons 299–300
Birkenhead, Lord 117, 293
Bismarck, Otto von 136, 322
Black and Tans 30
Blackett, Sir Basil 159
Blair, Tony 395, 403, 404
Blitz 226, 257, 259–60, 261, 262, 265, 280
Blitzkrieg 253–4, 262
Blok, Alexander 42
Blue Rider 164

Blueshirts 79

Blum, Léon 54

Blunden, Edmund 343–6, 347, 348, 360, 377
  Undertones of War 344

Blunt, Wilfrid Scawen 166

Boccioni, Umberto 163, 165, 167

Boer War 22, 25, 105

Bolshevism
  and Britain 59–60, 62–3, 64
  Churchill and 72–3
  and Europe 11–12, 14, 42, 46, 138
  and nationalism 9
  in Russia xxii, 42, 44, 210
  reinterpretations of 320, 392

Bomber Command 259

Bomberg, David 170

Bonar Law, Andrew 20, 26, 173

Bone, Muirhead 171–2, 173, 349

Bonham Carter, Violet 159

Bonn 388

Boot, Max 391

Boothby, Robert 157

Borden, Sir Robert 106

'Bore War' 233, 249

Bose, Subhas Chandra 119

Bosnia 298

Bosnia-Herzegovina 393

Botha, Louis 122

Bottomley, Horatio 56

Bradley, David 304

Bradley, Leslie 244

Braque, Georges 163–4, 167

Brereton, Frederick, *An Anthology of War Poems* 343–5

Brezhnev, Leonid 307

The Bridge on the River Kwai (film) 313

Bridges, Sir Edward 279

Britain
  1930s defence debate 230–1
  abdication crisis 73
  American loans 129–30, 146
  animosity to aliens and Jews 56
  aristocracy 74–5

Britishness, sense of 5, 17–18, 24, 33, 86, 111, 217, 402, 423
  case for war xix, 21–3, 291, 421–2, 427
  civic nationalism 16, 17
  coalition governments xx, 21, 26, 58, 65, 69–70, 70, 72, 73, 145, 148, 152, 158, 224, 228, 230, 252
  communism 59–60, 62, 63, 64
  defence spending 232, 312
  economic crises 69, 71, 72, 132, 141, 149, 425
  EEC membership 329, 372
  emigration 109–10
  and European integration 328–9
  financial services, global 130, 131, 133
  first-past-the-post system 63
  fiscal policy 146, 147, 149
  franchise enlargement 18, 46–9, 57–9, 68, 72, 424–5
  General Strike 66, 73
  and the gold standard 127–8, 141, 142, 145, 146, 148, 149, 153, 425
  industrial output 143, 150–1
  isolationist sentiments 220, 221, 222
  Labour governments 64–5, 148, 153, 217
  labour relations 59–61, 62, 66, 143–4, 148
  marginalization, fear of 328–9
  maritime power 87, 123, 125, 232
  military-industrial sector 232
  monarchy 16, 57, 75–6
  monetary policy 149, 150
  parliamentary government 16, 47
  peace movement 217–18, 218, 220–1, 223, 240, 243, 427
  post-war consensus 311
  post-war stability xvi, 60, 61, 65, 68, 70, 72, 74, 150, 152, 159
  rearmament 229–30, 232–3, 241

reconstruction booms 142–3
redrawing of constituency
    boundaries 65
remembrance of war 213, 309–10,
    325, 330–51, 376–7, 397, 421,
    426, 428, 429–30
security perimeter 224–5
Slump 141, 146, 159, 217, 263, 425
socialism 42, 64–5, 70, 80, 81
'special relationship' 277
sterling crisis 69, 132, 144
Sykes-Picot Agreement 97, 98, 100
taxation 75, 146, 147
transatlantic alliance 277, 329
two-party system 42, 63
unemployment 141, 143, 144, 148,
    152, 158
war funding 146, 147
welfare system 144, 145–6, 147,
    311
working-class solidarity 61, 81
see also United Kingdom
British Army
    caste system 107, 108
    conscription 56, 96
    imperial troops 87–8, 112, 185,
        431
    mutinies 59, 96
    volunteers 96, 360, 422
British Empire 17, 86–7
    colonies of conquest 87, 102, 112
    commercial network 87, 104, 109
    contraction of 312, 329
    crisis of empire 423
    decentralization 104
    expansion of xvi, 86, 103, 423
    global overstretch 93, 96, 97
    imperial loyalty 110
    imperium et libertas dilemma 105
    mandates 94–5
    Middle East 92, 98–102, 103
    nationalism, management of 103–4,
        107
    racial coding 111–12

settler colonies 87, 104, 105–6, 112,
    203
    see also Commonwealth; Dominions;
        and individual countries
British Expeditionary Force (BEF) 230,
    252
    Dunkirk evacuation 256, 257, 260,
        261, 265
    Great War 255, 422
    Second World war 256, 269
British Union of Fascists (BUF) 71–2
British War Memorials Committee
    (BWMC) 173
Brittain, Vera 218, 255
Britten, Benjamin, War Requiem 347,
    417
Brooke, Sir Alan 270, 271
Brooke, Rupert 85, 188, 189, 191,
    195, 258, 344
Bruce, Stanley 110, 112
Brüning, Heinrich 139–40, 145
'brutalization' thesis 384
    see also atrocities
Bryce Report 283, 284
Buchan, John 335
Buchenwald 287, 288
Buckles, Frank W. 416
Bulgaria 53
Bundy, McGeorge 303
Burne-Jones, Edward 66
Burns, Robert 18
Bush, George H.W. 389–90
Bush, George W. 391
Butler, R.A.B. 310
Byelorussia 12
Byng, Field Marshal Sir Julian 111

Cadogan, Sir Alexander 234–5
Cadorna, General Luigi 48
Calwell, Arthur 372
Cameroons 89
Camp Ashcan 295
Campaign for Nuclear Disarmament
    (CND) 337

Campbell, Alec 416

Canada
  as British Dominion 87, 88, 104, 105
  in Great War 106–7, 108, 109,
    110–11, 120
  and USA 130
  and war remembrance 111, 174

Canakkale 401

capitalism
  crisis of 51, 127–60
  Keynesian critique of 159–60
  laissez-faire capitalism 157, 158

Caporetto/Kobarid xxii, 48, 397

car industry 129, 132, 150–1, 152, 154

Carr, E.H. 279

Carroll, Sydney 203

Carson, Sir Edward 20, 26, 58

cash and carry trade 240, 242

Cassino 271–2

casualties
  aerial bombing 260
  American xvii, 34–5, 185, 308
  Australian 373
  Belgian 282–3
  British and Irish xvii, xx, 27–8, 34,
    161, 260, 262, 271, 272
  French xix, xx, 34, 260, 282–3
  German xx, 161, 260
  Italian 48
  poison gas 299
  Russian/Soviet 210, 272, 305, 306,
    391
  Second World War 260, 262, 272,
    303
  Serbian 34

Cather, Willa, One of Ours 204

Catholic Church 78, 79, 352

Catt, Carrie Chapman 236, 237

Cavendish-Bentinck, Victor 284–5

Cecil, Lord Robert 183, 184, 220–1

Cenotaph 179–80

Cézanne, Paul 165

Chagall, Marc 168

Chamberlain, Austen 220, 290–1

Chamberlain, Joseph 66

Chamberlain, Neville 67, 70, 148,
    152–3, 228, 262, 424
  announces Britain at war 248
  and Churchill 251–2
  and Guilty Men 262–3
  Munich agreement 228–9
  and rearmament 230, 232–3
  resignation 251

Channel Tunnel 220

The Charge of the Light Brigade (film)
    369n

Charteris, General John 171

Chechens 306

Chelmsford, Lord 114

Chetwode, General Sir Philip 96

Chiaureli, Mikhail 306

Chifley, Ben 372

China 86, 87, 88, 432
  May Fourth Movement 94
  nationalism 94, 432

Christian Democrats 326

Churchill, Winston 19, 20, 21, 22, 31,
    72–3, 125, 188, 350, 425, 432,
    435
  1945 election 310
  anti-Bolshevism 72–3, 74
  and the Atlantic Charter 275
  attrition strategy 271
  death of 330
  on disarmament 219
  economic policies 142
  and fascism 73, 74
  and the fall of Tobruk 269–70
  and Great War strategy 255
  and India 115, 117–18
  'Iron Curtain' speech 277
  myth-making 258, 259
  on war cemeteries 183–4, 435
  oratory 247, 258, 271
  on the peace movement 222
  on rearmament 233
  reluctance for cross-Channel attack
    269, 272–3

residual Liberalism 73
returns to government 251–2
strategic bombing, faith in 259, 269
on tank warfare 251
Teheran Conference 272–3
on trying the Kaiser 290
votes of no confidence in 271
on war crimes trials 296
war memoirs 21, 254, 279–80, 304, 323, 335, 432
civic nationalism 5, 16, 17, 35, 90, 122, 123
civilization, debates around 198–9
Clark, Alan 315, 330–1
   The Donkeys 315, 330–1
Clark, Kenneth 330, 348, 349
Clemenceau, Georges 93, 135, 169, 274, 291
Clynes, John 63
coal mines, nationalization of 310–11
coalition politics 70, 72
   see also Britain: coalition governments
Cold War xvii, xviii, 266, 277, 298, 309, 312, 387, 421, 429
   Cuban missile crisis 304, 309, 317–18, 329
   roots of 320, 390
collaborationists 324
Collins, Michael 77
Colman, Ronald 276
Committee of Unity and Progress (CUP) 90
Common Market see European Economic Community (EEC)
Commonwealth 105, 109, 111
Commonwealth War Graves Commission 434
communism 42, 45, 46, 51, 54, 55, 62, 63, 74, 82, 127, 128, 156–7
see also Bolshevism; Soviet Union
Conant, James 302–3
concentration camps 284, 287–8

Connolly, James 27
conscientious objectors 224, 236, 243
conscription
   Australia 107, 373
   Britain xx, 29, 56, 96, 192, 224, 261, 311, 422, 427
   France 422
   Germany 422
   Russia 8
   Second World War 261, 427
   United States 422
Conservative Party, British 19, 63, 70, 116
   revival in 1920s 65–8, 424
   post-1945 310, 311, 403
   progressives in 1930s 157–8
   and women voters 68
   see also Unionist Party
Constantinople 90, 92
consumer debt 129, 151
consumer revolution 129, 132, 150, 151
Cooksey, Jon, Pals 367–8
Cooper, James 341
Cosgrave, William 76, 77–8, 79
Cot, Pierre 224
Cousins, Norman 302
Coventry Cathedral 347
Cowan, William 19
Cowper, William 192
Craig, Sir James 33
Creel, George xvi, 284
Crimean War 215
Croatia 393
Croix de Feu 54
Crossman, Richard 330
Cru, Jean Norton, Témoins 380
Cruttwell, Charles, A History of the Great War 335
Cuban missile crisis 304, 309, 317–18, 329
Cumann na nGaedheal (CnaG) 76, 77, 79
Curragh Mutiny 20

currency controls 131
Currie, Arthur 108
Curtis, Lionel 106
Curzon, Lord 59, 92, 93, 97, 103, 116, 290
Cymru Fydd 19, 22
Czech Legion 8–9
Czechoslovakia 4, 6, 9–10, 14, 212, 228, 393, 429
  and Duchy of Teschen partition 13
  ethnic animosities 14, 15
  invasion of, 1939 233
  land reform 15
  liberal democracy 54
  nationalism 6
  velvet revolution 10

D-Day 272, 273, 308, 329
Dachau 287
Dahrendorf, Ralf 311
Daily Express 286
Daily Mail 68, 71
Daily Mirror 178, 264
Daladier, Edouard 214
Dalton, Hugh 157
Daniels, Josephus 277
d'Annunzio, Gabriele 48–9
Dardanelles 90, 400
Davidson, J.C.C. 70
Davis, Forrest 267
Dawes Plan 139
de Valera, Éamon 28–9, 77, 78, 79, 115, 351–2, 353
Debs, Eugene 80, 81
Declaration of Independence 123
Defence Requirements Committee (DRC) 229–30
demobilization 45, 59
democracy
  constitutions 47
  embattled idea 42, 55, 83
  liberal democracy 42, 54, 83
  mass democracy 18, 46–9, 57–9, 68, 72, 424–5

new democratic mood 184
'property-owning democracy' 67
Wilsonian promotion of 83, 390, 391
see also self-determination
Depression 126, 128
  and Britain 70–1, 141, 146, 159, 217, 263, 402, 425
  and France 149–50, 425
  and Germany 51, 70–1, 139–40, 425
  and USA 126, 132–4, 140, 425
deterrence policy 230
Detzer, Dorothy 237
Die Brücke (The Bridge) 164
Diggers 372, 373, 374
Dilke, Charles 105
Dimbleby, Richard 281–2, 285
disability payments 215, 216
disarmament debate 124, 219, 220, 235, 237
Dix, Otto 167, 168, 178, 399, 426
Doenitz, Admiral Karl 295
Dominions 31, 88, 105, 106–11
  see also individual countries
Douglas, James 341
Douglas, Keith 342, 343
Dresden 211
Du Bois, W.E.B. 85, 111
Ducasse, André, Vie et mort des français 1914–1918 381
Duffy, Carol Ann 385, 417–18
  'Last Post' 417–18
Duhamel, Georges 162, 357
Dunkerley, William 192
Dunkirk evacuation 256, 257, 260, 261, 265
Dunn, Harvey 169
dyarchy 105, 116
Dyer, General Reginald 114, 115

Easter Rising xvi, 26–7, 28, 33, 77, 317, 352, 423, 429
  memorialization of 317, 351, 353–4, 355, 404

Eastern Front
    1914–18 xii, 8, 268, 432
    1941–5 268–9, 342
Eden, Anthony 296
Edward VIII 73, 76
Egypt 112
    British protectorate 87, 94, 97
    independence 97
    nationalism 96, 97
    Ottoman tributary 97
Eichmann, Adolf 288, 322
Eisenhower, General Dwight D. 273, 288
Eliot, T.S. 188, 196–7, 260, 301, 348
    'Little Gidding' 260
    The Waste Land 196–7
Elizabeth II, Queen 405
Emergency Peace Campaign 237
Enniskillen bombing 404
Entente Powers see Britain; France; Russia
Enver, Ismail 90
Erhard, Ludwig 327
Erzberger, Matthias 289–90
Esher, Lord 57, 76
Essex, Tony 338, 339, 340, 342
estate duties 75
Estonia 10, 54, 393, 394–5
ethnic nationalisms 5, 6, 23
European balance of power 389
European Coal and Steel Community (ECSC) 327, 328
European Economic Community (EEC) 325, 327–8, 329–30, 352, 428
European integration 327, 328, 429
European monetary union 389, 390, 429
European Union 388, 395
evacuation plans 249
Ewer, W.N., '1814–1914' 419–20
extermination camps 281–2, 284–7, 298, 310, 343

Fabian socialism 155, 157
The Fall of Berlin (film) 306
Family History Tree (magazine) 367
Farrar-Hockley, Anthony 361
fascism 42, 47, 285, 324, 355, 424
    and Britain 71–2
    in Germany 47, 49–52
    and Ireland 79
    in Italy 47–50, 52, 73
    leadership cult 52–3, 424
Faulks, Sebastian, Birdsong 412–14, 415
Fay, Sidney B. 201
Federal Republic of Germany (FRG) see West Germany
Federal Reserve 133, 134
federalism 106, 118
Federation of Family History Societies 367
Feisal I of Iraq 100
Ferguson, Niall, The Pity of War 408–9
Ferro, Marc 357
Fianna Fáil 77, 78, 79, 352
fictional accounts of war 411–16
film-making
    American 203, 204–5, 309
    Australian 375
    British 171, 312–13, 333, 340–1
    French 203–4, 324, 357
    German 53, 203–4, 211
    Soviet 306–7
Fine Gael 79
Finland 6, 10, 12, 54
    civil war 12, 32
First World War see Great War
Fischer, Fritz 321–2, 336, 382–3, 409
Fitzgerald, Scott
    The Great Gatsby 430
    Tender Is the Night 205
Foot, Michael 262
Ford, Henry 129, 151
France
    Anglo-French alliances 219–20
    anti-Semitism 324

France – *continued*
  army mutiny xxi, 44
  the arts 167–8, 169–70
  collaborationists 324
  Communist Party (PCF) 46, 54
  fall of France (1940) 251, 256, 257, 268
  fear of bombing 227–8
  foreign investment 87
  franchise enlargement 46, 47
  Franco–British alliance 249–50
  Franco-German industrial
      cooperation 326
  Franco–Russian alliance 21, 220
  and the gold standard 149, 150
  imperialism 89, 97, 101, 103, 104
  liberation of 273
  merchant navy 87
  monetary policy 149–50
  nationalism in 5, 168, 243
  peace movement 221, 223–4
  political polarization 42, 54, 149
  Popular Front 54, 150, 233
  rearmament 233
  remembrance of war 213, 323–5,
      357, 380–1, 382, 428
  student revolt 324
  Sykes-Picot Agreement 97, 98, 100
  Vichy regime 323, 324
  war debt 149
  war reparations 136, 137
Franco, General Francisco 55
Franco-German treaty (1963) 328
Franco-Prussian war 14, 283
francs-tireurs 283
Frankfurt, Treaty of 136
Franz Joseph, Emperor 6
Free French 323
free trade 104, 120, 152, 153
Freikorps 212, 214
French, Field Marshal Sir John 254,
    300, 331, 334
French Resistance 323, 324, 326
French West Africa 104
Freud, Sigmund 198

Fromelles 373
Fry, Roger 165
Fukuyama, Francis 390
Fussell, Paul 377, 382
  The Great War and Modern Memory
      377–80, 409

Gaelic Athletic Association 354
Gaelic League 18
Gallacher, Willie 62
Gallipoli 90–1, 106, 371, 372, 374, 400–1
Gallipoli (film) 375
Gamelin, General Maurice 54
Gammage, Bill 375
  The Broken Years 373–5
Gandhi, Mohandas 113–16, 117, 119
Gardner, Brian 360
  Up the Line to Death 345–6
Gasperi, Alcide De 326–7
Gaudier-Brzeska, Henri 170
Gauguin, Paul 165
Gaulle, Charles de 323, 324, 325, 328,
    329
Geiss, Imanuel 322
General Strike 66, 73, 148
Geneva disarmament conference 219,
    220, 227, 235, 237
Genscher, Hans-Dietrich 388
geopolitics 91–2, 224–5, 243
George V 57, 64, 69, 75–6, 180, 209,
    290
George VI 76, 229, 260
Georges-Picot, François 97
Georgia 92
Georgians (poets) 188–9, 195, 197
German Democratic Republic (GDR)
    320–1, 387
German East Africa 89
German South-West Africa 89, 95
Germany
  army mutiny 44
  the arts 167
  Communist Party (KPD) 45, 46, 51
  debt dependence 139

'defensive war' justification 200–1, 201

Depression 51, 70, 134, 139–40, 425

ethnic nationalism 5

franchise enlargement 46–7, 68–9

Franco-German industrial cooperation 326

Franco-German treaty (1963) 328

hyperinflation 138, 147, 425

imperialism 86, 89, 95

industrial production 129, 139

Lebensraum 325

nationalism in 5, 167, 243

naval mutiny xxiii

Nazi-Soviet Pact 234, 393

Nazism 51, 52, 53, 69, 70, 140, 321

oligarchic ethos 120

parliamentary government 47

peace movement 219, 223

rearmament 220, 227, 229, 233–4

remembrance of war 211, 212, 321, 382–4

reparations payments 135–6, 137–8, 139, 140

'silent generation' xviii, 322

social unrest 45, 138

socialism 45, 80, 81

spring offensives, 1918 xxii, 26, 50, 192, 254–5

'stab in the back' mythology 50, 140

territorial losses 14, 34

trade war 137

unification 12, 387, 389.390

war funding 146

'war guilt' 135, 211, 289–94, 320, 321, 383

war weariness 212

Weimar Republic 50–1, 137, 214, 215, 311

welfare system 139, 145, 215, 311

women's suffrage 68–9

see also German Democratic Republic (GDR); West Germany

Gettysburg oration 36, 186

GI Bill 308

Gibraltar 87

Gill, Eric 182–3

Gleizes, Albert 164

Gloag, John 226

Gobineau, Arthur de 120

Goebbels, Joseph 53, 295

Gogh, Vincent van 165

gold reserves 131

gold standard 127, 130, 131, 148–9
    and Britain 69, 127, 131, 132, 141–2, 145, 146, 148–9, 153, 425
    and France 149–50, 425

Gompers, Samuel 80–1

Goncharova, Natalia 168–9

Good Friday agreement 404

Gorbachev, Mikhail 388, 389

Gotha raids 225

Grant, Ulysses S. 273

Graves, Robert 187, 206, 264, 343, 345
    Goodbye to All That 201, 380

Great Patriotic War 211, 257, 268–9, 272, 307

Great War
    Anglo-French crises during 254–6
    anniversaries of 211, 315, 356, 426, 427, 428–9
    Balkan roots 431–2
    demobilization 45, 59
    economic costs of xx, xxi
    global repercussions xvi–xvii, 86, 432
    impacts on 1920s and 1930s 3–209
    July crisis xix, 23, 201
    'learning curve' thesis xxiii, 407, 408–9
    midpoint 271
    mobilization 44–5
    phases xix–xxiii
    popular mythology and 264
    post-war cartography of Europe 4, 10
    post-war years xvi, 3–244, 420–1

Great War – *continued*
  renamed as First World War xvii,
      247, 278–9, 427
  revisionist discourse 201, 238, 240,
      258, 265, 284, 302, 336
  technology of warfare 408
  see also remembrance of war, writings
      about the Great War *and under*
      individual countries
The Great War TV series 337–40, 342,
    354
Grey, Sir Edward 21, 38
Griffith, Arthur 18, 76–7
Grigg, John 330
Grosz, George 167
Guilty Men ('Cato') 262–3
Gurney, Ivor 345, 347, 426
  'Photographs' 433–4

Haber, Fritz 300
Habsburg Empire xix, 6–7, 44
  collapse of xxiii, 9, 86
  Dual Monarchy 6, 18
Haig, Field Marshal Sir Douglas 172,
    213
  'Backs to the wall' order, 1918
      254–5
  reputation of 331, 334, 338, 361
  and Somme xx, 108, 339
  'Hundred Days', 1918 xxiii, 270,
      271, 406
Hailey, Sir Malcolm 119
Halbwachs, Maurice 316
Halder, General Fritz 253, 257
Haley, Alex, *Roots: The Saga of an*
    American Family 367
Halifax, Lord 117, 252, 256–7
Halls of Montezuma (film) 309
Hankey, Maurice 103
Hara Kei 121
Hardy, Thomas 18, 195n, 343
  'The Dynasts' 420
  'Men Who March Away' 420
Harris, John

Covenant with Death 362
The Somme: Death of a Generation
    360–1
Harrison, Austin 294
Harte, Paddy 405
Hashemites 98, 100, 102
Hawaii 122
Hawke, Bob 375, 399, 400
Hawkins, Jack 313
Hayden, Mary 79
Haykal, Muhammad 94
Heller, Joseph 378
Hemingway, Ernest 238
  A Farewell to Arms 205
Henderson, Arthur 61, 62–3, 144
heroic narrative of war 258–9, 260,
    330, 377
Hersey, John 302
Hess, Rudolf 53
Himmler, Heinrich 295
Hind, Lewis 175–6
Hindenburg, Paul von 53, 70–1, 76,
    211, 289, 293
Hirohito, Emperor 122
Hiroshima 301, 302, 303, 347
Historial de la Grande Guerre, Péronne
    398–9
Hitchcock, Alfred 333
Hitler, Adolf 46, 47, 50, 51–2, 52–3,
    69, 70, 212, 220, 223, 266
  annexation of Rhineland 223
  expansionism 322
  Führer 52–3, 254
  Mein Kampf 212, 383
  Munich agreement 228–9
  and rearmament 234
  rise to power 69, 140, 425
  suicide 295, 351
Hlinka, Father Andrej 15
Ho Chi Minh 115
Hoare, Sir Samuel 222
Hodges, Frank 63
Hoess, Rudolf 298
Hoffmann, Max 330–1

Hohenzollern empire 14, 86
Holocaust 282, 284–5, 287, 288, 298, 320, 395
  memorialization of 395–7
Holy Roman Empire 327
home fronts 172, 249, 251, 430–1
Home Guard 261
home ownership 67–8
Hoover, Herbert 140
housing
  British housing boom 151
  owner-occupancy 67–8
Howard, John 399–400
Hughes, Billy 95, 106–7, 110, 121–2, 290
Hughes, Charles Evans 124
Hulme, T.E. 188
Hundred Days, 1918 xxiii, 271, 406
Hungary 6, 10, 14, 15, 45
  fascism 53
  Hungarian Soviet Republic 45–6
Hunger Marches 141
Hurricane 231, 232
Hussein bin-Ali 97
Hussein, Saddam 102
Hussey, Maurice, Poetry of the First World War 346–7
Huxley, Aldous 223
Hyde, Douglas 18
hydrogen bomb 304
hyperinflation 138, 147

Imagists 188, 189
imperial legacies of war 86–90
Imperial War Cabinet 290, 291
Imperial War Graves Commission 181, 185, 186, 217
Imperial War Museum 170, 179, 209, 244, 348, 350–1
imperialism
  client regimes 92, 100
  imperial loyalty 110
  imperium et libertas dilemma 105
  new imperialism 119, 120–1

post-Ottoman settlement 90–103
war imperialism 86, 93, 97, 116, 312
Wilsonian constraints on 93, 96
see also British Empire, and under France; Germany
income tax 75
India 73, 86, 87, 92, 105, 112–19, 423
  Afghan invasion of 96
  civil disobedience 114–15, 117, 118
  Dominion status 117
  franchise 118
  Gandhi–Irwin Pact 117–18
  Government of India Act 116, 118, 119
  Great War 88, 112, 185
  industrial production 128
  nationalism 94, 113, 114, 116
  provincial devolution 118
Indian National Congress 112–13, 118–19
industrial production
  Britain 143, 150–1
  collective bargaining 143
  diffusion of 128–9
  Germany 129, 139
  labour relations 59–61, 62, 66, 143–4, 148
  pay deals 144
  rationalization 152
  US 128, 129, 131–2, 154
  working hours 143
Industrial Workers of the World (IWW) 82
influenza pandemic xvii, 35, 185–6
Insurrection (TV) 353–4, 429
interest rates 132, 143, 147
international criminal court 298
international economy, post-war, instabilities of 127–30
international security concept see League of Nations; United Nations
Iraq 86, 97, 101, 102
Iraq war 391

Ireland
    administrative structure 16–17
    Anglo-Irish Treaty 31, 76
    Catholic population 18, 20, 354, 355
    civil war 31–2, 76, 402, 423
    conscription crisis 29, 33
    cultural renaissance 18
    Dominion status 111
    Easter Rising see Easter Rising
    EEC membership 352
    emigration 352
    and fascism 79
    Great War xvi, 25–6, 27–8, 29, 33,
        404, 424
    Home Rule 19, 20–1, 25, 27, 65,
        106, 402, 423–4
    martial law 31
    nationalism 16, 18–19, 26, 29, 32,
        404
    Northern Ireland 33
    parliamentary democracy 80
    partition 31, 32, 33, 76
    proportional representation (PR) 32
    Protestant Ascendancy 17
    remembrance of war 405–6
    Second World War 351–2
    trade war 78, 79
    Unionists 20, 26, 28, 32–3, 354,
        424
    war of independence 29–31, 76, 96,
        402
    see also Irish Free State; Northern
        Ireland; Ulster
Irish Free State 32, 76, 77
Irish Parliamentary Party (IPP) 20, 25,
    29
Irish Republican Army (IRA) 29–31,
    76, 77, 79, 96, 352, 355, 404
Irish Volunteers 20, 25
Iron Curtain 277, 390
The Iron Hindenburg (film) 211
Ischinger, Wolfgang 388
Island of Ireland Peace Tower xviii,
    405, 429

isolationism
    American 240, 277, 302
    British 220, 221, 222
Isonzo River battles 48, 397
Italy
    fascism 42, 47–8, 49–50, 52, 71, 73
    franchise enlargement 46, 47, 49, 63
    Great War 47–8, 56
    invasion of Abyssinia 222–3
    parliamentary government 47
    proportional representation (PR) 49,
        63
    Second World War 257
Iwo Jima Memorial 309, 386

Jabotinsky, Vladimir 99
Jackson, Robert 297
Japan 88, 94, 95, 119, 432
    Anglo-Japanese alliance 120–1, 124,
        125
    Anglophilia 120
    capitulation in 1945 301, 302
    Great War 88, 120–1
    Hiroshima and Nagasaki 301, 302,
        303
    imperialism 120
    industrial production 128
    navy 120–1, 123–4
    oligarchic ethos 120
    Second World War 257, 268, 300,
        301, 302, 303
    Tokyo fire-bombing 301
Jerusalem 91
Joad, Cyril 228
Joffre, General Joseph 254, 336
John, Augustus 165
Johnson, Lyndon Baines 319
Joint Intelligence Committee 284
Joint Planning Committee (JPC) 225,
    226
Jones, David, In Parenthesis 235, 264
Jones, Tom 71
Joyce, James 78, 188
July crisis xix, 23, 201

Kaltenborn, H.V. 301
Kandinsky, Wassily 165, 168
Kaplan, Laurence F. 391
Karl, Emperor xxiii
Keating, Paul 362, 375, 399
Keegan, John
   The Face of Battle 365–6, 372
   The First World War 408
Keitel, Field Marshal Wilhelm 295
Kellogg–Briand Pact 236, 297
Kennedy, John F.
   assassination of 319
   Cuban missile crisis 317
   and *The Guns of August* 318
   and Vietnam 318–19
Kettle, Thomas 28
Keyes, Sidney 342
Keynes, John Maynard 127, 128, 135,
    142, 145, 149
   The General Theory of Employment,
    Interest and Money 159–60
   The Economic Consequences of
    Mr Churchill 141–2
   The Economic Consequences of the Peace
    135, 262, 274
Khrushchev, Nikita
   Cuban missile crisis 317
   destalinization 306, 307
Kiel mutiny 45
Kindleberger, Charles 133
Kipling, Rudyard 66, 183, 185, 191,
    343
   Epitaphs of the War 183
Kirkpatrick, Jeane 391
Klemperer, Victor 138
'knockout blow' concept 225, 234,
    249, 250, 269
Knox, Alexander 276, 309n
Kocka, Jürgen 383
Kohl, Helmut 388, 389
Korean War 312
Kosovo 393, 395
Kosovo Polje, battle of 7, 394
Krauthammer, Charles 391

Kun, Bela 45–6
Kurds 102
Kut 91

Labour Party, British 58, 61, 62, 63,
    64, 70, 128, 152, 243
   1945 landslide victory 263–4, 310
   communism, attitude to 156–7
   cultural conservatism 74
   ideology 424
   Labour governments 64–5, 148, 153,
    217
   and nationalization 128
Laemmle, Carl 203
Lancaster bomber 232
Lansbury, George 64
Lansdowne, Lord xxi, 27, 183
Lansing, Robert 38, 292
Larkin, Philip 359–60
   'MCMXIV' 359–60, 377
Laski, Harold 156
Lasswell, Harold 199–200
Latvia 10, 54, 393
Lawrence, D.H. 188
Lawrence, Susan 58
Le chagrin et la pitié (film) 324
Le Fauconnier, Henri 164
League of Nations 220, 236, 427
   Germany and 220
   mandates system 94–5, 123
   racial equality clause 121–2
   Roosevelt on 239, 274–5
   Wilson and 38–9, 94, 123, 276–7,
    278
League of Nations Association (LNA)
   236
League of Nations Union (LNU)
   220–1, 222, 223, 236
Leahy, Admiral William 300
'learning curve' xxiii, 345, 406–7
Lebanon 86, 97, 101, 102
Léger, Fernand 165, 168
Leipzig war trials 294
Lejeune, Max 398

Lemass, Sean 352–3, 355, 356
Lend-Lease 241n, 266, 267, 272
Lenin, Vladimir Ilyich 9, 42, 44
Leninism 73, 94, 129, 391
Les Croix de bois (film) 204
Levin, N. Gordon, Woodrow Wilson and World Politics 320
Lewis, Percy Wyndham 166, 170, 173, 174–5, 177, 178, 188, 351, 426
  A Battery Shelled 174–5
Liberal Party, British 20, 21, 63, 72
liberalism, Anglo-American 243, 390
Liddell Hart, Basil 250–1, 253, 335, 339, 407
  The Real War 335
Life 267, 281, 288, 289, 301
Ligue internationale des combattants de la paix (LIPC) 223–4
Lin, Maya 385–6
Lincoln, Abraham 36, 186
Lippmann, Walter 267
  U.S. Foreign Policy: Shield of the Republic 268
Lithuania 10, 393
Littlewood, Joan 331, 334
  Oh What a Lovely War 315, 331–4
Lloyd, Bertram, Poems Written during the Great War 343
Lloyd George, David 3, 21, 22–3, 42, 56, 60, 63, 70, 72, 73, 75, 85, 91, 92, 99, 124, 135, 136, 159, 173, 179, 186, 203, 290, 334, 425
  1918 election victory 310
  at Paris peace conference 93
  and Irish Home Rule 27, 31
  on the July crisis 201
  on trying the Kaiser 290, 292
  on war crimes trials 293
Locarno Treaty 220
Lodge, Henry Cabot 39, 276
London Ultimatum 136, 137
The Longest Day (film) 309
Loos 330
Louvain 22, 172, 282–3

Love on the Dole (film) 263
Low, David 260
Luce, Henry 267
Ludendorff, General Erich von xxii, xxiii, 50, 56, 293, 330–1, 336
Luftwaffe 227, 242
Lusitania, sinking of 22, 172, 239, 283
Lutyens, Sir Edwin 179, 180, 184–5, 186, 187
Luxembourg 327
Lyttleton, Oliver 333

Maastricht Treaty 389, 390, 398
McAleese, Mary 405
MacDermot, Frank 79
MacDiarmid, Hugh 260
Macdonald, Lynn 412
  They Called It Passchendaele 368–9
MacDonald, Ramsay 64–5, 69, 70, 74, 127, 144, 145, 155, 252, 262, 424
Macke, August 166
Maclean, John 62
MacLeish, Archibald 265
McMahon, Sir Henry 97–8, 99
Macmillan, Harold 157, 158, 160, 226, 329
Magyars 6
Mahon, Charlotte B. 275
Mailer, Norman 378
Major, John 390, 404
Malaviya, Madan Mohan 113
Malraux, André 323
Manchuria, Soviet invasion of 301
mandates 94–5, 101
Mann, Thomas 45, 388
Manstein, General Erich von 252
Manstein plan 253–4
Mao Zedong 94
Marc, Franz 163, 166
Marie, Queen of Romania 37
Marinetti, Filippo 165, 166, 175
Maronites 101
marriage rates, wartime 249
Marsh, Edward 188

Marshall, General George C. 300, 303–4
Marshall Plan 326
Marwick, Arthur, *The Deluge* 382
Marxism 62
  see also communism
Masaryk, Tomáš 9–10, 11, 12, 15, 99, 393
Masefield, John 191
Massey, William 110
Masterman, Charles 75, 170, 171–3, 199
Matisse, Henri 165, 350
Mauriac, François 387
Maxton, Jimmy 62
May Fourth Movement 94
Mayer, Arno, *Wilson vs Lenin* 320
Mediterranean theatre 271–2
memorials 111, 173, 179–80, 181, 184, 185, 211, 218, 309, 385–7
  see also Tomb of the Unknown Warrior; war cemeteries
memory
  collective memory 316
  communicative remembrance 316
  composing 370
  cult of xv, xviii
  cultural memory 316, 317
  national memory 386
  sites of memory 211, 386, 387, 416, 426, 434
  social construction of 317
  transnational memorialization 397–8
  see also remembrance of war
memory wars 394, 397
Mennonites 235
Menzies, Robert 372
Mesopotamia 92, 100, 101, 102, 103, 112
Metzinger, Jean 164
Meuse-Argonne offensive 35
Meyer, Jacques, *Vie et mort des français 1914–1918* 381
Middle East

Anglo-French compromise 100
British policies 92, 98–102, 103
client regimes 92
imperial legacies of war 89–90
mandates 101
oil interests 91, 103
successor states 101
theatre of war 90–1
middle way politics 158–9
Middlebrook, Martin, *The First Day on the Somme* 361–5, 366, 367, 413
Middleton Murry, John 161, 189
Milestone, Lewis 309
Mills, John 333
Milne, General Sir George 231
Milner, Lord 91
Milošević, Slobodan 394
Ministry of Information (MOI) 173, 284
Miracle on the Marne 254
Miracle on the Vistula 12
Mitchum, Robert 309
Mitterrand, François 388–9, 390
modernism 162–3, 176, 348, 349–51
monarchy, British 16, 57, 75–6
Monash, John 108
Monet, Claude 169–70
Monnet, Jean 326
Monroe Doctrine 267, 292
Montagu, Edwin 100
Montgomery, General Bernard 270–1
Moore, Henry 349–50
moral cause for war 22, 23, 291
Moreau, Emile 131
Morgan, J.P. 237
Morgenthau, Henry 296
Mosley, Sir Oswald 71, 72, 424
Mosse, George, *Fallen Soldiers* 383–4
Mosul 100
Mothers' Union 218
Mottram, Ralph Hale 217
Moulin, Jean 323
Mouvement républicain populaire (MRP) 326

Mowat, Charles, *Britain Between the Wars* 264
Munich agreement 228–9
Munich putsch 51
munitions industry 237–8, 240–1
Murrow, Edward R. 265, 287–8
Muslim League 113
Mussolini, Benito 42, 48, 49–50, 52, 71, 73, 257
  invasion of Abyssinia 222–3
March on Rome 52
Mustafa Kemal Ataturk 89, 401

Nagasaki 301, 303
Namur 254
Napoleonic wars 21, 136, 419–20, 420
Nash, Paul 172, 176–7, 178, 194, 348, 349, 351, 426
nation-states 5–6, 86
national consciousness 5, 8–9, 12, 15
  see also nationalism
National Council for the Prevention of War (NCPW) 237
National Grid 151
National Health Service 311
National Insurance schemes 144
nationalism 5–16, 10, 103–4, 107, 110, 394, 395, 403, 423
  civic nationalism 5, 16, 17, 35, 37, 90, 122, 123
  cultural nationalism 190
  ethnic nationalism 5, 6, 23
  see also under individual countries
nationalization 64, 70, 128, 157–8, 310–11
NATO 277
naval blockade xxii, 407
naval power
  Britain 87, 123, 125, 232
  Japan 120–1, 123–4
  parity principle 124–5
  USA 123, 124–5, 126
Nazi-Soviet Pact 234, 393
Nazism 51, 52, 53, 69, 70, 140, 321

négritude 125
Nehru, Jawaharlal 115, 117
neo-conservatism 93, 390–1
Netherlands 275, 327
Neutrality Acts 238, 239, 240, 242
'never again' 210, 211, 218, 247, 263, 280
Nevinson, C. Richard W. 172, 175–6, 177, 178, 348, 351, 426
  The Harvest of Battle 176
  La Mitrailleuse 175–6
New Deal 159
New Guinea 88, 95
New Left historians 320
New Zealand
  as British Dominion 104, 105, 110, 111
  and Great War 88, 89, 95, 376, 400
Newbolt, Sir Henry 161, 189, 207
Next Five Years Group 158
Nicholas II, Tsar 8, 43–4
Nicolson, Harold 45, 75
Niebuhr, Reinhold 130, 302
Niemeyer, Otto 146
Nietzsche, Friedrich 52, 53, 72
Nigeria 87
Ninkovich, Frank 390–1
Nipperdey, Thomas 5
Nivelle, General Robert xxi
Nora, Pierre 386–7, 395
Norman, Montagu 131, 149
Normandy landings 272, 273
North Atlantic Treaty 326
Northcliffe, Lord 130, 199
Northern Ireland 32, 354
  Catholic population 354, 355
  peace process 404
  'Troubles' 356, 404, 429
  Ulster Protestants 355–6
Norway 252, 275
Noske, Gustav 293
Nuremberg war trials 282, 295–8
Nuremberg Party Rally 53
Nye, Gerald P. 237
Nye Committee 237–8, 239, 241

O'Brien, Conor Cruise 78, 356
O'Duffy, Eoin 79
Oh What a Lovely War (play/film) 315,
    331–4
oil interests 91, 103
Olivier, Laurence 333
O'Neill, Terence 354–5, 356
Operation Barbarossa 257, 268, 269
Operation Georgette 255
Operation Michael 255
Ophüls, Marcel 324
oral and family history, vogue for 317,
    370, 405, 414, 416
Orange River 105
Orpen, William 165, 172, 176
Orwell, George 285
Othering 5, 7, 17, 24, 83, 111
Ottoman Empire xix–xx, xxii, 7,
    89–91
  civic nationalism 90
  collapse of 9, 86, 88, 89
  see also Turkey
Ottowa economic conference (1932)
    153
Owen, Wilfred 207, 409, 411
  as canonical 'war poet' xv, 187, 342,
    345, 347–8, 377, 382
  poetry 192–3, 195, 197, 258, 343,
    380, 426
  war service 192–3, 406
  writings
    'Agnus Dei' 417
    'Anthem for Doomed Youth'
      347
    'Dulce et Decorum Est' 192, 299,
      417
    'Exposure' 192
    'Strange Meeting' 347, 413
Oxenham, John 192

pacifism 203, 223, 224
  see also conscientious objectors;
      peace movement
Paisley, Revd Ian 355–6

Pakistan 119
Palestine 86, 91, 92, 99, 100–2, 112
  Balfour Declaration 98, 100
  British mandate 100, 102
  Zionism 98, 99, 101, 102
Palmer, A. Mitchell 82
Palmer raids 82
Palmerston, Lord 104
Pals battalions 308, 363, 366, 367–8
pan-Celtic revivalism 18
pan-Slavism 7
Papen, Franz von 51–2, 145
paramilitary groups 9, 30, 49, 54, 214
Paris peace conference 3, 10, 13, 38,
    93, 95, 109, 120
Parsons, I.M., *Men Who March Away*
    346
Passchendaele 272, 336, 368, 417
Patch, Harry 417
Patton, General George 288
Peace Ballot 221–2, 227, 240, 243, 427
peace movement 200, 225, 227
  American 235–7, 240, 243
  British 217–18, 220–1, 223, 240,
      427
  disarmament debate 124, 219, 220,
      227, 235, 237
  French 221, 223–4
  German 219, 223
  religious roots 224, 235
  women participants 218, 221–2,
      236
  see also League of Nations
Peace Pledge Union (PPU) 223, 227
Pearl Harbor 257, 267–8
Pearse, Padraig 26, 352
peasant agriculture 96–7
Péricard, Jacques, *Verdun* 380
Perle, Richard 391
Perreux, Gabriel, *Vie et mort des français
    1914–1918* 381–2
Pershing, John J. 34–5
Persia 92, 103
Pétain, Marshal Philippe 323

Peterloo 420
Petrie, Flinders 198
Phelan, James 122
Philippines 122, 123, 124
Phillips, Stephen 188
Philpott, William, *Bloody Victory* 407
phoney war 233, 249
photography, war 171
Picasso, Pablo 163–4, 165, 167–8, 350
Piłsudski, Jósef 10–11, 12, 26, 53
Pineau, Christian 325
Piper, John 348
Pitcairn 87
Plaid Cymru 24, 402
Plunkett, Joseph 26
poetry 187–98, 203, 419–20, 431
    anthologies 190, 343–7, 357
    anti-war poetry 187
    Georgian poetry 188–9, 195, 197
    Imagist poetry 188, 189
    patriotic 189–90, 191–2, 343, 344,
        345
    Second World War 342–3
    see also entries for individual poets
poilus xix, 380
Poincaré, Raymond 138, 149
poison gas 299–300
Poland 4, 6, 8, 9, 14, 34, 277
    and Duchy of Teschen 13
    ethnic animosities 14, 15
    invasion of, 1939 244
    nationalism 9, 10
    post-1918 revival 10–12, 53
Polish Legion 8, 11
Polish–Lithuanian Commonwealth 11
Political and Economic Planning (PEP)
    159
political polarization 42, 53, 54–5,
        56–7, 149, 159, 424
Pompidou, Georges 329
Ponsonby, Arthur 200, 207
    Falsehood in War-Time 200
Ponticelli, Lazare 416–17
Poppy Appeal 213

populist inclusivity of national narrative
    261–2
post-war consensus 311
Pound, Ezra 166, 188, 189, 195–6,
    197, 348
Hugh Selwyn Mauberley 195–6
Powell, William 276
Pownall, Colonel Henry 231, 234
Pozières 373
Poznan 14
Prague Declaration on European
    Conscience and Communism 396
Priestley, J.B. 206, 261
Primo de Rivera, General Miguel 55
prisoners of war 290
propaganda 170, 171, 172, 173, 199,
    200–1
    atrocity propaganda 284, 288
    public allergy to 284
proportional representation (PR) 32,
    49, 63
Prost, Antoine 382
protectionism 152–3, 327, 328
    see also tariffs
Protestant dissenting tradition 243
Public Broadcasting System (PBS)
    *1914–18: The Great War and the
        Shaping of the Twentieth Century*
        409–11
    Birdsong 415
Pugsley, Christopher 376
Pynchon, Thomas 378

Quakers 224, 235

radar 231, 232
Rawlinson, Sir Henry 364
rearmament
    British 229–30, 232–3, 241
    French 233
    German 220, 227, 229, 233–4
Red Army 268, 273, 287, 301, 305,
    393
Red Clydeside 60, 62

Redgrave, Sir Michael 338
Redgrave, Vanessa 333
Redmond, John 25, 26, 27, 113–14
Redmond, Willie 28
Reichsbanner 214
Reichsbund 212
Reims 172, 328
Remarque, Erich Maria 206, 212
    All Quiet on the Western Front 202–3
remembrance of war xv, 111, 179–87,
    387
    1960s revisiting 331–51, 408
    1990s revisiting 414
    post-Cold War 387–402, 429
    see also memorials, *and under*
        individual countries
Remembrance Sunday 376, 404
Renan, Ernest 5
Renouvin, Pierre, *La crise européenne et
    la Grande Guerre* 380–1
reparations payments 135–6, 137–8,
    139, 140
Repington, Colonel Charles 161, 279
republicanism 76, 355
Returned and Services League (RSL)
    371
Rhineland 34, 223, 325
Ribbentrop, Joachim von 295
Ridley, Nicholas 389
Riefenstahl, Leni 53
Riga, Treaty of 12
Ritter, Gerhard 322
Roberts, William 170, 173
Rocque, François de la 54
Romains, Jules 357
Romania 14, 34, 53, 53–4
Romanovs 7, 42, 44, 86
Rome, Treaty of 325, 327
Rome–Berlin Axis 257
Rommel, Field Marshal Erwin 48,
    270
Roosevelt, Franklin D. 83, 159, 216,
    238–9, 240
    on air warfare 241–2

Atlantic perspective 267, 268, 275
    on biological and chemical weapons
        300
    death of 277, 351
    and economic rights 308
    international security, concept of 273
    on the League of Nations 239,
        274–5
    and national security 242–3, 266–7
    Teheran Conference 272–3
    unconditional surrender demand 274
    war diplomacy 240, 241, 242–3, 266
Roosevelt, Theodore 274
Rosenberg, Isaac 434
Rosenthal, Joe 309
Rothermere, Lord 68, 71–2
Round Table group 106, 109
Royal Air Force 230, 231–2, 258–9
Royal British Legion 213, 214, 217,
    416
Royal Irish Constabulary (RIC) 29–30,
    77
Royal Navy 88, 124, 125, 232
Ruhr 138, 139, 325
Russell, Bertrand 223, 226
Russia
    1905 revolution 8
    1917 revolution 42–3, 44, 45
    armed forces mutinies 45
    civil war 9, 10, 72, 210
    epidemics and famines 210
    Great War 44, 211
    nationalism 8
    remembrance of war 210–11
    Russo–German antagonism 14
    Tsarism, collapse of 42–4, 57
    see also Bolshevism; Soviet Union
Russolo, Luigi 165
Rwanda 298
Ryan, Henry 216

'sacrifice', concept of 28, 207, 217, 426
Sakuzo, Yoshino 121
Salt March 117

Samoa 88, 95
Samuel, Herbert 100n
Sandburg, Carl 247
Sant'Elia, Antonio 167
Sarajevo 410
    Sarajevo assassination 7, 21
    siege of 393
Sargent, John Singer 178, 299, 351
    Gassed 178, 299
Sargent, Sir Orme 249–50
Sassoon, Siegfried 184, 209, 258, 342,
        344, 360, 378, 382, 411
    as canonical 'war poet' 187, 264, 343
    war service 193, 411
    writings
        'Base Details' 346
        Counter-Attack 345
        Memoirs of a Fox-Hunting Man
            201–2
        The Old Huntsman 345
satyagraha 113, 114
Schacht, Hjalmar 234
Schindler's List (film) 395–6
Schleicher, Kurt von 52
Schlieffen Plan 252
Schmidt-Rottluff, Karl 167
Schuman, Robert 326, 327
Scotland
    administrative structure 16
    Britishness and 24, 402
    devolution 403–4
    Home Rule 19, 21, 423
    nationalism 18, 24, 402, 403
    radicalism 62
    war dividend 24, 402
Scott, Sir Walter 191
Scottish Nationalist Party (SNP) 402,
        403, 404
Second World War 247–80
    1940–1 turning point 262–8
    as continuation of Great War 249,
        250
    fall of France 251, 256, 257, 268
    midpoint 271, 337, 427

Munich agreement 228–9
    new British national myth 264
    'people's war' 261–2, 264
    phoney war 233, 249
    rearmament 220, 227, 229–30,
        232–3, 233–4
    Second Front plans 269, 274
Secret Agent (film) 333
Sedan 253
Seeckt, Hans von 211–12
Seeley, John 105, 110–11, 112
Selborne, Lord 58
self-determination 9, 11, 14, 15, 29,
        36, 38, 93, 94, 99
    Wilsonian doctrine of 38, 86, 93, 94,
        96, 100, 117
September 11 2001 terrorist attacks 391
Serbia xix, 7, 15, 23, 34
Sergeant York (film) 205
Sevareid, Eric 265
Seydoux, Jacques 326
Shakespeare, William, Henry V 181,
        369–70
Shandong 94
Shaw, George Bernard 72
Sheffield, Gary, Forgotten Victory 406–7
Sheppard, Revd Dick 223
Sherman, Alfred 156
Sherriff, R.C. 206
    Journey's End 206, 339
Sherwood, Robert 239
Shia Muslims 102
Shinwell, Emanuel 62
Sholokhov, Mikhail 307
Sichelschnitt 253, 257
Sieff, Israel 159
Simon, Sir John 233, 296
Simpson, John 374
Singapore 125, 371
Sinn Féin 18, 28, 29, 96, 354
Slovakia 393
Slovenia 392–3, 397
Smith, Maggie 333
Smuts, Jan 89, 95, 109

Snowden, Philip 70
Sobibor 298
socialism 45, 46, 48, 54, 55
    in Britain 42, 64–5, 70, 73, 155,
        157
    in USA 80–1
Socialist Party (American) 80
Socialist Party (German) 214
Société des nations 221
Solzhenitsyn, Alexander 307
Sombart, Werner 81
Somme, battle of
    Britain and 27–8, 338–9, 407,
        427–8, 430
    casualties xx, 271, 332, 365
    fictional accounts of 413
    Germany and 271, 338, 407
    historians' interpretations of 336–7,
        360–7, 368–9, 406–7
    museum about 398–9
Sorley, Charles 344
South Africa 89, 104, 105, 106, 109,
    111
    Boer War 22, 25, 105
    Great War 88
Soviet Union
    1930s 153–4
    Cold War 304, 309, 317–18, 329
    collectivism 154
    destalinization 306–7
    disintegration of 387
    entry into Asian war 301, 303
    famines 156, 305
    Five Year Plans 154, 307
    German invasion of 257, 268, 269
    Great Patriotic War 211, 257, 268–9,
        272, 307
    industrial output 154
    Nazi-Soviet Pact 234
    post-war adjustment 305–6
    purges and show trials 156, 306
    remembrance of war 210–11, 307,
        356–7, 391–2, 428
    Stalinism 153–6

    see also Bolshevism; Russia
Spain, civil war 54–5, 73, 223
Spanish–American war 122–3
Spender, Percy 371
Spender, Stephen 197
Spengler, Oswald 198
Spielberg, Steven 395
Spitfire 231, 232
Spitfire Fund 261
Stahlhelm 50, 214
Stalin, Josef 129, 153, 154, 156, 269,
    272–3, 306, 342
Stalingrad 271n, 407
Stanley, Oliver 157
state-building 9–13
Statute of Westminster 109, 111
Stenger, General Karl 294
sterling crisis 142, 144, 148, 149
Stevenson, Frances 341
Stevenson, Robert Louis 191
Stimson, Henry 296–7, 298–9, 302,
    303
Stinnes, Hugo 138
Strachey, St Loe 71
strategic bombing 251, 259, 293, 299
Stresemann, Gustav 138
Strong, Benjamin 133–4
submarine warfare, unrestricted xxi, 37,
    291, 293, 299
suburbanization 151
Suez Canal 97
Sunni Muslims 102
Super Tax 75
Sutherland, Graham 348
Swing, Raymond Gram 238, 304
Sykes, Sir Mark 97
Sykes–Picot Agreement 97, 98, 99, 100
Synge, J.M. 18
Syria 86, 92, 93, 97, 99, 100, 101, 102

Tallinn 394–5
tanks 250, 251, 253
Tannenberg 211
Tannenberg (film) 211

tariffs 66–7, 133, 152–3
Tatars 306
Tate Gallery 350
taxation 75, 146, 147, 149
Taylor, A.J.P 173
    *The First World War: An Illustrated
        History* 334–5, 335–7, 357
    The Origins of the Second World War
        334
    The Struggle for Mastery of Europe 336
Teheran Conference 272–3
Tennyson, Alfred, Lord 195n
Terkel, Studs 309
Terraine, John 338, 339, 410
    The Educated Soldier 338
Teschen, Duchy of 13
Thatcher, Margaret 311, 389–90, 403
'The Few' *see* Royal Air Force
Thiepval Memorial 184–5, 186, 386,
    415–6
Thiepval Ridge 27–8
Third Balkan War 431
Third Geneva Convention 300
Third World War 302
Thomas, Edward 194, 197, 343, 385,
    411, 426
Thomas, Jimmy 64
Thompson, Dorothy 265
Thomson, Alistair, *Anzac Memories* 370
Tilsit, Treaty of 136
Time 301
The Times 98, 170, 179, 189, 250, 258,
    260, 261, 294, 341, 349
Tito, Josef Broz 392
Tobruk, fall of 269–70
Todd, Richard 309, 313
Togoland 89
Tokyo fire-bombing 301
Tomb of the Unknown Warrior
    Australia 375
    Britain 180
    France 180
    New Zealand 376
    Soviet Union 307

    USA 180, 309
'Tommies' 359n
total war xx, 135, 399
Toynbee, Arnold 153, 198, 226–7
    Study of History 198
trades unions 60, 66, 80–1, 82
Transjordan 86, 100, 101, 102
Transvaal 105
Transylvania 14
Treblinka 298
Trenchard, Sir Hugh 293–4
Trentino 48
Trevelyan, G.M. 419, 433
Triumph of the Will (film) 53
triumphalism 390
Truman, Harry S. 303–4, 304
Truman Doctrine 266
Tsingtao 88
Tuchman, Barbara, *The Guns of August*
    317–18
Turkey 90, 400–1
    see also Ottoman Empire
two-minute silence 179, 217, 416
Tyne Cot 186

U-boat warfare xxi, 37, 291, 293
Übermensch 52
Ukraine 8, 10, 11, 12, 14, 15, 393,
    394, 396, 429
Ulster 20, 32, 33, 402, 424
    see also Northern Ireland
Ulster Volunteers 20, 28
unemployment 51, 134, 139, 141, 142,
    143, 144, 145, 148, 152, 158
unemployment benefits 69, 137, 144, 149
Union Fédérale (UF) 214
Union nationale des combattants
    (UNC) 214
Union of Democratic Control 200
United Nations 275, 277
Unionist Party 19, 20, 21, 63
United Kingdom, unity of 16–33,
    401–6, 423
United Nations 275, 277

United States
  air power 241, 242, 273–4
  anti-communism 42, 320, 424
  Atlanticist ideology 267–8, 277
  atomic bomb 274, 282, 299, 301–5,
    312, 343
  civic nationalism 35–6, 37, 40, 122,
    123
  Civil Rights Movement 356
  Civil War xvii, 35, 36, 186, 273,
    308, 410
  Cold War xvii 304, 309, 317–18,
    319, 320, 329
  communist movement 82
  Depression 132, 134, 278, 425
  and European integration 329
  franchise enlargement 46–7, 80,
    82
  GDP 274
  global finance and 129–30, 131,
    133–4, 139
  Great War xvii, xxii–xxiv, 34–5,
    36–7, 83, 185–6
  hyper-patriotism 424
  immigrants 81–2, 122–3
  imperialism 120
  industrial militancy 80–1, 82
  industrial production 128, 129,
    131–2, 154
  isolationism 240, 277, 302
  naval supremacy, bid for 123, 124–5,
    126
  neutrality xxi, 36–7, 238
  New Deal 159
  peace movement 235–7, 240, 243
  racism 37, 81, 120, 122–3
  radicalism, failure of 42, 80, 82
  Red Scare 80, 82, 216, 243, 320,
    424
  remembrance of war 213, 307–9,
    421, 428
  Second World War xvii, 256–7,
    264–6, 272, 273–5, 278, 421
  social mobility 81
  socialism, failure of 80–2
  Soviet non-recognition policy 83
  'special relationship' 277
  two-party system 80, 82
  Vietnam War 318–19, 378
  war art 169
  war atrocity stories, impact of 283–4,
    287–9
  war dividend 82, 129, 278
  wars of independence 35

V-weapons 226, 280
Vandenberg, Arthur 238, 242
Vansittart, Sir Robert 220
Vaughan Williams, Ralph 18
Vaughan-Thomas, Wynford 282
Verdun xx, xxi, 323, 398
Versailles, Treaty of 135, 137, 179
  'war guilt' clauses 135, 200, 289,
    289–90
veterans' groups
  American 215–17, 308
  Australian 400
  British 213, 214, 217, 427
  deaths of last veterans 416–17
  disabled veterans 215, 216
  French 54, 214
  German 50, 213–14
  Soviet 306
  war pensions 214–15
Veterans of Foreign Wars 216
Vichy regime 323, 324
Vickers 240–1
Victoria, Queen 75, 182
Vietnam Veterans Memorial 385–6
Vietnam War 318–19, 378
Vimy Ridge 106, 111, 186
Vorticism 166, 170, 174, 175, 188

Wales
  administrative structure 16
  Anglican church disestablishment 19,
    21, 23, 423
  devolution 403–4

Wales – *continued*
  nationalism 18, 19, 24, 402
  Welsh language 403
Wallace, William 18
War Artists Advisory Committee
  (WAAC) 348, 349
war cemeteries 179, 180–5, 186–7,
  194–5, 210, 434–5
war crimes trials 291–8, 322
  Great War 294
  Nuremberg war trials 282, 295–8
  proposed trial of the Kaiser 289,
    290–1, 292–3
'war guilt' 135, 211, 289, 320, 321,
  383
war loans 24
war pensions 214–15
war weariness 212
Ward, Sir Joseph 106
Ware, Sir Fabian 181, 182, 184, 217,
  434
Washington Conference 124–5
Waterloo 182, 419–20, 427
Wayne, John 309
weapons of mass destruction 298–301
  see also atomic bomb
Webb, Beatrice 127, 155–6
Webb, Sidney 155–6
Wehler, Hans-Ulrich 322
Weir, Peter 375
Weizmann, Chaim 99
welfare systems 139, 144, 145–6, 147,
  215, 311
Wells, H.G. 41, 57, 217
West Germany 277, 320–1, 324,
  382–3, 387
West Prussia 14
Western Front 90, 268, 299, 335, 342,
  365, 378–9, 382, 404–5, 406, 430
  see also specific offensives
  casualties 272
Westfront 1918 (film) 204
Wharton, Edith, *A Son at the Front* 204
wheat production 128

Whitaker, T.K. 352
White Book 283
Whitlam, Gough 375
Whitman, Walt 186, 188
Wilde, Oscar 75
Wilhelm II, Kaiser 91, 289
  abdication and exile xxiii, 45, 292
  proposed trial of 289, 290–1, 292–3
Williams, William Appleman, *The
    Tragedy of American Diplomacy*
    319–20
Wilson, Edith 3–4
Wilson, Edmund 134
Wilson, Sir Henry 59, 96
Wilson, Woodrow 10, 76, 83, 123, 124
  critiques of, 1920s 135–6, 199
  Fourteen Points 9, 11
  in Great War 36–42
  and League of Nations 38–9, 94,
    239, 277
  New Left interpretations of 320
  and Paris peace conference 3, 4, 13,
    38, 93–4, 95
  rehabilitation of 275–7
  and self-determination 9, 38, 86, 93,
    94, 96, 100, 117
  stroke 239, 277
  on war crimes trials 292
Wilson (film) 276–7
Wilson Foundation 275
Windsor, House of 57, 76
Winter, Jay 398
  *1914–18: The Great War and the
    Shaping of the Twentieth Century*
    409–11
Wirth, Joseph 137
women
  in peace movements 218, 221–2, 236
  in political life 218
  suffrage 47, 57, 58–9, 68, 68–9, 82
  war work 58–9
Women's International League for
  Peace and Freedom (WIL) 218,
  236

Woolf, Virginia, *To the Lighthouse* 202
World War Veterans 216
writings about the Great War
   emotionalism 362, 365, 373,
      379–80
   lack of a clear narrative 334–6
   oral history, problems of 368–70
   orthodox military history xv, 365,
      367, 372, 380–1
   revisionist military history xxiii, 406–7
   soldier's experience, focus on
      361–70, 372, 373, 380, 381
   'structuralist' social history 383
   see also entries for individual authors

Yalta Conference 277

Yeats, W.B. 18, 26, 28
York, Alvin 205
Young Scots 19
Young Turks 89, 90
Young Wales 19, 22
Ypres 184, 299
   Menin Gate 184, 386
Yugoslavia 4, 10, 14, 15, 53, 392, 394,
     429, 431

Zanuck, Darryl F. 276, 309
Zborov 8–9
Zhukov, Marshal Georgy 306
Zimmern, Alfred 221
Zionism 98, 99, 101, 102
Zyklon B gas 300